BARRON'S

GMAT®

GRADUATE MANAGEMENT ADMISSION TEST

14TH EDITION

Eugene D. Jaffe, M.B.A., Ph.D.
Professor and Head, M.B.A. Program
Ruppin Academic Center
School of Social Sciences and Management

Stephen Hilbert, Ph.D.
Professor of Mathematics
Ithaca College

BARRON'S

® GMAT is a registered trademark of the Graduate Management Admission Council, which does not endorse this book.

For Liora, Iris and Nurit and for Susan

All inquiries should be addressed to:
Barron's Educational Series, Inc.
250 Wireless Boulevard
Hauppauge, New York 11788
www.barronseduc.com

ISBN-13: 978-0-7641-3362-6 (Book)
ISBN-10: 0-7641-3362-4 (Book)
ISBN-13: 978-0-7641-7900-6 (Book/CD Package)
ISBN-10: 0-7641-7900-4 (Book/CD Package)

ISSN: 1931-616X

PRINTED IN THE UNITED STATES OF AMERICA
9 8 7 6 5 4 3 2 1

Contents

PRE-TEST REVIEW

TEST YOURSELF

BUSINESS SCHOOL BASICS

APPENDIX

Preface

Barron's *Graduate Management Admission Test (GMAT)* is designed to assist students planning to take the official Graduate Management Admission Test administered by the Educational Testing Service of Princeton, New Jersey. Since the results of the GMAT are used by many graduate schools of business as a means for measuring the qualifications of their applicants, it is important that the prospective student do as well as possible on this exam. Admission to business school may well depend on it.

A study guide, although not able to guarantee a perfect score, can provide a good deal of assistance in test preparation by enabling students to become familiar with the material they will encounter on the exam and supplying them with ample opportunity for practice and review. With this in mind, we have developed a study guide that goes further than the simple simulation of the official GMAT in its effort to offer a sound basis of test preparation. Besides containing three practice tests with questions (and answers) similar to those students will encounter on the actual exam, it offers invaluable advice on *how* to prepare for the exam, ranging from a general discussion of the purpose and various formats of the GMAT to a step-by-step program of subject analysis and review designed to help students discover their weak points and take measures to correct them. A tactics section is included that covers every question type. These tactics give students practical instructions and hints on how to analyze and answer each question.

Review sections for each subject area appearing on the exam have been especially developed to meet the specific needs of students who may feel a deficiency in any of these areas. Each review provides both an explanation of the material and exercises for practical work. The practice exams included in the guide have self-scoring tables to help students evaluate their results and check their progress. All answers to the test questions are fully explained to ensure complete understanding.

The authors would like to extend their appreciation to Mrs. Susan Hilbert and Ms. Dawn Murcer for their excellent job in typing the manuscript, to Professor Shirley Hockett for several helpful discussions, and to Professor Justin Longenecker for his generous advice.

How to Use This Guide

The step-by-step study program appearing below outlines the recommended study plan you should follow when preparing for the GMAT. By making use of this procedure, you will be able to take full advantage of the material presented in this guide.

1. Familiarize yourself with the purpose and format of the GMAT Computer-Adaptive Test (CAT) (Chapter One).

2. Study the analysis of each type of question on the exam (Chapter Two).

3. Take the GMAT Diagnostic Test (Chapter Three) and use the Self-Scoring Table at the end of the test to evaluate your results.

4. Study the review sections (Chapters Four, Five, Six, Seven, and Eight), spending more time on areas where you scored poorly on the Diagnostic Test.

5. Take the two sample GMAT sections (Chapter Nine) and evaluate your results after completing each one.

6. Review again any areas you discover you are still weak in after you have evaluated your section results.

7. Take the two sample GMAT tests (Chapters 10 and 11) and evaluate your results after completing each one.

8. Review again any remaining weak areas.

Acknowledgments

The authors gratefully acknowledge the kindness of all organizations concerned with granting us permission to reprint passages, charts, and graphs. The copyright holders and publishers of quoted passages are listed on this and the following page.

Sources and permissions for charts and graphs appear on the appropriate pages throughout the book through the courtesy of the following organizations: the New York Times Company; U.S. Department of Labor; Dow Jones & Company, Inc.; U.S. Department of Health, Education, and Welfare; United Nations Economics Bulletin for Europe; Social Security Bulletin, Statistical Abstract of the U.S., U.S. Department of Commerce, Bureau of Economic Analysis; Federal Reserve Bank of New York; European Economic Community; U.S. Department of Commerce, Bureau of the Census; New York State Department of Labor; Federal Power Commission; U.S. Treasury Department; U.S. Bureau of Labor Statistics; Institute of Life Insurance; and the Statistical Abstract of Latin America.

PAGE 22, SAMPLE PASSAGE: Reprinted with permission of the author, Virgil Thomson.

PAGE 66, PASSAGE: Bob Doyle, "Is There a 10th Planet," *Cumberland Times-News,* September 14, 2005. © 2006 *Cumberland Times-News.* Reprinted with the permission of the *Cumberland Times-News.*

PAGE 68, PASSAGE: Michael Useem, Professor of Sociology, Boston University, "Government Patronage of Science and Art in America," from *The Production of Culture,* Richard A. Peterson, ed., © 1976 Sage Publications, Inc. Reprinted by permission of the author and the publisher.

PORTIONS OF THE "ESSAY WRITING REVIEW": George Ehrenhaft, *How to Prepare for SAT II: Writing,* © 1994 Barron's Educational Series, Inc., Hauppauge, N.Y.

PORTIONS OF THE "READING COMPREHENSION REVIEW": Eugene J. Farley, *Barron's How to Prepare for the High School Equivalency Examination Reading Interpretation Test,* © 1970 Barron's Educational Series, Inc., Hauppauge, N.Y.

PAGE 122, EXAMPLE: "Skye, Lonely Scottish Isle," *Newark Sunday News,* June 9, 1968, C 16, Sec. 2.

PAGE 124, EXAMPLE: David Gunter, "Kibbutz Life Growing Easier," *Newark News,* May 6, 1968, p. 5.

PAGE 129, EXAMPLE: Reprinted with permission from "Understanding Foreign Policy," by Saul K. Padover, *Public Affairs Pamphlet #280.* Copyright, Public Affairs Committee, Inc.

PAGES 133–134, EXERCISE B: Marina Gazzo and Catherine Browne, "Venice Rising," *Europe,* November–December, 1975, pp. 15–16. © The European Community, 1975.

PAGE 337, PASSAGE: The Economist Global Agenda, "A Darkening Mood Over Doha," *The Economist,* April 24, 2006. © 2006 *The Economist.* Reprinted with the permission of *The Economist.*

PAGE 340, PASSAGE: Benedict Carey, "Analyze These," *New York Times,* April 25, 2006. © 2006 *New York Times.* Reprinted with the permission of the New York Times Company.

PAGE 380, PASSAGE 1: From *Our Dynamic World: A Survey in Modern Geography by A. Joseph Wraight,* © 1966 by the author. Reproduced by permission of the publisher, Chilton Book Company, Radnor, Pennsylvania.

PAGES 382–383, PASSAGE 3: Jean Hollander, "Cops and Writers," Reprinted from *The American Scholar,* Volume 49, No. 2, Spring 1980. Copyright 1980 by the author.

PAGE 417, PASSAGE 1: *Improving Executive Development in the Federal Government,* copyright 1964 by the Committee for Economic Development.

PAGE 421, PASSAGE 1: "Open Admissions Assessed: The Example of The City University of New York, 1970–1975" by Irwin Polishook, Professor of History, Lehman College, CUNY. "Open Admissions Assessed" originally appeared in *Midstream* (April, 1976), © 1976, The Theodor Herzl Foundation.

PAGE 424, PASSAGE: "The Brains Business," *The Economist.* © 2006 *The Economist.* Reprinted with the permission of *The Economist.*

PAGES 445–482, BUSINESS SCHOOL BASICS: Eugene Miller and Neuman F. Pollack, *Guide to Graduate Business Schools,* 14th Edition. © 2005 Barron's Educational Series, Inc.

VARIOUS SENTENCE CORRECTION QUESTIONS (WITH EXPLAINED ANSWERS): Samuel C. Brownstein and Mitchel Weiner, *Barron's How to Prepare for College Entrance Examinations (SAT),* © 1980 Barron's Educational Series, Inc., Hauppauge, N.Y.; Sharon Green and Mitchel Weiner, *Barron's How to Prepare for the Test of Standard Written English,* © 1982 Barron's Educational Series, Inc., Hauppauge, N.Y.; Murray Rockowitz et al., *Barron's How to Prepare for the New High School Equivalency Examination (GED),* © 1979 Barron's Educational Series, Inc., Hauppauge, N.Y.

WHAT YOU NEED TO KNOW ABOUT THE COMPUTER-ADAPTIVE GMAT

An Introduction to the Computer-Adaptive GMAT

The Graduate Management Admission Test (GMAT) is no longer given in pencil and paper format (except in a few countries outside the United States). Instead, a computer-adaptive test (CAT) format is now used. This change in the test format means that previous test-taking strategies will have to be changed. The following sections explain how the computerized test works and how to prepare for it.

The following discussion centers on the purpose behind the Graduate Management Admission Test and answers basic questions about the general format and procedures used on the GMAT.

THE PURPOSE OF THE GMAT

The purpose of the GMAT is to measure your ability to think systematically and to employ the verbal and mathematical skills that you have acquired throughout your years of schooling. The types of questions that are used to test these abilities are discussed in the next chapter. It should be noted that the test does not aim to measure your knowledge of specific business or academic subjects. No specific business experience is necessary, nor will any specific academic subject area be covered. You are assumed to know basic algebra (but not calculus), geometry, and arithmetic, to know the basic conventions of standard written English, and to be able to write an analytical essay.

In effect, the GMAT provides business school admission officers with an objective measure of academic abilities to supplement subjective criteria used in the selection process, such as interviews, grades, and references. Suppose you are an average student in a college with high grading standards. Your overall grade average may be lower than that of a student from a college with lower grading standards. The GMAT allows you and the other student to be tested under similar conditions using the same grading standard. In this way, a more accurate picture of your all-around ability can be established.

WHERE TO APPLY

Unlike the pencil and paper GMAT exam which was scheduled on fixed dates four times a year, the Computer Adaptive Test may be taken three weeks per month, six days a week, ten hours a day at 400 testing centers in the United States and Canada and major cities throughout the world. The test-taker will be seated in a testing alcove with only a few others present at the same time. One may register for a test a few days before a preferred time. To schedule a test, simply call the ETS toll-free number 1-800-GMAT-NOW or go online at http://www.mba.com. Payment may be made by credit card, check, or money order. It is wise to schedule your exam early to ensure that the schools to which you are applying receive your scores in time.

Information about the exact dates of the exam, fees, testing locations, and a test registration form can be found in the "GMAT Bulletin of Information" for candidates published by ETS. You can obtain a copy by writing:

Graduate Management Admission Test
Educational Testing Service
P.O. Box 6103
Princeton, New Jersey 08541-6103
http://www.mba.com

WHAT IS A COMPUTER-ADAPTIVE TEST (CAT)?

In a computer-adaptive test, each question is shown on a personal computer screen one at a time. On the test, questions are of high, medium, and low difficulty. The first question on a test is of medium difficulty; the relative difficulty of the next question depends on your answer to the first question. If you answered correctly, the next question will be of greater difficulty. If your answer was incorrect, the next question will be less difficult, and so on. However, the choice of subsequent questions is not only based on whether the preceding answer was correct or incorrect, but also on the difficulty level of the preceding question, whether previous questions have covered a variety of question types, and specific test content. This procedure is repeated for each of your answers. In this way, the CAT adjusts questions to your ability.

The Computer-adaptive GMAT will have three parts: a writing section which consists of writing two essays, a quantitative test and a verbal test.

You will have 30 minutes to write each essay.

The quantitative test will be composed of Problem Solving and Data Sufficiency type questions. There will be 37 questions and you will have 75 minutes to finish this section.

The verbal test will be composed of Reading Comprehension, Critical Reasoning and Sentence Correction type questions. There will be 41 questions and you will have 75 minutes to finish this section.

There is an optional five-minute break between each section of the exam.

Before you start the exam you will be given time to become acquainted with the computer system. There is an interactive tutorial to help you practice your computer skills. You can try using the mouse and scrolling through text. You will be able to choose and confirm answers as well as use the word processor you will need to write your essays. Make sure you are thoroughly familiar with the system before you start the exam.

It is possible that your tests may contain some experimental questions. These questions may or may not be labeled experimental. You should do your best on any question that is not labeled experimental. Experimental questions are **not** counted in your scores.

In the CAT version of the GMAT once you enter and confirm your answer you **cannot** change the answer. You can't go back and work on previous questions if you finish a section early. Furthermore, you must answer each question before you can see the next question. (You will not be able to skip any questions.)

There are some pros and cons of the CAT compared to the previous paper and pencil version of the GMAT. Here is a list:

You've Answered the First Question: What's Next?

Suppose that you answered that first question correctly and then get a more difficult one that you also answer correctly and then an even harder one that you answer incorrectly. Will you get a lower score than say a candidate that answers the first question incorrectly and then gets an easier one that is answered correctly? No, because difficult questions are worth more points than easier ones. So, in the end, the mixture of questions that each candidate gets should be balanced to reflect his or her ability and subsequently their performance. There is little possibility that a candidate will have a higher score because he or she answered more easy questions correctly.

Pros and Cons of Computer-Adaptive Test

Pros	Cons
You can take the test at a time that is convenient for you throughout the year.	You cannot make notes on the computer screen and must rely only on scratch paper.
You may register for the test by phone, fax, online, or mail and pay with a credit card.	You cannot skip a question.
More personal — only a few people will be taking the test at the same time in individualized testing alcoves.	You cannot return to a question once you have confirmed your answer.
You know your score (verbal and quantitative) immediately after the test. Official complete scores are available after ten days	Those who have more experience using a word processor should have an advantage in using the terminal.
You may cancel scores immediately after the test by indicating your decision on the computer screen.	You cannot see all of the Reading Comprehension test, but must scroll. The same is true for graphs and charts.
A timer is available on screen so that you can better pace yourself.	

These rules apply to both the quantitative (problem solving and data sufficiency) and qualitative (reading comprehension, sentence correction, and critical reasoning) multiple-choice type questions. The Analytical Writing Assessment (AWA) will be written using the computer, but it will not be adaptive. Test-takers will write essays in response to two questions as was the case in the paper and pencil test. The overall quality of your thinking and writing will be evaluated by faculty members from a number of academic disciplines, including management. It will also be rated by an automated essay scoring system, developed by ETS, called an e-rater™. After extensive testing, the e-rater™ system was found to have a 92% agreement with human readers, which is about the same rate at which two human readers agree.

Another fact about the CAT is that questions cannot be skipped. You must answer the present question in order to proceed to the next one. This means that if you do not know the answer, you must guess (tips for guessing are given on page 8.) Answering a question means entering your choice by clicking the mouse next to the alternative you have chosen and then pressing the confirmation button by clicking the mouse on the "confirm" icon (see page 10). Once you have confirmed your answer, you cannot go back to check a previous question or change an answer.

What is the logic behind the no skipping of questions and no changing of answer policy? Suppose that you gave a wrong answer to a question. The next question will be an easier one—one that say, you answer correctly. If you were able to go back and change the previous wrong answer and this time get it right, you should have received an equally or more difficult question, rather than the easy question that was answered correctly and scored accordingly. Thus, if it were possible to change answers, the scoring system would be destroyed. Likewise, if question skipping were allowed, the system would have no basis for determining the difficulty level of the next question.

What Computer Skills Are Necessary?

Only basic computer skills are necessary for navigating the CAT. This means that you have to know how to use a mouse and how to scroll (navigate). You can download free test tutorials from www.mba.com. These will help you to review the basic skills of taking a computer-adaptive test, such as entering answers and accessing HELP. You should review these procedures before you arrive at the test center, because any time that you use to review HELP screens will mean less time for you to work on the test questions.

THE TEST FORMAT

The test format includes both multiple-choice verbal test questions: sentence correction, reading comprehension, and critical reasoning; and multiple-choice quantitative test questions: problem solving and data sufficiency. In the CAT, all verbal-type questions are mingled. The same is true for the two quantitative-type questions. In the former pencil and paper GMAT, each question type section was given separately. The total test time is approximately four hours including the two essay questions. A typical CAT is formatted as follows:

Question Type	Number of Questions	Time (Min)
Analytical Writing		
Analysis of an Issue	1 Topic	30
Analysis of an Argument	1 Topic	30
Optional break	Not relevant	5
Quantitative		
Problem Solving	19	
Data Sufficiency	18	75 (for all questions)
Optional break	Not relevant	5
Verbal		
Sentence Correction	15	
Reading Comprehension	15	
Critical Reasoning	11	75 (for all questions)
		Total: about 4 hours

In addition to the question types noted, a test may include identified and/or unidentified experimental sections. Identified experimental sections will usually be the last section of the exam. Unidentified sections can appear anywhere. However, answers (either correct or incorrect) will not affect your final score.

Note that aids such as hand-held calculators, watch calculators, pens, watch alarms, dictionaries, translators, electronic devices, beepers, will not be allowed in the testing room. You may not bring scratch paper to the test, but it will be handed out by the test administrator as needed. If you have some questions about procedures during the test, there is a HELP function that may be utilized. However, remember that the time spent with the HELP function will be at the expense of test time. Therefore, it is best to familiarize yourself with the computer procedures as much as possible before taking the test.

YOUR SCORES AND WHAT THEY MEAN

One benefit to the CAT test-takers is that unofficial scores on the verbal and quantitative parts of the test will be available upon completion. Official scores, including the AWA, will be mailed out within ten days. Scores are based on the number of questions answered correctly as well as performance on a particular type of question. Some correct answers to some questions are worth more than others because of different degrees of difficulty. Thus, a correct answer to a difficult question is worth more than a correct answer to an easy question. The total score ranges from 200 to 800.

In general, no particular score can be called good or bad, and no passing or failing grade has been established. Scores above 750 or below 250 are unusual. In recent years, about two thirds of all scores have fallen between 390 and 620, with the average about 530.

IMPORTANCE OF THE GMAT

Students often ask what is an adequate GMAT score. The answer is that every university and college requiring the GMAT sets its own requirements. Average scores throughout the United States are reported by the Educational Testing Service. For example, the average GMAT score of all test-takers in the United States during 2002–2003 was 524.

Average grades on the GMAT also differed by undergraduate major, with physics majors scoring 614, computer science majors 566, English majors 563, political science majors 543, and business majors 506.

Most college catalogs do not state what the minimum GMAT requirement is, but the annual reports of most MBA programs do note the average GMAT score of the last incoming student body. This is probably a good indication of the necessary ball-park figure for admission. However, obtaining a score somewhat below that figure does not mean that acceptance is not possible. First of all, it is an average figure. Some scored below, but were accepted. The GMAT is only one of a number of criteria for admission. Students who obtain a score below some required average may nevertheless make up for this by their undergraduate grade average or by writing a very good essay as part of the application process. In some cases, doing well in the personal interview with an admissions officer or other university representative may be just as, or even more, important. So, while scoring high on the GMAT is a desired goal and should be pursued with all the means possible, it is not the only requirement for admission to an MBA program. Before applying to a college or university, determine what criteria are considered for admission and how these criteria are ranked by order of importance. Directors of MBA programs, admissions officers, college catalogs, and annual reports should provide this information.

Your score on the GMAT is only one of several factors examined by admissions officers. Your undergraduate record, for example, is at least as important as your GMAT score. Thus, a low score does not mean that no school will accept you, nor does a high GMAT score guarantee acceptance at the school of your choice. However, since your score is one important factor, you should try to do as well as you can on the exam. Using this book should help you to maximize your score.

HOW TO PREPARE FOR THE CAT GMAT

You should now be aware of the purpose of the GMAT and have a general idea of the format of the CAT test. With this basic information, you are in a position to begin your study and review. The rest of this guide represents a study plan that will enable you to prepare for the GMAT. If used properly, it will help you diagnose your weak areas and take steps to remedy them.

Begin your preparation by becoming as familiar as possible with the various types of questions that appear on the exam. The analysis of typical GMAT questions in the next chapter is designed for this purpose. Test-taking tactics provide hints on how to approach the different types of questions.

Next, be familiar with the CAT system. Make sure you know how everything works (e.g., scrolling) before you start the exam. Pace is very important. Losing time because of unfamiliarity with the CAT is avoidable with practice using this manual and other tools.

When you feel you understand this material completely, take the Diagnostic Test that follows and evaluate your results. A low score in any area indicates that you should spend more time reviewing that particular material. Study the review section for that area until you feel you have mastered it and then take one of the sample GMAT tests. Continue the pattern until you are completely satisfied with your performance. For best results, try to simulate exam conditions as closely as possible when taking sample tests: no unscheduled breaks or interruptions, strict adherence to time limits, and no use of outside aids (with the exception of scratch paper).

TEST-TAKING STRATEGIES

1. **The first five or so questions count more than later questions.** Budget a little more time for these questions. You have about $1\frac{3}{4}$ minutes for each verbal question and 2 minutes for each quantitative question. So, be prepared to spend more time with the initial questions.

2. **Answer as many questions as possible.** While there is no minimum number to answer in order to get a score, your score will be lower if fewer questions are answered.

3. **If you are not sure, guess.** Unlike the former GMAT version, there is no penalty for a wrong answer, so if you are running out of time, guess. Also, since you have to give an answer in order to proceed to the next question, guessing may be necessary. For some tips see the Guessing section that follows.

4. **Pace yourself and be aware of remaining time.** Be aware of the number of questions and remaining time. How much time is left in a test section can be determined by pressing the time icon and a clock will appear on the upper left hand side of the screen.

5. **Confirm your answer only when you are confident that it is correct.** Remember, you cannot return to a previous question and you must confirm your answer in order to move on to the next question.

6. **Be careful about section exit and test quit commands.** Once you confirm a section exit command you cannot go back. Confirming the test quit command automatically ends the session with no chance of continuing.

GUESSING

Two elements should be considered in addressing the area of guessing. First, consider the way your score is determined by the Educational Testing Service, the administrators of the GMAT. If you do not answer a question, you cannot proceed to the next one. So, if you are stuck it helps to guess. Or, if you are near the end of a test section and time is running out, you have two options. You can guess the answers to questions that you are unsure of the correct answer, or you can quit the section when time runs out. As we pointed out before, it is best to spend more time with the first five questions and less time with the remaining ones. So, guessing becomes an important strategy when time is critical. The probability of selecting the correct answer by random guessing is 1 out of 5, or 0.20, which is rather low. However, suppose that you have had time to read the question and have been able to eliminate two answer alternatives, but are still unsure of the correct answer. Now, a random guess of the correct answer among the remaining alternatives has a probability 0.33. Obviously, if you are able to eliminate three alternatives, you then have a 50–50 chance of guessing the correct answer. Assuming that time has run out, guessing in this situation is a very low risk.

So, there is a difference between random and educated guessing. An educated guess occurs when you have eliminated three alternatives and now have a reasonable chance of selecting the correct answer. Elimination of three alternatives should be possible for most questions. Here are some examples of how to do this. The first example is a critical reasoning question:

EXAMPLE

The college tenure system provides long-term job security for established professors, but at the same time prevents younger instructors from entering the system. But instructors are familiar with current teaching material and therefore may provide students with a better education. Thus, it is a shame that many students are unable to be taught by instructors who cannot find employment because of the tenure system.

Which of the following is an assumption made in the argument above?

(A) Most tenured professors do not make an effort to provide quality education.
(B) Most instructors are against the tenure system.
(C) University students generally prefer to be taught by instructors.
(D) Instructors have received their graduate degrees more recently than professors.
(E) Tenured professors are not familiar with current teaching material.

In questions of this type, the assumption is usually one of the answer alternatives rather than part of the text. In any case, let us see how several alternatives may be readily eliminated. The fourth alternative (D), is true by definition, but is not even remotely a subject of the text, nor an assumption. Alternative (C) cannot be assumed; there is simply no evidence pointing in this direction. Likewise, there is no evidence for alternative (B). By process of elimination, alternatives (A) and (E) remain. Alternative (A), if true, would certainly buttress the claim that it is a shame that students cannot be taught by new instructors, rather than by tenured professors. But this assumes that instructors are better teachers than professors, either because professors do not make an effort to provide quality education (A) or because they are unfamiliar with up-to-date teaching material (E). So, both alternatives are plausible, and if we have to guess, we have a 50–50 chance of answering correctly. However, the claim above is that instructors are "familiar" with teaching material, but that professors are not familiar (E). So, (E) is the assumption made. The argument runs like this:

1. Instructors are familiar with teaching material and can thus provide students with a better education than professors.
2. The college tenure system . . . prevents instructors from entering the system.
3. Professors are not familiar with current teaching materials.
4. It is a shame for students that they cannot be taught by instructors.

The conclusion, "it is a shame that many students are unable to be taught by instructors" is buttressed by the addition of the premise (3) that professors are not familiar with current teaching materials.

Another example of how two or three alternatives may be quickly eliminated may be demonstrated by taking the reading comprehension passage concerning the "land bridge" on page 16 and question number 1 on page 17:

1. According to the passage, the major alternative to a U.S. land bridge is the

    (A) Panama Canal
    (B) Suez Canal
    (C) air-freight system
    (D) all-land route
    (E) military transport system

Alternative (C) may be quickly eliminated because it is not mentioned. Also (E), military transport system, can be eliminated because it is a user and not an alternative. An all-land route (D) is analogous to the U.S. land bridge, and so cannot be an alternative. So, three alternative answers have been quickly eliminated. The choice is between (A) or (B). If we read the passage carefully, we note that the Suez Canal (B) is not mentioned. However, the Panama Canal (A) is noted as the existing alternative to a land bridge.

MANEUVERING THE GMAT CAT PC SCREEN

While you will have the opportunity to try out the so-called "Testing Tools" of the CAT before taking the test, you will have an advantage if you are already familiar with them beforehand. These testing tools consist of a number of icons or commands by which you navigate the test. For the verbal and quantitative tests you will have a PC screen that looks like this:

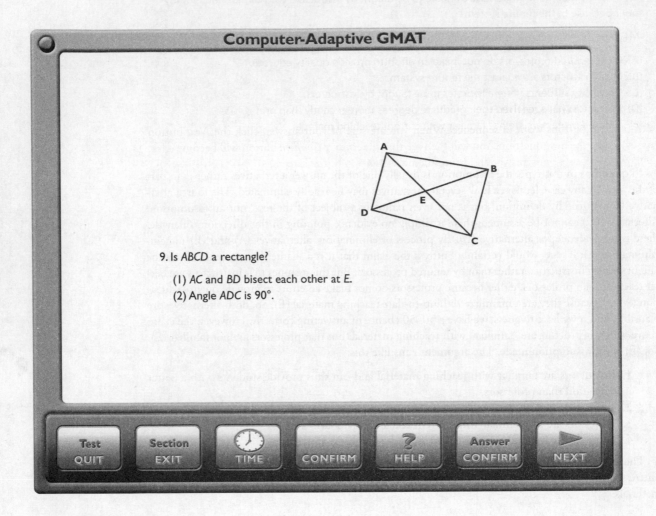

Test Quit

If you click this, you terminate the test. Only do this if you have completed the entire test.

Section Exit

Clicking this button terminates a test section and enables you to go on to the next test section. If you have used up all your time, the program will exit automatically. So, this button should be activated only if you have completed the section in less than the allotted time period. If you still have some time remaining and you click this button, you will be able to reverse your decision by pressing the "Return to Where I Was" command that appears on the bottom of the screen.

Time

Clicking this icon will show you how much time (shown in hours, minutes, and seconds) remains on the test. In any case, the time will appear in a flashing mode when your allotted time is nearly up.

? Help

Clicking this button will activate the help function. The help function contains directions for the question you are working on, directions for the section you are working on, general directions, how to scroll, and information about the testing tools. When you want to exit the help function, click the "Return to Where I Was" tool with the mouse.

Next and Answer Confirm

Both of these buttons work in sequence. When you are sure of your answer, click the *Next* button to move on to the next question. You will then see that the *Answer Confirm* button will become dark. Clicking it will save your answer and bring the next question to the screen.

You should also practice the word processing tools needed for the Analytical Writing Assessment (AWA). They are similar to those used on typical word processing programs such as Word for Windows or WordPerfect. The typing keys available are as follows:

Page up — moves the cursor up one page.

Page down — moves the cursor down one page.

Backspace — removes the text to the left of the cursor.

Delete — removes text to the right of the cursor.

Home — moves the cursor to the beginning of a line.

End — moves the cursor to the end of a line.

Arrows —moves the cursor up, down, left and right.

Enter — moves the cursor to the beginning of the next line.

There are also *Cut*, *Paste*, and *Undo* functions.

AFTER YOU TAKE THE EXAM

You can see your score on the verbal and quantitative parts of the exam immediately after the test. Official scores, including the AWA, will arrive by mail within approximately ten days.

You may repeat the test once per calendar month. However, if you repeat the test, your scores from that and the two most recent previous test results will be sent to all institutions you designate as score recipients. Many schools average your scores if you take the test more than once. So unless there is a reason to expect a substantial improvement in your score, it usually is *not* worthwhile to retake the exam.

You can cancel your scores if you act *before* leaving the test center. If you wish to cancel your scores, you must indicate this on the computer screen after completing the test. If you cancel your scores, the fact that you took the test will be reported to all the places you designated as score recipients. Thus, it is generally not advantageous to cancel your scores unless there is reason to believe that you have done substantially worse on the test than you would if you took the test again; for example, if you became ill while taking the exam. Once a score is canceled from your record it cannot be put back on your record or reported at a later date.

THE SELF-SCORING TABLES

The Self-Scoring Tables for each sample test in this guide can be used as a means of evaluating your weaknesses in particular subject areas and should help you plan your study program most effectively.

After completing a sample test, turn to the Answers section which immediately follows each test. Determine the number of *correct* answers you had for each section. This is your correct score for that section. Now turn to the section Evaluating Your Score, which follows the Answers Explained section of each test. Record your scores in the appropriate score boxes in the Self-Scoring Table as shown below.

Self-Scoring Table

Section	Score	Rating
Quantitative	13	Poor
Verbal	27	Good

Use the Rating scale to find your rating for each section.

Typical GMAT Questions and How to Approach Them

A logical first step in preparing for the GMAT is to become as familiar as possible with the types of questions that usually appear on this exam. The following analysis of typical GMAT questions explains the purpose behind each type and the best method for answering it. Tactics for handling each of the different types of questions are also given. These tactics provide practical tools and advice to help you prepare for the exam and take it more efficiently. Samples of the questions with a discussion of their answers are also included. More detailed discussions and reviews for each section of the test are presented in the Correct Your Weaknesses part of this book.

ANALYTICAL WRITING ASSESSMENT

The Analytical Writing Assessment section is designed to assess your ability to think critically and to communicate complex ideas. The writing task consists of two sections that require you to examine the composition of an issue, take a position on the basis of the details of the issue, and present a critique of the conclusion derived from a specific way of thinking. The issues are taken from topics of general interest related to business or to other subjects. There is no presumption of any specific knowledge about business or other areas.

Types of Analytical Writing Assessment Tasks

There are two types of Analytical Writing Assessment tasks: *Analysis of an Issue* and *Analysis of an Argument*. Following is an example of each:

EXAMPLE

Analysis of an Issue

Some analysts complain that consumers do not receive enough information to make rational purchase decisions. When the consumer is unable to make rational decisions, the economy suffers. Behavioral scientists contend that emotional and psychological factors play an important role in the satisfaction of consumer wants and that the measurable quantitative information being proposed by others is not as relevant for consumer decision-making as purported to be.

Which do you find more convincing: the complaint of the analysts or the contention of the behavioral scientists? State your position using relevant reasons and examples from your own experience, observation, or reading.

Test-Taking Tactics

1. **Identify the issue or argument.**   For additional practice doing this, read the Critical Reasoning Review on pages 159–171.

   In the example, the claim or conclusion is that the economy suffers when consumers cannot make rational decisions. Consumers cannot make rational decisions whenever information is lacking. The counter view is that consumer decision-making is based more on emotion than on rational reasoning. If that is the case, then information is not so important.

2. **Outline your ideas.**   You are asked to take sides. If you believe that consumers make decisions mainly on a rational basis, you will have to support your view by giving examples based on experience or on the facts that you have acquired from study or reading. You must state why you support this view and not the other. Do you have any facts on the issue? If so, list them along with examples. If you do not have facts, you will need to deal with the issue inferentially—by reasoning inductively. Here, experience and observation will be important to buttress your claims.

   Another possibility in this case is that consumer decision-making depends on the sort of product. When it comes to purchasing a house or making a similar capital investment, the decision is mainly rational, and so it depends on a good deal of information. Most consumer purchases, however, are not of this kind; for example, clothing, food, leisure activities—whose motivation is largely emotional. Thus, for most purchases, a lot of information is not necessary, and so the economy does not suffer as is claimed.

EXAMPLE

Analysis of an Argument

The computerized water-irrigation system to be installed by farmers will prevent crops from drying out. The soil moisture is measured by sensors in the ground that send signals back to the irrigation control system. On the basis of this information, the system automatically regulates the amount and time of irrigation.

Discuss how logically persuasive you find this argument. In presenting your point of view, analyze the sort of reasoning used and its supporting evidence. In addition, state what further evidence, if any, would make the argument more sound and convincing or would make you better able to evaluate its conclusion.

Test-Taking Tactics

1. **Identify the parts of the argument.**   For additional practice doing this, read the Critical Reasoning Review on pages 159–171.

2. **State how convincing (or unconvincing) you find the argument.**   The persuasiveness of an argument depends on its logic; that is, on whether the conclusion follows from the evidence presented. You are also asked to discuss what would make the argument more sound and persuasive or would help to evaluate its conclusion. To make an argument more sound, it is necessary to provide more evidence that will buttress the conclusion.

   In the example, the conclusion is found in the first sentence: the irrigation system will prevent crops from drying out. What evidence is given that the irrigation system will indeed perform this task? Overall, the argument is sound and convincing, assuming that proper irrigation is all that is needed to keep crops from drying out. What then could strengthen the conclusion? Evidence that systems similar to the one described are already in place and working. This last point is important because we have no evidence about the reliability of the system. Moreover, there may be a question of cost-effectiveness. Will farmers be willing to adopt such a system? If evidence of these factors could be provided, the conclusion would be strengthened.

READING COMPREHENSION

The Reading Comprehension questions test your ability to analyze written information and include passages from the humanities, the social sciences, and the physical and biological sciences. The typical Reading Comprehension portion of a verbal section consists of three passages of approximately 350 words with a total of approximately 15 questions. You will be allowed to scroll through the passages when answering the questions. However, many of the questions may be based on what is *implied* in the passages, rather than on what is explicitly stated. Your ability to draw inferences from the material is critical to successfully completing this section. You are to select the best answer from five alternatives.

Major Types of Reading Comprehension Questions

Reading comprehension questions usually fall into several general categories. In most questions, you will be asked about one of the following:

Main Idea

In this type of question you may be asked about the main idea or theme of the passage, about a possible title, or about the author's primary objective. Usually the main idea refers to the passage as a whole, not to some segment or part of the passage. The main idea is typically (but not always) found in the first paragraph. It will be a statement that gives the overall theme of the passage. In many cases, it will be in the form of an argument, including a premise and conclusion. (For the identification of the structure of an argument, see the Critical Reasoning Review later in this book.)

A frequent question on Reading Comprehension tests asks you to select the title or theme that best summarizes the passage.

EXAMPLE

Government policy in Frieland has traditionally favored foreign investment. Leaders of all political parties have been virtually unanimous in their belief that foreign investment in Frieland would contribute to speeding that country's economic development, a major
Line priority of both the ruling coalition and opposition parties. Of special interest to the gov-
(5) ernment were those industries that exported a significant share of their total output. Since Frieland had a relatively small population, there was a limit to the amount of goods that could be produced for the local market. Also, the government did not want to encourage foreign investors to compete with local industry, even though new industries might alleviate the already high unemployment rate.

1. The best possible title of the passage is

   (A) Government Policy in Frieland.
   (B) How to Provide Employment.
   (C) Attracting Foreign Investment.
   (D) The Economics of Developing Countries.
   (E) Foreign Investment and Economic Development.

All of the above alternatives can be found in the passage, with the exception of (D)—we don't know if Frieland is a developing country. However, note that the words "foreign investment" are mentioned three times in the passage, and in lines 5–6 it is linked with economic development. Clearly then, the main idea or subject is foreign investment, and the appropriate answer is (E).

Additional questions may ask you to identify the author's purpose in writing the passage.

EXAMPLE

2. It can be concluded that the aim of the author is to

(A) increase foreign investment.
(B) protect local industry from foreign competition.
(C) increase unemployment benefits for workers.
(D) develop a theory of foreign investment.
(E) increase the indigenous population of Frieland.

The most appropriate answer to the above question is (A). The author gives some of the reasons and under what conditions foreign investment would be beneficial to Frieland.

Supporting Ideas

In this type of question, you may be asked about the idea expressed in one part of the passage, rather than about the passage as a whole. Questions of this type test your ability to distinguish between the main idea and those themes that support it, some of which may be implicit or implied rather than explicitly stated.

EXAMPLE

Some economists believe that the United States can be utilized as a "land bridge" for the shipment of containerized cargo between Europe and the Far East. Under the land-bridge concept, containerized freight traveling between Europe Line and the Far East would be
(Line)
(5) shipped by ocean carrier to the United States East Coast, unloaded and placed on special railway flatcars, and shipped via railroad to a West Coast port. At this port, the containers would then be loaded on ships bound to a Far East port of entry. This procedure would be reversed for material traveling in the opposite direction. Thus, a land transportation system would be substituted for marine transportation during part of the movement of goods between Europe and the Far East.
(10)   If a land-bridge system of shipment were deemed feasible and competitive with alternative methods, it would open a completely new market for both United States steamship lines and railroads. At present, foreign lines carry all Far East-Europe freight. American carriers get none of this trade, and the all-water route excludes the railroads.
        The system established by a land bridge could also serve to handle goods now being
(15) shipped between the United States West Coast and Europe, or goods shipped between the Far East and the United States Gulf and East Coasts. Currently, there are 20 foreign lines carrying West Coast freight to Europe via the Panama Canal, but not one United States line. Thus, in addition to the land bridge getting this new business for the railroads, it also gives the United States East Coast ships an opportunity to compete for this trade.
(20)   While this method of shipment will probably not add to the labor requirements at East and West Coast piers, it does have the potential of absorbing some of the jobs that the containerization of current cargo has eliminated or could eliminate. Thus, the possibility of creating new jobs for longshoremen is not an expected benefit of such a system, but it will most certainly create other labor requirements. The land-bridge concept has the
(25) potential of offering new job openings for United States railway workers and seamen. In addition, there would be expansion of labor requirements for people in the shipbuilding and container manufacturing business.
        By making United States rail transportation an export service, the land-bridge system would have a favorable effect on our balance of payments.

The main idea in this passage is that the United States may be utilized as a land bridge for the shipment of containerized cargo between Europe and the Far East. This is evidenced by the first sentence in the passage. Supporting ideas would include any facts or arguments that buttress the main idea. A number of these may be found in the passage:

1. The opening of a new market. (paragraph 2)
2. Obtaining new business. (paragraph 3)
3. Creating labor requirements. (paragraph 4)

EXAMPLE

1. According to the passage, if a land-bridge system were feasible, it would

   (A) create employment in the bridge-building industry
   (B) decrease the amount of air freight
   (C) create a new market for steamship lines and railroads
   (D) make Amerian railroads more efficient
   (E) increase foreign trade

2. The author implies that which of the following would be provided employment by the development of a land bridge?

   I. Dock workers
   II. U.S. railway workers
   III. U.S. sailors

   (A) I only
   (B) III only
   (C) I and II only
   (D) II and III only
   (E) I, II, and III

The answer to question 1 is alternative (C), which refers to supporting idea (1) listed above and summarized in paragraph 2 of the passage. A land bridge would create a new market for U.S. steamship lines and railroads.

Question 2 is developed from an idea *implied* in the passage. Answer choice (D) is correct, because, in paragraph 4, it is argued that new jobs will be created for U.S. railway workers and sailors, but not for dock workers.

Drawing Inferences

Questions of this sort ask about ideas that are not explicitly stated in a passage. These questions refer to meanings *implied* by the author based on information given in the passage. Typical questions are:

1. The author feels (believes) that . . .
2. In reference to (event) it may be inferred that . . .

EXAMPLE

Refer to the land bridge passage on page 16.

Which of the following might least benefit from a land bridge?

(A) U.S. railway workers.
(B) U.S. sailors.
(C) U.S. scheduled shipping lines.
(D) U.S. unscheduled shipping lines.
(E) U.S. government.

The author specifically gives reasons why each of the factors mentioned in all alternative answers might benefit from a land bridge. However, the author states in the last paragraph that some one half of the total income of scheduled shipping lines is subsidized by the government. A land bridge would provide increased business for these lines, enabling the government to shift subsidies from scheduled to unscheduled lines. Thus, it may be inferred that the increased traffic will replace subsidized income. Therefore, scheduled shipping lines might *least* benefit from the land bridge, and answer choice (C) is correct.

Specific Details

In this type of question you may be asked about specific facts or details the author has stated explicitly in the passage. This sort of question may take the following forms:

1. Which of the following statements is mentioned by the author?
2. All of the following are given as reasons for (   ) except:
3. The author argues that . . .

EXAMPLE

Refer to the land bridge passage on page 16.

1. According to the passage, the major alternative to a U.S. land bridge is the

   (A) Panama Canal
   (B) Suez Canal
   (C) air-freight system
   (D) all-land route
   (E) military transport system

2. The passage states that a land bridge would improve United States

   (A) foreign trade
   (B) balance of payments
   (C) railroad industry
   (D) international relations
   (E) gold reserves

3. A land bridge would not

   (A) aid U.S. steamship lines
   (B) handle goods shipped between Europe and the Far East
   (C) create new jobs for dock workers
   (D) supply new business for U.S. railroads
   (E) create business for unscheduled shipping lines

The answer to specific detail questions may always be found in the passage. These questions do not deal with implications or inferences. The answer to question 1 above is (A); paragraph 3 discusses use of the Panama Canal as a route for freight lines. The answer to question 2 is (B), which is given in paragraph 5. The answer to question 3 is (C); in paragraph 4, it is specifically stated that dock workers would not benefit from a land bridge.

Applying Information from the Passage to Other Situations

These questions ask you to make an analogy between a situation described in the passage and a similar situation or event listed in the question. Unlike other types of questions, these describe situations *not* given in the passage, but rather those that are analogous to those in the passage. In order to answer a question of this kind, you must be able to draw a parallel between the situation in the question and its counterpart in the passage.

EXAMPLE

The Danes are widely renowned for their business orientation, which is reflected in their export promotion policies. Without any raw materials of their own, except for agricultural produce, the Danes obtain a third of their GNP from their export trade. This magnitude
Line has been achieved only through a thorough exploitation of export potential and the
(5) implementation of a wide range of promotional activities. The latter emphasize the practical rather than the theoretical, and actual business encounters rather than such indirect, and previously popular, means as cultural events and Danish weeks.

1. Which of the following countries should succeed in exporting?

   (A) Countries without domestic raw materials.
   (B) Countries with a growing GNP.
   (C) Countries with a practical approach to business.
   (D) Countries with a thoroughly produced and diverse promotional campaign.
   (E) Countries with some export potential based on a wide range of products.

This question asks you to project the Danish experience to similar events in other countries. The analogy, of course, is "what helped the Danes to export will help other countries as well." And what helped the Danes in this case was the "implementation of a wide range of promotional activities." The correct answer is (D). Note that you were not asked to comment on the validity of the analogy, but only to identify the parallel case.

Tone or Attitude of the Passage

These questions concentrate on the author's style, attitude, or mood. In order to determine this attitude, look for key words, such as adjectives that reveal if the author is "pessimistic," "critical," "supportive," or "objective" about an event, idea, or situation in the passage.

Typical questions are:

1. For what audience is the passage intended?

2. The passage indicates that the author expresses a feeling of

   (A) Hope
   (B) Confidence
   (C) Enthusiasm
   (D) Instability
   (E) Pleasure

3. It can be concluded that the author of the passage is

(A) sympathetic to John Doe's ideas
(B) uncritical of John Doe's interpretation of history
(C) politically conservative
(D) a believer in mysticism
(E) a political dilettante

Technique Used by the Author in the Passage

A reader can detect certain techniques used by authors, depending on the subject matter of the material.

If the subject matter of the passage is from the *social studies*, authors tend to

• make comparisons ("The ABC company uses a production process that can be likened to. . .")
• describe cause and effect relationships ("The development of the harbor can be attributed to. . .")
• opinionate or reason ("The author belongs to which of the following schools of thought?")

If the subject matter is from the *sciences,* writers deal with

• problem solving ("Serious unemployment leads labor groups to demand . . .")
• cause and effect ("Government investment in industry should result in . . .")
• classification of things and events ("According to the passage, the waves occur most frequently in the area of . . .")
• experimentation ("Given present wave tracking systems, scientists can forecast all of the following except:")

If the subject matter is *literature*, authors tend to

• create moods ("Which of the following best describes the author's tone in the passage?")
• narrate events ("The author's treatment of the topic can be best described as . . .")
• describe settings and characters ("The main character is a person attempting to . . .")

The Logical Structure of the Passage

These types of questions test your understanding of the overall meaning, logic, or organization of a passage. You may be asked how several ideas in a passage are interrelated or how a passage is constructed, classifies, compares, describes events, or situations. You may be asked about the strengths or weaknesses of the argument the author is making, to identify assumptions, or to evaluate counterarguments.

Typical questions are:

1. John Doe's judgment that he failed was based on an assumption. Which of the following could have served as that assumption?

2. Which of the following, if true, weaken the above argument?

3. If the statement in the passage is true, which of the following must also be true?

4. Which of the following conclusions can be drawn from the passage?

Determining the Meaning of Words from the Context

When a question asks for the meaning of a word, it can usually be deduced from the context of the passage. Remember, you are not required to know the meaning of technical or foreign words.

EXAMPLE

During the 1980 campaign to clean the streets of undesirables and criminal elements, a force of 10,000 special police was used to maintain order. Nevertheless, many of the hunted crime figures fought back with live weapons and the streets looked like a battle-
Line   field. Almost as many policemen were injured as criminals. This year's *aktion* will have to
(5)   be better planned.

1. The planned *aktion* can be described as a

    (A) police offensive
    (B) political campaign
    (C) battle
    (D) law and order
    (E) none of the above.

The passage tells us that that this year's *aktion* will have to be planned better. From this, we know that it is being compared to something that happened before, which in the passage was during 1980. That was the campaign to clean the streets. Therefore, the best answer choice is (A) and we know that the meaning of *aktion* is the police offensive described in the passage.

Test-Taking Tactics

1. **Answer passages with familiar subject matter first.** You may encounter a passage that contains familiar material, perhaps subjects you have studied or read. You should be able to do better on these or at least read the passage more quickly. However, even though you have some familiarity with the subject of a passage, do not let your knowledge influence your choice of answer alternatives. You must answer the questions only on what is written or implied in the passage.

2. **Read the question first, then the passage.** Reading the question first enables you to identify the question *type*. However, do not read the answer alternatives at this time. If you are familiar with the question type, such as identifying a main idea or drawing inferences, you know what to look for in the passage. After you know the question type, carefully read the passage.

   Read as quickly as you can, but not in haste. Each Reading Comprehension passage contains about 500 words, so even if you read at a medium rate of 300 words a minute, you will read the passages in approximately 2 minutes, leaving 23 minutes for answering the questions, or approximately 1.5 minutes per question.

   If the question asks you to identify the main idea, remember that often it will be found in the opening sentences or in the summary part of the passage. In order to identify the main idea, first determine the object, person, or thing that is the subject of the passage. Ask yourself: "What is the main point the author is making?"

3. **Read all the answer alternatives.** Read *all* the answer choices. Never assume you have found the correct answer until you have considered all the alternatives. Choose the best possible answer on the basis of what is written in the passage and not on your own knowledge from other sources.

4. **Learn to identify the major question types.** Before taking a Reading Comprehension test, make sure that you are thoroughly familiar with the major question types. This will save you time on the test and increase your effectiveness in choosing the correct answer. Time will be saved because you will know in advance what to look for and how to read the passage. You will be more effective because you will immediately know what reading tactic to apply. To become familiar with the various question types be sure to read the "Major Types of Reading Comprehension Questions" earlier in this chapter.

Sample Passage and Questions

The following passage will give you an idea of the format of the Reading Comprehension section. Read the passage through and then answer the questions, making sure to leave yourself enough time to complete them all.

TIME: 10 minutes

Political theories have, in fact, very little more to do with musical creation than electronics theories have. Both merely determine methods of distribution. The exploitation of these methods is subject to political regulation and is quite rigidly regulated in many countries.

Line
(5)
The revolutionary parties, both in Russia and elsewhere, have tried to turn composers on to supposedly revolutionary subject-matter. The net result for either art or revolution has not been very important. Neither has official fascist music accomplished much either for music or for Italy or Germany.

Political party-influence on music is just censorship anyway. Performances can be forbidden and composers disciplined for what they write, but the creative stimulus comes from else-
(10) where. Nothing really "inspires" an author but money or food or love.

That persons or parties subventioning musical uses should wish to retain veto power over the works used is not at all surprising. That our political masters (or our representatives) should exercise a certain negative authority, a censorship, over the exploitation of works whose content they consider dangerous to public welfare is also in no way novel or surprising. But that
(15) such political executives should think to turn the musical profession into a college of political theorists or a bunch of hired propagandists is naïve of them. Our musical civilization is older than any political party. We can deal on terms of intellectual equality with acoustical engineers, with architects, with poets, painters, and historians, even with the Roman clergy if necessary. We cannot be expected to take very seriously the inspirational dictates of persons or of groups
(20) who think they can pay us to get emotional about ideas. They can pay us to get emotional all right. Anybody can. Nothing is so emotion-producing as money. But emotions are factual; they are not generated by ideas. On the contrary, ideas are generated by emotions; and emotions, in turn, are visceral states produced directly by facts like money and food and sexual intercourse. To have any inspirational quality there must be present facts or immediate anticipations, not
(25) pie-in-the-sky.

Now pie-in-the-sky has its virtues as a political ideal, I presume. Certainly most men want to work for an eventual common good. I simply want to make it quite clear that ideals about the common good (not to speak of mere political necessity) are not very stimulating subject-matter for music. They don't produce visceral movements the way facts do. It is notorious
(30) that musical descriptions of hell, which is something we can all imagine, are more varied and vigorous than the placid banalities that even the best composers have used to describe heaven; and that all composers do better on really present matters than on either: matters like love and hatred and hunting and war and dancing around and around.

The moral of all this is that the vetoing of objective subject-matter is as far as political
(35) stimulation or censorship can go in advance. Style is personal and emotional, not political at all. And form or design, which is impersonal, is not subject to any political differences of opinion.

1. The author is making a statement defending

   I. intellectual freedom
  II. the apolitical stance of most musicians
 III. emotional honesty

  (A) I only
  (B) II only
  (C) I and II only
  (D) I and III only
  (E) I, II, and III

2. The tone of the author in the passage is

   (A) exacting
   (B) pessimistic
   (C) critical
   (D) optimistic
   (E) fatalistic

3. The author's reaction to political influence on music is one of

   (A) surprise
   (B) disbelief
   (C) resignation
   (D) deference
   (E) rancor

4. According to the author, political attempts to control the subject matter of music

   (A) will be resisted by artists wherever they are made
   (B) may succeed in censoring but not in inspiring musical works
   (C) will succeed only if the eventual goal is the common good
   (D) are less effective than the indirect use of social and economic pressure
   (E) have profoundly influenced the course of modern musical history

5. The author refers to "musical descriptions of hell" (line 30) to make the point that

   (A) musical inspiration depends on the degree to which the composer's imagination is stimu-
       lated by his subject
   (B) composers are better at evoking negative emotions and ideas than positive ones
   (C) music is basically unsuited to a role in support of political tyranny
   (D) religious doctrines have inspired numerous musical compositions
   (E) political ideals are a basic motivating force for most contemporary composers

6. The author implies that political doctrines usually fail to generate artistic creativity because
   they are too

   (A) naïve
   (B) abstract
   (C) rigidly controlled
   (D) concrete
   (E) ambiguous

Answers

   1. (**D**)   3. (**C**)   5. (**A**)
   2. (**C**)   4. (**B**)   6. (**B**)

Analysis

1. (**D**) The author is arguing that musicians will not conform to any control over their creativity. Thus, they want to be intellectually free and emotionally honest. It does not mean that
   they could not be active in politics (apolitical).
2. (**C**) The author is critical of attempts to censor the arts, especially music.
3. (**C**) The author does not find censorship surprising (lines 11–12), nor does he take it seriously
   (lines 19–21). He is resigned to attempts at censorship, although he does not believe it can
   inspire creativity.
4. (**B**) See paragraph 2.

5. **(A)** See lines 30–32.
6. **(B)** See paragraph 4, in which the author states that "ideals" do not inspire music as "facts" do; and also see lines 9–10 and 24–25.

Now that you have reviewed the answers, look at the same passage marked with cues to the major question types.

MI Political theories have, in fact, very little more to do with musical creation than electronics theories have. Both merely determine methods of distribution. The exploitation of these methods is subject to political regulation and is quite rigidly regulated in many countries.

Line The revolutionary parties, both in Russia and elsewhere, have tried to turn composers on to

(5) supposedly revolutionary subject-matter. The (net result) for either art or revolution has not been very important. Neither has official fascist music accomplished much either for music or for Italy or Germany.

SI <u>Political</u> party-influence on music is just censorship anyway. Performances can be forbidden and composers disciplined for what they write, but the creative stimulus comes from else-

(10) where. Nothing really "inspires" an author but money or food or love.

SD (That) persons or parties subventioning musical uses should wish to retain veto power over the

SI works used is not at all surprising. (That) our <u>political masters</u> (or our representatives) should exercise a certain negative authority, a censorship, over the exploitation of works whose con-

SI tent they consider dangerous to public welfare is also in no way novel or surprising. (But that)

(15) such <u>political executives</u> should think to turn the musical profession into a college of <u>political theorists</u> or a bunch of hired propagandists is naïve of them. Our musical civilization is older than any <u>political party</u>. We can deal on terms of intellectual equality with acoustical engineers, with architects, with poets, painters, and historians, even with the Roman clergy if necessary. We cannot be expected to take very seriously the inspirational dictates of persons

(20) or of groups who think they can pay us to get <u>emotional about</u> ideas. They can pay us to get <u>emotional</u> all right. Anybody can. Nothing is so <u>emotion-producing</u> as money. (But) emotions are factual; they are not generated by ideas. (On the contrary,) ideas are generated <u>by emotions</u>; and <u>emotions, in turn</u>, are visceral states produced directly by facts like money and food and sexual intercourse. To have any inspirational quality there must be present facts or immedi-

(25) ate anticipations, not pie-in-the-sky.

SI (Now) pie-in-the-sky has its virtues as a political ideal, I presume. Certainly most men want

SI to work for an eventual common good. I simply want to make it quite clear that ideals about the common good (not to speak of mere political necessity) are not very stimulating subject-matter for music. They don't produce visceral movements the way facts do. It is notorious

(30) that musical descriptions of hell, which is something we can all imagine, are more varied and

SI vigorous than the placid banalities that even the best composers have used to describe heaven; and that all composers do better on really present matters than on either: matters like love and hatred and hunting and war and dancing around and around.

   (The moral) of all this is that the vetoing of <u>objective subject</u>-matter is as far as <u>political stim-</u>

(35) <u>ulation</u> or censorship can go in advance. Style is <u>personal and emotional, not political</u> at all. And form or design, which is impersonal, is not subject to any <u>political differences</u> of opinion.

Note the marked passage above. Cue words have been circled, and major question types have been marked in the margins. For example, in the first paragraph the cue words "net result" have been circled. These words refer to the sentences above and to the main idea (MI)—found in the first sentence—that politics and the arts are foreign to each other and that political regulation of music and the arts does nothing for them.

In the second paragraph there are a supporting idea (SI) and a specific detail (SD). The word "that," which appears three times at the beginning of the third paragraph, signals that a statement is to be made. The first two introduce a supporting idea to the effect that it is not surprising to find censorship of artistic works considered to be dangerous to a (totalitarian) state. The "But" before the third "that" signals a different thought: that while censorship may be applied, it will not politicize the musical profession. A second "But" and the phrase "On the contrary" signal that the following ideas or details present a contrasting argument to what was previously presented.

The word "Now" at the beginning of the fourth paragraph clues us to the introduction of another idea, namely, that inspiration, contrary to political ideals, is based on the happenings of everyday life and not on theory.

The cue word "moral" in the last paragraph signals a summing up or a conclusion. The conclusion of the passage is that, while censorship of objective subject matter is possible, the arts cannot be politicized.

Since the main idea is concerned with the politicizing of the arts, the word "political" was underlined every time it appeared. Since musical or artistic creation is also a subject of the passage, the word "emotional" was underlined. As can be seen from the marked passage, underlining was done very sparingly.

Looking now at the passage as a whole, we can see that the first paragraph contains the main idea, the second, third, and fourth paragraphs contain supporting ideas and details buttressing (or, in other passages, sometimes negating) the main idea, while the last paragraph sums up and gives a conclusion. This is a typical structure of a Reading Comprehension passage. You will find that questions will usually follow this order.

SENTENCE CORRECTION

The Sentence Correction part of the Verbal section tests your understanding of the basic rules of English grammar and usage. To succeed on these questions, you need a command of sentence structure including tense and mood, subject and verb agreement, proper case, parallel structure, and other basics. No attempt is made to test for punctuation, spelling, or capitalization.

In the Sentence Correction part of the section you will be given sentences in which all or part of the sentence is underlined. You will then be asked to choose the best phrasing of the underlined part from five alternatives. (A) will always be the original phrasing.

Test-Taking Tactics

1. **Remember that any error in the sentence must be in the underlined part.** Do not look for errors in the rest of the sentence.

2. **If you determine that there is an error in the underlined part of the sentence, immediately eliminate answer choice (A),** which always repeats the wording of the original sentence. Also eliminate any other answer alternatives that repeat the specific error. Then, concentrate on the remaining answer alternatives to choose your answer.

3. **Do not choose as an answer any alternative that changes the meaning of the original sentence.**

4. **Determine if the parts of the sentence are linked logically.** Are the clauses of a sentence equal ("and," "or," etc.) or is one clause subordinate to another ("because," "since," "who," etc.)?

5. **Look at the changes made in the answer alternatives.** This will tell you what specific error or usage problem is being tested. This can be particularly helpful if you know that there is an error in the original sentence—your ear tells you the sentence is wrong—but you cannot pinpoint the error. Noticing what you have to choose between will help you identify the error and then select what you think is correct.

6. **Be aware of the common grammar and usage errors tested on the GMAT.** Among the most common errors are errors in verb tense and formation and errors in the use of infinitives and gerunds in verb complements; errors in pronoun case and agreement with subject-object; errors in use of adjectives and adverbs, especially after verbs of sense; errors in comparatives, connectors, parallel construction, and unnecessary modifiers.

   There are also commonly confused words—for example, affect and effect, afflict and inflict, prescribe and proscribe. Be sure you know the meaning and spelling of these words and check that they are used correctly in the sentence.

Chapter Six—Sentence Correction Review—reviews those errors in grammar and usage commonly found on the GMAT. Examples of incorrect and correct sentences are given and a list of frequently misused words and prepositional idioms is provided.

Sample Question

Since the advent of cable television, at the beginning of <u>this decade, the video industry took</u> a giant stride forward in this country.

(A) this decade, the video industry took
(B) this decade, the video industry had taken
(C) this decade, the video industry has taken
(D) this decade saw the video industry taking
(E) the decade that let the video industry take

Answer

(**C**)

Analysis

The phrase "Since the advent . . ." demands a verb in the present perfect form; thus, *has taken*, not *took*, is correct. Choice (E) changes the meaning of the original sentence.

CRITICAL REASONING

The Critical Reasoning part of the Verbal section is designed to test your ability to evaluate an assumption, inference, or argument. Each question consists of a short statement followed by a question or assumption about the statement. Each question or assumption has five possible answers. Your task is to evaluate each of the five possible choices and select the best one.

Types of Critical Reasoning Questions

There are a number of different question types.

Inference or Assumption

These questions test your ability to evaluate an assumption, inference, or argument. You will be given a statement, position, argument, or fact and will be asked to identify a conclusion or claim and the premise on which it is based.

EXAMPLE

Four years ago the government introduced the Youth Training Program to guarantee teenagers leaving school an alternative to the dole. Today, over 150,000 16- and 17-year-olds are still signing on for unemployment benefits.

Each of the following, if true, could account for the above except

(A) The program provides uninteresting work.
(B) It is difficult to find work for all the program's graduates.
(C) The number of 16- and 17-year-old youths has increased over the past four years.
(D) Unemployment benefits are known while future salaries are not.
(E) Youths are unaware of the program's benefits.

The correct answer is (C). The fact that the number of 16- and 17-year-old youths has increased does not explain *why* unemployed high school graduates do not opt for the training program. All other answer alternatives do give possible reasons.

Flaws

In this type of question you are asked to choose the best alternative answer that either represents a flaw in the statement position, or if true, would weaken the argument or conclusion.

EXAMPLE

"Many people are murdered by killers whose homicidal tendencies are triggered by an official execution. Since 1977, for each execution there were about four homicides. . . . If each of the 1,788 death row prisoners were to be executed, up to 7,152 additional murders would be one of the results."

Which of the following, if true, would weaken the above argument?

(A) The rate of murders to executions is 1 to 1.66
(B) There is no relation between executions and murders.
(C) Executions result from the higher incidence of violent crime.
(D) The death penalty will be abolished.
(E) Not all death row prisoners will be executed.

The correct answer is (B). The author's assumption is that there is a relation between executions and homicides. As executions increase, so will homicides—at a given rate. Of course, if (D) occurred, presumably the homicide rate, according to the author's argument, will decline. However, (B) is the strongest argument—if true—against the author's premise.

Statements of Fact

With this type of question, you will be asked to find the answer that best agrees with, summarizes, or completes the statement.

EXAMPLE

When Herodotus wrote his history of the ancient world, he mixed the lives of the famous with those of the everyday. He wanted not only to record the events that shaped his world but also to give his readers a taste of life in past times and faraway places.

Which of the following best summarizes the above?

(A) Herodotus performed the tasks of both historian and journalist.
(B) Historians alone cannot reconstruct times and social circles.
(C) Herodotus relied on gossip and hearsay to compile his essays.
(D) Herodotus's history was based on scanty evidence.
(E) Herodotus preferred writing about the elite, rather than the lower classes.

The correct answer is (A). Herodotus wrote about all classes of people, recording not only momentous events but also the mundane. Therefore, he could be classified as a historian and as a journalist.

Test-Taking Tactics

1. **First, read the question and then read the passage.**   If you can identify the question type, you will know what to look for in the passage.

2. **Learn to spot major critical reasoning question types.**   The categories of questions and how to identify them were discussed. If you are able to recognize what a question is asking, you will know what reasoning tactic to apply. For example, if you recognize a question to be the flaw type, you are alerted to the fact that you must identify the argument and conclusion in the passage. If the question is "Which of the following, if true, would weaken the above argument?," your task is to find the author's argument by identifying the premise(s) and conclusion.

   In the factual type of question—for example, "Which of the following best summarizes the statement above?" or "If the information in the statement is true, which of the following must also be true?"—you look for the main facts, and what is claimed from the facts. The next step is to determine to what extent the conclusion is substantiated by the facts. In making your judgment as to whether or not the conclusion is substantiated rely only on the facts presented in the passage and not on any outside information. Moreover, assume that the facts are true, without making any value judgment.

3. **Look for the conclusion first.**   Critical reasoning questions are preceded by an argument or statement that has a conclusion or claim. While it may seem logical that a conclusion appears at the end of a passage, it might be given at the beginning or in the middle. Clues to help you find the conclusion are given in the Critical Reasoning Review.

4. **Find the premises.**   Premises are facts or evidence. Determine whether or not the conclusion follows logically from the premises or whether it is merely alleged. A conclusion may not follow, even though premises may be true. You must determine the legitimacy of assumptions and final conclusions. A number of methods for doing this are given in the Review.

   A typical question might ask you to attack or find a fact that weakens an argument. You must find the premise (one of the answer alternatives) that defeats the author's assumption.

EXAMPLE

"The United States gives billions of dollars in foreign aid to Balonia. Leaders of Balonia resent foreign aid. The United States should discontinue direct foreign aid to developing countries."

Which of the following statements, if true, would weaken the above argument?

(A) Balonia doesn't need foreign aid.
(B) Balonia isn't a developing country.
(C) Balonia is ruled by a dictator.
(D) Balonia's balance of payments is in surplus.
(E) Balonia's economy is growing.

In the above argument, only one example (that of Balonia) was used as a premise for reaching the conclusion that foreign aid should be discontinued. If it could be shown that Balonia is not a developing country (Choice B), then the premise is false and the conclusion invalid.

---

5. **Do not be opinionated.**   The statement given in a question may contain a specific point of view. Do not form an opinion about the statement or its claim. Concentrate on the structure of the argument and whether or not the structure and logic is valid. Accept each statement, argument, or trend as fact and proceed accordingly.

6. **Do not be overwhelmed by unfamiliar subjects.** You are not expected to be familiar with subject matter in a particular field—say, economics or political history. Most scientific and technical words will be explained.

PROBLEM SOLVING

The Problem Solving part of the Quantitative section is designed to test your ability to work with numbers. There are a variety of questions dealing with the basic principles of arithmetic, algebra, and geometry. These questions may take the form of word problems or require straight calculation. In addition, questions involving the interpretation of tables and graphs may be included.

The Quantitative section of the GMAT will contain Problem Solving-type questions. Based upon past tests about 60 percent of the questions in a Quantitative section will be Problem Solving questions.

The Problem Solving and Data Sufficiency section consists of 37 questions that must be answered within a time limit of 75 minutes. These questions range from very easy to quite challenging. Make sure you budget your time so that you can try each question.

Test-Taking Tactics

1. **Answer the question that is asked.** Read the question carefully. If your answer matches one of the choices given, your answer is not necessarily correct. Some of the choices given correspond to answers you would obtain by making simple errors, such as adding instead of subtracting or confusing area and perimeter.

EXAMPLE 1

If $x + y = 2$ and $x = 4$, then $x + 2y$ is

(A) –4 (B) –2 (C) 0 (D) 2 (E) 8

Since $x = 4$, then $x + y = 2$ means that y must be –2, and choice (B) is –2. But (B) is not the answer to the question. The question asked for the value of $x + 2y$, not for the value of y. The correct answer is (C), since $x + 2y$ is $4 + 2(-2) = 0$. If you forgot the minus sign and used $y = 2$ in evaluating $x + 2y$, your answer would be 8, which is choice (E).

To give you practice in avoiding these types of mistakes, some of the choices given on the sample tests in this book will be answers you would obtain if you made simple errors. After you have worked through the tests, you will know how to avoid errors of this kind.

EXAMPLE 2

How much will it cost to fence in a field that is 12 feet long and 42 feet wide with fence that costs $10 a yard?

(A) $180 (B) $360 (C) $504 (D) $540 (E) $1,080

If you multiply 12×42, you get 504; however, this is the area of the field in square feet. What you need to determine to answer this question is the perimeter of the field. The perimeter of the field is $12 + 12 + 42 + 42 = 108$ feet. If you multiply 108 by $10, you get $1,080, or (E). However, this is incorrect. The price is $10 *per yard*. You must change the perimeter to yards before calculating the price. 108 feet ÷ 3 = 36 yards (there are 3 feet in 1 yard). 36 yards multiplied by $10 per yard equals $360, which is answer choice (B).

2. Don't perform unnecessary calculations.   If you can, answer the question by estimating or doing a rough calculation rather than by figuring it out exactly. The time you save can be used to check your answers.

EXAMPLE

Find the value of $2x + 2y$ if $x + 2y = 6$ and $x + y = 10$.

(A) –4   (B) 6   (C) 10   (D) 14   (E) 20

You could solve for x and y and then evaluate $2x + 2y$. It is much faster to use the fact that $2(x + y)$ is $2x + 2y$ so the correct answer is 2(10) or 20.

---

3. Look at the answer choices before you start to work on the problem.   For some questions, it may be easier and quicker to check the answers than to solve the problem.

EXAMPLE

Which of the following numbers is the closest to the square root of .0017?

(A) .005   (B) .05   (C) .13   (D) .4   (E) .04

To answer this question, do not try to find the exact square root of .0017 and then see which of the choices is closest to your answer. Instead simply square each answer choice and then determine which is closest to .0017. (E) is the correct answer (.04 × .04 = .0016, which is closer to .0017 than the square of any of the other choices).

---

4. Use intelligent guessing to improve your score.   You have to answer each question in order to see the next question, so if you have no idea of the correct answer you must make a random guess. However, in most cases you should be able to eliminate at least one answer choice. After eliminating all the incorrect choices that you can, you should guess one of the remaining choices.

However, if you can eliminate even a single choice, you should guess one of the remaining answers. In problem solving, you may be able to eliminate one or two choices by performing a quick estimate. Look at each choice offered. Some choices may obviously be incorrect. This tactic can be very useful for inference questions.

EXAMPLE

If xy is positive, then which of the following conclusions is valid? (x and y are integers.)

    I. x must be positive.
   II. x is not zero.
   III. x must be negative.

(A) Only I
(B) Only II
(C) I and II only
(D) II and III only
(E) I, II, and III

Since 0 times any number is 0 it is easy to see that II is valid. Even if you can't go any further on this problem you know that the correct answer must be a choice that has II as part of the answer. So you know that (A) is incorrect. Guess one of the remaining choices.

EXAMPLE

What is the product of 21.84×32.78?

(A) 615.9152

(B) 715.8152

(C) 715.902

(D) 715.9152

(E) 725.9152

Since the product asked for will be greater than 21×32, which is 672, you can eliminate choice (A). Also each term has two decimal places, so the answer must have four decimal places and since $8 \times 4 = 32$, the correct answer must have 2 in the fourth decimal place; therefore you can eliminate choice (C). If you can't do the calculation, then guess (B), (D), or (E). The correct answer is (D).

5. **Use your scrap paper to copy diagrams and mark up the diagrams.** You will be provided with scrap paper. Make copies of diagrams and make whatever marks will help you to answer questions. If you are given the dimension of part of a diagram, write it on the diagram. If you are told parts are equal, mark them as equal. Cross out answers you have eliminated as you work on a problem. If a diagram is not supplied, draw a picture wherever possible.

6. **Hold the edge of the scrap paper up to the screen as a ruler.**

7. **Check your work if you can.** If you can check your work quickly, do so. This will help you avoid silly mistakes. For example, if you are asked to solve an equation, check that your answer actually does satisfy the equation. In many questions, you can catch an obvious error by simply asking if your answer makes sense or by looking at an easy case of the problem.

EXAMPLE

What is the solution set to the inequality $2x > 5x - 18$?

(A) $x > 6$

(B) $x < 6$

(C) $x > -6$

(D) $x < -6$

(E) $x > \dfrac{18}{7}$

The correct answer is (B). However, a mistake in algebra could give one of the other choices. For instance if you thought the answer was (C) try $x = -5$ and see if it works and try $x = -7$ and see if it doesn't work. Since $x = -7$ satisfies $2x > 5x - 18$ answer (C) must not be correct. If you thought (A) was the answer then check that $x = 7$ works and $x = 5$ doesn't work, etc. Remember, an incorrect answer at the beginning of the test can have a larger effect on your score than an incorrect answer did on the old paper and pencil GMAT.

8. **If a problem involves units, keep track of the units. Make sure your answer has the correct units.** If a problem asks for the area of a figure, then your answer should be in square inches or some *square measurement*. Volumes should be in *cubic measurements*. Speed is measured in *miles per hour* or *feet per second*, etc.

EXAMPLE

How much fence will be needed to enclose a rectangular field that is 20 feet long and 100 feet wide?

(A) 120 feet   (B) 140 feet   (C) 200 feet   (D) 240 feet   (E) 2,000 feet

The correct answer is 240 feet, which is the perimeter of the field. If you made a mistake and multiplied length × width (i.e., you found the area of the field), then your answer would be 20 feet × 100 feet = 2,000 square feet, which is not the same as choice (E). If you only looked at the number 2,000 you might have made the wrong choice.

---

9. **Use numerical values to find or check answers that involve formulas.** Some questions will have answers that use given quantities whose numerical value is not given. For example, a question may ask for the cost of making y objects and the answer choices will all involve y. In such problems, assigning a value that is easy to compute with can simplify the problem and enable you to check your answer.

EXAMPLE

The first 100 copies of a poster cost x cents each; after the first 100 copies have been made, extra copies cost $\frac{x}{4}$ cents each. How many cents will it cost to make 300 copies of the poster?

(A) 100x   (B) 150x   (C) 200x   (D) 300x   (E) 400x

The correct answer is 100x plus 200($\frac{x}{4}$) or 150x which is (B). Let x = 8. (Since the problem has $\frac{x}{4}$, choose a number divisible by 4.) Then the first 100 copies cost 800 cents and extra copies cost $\frac{8}{4}$ = 2 cents each. 200 extra copies will cost 200 × 2 = 400 cents. The total cost is 800 + 400, or 1,200. Letting x = 8, the possible answers are 800, 1,200, 1,600, 2,400, and 3,200, so (B) is correct.

When assigning variables avoid the values 0 or 1, since 0 times any number is 0 and 1 times a number does not change the number. If there is more than one unknown quantity in the answer, assign different numbers to each quantity.

This technique can sometimes help you eliminate answers to a problem so that you can make an intelligent guess.

In many cases you can eliminate all the incorrect choices by this technique. Start with the easiest formula to compute and work toward the hardest. If the formulas are complicated, this approach may take too much time. So be sure to check the time left and the number of questions left in the section before you use this approach on complicated formulas.

EXAMPLE

Box seats for a ball game cost $b each and general admission seats cost $g each. If 10,000 seats are sold, and x of the seats are box seats, which expression gives the fraction of money made on seat sales that came from box seats?

(A) $\dfrac{bx}{bx+(10,000-x)g}$

(B) $1+(10,000-x)g$

(C) $\dfrac{bx}{10,000}$

(D) $\dfrac{b}{(b+g)}$

(E) $\dfrac{x}{10,000}$

Since $10,000-x$ general admission tickets are sold, the total from seat sales is $bx+(10,000-x)g$.

Thus, the fraction made on box seats sales is $\dfrac{bx}{bx+(10,000-x)g}$ or (A). If you couldn't solve

this problem, assign values to each quantity. For instance, let $b=20$, $g=10$ and $x=2,000$ (note $x=5,000$ is not a good choice since then the number of box seats and general admission seats will be identical). Then 2,000 box seats were sold and 8,000 general admission seats were sold. The total from box seats is $2,000 \times 20 = 40,000$ and the total from general admission is $8,000 \times 10 = 80,000$. So the total from ticket sales is 120,000, and 40,000 came from box seats;

therefore, the answer is $\dfrac{40,000}{120,000}=\dfrac{1}{3}$. The value of answer (C) is $\dfrac{40,000}{10,000}=4$, so (C) is wrong;

the value of (D) is $\dfrac{20}{(20+10)}=\dfrac{2}{3}$, which is wrong; and the value of (E) is $\dfrac{2,000}{10,000}=\dfrac{2}{10}$, which

is wrong. The value of (B) is $1+(8,000)(10)=80,001$, which is incorrect. So the only possible answer

is (A). When you substitute the values into choice (A), the result is $\dfrac{40,000}{[40,000+(8,000)10]}=$

$\dfrac{40,000}{120,000}=\dfrac{1}{3}$, which agrees with the correct answer. So the correct answer is (A).

WARNING
If you use this method and one choice gives you the correct answer
be sure to check the remaining choices. Different formulas may
give the same result for one assignment of quantities.

---

10. **Always remember that x or y could be negative, especially if you need to know whether it is "larger than" or "smaller than."** For example, if $x = 3y$, this does not imply that x is greater than y, since if $y = -1$, then x is -3, which is less than -1.

11. **Always remember that there are a positive and a negative root to $x^2 = a$.** For example, $x^2 = 4$ does not mean that $x = 2$. You only know that $x = 2$ or $x = -2$.

12. **Translate the information you are given into numerical or algebraic equations to start working a problem.** If there is more than one variable in the problem, keep track of what each variable represents. It is helpful to use variables that suggest what the variable represents. For example, if you have the equation Profit = Revenue − Cost, use the variables P = Profit, R = Revenue, and C = Cost. The equation becomes $P = R - C$, which is much more informative than $x = y - z$.

Long-Term Strategy for Problem Solving

1. **Practice arithmetic.** Most Problem Solving sections contain one or two basic computational questions, such as multiplying two decimals or finding the largest number in a collection of fractions. If you are used to using a calculator to do all your arithmetic, these easy questions may be difficult for you. *You cannot use a calculator on the GMAT,* so practice your arithmetic before you take the exam. You already know how to do basic computation; you just need to practice to improve your speed and accuracy. See the Math Review for computational details and practice.

2. **Try to think quantitatively.** If you want to be a good reader, you should read a lot. In the same way, if you want to improve your quantitative skills, you should exercise them frequently. When you go grocery shopping, try to figure out whether the giant size is cheaper per ounce than the economy size. When you look at the news, try to make comparisons when figures are given. If you get used to thinking quantitatively, the Problem Solving sections will be much easier for you and you will feel more confident about the entire exam.

Sample Problem Solving Questions

Solve the following sample questions, allowing yourself 12 minutes to complete all of them. As you work try to use the above tactics. Any figure that appears with a problem is drawn as accurately as possible. All numbers used are real numbers. The analysis of each of these questions will include a difficulty score ranging from 3 (easiest) to 9 (hardest). An average question will have a difficulty level of 6.

TIME: 12 minutes

1. A train travels from Albany to Syracuse, a distance of 120 miles, at the average rate of 50 miles per hour. The train then travels back to Albany from Syracuse. The total traveling time of the train is 5 hours and 24 minutes. What was the average rate of speed of the train on the return trip to Albany?

   (A) 60 mph
   (B) 50 mph
   (C) 48 mph
   (D) 40 mph
   (E) 35 mph

2. A parking lot charges a flat rate of X dollars for any amount of time up to two hours, and $\frac{1}{6}X$ for each hour or fraction of an hour after the first two hours. How much does it cost to park for 5 hours and 15 minutes?

   (A) $3X$
   (B) $2X$
   (C) $1\frac{2}{3}X$
   (D) $1\frac{1}{2}X$
   (E) $1\frac{1}{6}X$

3. How many two-digit numbers are divisible by both 5 and 6?

   (A) none
   (B) one
   (C) two
   (D) three
   (E) more than three

4. What is 1 percent of .023?

   (A) .00023
   (B) .0023
   (C) .23
   (D) 2.3
   (E) 23

5. A window has the shape of a semicircle placed on top of a square. If the length of a side of the square is 20 inches, how many square inches is the area of the window?

   (A) 400
   (B) 200π
   (C) $50(8 + \pi)$
   (D) $200(2 + \pi)$
   (E) $400(1 + \pi)$

20

6. Which of the following sets of values for w, x, y, and z, respectively, are possible if ABCD is a parallelogram?

   I.   50, 130, 50, 130
   II. 60, 110, 70, 120
   III. 60, 150, 50, 150

   (A) I only
   (B) II only
   (C) I and II only
   (D) I and III only
   (E) I, II, and III

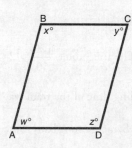

7. John weighs twice as much as Marcia. Marcia's weight is 60% of Bob's weight. Dave weighs 50% of Lee's weight. Lee weighs 190% of John's weight. Which of these 5 persons weighs the least?

   (A) Bob
   (B) Dave
   (C) John
   (D) Lee
   (E) Marcia

8. There were P people in a room when a meeting started. Q people left the room during the first hour, while R people entered the room during the same time. What expression gives the number of people in the room after the first hour as a percentage of the number of people in the room who have been there since the meeting started?

(A) $\dfrac{(P-Q)}{(P-Q+R)}$

(B) $100 \times \dfrac{(P-Q+R)}{(P-Q)}$

(C) $\dfrac{(P+R)}{(P-Q)}$

(D) $100 \times \dfrac{(P-Q)}{(P-Q+R)}$

(E) $100 \times \dfrac{(P+R)}{(P-Q)}$

Answers

1. **(D)**   3. **(D)**   5. **(C)**   7. **(E)**
2. **(C)**   4. **(A)**   6. **(A)**   8. **(B)**

Analysis

Difficulty Level

1. **(D)** The train took $\dfrac{120}{50} = 2\dfrac{2}{5}$ hours to travel from Albany to Syracuse. Since the total traveling time of the train was $5\dfrac{2}{5}$ hours, it must have taken the train 3 hours for the trip from Syracuse to Albany. Since the distance traveled is 120 miles, the average rate of speed on the return trip to Albany was $(\dfrac{1}{3})(120)$ mph = 40 mph.

Difficulty Level

2. **(C)** It costs X for the first 2 hours. If you park 5 hours and 15 minutes there are 3 hours and 15 minutes left after the first 2 hours. Since this time is charged at the rate of $\dfrac{X}{6}$ for each hour or fraction thereof, it costs $4\left(\dfrac{X}{6}\right)$ for the last 3 hours and 15 minutes. Thus the total $X + \dfrac{4}{6}X = 1\dfrac{2}{3}X$.

Difficulty Level

3. **(D)** Since 5 and 6 have no common factors any number divisible by both 5 and 6 must be divisible by the product of 5 times 6 or 30. The only two digit numbers divisible by 30 are 30, 60, and 90. So, the correct answer is (D).

Difficulty Level

4. **(A)** Remember that the decimal equivalent of 1 percent is .01. To find 1 percent of .023 you simply multiply .023 by .01. The answer must have five decimal places since .023 has three decimal places and .01 has two decimal places. Therefore, the correct answer is .00023 or choice (A). This is an example of the type of simple calculation that many versions of the GMAT will have in one question in the Quantitative section.

5. **(C)** Copy the diagram onto scrap paper and mark up the diagram by dividing the given figure into a square and a semicircle as shown below. Label all the lengths that you are given.

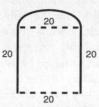

The area of the window is the area of the square plus the area of the semicircle. The area of the square is 20^2 or 400 square inches. The area of the semicircle is $\frac{1}{2}$ of πr^2 where r is the radius of the semicircle. Since the side of the square is a diameter of the semicircle, the radius is $\frac{1}{2}$ of 20, or 10 inches. The area of the semicircle is $\frac{1}{2} \times \pi \times 100 = 50\pi$ square inches. Therefore, the area of the window is $400 + 50\pi = 50(8 + \pi)$ Note that you must be able to change your answer into the correct form to answer this question.

6. **(A)** The sum of the angles of a parallelogram (which is 4-sided) must be $(4 - 2)180° = 360°$. Since the sum of the values in III is 410, III cannot be correct. The sum of the numbers in II is 360, but in a parallelogram opposite angles must be equal so x must equal z and y must equal w. Since 60 is unequal to 70, II cannot be correct. The sum of the values in I is 360 and opposite angles will be equal, so I is correct.

7. **(E)** John weighs twice as much as Marcia, so John cannot weigh the least. Marcia's weight is less than Bob's weight, so Bob's weight is not the least. Dave's weight is $\frac{1}{2}$ of Lee's weight, so Lee can't weigh the least. The only possible answers are Marcia or Dave. So only (B) and (E) are possible; if you can't get any further, you should choose one of the two as your answer, since you have eliminated three choices. Let J, M, B, D, and L stand for the weights of John, Marcia, Bob, Dave, and Lee respectively. Then $D = .5L = .5(1.9)J$. So $D = .95J$. Since $J = 2M$, we know $M = .5J$. Therefore Marcia weighs the least. It may help to write the 5 names (or initials) on your paper and cross out each incorrect choice as you work through the problem.

8. **(B)** Although this problem looks difficult, it is fairly simple if you approach it in a step-by-step manner. First, express the number of people in the room after the first hour. There were P to begin with and Q left while R entered, so after the first hour there were $P - Q + R$ in the room. Second, express the number of people who have been in the room since the meeting started. R people entered while the meeting was in progress, so $P - Q$ people were in the room the entire hour. Therefore $\frac{(P - Q + R)}{(P - Q)}$ is the desired expression. But the question asks for a percentage. To change a number (fraction) into a percentage, simply multiply the number by 100. The correct answer is (B). If you can't work this out, you can let $P = 100$, $Q = 40$ and $R = 20$. For these values, 80 people are in the room after the first hour and there are 60 people left in the room at the end of the hour who were there at the start. So $80/60 = 133$ and $1/3\%$ is the correct answer. Now eliminate the answers which give an incorrect result. (A) gives $60/80$, (C) gives $120/60 = 2$, (D) gives $100 \times (60/80) = 75$ and (E) gives $100 \times (120/60) = 200$ so (B) must be the correct answer.

The total possible score for these questions is 47.

DATA SUFFICIENCY

This type of question, which also appears in the Quantitative section, is designed to test your reasoning ability. Like the Problem Solving questions, they require a basic knowledge of the principles of arithmetic, algebra, and geometry. Each Data Sufficiency question consists of a mathematical problem and two statements containing information relating to it. You must decide whether the problem can be solved by using information from: (A) the first statement alone, but not the second statement alone; (B) the second statement alone, but not the first statement alone; (C) both statements together, but neither alone; or (D) either of the statements alone. Choose (E) if the problem cannot be solved, even by using both statements together. About 40 percent of the questions on a Quantitative test will be Data Sufficiency problems. Approaching these problems properly will help you achieve a high score. As in the Problem Solving section, time is of the utmost importance. Approaching Data Sufficiency problems properly will help you use this time wisely.

Test-Taking Tactics

1. **Make sure you understand the directions.** Reread the paragraph above. Make sure you know what is being asked. If you have never seen this type of question before, make sure you do the practice problems that follow. At first, these questions may seem difficult, but once you have worked through several examples, you will start to feel comfortable with them.

2. **Don't waste time figuring out the exact answer.** Always keep in mind that you are never asked to supply an answer for the problem; you are only asked to determine if there is sufficient data available to find the answer. Once you know whether or not it is possible to find the answer from the given information, you are done. If you waste time figuring out the exact answer, you may not be able to finish the entire section.

EXAMPLE

The profits of a company are the revenues the company receives minus the costs that the company pays. How much were the profits of the XYZ Company in 1999?

(1) The XYZ Company had revenues of $112,234,567 in 1999.
(2) The costs of the XYZ Company were $102,479,345 in 1999.

The information given states that to find the profit you need to know both the revenues and the costs. So it is easy to see that both (1) and (2) are needed and that the profit could be determined using (1) and (2). So the answer is (C). Do not compute the profit. If you perform the subtraction needed to compute the profit, you are just wasting time that could be spent on other problems.

3. **Draw a picture whenever possible.** Make a copy of any diagrams on your paper and mark them up. If a diagram is not supplied, draw one on your paper. Pictures can be especially helpful in any question that involves geometry.

4. **Don't make extra assumptions.** You are only allowed to use the information given and facts that are always true (such as the number of hours in a day) to answer these questions. Do not make assumptions about things such as prices rising every year. If you are given a diagram don't assume two lines that appear to be perpendicular are perpendicular unless you are given specific information that says the lines are perpendicular. If an angle looks like a 45° angle don't assume it is 45° unless you are given that fact.

5. Use a system to work through the questions. Try to adopt a consistent approach to these types of problems. The system that follows will help you to answer the questions and also let you guess intelligently, if you can't complete the problem. You will have to invest some time to understand the method, but once you have done so, you should be much better prepared for these types of questions.

System for Data Sufficiency Questions

A systematic analysis can improve your score on Data Sufficiency sections. By answering three questions, you will always arrive at the correct choice. In addition, if you can answer any one of the three questions, you can eliminate at least one of the possible choices so that you can make an intelligent guess.

The three questions are:

    I. Is the first statement alone sufficient to solve the problem?
   II. Is the second statement alone sufficient to solve the problem?
  III. Are both statements together sufficient to solve the problem?

As a general rule try to answer the questions in order I, II, III, since in many cases you will not have to answer all three to get the correct choice.

Here is how to use the three questions:

If the answer to I is YES, then the only possible choices are (A) or (D). Now, if the answer to II is YES, the choice must be (D), and if the answer to II is NO, the choice must be (A).

If the answer to I is NO then the only possible choices are (B), (C), or (E). Now, if the answer to II is YES, then the choice must be (B), and if the answer to II is NO, the only possible choices are (C) or (E).

So, finally, if the answer to III is YES, the choice is (C), and if the answer to III is NO, the choice is (E).

A good way to see this is to use a decision tree.

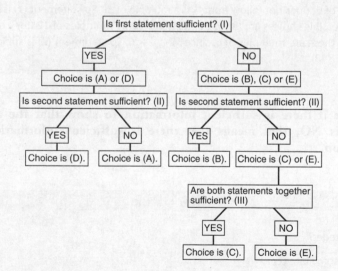

To use the tree simply start at the top and by answering YES or NO move down the tree until you arrive at the correct choice. For example, if the answer to I is YES and the answer to II is NO, then the correct choice is (A). (Notice that in this case you don't need to answer III to find the correct choice.)

The decision tree can also help you make intelligent guesses. If you can only answer one of the three questions, then you can eliminate the choices that follow from the wrong answer to the question.

EXAMPLE 1:   You know the answer to I is YES. You can eliminate choices (B), (C), and (E).

EXAMPLE 2:   You know the answer to II is NO. You can eliminate choices (D) and (B) since they follow from YES for II.

EXAMPLE 3:   You know the answer to III is YES. You can eliminate choice (E) since it follows from NO for III.

EXAMPLE 4:   You know the answer to I is NO and the answer to III is YES. You can eliminate (E) since it follows from NO to III. You also can eliminate (A) and (D) since they follow from YES to I.

Practice this system to improve your ability to solve as well as make educated guesses for Data Sufficiency problems.

There is an additional practice section of Data Sufficiency questions following the Math Review on pages 303–305. The analysis of these exercises (on pages 314–317) gives worked-out solutions using this system.

6. **In many cases you can use simple values to check quickly whether a statement follows from a given statement.** This can be especially useful in deciding that a statement does *not* follow from a given statement.

EXAMPLE

Is k a multiple of 6?

(1) k is a multiple of 3.
(2) k is a multiple of 12.

Write out some simple multiples of 3 ($3 \times 1 = 3$, $3 \times 2 = 6$, etc.). Since 3 is not a multiple of 6, "k is a multiple of 6" does not follow from "k is a multiple of 3." So statement (1) is not sufficient, and the only possible choices are (B), (C), or (E). Write some multiples of 12 (for example, 12, 24, 36, 48, . . .). All these are multiples of 6, since 12 is 2×6. So statement (2) is sufficient, and the correct answer is (B).

---

7. **Remember if there is sufficient information to show that the answer to the question is NO, that means that there is sufficient information to answer the question.**

EXAMPLE

Is n an even integer?

(1) $n = 3k$, for some integer k.
(2) $n = 2j + 1$, for some integer j.

The first statement is not sufficient, since 3×2 is 6, which is even, but 3×3 is 9, which is odd. The second statement is sufficient, since it means that n is odd. This means that the answer to the main question is "no," and therefore (B) is the correct choice.

LONG-TERM STRATEGY FOR DATA SUFFICIENCY QUESTIONS

Practice Working Data Sufficiency Questions.   Most people have not had much experience with these types of questions. The more examples you work out the better you will perform on this section of the test. By the time you have finished the sample exams, you should feel confident about your ability to answer Data Sufficiency questions.

Sample Questions

Read the following directions carefully and then try the sample Data Sufficiency questions below. Allow yourself 8 minutes total time. All numbers used are real numbers. A figure given for a problem is intended to provide information consistent with that in the question, but not necessarily consistent with the additional information contained in the statements. The analysis for each question will include a difficulty grade ranging from 3 (easiest) to 9 (hardest) with 6 indicating a question of average difficulty.

TIME: 8 minutes

Directions: Each of the following problems has a question and two statements which are labeled (1) and (2). Use the data given in (1) and (2) together with other available information (such as the number of hours in a day, the definition of *clockwise*, mathematical facts, etc.) to decide whether the statements are *sufficient* to answer the question. Then choose

(A) if you can get the answer from **(1) ALONE** but not from (2) alone
(B) if you can get the answer from **(2) ALONE** but not from (1) alone
(C) if you can get the answer from **BOTH (1) and (2) TOGETHER,** but not from (1) alone or (2) alone
(D) if **EITHER** statement **(1) ALONE OR** statement **(2) ALONE** suffices
(E) if you **CANNOT** get the answer from statements **(1) and (2) TOGETHER,** but need even more data

All numbers used are real numbers. A figure given for a problem is intended to provide information consistent with that in the question, but not necessarily consistent with the additional information contained in the statements.

1. A rectangular field is 40 yards long. Find the area of the field.

   (1) A fence around the entire boundary of the field is 140 yards long.
   (2) The field is more than 20 yards wide.

2. Is X a number greater than zero?

   (1) $X^2 - 1 = 0$
   (2) $X^3 + 1 = 0$

3. An industrial plant produces bottles. In 2001 the number of bottles produced by the plant was twice the number produced in 2000. How many bottles were produced altogether in the years 2000, 2001, and 2002?

   (1) In 2002 the number of bottles produced was 3 times the number produced in 2000.
   (2) In 2003 the number of bottles produced was one half the total produced in the years 2000, 2001, and 2002.

4. A man 6 feet tall is standing near a pole. On the top of the pole is a light. What is the length of the shadow cast by the man?

   (1) The pole is 18 feet high.
   (2) The man is 12 feet from the pole.

5. Find the length of *RS* if *z* is 90° and *PS* = 6.

   (1) *PR* = 6
   (2) *x* = 45°

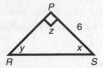

6. Working at a constant rate and by himself, it takes worker *U* three hours to fill up a ditch with sand. How long would it take for worker *V* to fill up the same ditch working by herself?

   (1) Working together but at the same time U and V an fill in the ditch in 1 hour $52\frac{1}{2}$ minutes.

   (2) In any length of time worker *V* fills in only 60% as much as worker *U* does in the same time.

7. Did John go to the beach yesterday?

   (1) If John goes to the beach, he will be sunburned the next day.
   (2) John is sunburned today.

Answers:

1. **(A)**   3. **(E)**   5. **(D)**   7. **(E)**
2. **(B)**   4. **(C)**   6. **(D)**

Analysis:

1. **(A)** The area of a rectangle is the length multiplied by the width. Since you know the length is 40 yards, you must find out the width in order to solve the problem. Since statement (2) simply says the width is greater than 20 yards you cannot find out the exact width using (2). So (2) alone is not sufficient. Statement (1) says the length of a fence around the entire boundary of the field is 140 yards. The length of this fence is the perimeter of the rectangle, the sum of twice the length and twice the width. If we replace the length by 40 in $P = 2L + 2W$ we have $140 = 2(40) + 2W$, which can be solved for *W*. On the test don't waste time calculating *W* or the area. At this point you know that (1) alone is sufficient. So the correct choice is (A).

2. **(B)** Statement (1) means $X^2 = 1$, but there are two possible solutions to this equation, $X = 1, X = -1$. Thus using (1) alone you cannot deduce whether *X* is positive or negative. Statement (2) means $X^3 = -1$, but there is only one possible (real) solution to this, $X = -1$. Thus *X* is not greater than zero, which answers the question. And (2) alone is sufficient.

3. **(E)** *T*, the total produced in the three years, is the sum of $P_0 + P_1 + P_2$, where P_0 is the number produced in 2000, P_1 the number produced in 2001, and P_2 the number produced in 2002. You are given that $P_1 = 2P_0$. Thus $T = P_0 + P_1 + P_2 = P_0 + 2P_0 + P_2 = 3P_0 + P_2$. So we must find out P_0 and P_2 to answer the question. Statement (1) says $P_2 = 3P_0$; thus, by using (1) if we can find the value of P_0 we can find *T*. But (1) gives us no further information about P_0. Statement (2) says $^1/_2 \, T$ equals the number produced in 2003, but it does not say what this number is. Since there are no relations given between production in 2003 and production in the individual years 2000, 2001, or 2002 you cannot use (2) to find out what P_0 is. Thus, (1) and (2) together are not sufficient.

4. **(C)** Sometimes it may help to draw a picture. By proportions or by similar triangles the height of the pole, h, is to 6 feet as the length of shadow, s, + the distance to the pole, x, is to s.

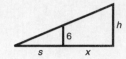

So $\dfrac{h}{6} = \dfrac{(s+x)}{s}$. Thus, $hs = 6s + 6x$ by cross-multiplication.

Solving for s gives $hs - 6s = 6x$, or $s(h-6) = 6x$, or, finally, we have $s = \dfrac{6x}{(h-6)}$.

Statement (1) says $h = 18$; thus $s = \dfrac{6x}{12} = \dfrac{x}{2}$, but using (1) alone we cannot deduce the

value x. Thus (1) alone is not sufficient. Statement (2) says x equals 12; thus, using (1) and

(2) together we deduce $s = 6$, but using (2) alone all we can deduce is that $s = \dfrac{72}{(h-6)}$, which

cannot be solved for s unless we know h. Thus using (1) and (2) together we can deduce the answer but (1) alone is not sufficient nor is (2) alone.

5. **(D)** Since z is a right angle, $(RS)^2 = (PS)^2 + (PR)^2$, so $(RS)^2 = (6)^2 + (PR)^2$, and RS will be the positive square root of $36 + (PR)^2$. Thus, if you can find the length of PR the problem is solved. Statement (1) says $PR = 6$, thus $(RS)^2 = 36 + 36$, so $RS = 6\sqrt{2}$. Thus, (1) alone is sufficient. Statement (2) says $x = 45°$ but since the sum of the angles in a triangle is 180° and z is 90° then $y = 45°$. So, x and y are equal angles and that means the sides opposite x and opposite y must be equal or $PS = PR$. Thus, $PR = 6$ and $RS = 6\sqrt{2}$ so (2) alone is also sufficient.

6. **(D)** (1) says U and V together can fill in the ditch in $1\dfrac{7}{8}$ hours. Since U can fill in the

ditch in 3 hours, in 1 hour he can fill in one-third of the ditch. Hence, in $1\dfrac{7}{8}$ hours U

would fill in $\left(\dfrac{1}{3}\right)\left(\dfrac{15}{8}\right) = \dfrac{5}{8}$ of the ditch. So V fills in $\dfrac{3}{8}$ of the ditch in $1\dfrac{7}{8}$ hours. Thus,

V would take $\left(\dfrac{8}{3}\right)\left(\dfrac{15}{8}\right) = 5$ hours to fill in the ditch working by herself. Therefore, statement

(1) alone is sufficient. According to statement (2) since U fills the ditch in 3 hours, V will fill

$\dfrac{3}{5}$ of the ditch in 3 hours. Thus, V will take 5 hours to fill in the ditch working alone.

7. **(E)** Obviously, neither statement alone is sufficient. John *could* have gotten sunburned at the beach, but he might have gotten sunburned somewhere else. Therefore, (1) and (2) together are not sufficient. This problem tests your grasp of an elementary rule of logic rather than your mathematical knowledge.

The total score for all these questions is 37.

A SHORT SAMPLE OF A CAT QUANTITATIVE TEST

This test is based on the 8 sample questions that were given in the Problem Solving section and the 7 sample questions that were given in the Data Sufficiency section. These questions will be labeled PS1, PS2, . . . , PS8 and DS1, DS2, . . . , DS7. Once a question is used it will not reappear on the test.

First question: Possible choices are PS3 or PS6 or DS3 or DS5 or DS6.

If the first question is answered correctly, possible choices for question 2 are: PS5, DS7.

If the first question is answered incorrectly, possible choices for question 2 are: PS2, DS4.

If the first two questions are answered correctly, possible choices for the third question are: PS7, PS8.

If the first question was answered correctly, but the second was not, then choices for the third question are: PS3, PS6, DS3, DS5, or DS6.

If the first question was answered incorrectly but the second was answered correctly, then choices for the third question are PS3, PS6, DS3, DS5 or DS6.

If the first two questions were answered incorrectly, then possible choices for the third question are: PS1, DS2.

Someone with a potentially high score might have had questions PS3 then DS7 followed by PS7. In terms of the difficulty scale that appeared with the problems, the first question was level 6, followed by level 7 and then level 8. Someone with a potentially low score might have also started with PS3 but then had DS4 followed by PS1. In terms of the difficulty scale, the first question was level 6, followed by level 5, and then level 4.

DIAGNOSE YOUR PROBLEM

Answer Sheet

DIAGNOSTIC TEST

Quantitative Section

1 Ⓐ Ⓑ Ⓒ Ⓓ Ⓔ	11 Ⓐ Ⓑ Ⓒ Ⓓ Ⓔ	21 Ⓐ Ⓑ Ⓒ Ⓓ Ⓔ	31 Ⓐ Ⓑ Ⓒ Ⓓ Ⓔ
2 Ⓐ Ⓑ Ⓒ Ⓓ Ⓔ	12 Ⓐ Ⓑ Ⓒ Ⓓ Ⓔ	22 Ⓐ Ⓑ Ⓒ Ⓓ Ⓔ	32 Ⓐ Ⓑ Ⓒ Ⓓ Ⓔ
3 Ⓐ Ⓑ Ⓒ Ⓓ Ⓔ	13 Ⓐ Ⓑ Ⓒ Ⓓ Ⓔ	23 Ⓐ Ⓑ Ⓒ Ⓓ Ⓔ	33 Ⓐ Ⓑ Ⓒ Ⓓ Ⓔ
4 Ⓐ Ⓑ Ⓒ Ⓓ Ⓔ	14 Ⓐ Ⓑ Ⓒ Ⓓ Ⓔ	24 Ⓐ Ⓑ Ⓒ Ⓓ Ⓔ	34 Ⓐ Ⓑ Ⓒ Ⓓ Ⓔ
5 Ⓐ Ⓑ Ⓒ Ⓓ Ⓔ	15 Ⓐ Ⓑ Ⓒ Ⓓ Ⓔ	25 Ⓐ Ⓑ Ⓒ Ⓓ Ⓔ	35 Ⓐ Ⓑ Ⓒ Ⓓ Ⓔ
6 Ⓐ Ⓑ Ⓒ Ⓓ Ⓔ	16 Ⓐ Ⓑ Ⓒ Ⓓ Ⓔ	26 Ⓐ Ⓑ Ⓒ Ⓓ Ⓔ	36 Ⓐ Ⓑ Ⓒ Ⓓ Ⓔ
7 Ⓐ Ⓑ Ⓒ Ⓓ Ⓔ	17 Ⓐ Ⓑ Ⓒ Ⓓ Ⓔ	27 Ⓐ Ⓑ Ⓒ Ⓓ Ⓔ	37 Ⓐ Ⓑ Ⓒ Ⓓ Ⓔ
8 Ⓐ Ⓑ Ⓒ Ⓓ Ⓔ	18 Ⓐ Ⓑ Ⓒ Ⓓ Ⓔ	28 Ⓐ Ⓑ Ⓒ Ⓓ Ⓔ	
9 Ⓐ Ⓑ Ⓒ Ⓓ Ⓔ	19 Ⓐ Ⓑ Ⓒ Ⓓ Ⓔ	29 Ⓐ Ⓑ Ⓒ Ⓓ Ⓔ	
10 Ⓐ Ⓑ Ⓒ Ⓓ Ⓔ	20 Ⓐ Ⓑ Ⓒ Ⓓ Ⓔ	30 Ⓐ Ⓑ Ⓒ Ⓓ Ⓔ	

Verbal Section

1 Ⓐ Ⓑ Ⓒ Ⓓ Ⓔ	12 Ⓐ Ⓑ Ⓒ Ⓓ Ⓔ	23 Ⓐ Ⓑ Ⓒ Ⓓ Ⓔ	35 Ⓐ Ⓑ Ⓒ Ⓓ Ⓔ
2 Ⓐ Ⓑ Ⓒ Ⓓ Ⓔ	13 Ⓐ Ⓑ Ⓒ Ⓓ Ⓔ	24 Ⓐ Ⓑ Ⓒ Ⓓ Ⓔ	36 Ⓐ Ⓑ Ⓒ Ⓓ Ⓔ
3 Ⓐ Ⓑ Ⓒ Ⓓ Ⓔ	14 Ⓐ Ⓑ Ⓒ Ⓓ Ⓔ	25 Ⓐ Ⓑ Ⓒ Ⓓ Ⓔ	37 Ⓐ Ⓑ Ⓒ Ⓓ Ⓔ
4 Ⓐ Ⓑ Ⓒ Ⓓ Ⓔ	15 Ⓐ Ⓑ Ⓒ Ⓓ Ⓔ	26 Ⓐ Ⓑ Ⓒ Ⓓ Ⓔ	38 Ⓐ Ⓑ Ⓒ Ⓓ Ⓔ
5 Ⓐ Ⓑ Ⓒ Ⓓ Ⓔ	16 Ⓐ Ⓑ Ⓒ Ⓓ Ⓔ	27 Ⓐ Ⓑ Ⓒ Ⓓ Ⓔ	39 Ⓐ Ⓑ Ⓒ Ⓓ Ⓔ
6 Ⓐ Ⓑ Ⓒ Ⓓ Ⓔ	17 Ⓐ Ⓑ Ⓒ Ⓓ Ⓔ	28 Ⓐ Ⓑ Ⓒ Ⓓ Ⓔ	40 Ⓐ Ⓑ Ⓒ Ⓓ Ⓔ
7 Ⓐ Ⓑ Ⓒ Ⓓ Ⓔ	18 Ⓐ Ⓑ Ⓒ Ⓓ Ⓔ	29 Ⓐ Ⓑ Ⓒ Ⓓ Ⓔ	41 Ⓐ Ⓑ Ⓒ Ⓓ Ⓔ
8 Ⓐ Ⓑ Ⓒ Ⓓ Ⓔ	19 Ⓐ Ⓑ Ⓒ Ⓓ Ⓔ	30 Ⓐ Ⓑ Ⓒ Ⓓ Ⓔ	
9 Ⓐ Ⓑ Ⓒ Ⓓ Ⓔ	20 Ⓐ Ⓑ Ⓒ Ⓓ Ⓔ	31 Ⓐ Ⓑ Ⓒ Ⓓ Ⓔ	
10 Ⓐ Ⓑ Ⓒ Ⓓ Ⓔ	21 Ⓐ Ⓑ Ⓒ Ⓓ Ⓔ	32 Ⓐ Ⓑ Ⓒ Ⓓ Ⓔ	
11 Ⓐ Ⓑ Ⓒ Ⓓ Ⓔ	22 Ⓐ Ⓑ Ⓒ Ⓓ Ⓔ	34 Ⓐ Ⓑ Ⓒ Ⓓ Ⓔ	

Diagnostic Test with Answers and Analysis

Now that you have become familiar with the various types of questions appearing on the GMAT and have had a chance to sample each type, you probably have an idea of what to expect from an actual exam. The next step, then, is to take a sample test to see how you do.

The Diagnostic Test that follows has been designed to help you with the types of questions that will appear on the new GMAT. When taking it, try to simulate actual test conditions as closely as possible. For example, time yourself as you work on each section so that you don't go over the allotted time limit for that section. After you have completed the test, check your answers and use the self-scoring chart to evaluate the results. Use these results to determine which review sections you should spend the most time studying before you attempt the 2 sample GMATs at the end of the book. To assist you in your review, all answers to problem solving questions are keyed so that you can easily refer to the section in the Mathematics Review that discusses the material tested by a particular question.

In the CAT GMAT, the quantitative test will contain two types of questions: Problem Solving and Data Sufficiency. The verbal test will be made up of three types of questions: Reading Comprehension, Critical Reasoning, and Sentence Correction. There will also be an Analytical Writing section. After you have finished using this book, you will be so familiar with the structure of each type of question that you will be able to identify it according to the passage or the structure of the question, and to solve it using the techniques that you learned by taking the tests in this book.

WRITING ASSESSMENT

Part I TIME: 30 MINUTES

Directions: Write a clear, logical, and well-organized response to the following issue or argument. Your response should be in the form of a short essay, following the conventions of standard written English. Your answer should fit on three pages of lined 8½" × 11" paper or equivalent on your PC. Write legibly. Essays that are illegible or that are written on a topic other than the one outlined in the question will not be scored.

The Japanese always have to consult a companion or call a conference to solve even the most trivial things. In India, there are definite rules for family members (and this is also true for other social groups), so that when one wants to do something, one knows whether it is all right by following those rules. Because of the rule system, things get done more quickly in India.

Discuss how logically persuasive you find the argument. In presenting your point of view, analyze the sort of reasoning used and its supporting evidence. In addition, state what further evidence, if any, would make the argument more sound and convincing or would make you better able to evaluate its conclusion.

Part II TIME: 30 MINUTES

Directions: Write a clear, logical, and well-organized response to the following issue or argument. Your response should be in the form of a short essay, following the conventions of standard written English. Your answer should fit on three pages of lined 8½" × 11" paper or equivalent on your PC. Write legibly. Essays that are illegible or that are written on a topic other than the one outlined in the question will not be scored.

The economic penetration by multinational corporations shapes and distorts cultural patterns in developing countries. The Westernization, particularly the Americanization, of culture presents a formidable threat to the cultural integrity of the non-Western world. Nevertheless, the know-how of these corporations is necessary to fuel the economic development of developing countries.

Which of the attributes of the multinational corporation do you agree with: a contributor to growth or a threat to culture? Support your point of view with specific reasons or examples that you have observed or read about.

IF THERE IS STILL TIME REMAINING, YOU MAY REVIEW YOUR ANSWER. AFTER YOU HAVE CONFIRMED YOUR ANSWER, YOU CANNOT RETURN TO THIS QUESTION.

QUANTITATIVE SECTION

TIME: 75 MINUTES

37 QUESTIONS

This section consists of two types of questions: Problem Solving and Data Sufficiency.

Problem Solving
Directions: Solve each of the following problems; then indicate the correct answer.

NOTE: A figure that appears with a problem is drawn as accurately as possible so as to provide information that may help in answering the question.
Numbers in this test are real numbers.

Data Sufficiency
Directions: Each of the following problems has a question and two statements which are labeled (1) and (2). Use the data given in (1) and (2) together with other available information (such as the number of hours in a day, the definition of *clockwise*, mathematical facts, etc.) to decide whether the statements are *sufficient* to answer the question. Then fill in space

(A) If you can get the answer from (1) **ALONE** but not from (2) alone
(B) If you can get the answer from (2) **ALONE** but not from (1) alone
(C) If you can get the answer from **BOTH (1) and (2) TOGETHER** but not from (1) alone or (2) alone
(D) If **EITHER** statement (1) **ALONE OR** statement (2) **ALONE** suffices
(E) If you **CANNOT** get the answer from statements (1) and (2) **TOGETHER** but need even more data

All numbers used in this section are real numbers.

A figure given for a problem is intended to provide information consistent with that in the question, but not necessarily with the additional information contained in the statements.
All figures lie in the plane unless you are told otherwise.
Figures are drawn as accurately as possible; straight lines may not appear straight on the screen.

1. If the length of a rectangle is increased by 20 percent and the width is decreased by 20 percent, then the area

   (A) decreases by 20%
   (B) decreases by 4%
   (C) stays the same
   (D) increases by 10%
   (E) increases by 20%

2. It costs x dollars each to make the first 1,000 copies of a compact disc and y dollars to make each subsequent copy. If z is greater than 1,000, how many dollars will it cost to make z copies of the compact disc?

   (A) $1,000x + yz$
   (B) $zx - zy$
   (C) $1,000\,(z - x) + xy$
   (D) $1,000\,(z - y) + xz$
   (E) $1,000\,(x - y) + yz$

3. How many two-digit integers satisfy the following property? The last digit (units digit) of the square of the two-digit number is 8,

   (A) none
   (B) 1
   (C) 2
   (D) 3
   (E) more than 3

4. Ms. Taylor purchased stock for $1,500 and sold $\frac{2}{3}$ of it after its value doubled.

   She sold the remaining stock at 5 times its purchase price. What was her total profit on the stock?

   (A) $1,500
   (B) $2,000
   (C) $2,500
   (D) $3,000
   (E) $4,500

5. City B is 8 miles east of City A. City C is 6 miles north of city B. City D is 16 miles east of city C, and city E is 12 miles north of city D. What is the distance from city A to city E?

   (A) 10 miles
   (B) 20 miles
   (C) 24 miles
   (D) 30 miles
   (E) 42 miles

6. If x is a number satisfying $2 < x < 3$ and y is a number satisfying $7 < y < 8$, which of the following expressions will have the largest value?

   (A) $x^2 y$
   (B) xy^2
   (C) $5xy$

   (D) $\dfrac{4x^2 y}{3}$

   (E) $\dfrac{x^2}{y}$

(A) If you can get the answer from **(1) ALONE** but not from **(2)** alone
(B) If you can get the answer from **(2) ALONE** but not from **(1)** alone
(C) If you can get the answer from **BOTH (1)** and **(2) TOGETHER** but not from **(1)** alone or **(2)** alone
(D) If **EITHER** statement **(1) ALONE OR** statement **(2) ALONE** suffices
(E) If you **CANNOT** get the answer from statements (1) and (2) **TOGETHER** but need even more data

7. The median salary of the employees in the sales department in 1999 was x. The average raise for the next year was $800 per employee. What was the median salary of the employees in the sales department in 2000?

   (1) $x = 48,000$

   (2) The range of the salaries in the sales department in 2000 was $12,000.

8. If 50 apprentices can finish a job in 4 hours and 30 skilled workers can finish the same job in $4\frac{1}{2}$ hours, how much of the job should be completed by 10 apprentices and 15 skilled workers in 1 hour?

   (A) $\dfrac{1}{9}$

   (B) $\dfrac{29}{180}$

   (C) $\dfrac{26}{143}$

   (D) $\dfrac{1}{5}$

   (E) $\dfrac{39}{121}$

9. If the shaded area is $\dfrac{1}{2}$ the area of triangle ABC and angle ABC is a right angle, then the length of line segment AD is

   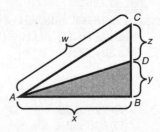

   (A) $\left(\dfrac{1}{2}\right)w$

   (B) $\left(\dfrac{1}{2}\right)(w + x)$

   (C) $\sqrt{2x^2 + z^2}$

   (D) $\sqrt{w^2 - 3y^2}$

   (E) $\sqrt{y^2 + z^2}$

(A) If you can get the answer from (1) **ALONE** but not from (2) alone
(B) If you can get the answer from (2) **ALONE** but not from (1) alone
(C) If you can get the answer from **BOTH** (1) **and** (2) **TOGETHER** but not from
   (1) alone or (2) alone
(D) If **EITHER** statement (1) **ALONE OR** statement (2) **ALONE** suffices
(E) If you **CANNOT** get the answer from statements (1) and (2) **TOGETHER** but
   need even more data

10. There are 4 quarts in a gallon. A gallon of motor oil sells for $12 and a quart of the
    same oil sells for $5. The owner of a rental agency has 6 machines and each machine
    needs 5 quarts of oil. What is the minimum amount of money she must spend to
    purchase enough oil?

    (A) $84
    (B) $94
    (C) $96
    (D) $102
    (E) $150

11. A store has a parking lot which contains 70 parking spaces. Each row in the parking lot
    contains the same number of parking spaces. The store has bought additional property
    in order to build an addition to the store. When the addition is built, 2 parking spaces
    will be lost from each row; however, 4 more rows will be added to the parking lot. After
    the addition is built, the parking lot will still have 70 parking spaces, and each row will
    contain the same number of parking spaces as every other row. How many rows were in
    the parking lot before the addition was built?

    (A) 5
    (B) 6
    (C) 7
    (D) 10
    (E) 14

12. A piece of wood 5 feet long is cut into three smaller pieces. How long is the longest
    of the three pieces?

    (1) One piece is 2 feet 7 inches long.

    (2) One piece is 7 inches longer than another piece and the remaining piece is
        5 inches long.

13. *AC* is a diameter of the circle. *ACD* is a straight line. What is the value of *x*?

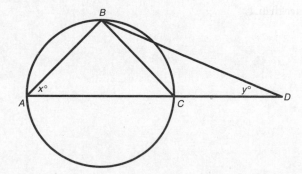

    (1) *AB* = *BC*

    (2) *x* = 2*y*

14. What is the value of y?

    (1) $x + 2y = 6$

    (2) $y^2 - 2y + 1 = 0$

15. Two pipes, A and B, empty into a reservoir. Pipe A can fill the reservoir in 30 minutes by itself. How long will it take for pipe A and pipe B together to fill up the reservoir?

    (1) By itself, pipe B can fill the reservoir in 20 minutes.

    (2) Pipe B has a larger cross-sectional area than pipe A.

16. AB is perpendicular to CO. Is A or B closer to C?

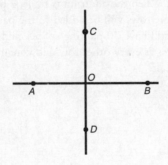

    (1) OA is less than OB.

    (2) $ACBD$ is not a parallelogram.

17. Is xy greater than 1? x and y are both positive.

    (1) x is less than 1.

    (2) y is greater than 1.

18. Does $x = y$?

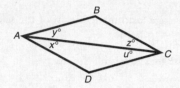

   (1) $z = u$

   (2) $ABCD$ is a parallelogram.

19. Train T leaves town A for town B and travels at a constant rate of speed. At the same time, train S leaves town B for town A and also travels at a constant rate of speed. Town C is between A and B. Which train is traveling faster? Towns A, C, and B lie on a straight line.

   (1) Train S arrives at town C before train T.

   (2) C is closer to A than to B.

20. Does $x = y$?

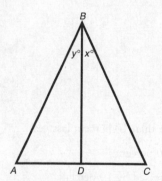

   (1) BD is perpendicular to AC.

   (2) AB is equal to BC.

21. What is the value of $x + y$?

   (1) $x - y = 4$

   (2) $3x + 3y = 4$

(A) If you can get the answer from (1) **ALONE** but not from (2) alone
(B) If you can get the answer from (2) **ALONE** but not from (1) alone
(C) If you can get the answer from **BOTH** (1) **and** (2) **TOGETHER** but not from (1) alone or (2) alone
(D) If **EITHER** statement (1) **ALONE OR** statement (2) **ALONE** suffices
(E) If you **CANNOT** get the answer from statements (1) and (2) **TOGETHER** but need even more data

22. Did the XYZ Corporation have higher sales in 1988 or in 1989? Assume sales are positive.

    (1) In 1988, the sales were twice the average (arithmetic mean) of the sales in 1988, 1989, and 1990.

    (2) In 1990, the sales were 3 times those in 1989.

23. Is *ABDC* a square?

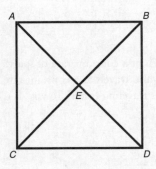

    (1) *BC* is perpendicular to *AD*.

    (2) *BE* = *EC*.

24. *k* is an integer. Is *k* divisible by 12?

    (1) *k* is divisible by 4.

    (2) *k* is divisible by 3.

25. Did the price of lumber rise by more than 10 percent last year?

    (1) Lumber exports increased by 20 percent.

    (2) The amount of timber cut decreased by 10 percent.

26. What was the price of a dozen eggs during the 15th week of the year 2004?

    (1) During the first week of 2004 the price of a dozen eggs was 75¢.

    (2) The price of a dozen eggs rose 1¢ a week every week during the first four months of 2004.

(A) If you can get the answer from (1) **ALONE** but not from (2) alone

(B) If you can get the answer from (2) **ALONE** but not from (1) alone

(C) If you can get the answer from **BOTH (1) and (2) TOGETHER** but not from (1) alone or (2) alone

(D) If **EITHER** statement (1) **ALONE OR** statement (2) **ALONE** suffices

(E) If you **CANNOT** get the answer from statements (1) and (2) **TOGETHER** but need even more data

27.   Is *DE* parallel to *BC*? *DB = AD*.

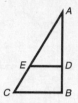

(1)   *AE = EC*

(2)   *DB = EC*

28.   If the area of a rectangle is equal to the area of a square, then the perimeter of the rectangle must be

(A)   one half of the perimeter of the square

(B)   equal to the perimeter of the square

(C)   equal to twice the perimeter of the square

(D)   equal to the square root of the perimeter of the square

(E)   none of the above

29.   Which of the following are possible values for the angles of a parallelogram?

  I.   90°, 90°, 90°, 90°

 II.   40°, 70°, 50°, 140°

III.   50°, 130°, 50°, 130°

(A)   I only

(B)   II only

(C)   I and III only

(D)   II and III only

(E)   I, II, and III

30.   For every novel in the school library there are 2 science books; for each science book there are 7 economics books. Express the ratio of economics books to science books to novels in the school library as a triple ratio.

(A)   7 : 2 : 1

(B)   7 : 1 : 2

(C)   14 : 7 : 2

(D)   14 : 2 : 1

(E)   14 : 2 : 7

31. There are 50 employees in the office of ABC Company. Of these, 22 have taken an accounting course, 15 have taken a course in finance, and 14 have taken a marketing course. Nine of the employees have taken exactly two of the courses, and one employee has taken all three of the courses. How many of the 50 employees have taken none of the courses?

    (A) 0
    (B) 9
    (C) 10
    (D) 11
    (E) 26

32. If $x + y = 4$ and $x - y = 3$, then $x + 2y$ is

    (A) $\dfrac{1}{2}$

    (B) 3.5
    (C) 4

    (D) $4\dfrac{1}{2}$

    (E) $7\dfrac{1}{2}$

33. How much interest will $2,000 earn at an annual rate of 8 percent in 1 year if the interest is compounded every 6 months?

    (A) $160.00
    (B) $163.20
    (C) $249.73
    (D) $332.80
    (E) $2,163.20

34. If BC is parallel to AD and CE is perpendicular to AD, then the area of $ABCD$ is

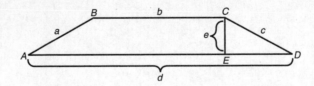

    (A) bd
    (B) $bd + ac$
    (C) ed
    (D) $e(b + d)$
    (E) $.5eb + .5ed$

35. If the price of steak is currently $1.00 a pound, and the price triples every 6 months, how long will it be until the price of steak is $81.00 a pound?

    (A) 1 year
    (B) 2 years

    (C) $2\frac{1}{2}$ years

    (D) 13 years

    (E) $13\frac{1}{2}$ years

36. If $\frac{x}{y} = \frac{2}{3}$, then $\frac{y^2}{x^2}$ is

    (A) $\frac{4}{9}$

    (B) $\frac{2}{3}$

    (C) $\frac{3}{2}$

    (D) $\frac{9}{4}$

    (E) $\frac{5}{2}$

37. What is the maximum number of points of intersection of two circles that have unequal radii?

    (A) none
    (B) 1
    (C) 2
    (D) 3
    (E) infinite

STOP

IF THERE IS STILL TIME REMAINING, YOU MAY REVIEW YOUR ANSWERS. AFTER YOU HAVE CONFIRMED YOUR ANSWERS, YOU CANNOT RETURN TO THESE QUESTIONS.

VERBAL SECTION

TIME: 75 MINUTES

41 QUESTIONS

Reading Comprehension
Directions: This section contains three reading passages. You are to read each one carefully. When answering the questions, you *will* be allowed to refer back to the passages. The questions are based on what is *stated* or *implied* in each passage.

Critical Reasoning
Directions: For each question in this section, choose the best answer among the listed alternatives.

Sentence Correction
Directions: This part of the section consists of a number of sentences in each of which some part or the whole is underlined. Each sentence is followed by five alternative versions of the underlined portion. Select the alternative you consider both most correct and most effective according to the requirements of standard written English. Answer (A) is the same as the original version; if you think the original version is best, select answer (A).

In considering the answer choices, be attentive to matters of grammar, diction, and syntax, as well as clarity, precision, and fluency. Do not select an answer that alters the meaning of the original sentence.

1. Typically, the entrepreneur is seen as an individual who owns and operates a small business. But, simply to own and operate a small business—or even a big business—does not make someone an entrepreneur. If this person is a true entrepreneur, then new products are being created and new ways of providing services are being implemented.

   Which of the following conclusions can best be drawn from the above passage?

   (A) An owner of a large business may be an entrepreneur.
   (B) Someone who develops an enterprise may be considered an entrepreneur.
   (C) Entrepreneurs do not own and operate small businesses.
   (D) Entrepreneurs are the main actors in economic growth.
   (E) Entrepreneurs are investors.

2. The principal reason for our failure was quite apparent <u>to those whom we had brought</u> into the venture.

   (A) to those whom we had brought
   (B) to them whom we had brought
   (C) to the ones whom we had brought
   (D) to those who we had brought
   (E) to those who we had brung

Questions 3–6 are based on the following passage.

It is easy to accept Freud as an applied scientist, and, indeed, he is widely regarded as the twentieth century's master clinician. However, in viewing Marx as an applied social scientist the stance needed is that of a Machiavellian operationalism. The objective is neither
Line to bury nor to praise him. The assumption is simply that he is better understood for being
(5) understood as an applied sociologist. This is in part the clear implication of Marx's *Theses on Feurbach*, which culminate in the resounding 11th thesis: "The philosophers have only interpreted the world in different ways; the point, however, is to change it." This would seem to be the tacit creed of applied scientists everywhere.

Marx was no Faustian, concerned solely with understanding society, but a Promethean
(10) who sought to understand it well enough to influence and to change it. He was centrally concerned with the social problems of a lay group, the proletariat, and there can be little doubt that his work is motivated by an effort to reduce their suffering, as he saw it. His diagnosis was that their increasing misery and alienation engendered endemic class struggle; his prognosis claimed that this would culminate in revolution; his therapeutic prescrip-
(15) tion was class consciousness and active struggle.

Here, as in assessing Durkheim or Freud, the issue is not whether this analysis is empirically correct or scientifically adequate. Furthermore, whether or not this formulation seems to eviscerate Marx's revolutionary core, as critics on the left may charge, or whether the formulation provides Marx with a new veneer of academic respectability, as critics on
(20) the right may allege, is entirely irrelevant from the present standpoint. Insofar as Marx's or any other social scientist's work conforms to a generalized model of applied social science, insofar as it is professionally oriented to the values and social problems of laymen in his society, he may be treated as an applied social scientist.

Despite Durkeim's intellectualistic proclivities and rationalistic pathos, he was too much
(25) the product of European turbulence to turn his back on the travail of his culture. "Why strive for knowledge of reality, if this knowledge cannot aid us in life," he asked. "Social science," he said, "can provide us with rules of action for the future." Durkheim, like Marx, conceived of science as an agency of social action, and like him was professionally oriented to the values and problems of laymen in his society. Unless one sees that Durkheim was in
(30) some part an applied social scientist, it is impossible to understand why he concludes his monumental study of *Suicide* with a chapter on "Practical Consequences," and why, in the *Division of Labor*, he proposes a specific remedy.

3. Which of the following best describes the author's conception of an applied social scientist?

   (A) A professional who listens to people's problems
   (B) A professional who seeks social action and change
   (C) A student of society
   (D) A proponent of class struggle
   (E) A philosopher who interprets the world in a unique way

4. According to the author, which of the following did Marx and Durkheim have in common?

   (A) A belief in the importance of class struggle
   (B) A desire to create a system of social organization
   (C) An interest in penology
   (D) Regard for the practical applications of science
   (E) A sense of the political organization of society

5. It may be inferred from the passage that the applied social scientist might be interested in all of the following subjects *except*

   (A) the theory of mechanics
   (B) how to make workers more efficient
   (C) rehabilitation of juvenile delinquents
   (D) reduction of social tensions
   (E) industrial safety

6. Which of the following best summarizes the author's main point?

   (A) Marx and Durkheim were similar in their ideas.
   (B) Freud, Marx, and Durkheim were all social scientists.
   (C) Philosophers, among others, who are regarded as theoreticians can also be regarded as empiricists.
   (D) Marx and Durkheim were applied social scientists because they were concerned with the solution of social problems.
   (E) Pure and applied sciences have fundamentally similar objectives.

7. During the incumbent president's term of office he succeeded in limiting annual increases in the defense budget by an average of 5 percent. His predecessor experienced annual increases of 8 percent. Therefore, the incumbent president should be given credit for the downturn in defense outlays.

   Which of the following statements, if true, would most seriously weaken the above conclusion?

   (A) Some generals have claimed that the country's defenses have weakened in the past year.
   (B) More soldiers were drafted during the former president's term of office.
   (C) The incumbent president advocates peaceful resolution of international disputes.
   (D) The average annual inflation rate during the incumbent president's term was 4%, while during his predecessor's term it was 10%.
   (E) A disarmament treaty with a major adversary was signed by the incumbent president.

8. Ira is taller than Sam.
   Elliot is taller than Harold.
   Harold is shorter than Gene.
   Sam and Gene are the same height.

   If the above are true, which of the following conditions must also be true?

   (A) Elliot is taller than Gene.
   (B) Elliot is taller than Ira.
   (C) Sam is shorter than Elliot.
   (D) Ira is taller than Harold.
   (E) Sam is shorter than Harold.

9. Although he was the most friendly of all present and <u>different from the others, he hadn't hardly any friends except me.</u>

   (A) different from the others, he hadn't hardly any friends except me
   (B) different than the others, he had hardly any friends except me
   (C) different from the others, he had hardly any friends except me
   (D) different than the others, he hadn't hardly any friends except I
   (E) different from the others, he hardly had any friends except I

10. It was <u>us who had left before he arrived.</u>

    (A) us who had left before he arrived
    (B) we who had left before he arrived
    (C) we who had went before he arrived
    (D) us who had went before he arrived
    (E) we who had left before the time he had arrived

11. Buy Plenty, a supermarket chain, had successfully implemented an in-store promotional campaign based on video messages flashed on a large screen. The purpose of the campaign was to motivate customers to purchase products they had not planned to buy before they entered the store. The sales manager of Build-It Inc., a chain of do-it-yourself hardware stores, saw the campaign and plans to introduce it at Build-It locations.

    The sales managers plan assumes that

    (A) supermarket and hardware products are the same
    (B) products cannot be sold successfully without a video sales campaign
    (C) supermarket chains do not sell hardware products
    (D) consumer decision making to buy products does not differ substantially when it comes to both supermarket and hardware products
    (E) in-store campaigns are more effective than out-of-store advertising and sales promotion

Questions 12–16 are based on the following passage.

In the 1970s, Charles Kowal at Mount Palomar Observatory discovered Chiron, an asteroid whose orbit was in the vicinity of Saturn and Uranus, far from other known asteroids.

In the 1990s, robotic telescopes began to comb the Kuiper Belt, the region of the solar
Line system beyond the orbit of Neptune. More than 400 objects were discovered there, with the
(5) biggest object about half the size of Pluto.

Last year, the farthest asteroid to date was found: Sedna, named after an Inuit goddess who dwells in a cave at the bottom of the Arctic Ocean. Sedna has a very eccentric orbit that takes it nearly 1,000 times farther from the Sun than Pluto and outside the Kuiper Belt.

In early January 2005, the same team that discovered Sedna found a larger body. From
(10) its light and absence of infrared radiation, the team of Brown, Trujillo, and Rabinovitz are certain that the object's size is between that of Pluto (1,485 miles across) and our moon (2,160 miles across).

Its temporary name is 2003 UB313. Presently, the object is 9 billion miles from the sun, about three times as far as Pluto. At this distance from the Sun, 2003 UB313 has a surface
(15) temperature of 415° below zero.

This Kuiper Belt object takes 560 Earth years to orbit the Sun. 2003 UB313's orbit has a tilt of 44 degrees to the plane of the solar system, more than twice the tilt of Pluto (the previous planet record holder). Its minimum solar distance is 3.3 billion years, close to the edge of Neptune's orbit.

(20) 2003 UB313's orbit is well known due to its being captured on wide angle photographs taken in 2003 by the 4-foot-wide Schmidt telescope on Mount Palomar.

Will UB313 be called the tenth planet? The decision is up to the International Astronomical Union.

Asteroids are mini-planets, most of which are located in the asteroid belt, between the
(25) orbits of Mars and Jupiter. The largest of the belt asteroids is Ceres, about 700 miles across (i.e., roughly the size of Texas). Most asteroids are much smaller, typically less than a mile across.

While most asteroids keep their distance from Earth, there are probably 1,000 asteroids that are located in the inner solar system and may cross Earth's orbit.

(30) Last summer, a robotic telescope discovered a 1,000-foot-wide asteroid that crosses Earth's orbit. The object is 99942 Apophis. Once Apophis' orbit was determined, its future positions decades ahead were generated by computer.

There was a shock when an early study showed Apophis to be on a collision course with Earth in 2029. More early observations were utilized to refine Apophis' orbit; new calcula-
(35) tions showed that on April 13, 2029, Apophis would instead pass 22,000 miles from Earth, which is a little less than three Earth diameters. Apophis will then be visible to the naked eye from Europe and western Africa.

12. The author provides information that would answer which of the following questions?

    (A) What are some of the causes of asteroids?
    (B) Who is Charles Kowal?
    (C) What are asteroids?
    (D) When will Neptune collide with Earth?
    (E) How far are asteroids from the sun?

13. It may be concluded from the passage that

    (A) the Kuiper Belt includes 1,000 asteroids
    (B) there is a chance that Apophis may collide with Earth
    (C) most asteroids are dangerously close to Earth
    (D) there is no inherent danger from falling asteroids
    (E) asteroid research is not very advanced scientifically

14. The passage mentions that

    (A) the decision to name new asteroids is made by their discovers
    (B) Sedna is the farthest asteroid from Earth
    (C) the largest asteroid is Pluto
    (D) Apophis is about the size of Pluto
    (E) UB313 will be named after Brown, Trujillo, and Rabinovitz

15. Which of the following titles best describes the contents of the passage?

    (A) "The Impact of Asteroids on the Solar System"
    (B) "What Is the Tenth Planet?"
    (C) "How Asteroids Are Discovered"
    (D) "The Search for Asteroids"
    (E) "The Discoveries of Charles Kowal"

16. According to the author, all of the following are asteroids *except*

    (A) Inuit
    (B) Sedna
    (C) Ceres
    (D) Apophis
    (E) UB313

17. She is the <u>sort of person who I feel would be capable of making these kind of</u> statements.

    (A) sort of person who I feel would be capable of making these kind of
    (B) sort of a person who I feel would be capable of making these kind of
    (C) sort of person who I feel would be capable of making these kinds of
    (D) sort of person whom I feel would be capable of making these kinds of
    (E) sort of person whom I feel would be capable of making this kind of

18. The movement to ownership by unions is the latest step in the progression from management ownership to employee ownership. Employee ownership can save depressed and losing companies.

    All of the following statements, if true, provide support for the claim above *except*

    (A) Employee-owned companies generally have higher productivity.
    (B) Employee participation in management raises morale.
    (C) Employee union ownership drives up salaries and wages.
    (D) Employee union ownership enables workers to share in the profits.
    (E) Employee union ownership makes it easier to lay off redundant workers.

19. The burning of coal, oil, and other combustible energy sources produces carbon dioxide, a natural constituent of the atmosphere. Elevated levels of carbon dioxide are thought to be responsible for half of the greenhouse effect. Enough carbon dioxide has been sent into the atmosphere already to cause a significant temperature increase. Growth in industrial production must be slowed, or production processes must be changed.

    Which of the following, if true, would tend to weaken the strength of the above conclusion?

    (A) Many areas of the world are cold anyway, so a small rise in temperature would be welcome.
    (B) Carbon dioxide is bad for the health.
    (C) Most carbon dioxide is emitted by automobiles.
    (D) Industry is switching over to synthetic liquid fuel extracted from coal.
    (E) A shift to other energy sources would be too costly.

Questions 20–24 are based on the following passage.

The institutions engaged in artistic or scientific activity are centrally concerned with the maintenance and extension of cultural systems. The growth of government patronage of these areas suggests that facilitation and production of culture has become a major state
Line activity in the United States. The objectives underlying this state intervention are not well
(5) understood. The central purpose of this paper is to evaluate the relative strengths of several alternative explanations for the government's involvement in the production of culture. A second purpose is to suggest the likely impact of government patronage on the physical sciences, social sciences, and arts in America.

Four distinct models for explaining the state's growing interest in the production of cul-
(10) ture can be identified. One model emphasizes the value of patronage for the maintenance of the cultural institutions in question. A second model stresses the utility of the investment for capital accumulation. A third model points toward the value of supporting science and art for the administration of government programs. The fourth model identifies the ideological potential of science and art as a primary reason for government patronage.

(15)   *Science and art for their own sake.* The first model of government patronage is predicated on the structural-functionalist assumption that the government is a relatively neutral instrument for the articulation and pursuit of collective goals in a society with relatively autonomous subsystems. Pure science and art are vital societal subsystems, and the government moves to protect and develop these areas to ensure the continued production of cul-
(20) ture for the benefit of all members of society. Thus, the government intervenes directly as the final patron of public goods that would otherwise be unavailable.

Two important corollaries follow from this formulation, which makes it empirically testable. First, the timing of government intervention should primarily be related to economic crises faced by the arts and sciences themselves, not to crises in the political system,
(25) economy, or elsewhere. Second, government intervention should generally take the form of protecting the paradigm of the arts and sciences. Specifically, federal funding should be allocated to the most creative artists and organizations, as defined by the relevant artistic community. Similarly, funding should be preferentially bestowed on scientists whose research is making the greatest contribution to the advance of the scientific discipline, regardless of its
(30) relevance for outside problems or crises.*

*Reprinted from Michael Useem, "Government Patronage of Science and Art in America," pp. 123–142 in Richard A. Peterson, ed., *The Production of Culture,* © Sage Publications, Inc.

20. Which of the following best summarizes the four culture production models mentioned in the passage?

(A) They are based on economic criteria.
(B) They explain why government should support cultural activities.
(C) They argue against government intervention.
(D) They are not well understood.
(E) They argue for a separation of government and the arts.

21. The major objective of the passage is to

(A) increase appreciation for the arts
(B) provide an ideological basis for artistic funding
(C) explain why government supports cultural activities
(D) argue for more government support of the arts and sciences
(E) demonstrate cultural activities in the United States

22. A corollary of the science and art for government programs is

    (A) funding should be provided by government only as a last resort
    (B) funding will be geared to projects of value to the government
    (C) funding is to be provided only to nongovernmental employees
    (D) funding by the government is self-defeating
    (E) funding by the government is inflationary

23. A conclusion reached by the author of the passage is that

    (A) the arts and sciences have been funded by the government for different reasons.
    (B) government is a neutral observer of the arts and sciences.
    (C) government intervention in the arts and sciences is declining.
    (D) the arts and sciences are not dependent on government funding.
    (E) politics and science go together.

24. The idea that government should support the arts and sciences only when the market does not provide enough funds belongs to which school?

    (A) "their own sake"
    (B) "business application"
    (C) "government programs"
    (D) "ideological control"
    (E) all of the above

Questions 25 and 26 are based on the following passage.

Contrary to charges made by opponents of the new trade bill, the bill's provisions for taking action against foreign countries that place barriers against American exports is justified. Opponents should take note that restrictive trade legislation in the 1930s succeeded in improving the U.S. trade balance even though economists were against it.

25. The author's method of rebutting opponents of the new trade bill is to

    (A) attack the patriotism of its opponents
    (B) attack the opponents' characters rather than their claims
    (C) imply an analogy between the new trade bill and previous trade legislation
    (D) suggest that economists were against both pieces of legislation
    (E) imply that previous legislation also permitted retaliatory action against foreign countries

26. Opponents of the new legislation could defend themselves against the author's strategy by arguing that

    (A) the fact that past trade legislation improved the trade balance does not mean that the present bill will do the same
    (B) economists are not always right
    (C) the United States had a trade deficit both in the 1930s and at the time of the new bill
    (D) the new law is not as strong as the 1930s bill
    (E) America's new trading partners have also passed similar legislation

27. Beside me, there were many persons who were altogether aggravated by his manners.

    (A) Beside me, there were many persons who were altogether aggravated
    (B) Beside me, there were many persons who were all together aggravated
    (C) Besides me, there were many persons who were altogether aggravated
    (D) Besides me, there were many persons who were altogether irritated
    (E) Beside me, there were many persons who were all together irritated

28. The owner, who was a kind man, spoke to the boy and he was very rude.

    (A) , who was a kind man, spoke to the boy and he
    (B) was a kind man and he spoke to the boy and he
    (C) spoke to the boy kindly and the boy
    (D) , a kind man, spoke to the boy who
    (E) who was a kind man spoke to the boy and he

29. Because we cooperated together, we divided up the work on the report that had been assigned.

    (A) together, we divided up the work on the report that had been assigned
    (B) together, we divided the work on the report that had been assigned
    (C) , we divided up the work on the report that was assigned
    (D) , we divided the work on the assigned report
    (E) we divided up the work on the assigned report

30. During 1999, advertising expenditures on canned food products increased by 20 percent, while canned food consumption rose by 25 percent.

Each of the following, if true, could help to explain the increase in food consumption *except*

    (A) Advertising effectiveness increased
    (B) Canned food prices decreased relative to substitutes
    (C) Canned food product were available in more stores
    (D) Can opener production doubled
    (E) Per-capita consumption of frozen foods declined

31. Inflation rose by 5.1 percent over the second quarter, up from 4.1 percent during the first quarter of the year, and higher than the 3.3 percent recorded during the same time last year. However, the higher price index did not seem to alarm Wall Street, as stock prices remained steady.

Which of the following, if true, could explain this reaction to Wall Street?

    (A) Stock prices were steady because of a fear that inflation would continue.
    (B) The president announced that he was concerned about rising inflation.
    (C) Economists warned that inflation would persist.
    (D) Much of the quarterly increase in the price level was due to a summer drought's effect on food prices.
    (E) Other unfavorable economic news had overshadowed the fact of inflation.

32. "Ever since I arrived at the college last week, I've been shocked by the poor behavior of students and the unfriendly attitude of the townspeople, but the professors are very erudite and genuinely helpful. Still, I wonder if I should have come here in the first place."

    Which of the following, if true, would weaken the above conclusion?

    (A) Professors are not always helpful to students.
    (B) The college has more than 50,000 students.
    (C) The college is far from the student's home.
    (D) Not all professors have doctorates.
    (E) The narrator was unsure of staying at the college.

33. The senator <u>rose up to say that, in her opinion, she thought the bill should be referred back</u> to committee.

    (A) rose up to say that, in her opinion, she thought the bill should be referred back
    (B) rose up to say that she thought the bill should be referred back
    (C) rose up to say that she thought the bill should be referred
    (D) rose up to say that, in her opinion, the bill should be referred
    (E) rose to say that she thought the bill should be referred

34. I don't know <u>as I concur with your decision to try and</u> run for office.

    (A) as I concur with your decision to try and
    (B) that I concur in your decision to try to
    (C) as I concur in your decision to try and
    (D) that I concur in your decision to try to
    (E) as I concur with your decision to try, to

35. Jones, the president of the union and <u>who is also a member of the community group,</u> will be in charge of the negotiations.

    (A) who is also a member of the community group
    (B) since he is a member of the community group
    (C) a member of the community group
    (D) also being a member of the community group
    (E) in addition, who is a member of the community group

36. A local garbage disposal company increased its profitability even though it reduced its prices in order to attract new customers. This was made possible through the use of automated trucks, thereby reducing the number of workers needed per truck. The company also switched from a concentration on household hauling to a concentration on commercial hauling. As a result of its experience, company management planned to replace all its old trucks and increase the overall size of the truck fleet, doubling hauling capacity.

    The company's plan, as outlined above, takes into consideration each of the following *except*

    (A) Commercial clients have more potential than household customers.
    (B) The demand for garbage removal services is sensitive to price.
    (C) Demand for garbage removal services would increase in the future.
    (D) Doubling of capacity would not necessitate a substantial increase in the workforce.
    (E) Doubling of capacity would not cause bottlenecks, leading to a decrease in productivity.

37. Every town with a pool hall has its share of unsavory characters. This is because the pool hall attracts gamblers and all gamblers are unsavory.

    Which of the following, if true, cannot be inferred from the above?

    (A) All gamblers are unsavory.
    (B) All pool halls attract gamblers.
    (C) Every town has unsavory characters.
    (D) All gamblers are attracted by pool halls.
    (E) An explanation of what attracts gamblers.

38. In an August 2000 poll, 36 percent of voters called themselves Republican or said they were independents leaning toward being Republicans. In November 2004, the Republican figure rose to 47 percent. But in a later survey, the Republicans were down to 38 percent. Therefore, the Democrats are likely to win the next election.

    Which of the following, if true, would most seriously weaken the above conclusion?

    (A) Republicans were a minority in 2004, but a Republican president was elected.
    (B) People tend to switch their votes at the last minute.
    (C) People vote for the best candidate, not for a political party.
    (D) No one can predict how people will vote.
    (E) It has been shown that 85% of Republicans vote in an election, compared to 50% of the Democrats.

39. Average family income is right where it was 20 years ago, even though in most families these days, both husbands and wives are working.

    The above statement implies all of the following *except*

    (A) Even though nominal family income may have increased, inflation has risen at an equal rate.
    (B) More husbands and wives are working today than 20 years ago.
    (C) It was more prevalent for only one spouse to work 20 years ago than it is today.
    (D) Wives earn more than husbands today.
    (E) The price level was lower 20 years ago.

40. The instructor told the student to hold the club lightly, keeping his eye on the ball, and drawing the club back quickly, but that too much force should not be used on the downward stroke.

    (A) to hold the club lightly, keeping his eye on the ball, and drawing the club back quickly, but that too much force should not be used
    (B) to hold the club lightly, keep his eye on the ball, and drawing the club back quickly, and that too much force should not be used
    (C) to hold the club lightly, keep his eye on the ball, draw the club quickly back, and not use too much force
    (D) to hold the club lightly, keep his eye on the ball, draw the club back quickly and that too much force should not be used
    (E) he should hold the club lightly, keeping his eye on the ball, drawing the club back quickly, and not using too much force

41. The <u>horse, ridden by the experienced jockey with the broken leg, had</u> to be destroyed.

    (A) horse, ridden by the experienced jockey with the broken leg, had
    (B) horse ridden by the experienced jockey with the broken leg had
    (C) horse with the broken leg ridden by the experienced, jockey had
    (D) horse with the broken leg ridden by the experienced jockey, had
    (E) horse with the broken leg, ridden by the experienced jockey, had

*IF THERE IS STILL TIME REMAINING, YOU MAY
REVIEW YOUR ANSWERS. AFTER YOU HAVE CONFIRMED
YOUR ANSWERS, YOU CANNOT RETURN TO THESE QUESTIONS.*

Answer Key
DIAGNOSTIC TEST

Quantitative Section

1. B	11. D	21. B	31. C
2. E	12. D	22. A	32. D
3. A	13. A	23. E	33. B
4. D	14. B	24. C	34. E
5. D	15. A	25. E	35. B
6. B	16. A	26. C	36. D
7. E	17. E	27. A	37. C
8. B	18. C	28. E	
9. D	19. C	29. C	
10. B	20. C	30. D	

Verbal Section

1. B	12. C	23. A	34. B
2. A	13. B	24. A	35. C
3. B	14. B	25. C	36. E
4. D	15. B	26. A	37. C
5. A	16. A	27. D	38. E
6. D	17. C	28. D	39. D
7. D	18. C	29. D	40. C
8. D	19. C	30. D	41. E
9. C	20. B	31. D	
10. B	21. C	32. B	
11. D	22. B	33. E	

Analysis

Self-Scoring Guide—Analytical Writing

Evaluate your writing tests (or have a friend or teacher evaluate them for you) on the following basis. Read each essay completely, paying special attention to its logical organization and use of examples and facts to buttress its claims or position. Assign a holistic score between 0 and 6, using the scale below. Your writing score will be the average of the scores of the two essays.

6 Outstanding — Cogent, well-articulated analysis of the issue or critique of the argument. Develops a position with insightful reasons and persuasive examples. Well organized. Superior command of language and variety of syntax. Only minor flaws in grammar, usage, and mechanics.

5 Strong — Well-developed analysis or critique. Develops a position with well-chosen examples or reasons. Generally well organized. Clear control of language and variety of syntax. Minor flaws in grammar, usage, and mechanics.

4 Adequate — Competent analysis or critique. Develops a position with relevant reasons or examples. Adequately organized. Adequate control of language, but may lack syntactic variety. May have some flaws in grammar, usage, and mechanics.

3 Limited — Competent but clearly flawed analysis or critique. Vague or limited in developing a position. Poorly organized. Weak in using relevant examples or reasons. Language used imprecisely or lacking in sentence variety. Contains major errors or frequent minor errors in grammar, usage, and mechanics.

2 Seriously Flawed — Serious weaknesses in analysis and organization. Unclear or seriously limited in presenting or developing a position. Disorganized. Few relevant examples or reasons. Frequent serious problems in language and sentence structure. Numerous errors in grammar, usage, or mechanics that interfere with meaning.

1 Fundamentally Deficient — Little evidence of ability to organize and develop a coherent response to issue or argument. Severe and persistent errors in language and sentence structure. Pervasive pattern of errors in grammar, usage, and mechanics that severely interfere with meaning.

0 Unscorable — Illegible or not written in the assigned topic.

ANSWERS EXPLAINED

Quantitative Section

1. **(B)** Let L be the original length and W the original width. The new length is 120 percent of L, which is $1.2L$; the new width is 80 percent of W, which is $.8W$. The area of a rectangle is length times width, so the original area is LW and the new area is $(1.2L)(.8W)$ or $.96LW$. Since the new area is 96 percent of the original area, the area has decreased by 4 percent. (I-4)

2. **(E)** The first 1,000 copies cost x dollars each, so altogether they will cost $1,000x$ dollars. Since z is greater than 1,000, there are $z - 1,000$ copies left, which each cost y dollars. Their cost is $(z - 1,000)y$. Thus the total cost is $1,000x + (z - 1,000)y$. However, this is not one of the answer choices. But $(z - 1,000)y = zy - 1,000y$, so the total cost is $1,000x - 1,000y + yz$ or $1,000(x - y) + yz$, which is choice (E). If you want to check your work, let $x = 5$, $y = 2$, and $z = 3,000$. (II-3)

3. **(A)** When two integers are multiplied, the units digit of the product is the last digit of the product of the last digit of each of the integers. For example, the product of 22×18 is 396. The last digit of 396 is 6. And 6 is also the last digit of 16 which is the product of 2 (the last digit of 22) times 8 (the last digit of 18). When an integer is squared, the last digit of the square is the last digit of the square of the last digit. Squaring an odd number gives an odd number, and odd numbers cannot end in 8. Squaring a number that ends in 0 gives a number that ends in 0. Squaring a number that ends in 2 or 8 gives a number that ends in 4. Squaring a number that ends in 4 or 6 results in a number that ends in 6. So no integer squared ends in 8. Therefore, the correct choice is (A). (I-1)

4. **(D)** Two-thirds of the stock cost $\frac{2}{3}$ of \$1,500, or \$1,000. So, when its value doubled, it was worth \$2,000. The profit on this part of the stock is \$2,000 − \$1,000 = \$1,000. The remaining stock cost \$1,500 − \$1,000 = \$500. Five times the purchase price for this part of the stock is $5 \times \$500 = \$2,500$. The profit on this part is \$2,500 − \$500 = \$2,000. So the total profit is \$1,000 + \$2,000 = \$3,000, which is choice (D). (II-3)

5. **(D)** Drawing a picture makes this problem easy. One way to solve the problem is to use coordinate geometry. Let A have coordinates $(0,0)$; then the coordinates for B, C, D, and E are $(8,0)$, $(8,6)$, $(24,6)$, and $(24,18)$, respectively. So the distance from A to E is the square root of $24^2 + 18^2 = \sqrt{576 + 324} = \sqrt{900}$, which is 30. (III-9)

6. **(B)** From the information given you know that x and y are both positive and that $x < y$. So, we know that xy is positive. Since $xy = xy$ and $x < y$, we have that $x(xy) < y(xy)$, so (A) < (B).

Since $5 < 7 < y$, we know that $5(xy) < y(xy)$, so (C) < (B). Since $x < 3$, we know $\left(\frac{4}{3}\right)x < 4$ so $\left(\frac{4}{3}\right)x(xy) < 4xy$ so (D) < (B). Since $y > 7$ and $x < 3$, (E) is obviously less than (B). Therefore, (B) has the greatest value and is the correct choice. (II-7)

7. **(E)** STATEMENT (1) alone is not sufficient. If every employee received a raise of \$800, then the median in 2000 would be $x + 800$, but raises could be distributed in several different ways and still have the average raise equal to \$800. For example, if the top 10 percent received all the increases and everyone else received no increase, the median would not change from 1999. Information about only the range gives us the difference between the largest and smallest salaries; this does not let us find the middle salary, which is what we need for the median. So STATEMENT (2) along with STATEMENT (1) is not sufficient. (I-7)

8. **(B)** Since 10 is $\frac{1}{5}$ of 50, the 10 apprentices should do $\frac{1}{5}$ as much work as 50 apprentices.

Since 50 apprentices did the job in 4 hours, in 1 hour 50 apprentices will do $\frac{1}{4}$ of the job.

Therefore, 10 apprentices should do $\frac{1}{5}$ of $\frac{1}{4} = \frac{1}{20}$ of the job in an hour.

Since 15 is $\frac{1}{2}$ of 30, 15 skilled workers will do half as much work as 30 skilled workers.

The 30 skilled workers finished the job in $4\frac{1}{2}$ hours, which is $\frac{9}{2}$ hours, so in 1 hour they

will do $\frac{2}{9}$ of the job. Therefore, 15 skilled workers will do $\frac{1}{2}$ of $\frac{2}{9} = \frac{1}{9}$ of the job in

1 hour. So both groups will do $\frac{1}{20} + \frac{1}{9} = \frac{9}{180} + \frac{20}{180} = \frac{29}{180}$ of the job in 1 hour. (II-3)

9. **(D)** Since angle *ABC* is a right triangle, we know that the length of *AD* squared is equal to

the sum of y^2 and x^2. However, none of the answers given is $\sqrt{x^2 + y^2}$. The area of

triangle *ABC* is $\left(\frac{1}{2}\right)x(y + z)$, and the area of triangle *ABD*, which is $\left(\frac{1}{2}\right)xy$, must be one half

of $\left(\frac{1}{2}\right)x(y + z)$. So $\left(\frac{1}{4}\right)xy + \left(\frac{1}{4}\right)xz = \left(\frac{1}{2}\right)xy$, which can be solved to give $y = z$. Since angle

ABC is a right triangle, $w^2 = (y + z)^2 + x^2 = (2y)^2 + x^2$. So $w^2 = 4y^2 + x^2$. Since we want

$x + y$, we subtract $3y^2$ from each side to get $w^2 - 3y^2 = y^2 + x^2$. Therefore, the length of *AD*
squared is $w^2 - 3y^2$. (III-4, III-7)

10. **(B)** The total amount of oil needed is $6 \times 5 = 30$ quarts, or 7 gallons and 2 quarts. Since
the cost of oil per quart is cheaper when you purchase by the gallon, the owner should buy
at least 7 gallons of oil. However, in order to get the remaining 2 gallons, it is cheaper
to buy 2 quarts individually rather than another gallon. So the minimum amount is
$7 \times \$12 + 2 \times \$5 = \$84 + \$10 = \$94$. The correct answer is (B). (II-3)

11. **(D)** Call *s* the number of spaces in each row and *r* the number of rows in the parking lot
before the addition is built. The parking lot had 70 parking spaces, so $sr = 70$. Since after the
addition is built there will be 4 more rows, 2 fewer spaces in each row, and a total of 70
spaces, we know that $(s - 2)(r + 4) = 70$. You could solve these two equations by algebra, but
it would be rather lengthy and there is a faster method. Since the number of rows and the
number of spaces must be positive integers, you are looking for a way to write 70 as the
product of two factors *s* and *r* with the additional property that $s - 2$ and $r + 4$ also have
70 as their product. Writing 70 as a product of primes, we get $70 = 2 \times 35 = 2 \times 5 \times 7$.
Therefore, the only possibilities for *s* and *r* are listed here:

s	r	s	r
1	70	10	7
2	35	14	5
5	14	35	2
7	10	70	1

Now just check whether any pair of solutions (s, r) has the property that $s - 2$ and $r + 4$ is a solution. For example, if $s = 5$ and $r = 14$, then $s - 2 = 3$ and $r + 4 = 18$, which are not solutions. But if $s = 7$ and $r = 10$, then $s - 2 = 5$ and $r + 4 = 14$, which is also a solution. It is easy to see this is the only solution that works. So before the addition was built, there were 10 rows, each with 7 spaces. (I-1)

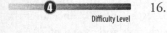

12. **(D)** STATEMENT (1) alone is sufficient. Since 2 feet 7 inches is more than half of 5 feet, the piece that is 2 feet 7 inches long must be longer than the other two pieces put together.

STATEMENT (2) alone is sufficient. Since one piece is 5 inches long, the sum of the lengths of the remaining two pieces is 4 feet 7 inches. Since one piece is 7 inches longer than the other, $L + (L + 7 \text{ inches}) = 4$ feet 7 inches, where L is the length of the smaller of the two remaining pieces. Solving the equations yields $L + 7$ inches as the length of the longest piece. (II-2)

13. **(A)** Since AC is a diameter, angle ABC is inscribed in a semicircle and is therefore a right angle.

STATEMENT (1) alone is sufficient since it implies that the two other angles in the triangle must be equal. Since the sum of the angles of a triangle is 180°, we can deduce that $x = 45$.

STATEMENT (2) alone is not sufficient. There is no information about the angle ABD; so STATEMENT (2) cannot be used to find the angles of triangle ABD. (III-6)

14. **(B)** STATEMENT (2) alone is sufficient, $y^2 - 2y + 1 = (y - 1)^2$, and the only solution of $(y - 1) = 0$ is $y = 1$.

STATEMENT (1) alone is not sufficient. $x + 2y = 6$ implies $y = 3 - \dfrac{x}{2}$, but there are no data given about the value of x. (II-2)

15. **(A)** STATEMENT (1) alone is sufficient. Pipe A fills up $\dfrac{1}{30}$ of the reservoir per minute.

STATEMENT (1) says pipe B fills up $\dfrac{1}{20}$ of the reservoir per minute, so A and B together fill up $\dfrac{1}{20} + \dfrac{1}{30}$ or $\dfrac{5}{60}$ or $\dfrac{1}{12}$ of the reservoir.

You should not waste any time actually solving the problem. Remember, you only have to decide if there is enough information to let you answer the question.

STATEMENT (2) alone is not sufficient. There is no information about how long it takes pipe B to fill the reservoir. (II-3)

16. **(A)** STATEMENT (1) alone is sufficient. Draw the lines AC and BC; then AOC and BOC are right triangles since AB is perpendicular to CO. By the Pythagorean theorem, $(AC)^2 = (AO)^2 + (CO)^2$ and $(BC)^2 = (OB)^2 + (CO)^2$; so if AO is less than OB, then AC is less than BC.

STATEMENT (2) alone is not sufficient. There is no restriction on where the point D is. (III-5, III-4)

17. **(E)** STATEMENTS (1) and (2) together are not sufficient. If $x = \dfrac{1}{2}$ and $y = 3$, then xy is greater than 1, but if $x = \dfrac{1}{2}$ and $y = \dfrac{3}{2}$, then xy is less than 1. This is a good example of the use of specific values for x and y to decide whether the given statements are sufficient to deduce the desired conclusion. (II-7)

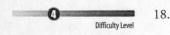

18. **(C)** STATEMENT (1) alone is not sufficient. By moving the point B along the original side BC, we can have either $x = y$ or $x \neq y$ and still have $z = u$.

STATEMENT (2) alone is not sufficient. It implies that $x = z$ and $y = u$, but gives no information to compare x and y.

STATEMENTS (1) and (2) together, however, yield $x = y$. (III-5)

19. **(C)** STATEMENT (1) alone is not sufficient. If town *C* were closer to *B*, even if *S* were going slower than *T*, it could arrive at *C* first. But if you also use STATEMENT (2), then train *S* must be traveling faster than train *T* since it is further from *B* to *C* than it is from *A* to *C*.

So STATEMENTS (1) and (2) together are sufficient.

STATEMENT (2) alone is insufficient since it gives no information about the trains. (II-3)

20. **(C)** STATEMENT (2) alone is not sufficient since *D* can be any point on the line *AC* if we assume only STATEMENT (2).

STATEMENT (1) alone is not sufficient. Depending on the position of point *C*, *x* and *y* can be equal or unequal. For example, in both of the following triangles *BD* is perpendicular to *AC*.

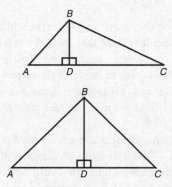

If STATEMENTS (1) and (2) are both true, then $x = y$. The triangles *ABD* and *BDC* are both right triangles with two pairs of corresponding sides equal; the triangles are therefore congruent and $x = y$. (III-4)

21. **(B)** STATEMENT (2) alone is sufficient since $3x + 3y$ is $3(x + y)$. (Therefore, if $3x + 3y = 4$, then $x + y = \frac{4}{3}$.)

STATEMENT (1) alone is not sufficient, since you need another equation besides $x - y = 4$ to find the values of *x* and *y*. (II-2)

22. **(A)** STATEMENT (1) alone is sufficient. We know that the total of sales for 1988, 1989, and 1990 is three times the average and that sales in 1988 were twice the average. Then the total of sales in 1989 and 1990 was equal to the average. Therefore, sales were less in 1989 than in 1988.

STATEMENT (2) alone is insufficient since it does not relate sales in 1989 to sales in 1988. (I-7)

23. **(E)** STATEMENTS (1) and (2) together are not sufficient since points *A* and *D* can be moved and STATEMENTS (1) and (2) will still be satisfied. (III-5)

24. **(C)** List the first few numbers that are divisible by 4, such as 4, 8, 12, 16, 20, 24, . . ., and list the first few numbers that are divisible by 3, such as 3, 6, 9, 12, 15, 18, 21, 24, ... Notice that the integers that appear in both lists are divisible by 12. STATEMENT (1) alone is not sufficient, since 24 and 16 are both divisible by 4 but only 24 is divisible by 12.

STATEMENT (2) alone is not sufficient since 24 and 15 are divisible by 3 but 15 is not divisible by 12.

STATEMENT (1) implies that $k = 4m$ for some integer *m*. If you assume STATEMENT (2), then since *k* is divisible by 3, either 4 or *m* is divisible by 3. Since 4 is not divisible by 3, *m* must be. Therefore, $m = 3j$, where *j* is some integer and $k = 4 \times 3j$ or $12j$. So *k* is divisible by 12. Therefore, STATEMENTS (1) and (2) together are sufficient. (I-1)

③ Difficulty Level

25. **(E)** Both statements give facts that *might* explain why the price of lumber rose. However, even using both statements you have no information about the price of lumber.

③ Difficulty Level

26. **(C)** You need (1) to know what the price was at the beginning of 2004. Using (2) you could then compute the price during the 15th week. Either statement alone is insufficient. You should not actually compute the price since it would only waste time. (II-6)

⑦ Difficulty Level

27. **(A)** (1) alone is sufficient since the line connecting the midpoints of two sides of a triangle is parallel to the third side. (2) alone is insufficient. In an isosceles triangle statement (2) would imply that *ED* is parallel to *BC*, but in a nonisosceles triangle, (2) would imply that *ED* and *BC* are not parallel. (III-4)

⑧ Difficulty Level

28. **(E)** Let *L* be the length and *W* be the width of the rectangle, and let *S* be the length of a side of the square. It is given that $LW = S^2$. A relation must be found between $2L + 2W$ and $4S$. It is possible to construct squares and rectangles so that each of (A), (B), (C), and (D) is false, so (E) is correct. For example, if the rectangle is a square, then the two figures are identical and (A), (C), and (D) are false. If the rectangle is not equal to a square, then the perimeter of the rectangle is larger than the perimeter of the square, so (B) is also false. (III-7)

⑦ Difficulty Level

29. **(C)** Since a parallelogram is a four-sided polygon, the sum of the angles of a parallelogram must be $(4 - 2)180° = 360°$. (A diagonal divides a parallelogram into two triangles, and the sum of each triangle's angles is 180°.) Since the sum of the angles in II is not 360°, II is not possible. But I and III both consist of angles whose sum is 360°. Also, since in both I and III opposite angles are equal, (C) is the correct choice. Note that a rectangle is also a parallelogram, so I does give possible values for the angles of a parallelogram. (III-3, III-5)

⑧ Difficulty Level

30. **(D)** If you know two ratios, *A* : *B* and *B* : *C*, you can combine them into a triple ratio if *B* is the same number and represents the same quantity in both ratios. We know that the ratio of economics books to science books is 7 : 1 and that the ratio of novels to science books is 1 : 2. However, we can't combine this into the triple ratio 7 : 1 : 2 since 1 in the first ratio represents science books and 1 in the second ratio represents novels. We need science books as the middle term in the triple ratio, so we express the second ratio as: The ratio of science books to novels is 2 : 1. Now, the ratio of economics books to science books is 7 : 1 and the ratio of science books to novels is 2 : 1. Since a ratio is unchanged if both sides are multiplied by the same positive number, we can also express the ratio of economics books to science books as 14 : 2. Finally, we can combine these into the triple ratio 14 : 2 : 1 of economics books to science books to novels. (II-5)

⑦ Difficulty Level

31. **(C)** A diagram helps.

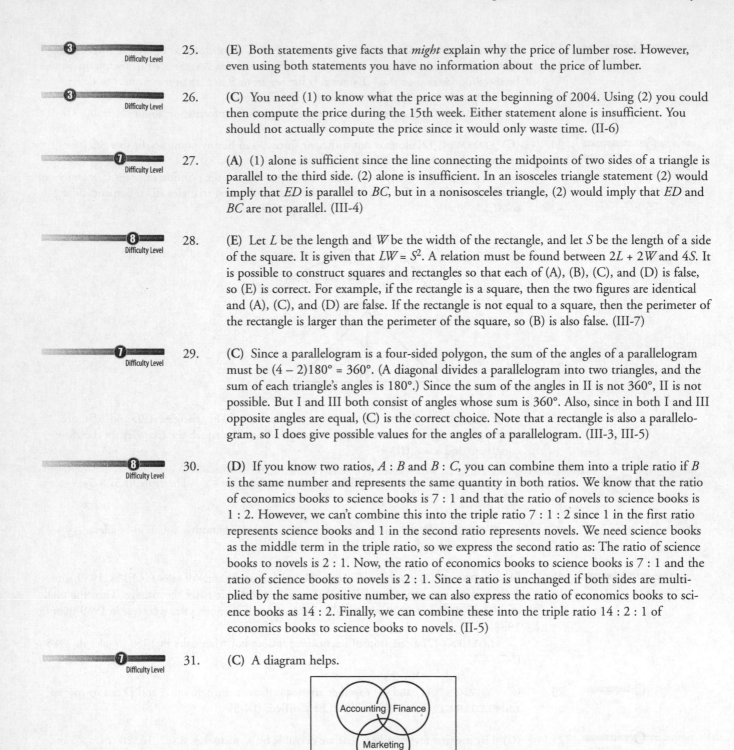

We want to know how many people are not in any of the sets. The easy way to do this is to find the number in at least one of the sets and subtract this number from 50. To find the number of employees in at least one set, *do not count the same employee more than once*. If you add 22, 15, and 14, an employee who took exactly two of the courses will be counted twice, and employees who took all three courses will be counted three times. So the number who took at least one course is the number in accounting plus the number in finance plus the number in marketing minus the number who took exactly two courses minus 2 times

the number who took all three courses = $22 + 15 + 14 - 9 - (2 \times 1) = 51 - 9 - 2 = 40$.
Since 40 of the employees took at least one course, $50 - 40 = 10$ took none of the courses.
(II-4)

32. **(D)** Add $x + y = 4$ to $x - y = 3$ to obtain $2x = 7$. Therefore, $x = 3\frac{1}{2}$. Since $x + y = 4$, y must

be $4 - 3\frac{1}{2} = \frac{1}{2}$. So $x + 2y = 3\frac{1}{2} + 2\left(\frac{1}{2}\right) = 4\frac{1}{2}$. (II-2)

33. **(B)** The interest is compounded every 6 months. At the end of the first 6 months, the

interest earned is $\$2{,}000(.08)\left(\frac{1}{2}\right) = \$80$. (Don't forget to change 6 months into $\frac{1}{2}$ year

since 8 percent is the annual—yearly—rate.) Since the interest is compounded, $2,080 is the
amount earning interest for the final 6 months of the year. So the interest earned during

the final 6 months of the year is $\$2{,}080(.08)\left(\frac{1}{2}\right) = \$83.20$. Therefore, the total interest

earned is $\$80 + \$83.20 = \$163.20$. (I-4)

34. **(E)** Since BC is parallel to AD, the figure $ABCD$ is a trapezoid. The area of a trapezoid is
the average of the parallel sides times an altitude. Since CE is perpendicular to AD, e is an

altitude. So the area is $e\left(\frac{1}{2}\right)(b + d) = \left(\frac{1}{2}\right)eb + \left(\frac{1}{2}\right)ed$. Since $\frac{1}{2} = .5$, (E) is the correct

answer. (III-7)

35. **(B)** The price will be $3.00 a pound 6 months from now and $9.00 a pound 1 year from
now. The price is a geometric progression of the form 3^j, where j is the number of 6-month
periods that have passed. Since $3^4 = 81$, after 4 six-month periods the price will be $81.00 a
pound. Therefore, the answer is 2 years since 24 months is 2 years. (II-6, I-8)

36. **(D)** Since $\frac{x}{y} = \frac{2}{3}$, $\frac{y}{x}$, which is the reciprocal of $\frac{x}{y}$, must be equal to $\frac{3}{2}$. Also,

$\frac{y^2}{x^2}$ is equal to $\left(\frac{y}{x}\right)^2$, so $\frac{y^2}{x^2}$ is equal to $\left(\frac{3}{2}\right)^2 = \frac{9}{4}$. (I-2, I-8)

37. **(C)** Since the radii are unequal, the circles cannot be identical, thus (E) is incorrect. If two
circles intersect in three points, they must be identical, so (D) is also incorrect. Two different
circles can intersect at 2 points without being identical, so (C) is the correct answer. (III-6)

Verbal Section

1. **(B)** Answer (B) is the best choice. Note the cue word "then" before "new products" and "new ways." An entrepreneur is one who creates or implements change, not necessarily an inventor, as in answer (E). Answer (A) is true (the owner of a large business may be an entrepreneur), but it is not the best conclusion that can be drawn from the passage. It is a necessary but insufficient condition. Note that the text states that to own a small or large business does not make someone an entrepreneur. Answer (C) is not supported by the passage and not enough information is given to conclude answer (D).

2. **(A)** No error.

The passage for questions 3–6 appears on page 63.

3. **(B)** Lines 6–7 quote Marx as saying that philosophers only want to interpret the world, when what should be done is to change it. Change, the author states in line 8, is "the creed of applied scientists everywhere."

4. **(D)** Durkheim also valued the application of science rather than theoretical constructs alone. See paragraph 4.

5. **(A)** Items (B) through (E) deal with *applied* problems, which are the main concern of the social scientist, according to the passage.

6. **(D)** This point is stressed in lines 4–6, 10–11, and 28–29.

7. **(D)** If inflation averaged 4 percent and spending increased 5 percent, the *real* value of defense outlays actually increased 25 percent. During the former president's term, outlays actually declined faster than inflation, indicating a real decrease of 25 percent. The passage and the conclusions concern defense outlays only; the strength of the defenses (A), number of draftees (B), presidential views (C), or international treaties (E) are not mentioned in the passage and no direct inferences can be made; therefore all other alternatives are not relevant. The argument may be summarized as follows:

(1) Annual increases of incumbent were 5 percent.
(2) Annual increases of predecessor were 8 percent.

These two premises lead to a conclusion: 5% < 8%. However, converting the nominal to real increases, as we showed above, weakens the conclusion.

8. **(D)** As Harold is shorter than Gene, and as Gene is the same height as Sam, Harold is also shorter than Sam. As Ira is taller than Sam, Ira must also be taller than Harold. Therefore, (D) is the best answer. Choices (A), (B), and (C) might be inferred if one knew more about Elliot's height in relation to the height of the others. Choice (E) cannot be inferred from the information given. The following diagram helps make the situation clear:

$$I > S = G > E > H$$

9. **(C)** This corrects the double negative (*hadn't hardly*). *Different from* is the correct idiom. *Me* is the correct form of the pronoun after the preposition *except*.

10. **(B)** *We* is correct; a predicate pronoun is in the nominative case. *Had went* is an incorrect verb form (either *went* or *had gone*). (E) is not only wordy, but the tense sequence also is wrong (the *leaving* occurred before the *arriving*).

8 Difficulty Level

11. **(D)** Build-It's sales manager assumes via analogy that consumers behave the same way when it comes to buying do-it-yourself hardware products as they behave in a supermarket even though no evidence for this is given in the passage. Choice (A) cannot be inferred, and there is no evidence to support choice (B), (C), or (E).

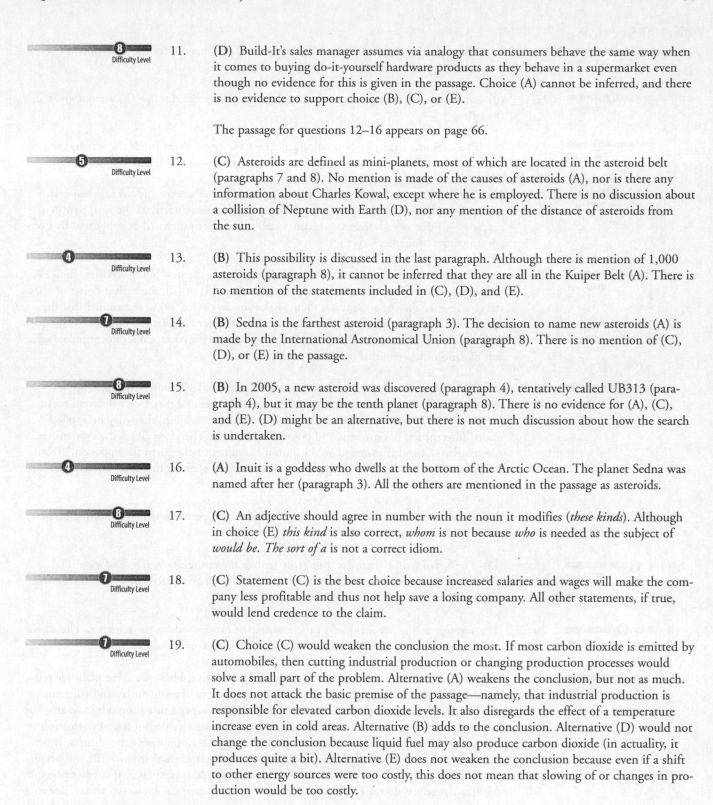

The passage for questions 12–16 appears on page 66.

5 Difficulty Level

12. **(C)** Asteroids are defined as mini-planets, most of which are located in the asteroid belt (paragraphs 7 and 8). No mention is made of the causes of asteroids (A), nor is there any information about Charles Kowal, except where he is employed. There is no discussion about a collision of Neptune with Earth (D), nor any mention of the distance of asteroids from the sun.

4 Difficulty Level

13. **(B)** This possibility is discussed in the last paragraph. Although there is mention of 1,000 asteroids (paragraph 8), it cannot be inferred that they are all in the Kuiper Belt (A). There is no mention of the statements included in (C), (D), and (E).

7 Difficulty Level

14. **(B)** Sedna is the farthest asteroid (paragraph 3). The decision to name new asteroids (A) is made by the International Astronomical Union (paragraph 8). There is no mention of (C), (D), or (E) in the passage.

8 Difficulty Level

15. **(B)** In 2005, a new asteroid was discovered (paragraph 4), tentatively called UB313 (paragraph 4), but it may be the tenth planet (paragraph 8). There is no evidence for (A), (C), and (E). (D) might be an alternative, but there is not much discussion about how the search is undertaken.

4 Difficulty Level

16. **(A)** Inuit is a goddess who dwells at the bottom of the Arctic Ocean. The planet Sedna was named after her (paragraph 3). All the others are mentioned in the passage as asteroids.

8 Difficulty Level

17. **(C)** An adjective should agree in number with the noun it modifies (*these kinds*). Although in choice (E) *this kind* is also correct, *whom* is not because *who* is needed as the subject of *would be*. *The sort of a* is not a correct idiom.

7 Difficulty Level

18. **(C)** Statement (C) is the best choice because increased salaries and wages will make the company less profitable and thus not help save a losing company. All other statements, if true, would lend credence to the claim.

7 Difficulty Level

19. **(C)** Choice (C) would weaken the conclusion the most. If most carbon dioxide is emitted by automobiles, then cutting industrial production or changing production processes would solve a small part of the problem. Alternative (A) weakens the conclusion, but not as much. It does not attack the basic premise of the passage—namely, that industrial production is responsible for elevated carbon dioxide levels. It also disregards the effect of a temperature increase even in cold areas. Alternative (B) adds to the conclusion. Alternative (D) would not change the conclusion because liquid fuel may also produce carbon dioxide (in actuality, it produces quite a bit). Alternative (E) does not weaken the conclusion because even if a shift to other energy sources were too costly, this does not mean that slowing of or changes in production would be too costly.

The passage for questions 20–24 appears on page 68.

6 Difficulty Level

20. **(B)** Note in the second paragraph that the first model emphasizes the "value of patronage," the second model stresses the "utility of the investment," the third model mentions the "value of supporting science and art," and the fourth model "identifies the ideological potential." "Utility" is an economic concept, but "value" is not necessarily so.

21. **(C)** The author's objective is to provide "alternative explanations for the government's involvement in the production of culture" (paragraph 1).

22. **(B)** Alternative (A) belongs to the first model; alternatives (C) through (E) are not given in the passage.

23. **(A)** The author is trying to show empirically how the government funds the arts and sciences, but for different reasons, i.e., as a consumer, as an influencer, and as a subsidizer.

24. **(A)** The idea expressed in the question is suggested by the "science and art for their own sake" model, in the sentence ". . . the government intervenes directly as the final patron of public goods that would otherwise be unavailable," i.e., not purchased or supported by nongovernmental or market forces.

25. **(C)** The author refers to 1930s trade legislation to justify the new bill. Therefore, choice (C) is the best answer. There is no information to conclude (A) or (B); the author does not attack the character of the opposition, nor their patriotism. In choice (D), it is assumed that the opposition infers that economists were against both pieces of legislation, but there is no evidence of this in the passage. Choice (E) is wrong because the passage does not stipulate what sort of action was permitted by the earlier legislation.

26. **(A)** The opponents could argue that two similar pieces of legislation passed and implemented at different times may not have the same effect because they face a different set of circumstances. Even though both bills may have similar provisions, they may be applied under different sets of economic and political conditions. Therefore, (A) is the best answer. Alternatives (C) and (E) strengthen the author's argument rather than the opponent's rebuttal. Alternative (B) may be so, but it does not necessarily apply in this case. There is not enough information to conclude (D).

27. **(D)** *Besides* means "*in addition to.*" *Irritated* is correct. A person is irritated; a situation or condition is aggravated.

28. **(D)** The appositive, *a kind man*, can easily replace the clause *who was a kind man*. The words *and he*, where the antecedent of *he* is vague, should be replaced by *who*, which refers specifically to the boy.

29. **(D)** *Together* and *up* are included in the meaning of other words in the sentence. The adjective *assigned* is preferable stylistically to the adjective clause *which was assigned*.

30. **(D)** The problem in this example is finding cause and effect. However, some plausible relationships exist. Assuming a positive relationship between advertising outlay and consumption, if advertising is more effective, a smaller increase in expenditure should lead to an increase in consumption, the conclusion in (A), even though we do not have information about the absolute, base amounts of either advertising or consumption expenditures. If people buy more of a substitute product when its price is lower, then alternative (B) will occur. If canned food is made more available, consumption should increase (C). If consumption of substitute products decrease (E); canned products should increase. However, an increase in can opener production may be a result of increased canned food consumption (D), and not the other way around.

31. **(D)** Answer (D) is most appropriate. If most of the quarterly inflation was due to a rise in food prices caused by a drought, then other prices rose less or no more than in the last quarter. Because the drought is probably a temporary phenomenon, it may be expected that the price level will decline next quarter. A fear that inflation would continue (A), an announcement by the president that he was concerned about inflation (B), economists' warnings about

The difficulty levels shown on the left are: 21. 5, 22. 7, 23. 8, 24. 7, 25. 5, 26. 6, 27. 5, 28. 5, 29. 6, 30. 6, 31. 7.

inflation (C), and other unfavorable economic news (E) would all tend to cause stock prices to decline and cause alarm on Wall Street.

32. **(B)** If, as the passage states, the narrator spent only a week at a college that has more than 50,000 students, how could he or she possibly draw a conclusion about the entire group. This is an example of an overgeneralization, so choice (B) is correct. Choice (A) would support the conclusion. Choices (C), (D), and (E) are irrelevant to the issue.

33. **(E)** The words *up, in his opinion,* and *back* are unnecessary.

34. **(B)** *As* is an incorrect vulgarism after the verb *know*. One concurs in a decision. The infinitive *try* should be followed by *to*.

35. **(C)** Nouns in apposition must be parallel to one another: "Jones, the *president* . . . and a *member* . . ."

36. **(E)** There is no evidence that the doubling of capacity is linked to productivity. All other answer choices can be inferred. Choice (A) is inferred from the fact that the company switched from household to commercial customers. Choice (B) is inferred from the company's decision to lower charges, which will result in greater demand for its services. Choices (C) and (D) are inferred from the decision to switch to labor-saving trucks.

37. **(C)** The statement's conclusion is that all towns have unsavory characters. This conclusion is false. According to the passage, only towns with pool halls have unsavory characters; and since we cannot infer that all towns have pool halls, conclusion (C) is wrong. Alternatives (A) and (B) are stated in the passage, while alternatives (D) and (E) can be deduced. A diagram will help:

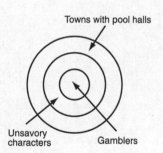

The argument may be summarized as follows:

1. Pool halls attract gamblers.
2. Gamblers are unsavory.
3. *Therefore,* towns with pool halls have unsavory characters.

Check this argument and the diagram with alternative statements in this question.

38. **(E)** 85 percent of 38 percent is 32 percent, while 50 percent of 62 percent is 31 percent; therefore, it can be expected that more Republicans will vote. Alternative (A) shows that even though 47 percent of the voters called themselves Republicans, the Republican Party won the election. In the latest poll, the proportion of Republicans declined to 38 percent. (A) weakens the conclusion but not as strongly as (E). Alternatives (B) and (C) hold equally for both Republicans and Democrats. Alternative (D) weakens the conclusion but not as much as (E); the fact that no one can predict how people will vote does not imply that results cannot be forecast with a high probability.

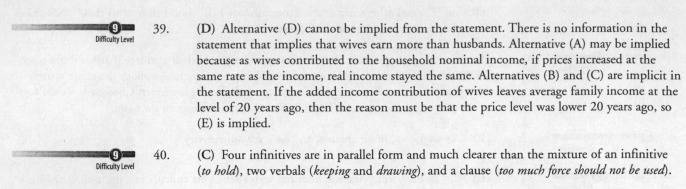

39.   **(D)** Alternative (D) cannot be implied from the statement. There is no information in the statement that implies that wives earn more than husbands. Alternative (A) may be implied because as wives contributed to the household nominal income, if prices increased at the same rate as the income, real income stayed the same. Alternatives (B) and (C) are implicit in the statement. If the added income contribution of wives leaves average family income at the level of 20 years ago, then the reason must be that the price level was lower 20 years ago, so (E) is implied.

40.   **(C)** Four infinitives are in parallel form and much clearer than the mixture of an infinitive (*to hold*), two verbals (*keeping* and *drawing*), and a clause (*too much force should not be used*).

41.   **(E)** *With the broken leg* is a misplaced modifier. Commas are needed to set off the nonrestrictive clause *ridden by the experienced jockey*.

EVALUATING YOUR SCORE

Tabulate your score for each section of the Diagnostic Test according to the directions on page 12 and record the results in the Self-Scoring Table below. Then find your rating for each score on the Self-Scoring Scale and record it in the appropriate blank.

Self-Scoring Table

Section	Score	Rating
Quantitative		
Verbal		

Self-Scoring Scale—RATING

Section	Poor	Fair	Good	Excellent
Quantitative	0–15	15–25	26–30	31–37
Verbal	0–15	15–25	26–30	31–41

The following Review sections cover material for each type of question on the GMAT. Spend more time studying those sections for which you had a rating of FAIR or POOR on the Diagnostic Test.

CORRECT YOUR WEAKNESSES

Essay Writing Review

CHAPTER 4

THE GMAT ANALYTICAL WRITING ASSESSMENT

The Analytical Writing Assessment (AWA) consists of two essay questions, each of which is allotted 30 minutes.

In general, the addition of the essay questions (and the reduction of the number of multiple-choice questions) will probably favor persons accustomed to expressing their thoughts in concise and well-organized written English. The Analytical Writing Assessment will be the first portion of the test administered, so be prepared to start when you are fresh.

Each essay will be scored by two graders, who are college and university instructors from various schools and departments experienced in teaching and evaluating writing. Each essay will be scored "holistically," which means that it will be assigned one score (between 0 and 6, with 0 being the lowest and 6 the highest) by each reader, based on its overall quality. The two scores for each essay are averaged, and then the two average scores (one for each essay) are averaged again to produce the writing score, which is reported on a scale of 0 to 6, rounded off to the nearest half point.

Writing an Essay

Many students dread the thought of writing an essay on an assigned topic, but it need not be that difficult. Writing an essay that will receive a holistic score of 4, 5, or even 6 requires no more than some common sense, a little on-the-spot planning, familiarity with the standards of written English, and a healthy amount of practice. Indeed, the best way to improve your writing ability is through practice. The more you write, the more comfortable and confident you become with the process.

This chapter cannot substitute for a writing course or for a lifetime of practice, but it will outline some helpful points and strategies for improving your writing and scoring higher on the GMAT Analytical Writing Assessment.

Types of Questions

The essay questions on the GMAT fall into two types: the analysis of an issue and the analysis of an argument. Both types of questions expect you to explore some complexities of the topic, to take a position, and to demonstrate critical reasoning abilities. The questions will not require you to have any pre-existing knowledge of the subject or any specific business training or experience. Some topics may relate to business, but others will be about areas of general interest or current events and issues.

General Strategy

The most important thing your essay must do is take a position. Even if you are not entirely sure that you would always agree with that position, *take a position*. You are not deciding on an irrevocable course in life—you are writing an essay to be assessed on the basis of how well it is written. Support your position with examples organized in a logical order; restate your position in a conclusion. Remember that there are no right or wrong answers to these questions, just well-written or poorly written ones. Don't try to guess what the graders' feelings about the issue might be so you can agree. Take a position upon which you can develop examples and supportive arguments. Make it a specific position; don't try to be too broad: it is much easier to put together ideas about banning automatic assault rifles than it is to discuss the use or misuse of firearms in general.

The second most important thing your essay needs is good organization. Stop and plan before you begin writing. Place your arguments or examples in the most logical order and provide reasonable transitions between them. Usually, three examples are enough.

Finally, you need to concentrate on writing a good beginning and a good conclusion. Your opening sets the stage and draws the reader in; your conclusion clinches your point and leaves your argument fresh in the graders' minds when they assign a score.

OVERALL STRATEGY

1. Narrow the topic.
2. Take a position.
3. Use three examples or points and connect them logically.
4. Write a good, interesting opening and a strong, memorable conclusion.

HOW TO WRITE AN ESSAY IN 30 MINUTES

Don't be misled by the title of this section. It promises more than it can deliver. For one thing, writing an essay in 30 minutes may be a contradiction in terms. An essay is essentially the product of a writer's thinking about a topic. It expresses a point of view arrived at after reflection, analysis, or interpretation of a subject or issue. When you are given an assignment only 30 minutes before the essay is due, you can't expect to pore over the topic for long. If you think too deeply, before you know it you'll have thought the allotted time away.

A second reason to distrust the title is that no one learns to write well by reading a "how-to" book on the subject. You learn essay writing by taking a pen in hand, by messing around with ideas and words, and by experimenting, practicing, and doing. Many of the in-class essays you've had to produce for social science or humanities courses have probably been good training for the kind of instant essay required by the GMAT Analytical Writing Assessment. In your classes, though, success was often determined by how closely your essay resembled what the teacher had in mind. That's not true on the GMAT, which won't give you a topic with a predetermined answer. You can't study for this essay writing test the way you can study calculus or Spanish. What you need to know is already lodged inside you. The task you face on test day is to organize your ideas and put them into readable form on a piece of paper, which takes practice, practice, practice. Just as athletic skills improve with repetition, so do essay writing skills. All you need each time you schedule a writing session is 30 minutes.

The next several pages will take you inside essay writing. By entering the territory, you won't become a world-class author of essays, but you'll see what most good writers do as they write essays. You'll be shown what works and what to watch out for.

A Dozen Principles of Good Writing

Success in essay writing depends in large measure on how completely you can master these 12 guidelines:

1. Study the topic closely.

2. Narrow the topic.

3. Decide what point(s) to make about the topic.

4. Collect ideas and put them in order.

5. Start with an appealing and informative introduction.

6. Develop your ideas with specific examples and details.

7. Guide readers with transitions.

8. Use plain, precise, lively, and fresh words.

9. Omit needless words.

10. Vary your sentences.

11. End your essay unforgettably.

12. Follow the conventions of standard English.

Refer to these guidelines often. If your writing usually demonstrates mastery of these 12 principles, you're undoubtedly a terrific writer. To be a still better one, though, you must know that occasionally one or more of the principles ought to be set aside. When a principle leads you to say something barbaric, ignore it for the time being. Let your intuition and good judgment guide you instead. The principles, after all, merely describe what most good writers do; they are not commandments.

Through experience, accomplished and experienced essayists have absorbed good writing habits into their craft. Professionals needn't be reminded, for example, to cut needless words from their writing or to prefer the plain word to the pompous one.

The Process of Writing an Essay

To start, plan what to do during each stage of the process. The first stage, *prewriting*, consists of all you do before you actually begin writing the text of your essay. During the second stage, *composing*, you are choosing the words and forming the sentences that contain your thoughts. And finally, during the *revising and proofreading* stage, polish and refine the text of your essay word by word, making it true, clear, and graceful. Actually, the lines between the stages are not at all distinct. Sometimes it helps to put words on paper during the prewriting stage. Writers compose, revise, and proofread simultaneously. New ideas may sprout at any time. No stage really ends until the final period of the last sentence is securely in place—or until time is up.

In spite of the blurry boundaries between the stages of the writing process, it pays to keep the functions of each stage in mind as you study in detail how the dozen principles of good writing contribute to the growth of a successful essay.

1. Study the Topic Closely

Obviously, your work on the GMAT essay question should start with a meticulous reading of the topic. Read it more than once, underscoring key ideas and words until you know it intimately. If in doubt, read it again.

Here is a typical essay topic for your scrutiny.

EXAMPLE

Concerned about the survival of democracy, the president of the University of Chicago, Robert Maynard Hutchings, once wrote, "The death of democracy is not likely to be an assassination from ambush. It will be a slow extinction from apathy, indifference, and undernourishment."

While democracy may still be alive and well, situations often arise that do not coincide with the democratic principles on which America was founded. Using examples based on your studies, reading, or on personal experience, write an essay that illustrates your view on the current health of democracy.

Before reading the explanation, briefly write your understanding of what the topic asks you to do:

_____

_____

_____

_____

Explanation: The basic task is clearly spelled out in the last clause: *write an essay that illustrates your view on the current health of democracy*. The prompt and everything else merely creates a context for the task and provides some general clues to the meaning of "health of democracy." Other essential information is that the essay must use examples drawn from your studies—that is, course work or independent study; your reading, which includes fiction and nonfiction read for school or on your own; or relevant personal experiences.

All told, the topic gives students considerable leeway for interpretation. In fact, lengthy and complicated topics like this one often encourage students to blaze their own trails. Shorter topics, on the other hand, often tighten the reins on creativity.

Although writing about one's experience has a lot of merit, not every GMAT question allows students to write a personal response. But when possible, it's an option that may be too good to refuse, especially when the topic leaves you cold. Students are leading authorities on their own life and times. With a little finesse, almost any topic on the GMAT can be shaped into an interesting and readable personal essay.

2. Narrow the Topic Unmercifully

Because a GMAT topic must suit a multiethnic, multicultural, and multitalented student audience, it is bound to be very broad. Your first job is to reduce it to a size snug enough to fit the time and space allotted. In fact, the quality of the essay you write could depend on how narrowly you define the topic. Think small. A cosmic approach won't work, and you are not likely to err by narrowing the topic too much. If you were to run out of things to say about a narrowed topic, the simple solution would be to expand the main idea in midstream, a far easier task than hacking away at an overweight topic after you've already filled most of a page.

It would be beyond the hope and talent of most students to compose a substantive 300 or 400 word essay on such topics as *democracy*, *psychology*, or *jazz*—subjects so vast you could probably fill a barn with books about them. The same holds true for any general subject, from *alcoholism* to *zoology*. Therefore, to keep your essay from being stuck in a mess of generalities, narrow the topic ruthlessly.

Try building a ladder of abstraction. Start at the top with the most general word. As you descend the ladder, make each rung increasingly specific. When you reach the bottom, you may have a topic sufficient for a short essay. Here are some examples:

SUBJECT: *Democracy*

Democracy	*Highest level of abstraction*
Democracy in conflict with totalitarianism	*Too broad for a short essay*
People's rights vs. government control	*Still too broad*
Freedom of press vs. government restrictions	*Still too broad*
The right to print opinions vs. censorship	*Still broad, but getting there*
The right to print a scandalous story in a school newspaper	*Possible topic for a short essay*
What happened to Pete when *The Globe* published a story about incompetent teachers	*Distinct possibility for an essay*

SUBJECT: *Alcoholism*

Alcoholism	*Highest level of abstraction*
The effects of alcoholism on society	*Extremely broad for a short essay*
Family problems resulting from alcoholism	*Still too broad*
Alcoholism as a cause of broken families	*Very broad, but getting closer*
The effects of alcoholism on children from broken homes	*Good only for a lengthy research paper*
The experience of Betsy G., the daughter of an alcoholic	*A definite topic for a short essay*

Each subject has been pared down to a scale appropriate for a GMAT essay. Topics on the bottom rungs offer students a chance to write a thorough essay. Focusing on a single idea may deny them the chance to demonstrate the scope of their knowledge. The GMAT, however, is not a place to show off breadth, but rather to display depth. Business school applications show breadth. For the present, it's depth that counts.

PRACTICE IN NARROWING TOPICS

Reduce several of the following subjects to a level of specificity concise enough to be used for a GMAT essay. Try constructing a ladder of abstraction for each one. Put the broadest topic on the top. Don't stop descending until you have a topic suitable for a short essay.

Youth and Age	Calamities
Procrastination	Probability
Jealousy	Truth
Taking Risks	Style
Change vs. Permanence	Wonder

SUBJECT: *Zoology*

Zoology	*Highest level of abstraction*
The study of mammals	*Too broad*
The study of primates	*Still very broad*
Researching the behavior of chimpanzees	*Still too broad*
Teaching of chimps	*Still rather broad*
Training chimps to distinguish colors	*A reasonable topic*
My job in the primate lab working on the color recognition project	*A fine topic for a short paper*

3. Decide What Point(s) to Make About the Topic

An essay needs a point. Nothing will disappoint a reader more than arriving at the end only to discover that the essay lacks a point. Essays may be written with beautiful words, contain profound thoughts, and make readers laugh or weep. But without a point, sometimes called a *main idea* or a *thesis*, an essay remains just words in search of a meaning. After they've finished, readers may scratch their heads, say "Huh?" and resent having wasted their time. Don't confuse the topic of an essay with its point, for even a pointless essay is likely to be about something. But a topic isn't enough. An essay must also say something about its topic. It can be basically factual, but it should express a point of view about an issue.

Finding a Point for Your GMAT Essay

TOPIC: The topic will be given to you in the instructions for writing the essay.

Purpose: The purpose of the essay will be explained by the wording of the topic. Look for such words as *describe, compare, contrast, persuade, explain, report, analyze,* and *interpret.* Each requires a slightly different response. Or the purpose of the essay may be left up to you.

Point: The point is the essay's main idea or thesis, or what the essay demonstrates, proves, or argues.

Even if you have no particular opinion on an issue or topic, the hard fact is that you must still try to create the illusion that you care deeply about the issue. Doing so may rub your conscience the wrong way, but rather than raise a stink, which won't get you anywhere, make the best of it. This time go along to get along. Don't regard it as a cop-out. Rather, consider it a survival tactic, a challenge to your resilience and creativity, qualities that schools and businesses seek and admire.

Faced with the prospect of writing an essay about a topic that leaves you cold, you have some choices to make: Fake it, fight it, drop it, or psych yourself to do the best you can.

1. **Fake it.** Writing to say something even when you have nothing to say inevitably leads to words on a page that sound forced, like a conversation you might have with an aging aunt at Thanksgiving. Not a good choice.

2. **Fight it.** Some resentful students turn on the test or the test makers by attacking the admissions testing system in America. They write statements declaring their refusal to participate in a dehumanizing charade that fails to take into account each student as a unique individual. After the test, such students may feel relieved for having spoken their minds, but their position also will have irreparably damaged their chances of being admitted to the school of their choice. While admissions officials generally approve of individual initiative and an independent spirit, they won't bother with students who respond defiantly to a GMAT essay question. Not a good choice.

3. **Drop it.** Although this is the only foolproof way to keep yourself from writing a pointless essay, it's not a viable option when you're striving for good grades and high test scores. Not a good choice.

4. **Psych yourself.** This is the most promising solution. Begin by asking yourself ten or a dozen questions about the topic. Start with easy questions and work toward the harder ones.

Here, for example, are questions on the general topic

> *Dangerous Pursuits:*
> *What are some dangerous pursuits?*
> *Why do some people go bungee jumping?*
> *Why don't I go bungee jumping?*
> *Why does my cousin Henry go?*

After a while, the questions and answers become more provocative:

> *When is it okay to gamble with your life?*
> *Does the state have the right to forbid you from*
> *risking your life?*
> *At what point in lawmaking does the government*
> *overstep its bounds?*

Obviously, at the beginning of a 30-minute essay test, you won't have time to ask and answer dozens of questions, but the more thoughts you can generate, the richer your writing will be.

If self-psyching fails to work, try this alternative: As rapidly as possible write a list of anything, literally anything, that might qualify as a response to the topic. Like pulling a stopper, making a list often starts the flow of ideas. Your mind makes connections as one idea calls up memories of another, and then another. Don't be particular. After a short time, review the list and choose the idea that holds promise for your essay. Even if the list doesn't thrill you, pick the least objectionable item and begin to write on it. Who knows, you may have accidentally stumbled upon a rich lode of ideas. Writers often discover what they really want to say only after they've written for a while, even as long as 10 minutes. After that, time and space won't permit a complete rewrite, but a few crucial sentences could change the emphasis of what they've written, and they can quickly relocate ideas and restructure their essays with neatly drawn arrows.

Sometimes a better thesis suddenly swims into view halfway through the test. Should you change course or stick with what you have? It takes courage to return to "Go" and to start over. Because of time and space restraints on the GMAT, a switch could be fatal. In general, the new idea ought to be out of this world to justify trashing what you've written.

If you find yourself in such a predicament, don't switch unless you'll never again be able to look yourself in the eye. Grit your teeth and finish what you began. Resist the temptation to shift from your original idea even if you don't believe in it anymore. You won't be penalized for hypocrisy, but you will surely damage your essay with a confusing or ambivalent presentation.

Normally, the wording of a GMAT essay question forces you to take a position on the issue or topic. It might say to you directly, "State your opinion," or ask "Do you agree or disagree?" Your view then becomes the point, or thesis, of your essay. In the essay itself the thesis is usually stated outright in a simple declarative sentence, as in these examples:

TOPIC: Democracy   Thesis: Democracy is a far more cumbersome form of govern-
                                    ment than dictatorship.
TOPIC: Psychology   Thesis: In the discipline of children, instilling a fear of punishment
                                    is more effective than promising a reward.
TOPIC: War   Thesis: War is hell.

On the other hand, the thesis of an essay may be so strongly implied by the cumulative weight of evidence that stating the thesis is unnecessary. Whichever way you decide to inform the reader of your essay's thesis—by announcing it directly or by weaving it subtly into the fabric of the text—be sure to lock onto it as you write. Let it guide you from the opening lines to your conclusion. Omit material that causes the essay to wander from its point. Readers will appreciate an essay that rarely deviates from a well-defined path.

4. Collect Ideas and Arrange Them in Order

Unless you are blessed with a lightning-quick mind that instantly analyzes issues and draws conclusions in a logical sequence, you'll have to gather and organize ideas for your essay the way ordinary mortals do. You'll search your knowledge and experience for ideas and examples to support your thesis. You'll keep them in mind as you write, note them on paper as you think of them, or prepare a sketchy outline. Jotting down a brief list of ideas that occur to you, or possibly preparing a sketchy outline, is all it takes.

While you reflect on your jottings, a better thesis may come to mind, or you may run into new ideas that bolster your first one. Before you write a word on your answer sheet, though, you probably should devote at least a few minutes to collecting your thoughts. Obviously, on the GMAT, you'll have to think rapidly, but better in haste than not at all.

The Formula

Most essays are variations and adaptations of the formula. Using the formula will not make your prose immortal, but it could help turn a muddle of words into a model of clear thinking. The formula is simply an all-purpose plan for putting ideas into a clear, easy-to-follow order. It uses a beginning, a middle, and an end. It's not sensational, but it works for virtually any essay. Its greatest virtue is simplicity. Each part has its place and purpose within the essay:

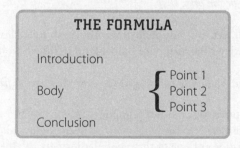

The formula prescribes a three-stage structure for an essay. It also requires a body consisting of three points. Why three? Mainly because three is a number that works. If you can make three different statements about a topic, you probably know what you're talking about. One is too simple, two is better but is still shallow. Three, however, is thoughtful. It suggests depth. Although every short essay needn't include three points to support its thesis, three carries a voice of authority. If you can't think of three, stick with two, and don't make up a third that is simply a rehash of one of the first two disguised as something new. Psychologically, three also creates a sense of wholeness for the reader, like the beginning, middle, and end of a story. It's no accident that the number three recurs in all literature, from *The Three Little Pigs* to *The Bible*.

The order of ideas is important too. What comes first? Second? Third? The best order is the clearest order, the arrangement that readers can follow with the least effort. No plan is superior to another provided you have a valid reason for using it. The plan least likely to succeed is the aimless one, the one in which you state and develop ideas in the random order they happened to come to mind. It's better to rank your ideas in the order of importance. Decide which provides the strongest support of your thesis. Although your best argument may be listed first in your notes, save it for last on the essay. Giving it away at the start is self-defeating, because everything that follows will be anticlimactic. In other words, work toward your best point, not away from it. An excellent way to plot three good ideas is to lead with your second best, save your best for the end, and sandwich your least powerful idea between the others. This structure recognizes that the end and the beginning of an essay are its critical parts. A good opening draws the reader in and creates an all-important first impression, but a memorable ending, coming last, is what readers have fresh in their minds when they assign you a grade.

5. Start With an Appealing and Informative Introduction

The opening lines of an essay tell readers what to expect. If the opening is dull or confusing, readers will brace themselves for a less than thrilling reading experience. Some essays become clear and engaging by the second paragraph, but an essay with an unimaginative start begins with a handicap, and the writer will have to work that much harder to overcome the reader's first impressions.

It pays, therefore, to write an opening that stops readers in their tracks. Begin with something to lure the reader into the piece. Use a hook—a phrase, sentence, or idea to grab your readers so firmly that they'll desperately want to read on. Hooks must be very crisp, very clean. They must surprise, inform, or tickle the reader in an instant, and say "Read on; you'll be glad you did." A dull hook just won't do. In a short essay, a hook can't take up more than a couple of lines. Anything longer will erode the heart of the essay.

A concise one-sentence opening is probably harder to write than a longer one. In other words, you can't fool around when space is tight. It's not unheard of for students, smitten with an inventive idea, to write half a page before they start to deal directly with the topic. Some students need that much space to put their thoughts in order. Either way, on the GMAT, beware of an introduction that drags on.

Beware also of openings that are too cute or too precious, as in

> *Little did George Washington know as he sat sipping a brew on the veranda at Mount Vernon with his little woman Martha beside him, that . . .*

Be thoughtful and clever, yes, but not obnoxious. Above all, steer clear of an all-inclusive opening that grandiloquently reviews the history of humankind in fifteen words or less, as in

> *Throughout recorded time, humanity has struggled to keep the flame of freedom alive, . . .*

Be intelligent and perceptive, yes, but not pompous.

Techniques for pulling readers into the body of an essay are unlimited. Yet many successful openings are merely unique variations of one of these popular formats:

1. Begin with a brief incident or anecdote that relates to the point of your essay.

   When Joan S. entered Springdale College early last September, she didn't know that she had left her constitutional rights at the campus gate.

2. State a provocative idea in an ordinary way or an ordinary idea in a provocative way. Either will arrest the reader's interest.

   That a person is supposed to be innocent until proven guilty is an alien concept in my university.

3. Use a quote from the test question, Bruce Springsteen, or any other source—maybe even your grandmother. But be sure the quote relates to the topic of your essay and says it better than you can.

   "All animals are equal, but some animals are more equal than others." George Orwell said that.

4. Knock down a commonly held assumption or define a word in a new and startling way.

   When Ulov, a Russian immigrant, arrived in Shaftsbury, Vermont, he learned that freedom does not mean cutting down a neighbor's maple tree.

5. Ask an interesting question or two, which you will answer in your essay.

   Is true democracy possible? Or is it just an ideal to work for?

6. Make an unexpected connection between your topic and a bit of culture. By offering readers a second layer of meaning, your writing is enriched.

   We'll get by with a little help from our friends. That, at least, was the hope of Hurricane Andrew's victims after the winds died down.

7. Create suspense by waiting until the end of your opening passage to reveal your topic.

   Michael Jackson takes his everywhere, while Julia Roberts takes hers to bed. Rob Lowe keeps one in each Porsche, and Jennifer Jason-Leigh has one made of gold. Happiness, for all these stars, depends on having a telephone at their fingertips.

If none of these techniques works for you, or if you don't have time on the GMAT to devise a good hook, rely on the direct approach. Just declare your thesis right up front. But don't phrase it like an announcement, as in "In this essay, I am going to prove that democracy is not dead." State your point, as in "Democracy is far from dead," and take it from there.

If at first you can't find a suitable opening, don't put off writing the rest of your essay. Just skip a few lines and begin with the body of your essay. As you write, a pleasing opening idea might strike you. Add it later. Whatever you do, though, be sure that your opening fits your writing style and personality. Work hard to get it right, but not so hard that it will seem forced or too cute or too long. Ideally, it should introduce your topic so naturally and unobtrusively that readers will not even realize that they are being enticed into reading past the first sentence.

6. Develop Your Ideas Fully With Examples and Details

Precise, well-documented information is far more convincing than general and unsubstantiated opinion. In an essay, the information used to give credence to the writer's main point is commonly called *development*. Because development indicates how deeply a student can think—a matter of great concern to business schools—it counts heavily in grading GMAT essays. Development does not mean number of words. An essay of a thousand words can still be underdeveloped. Some students, unaware of the difference between development and throwing the bull, fill their essays with verbal waste. They write even when they have nothing to say. Perhaps you've done it yourself on occasion. Be assured that essays short on development but long on refuse will be found wanting by GMAT readers, who know bull when they see it.

Nor is development simply the range of evidence summoned to uphold a thesis. Not every good essay needs, say, three or five or a dozen supporting ideas. The fact is that superior development skills can be demonstrated on the GMAT with a single vivid example. It's depth that counts.

Each paragraph in your essay should contribute to the development of the main idea. It should contain facts, data, arguments, examples—testimony of all kinds to corroborate the thesis. If you are unsure how a particular paragraph lends support to the thesis, cross it out or revise it. If you're perplexed, just imagine how your readers will feel. Be merciless with your writing. Even though you may admire a paragraph, give it the boot if it doesn't help to make your case.

A paragraph indentation ordinarily signals readers to get ready for a change in thought or idea. Yet not every new paragraph signals a drastic change in direction. It may simply move the essay ahead one small step at a time. Paragraphs also permit readers to skim your writing. Readers in a hurry focus on opening and closing sentences and skip what lies between, but you can force readers to slow down by varying the location of the most important idea in each paragraph, usually called the *topic sentence*.

While topic sentences come in assorted guises, they share a common trait. They are helpful in keeping both writers and readers on the track. When you write, assume that readers have a poor sense of direction. Given half a chance, they'll lose their way. Therefore, remind them often of where they are. Lead them with topic sentences, but be sure that whatever you say in the rest of the paragraph supports what the topic sentence says.

7. Guide Readers With Transitions

Readers need to be guided through an essay. Consider them visitors in a strange place. As the writer you must show them around by setting up verbal guideposts. Tell them where they are going, show them their progress, and remind them often of the destination. If you've done your job, they should be ready for what they find at the end. By repeatedly alluding to the main idea, you'll not only compel readers to focus on your point, but you'll keep readers at your side from start to finish.

Help readers along, too, by choosing words that establish relationships between one thought and the next. This can be done with words such as *this*, which happens to tie the sentence you are reading to the one before. (The word *too* in the first sentence of this paragraph serves the same function; it serves as a link between this and the earlier paragraph.) The English language is rich with words and phrases that serve to tie sentences and ideas together. Here is a brief thesaurus of common transitions grouped according to their customary use. With a bit of thought, you probably can think of others.

When you **ADD** ideas	*in addition, furthermore, moreover, further, besides, too, also, and then, then too, again, next, secondly, equally important*
When you **COMPARE or CONTRAST**	*similarly, likewise, in comparison, in like manner, however, in contrast, conversely, on the other hand, but, nevertheless, and yet, even so, still*
When you cite an **EXAMPLE**	*for example, for instance*
When you **REINFORCE** an idea	*indeed, in fact, as a matter of fact, to be sure, of course, in any event, by all means*
When you show **RESULTS**	*as a result, as a consequence, consequently, therefore, thus, hence, accordingly*
When you express a **SEQUENCE** or the passing of **TIME**	*soon after, then, previously, meanwhile, in the meantime, later, at length, after a while, immediately, next*
When you show **PROXIMITY**	*here, nearby, at this spot, near at hand, in this vicinity, on the opposite side, across from, adjacent to, not far from*
When you **CONCLUDE**	*finally, in short, in other words, in a word, to sum up, in conclusion, in the end*

Not every sentence needs to be tied to the previous one with a particular transitional word or phrase. The ideas themselves sometimes create a natural link.

Whenever you use a transition to tie one sentence to another, you do your readers a favor. You guarantee them a smooth trip through your essay. Otherwise, each sentence stands like a disconnected link in a chain, and readers bump along, often losing the point you are trying to make.

Although many sentences won't contain transitions, three or four sentences in succession without a link of some sort may leave readers doubting that this trip is worth taking.

8. Choose Plain, Precise, Lively, and Fresh Words

Use Plain Words

That's a principle easy to say but hard to live by when you're hoping to impress readers with your intellect and sophistication. Yet nothing, truly nothing, conveys your erudition better than plain words. However big your vocabulary, never use a complex word on the GMAT essay to show off. You'll get no extra credit for an essay crammed with ornate, multisyllabic words used for no other purpose than to sound ornate and multisyllabic. There's always a risk, in fact, that words that sound profound to you may seem pompous to your readers. Or worse, they could make you appear foolish.

The student who wrote, "I am of the opinion that a prerequisite for parenthood includes disbursement of penal adjudication among siblings with an even, dispassionate hand," needs a basic lesson in plain writing. How much clearer to have written, "I think that good parents should know how to be fair in disciplining their children" or "I think that being equally strict with all their children is a prerequisite of being good parents." Words should be like gifts, carefully chosen to give pleasure to someone you like. High gloss is not a measure of value. You won't gain much by dressing ordinary ideas in fancy robes or from trying to appear more impressive than you already are.

This admonition to use plain words, however, shouldn't be regarded as a license to use current, everyday slang or street talk in your essays. Spoken language, which contains many colorful words and expressions like *chill*, *pig out*, *dissed*, and *freak out*, has its place, but its place is not in a GMAT essay unless you definitely need current lingo to create an effect that you can't get any other way. If you must write slang terms, don't highlight them with quotation marks. Why call attention to the fact that you can't think of standard or more original words?

Use plain words even for profound thoughts—correction, *especially* for profound thoughts. By writing "I think. Therefore, I am," the seventeenth-century philosopher René Descartes reshaped the way humans think about existence. He could have used more exotic words, of course, words more in keeping with the florid writing style of his time, but his statement probably derives its power from its simplicity. A sign of true intelligence is the ability to convey deep meanings with simple words.

Simple doesn't necessarily mean short. It's true that the plain words tend to be the short ones, but not always. The word *fid* is short, but it's not plain, unless you are a sailor, in which case you'd know that a fid supports the mast on your boat or is used to pry open a tight knot in your lines. On the other hand, *spontaneously* is five syllables long. Yet it is a plain and simple word because of its frequent use. It springs, well, spontaneously from the mouth.

For any GMAT essay, a plain, conversational style is appropriate. The language should sound like you. In formal writing, custom requires you to remove yourself from stage center and focus on the subject matter. At some point in your schooling, you may have been warned never to use "I" in an essay. That caveat may apply to some forms of exposition, but not to GMAT essays. In fact, GMAT topics often encourage first-person responses by asking you to state your opinion or preference. How do you do that without using "I"? It can be done, of course, by using pronouns like *one*, as in "When *one* is getting ready for graduate school, *one* sometimes writes funny," or *you*, as in "Sometimes *you* feel like a dope," or by avoiding pronouns altogether. But an essay that expresses the writer's personal opinion will sound a lot more natural when cast in the first-person singular.

GMAT essay readers are old hands at rooting pretense out of student writing. Unless students are exceptionally astute, they usually give themselves away by using elaborate words that fall a mite short of precise diction. Writers who leave no clue that they are posing as bright, witty, clever, articulate people, on the other hand, are probably bright, witty, clever, and articulate enough to write essays in their natural voice, so why pretend?

The point is, don't be phony! Just let your genuine voice ring out, although the way you speak is not necessarily the way you should write. Most speaking is vague, clumsy, confused, and wordy. Consider writing as the casual speech of someone who speaks exceedingly well. It's grammatically correct and is free of pop expressions and clichés. Think of it as the kind of speech expected of you in an interview. Or maybe even the way this paragraph sounds. You could do a lot worse!

Choose Precise Words

Hazy, vague, and abstract words fade as quickly from a reader's memory as last night's dream. They indicate a lack of clear and precise thinking. How much easier it is to say that a book is *good, interesting,* or *exciting* than to search for words that will precisely describe the book's appeal. Similarly, it's more convenient to resort to words like *nice, fine, stupid, boring,* and *pretty* than to explain in detail what you mean by each word. But to write something that will stick in a reader's mind, use well-defined, hard-edged words. Exact words help you express exact thoughts. To write precisely is to write with pictures, sounds, and actions that are as vivid in words as in reality. Exact words leave a distinct mark; general ones, only a blurry impression.

Good writers often experience the world more intensely than other people. Like artists, they think visually. They listen hard to the sounds and voices around them and are extra-sensitive to smells, to tastes, and to the feel of things. They keep their senses at full throttle in order, as the writer James Baldwin once said, "to describe things which other people are too busy to describe." They understand that good writing must sometimes appeal to their readers' senses.

To evoke a strong response from your readers, make use of the principle that a picture is worth a thousand words. Actually, whether it's more or less than a thousand is debatable, but the point is clear: words should help readers *see.* Therefore, *show* more than you *tell!* Instead of describing your uncle as "absent-minded," show him stepping into his morning shower with his pajamas on. Rather than saying that your room is a "mess," show the pile of wrinkled clothes in the corner and the books and Snickers wrappers scattered on the floor next to your unmade bed. The same principle applies to smells: "Her breath was foul with a stale whiskey stench"; to sounds: "the hum and throb of big machines in the distance"; to touch: "the feel of cool, linen bedsheets"; and to tastes: "a cold, sweet drink of clear water on a hot day." In short, by writing vividly, you prevent readers from misinterpreting what you have to say.

Essays bogged down in detail no doubt grow tedious both to read and to write. Authors need to choose what readers need to see and know. Excessive analysis is boring, but so is too little. A balance is best. No one can tell you precisely how to achieve the balance. The feel of what seems right takes time and practice. In the end, the content and purpose of an essay will have to determine how detailed it needs to be. Every time you mention a meal, it's not necessary to recite the menu unless there's a good reason for doing so. When you use an abstract word, ask what is more important, to give details to readers or to push on to other matters? The context, as well as your judgment and experience as a writer, will determine what you can expect readers to understand. To get the knack a little more quickly, reread any interesting passage from a book or other publication. Pick out the details and the broad statements. What did the passage show, and what did it tell? Since the passage held your interest, perhaps you will have found a model worth emulating in your own writing.

By no means does this plea for verbal precision suggest that abstract words be eliminated from the language. After all, we need them to talk to each other about *beauty, love, fairness, satisfaction, power, enlightenment,* and thousands of other notions that exist in our hearts and minds. The ability to think abstractly, to invent theories, to express feelings, and to articulate ideals and lofty principles is a gift that separates human beings from all other creatures, and we should delight in it, but remember that most readers are an impatient lot. They will reject essays that don't, at some point, come down to earth.

Use Lively Language

Active and Passive Verbs: Unlike the machine-scored multiple-choice questions, your GMAT essay will be read by people—real people with feelings, moods, likes and dislikes, and the capacity to laugh, grow angry, and be moved. They are usually teachers who know that student writing can be lively, interesting, and clear. Like any readers, they will be put off by writing that is dull.

The most efficient way to inject life into your writing is to pay close attention to your choice of verbs. Verbs, as you've no doubt been taught, show action or state of being. To a writer, the fact that verbs show action is extremely important. Active verbs stimulate interest by waking up the language. They create movement, perform, stir things up, and move around. They excel all other words in their power to restore life to lifeless prose. They add energy and vitality to sentences, and, as a bonus, they help you to write more economically.

While *active* verbs are full of life, *being* verbs are not. They stagnate. They don't do anything but connect one thought to another, especially forms of the verb *to be*: *is, are, was, were, am, has been, had been, will be*. When used in sentences, each of these being verbs joins a subject to a predicate, and that's all. In fact, the verb *to be* in all its forms acts much like a verbal equal sign, as in "Seven plus three *is* ten" (7 + 3 = 10) or "Sam *is* a genius" (Sam = genius), or "Your GMAT score *is* going up" (That = good news!). Because *being* verbs (and equal signs) show little life, use active verbs whenever possible.

Here are some ways to pump life into sluggish sentences:

1. Try to substitute an active verb drawn from another word in the sentence.

> BEING VERB: Monica and Phil *were* the highest scorers on the GMAT practice test.
> ACTIVE VERB: Monica and Phil *scored* highest on the GMAT practice test.
> The verb *scored* has been drawn from the noun *scorers.*
> Active verbs may also be extracted from adjectives:

> BEING VERB: Achievement *is* the determining factor in GMAT grades.
> ACTIVE VERB: Achievement *determines* GMAT grades.

The verb *determines* has been drawn from the adjective *determining*.

2. Sometimes it's preferable to find an altogether new verb:

> BEING VERB: It *is* logical that admission to business school is the result of a student's effort and achievement.
> ACTIVE VERB: Logic *dictates* that a student's effort and achievement lead to business school admission.

Being verbs are perfectly acceptable in speech and writing. We can hardly get along without them. But use them sparingly in your essays. As a rule of thumb, if more than one in four of your sentences relies on a form of the verb *to be* as its main verb, you may be depending excessively on passive verbs.

When you start to weed *being* verbs out of your writing, you're likely to find that some sentences resist easy change. Some need to be thoroughly recast. Subjects become verbs, verbs turn into nouns, unnecessary phrases are eliminated entirely—alterations that result in sentences that bear little resemblance to the original. At the same time, though, your writing may get an unexpected lift. Verb-swapping tends to eliminate needless words, thereby improving your writing.

Once you get into the habit of clearing dead verbs out of your prose, you may notice that certain nouns limit your options for using active verbs. That is, certain nouns, when used as the subject of a sentence, determine your chances for finding a lively verb. Some abstract nouns, in fact, cut the choices drastically. Take, for example, sentences starting with "The reason," as in "The reason for taking the GMAT is . . ." Verb choices are also severely reduced by subject nouns like *thought, idea, issue, way, notion, concept*, or any other essentially abstract nouns. The same holds true for sentences that begin with "There," as in "There are 2,400 colleges in America," and often for sentences that begin with "It," as in "It is difficult to choose just one." On the other hand, nouns that name people, places, concrete objects, or events almost cry out for active verbs. When the subject can perform an action, like a person, for instance, you'll never run out of verb choices.

As these examples illustrate, whenever you insert a concrete, easy-to-define noun in place of an abstraction, you are apt to write a tighter, more energetic, and more readable sentence.

> ABSTRACT: The *cause* of the strike was the students' demand for freedom.
> DEFINITE: The *students* struck for freedom.

> ABSTRACT: The *way* to the dean's office is down the next corridor.
> DEFINITE: The next *corridor* goes to the dean's office.

> ABSTRACT: *There* are students who are good in chemistry but not in physics.
> DEFINITE: Some *students* excel in chemistry but not in physics.

Being verbs are not the only verbs that sap the life out of sentences. They share that distinction with several other verbs, such as any form of *to have, to come, to go, to make, to move,* and *to get.* They are convenient and versatile, but because of constant use, such verbs pale next to more animated verbs. But, like *being* verbs, they are indispensable. When they show up in your writing, stick with them only if you can swear that no other words will do. Unless they fit perfectly, however, trade them in for better, livelier ones.

DULL: The line to the lunch counter *moved* very slowly.
LIVELY: The line *crept* (crawled, poked, inched) to the lunch counter.

Note that by using a more animated verb, you eliminate the need for "very slowly," which would be redundant.

DULL: The dean *gave* permission to the students to eat in the staff room.
LIVELY: The dean *permitted* the students to eat in the staff room.

Active and Passive Sentences

To write lively prose, also keep in mind the distinction between *active* and *passive* sentences. A passive sentence is one in which the performer of the action is not mentioned until late in the sentence or is left out altogether. Any time you restructure passive sentences, you pep up the prose.

PASSIVE: This book was recommended by my teacher.
ACTIVE: My teacher recommended this book.

PASSIVE: It was bought for me by my mother.
ACTIVE: My mother bought it for me.

Although active sentences usually sound more natural and interesting, sometimes a passive sentence will work better. When it's immaterial who performed an action, for example, or when the actor can't be identified, passive voice makes perfect stylistic sense.

ACTIVE: The exam proctor gave the starting signal at 8:30.
PASSIVE: The starting signal was given at exactly 8:30.

In the passive version the important fact is the starting time. Who gave the signal is secondary.

Use Fresh Language

Here's your chance to do yourself and your readers a favor. Instead of relying on safe, customary language, take a chance now and then and give your readers a verbal surprise. GMAT essay readers, especially after reading hundreds of predictable essays on the same topic, will do cartwheels for something fresh, something new—a word, a phrase, a sentence still wet behind the ears. A pleasant verbal surprise or two will give your readers, as well as your essay, a boost.

A verbal surprise is simply a unique and interesting choice of words. You don't have to turn exotic phrases in order to dazzle your reader. Common words, deftly used, will do the job just as well—better, probably, for they will sound more natural than something forced onto the page just to sound unusual.

ORDINARY: He wrote a magnificent essay on baseball.
SURPRISING: He pitched a magnificent essay on baseball.

Since essays are not normally *pitched,* the unexpected shift from *wrote* to *pitched* is modestly surprising. The verb *pitched* works well only because the topic is baseball. It might be silly in an essay on another topic.

ORDINARY: The shark bit the swimmers.
SURPRISING: The shark dined on the swimmers.

Changing *bit* to *dined* suggests good manners and gentility, qualities that sharks rarely enjoy.

ORDINARY: The gunshot frightened the pigeons, which flew away.
SURPRISING: The gunshot filled the sky with frightened pigeons.

The ordinary sentence states literally what happened: the sound of the gunshot scared the pigeons silly. In the second version, though, the shot becomes a vital force with the power to fill the sky. Both the pigeons and the sentence have sprung to life.

Surprise with Comparisons

Does this sound familiar? You can't find the words to express a feeling that you have inside you. You know what you want to say, but the words won't come. Although our language is filled with wonderful words to describe virtually anything, sometimes emotions and experiences seem almost inexpressible. How, for instance, do you show the look you got from the bus driver when you didn't have the exact fare? How do you describe street sounds at 5 o'clock on a summer morning or the feel of clean bedsheets?

Comparisons are economical. They condense a lot of thought and feeling into a few words. Ernie Pyle, a famous newspaper correspondent in World War II, reported his stories as though they were being told by the average GI lying in a foxhole. He said, "I write from a worm's eye point of view." What a terrific comparison! Who ever thought that worms have eyes, much less a point of view? The idea gives a fresh slant to the old expression "bird's eye view" and cleverly emphasizes Pyle's position on the battlefield.

Similes ("Norma babbles like a brook") and *metaphors* ("Norma is a babbling brook") compare something known (a babbling brook) to something unknown (Norma). Little kids use such figures of speech instinctively. Because their vocabularies are limited, they compare what they know with what they can't yet express. "When my foot is asleep, it feels like seltzer," says a boy to his daddy, or "Today is chocolate sunshine." As people grow up, they lose the knack of making colorful comparisons and have to relearn it. When you actively look for comparisons, they sprout, like weeds in the garden, all around.

Every familiar combination of words, such as "I couldn't care less," or "you've got to be kidding," or "what a bummer," was once new, cool, or poetic. But constant repetition turned them into clichés, and clichés, by definition, have lost their zing and their power to surprise. Still, clichés crowd our conversations, swamp our airwaves, and deluge the media. Like the air we breathe (a cliché), we hardly notice them. In an essay, however, especially one that is supposed to demonstrate your unique cast of mind, you must avoid clichés like the plague. "Like the plague," in fact, is one you should avoid, along with other secondhand phrases and expressions like *the bottom line, how does that sit with you, to touch base with, off the top of my head, I'm outta here, a point well taken, two sides of the same coin, getting psyched, go off the deep end, life in the fast lane, for openers, flipped out, get off my back, get a life!, super, so amazing, at the cutting edge of,* and would you believe, *would you believe?* Using such trite phrases and expressions declares that you'd rather borrow what someone else has said than think of something on your own. Spewing one cliché after another is also the sign of a poverty-stricken mind.

Expunge clichés that sneak into your prose *when your back is turned, when your defenses are down,* and *when you least expect them.* Be vigilant, and purge them from your prose. Don't use an expression that you've ever heard or seen before. If you've written a phrase with a familiar ring, drop it, not *like a hot potato,* but just as quickly.

Your GMAT essay won't be penalized for an absence of inventive and scintillating expressions, but it is sure to suffer if infested with clichés. Get into the habit of expelling all trite phrases from your writing vocabulary. *Half the battle,* as they say, is knowing a cliché when you see one. The other half—removing them—is still to be fought and won.

9. Omit Needless Words

In *Hamlet*, the old windbag Polonius knew what he was talking about when he said "Brevity is the soul of wit." What he meant, in brief, is that Brief is Better. Never use two words when one will do. Readers want to be told quickly and directly what you have to say. They value economy and resent reading more words than necessary.

Here's a word to the wise:

Work through all the sentences you write by examining each one and crossing out all the words you don't definitely need.

Actually, that's 21 words to the wise—probably more than are needed.

Go through every sentence you write and cross out unnecessary words.

That's better—11 words of free advice, but still too many. The sentence could be trimmed still further:

Cut extra words out of every sentence.

Aha! This streamlined version contains just 7 words, one third of the original. If you can regularly trim that proportion of words from your writing without changing meaning or intent, you will have gone about as far as you can to make your writing interesting, although a ruthless, sharp-eyed editor might cut even more:

Omit unnecessary words.

The ultimate goal in economical writing is to make every word count, so that omitting a single word will alter or distort the meaning.

Sentences are trimmed by squeezing them through various wringers.

Wringer #1. Look for repetition. Then combine sentences.

FAT: In his last and final year in college, Bill was elected to be the head of the statewide SADD organization. As head of the statewide organization, he learned about the details of laws dealing with DWI convictions and had many experiences talking in public to large groups of people. (49 words)

TRIMMED: Elected head of the statewide SADD organization in his senior year, Bill learned about DWI laws and spoke often to large groups. (21 words)

Wringer #2. Look for telltale words like *which, who, that, thing, all*. They sometimes indicate the presence of fat.

FAT: Football is a sport that millions of fans enjoy. (9 words)

TRIMMED: Millions of fans enjoy football. (5 words)

Wringer #3. Look for phrases that add words but little meaning.

FAT: *By that point in time*, people will be ready for a change. (12 words)

TRIMMED: By then, people will be ready for a change. (9 words)

FAT: Hamlet returned home *as a result of* his father's death. (10 words)

TRIMMED: Hamlet returned home because his father died. (7 words)

FAT PHRASES	TRIMMED
what I mean is	I mean
on account of	} because
due to the fact that	
in the final analysis	} finally
the bottom line is	
few and far between	} few
insignificant in number	
each and every one	each
this is a subject that	this subject
ten in number	ten
at the age of six years old	at age six
most unique	unique
true fact	fact
biography of his life	biography
in regard to	} about
with regard to	
in relation to	
with reference to	

Wringer #4. Search for redundancies. Countless words are wasted on reiteration of what has already been said, on restating the obvious, on repeating the same ideas, on saying the same darn thing again and again.

> FAT: While carefully scrutinizing her patient's medical history, the doctor seemed fully absorbed by what she was reading. (17 words)

Because scrutinize means "to study carefully," the word "carefully" is unnecessary. Also, *absorbed by what she was reading* repeats what has already been stated.

> TRIMMED: While scrutinizing her patient's medical history, the doctor seemed absorbed. (10 words)

After you've pared your sentences to the bone, study the remains. Cut away still more by tracking down little words like *the, a, an, up, down, its,* and *and.* Don't remove whatever gives writing its energy and character, but neither should you spare yourself the pain of removing what you worked hard to put in. Throwing away your precious words may feel sometimes as though you are chopping off your hand, but count on it, your writing will gain life and strength without unnecessary words.

10. Vary Your Sentences

In writing, it's easy to fall into a rut by repeatedly using the same sentence pattern. To avoid boring your readers to death, serve them a variety of sentences. Your prose will be invigorated and your readers will be happy. Because English is such a pliant language, sentences can be endlessly revised until you've got a mix that works.

You probably know that most simple declarative sentences start with the subject, followed by the verb:

The peaches (subject) *are* (verb) not yet ripe or ready to eat.
They (subject) *left* (verb) for the airport at dusk.
This policy (subject) *is* (verb) not easy to enforce.

Several sentences in a row with this subject-verb pattern will make writing sound like a chapter from a grade-school primer. Take steps to more mature prose by checking an essay you've recently written. If several of your sentences lead off with the subject, try starting some of them with a prepositional phrase, with an adverb or adjective, or with some other grammatical unit. By varying sentence openings, you make your writing bolder and more readable.

The following pairs of sentences illustrate ways in which a subject can be shifted from its customary position:

BEFORE THE SHIFT: Poison ivy thrives in the woods.
AFTER THE SHIFT: In the woods, poison ivy thrives.

After a prepositional phrase the subject of the sentence appears.

BEFORE: Poison ivy is apparently one of the most poisonous plants.
AFTER: Apparently, poison ivy is one of the most poisonous plants.

Obviously, the revised sentence begins with an adverb.

BEFORE: Many people still don't know what it looks like.
AFTER: Still, many people don't know what it looks like.

Well, here the sentence subject is snuck in after an opening connective.

BEFORE: People should keep their eyes peeled for an innocent-looking three-leaved plant on a single stem whenever they go out to the country.
AFTER: Whenever people are out in the country, they should keep their eyes peeled for an innocent-looking three-leaved plant on a single stem.

After introducing this sentence with a dependent clause, the writer named the subject and then added the rest of the sentence.

BEFORE: A prudent person should take a shower with plenty of soap and water as soon as possible after brushing up against the plant to guard against infection.
AFTER: To guard against infection after brushing up against the plant, a prudent person should take a shower with plenty of soap and water as soon as possible.

To revise this sentence the writer began with a *verbal,* in this case "to guard," the infinitive form of the verb. Verbals look and feel a lot like verbs (hence, their name), but are not. (The infinitive form of any verb, for example, cannot serve as the main verb of a sentence.) Verbals, though, come from verbs, which explains the resemblance.

BEFORE: Some people walk through patches of poison ivy without worrying, thinking that they are immune.
AFTER: Thinking that they are immune from poison ivy, some people walk through patches of the stuff without worrying.

Hoping to add diversity to sentence openings, the writer began this sentence with another kind of verbal, known as a *participle.* Most of the time the *-ing* ending is a clue that the word is a participle.

BEFORE: Such people, who were unconcerned about becoming infected, may be shocked to discover that their immunity has suddenly disappeared.
AFTER: Unconcerned about becoming infected, such people may be shocked to discover that their immunity has suddenly disappeared.

Determined to try something different, the writer picked an adjective that happens to sound like a verb because of its *-ed* ending.

Another variation to try occasionally is the sentence with a paired construction. Two equal and matched ideas are set against each other, often differing by only one or two words:

It wasn't that David caught poison ivy, it was poison ivy that caught him.
"Ask not what your country can do for you, ask what you can do for your country."
—John F. Kennedy, January 20, 1961

The strength of such a sentence lies in the balance of parallel parts. Each part could stand alone, but together the thought is expressed more vigorously.

No rule of thumb governs the proportion of sentences in an essay that should depart from the usual subject-verb word order. Much depends on the intent and content of the essay.

Don't deliberately scramble up sentence types just to make a sentence potpourri, for you may end up with a mess on your hands. Be guided always by what seems clearest and by what seems varied enough to hold reader interest.

Use of Repetition

Contrary to what this book has stated previously, repetition deserves a place in an essay writing repertoire. Some kinds of repetition are boring, true, but adept use of repetition lets a writer stress important ideas in an unusual way. People naturally repeat words for emphasis, anyway, as in "I love you. I love you very much," and "Knock it off. I said knock it off."

While effective repetition leaves its mark, accidental repetition can be annoying. Watch out for avoidable repetitions:

At the end of the hall stood a clock. The clock said five o'clock.
Columbus made three voyages. The voyages took him across the Atlantic.

Usually, combining such sentences will keep you from ending one sentence and starting the next one with the same words:

The clock at the end of the hall said five.
Columbus made three voyages across the Atlantic.

Occasionally sentences are plagued by a word or sound that won't let go. One student wrote:

Maybe some people don't have as much freedom as others, but the freedom they do have is given to them for free. Therefore, freedom is proof enough that the best things in life are free.

Another student wrote:

The members of the assembly remembered that November was just around the corner.

These authors weren't listening to the sound of their own words. Had they read their sentences aloud, their ears would probably have noticed that the record seemed to be stuck. In fact, reading your work aloud allows you to step back (Hold it! Those two words—aloud and allows—should not be allowed to stand. They sound sour, don't you agree?) Anyway, when you say your written words out loud, you gain perspective and notice repetitive bumps that need repair. Or better still, let your essay cool for a spell, then recruit a friend to read it to you. That's how to achieve real objectivity.

Short and Long Sentences

Sentences can be written in any length, from one word to thousands. A long sentence demands more from readers because, while stepping from one part of the sentence to the next, they must keep track of more words, modifiers, phrases (not to speak of parenthetical asides), and clauses without losing the writer's main thought, which may be buried amid any number of secondary, or less important, thoughts. Short sentences are easier to grasp. A brief sentence makes its point quickly and often with considerable force, as in this passage about a family trip:

For three days, my parents and I sat in our Toyota and drove from college to college, looking for the perfect place for me to spend the next four years. For 72 hours we lived as one person, sharing thoughts and dreams, stating opinions about each college we visited, taking guided tours, interviewing students and college officials, asking directions a hundred times, eating together in town after town, and even sleeping in the same motel rooms. But mostly, we fought.

The blunt closing sentence, particularly after a windy 46-word sentence, produces a mild jolt. To be sure, it's meant to shock, but placing a tight, terse sentence against a long one intensifies the effect. Like all stylistic techniques, this one mustn't be used too often. Overuse dilutes its impact, but when it works well, it's indelible.

Short and long sentences create the rhythm of writing. Because readers usually pause, subconsciously at least, at every period, short sentences slow the tempo. Long sentences may speed it up, but the pace depends a lot on the placement of clauses, the amount of parenthetical matter, and word choices.

In any case, a string of short, simple sentences can be as tiresome to read as series of long, complex ones strung end to end. A balance is best. A sequence of four or five equally short (or long) sentences should be given the fission-or-fusion treatment. That is, split the big ones and combine the others.

Passages consisting of short sentences can also be made more readable by fusing ideas.

When sentences are combined, words are excised and the writing often becomes livelier. Not only that, but when some ideas are subordinated to others, not every thought receives equal emphasis.

TO VARY YOUR SENTENCES—A SUMMARY

Start sentences with:

1. A prepositional phrase: *In the beginning, From the start, In the first place*
2. Adverbs and adverbial phrases: *Originally, At first, Initially*
3. Dependent clauses: *If you follow my lead, When you start with this*
4. Conjunctions: *And, But, Not only, Either, So, Yet*
5. Verbal infinitives: *To launch, To take the first step, To get going*
6. Adjectives and adjective phrases: *Fresh from, Introduced with, Headed by*
7. Participles: *Leading off, Starting up, Commencing with*
8. Inversions: *Unique is the writer who embarks . . .*

Use a variety of sentence types.
Balance long and short sentences.
Combine series of very short sentences.
Dismember very long sentences.

---

11. End Your Essay Unforgettably

When you reach the end of your GMAT or any other essay, you can lift your fingers from the keyboard and be done with it, or you can leave your readers a little gift to remember you by. What you leave can be a little piece of insight, wisdom, or humor to make readers glad that they stayed with you to the end. It may be something to tease their brains, tickle their funny bones, or make them feel smart.

Whatever you give, choose it carefully, and let it spring naturally from the text of your essay. A good essay can easily be spoiled by an ill-fitting ending. Also, don't be tempted to use an ending that is too coy, corny, or cute, such as *that's all, folks*; *it was a dream come true*; *a good time was had by all*; *tune in next week—same time, same station*; or *a nice place to visit, but I wouldn't want to live there*. These are outrageously trite endings that leave behind an impression that the writer was either too cheap to leave a better gift or too dull to think of something classier. Readers will appreciate almost any gift you give them, provided you've put some thought into its selection. Don't spoil a fresh essay with a stale conclusion.

Nor must you tack on an ending just for the sake of good form. The best endings grow organically out of the essay's content. Endings are so crucial in works of creative art that specific words have been designated to name them. A piece of music has a *coda*; a story or play, a *denouement*, a musical show, a *grand finale*. When an ending approaches, you sense it at hand and expect soon to be bathed with a feeling of satisfaction. Good endings please both heart and mind.

Choose the gift judiciously. Leave behind a memento of your thinking, your sense of humor, or your vision. Even an ordinary thought, uniquely presented, will shed an agreeable afterglow.

1. Have some fun with your ending. A reader may remember your sense of humor long after forgetting the essay that struck his funny bone.

   SUBJECT: Stricter gun control laws
   GIFT: On this issue, the legislature has taken a cheap shot at many law-abiding citizens.

2. End with an apt quotation taken from the essay, from the assigned topic or from some other source.

   SUBJECT: The nobility of the teaching profession
   GIFT: As a wise person once said, "Catch a fish and you feed a man his dinner, but teach a man to fish, and you feed him for life."

   SUBJECT: The costs of racial disharmony
   GIFT: Now, more than ever, Rodney King's question, "Can we all get along?" has a new meaning.

3. Finish by reviewing the paper's main point, but with new words. Add a short tag line, perhaps.

   SUBJECT: The low quality of art supplies used in school, arguing that money should be devoted to support the art program.
   GIFT: Colors fade rapidly when exposed to sunlight, a true indication of the paint's poor quality. How frustrating!

   SUBJECT: The purported death of democracy
   GIFT: Our victory over the forces of the communist menace must mean that democracy has the power to endure and must mean that it is healthy.

4. Project your readers into the future. What will happen in the months or years ahead?

   SUBJECT: Being adventurous
   GIFT: By late spring I had my fill of studying the river; it was time to get a raft and try the rapids myself.

   SUBJECT: The misuse of our environment
   GIFT: We must all do our part to save the planet, or there won't be a planet left to save.

A catchy conclusion isn't always needed, but some sort of ending is necessary to make readers feel they've arrived somewhere. They won't be satisfied with an essay that just evaporates. A short one is better than none at all. Stay away from summary endings, particularly when the essay is short, as on the GMAT. It's insulting, in fact, to review for the readers what is evident on the page in front of them. Readers are intelligent people. Trust them to remember what the essay says.

12. Follow the Conventions of Standard English

This book is too lean to house a complete handbook of standard English usage. For a full treatment of English usage, however, see the Sentence Correction Review in Chapter 6 or go to the library and check out one of the hefty books on the subject. Look, for instance, at H. W. Fowler's *Modern English Usage*, the definitive reference work, in which you can find a page-long discussion of such arcane usage questions as the difference between *farther* and *further*, or when to use *that*, as in "Is it my Mazda Miata *that* is parked illegally?" and when to use *which*, as in "Yes, your Mazda Miata, *which* is now being ticketed, is parked illegally." Numerous other books, such as *The New York Times Manual of Style and Usage* and *The Careful Writer* by Theodore M. Bernstein are packed with solutions to literally thousands of usage problems.

Unhappily, there is no particular logic to standard English usage. Like the famous definition of pornography, it's hard to define but easy to spot when you see it. Standard English is merely a badge of an educated person, the level of writing and speech expected of people who are literate and who, to some degree, must depend on their language skills to help them make their way in the world.

Essay Topics for Further Practice

> **Directions:** Write a clear, logical, and well-organized response to the following issue or argument. Your response should be in the form of a short essay, following the conventions of standard written English. Your answer should fit on three pages of lined 8½" × 11" paper; on your computer, the equivalent would be a word count of approximately 1,000.
>
> Eighteen topics are suggested for practice, but if you write on the same topic again and again, the number of topics is two, three, or even ten times as many. Since it's virtually impossible to write the same essay twice, you could try the same topic over and over without repeating yourself. Each time you write on the same topic, choose another point of view to defend. They say that one sign of erudition is the ability to argue both sides of an issue equally well. Then compare the results.

1. *Adlai Stevenson once commented, "It is often easier to fight for principles than to live up to them."*

   Based on your reading, observation, or experience, to what extent to you agree or disagree with Stevenson's words? Please give examples that support your point of view.

2. *The former secretary general of the United Nations, Dag Hammarskjöld wrote, "Never look down to test the ground before taking your next step: only he who keeps his eye fixed on the far horizon will find his right road."*

   While such a philosophy may be appropriate for the leader of the United Nations, it may not be an acceptable practice for ordinary individuals to follow as they go about their daily lives. What is your opinion? Support your position with illustrations from your observation, study, reading, or personal experience.

3. *The German poet Goethe once wrote, "Treat people as if they were what they ought to be and you help them to become what they are capable of being."*

   Goethe's statement could probably apply to schools, government, social services, business, even to families—anyplace, really, where people interact with each other. Is Goethe just expressing pretty-sounding, idealistic nonsense, or does his idea have real-life applicability? Based on your experience, observation, or reading, please comment on the usefulness of Goethe's statement as a realistic guide to human relationships.

4. *Some cultures view life as a line, extending from point A to point B. Others view life as a circle.*

   Explain which of these two views coincides with yours. If neither, what shape or form would you propose? Please explain.

5. *After rescuing a child from a burning building, Jim Smith, a fire fighter, commented, "Courage is just a matter of luck—of being in the right place at the right time."*

   Do you think that courage is common to most of us, but that most of us never have an opportunity to show it? Or is physical courage like Jim Smith's an unusual quality in most of us?

6. *Why are you such an awful procrastinator? Or why doesn't this question apply to you?*

   Explain your answer to one of the above questions. Use illustrations from your personal experience to support your views.

7. *"Ignorance of the law is no excuse for breaking it."*

   Do you agree or disagree with this legal principle? If you do, should exceptions ever be made? Under what circumstances? If you don't, why do you suppose such a principle exists? What would you propose as an alternative?

8. *There's an old proverb, "Spare the rod and spoil the child." To put it another way, fear of punishment keeps people in line.*

   Do you agree or disagree with this view of human nature? Is the hope of reward ever a better way to control behavior?

9. *There's an old proverb, "There's no great loss without some gain." Another way to put it is, "Every cloud has a silver lining."*

   Do you agree or disagree with this observation? Support your position with illustrations from your observation, studies, reading, or personal experience.

10. *An old English proverb says, "What you don't know can't hurt you."*

    Do you think that this proverb is generally true or generally false, or do you think that its validity lies somewhere in between? Defend your opinion using examples from life, literature, or your studies.

11. *Thomas Jefferson said, "When a man assumes a public trust, he should consider himself public property." In other words, public figures, such as a president and other government officials, should not expect to have the same right of privacy as ordinary citizens.*

    To what extent do you support or oppose this point of view? Be as specific as you can in explaining your position.

12. *On whom should the moral responsibility for battlefield atrocities lie? Does it rest on military leaders, soldiers who carry out orders, the makers of weapons, or on the people as a whole? Or do you think that no person has the right to hold another person morally responsible for anything—in wartime or any other time?*

Where do you stand on this issue? Please explain and defend your position.

13. *It has been said that a great leader cannot be overly cautious.*

To what extent do you agree or disagree with this statement? Support your point of view using examples from your observation, experience, reading, or study of history.

14. *By law, cigarettes and liquor may not be advertised on television. Some people think there should also be an advertising ban on foods that are unhealthy for children, such as candy and heavily sugared cereals. Opponents view such a ban as an infringement of basic freedoms.*

What is your opinion? Explain and defend your viewpoint, using examples from your observation, study, or experience.

15. *Two existing government organizations are the National Endowment for the Humanities, which supports art and culture, and the National Academy of the Sciences, which supports endeavors in the sciences. If you had the opportunity to propose the creation of a new organization to support a cause, it would be the National _____.*

Fill in the blank and explain why you would support such a venture.

16. *After some 16 years of schooling you are likely to have had some good teachers.*

In your view what makes a good teacher?

17. *In most colleges, students who fail a certain number of academic courses are ineligible to participate in intercollegiate athletics until their grades have improved.*

Do you believe it is proper to link participation in athletics to classroom performance? Write an essay in which you defend or criticize this policy.

18. *As a visitor from another planet, you have been observing humankind and its behavior on Earth. One of the oddest features you have observed is _____.*

Fill in the blank, and explain why you singled out that particular feature.

Sample Essays

Below are two sample essays.

Analysis of an Argument

> The following was published by a non-governmental organization (NGO).
>
> *Globalization shapes and distorts cultural patterns in developing countries. The Westernization, particularly the Americanization, of culture presents a formidable threat to the cultural integrity of the non-Western World.*
>
> Discuss how well reasoned the above argument is.

Popular sentiment against globalization has often been directed at one of its perceived engines — a Western consumer culture of fast food, gadgetry, and cinema imposed on the entire world.

The process of globalization is resulting in the marketing not only of consumer products, but even of culture and indigenous traditions of different societies. The globalization and westernization of culture is taken by traditional and ancient cultures as cultural aggression and a threat to the cultural and social values of such societies through media, information technology, and social and political changes.

Perhaps by far the most important far-reaching effect of cultural globalization is the commercialization of culture. Production and consumption of cultural goods and services have become commodities. In a way very similar to economic globalization, most people (and especially the poor) do not experience cultural globalization on terms they have decided for themselves. Culture—whether it is music, food, clothes, art, sport, images of age or youth, masculinity or femininity—has become a product sold in the market place.

The commercialization of culture has a disturbing impact on people. What once was an element of their way of life becomes a product, rather than something unique they had made to suit their own specific needs and circumstances. At the same time, people are increasingly bombarded with new images, new music, new clothes, and new values. The familiar and old are to be discarded. While there was cultural change long before globalization, there is a danger that much will be lost simply because it is not valued by global markets.

In conclusion, cultural globalization, or worldwide McDonaldization, destroys diversity and displaces the opportunity to sustain decent human life through an assortment of many different cultures. It is more a consequence of power concentration in the global media and manufacturing companies than the people's own wish to abandon their cultural identity and diversity.

Analysis of an Issue

"Most groups and organizations should work as teams in which everyone shares in the decision and responsibility for carrying them out. Giving one person central authority and responsibility for a project or task is a less effective means to get the job done."

State the extent to which you agree or disagree with the above issue. Support your viewpoint with examples taken from your work or school experiences, your reading, or your observations.

Organizations have undergone a shift from the individual climb up the corporate ladder to an increasing emphasis on work teams and groups. The shift to work teams is largely due to factors such as globalization, downsizing, and the need for technological efficiency. As companies expand and tasks become more complex, more and more specialists are needed within organizations. These specialists must learn to work together so that colleagues have an understanding of the role and responsibility of those whose skills differ from their own.

There are other reasons for the emergence of work teams as well. Stiff competition, particularly in technology-driven fields, requires teamwork with a concerted effort to keep the company as a whole on the cutting edge. Because technology-driven tasks have become far too complex for one person to handle alone, many organizations create work teams to accomplish collective goals.

There are many challenges that can affect teamwork. For example, members of a team can suffer from "groupthink," the belief that every member already knows what the others will propose as solutions. When this happens, teams can become paralyzed by inaction. Issues related to globalization create what are perhaps the most daunting challenges to teams. As national borders become transparent and economies intertwine, there is an increased risk of choosing solutions that isolate or marginalize some team members because the solutions are based on preconceived notions that do not apply across international borders.

While many managers and executives view teams as the most effective design for involving all employees in the success of a company, they may not be skilled in the group dynamics needed to run teams effectively. This, along with the fact that many people are initially more comfortable working alone, may cause executives to be skeptical about the value of work teams and hesitant to take the necessary steps to create them.

Reading Comprehension Review

A large proportion of the GMAT is designed to test your ability to comprehend material contained in reading passages. The Reading Comprehension review is preparation for not only the Reading Comprehension questions on the test but also the Critical Reasoning questions. The Reading Comprehension questions do allow you to turn back to the passages when answering the questions. However, many of the questions may be based on what is *implied* in the passages, rather than on what is explicitly stated. Your ability to draw inferences from the material is critical to successfully completing these questions. It is also critical to your success on the Critical Reasoning questions, which test your ability to evaluate assumptions, inferences, and arguments.

In each case, success depends on the extent of your reading comprehension skills. The following discussion is designed to help you formulate an approach to reading passages that will enable you to better understand the material you will be asked to read on the GMAT. Practice exercises at the end of this review will give you an opportunity to try out this approach.

BASIC READING SKILLS

A primary skill necessary for good reading comprehension and recall is the understanding of the meanings of individual words. Knowledge of a wide and diversified vocabulary enables you to detect subtle differences in sentence meaning that may hold the key to the meaning of an entire paragraph or passage. For this reason, it is important that you familiarize yourself with as many words as possible.

A second reading skill to be developed is the ability to discover the central theme of a passage. By making yourself aware of what the entire passage is about, you are in a position to relate what you read to this central theme, logically picking out the main points and significant details as you go along. Although the manner in which the central theme is stated may vary from passage to passage, it can usually be found in the title (if one is presented), in the "topic sentence" of a paragraph in shorter passages, or, in longer passages, by reading several paragraphs.

A third essential skill is the capacity to organize mentally how the passage is put together and determine how each part is related to the whole. This is the skill you will have to use to the greatest degree on the GMAT, where you must pick out significant and insignificant factors, remember main details, and relate information you have read to the central theme.

In general, a mastery of these three basic skills will provide you with a solid basis for better reading comprehension wherein you will be able to read carefully to draw a conclusion from the material, decide the meanings of words and ideas presented and how they in turn affect the meaning of the passage, and recognize opinions and views that are expressed.

APPLYING BASIC READING SKILLS

The only way to become adept at the three basic reading skills outlined above is to practice using the techniques involved as much as possible. Studying the meanings of new words you encounter in all your reading material will soon help you establish a working knowledge of many words. In the same manner, making an effort to locate topic sentences, general themes, and specific details in material you read will enable you to improve your skills in these areas. The following drills will help. After you have read through them and answered the questions satisfactorily, you can try the longer practice exercises at the end.

FINDING THE TOPIC SENTENCE

The term "topic sentence" is used to describe the sentence that gives the key to an entire paragraph. Usually the topic sentence is found in the beginning of a paragraph. However, there is no absolute rule. A writer may build the paragraph to a conclusion, putting the key sentence at the end. Here is an example in which the topic sentence is located at the beginning:

EXAMPLE 1

Line   The world faces a serious problem of overpopulation. Right now many people starve from
(2)   lack of adequate food. Efforts are being made to increase the rate of food production, but
         the number of people to be fed increases at a faster rate.

The idea is stated directly in the opening sentence. You know that the passage will be about "a serious problem of overpopulation." Like a heading or caption, the topic sentence sets the stage or gets your mind ready for what follows in that paragraph.

Before you try to locate the topic sentence in a paragraph you must remember that this technique depends upon reading and judgment. Read the whole passage first. Then try to decide which sentence comes closest to expressing the main point of the paragraph. Do not worry about the position of the topic sentence in the paragraph; look for the most important statement. Find the idea to which all the other sentences relate.

Try to identify the topic sentence in this passage:

EXAMPLE 2

         During the later years of the American Revolution, the Articles of Confederation govern-
         ment was formed. This government suffered severely from a lack of power. Each state dis-
         trusted the others and gave little authority to the central or federal government. The
Line   Articles of Confederation produced a government which could not raise money from
(5)   taxes, prevent Indian raids, or force the British out of the United States.

What is the topic sentence? Certainly the paragraph is about the Articles of Confederation. However, is the key idea in the first sentence or in the second sentence? In this instance, the *second* sentence does a better job of giving you the key to this paragraph—the lack of centralized power that characterized the Articles of Confederation. The sentences that complete the paragraph relate more to the idea of "lack of power" than to the time when the government was formed. Don't assume that the topic sentence is always the first sentence of a paragraph. Try this:

EXAMPLE 3

There is a strong relation between limited education and low income. Statistics show that unemployment rates are highest among those adults who attended school the fewest years. Most jobs in a modern industrial society require technical or advanced training. The

Line best pay goes with jobs that demand thinking and decisions based on knowledge. A few

(5) people manage to overcome their limited education by personality or a "lucky break." However, studies of lifetime earnings show that the average high school graduate earns more than the average high school dropout, who in turns earns more than the average adult who has not finished eighth grade.

Here, the first sentence contains the main idea of the whole paragraph. One more example should be helpful:

EXAMPLE 4

They had fewer men available as soldiers. Less than one third of the railroads and only a

Line small proportion of the nation's industrial production was theirs. For most of the war their

(3) coastline was blockaded by Northern ships. It is a tribute to Southern leadership and the courage of the people that they were not defeated for four years.

In this case you will note that the passage builds up to its main point. The topic sentence is the last one. Practice picking out the topic sentences in other material you read until it becomes an easy task.

FINDING THE GENERAL THEME

A more advanced skill is the ability to read several paragraphs and relate them to one general theme or main idea. The procedure involves careful reading of the entire passage and deciding which idea is the central or main one. You can tell you have the right idea when it is most frequent or most important, or when every sentence relates to it. As you read the next passage, note the *underlined* parts.

EXAMPLE 1

True democracy means direct rule by the people. A good example can be found in a modern town meeting in many small New England towns. All citizens aged 21 or over may vote. They not only vote for officials, but they also get together to vote on local laws (or ordi-

Line nances). The small size of the town and the limited number of voters make this possible.

(5)   In the cities, voters cast ballots for officials who get together to make the laws. Because the voters do not make the laws directly, this system is called indirect democracy or representative government. There is no problem of distance to travel, but it is difficult to run a meeting with hundreds of thousands of citizens.

          Representation of voters and a direct voice in making laws are more of a problem in

(10) state or national governments. The numbers of citizens and the distances to travel make representative government the most practical way to make laws.

Think about the passage in general and the underlined parts in particular. Several examples discuss voting for officials and making laws. In the first paragraph both of these are done by the voters. The second paragraph describes representative government in which voters elect officials who make laws. The last paragraph emphasizes the problem of size and numbers and says that representative government is more practical. In the following question, put all these ideas together.

The main theme of this passage is that

(A) the United States is not democratic
(B) citizens cannot vote for lawmakers
(C) representative government does not make laws
(D) every citizen makes laws directly
(E) increasing populations lead to less direct democracy

The answer is choice (E). Choices (B), (C), and (D) can be eliminated because they are not true of the passage. Choice (A) may have made you hesitate a little. The passage makes comments about *less direct* democracy, but it never says that representative government is *not democratic*.

The next three passages offer further practice in finding the main theme. Answer the question following each example and check the analysis to make sure you understand.

EXAMPLE 2

Skye, 13 miles off the northwest coast of Scotland, is the largest and most famous of the Hebrides. Yet fame has neither marred its natural beauty nor brought affectation to its inhabitants. The scene and the people are almost as they were generations ago.

Line   The first sight that impresses the visitor to Skye is its stark beauty. This is not beauty of
(5)   the usual sort, for the island is not a lush green "paradise." It is, on the other hand, almost devoid of shrubbery. Mountains, moorlands, sky, and sea combine to create an overpowering landscape. Endless stretches of rocky hills dominate the horizon. Miles of treeless plains meet the eye. Yet this scene has a beauty all its own.

And then cutting into the stark landscape are the fantastic airborne peaks of the
(10) Cuillins, rising into the clear skies above. The Cuillins are the most beloved mountains in Scotland and are frequently climbed. Their rugged, naked grandeur, frost-sculptured ridges and acute peaks even attracted Sir Edmund Hillary.

The main idea of this passage is

(A) the sky over Skye
(B) the lack of trees on Skye
(C) the natural beauty of Skye
(D) the lack of affectation on Skye
(E) the Cuillins in the skies of Skye

All of the answers have some truth to them. The problem is to find the best answer. Four of the choices are mentioned in the passage only by a small comment. But choice (C) is discussed throughout every part of the passage. The clue to the correct answer was how often the same theme was covered.

EXAMPLE 3

Trade exists for many reasons. No doubt it started from a desire to have something differ-ent. Men also realized that different men could make different products. Trade encour-aged specialization, which led to improvement in quality.

Line (5) Trade started from person to person, but grew to involve different towns and different lands. Some found work in transporting the goods or selling them. Merchants grew rich as the demand for products increased. Craftsmen were able to sell more products at home and abroad. People in general had a greater variety of things to choose.

(10) The knowledge of new products led to an interest in the lands which produced them. More daring persons went to see other lands. Others stayed at home, but asked many questions of the travelers. As people learned about the products and the conditions in other countries, they compared them with their own. This often led to a desire for better conditions or a hope for a better life. Trade was mainly an economic force, but it also had other effects.

The general theme of the passage is how

(A) trade makes everyone rich
(B) trade divides the world
(C) products are made
(D) trade changes people's lives
(E) people find new jobs

This is not easy, as you may feel that all the choices are good. Most of them were mentioned in some part of the passage. However, you must select the best choice. If you had trouble, let us analyze the passage.

Paragraph one emphasizes a "desire" for "something different" and "improvement." The sec-ond paragraph mentions "found work," "merchants grew rich," "craftsmen . . . sell more," and "greater variety of things to choose." The third paragraph covers "interest in the lands," "com-pared them with their own," "desire for better conditions," and "better life." All these are evidence of the same general theme of how trade brings changes in the lives of people. Choice (D) is the best answer.

Choice (A) is tempting because of the comment on merchants getting rich. However, this idea is not found all through the passage. Choice (B) may catch the careless thinker. Trade does not divide the world, even though the passage talks about dividing jobs. Choice (C) is weak. Some comment is made about making products, but not in all parts of the passage. Choice (E) is weak for the same reason as choice (C).

EXAMPLE 4

    The enormous problems of turning swamps and desert into fields and orchards, together with the ideal of share-and-share-alike, gave birth to the kibbutz.

    In those days, the kibbutz member had to plow the fields with a rifle slung over his shoulder.

Line

(5)

    Today security is still a factor in the kibbutz. Shelters are furrowed into the ground along every walk among the shade trees, near the children's house, where all the young children of the kibbutz live, and near the communal dining room.

    But the swamps have been conquered, and the desert is gradually becoming green. And while kibbutz members once faced deprivation and a monotonous diet, today they reap the harvest of hard work and success.

(10)

    One such kibbutz is Dorot, at the gateway to the Negev desert and typical of the average-size Israeli communal settlement.

    Life on the kibbutz has become more complex through growth and prosperity. While once the land barely yielded enough for a living, Dorot, like many other kibbutzim, now exports some of its crops. It also has become industrialized, another trend among these settlements. Dorot has a factory which exports faucets to a dozen countries, including the United States.

(15)

The main theme of this article is

(A) the manufacture of faucets is a sign of growth and prosperity in the kibbutz
(B) with the solving of agricultural problems the kibbutz has become a more complex society
(C) since security is a problem for the kibbutz, it has become industrialized
(D) Dorot is the prosperous gateway to the Negev desert
(E) kibbutzim are good places to live, although they are located in swamps and deserts

Choice (A) receives brief mention at the end of the passage. It is an idea in the passage, but certainly not the general idea of the passage. Choice (D) is the same kind of answer as choice (A)—it is too specific a fact. Choice (E) is unrelated to the passage. We now have choices (B) and (C) as possible answers. Choice (C) seems reasonable until you analyze it. Did the need for security *cause* the industrialization? Or are there better examples of how life has become more complex now that agricultural problems have been solved? The evidence leans more to choice (B).

In summary, in order to find the general theme:

1. Read at your normal speed.

2. Locate the topic sentence in each paragraph.

3. Note ideas that are frequent or emphasized.

4. Find the idea to which most of the passage is related.

FINDING LOGICAL RELATIONSHIPS

In order to understand fully the meaning of a passage, you must first look for the general theme and then relate the ideas and opinions found in the passage to this general theme. In this way, you can determine not only what is important but also how the ideas interrelate to form the whole. From this understanding, you will be better able to answer questions that refer to the passage.

As you read the following passages, look for general theme and supporting facts, words or phrases that signal emphasis or shift in thought, and the relation of one idea to another.

EXAMPLE 1

Candidates for election pay close attention to statements and actions that will make the voters see them favorably. In ancient Rome candidates wore pure white togas (the Latin word *candidatus* means "clothed in white") to indicate that they were pure, clean, and above any "dirty work." However, it is interesting to note that such a toga was not worn after election.

Line (5)

In more modern history, candidates have allied themselves with political parties. Once a voter knows and favors the views of a certain political party, he may vote for anyone with that party's label. Nevertheless, divisions of opinion develop, so that today there is a wide range of candidate views in any major party.

1. The best conclusion to be drawn from the first paragraph is that after an election

(A) all candidates are dishonest
(B) candidates are less concerned with symbols of integrity
(C) candidates do not change their ideas
(D) officials are always honest
(E) policies always change

You noted the ideas about a candidate in Rome. You saw the word "however" signal a shift in ideas or thinking. Now the third step rests with your judgment. You cannot jump to a conclusion; you must see which conclusion is reasonable or fair. Choices (A), (D), and (E) should make you wary. They say "all" or "always" which means without exception. The last sentence is not that strong or positive. Choices (B) and (C) must be considered. There is nothing in the paragraph that supports the fact that candidates do not change their ideas. This forces you into choice (B) as the only statement logically related to what the paragraph said.

2. A fair statement is that most candidates from the same political party today are likely to

(A) have the same views
(B) be different in every view
(C) agree on almost all points
(D) agree on some points and disagree on others
(E) agree only by accident

Here again, the burden rests on your judgment after following ideas and word clues. The paragraph makes the point that there is a wide range of views. That eliminates choice (A). Choice (B) is not logical because the candidates would not likely be in the same party if they disagree on every view. The remaining choices are different degrees of agreement. Choice (E) is weak because candidates are too interested to arrive at agreement only by accident. The wide range mentioned seems to oppose choice (C) and favor choice (D) as a little more likely. You may say that choice (C) sounds pretty good. Again we stress that you *are picking the very best choice*, not just a good choice. That is what we mean by reflecting carefully on all possibilities and selecting the best available choice.

EXAMPLE 2

In 1812 Napoleon had to withdraw his forces from Russia. The armies had invaded successfully and reached the city of Moscow. There was no question of French army disloyalty or unwillingness to fight. As winter came, the Russian army moved out of the way,
Line   leaving a wasted land and burned buildings. Other conquered European nations seized
(5)   upon Napoleon's problems in Russia as their chance to rearm and to break loose from French control.

According to the passage, it may be inferred that the main reason for Napoleon's withdrawal from Russia was the

(A) disloyalty of the French troops
(B) Russian winter
(C) burned buildings
(D) revolts in other countries
(E) Russian army

In this passage, only choice (A) is totally incorrect. Choice (E) is very weak because the Russian army was not able to stop the invasion. The choices narrow to which is the best of (B), (C), and (D). It seems that all three answers are supported by the passage. There needs to be some thought and judgment by you. Which of these could be overcome easily and which could be the strongest reason for Napoleon leaving Russia? The burned buildings could be overcome by the troops making other shelters. The Russian winter was severe and the army did not want to face it. However, marching out of Russia in the winter was also a great problem. Napoleon probably would have stayed in Moscow except for a more serious problem—the loss of the control he had established over most of Europe. Thus, answer (D) is best.

EXAMPLE 3

By 1915 events of World War I were already involving the United States and threatening its neutrality. The sinking of the British liner Lusitania in that year by a German submarine caused great resentment among Americans. Over a hundred United States citizens were
Line   killed in the incident. President Wilson had frequently deplored the use of submarines by
(5)   Germany against the United States. Since the United States was neutral, it was not liable to acts of war by another nation.

However, Wilson resolved to represent the strong feeling in the country (notably in the Midwest) and in the Democratic Party that United States neutrality should be maintained. He felt that the United States should have "peace with honor," if possible.
(10)   There were also people, mostly in the East, who wanted to wage a preventive war against Germany. Such leaders as Theodore Roosevelt bitterly attacked Wilson as one who talked a great deal but did nothing.

By 1917 Germany again used unrestricted submarine warfare and Wilson broke off relations with Germany. In February British agents uncovered the Zimmerman Telegram.
(15)   This was an attempt by the German ambassador to Mexico to involve that nation in a war against the United States. And in March several American merchant ships were sunk by German submarines. His patience at an end, Wilson at last took the position of a growing majority of Americans and asked Congress to declare war on Germany. Thus, the United States entered World War I.

1. This passage tries to explain that

   (A) Wilson wanted the United States to go to war against Germany
   (B) Wilson tried to avoid war with Germany
   (C) Germany wanted the United States to enter the war
   (D) other nations were pressuring the United States to enter the war
   (E) Mexico was our main enemy

2. We can conclude from the passage that most citizens of the United States in 1917 were

   (A) totally opposed to war with Germany
   (B) in favor of war before Wilson was
   (C) willing to accept war after Wilson persuaded them
   (D) neutral
   (E) trying to avoid war

3. The last event in the series of happenings that led to a declaration of war against Germany was

   (A) the Zimmerman Telegram
   (B) attacks on U.S. merchant ships
   (C) Wilson's war message to Congress
   (D) a change in public opinion
   (E) the sinking of the *Lusitania*

In question 1, the key is to note Wilson's actions discussed in paragraph two. Near the end of the passage there is a phrase about "his patience at an end." This describes a man who was trying to avoid a conflict, as in answer choice (B).

Question 2 rests on two ideas. There was a change in the feeling of the American people about war. The other idea is that Wilson responded after he felt that they had changed. The phrase "took the position of a growing majority of Americans" tells us that Wilson followed the change in opinion, as in answer choice (B).

In question 3, you need to check the sequence of events. The declaration of war followed the president's request.

MAKING INFERENCES

An inference is not stated. It is assumed by the reader from something said by the writer. An inference is the likely or probable conclusion rather than the direct, logical one. It usually involves an opinion or viewpoint that the writer wants the reader to follow or assume. In another kind of inference, the reader figures out the author's opinion even though it is not stated. The clues are generally found in the manner in which facts are presented and in the choice of words and phrases. Opinion is revealed by the one-sided nature of a passage in which no opposing facts are given. It is shown further by "loaded" words that reveal the author's feelings.

It is well worth noting that opinionated writing is often more interesting than straight factual accounts. Some writers are very colorful, forceful, or amusing in presenting their views. You should understand that there is nothing wrong with reading opinion. You should read varied opinions, but know that they are opinions. Then make up your own mind.

Not every writer will insert an opinion obviously. However, you can get clues from how often the same idea is said (frequency), whether arguments are balanced on both sides (fairness), and the choice of wording (emotional or loaded words). Look for the clues in this next passage.

EXAMPLE 1

Slowly but surely the great passenger trains of the United States have been fading from the rails. Short-run commuter trains still rattle in and out of the cities. Between major cities you can still find a train, but the schedules are becoming less frequent. The Twenti-
Line (5) eth Century Limited, The Broadway Limited, and other luxury trains that sang along the rails at 60 to 80 miles an hour are no longer running. Passengers on other long runs complain of poor service, old equipment, and costs in time and money. The long-distance traveler today accepts the noise of jets, the congestion at airports, and the traffic between airport and city. A more elegant and graceful way is becoming only a memory.

1. With respect to the reduction of long-run passenger trains, this writer expresses

   (A) regret
   (B) pleasure
   (C) grief
   (D) elation
   (E) anger

Before you choose the answer, you must deduce what the writer's feeling is. He does not actually state his feeling, but clues are available so that you may infer what it is. Choices (B) and (D) are impossible, because he gives no word that shows he is pleased by the change. Choice (C) is too strong, as is choice (E). Choice (A) is the most reasonable inference to make. He is sorry to see the change. He is expressing regret.

2. The author seems to feel that air travel is

   (A) costly
   (B) slow
   (C) streamlined
   (D) elegant
   (E) uncomfortable

Here we must be careful because he says very little about air travel. However, his one sentence about it presents three negative or annoying points. The choice now becomes fairly clear. Answer (E) is correct.

EXAMPLE 2

When the United States was founded at the end of the eighteenth century, it was a small and weak country, made up mostly of poor farmers. Foreign policy, reflecting this domestic condition, stressed "no entangling alliances." The State Department then had a staff of
Line less than half a dozen persons, whose total salary was $6,600 (of which $3,500 went to the
(5) Secretary of State), and a diplomatic service budget (July, 1790) of $40,000. Militarily, too, the country was insignificant. The first United States army, soon after the American Revolution, was made up of one captain (John Doughty) and 80 men. Clearly, the United States did not consider itself a real power and was not taken seriously by the rest of the world.

It was not until immense changes took place *inside* the United States that the country
(10) began to play an important role in foreign affairs. By the beginning of the twentieth century, the United States had ceased to be a predominantly agricultural nation and had become an industrial one. Its population had grown to more than 30 times its original number. George Washington was president of 3,000,000 Americans; Theodore Roosevelt, of 100,000,000.

1. A country today cannot expect to play an important part in world affairs unless it

   I. has wealth
   II. has a large population
   III. is strong internally

   (A) I only
   (B) III only
   (C) I and II only
   (D) II and III only
   (E) I, II, and III

This is a slightly different style of question. You must look at each of the answer choices in I, II, and III. As you consider the passage and what it suggests, you note that each of the answer choices in I, II, and III make good sense. Therefore, answer choice (E) is the best answer because it includes all of the correct statements. Again, this is not designed to trick you. The purpose of such a question is to be sure that you have read all the choices.

2. The writer seems to think that a major factor in making the United States a world power was

   (A) industrialization
   (B) the passing of time
   (C) a change in government policies
   (D) the presidency of Theodore Roosevelt
   (E) the avoidance of entangling alliances

The passage does not answer the question directly. You must infer what is meant by the author. However, there is a clue in the author's comment that changes inside a country make a big difference in its foreign policy. The big internal changes noted are the growth of America's population and industrial power. By correctly interpreting the passage, you will be led to choice (A) for this question.

In Example 3 you will find three short statements by three different writers. The questions will require that you make inferences about each writer and then make comparisons of one against the other two.

EXAMPLE 3

Writer I

No nation should tolerate the slacker who will not defend his country in time of war. The so-called conscientious objector is a coward who accepts the benefits of his country but
Line   will not accept the responsibility. By shirking his fair share, he forces another person to
(5)   assume an unfair burden.

Writer II

A democratic nation should have room for freedom of conscience. Religious training and belief may make a man conscientiously opposed to participation in war. The conscientious objector should be permitted to give labor service or some form of noncombat mil-
(10)   itary duty. His beliefs should be respected.

Writer III

The rights of the conscientious objector should be decided by each individual. No government should dictate to any person or require him to endanger his life if the person, in conscience, objects. There need be no religious basis. It is enough for a free individual to
(15)   think as he pleases and to reject laws or rules to which he conscientiously objects.

1. A balanced opinion on this subject is presented by

    (A) Writer I
    (B) Writer II
    (C) Writer III
    (D) all of the writers
    (E) none of the writers

2. We can conclude that the writer most likely to support a person who refuses any military service is

    (A) Writer I
    (B) Writer II
    (C) Writer III
    (D) all of the writers
    (E) none of the writers

3. An authoritarian person is most likely to agree with

    (A) Writer I
    (B) Writer II
    (C) Writer III
    (D) all of the writers
    (E) none of the writers

Look for clues in the language or choice of words that are loaded with feeling such as "slacker," "so-called," and "shirking" by Writer I and "dictate," "endanger," and "as he pleases" by Writer III. Compare them with the language used by Writer II. Then see if you can connect what these writers say with views you have heard or read. We are not asking you to accept any of these opinions. You are using your skill in reading what the writers think and adding it to your own knowledge. Then you make logical inferences. The correct answers are 1 (B), 2 (C), and 3 (A).

Now that you have spent time reviewing the three basic skills you should master for better reading comprehension ability, try the two practice exercises that follow. Answers to these exercises appear after Exercise B. You should also try to spend time using this reading approach as you read other material not related to the GMAT.

Practice Exercises

The following two reading passages are similar to the Reading Comprehension passages found on the GMAT. You should read each one and then answer the questions that follow according to the directions. Remember that in Reading Comprehension sections you are permitted to refer to the passage while answering the questions.

Exercise A

TIME: 9 minutes

> **Directions:** This part contains a reading passage. You are to read it carefully. When answering the questions, you *will* be able to refer to the passages. The questions are based on what is stated or *implied* in the passage. You have nine minutes to complete this part.

Above all, colonialism was hated for its explicit assumption that the civilizations of colonized peoples were inferior. Using slogans like *The White Man's Burden* and *La Mission Civilicatrice*, Europeans asserted their moral obligation to impose their way of life on
Line those endowed with inferior cultures. This orientation was particularly blatant among the
(5) French. In the colonies, business was conducted in French. Schools used that language and employed curricula designed for children in France. One scholar suggests that Muslim children probably learned no more about the Maghreb than they did about Australia. In the Metropole, intellectuals discoursed on the weakness of Arabo-Islamic culture. A noted historian accused Islam of being hostile to science. An academician wrote that Ara-
(10) bic—the holy language of religion, art and the Muslim sciences—is "more of an encumbrance than an aid to the mind. It is absolutely devoid of precision." There was of course an element of truth in the criticisms. After all, Arab reformists had been engaging in self-criticism for decades. Also, at least some Frenchmen honestly believed they were helping the colonized. A Resident General in Tunisia, for example, told an assemblage of Muslims
(15) with sincerity, "We shall distribute to you all that we have of learning; we shall make you a party to everything that makes for the strength of our intelligence." But none of this could change or justify the cultural racism in colonial ideologies. To the French, North Africans were only partly civilized and could be saved only by becoming Frenchmen. The reaction of the colonized was of course to defend their identity and to label colonial pol-
(20) icy, in the words of Algerian writer Malek Hadad, "cultural asphyxia." Throughout North Africa, nationalists made the defense of Arabo-Islamic civilization a major objective, a value in whose name they demanded independence. Yet the crisis of identity, provoked by colonial experiences, has not been readily assured and lingers into the post-colonial period. A French scholar describes the devasting impact of colonialism by likening it to
(25) "the role played for us (in Europe) by the doctrine of original sin." Frantz Fanon, especially in his *Studies in a Dying Colonialism*, well expresses the North African perspective.
Factors producing militant and romantic cultural nationalism are anchored in time. Memories of colonialism are already beginning to fade and, when the Maghreb has had a few decades in which to grow, dislocations associated with social change can also be
(30) expected to be fewer. Whether this means that the cultural nationalism characteristic of the Maghreb today will disappear in the future cannot be known. But a preoccupation with identity and culture and an affirmation of Arabism and Islam have characterized the Maghreb since independence and these still remain today important elements in North African life.
(35) A second great preoccupation in independent North Africa is the promotion of a modernist social revolution. The countries of the Maghreb do not pursue development in the same way and there have been variations in policies within each country. But all three spend heavily on development. In Tunisia, for example, the government devotes 20–25% of its annual budget to education, and literacy has climbed from 15% in 1956 to about
(40) 50% today. A problem, however, is that such advances are not always compatible with

objectives flowing from North African nationalism. In Morocco, for instance, when the government decided to give children an "Arab" education, it was forced to limit enrollments because, among other things, most Moroccans had been educated in French and the country consequently had few teachers qualified to teach in Arabic. Two years later, with literacy
(45) rates declining, this part of the Arabization program was postponed. The director of Arabization declared, "We are not fanatics; we want to enter the modern world."

1. Which of the following titles best describes the content of the passage?

   (A) *Education in the Levant*
   (B) *Nationalism in North Africa*
   (C) *Civilization in the Middle East*
   (D) *Muslim Science*
   (E) *Culture and Language*

2. Which of the following is not used to present the author's arguments?

   (A) Colonialism demoralized the local inhabitants.
   (B) Colonialism produced an identity crisis.
   (C) Cultural nationalism will soon disappear.
   (D) Decolonization does not always run smoothly.
   (E) Colonialists assumed that local cultures were inferior.

3. The author's attitude toward colonialism is best described as one of

   (A) sympathy
   (B) bewilderment
   (C) support
   (D) hostility
   (E) ambivalence

4. Which of the following does the author mention as evidence of cultural colonialism?

   (A) Native children in North Africa learned little about local culture.
   (B) Science was not taught in the Arabic language.
   (C) Colonial policy was determined in France.
   (D) Colonialists spent little on development.
   (E) Native teachers were not employed in public schools.

5. The author provides information that would answer which of the following questions?

   (A) What was the difference between French and German attitudes toward their colonies?
   (B) Why did Europeans impose their way of life on their colonies?
   (C) Why was colonialism bad?
   (D) Why was colonialism disliked?
   (E) When did colonialism end in North Africa?

Exercise B

TIME: 9 minutes

Directions: This part contains a reading passage. You are to read it carefully. When answering the questions, you will be able to refer to the passages. The questions are based on what is stated or implied in the passage. You have nine minutes to complete this part.

Line
(5)

Man and nature were the culprits as Venice sank hopelessly—or so it seemed—into the 177 canals on which the city is built. While nature's work took ages, man's work was much quicker and more brutal. But now man is using his ingenuity to save what he had almost destroyed. The sinking has been arrested and Venice should start rising again, like an oceanic phoenix from the canals.

The saving of Venice is the problem of the Italian Government, of course, but Venice is also a concern for Europe. And it happened that in the second half of 1975 Italy was in the chair of the European Council of Ministers. But the EC as such has no program for the salvation of Venice. "The Community is not a cultural community," explained one

(10)
Commission official. "There are some areas where it just does not have competence, the preservation of historical landmarks being one of them." So the efforts to save Venice have taken on a worldwide, rather than a Community-wide dimension.

Industrialization of the Porto Marghera area brought economic benefits to Venice, but it also raped the city as growing air and water pollution began to take their toll on the

(15)
priceless works of art and architecture. The danger of the imminent disappearance of Venice's cultural heritage was first brought to public attention in November 1966 when tides rose over six feet to flood Venice's canals and squares. Since then, various national and international organizations have sought ways and means to halt the destruction of the "queen of the Adriatic," though no one program has proved wholly satisfactory.

(20)
The US "Save Venice" group and the British "Venice in Peril" committee were formed to raise money for the restoration of priceless works of art and monuments. In 1967 the United Nations Educational, Scientific and Cultural Organization (UNESCO) took on the task of helping to save Venice by setting up a joint international advisory committee with the Italian Government. Such distant lands as Pakistan, no stranger to aid programs

(25)
itself, joined in the effort, giving UNESCO a gift of 10,000 postage stamps for "Venice in Peril." Even a group of famous cartoonists felt moved to draw attention to the fact that "Venice must be saved" and organized an exhibit in 1973, with the Council of Europe in Strasbourg, France, and this year a ballet festival drew people and funds to Venice.

Though Venice, the city of bridge-linked islands, was built in the fifth century, the land

(30)
on which it was built has been sinking "naturally" for a billion years. Movements of the earth's crust have caused the very slow and gradual descent of the Po Valley. And nature's forces aren't easily countered. Each year, Venice has been sinking about one millimeter into the lagoon which holds this Adriatic jewel. To add to Venice's peril, the slow melting of the polar cap causes the level of the sea to rise another millimeter. If nothing is done to

(35)
reverse nature's work, Venice is doomed to be another Atlantis, lost for ever beneath the murky sea.

Man's part in the sink-Venice movement has been for reasons mainly economic. For the last 400 years, the population of Venice has been drifting toward the mainland to escape the isolation and inconvenience of living on a series of islets. Between 1951 and

(40)
1971, Venice lost 63,000 inhabitants. To curtail this migration, new, artificial land areas, on the Dutch model, were added to the old Venice. Venice's original builders had not been far-sighted enough and set the ground level at only a few inches above what they expected to be the maximum tides. The combination of reclaimed land and Porto Marghera industrialization have "squeezed" the lagoon until its waters have no place to go but . . . . up.

(45)   As Porto Marghera grows as an industrial port, and more and deeper channels are added for larger ships, currents become faster and dikes make the ravaging tides even more violent. The "acqua alta" has always been a problem for Venice, but with increased industrialization, flooding has become more frequent, sometimes occurring 50 times a year. Added to the violent "scirocco" that blows up to 60 miles an hour, Venice is rendered all
(50) the more vulnerable.

Yet Venice is not crumbling. Despite the visible decay caused by repeated floods and despite pollution that peels the stucco off the palazzi and eats away at their bottom-most steps, the structures are solid. The Rialto Bridge still stands safely on its ancient foundations supported by 6,000 piles.

(55)   And something has been done to stop the damage done by water. Indeed, one simple measure has proved to work miracles; The ban on pumping from the thousands of artesian wells in and around the city—an easy source of water, but also a folly that caused a further descent of 5 millimeters a year—has been so effective that Venice should rise an inch in the next 20 years.

1. According to the passage, between 1951 and 1971, Venice lost approximately how many residents annually?

    (A) 475
    (B) 3,150
    (C) 6,300
    (D) 15,500
    (E) 63,000

2. The author's point of view is that Venice

    (A) cannot be saved from destruction
    (B) is in danger of imminent disappearance
    (C) is doomed to become another "Atlantis"
    (D) can be saved, but much work is necessary
    (E) must become a member of the EC

3. Which of the following conditions has *not* contributed to Venice's peril?

    (A) Movement of the earth's crust
    (B) Natural causes
    (C) Melting of the polar cap
    (D) Industrialization
    (E) Shipping on the canals

4. According to the passage, which of the following figures indicates the approximate year when Venice first began sinking?

    (A) 400 B.C.
    (B) A.D. 1400
    (C) A.D. 1966
    (D) A.D. 1970
    (E) None of the above

5. The author feels that Venice is an example of

    (A) a doomed city like Atlantis
    (B) uncontrolled conditions
    (C) a combination of natural and human destruction
    (D) international neglect
    (E) benign concern by international agencies

Answers and Analysis

Exercise A

1. **(B)** Clearly, the main subject of the passage is nationalism. This is given in the statement on line 1, "Above all, colonialism was hated . . ." and in lines 20ff, and 27ff.
2. **(C)** Choice (E) is given in lines 1–2, (D) in lines 12–24, (B) in lines 12–14, and (A) is implied throughout; while the opposite of (C) is found in lines 16–17.
3. **(D)** See, for instance, the reference to "cultural racism" in line 17, as well as the general tone of paragraph 1.
4. **(A)** This is mentioned in lines 5–6. The fact that children were taught very little about their own culture and history was due to cultural colonialism.
5. **(D)** This theme begins on line 1 and continues throughout much of the passage.

Exercise B

1. **(B)** 63,000 people were lost over a 20-year period (1951–1971), or approximately 3,150 annually.
2. **(D)** Venice can be saved, but much work is necessary. See lines 3–5.
3. **(E)** Answer (A) appears in line 31, (B) in 30, (C) in 33–35, and (D) in lines 43–44. Choice (E) is not mentioned.
4. **(E)** In line 30 it is stated that the land on which Venice is situated has been sinking for a billion years.
5. **(C)** The theme is given in the first line and repeated in lines 31, 34, 37, 43, 44, and 49.

Sentence Correction Review

The Sentence Correction questions of the GMAT test your understanding of the basic rules of English grammar and usage. This chapter reviews those errors in grammar and usage that appear most frequently on the GMAT.

On the GMAT you will be given sentences in which all or part of the sentence is underlined. You will then be asked to choose the best phrasing of the underlined part from five alternatives. (A) will always be the original phrasing.

EXAMPLE

Not having heard clearly, the speaker was asked to repeat his statement.

(A) the speaker was asked to repeat his statement.
(B) she asked the speaker to repeat again his statement.
(C) the speaker was asked to repeat his statement again.
(D) she asked the speaker to repeat his statement.
(E) she then asked the speaker again to repeat his statement.

Answer

(D) is the best choice.

REVIEW OF ERRORS COMMONLY FOUND IN THE SENTENCE CORRECTION SECTION

Since you need only *recognize* errors in grammar and usage for this part of the exam, this section of the book will review those errors most commonly presented in the GMAT and teach you *what to look for*. We will not review the *basic* rules of grammar, such as the formation and use of the different tenses and the passive voice, the subjective and objective cases of pronouns, the position of adjectives and adverbs, and the like. We assume that a candidate for the GMAT is familiar with basic grammar, and we will concentrate on error recognition based on that knowledge.

Verb Errors

1. Errors in Verb Tense

Check if the correct verb *tense* has been used in the sentence.

INCORRECT:	When I came home, the children still didn't finish dinner.
CORRECT:	When I came home, the children still hadn't finished dinner.
INCORRECT:	As we ate dinner, the phone rang.
CORRECT:	As we were eating dinner, the phone rang.

In REPORTED SPEECH, check that the rule of *sequence of tenses* has been observed.

INCORRECT:	She promised she will come.
CORRECT:	She promised she would come.
INCORRECT:	She said she doesn't know his phone number.
CORRECT:	She said she didn't know his phone number.
INCORRECT:	She claimed she has never been there.
CORRECT:	She claimed she had never been there.

2. Errors in Tense Formation

Check if the tense has been formed correctly. *Know* the past participle of irregular verbs!

INCORRECT:	He throwed it out the window.
CORRECT:	He threw it out the window.
INCORRECT:	Having just drank some water, I wasn't thirsty.
CORRECT:	Having just drunk some water, I wasn't thirsty.

3. Errors in Subject-Verb Agreement.

Check if the subject of the verb is singular or plural. Does the verb agree in number?
Multiple subjects will be connected by the word AND:

Ted, John, and I are going.

If a singular subject is separated by a comma from an accompanying phrase, *it remains singular*.

The bride, together with the groom and her parents, is receiving at the door.

INCORRECT:	There is many reasons why I can't help you.
CORRECT:	There are many reasons why I can't help you.
INCORRECT:	Sir Lloyd, accompanied by his wife, were at the party.
CORRECT:	Sir Lloyd, accompanied by his wife, was at the party.
INCORRECT:	His mastery of several languages and the social graces make him a sought-after dinner guest.
CORRECT:	His mastery of several languages and the social graces makes him a sought-after dinner guest.

4. Errors in Conditional Sentences.

In conditional sentences, the word *if* will NEVER be followed by the words *will* or *would*.
Here are the correct conditional forms:

FUTURE:	If I have time, I will do it tomorrow.
PRESENT:	If I had time, I would do it now.
PAST:	If I had had time, I would have done it yesterday.

Sentences using the words *when*, *as soon as*, *the moment*, etc., are formed like future conditionals:

I will tell him if I see him.
I will tell him when I see him.

The verb *to be* will ALWAYS appear as *were* in the present conditional:

If I were you, I wouldn't do that.
She wouldn't say so if she weren't sure.

NOTE: Not all sentences containing *if* are conditionals. When *if* appears in the meaning of *whether*, it may take the future:

I don't know if he will be there. (I don't know whether he will be there.)

INCORRECT:	If I would have known, I wouldn't have gone.
CORRECT:	If I had known, I wouldn't have gone.
INCORRECT:	You wouldn't be so tired if you weren't going to bed so late.
CORRECT:	You wouldn't be so tired if you didn't go to bed so late.
INCORRECT:	Call me the moment you will get home.
CORRECT:	Call me the moment you get home.
INCORRECT:	We could go to the beach if it wasn't so hot.
CORRECT:	We could go to the beach if it weren't so hot.

5. Errors in Expressions of Desire

Unfulfilled desires are expressed by the form "_____ had hoped that _____ would (or *could*, or *might*) do _____ ."

I had hoped that I would pass the exam.

Expressions with *wish* are formed as follows:

PRESENT:	I wish I knew him.
FUTURE:	I wish you could (would) come.
PAST:	I wish he had come. (or could have come, would have come, might have come)

NOTE: As in conditionals, the verb *to be* will ALWAYS appear as *were* in the present: I wish she were here.

INCORRECT:	I wish I heard that story about him before I met him.
CORRECT:	I wish I had heard (or could have heard or would have heard) that story about him before I met him.
INCORRECT:	She wishes you will be on time.
CORRECT:	She wishes you could (or would) be on time.

6. Errors in Verbs Followed by VERB WORDS

The following list consists of words and expressions that are followed by a VERB WORD (the infinitive without the *to*):

ask	prefer	requirement
demand	recommend	suggest
desire	recommendation	suggestion
insist	require	urge

It is essential/imperative/important/necessary that . . .

INCORRECT:	She ignored the doctor's recommendation that she stops smoking.
CORRECT:	She ignored the doctor's recommendation that she stop smoking.

| INCORRECT: | It is essential that you are on time. |
| CORRECT: | It is essential that you be on time. |

| INCORRECT: | He suggested that we should meet at the train. |
| CORRECT: | He suggested that we meet at the train. |

7. Errors in Negative Imperatives.

Note the two forms for negative imperatives:

A. Please don't do that.
B. Would you please not do that.

INCORRECT:	Would you please don't smoke here.
CORRECT:	Please don't smoke here.
	OR
	Would you please not smoke here.

8. Errors in Affirmative and Negative Agreement of Verbs.

Note the two correct forms for *affirmative* agreement:

A.   I am an American and so is she.
B.   I am an American and she is too.

A.   Mary likes Bach and so does John.
B.   Mary likes Bach and John does too.

A.   My father will be there and so will my mother.
B.   My father will be there and my mother will too.

INCORRECT:	I have seen the film and she also has.
CORRECT:	I have seen the film and so has she.
	OR
	I have seen the film and she has too.

Note the two correct forms for *negative* agreement:

A.   I'm not American and he isn't either.
B.   I'm not American and neither is he.

A.   Mary doesn't like Bach and John doesn't either.
B.   Mary doesn't like Bach and neither does John.

A.   My father won't be there and my mother won't either.
B.   My father won't be there and neither will mymother.

INCORRECT:	I haven't seen the film and she hasn't neither.
CORRECT:	I haven't seen the film and she hasn't either.
	OR
	I haven't seen the film and neither has she.

9. Errors of Infinitives or Gerunds in the Complement of Verbs

Some verbs may be followed by either an infinitive or a gerund:

I love swimming at night.
I love to swim at night.

Other verbs, however, may require either one *or* the other for idiomatic reasons. Following is a list of the more commonly used verbs in this category:

Verbs requiring an INFINITIVE:

agree	fail	intend	promise
decide	hope	learn	refuse
expect	want	plan	

Verbs requiring a GERUND:

admit	deny	quit
appreciate	enjoy	regret
avoid	finish	risk
consider	practice	stop

Phrases requiring a GERUND:

approve of	do not mind	keep on
be better off	forget about	look forward to
can't help	insist on	think about
count on	get through	think of

INCORRECT:	I intend learning French next semester.
CORRECT:	I intend to learn French next semester.

INCORRECT:	I have stopped to smoke.
CORRECT:	I have stopped smoking.

INCORRECT:	We are looking forward to see you.
CORRECT:	We are looking forward to seeing you.

10. Errors in Verbs Requiring HOW in the Complement

The verbs KNOW, TEACH, LEARN, and SHOW require the word *HOW* before an infinitive in the complement.

INCORRECT:	She knows to drive.
CORRECT:	She knows how to drive.

INCORRECT:	I will teach you to sew.
CORRECT:	I will teach you how to sew.

11. Errors in Tag Endings

Check for *three* things in tag endings:

A. Does the ending use the *same person* as the sentence verb?
B. Does the ending use the *same tense* as the sentence verb?
C. If the sentence verb is positive, is the ending negative; if the sentence verb is negative, is the ending positive?

It's nice here, isn't it?
It isn't nice here, is it?
She speaks French, doesn't she?
She doesn't speak French, does she?
They'll be here tomorrow, won't they?
They won't be here tomorrow, will they?

EXCEPTIONS:

I'm right, aren't I?
We ought to go, shouldn't we?
Let's see, shall we?

NOTE: If there is a contraction in the sentence verb, make sure you know what the contraction stands for:

| INCORRECT: | She's been there before, isn't she? |
| CORRECT: | She's been there before, hasn't she? |

| INCORRECT: | You'd rather go yourself, hadn't you? |
| CORRECT: | You'd rather go yourself, wouldn't you? |

12. Errors in Idiomatic Verb Expressions

Following are a few commonly used idiomatic verb expressions. Notice whether they are followed by a verb word, a participle, an infinitive, or a gerund. Memorize a sample of each to check yourself when choosing an answer:

A. *must have* (*done*)—meaning "it is a logical conclusion"

They're late. They must have missed the bus.
There's no answer. They must have gone out.

B. *had better* (*do*)—meaning "it is advisable"

It's getting cold. You had better take your coat.
He still has fever. He had better not go out yet.

C. *used to* (*do*)—meaning "was in the habit of doing in the past"

I used to smoke a pack of cigarettes a day, but I stopped.
When I worked on a farm, I used to get up at 4:30 in the morning.

D. *to be used to*—meaning "to be accustomed to"

to get used to

to become used to   } —meaning "to become accustomed to"

The noise doesn't bother me; I'm used to studying with the radio on.
In America you'll get used to hearing only English all day long.

E. *make* someone *do*—meaning "force someone to do"
have someone *do*—meaning "cause someone to do"
let someone *do*—meaning "allow someone to do"

My mother made me take my little sister with me to the movies.
The teacher had us write an essay instead of taking an exam.
The usher didn't let us come in until the intermission.

F. *would rather*—meaning "would prefer"

I would rather speak to her myself.
I would rather not speak to her myself.

But if the preference is for someone *other than the subject* to do the action, use the PAST:

I would rather you spoke to her.
I would rather you didn't speak to her.

Pronoun Errors

1. Errors in Pronoun Subject-Object

Check if a pronoun is the SUBJECT or the OBJECT of a verb or preposition.

| INCORRECT: | All of us—Fred, Jane, Alice, and me—were late. |
| CORRECT: | All of us—Fred, Jane, Alice, and I—were late. |

INCORRECT:	How could she blame you and he for the accident?
CORRECT:	How could she blame you and him for the accident?

2. Errors with WHO and WHOM

When in doubt about the correctness of WHO/WHOM, try substituting the subject/object of a simpler pronoun to clarify the meaning:

I don't know who/whom Sarah meant.

Try substituting *he/him*; then rearrange the clause in its proper order:

he/him Sarah meant / Sarah meant him

Now it is clear that the pronoun is the *object* of the verb *meant*, so *whom* is called for.

CORRECT:	I don't know whom Sarah meant.

ANOTHER EXAMPLE:

There was a discussion as to who/whom was better suited.

Try substituting *she/her*:

she was better suited / her was better suited

Here the pronoun is the *subject* of the verb *suited*:

CORRECT:	There was a discussion as to who was better suited.

3. Errors of Pronoun Subject-Verb Agreement

Check if the pronoun and its verb agree in number. Remember that the following are *singular:*

anyone	either	neither	what
anything	everyone	no one	whatever
each	everything	nothing	whoever

These are *plural:*

both	many	several	others
few			

INCORRECT:	John is absent, but a few of the class is here.
CORRECT:	John is absent but a few of the class are here.

INCORRECT:	Everyone on the project have to come to the meeting.
CORRECT:	Everyone on the project has to come to the meeting.

INCORRECT:	Either of those dresses are suitable for the party.
CORRECT:	Either of those dresses is suitable for the party.

INCORRECT:	Neither of them are experts on the subject.
CORRECT:	Neither of them is an expert on the subject.

NOTE: The forms "either . . . or" and "neither . . . nor" are singular and take a singular verb. For reasons of diction, however, if the noun immediately preceding the verb is plural, use a plural verb. An English speaker finds it difficult to pronounce a singular verb after a plural subject, as in ". . . they is coming," even though "they" is preceded by "Neither he nor . . ."

Either his parents or he is bringing it.
Either he or his parents are bringing it.
Neither his parents nor he was there.
Neither he nor his parents were there.

4. Errors of Possessive Pronoun Agreement

Check if possessive pronouns agree in *person* and *number*.

INCORRECT:	If anyone calls, take their name.
CORRECT:	If anyone calls, take his name.

INCORRECT:	Those of us who care should write to their congressman.
CORRECT:	Those of us who care should write to our congressman.

INCORRECT:	Some of you will have to come in their own cars.
CORRECT:	Some of you will have to come in your own cars.

5. Errors in Pronouns after the Verb TO BE

TO BE is an intransitive verb and will always be followed by a subject pronoun.

INCORRECT:	It must have been her at the door.
CORRECT:	It must have been she at the door.

INCORRECT:	I wish I were him!
CORRECT:	I wish I were he!

INCORRECT:	He didn't know that it was me who did it.
CORRECT:	He didn't know that it was I who did it.

6. Errors in Position of Relative Pronouns

A relative pronoun refers to the word preceding it. If the meaning is unclear, the pronoun is in the wrong position.

INCORRECT:	He could park right in front of the door, which was very convenient.

Since it was not the door which was convenient, the "which" is illogical in this position. In order to correct the sentence, it is necessary to rewrite it completely:

CORRECT:	His being allowed to park right in front of the door was very convenient.

INCORRECT:	The traffic was very heavy, which made me late.
CORRECT:	I was late because of the heavy traffic.
	OR
	The heavy traffic made me late.

7. Errors in Parallelism of Impersonal Pronouns

In forms using impersonal pronouns, use *either* "one . . . one's/his or her" *or* "you . . . your."

INCORRECT:	One should take your duties seriously.
CORRECT:	One should take one's/ his or her duties seriously.
	OR
	You should take your duties seriously.

INCORRECT:	One should have their blood pressure checked regularly.
CORRECT:	One should have one's/ his or her blood pressure checked regularly.
	OR
	You should have your blood pressure checked regularly.

Adjective and Adverb Errors

1. Errors in the Use of Adjectives and Adverbs

Check if a word modifier is an ADJECTIVE or an ADVERB. Make sure the correct form has been used.

An ADJECTIVE describes a noun and answers the question, *What kind?*

She is a good cook. (What kind of cook?)

An ADVERB describes either a verb or an adjective and answers the question, *How?*

She cooks well. (She cooks how?)

This exercise is relatively easy. (How easy?)

Most adverbs are formed by adding *-ly* to the adjective.

EXCEPTIONS

Adjective	*Adverb*
early	early
fast	fast
good	well
hard	hard (*hardly* means *almost not*)
late	late (*lately* means *recently*)

INCORRECT:	I sure wish I were rich!
CORRECT:	I surely wish I were rich!
INCORRECT:	The young man writes bad.
CORRECT:	The young man writes badly.
INCORRECT:	He's a real good teacher.
CORRECT:	He's a really good teacher.

2. Errors of Adjectives with Verbs of Sense

The following verbs of sense are intransitive and are described by ADJECTIVES:

be	look	smell	taste
feel	seem	sound	

INCORRECT:	She looked very well.
CORRECT:	She looked very good.

NOTE: "He is well" is also correct in the meaning of "He is healthy" or in describing a person's well-being.

INCORRECT:	The food tastes deliciously.
CORRECT:	The food tastes delicious.

NOTE: When the above verbs are used as transitive verbs, modify with an adverb, as usual: She tasted the soup quickly.

3. Errors in Comparatives

A. Similar comparison

ADJECTIVE: She is as <u>pretty</u> as her sister.
ADVERB: He works as <u>hard</u> as his father.

B. Comparative (of two things)

ADJECTIVE: She is <u>prettier</u> than her sister.
                     She is more <u>beautiful</u> than her sister.
                     She is less <u>successful</u> than her sister.
ADVERB: He works <u>harder</u> than his father.
                     He reads more <u>quickly</u> than I.
                     He drives less <u>carelessly</u> than he used to.

NOTE 1: A pronoun following *than* in a comparison will be the *subject pronoun*:

You are prettier than she (is).
You drive better than he (does).

NOTE 2: In using comparisons, adjectives of one syllable, or of two syllables ending in *-y*, add *-er*: smart, smarter; pretty, prettier. Other words of more than one syllable use *more*: interesting, more interesting. Adverbs of one syllable add *-er*; longer adverbs use *more*: fast, faster; quickly, more quickly.

NOTE 3: The word *different* is followed by *from*:

You are <u>different</u> from me.

C. Superlative (comparison of more than two things)

ADJECTIVE: She is the <u>prettiest</u> girl in her class.
                     He is the most <u>successful</u> of his brothers.
                     This one is the least <u>interesting</u> of the three.
ADVERB: He plays the <u>best</u> of all.
                     He speaks the most <u>interestingly</u>.
                     He spoke to them the least <u>patronizingly</u>.

EXCEPTIONAL FORMS		
good	better	best
bad	worse	worst
much/many	more	most
little	less	least

INCORRECT: This exercise is harder then the last one.
CORRECT: This exercise is harder than the last one.

INCORRECT: He works faster than her.
CORRECT: He works faster than she.

INCORRECT: She is the more responsible person of the three.
CORRECT: She is the most responsible person of the three.

INCORRECT: She was much different than I expected.
CORRECT: She was much different from what I expected.

INCORRECT: This year I'll have littler free time.
CORRECT: This year I'll have less free time.

4. Errors in Parallel Comparisons

In parallel comparisons, check if the correct form has been used.

INCORRECT: The more you practice, you will get better.
CORRECT: The more you practice, the better you will get.

INCORRECT: The earlier we leave, we will get there earlier.
CORRECT: The earlier we leave, the earlier we will get there.

INCORRECT: The busier you become, lesser time you have for reading.
CORRECT: The busier you become, the less time you have for reading.

5. Errors of Illogical Comparatives

Check comparisons to make sure they *make sense*.

INCORRECT: Alaska is bigger than any state in the United States.
CORRECT: Alaska is bigger than any other state in the United States. (If Alaska were bigger than *any state*, it would be bigger than itself!)

INCORRECT: That is the most important of any other reason.
CORRECT: That is the most important reason.

INCORRECT: Of the two books, this one is best.
CORRECT: Of the two books, this one is better.

6. Errors of Identical Comparisons

Something can be *the same as* OR *like* something else. Do not mix up the two forms.

INCORRECT: Your dress is the same like mine.
CORRECT: Your dress is like mine.
                OR
                Your dress is the same as mine.

7. Errors in Idioms Using Comparative Structures

Some idiomatic terms are formed like comparatives, although they are not true comparisons:

| as high as | as much as | as few as |
| as little as | as many as | |

INCORRECT: You may have to spend so much as two hours waiting.
CORRECT: You may have to spend as much as two hours waiting.

INCORRECT: It cost twice more than I thought it would.
CORRECT: It cost twice as much as I thought it would.

8. Errors in Noun-Adjectives

When a NOUN is used as an ADJECTIVE, treat it as an adjective. Do not pluralize or add *'s*.

INCORRECT: You're talking like a two-years-old child!
CORRECT: You're talking like a two-year-old child!

9. Errors in Ordinal and Cardinal Numbers

Ordinal numbers (first, second, third, etc.) are preceded by *the*. Cardinal numbers (one, two, three, etc.) are not.

We missed the first act.
We missed Act One.

NOTE: Ordinarily, either form is correct. There are two exceptions:

A. In *dates* use only *ordinal* numbers:
   May first (*not* May one)
   the first of May

B. In terms dealing with *travel*, use only *cardinal* numbers, as "Gate Three" may not actually be the third gate. It is Gate Number Three.

INCORRECT:	We leave from the second pier.
CORRECT:	We leave from Pier Two.

INCORRECT:	His birthday is on February twenty-two.
CORRECT:	His birthday is on February twenty-second.

10. Errors in Modifying Countable and Noncountable Nouns

If a noun can be preceded by a number, it is a countable noun and will be modified by these words:

a few	many, more	some
few, fewer	number of	

If it cannot be preceded by a number, it is noncountable and will be modified by these words:

amount of	little, less	some
a little	much, more	

INCORRECT:	I was surprised by the large amount of people who came.
CORRECT:	I was surprised by the large number of people who came.

INCORRECT:	You need only a little eggs in this recipe.
CORRECT:	You need only a few eggs in this recipe.

Errors in Usage

1. Errors in Connectors

There are several ways of connecting ideas. Do not mix the different forms:

and	also	not only . . . but also
too	as well as	both . . . and

INCORRECT:	She speaks not only Spanish but French as well.
CORRECT:	She speaks Spanish and French.

She speaks Spanish. She also speaks French.
She speaks Spanish and French too.
She speaks not only Spanish but also French.
She speaks both Spanish and French.
She speaks Spanish as well as French.

2. Errors in Question Word Connectors

When a question word such as *when* or *what* is used as a connector, the clause that follows is *not* a question. Do not use the interrogative form.

INCORRECT:	Do you know when does the movie start?
CORRECT:	Do you know when the movie starts?

INCORRECT:	I don't know what is his name.
CORRECT:	I don't know what his name is.

INCORRECT:	Did he tell you why hasn't he come yet?
CORRECT:	Did he tell you why he hasn't come yet?

3. Errors in Purpose Connectors

The word *so* by itself means *therefore*.

> It was too hot to study, so we went to the beach.
> *So that* means *in order to* or *in order that*.
> INCORRECT: We took a cab so we would be on time.
> CORRECT: We took a cab so that we would be on time.

4. Errors with BECAUSE

It is incorrect to say: *The reason is because* . . . Use: *The reason is that* . . .

INCORRECT:	The reason he was rejected was because he was too young.
CORRECT:	The reason he was rejected was that he was too young.
	OR
	He was rejected because of his young age.
	OR
	He was rejected because he was too young.

5. Errors of Dangling Modifiers

An introductory verbal modifier should be directly followed by the noun or pronoun that it modifies. Such a modifier will start with a gerund or participial phrase and be followed by a comma. Look for the modified noun or pronoun *immediately* after the comma.

INCORRECT:	Seeing that the hour was late, it was decided to postpone the committee vote.
CORRECT:	Seeing that the hour was late, the committee decided to postpone the vote.
INCORRECT:	Unaccustomed to getting up early, it was difficult for him to get to work on time.
CORRECT:	Unaccustomed to getting up early, he found it difficult to get to work on time.
INCORRECT:	Wanting to get feedback, a questionnaire was handed out to the audience.
CORRECT:	Since the speaker wanted to get feedback, she handed out a questionnaire to the audience.

6. Errors in Parallel Construction

In sentences containing a series of two or more items, check if the same form has been used for all the items in the series. Do *not* mix infinitives with gerunds, adjectives with participial phrases, or verbs with nouns.

INCORRECT:	The film was interesting, exciting, and it was made well.
CORRECT:	The film was interesting, exciting, and well made.
INCORRECT:	The purpose of the meeting is to introduce new members and raising money.
CORRECT:	The purpose of the meeting is to introduce new members and to raise money.
	OR
	The purpose of the meeting is introducing new members and raising money.
INCORRECT:	He died unloved, unknown, and without any money.
CORRECT:	He died unloved, unknown, and penniless.

INCORRECT:	He was popular because of his sense of humor, his intelligence, and he could get along with people.
CORRECT:	He was popular because of his sense of humor, his intelligence, and his ability to get along with people.

OR

He was popular because he had a sense of humor, was intelligent, and could get along with people.

7. Errors of Unnecessary Modifiers

In general, the more simply an idea is stated, the better it is. An adverb or adjective can often eliminate extraneous words.

INCORRECT:	She drove in a careful way.
CORRECT:	She drove carefully.

INCORRECT:	The problem was difficult and delicate in nature.
CORRECT:	It was a difficult, delicate problem.

Beware of words with the same meaning in the same sentence.

INCORRECT:	The new innovations were startling.
CORRECT:	The innovations were startling.

INCORRECT:	Would you please repeat again what you said?
CORRECT:	Would you please repeat what you said?

INCORRECT:	He left more richer than when he came.
CORRECT:	He left richer than when he came.

Beware of general wordiness.

INCORRECT:	That depends on the state of the general condition of the situation.
CORRECT:	That depends on the situation.

8. Errors of Commonly Confused Words

Following are some of the more commonly misused words in English:

to lie	lied	lied	lying	to tell an untruth
to lie	lay	lain	lying	to recline
to lay	laid	laid	laying	to put down

(*Idiomatic* usage: LAY THE TABLE, put dishes, etc., on the table; CHICKENS LAY EGGS; LAY A BET, make a bet)

to rise	rose	risen	rising	to go up; to get up
to arise	arose	arisen	arising	to wake up; to get up

(*Idiomatic* usage: A PROBLEM HAS ARISEN, a problem has come up)

to raise	raised	raised	raising	to lift; bring up

(*Idiomatic* usage: TO RAISE CHILDREN, to bring up children; TO RAISE VEGETABLES, to grow vegetables; TO RAISE MONEY, to collect funds for a cause)

to set	set	set	setting	to put down

(*Idiomatic* usage: SET A DATE, arrange a date; SET THE TABLE, put dishes, etc., on the table; THE SUN SET, the sun went down for the night; TO SET THE CLOCK, to adjust the timing mechanism of a clock)

to sit	sat	sat	sitting	to be in or get into a sitting position
to let	let	let	letting	to allow; to rent
to leave	left	left	leaving	to go away

formerly—previously
formally—in a formal way

to affect—to influence (verb)
effect—result (noun)

INCORRECT: He was laying in bed all day yesterday.
CORRECT: He was lying in bed all day yesterday.

INCORRECT: It had laid in the closet for a week before we found it.
CORRECT: It had lain in the closet for a week before we found it.

INCORRECT: The price of gas has raised three times last year.
CORRECT: The price of gas rose three times last year.
OR
The price of gas was raised three times last year.

INCORRECT: He raised slowly from his chair.
CORRECT: He arose slowly from his chair.

INCORRECT: We just set around the house all day.
CORRECT: We just sat around the house all day.

INCORRECT: His mother wouldn't leave him go with us.
CORRECT: His mother wouldn't let him go with us.

INCORRECT: All the men were dressed formerly.
CORRECT: All the men were dressed formally.

INCORRECT: My words had no affect on her.
CORRECT: My words had no effect on her.

9. Errors of Misused Words and Prepositional Idioms.

A. **in spite of; despite**

The two expressions are synonymous; use *either* one *or* the other.

INCORRECT: They came despite of the rain.
CORRECT: They came in spite of the rain.
OR
They came despite the rain.

B. **scarcely; barely; hardly**

All three words mean *almost not at all*; do NOT use a negative with them.

INCORRECT: I hardly never see him.
CORRECT: I hardly ever see him.

INCORRECT: He has scarcely no money.
CORRECT: He has scarcely any money.

C. Note and memorize the prepositions in these common idioms:

> agree/disagree with
> approve/disapprove of
> be afraid of
> be ashamed of
> be bored with
> be conscious of
> be equal to
> be interested in
> capable/incapable of
> compare to (point out similarities between things of a different order)
> compare with (point out differences between things of the same order)
> dependent on
> except for
> in the habit of
> independent of
> next to
> related to
> similar to

D. Confusion of words that *sound alike*:

> **adapt**—to change, to adjust
> **adept**—skilled
>
> **advice**—counsel (n.)
> **advise**—to give advice (v.)
>
> **affect**—to influence (v.)
> **effect**—result (n.)
>
> **afflicted**—stricken
> **inflicted**—caused or imposed something negative
>
> **affront**—to insult
> **confront**—to face
>
> **alteration**—a change
> **altercation**—argument
>
> **allude**—to refer to indirectly
> **elude**—to evade
>
> **allusion**—a reference to
> **illusion**—unreal image
> **delusion**—false belief
>
> **apprise**—to let know
> **appraise**—to estimate the value of
>
> **beside**—near
> **besides**—in addition
>
> **capital**—money; punishable by death; large form of letter
> **Capitol**—the U.S. house of legislature
>
> **caret**—a mark used in proofreading
> **carat**—unit of gem weight
> **carrot**—an orange vegetable
>
> **censor**—one who screens objectionable material
> **censure**—condemnation

cite—to quote
sight—vision
site—location

coherent—intelligible
inherent—a naturally included quality

collaborate—to work together
corroborate—to confirm

command—to order
commend—to praise

compile—to collect
comply—to consent

complement—to make complete
compliment—to praise

continual—happening often
continuous—happening uninterruptedly

conscientious—diligent
conscious—aware; awake

credible—believable
creditable—worthy of credit or praise
credulous—believing anything

depredation—a robbing
deprecation—disapproval

detain—to keep or hold up
retain—to keep in possession; to remember

detracted—taken away from
distracted—diverted

devise—to create
revise—to change; to improve

devolve—to deliver from one possessor to another
evolve—to develop

discouraging—seeming to be with no chance of success
disparaging—belittling

disinterested—having nothing personal to gain; impartial
uninterested—having no interest in

elegant—graceful; refined; with good taste
eloquent—persuasive; fluent (speech or writing)

elicit—to draw out
illicit—unlawful

emigrant—one who leaves a country to settle in another
immigrant—one who comes to a new country to settle

eminent—famous; prominent
imminent—impending
immanent—universal

epaulet—a shoulder decoration (usually on a uniform)
epithet—a descriptive word or phrase

epic—a long poem dealing with heroic deeds
epoch—a period of time marked by noteworthy people or events

flouting—scorning
flaunting—showing off provocatively

foreword—introduction to a book
forward—toward the front

gorilla—an ape
guerrilla—a soldier of the underground

horde—a crowd
hoard—to store up a supply

human—belonging to the race of man
humane—kind

immoral—without a sense of morality
immortal—able to live forever

imply—to hint
infer—to conclude from a known fact

in—within
inn—a pub or hostel

incandescent—glowing
clandestine—secret

incite—to urge to action
insight—quality of perceptiveness

incorporate—to include; to merge
incarcerate—to imprison

incredible—unbelievable
incredulous—doubting

ingenious—clever
ingenuous—frank

irrelevant—having no bearing on a matter
irreverent—lacking respect

loath—reluctant
loathe—to hate

luxuriant—growing thickly; highly ornamented
luxurious—rich; having an aura of wealth

perpetuate—to cause to continue
perpetrate—to do (something evil)

persecute—to affflict constantly in order to injure
prosecute—to institute legal proceedings against

personal—private
personnel—employees

perspective—appearance as determined by distance and position
prospective—likely

precede—to come before
proceed—to continue

prescribe—to order; to advise (as medicine)
proscribe—to outlaw

principal—the amount of a debt; the head of a school
principle—a fundamental law

profuse—excessive
profess—to declare

prophecy—prediction (n.)
prophesy—to predict (v.)

relay—to convey; a race between teams
relate—to tell; to connect

repel—to reject
repeal—to cancel

respectful—showing regard for
respective—particular

rightly—with good reason
rightfully—having a lawful claim
righteously—acting in a virtuous way

ruminating—meditating
fulminating—shouting
culminating—ending

sensual—of the body
sensuous—appealing to the senses

staple—basic commodity; a pin holding papers together
stable—firm; a shed for horses

stationary—immobile
stationery—writing materials

supplement—to add to something
supplant—to forcefully replace

temerity—boldness
timidity—shyness

their—belonging to them
there—in that place
they're—they are

troop—a group of people
troupe—a company of singers, dancers, or actors

weigh—to measure the weight of
way—road
whey—a part of milk that is separated from the curds in cheese making

weather—atmospheric conditions
whether—if

wholesome—healthful
fulsome—disgusting because of excessiveness

STRATEGY FOR SENTENCE CORRECTION QUESTIONS

The first step in the Sentence Correction part of the exam is to read the sentence carefully in order to spot an error of grammar or usage. Once you have found an error, eliminate choice (A) and ALL OTHER ALTERNATIVES CONTAINING THAT ERROR. Concentrate on the remaining alternatives to choose your answer. Do not select an alternative that has changed the *meaning* of the original sentence.

EXAMPLE 1

If I knew him better, I would have insisted that he change the hour of the lecture.

(A) I would have insisted that he change
(B) I would have insisted that he changed
(C) I would insist that he change
(D) I would insist for him to change
(E) I would have insisted him to change

Since we must assume the unmarked part of the sentence to be correct, this is a PRESENT CONDITIONAL sentence; therefore, the second verb in the sentence should read *I would insist*. Glancing through the alternatives, you can eliminate (A), (B), and (E). You are left with (C) and (D). Remember that the word *insist* takes a *verb word* after it. (C) is the only correct answer.

If you do not find any grammatical error in the underlined part, read the alternatives to see if one of them does not use a clearer or more concise style to express the same thing. Do not choose an alternative that changes the meaning of the original sentence.

EXAMPLE 2

The couple, who had been married recently, booked their honeymoon passage through an agent who lived near them.

(A) The couple, who had been married recently, booked their honeymoon passage through an agent who lived near them.
(B) The couple, who had been recently married, booked their honeymoon passage through an agent who lived not far from them.
(C) The newlyweds booked their honeymoon passage through a local agent.
(D) The newlyweds booked their passage through an agent that lived not far from them.
(E) The couple lived not far from the agent who through him they booked their passage.

Although (A), the original, has no real errors, (C) expresses the same thing more concisely, without distorting the original meaning of the sentence.

Remember: If you find no errors, and if you find that none of the alternatives improve the original, choose (A).

Practice Exercises

Directions: This exercise consists of a number of sentences, in each of which some part or the whole is underlined. Each sentence is followed by five alternative versions of the underlined portion. Select the alternative you consider both most correct and most effective according to the requirements of standard written English. Answer (A) is the same as the original version; if you think the original version is best, select answer (A).

In considering the answer choices, be attentive to matters of grammar, diction, and syntax, as well as clarity, precision, and fluency. Do not select an answer that alters the meaning of the original sentence.

1. A good doctor inquires not only about his patients' physical health, but about their mental health too.

   (A) but about their mental health too
   (B) but their mental health also
   (C) but also he inquires about their mental health
   (D) but also about their mental health
   (E) but too about their mental health

2. Knowing that the area was prone to earthquakes, all the buildings were reinforced with additional steel and concrete.

   (A) Knowing that the area was prone to earthquakes,
   (B) Having known that the area was prone to earthquakes,
   (C) Since the area was known to be prone to earthquakes,
   (D) Since they knew that the area was prone to earthquakes,
   (E) Being prone to earthquakes,

3. John would never have taken the job if he had known what great demands it would make on his time.

   (A) if he had known
   (B) if he knew
   (C) if he had been knowing
   (D) if he knows
   (E) if he was knowing

4. Anyone wishing to enroll in the program should send in their applications before the fifteenth of the month.

   (A) send in their applications
   (B) send their applications in
   (C) send in their application
   (D) send their application in
   (E) send in his application

5. Start the actual writing only after having thoroughly researched your subject, organized your notes, and you have planned an outline.

   (A) you have planned an outline
   (B) planned an outline
   (C) you having planned an outline
   (D) an outline has been planned
   (E) an outline was planned

Answers and Analysis

1. **(D)** The connective *not only* MUST be accompanied by *but also*. Eliminate (A), (B), and (E). (C) repeats *he inquires* unnecessarily. (D) is correct.

2. **(C)** *All the buildings* couldn't have known that the area was prone to earthquakes. Since the unmarked part of the sentence must be assumed to be correct, eliminate all alternatives beginning with a dangling modifier: (A), (B), and (E). In (D) the word *they* is unclear. Where there is no definite subject, the passive is preferable. (C) is correct.

3. **(A)** This is a past conditional sentence. (A) is correct.

4. **(E)** *Anyone* is singular. At one glance eliminate every choice but (E).

5. **(B)** Here is a series of three verbs: having *researched*, *organized*, and *planned*. (B) is correct.

Critical Reasoning Review

The principal object of the critical reasoning questions in the GMAT is to test skills in constructing and evaluating arguments. An argument is a sequence of two or more phrases, clauses, sentences or statements, one of which is a claim or conclusion, which follows the premises. For example:

"The ground was wet, so it must have been raining."

The first part of the sentence, "The ground was wet . . . ," is called a *premise*. The *conclusion* of the sentence, "it must have been raining," is based on the premise. Taken together, the premise and the conclusion form an *argument*. The method of reasoning in this example can be termed an *inference*. It is the inference that links the conclusion to the premise. Whether or not the argument and conclusion are valid is another question. In this case, the conclusion is not valid. The ground could have been wet for a variety of reasons, not necessarily connected with the weather.

IDENTIFYING THE PREMISE AND CONCLUSION

In evaluating an argument and its strength and validity, the first step is to identify the components—the premise and conclusion. There are several things to keep in mind when doing this.

Cue Words

Very often you will be helped in identifying the parts of an argument by the presence of cue words. Words such as "if," "given that," "since," "because," "for," " suppose," and "in view of" signal the presentation of evidence and reasons in support of a fact or claim. These cues identify premises. Conclusions, on the other hand, may often be preceded by words such as "thus," "hence," "so," and "therefore."

Without cue words, identifying and analyzing an argument become more difficult. For example, in conversation one might say:

"The roads were empty yesterday. It was Sunday."

This example seems to contain two simple assertions that do not necessarily constitute an argument. However, the juxtaposition of the two facts may indicate that one statement was intended to be a conclusion based on the fact stated in the other statement. In the example given, one is really saying:

"In view of the fact that it was Sunday, the roads were empty yesterday."

Fortunately, examples with no cue words at all are not common.

Position of Conclusion

Conclusions do not have to be at the end of an argument, as in the first example about wet streets and rain. Conclusions and premises may be reversed while the same meaning is conveyed. For example:

"David was talking during the lesson, so he didn't understand the teacher's instructions."
"David did not understand the teacher's instructions because he was talking during the lesson."

In both statements, the conclusion is "David did not understand the teacher's instructions."

Connecting Events to Draw Conclusions

Arguments frequently contain a number of premises and possibly more than one conclusion. Therefore, it is necessary to classify and connect things and events in order to analyze the arguments. To aid this analysis, think of events in terms of time sequence or causal relationships. For example:

"Sarah overslept, which caused her to be late leaving for school; therefore, she ran all the way, causing her to be out of breath."

Sometimes we predict future events, basing our prediction on regular sequences we have previously experienced. An example of such a sequence:

"The sun rose this morning. The sun rose yesterday. Therefore, it will rise tomorrow."

Note that we are not using our previous experience to prove anything, but rather applying our knowledge about what has happened before as a basis for our conclusion about what will happen in the future.

Determining What the Writer Is Trying to Prove

At first glance the analysis of some arguments looks difficult because of the absence of cue words. In these cases, ask yourself, "What is the writer trying to prove?" Once you have identified the main point of the argument, define it. Ask "How great a claim (or 'How limited a claim') is the author making?" "What precisely is the author talking about?" "What was the author's purpose in making the claim?"

To answer the first of these questions, look again for signal words—for instance "all," "none," "never," "always," "some," and "sometimes." There is a big difference, for example, between "all cars are red" and "some cars are red." The first statement is false. The second is most definitely true. Similarly, note the difference between "I have never seen him before" and "I have not seen him today."

Often the use of different verbs and adverbs can change the meaning of similar claims. Consider the first example used in this chapter: "The ground was wet, so it must have been raining." We can limit the claim by changing "must" to "probably." "The ground was wet. So it probably has been raining." The first statement stands more chance of being proven false. Anything else that can be shown to have made the ground wet limits the chance that it must have been the rain that caused the wetness. However, it could still have been raining, and there is always the probability, no matter how small, that it may have been.

Descriptive words, both nouns and adjectives, in a passage are also used to limit or expand claims made by another. Take the example:

"Teachers in New York deserve extra pay for the dangers they face in the classroom."

Here the claim is made about teachers; it cannot be extended (without further information) to members of any other occupation or to teachers from any other place, except New York.
Another example:

"Prisoners in San Quentin rioted today because they were angry about their conditions."

The author's choice of the word "Prisoners" indicates merely that more than one prisoner rioted. Maybe all or maybe only some prisoners rioted. Note also that the author claims to know the reason for the riot—namely, that the prisoners were angry about their conditions and for no other reason. However, you cannot assume that just because an author states a reason for a claim, he or she is correct in that assumption. And if an author makes a claim about the cause of some event, he or she may either endorse or condemn it. Endorsement of a claim without any supporting evidence is not a substitute for proof.

The use of assumptions is vital in evaluating an argument. We have seen earlier that the conclusion of one argument can act as the premise for a further argument. In practice, we do not extend arguments indefinitely, but we stop at the conclusion we set out to prove, having begun from what seems to be a convenient and secure starting point. The strength of the argument depends on the legitimacy of its assumptions.

DEDUCTIVE AND INDUCTIVE ARGUMENTS

An argument may be deductive or inductive, depending on how the conclusion follows or is inferred from the premises.

An argument may be defined as deductive if it is *impossible* for the conclusion to be false if all the premises are true. In other words, in a deductive argument, the premises necessitate the conclusion. An example of a deductive argument is:

All men are mortal.
Brian is a man.
Therefore, Brian is a mortal.

If both premises are true, then the conclusion follows automatically.

An argument is inductive if it is *improbable* that the conclusion is false if all premises are true. The premises do not necessitate but do make probable the conclusion. The conclusion may be false even if all the premises are true.

Determining if the conclusion in an argument has been arrived at through deductive reasoning or through inductive reasoning can often be discerned from the wording of the statement or sentence. Words such as "usually," "sometimes," and "generally," are usually signals of induction.

An example of an inductive argument is:

1. Freshmen usually find Economics I difficult.
2. Jones is a freshman.
3. Therefore, Jones finds Economics I difficult.

In the above statement, both premises are true. If the premises are true, does the conclusion automatically follow? No, because not all freshmen find Economics I difficult, and Jones may be one of the minority of freshmen who do not.

The distinction between deduction and induction should not be taken as a distinction between a good or superior way of arguing or reasoning and an inferior way. An inductive argument is not necessarily a bad argument. The two methods of argument serve different and complementary purposes. The distinction is in the manner by which a conclusion follows its premise(s).

TYPES OF INDUCTIVE ARGUMENTS

Inductive arguments may be based on examples, generalizations, analogy, causal connection or other grounds for belief. We shall discuss a few types of inductive arguments.

Argument by Example

Arguing by example means inferring conclusions from specific cases or examples. The number of cases or examples used may vary from one to several. Example:

The U.S. gives billions of dollars in foreign aid to Balonia. Leaders of Balonia resent foreign aid. The U.S. should discontinue direct foreign aid to developing countries.

In the above argument, only one example—that of Balonia—was used as a premise for reaching the conclusion that foreign aid should be discontinued. If it could be shown that Balonia is not a developing country, then one premise is false, and the argument and conclusion are invalid.

Assume for the moment that both premises are true. Is the conclusion then valid? Remember: only one example was given. One might argue that most developing countries welcome foreign aid and, therefore, that the single example given is irrelevant or atypical.

A typical critical reasoning question on the GMAT may ask you to select an answer that weakens an argument. In other words, you will be asked to select an answer that falsifies a premise or casts doubt on a generalization. One way to do this is to show that the specific example(s) given is (are) not typical or relevant and therefore cannot be the basis of a valid inductive argument in which examples are used to build a generalization.

Argument by Analogy

Arguing or reasoning by analogy consists of making a comparison between two similar cases, and inferring that what is true in one case is true in the other. A model for argument by analogy is as follows:

Two things A and B are alike in respect to $C1, \ldots Cn$.
A has characteristic $Cn + 1$.
Therefore, B will have characteristic $Cn + 1$.

This model may be illustrated by the following example:

1. The Conservative and Labor parties support a viable economy, including economic growth, industrialization, a fair wage policy, and unrestricted immigration.
2. The Conservative party endorsed free trade.
3. Therefore, the Labor party will endorse free trade.

In premise (1), both parties (A and B) have the same characteristics ($C1, \ldots Cn$). In premise (2), the Conservative Party (A) takes on an additional characteristic—that of endorsing free trade ($Cn + 1$). In the conclusion (3), it is claimed by analogy that the Labor Party (B) will also take on the characteristic ($Cn + 1$). This is an invalid argument by analogy—even though the arguer has shown that the two parties are similar in some ways. Because the Conservative and Labor parties are alike in some ways does not necessarily mean that they are alike in other ways.

In some arguments there is a lack of similar shared characteristics. For example:

1. France and England have nearly the same population size.
2. France has fluoridated drinking water.
3. England will have fluoridated drinking water.

The problem in the above example is that there are not enough points of similarity between France and England to lead to the conclusion. Critical differences might involve income, drinking habits, attitudes toward medicine, and many other things.

Causal Arguing

In causal arguing, one infers that an act or factor (cause) produces a result (effect). This may be illustrated as:

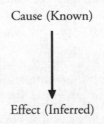

Cause (Known)

Effect (Inferred)

An *X* may be said to be a cause of *Y* if the occurrence of *X* is sufficient for the occurrence of *Y*. Whenever *X* occurs, *Y* follows, so that *X* determines *Y*. (Note here that factors other than *X* may also determine *Y* and that this does not alter the validity of the stated argument.)

DETERMINING THE LOGICAL SEQUENCE OF AN ARGUMENT

Having discussed types of arguments, we will now demonstrate in more detail how an argument can be identified and analyzed. You must be able to determine what the writer is trying to establish.

In order to identify an argument:

1. Find the conclusion first. This may be done by locating the cue that introduces the conclusion.
2. Find the premise(s). Again, locate the cue words (if present) that signal premises.
3. Determine if the premise(s) are true.
4. Determine the logical form of the argument.

A good way to check whether or not a conclusion follows from the premise(s) is to draw a Venn diagram, a device named after the British logician John Venn (1834–1923). A simplified form of the Venn diagram may consist of circles, one for each term of an argument. Take a simple argument:

"All weeds are plants; all daisies are weeds. Therefore, all daisies are plants."

We can now classify the various things (terms) in this argument and enclose each in a circle. Thus:

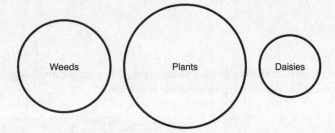

This deductive argument can be arranged to show the premises and conclusion, by showing that "daisies" are totally included in "weeds" and "weeds" are totally included in "plants."

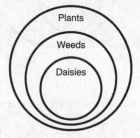

Since "daisies" are totally included in "plants," the conclusion of the argument is valid.

Venn diagrams can also be used to show if arguments are invalid. For example, take the argument:

"Because all dollars are money and all yen are money, then all dollars must be yen."

By placing dollars, money, and yen in circles and arranging them appropriately, we arrive at:

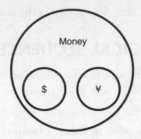

We can see that the conclusion—all dollars are yen—does not stand under scrutiny, since dollars and yen are not in the same small circle. All we can conclude is that both dollars and yen are money.

Using Venn Diagrams

Using examples, we shall now discuss the steps involved in using Venn diagrams to analyze the structure and logical sequence of an argument.

Study the following example.

1. All men are mortal.
2. Brian is a man.
3. Brian is a mortal.

Step One

The first premise states that all men belong to a term which is called mortality. Therefore, we need one circle to represent the term and another circle for "men."

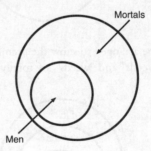

Step Two

The second premise states that Brian is a man. We draw a third circle for Brian. Brian's circle is within the circle of men.

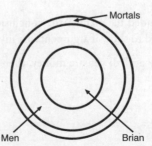

Step Three

Is the argument valid? Certainly, because we see that the conclusion—Brian is mortal—follows from the premises. Brian is in the "mortal" space, so he is mortal as well.

EXAMPLE

(1) Dr. Deutch's economics class is difficult.
(2) Dr. Jacque's economics class is difficult.
(3) Professor Sol's economics class is difficult.
(4) Therefore, all economic classes are difficult.

Step One. The first premise states that Dr. Deutch's economics class fits the term "difficult." This can be represented by two circles, one for the term "difficult," one for Dr. Deutch's class.

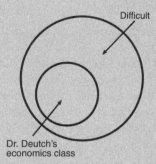

Step Two. Following step one, we are given two similar premises. We will add one circle for each.

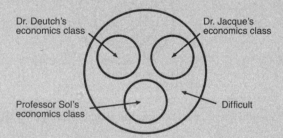

Step Three. Does the conclusion "all economics classes are difficult" follow the premises? The argument is inductive since we do not know if the three economics classes represent all, 90%, or 20% of all economics classes. If we know that they represent all economics classes, we could conclude that the conclusion follows from its premises. Since we do not know this, the conclusion is invalid.

ANALYZING THE LOGICAL SEQUENCE OF AN ARGUMENT

Now that we have reviewed the use of cue words, the logical sequence of arguments, and the use of Venn diagrams to check the structure of an argument, let us apply these concepts to some examples. The following letter was written to the columnist Ann Landers:

> Dear Ann Landers: I am a 21-year-old guy who is perfectly straight. I like to go to a gay bar in our neighborhood because the music is good and the people are very friendly.
>
> My dad sat me down last night and asked me if I was a switch-hitter. I told him absolutely not. He said he was very relieved because he had heard I was a steady at this place. When I explained I liked the ambiance, he advised me to find my fun someplace else because everyone assumes that a guy who goes to a gay bar is gay. I think he is wrong . . .[*]

[*]Copyright Field Newspaper Syndicate, 1977.

What is the reasoning shown in the letter? Clearly, the young man's father believes that his son is guilty by association. The father claims that anyone frequenting a gay bar will be associated with the company he (or she) keeps. What evidence is given for the claim? Searching for key words shows that "because" appears three times. First, in line 2 "because" explains why the son goes to a gay bar. Second, in line 4 "because" signals evidence that the son is a steady patron of the gay bar. Third, in line 6, "because" signals the important assumption that people frequenting a gay bar are presumed to be gay. The father's reasoning may be summarized as follows:

1. Any person frequenting a gay bar is presumed to be gay.
2. You are a person frequenting a gay bar.
3. *Therefore*, you are presumed to be gay.

Is the reasoning logical? Let us check it with a Venn diagram. Three terms are evident: "gay," "person frequenting a gay bar," and the subject, "you." We draw a circle for each of these terms as explained above. The rule for putting the circles together is that the outermost circle contains the term that appears in a premise and the conclusion. That term is "gay." Next, the middle circle contains the term that appears in both premises. That term is "person frequenting a gay bar." Finally, the innermost circle contains the term that appears in the middle premise and the conclusion. That term is "you." Therefore, we may conclude that the son (the "you") who frequents a gay bar will be presumed to belong to the term "gay."

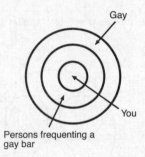

Now let us take another example, from a question that appeared on a recent exam.

EXAMPLE

A weapons-smuggling incident recently took place in country Y. We all know that Y is a closed society. So Y's government must have known about the weapons.

Which of the following is an assumption that would make the conclusion above logically correct?

(A) If a government knows about a particular weapons-smuggling incident, it must have intended to use the weapons for its own purposes.
(B) If a government claims that it knew nothing about a particular weapons-smuggling incident, it must have known everything about it.
(C) If a government does not permit weapons to enter a country, it is a closed society.
(D) If a country is a closed society, its government has a large contingent of armed guards patrolling its borders.
(E) If a country is a closed society, its government has knowledge about everything that occurs in the country.

The only cue word in the above passage is "so," which signals a conclusion: Y's government must have known about the weapons. What evidence is available to buttress this conclusion? The first premise is that "Y is a closed society." Now the question is, How can we link the premise with its conclusion? We need a second premise, but we do not have it in the passage. Surely, a "weapons-smuggling incident" is not the linkage. Therefore, we have what is called a "hidden" premise, one that is not given but must be assumed. However, in passages of this sort, the "hidden" premise is usually one of the answer alternatives. In fact, the question stem asks us to find the alternative that would make the conclusion logically correct. That alternative is (E). The complete argument is:

1. If a country is a closed society, its government has knowledge.
2. Y is a closed society.
3. *Therefore*, Y's government must have known about the weapons.

Is the reasoning logical? Let us draw a Venn diagram. The terms are "country Y," "closed society," and "government has knowledge." Again, the outer circle contains the term found in a premise and the conclusion: "government has knowledge" ("must have known"). The middle circle contains the term found in both premises: "closed society." Finally, the innermost circle contains the term found in the middle premise and the conclusion: "country Y." The Venn diagram shows that the reasoning is logical.

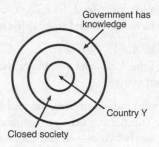

ATTACKING THE ASSUMPTIONS OF AN ARGUMENT

In the GMAT test, one often has to attack or find a fact that weakens an argument. The most effective way of doing this is to defeat the assumptions. Consider the following argument:

1. "Cooking classes take place on Tuesdays"
2. "Today is Tuesday"
3. "Therefore, cooking classes take place today."

We may be able to defeat this argument by analyzing the first premise. If we assume that cooking classes usually take place on a Tuesday, then there is a probability that if today is Tuesday it will be one of those Tuesdays when cooking classes are held, but this is obviously not certain. Premise (1) does not state that cooking classes take place every Tuesday; classes could be held every other Tuesday or every third Tuesday. Therefore, the third sentence, the conclusion of the argument *may* be false.

Often, the attack on the argument will not be so obvious because the assumptions on which the argument is built are hidden or concealed. Someone who is making a totally honest and correct argument will not explicitly acknowledge all of the assumptions he or she makes. These hidden assumptions may be open to attack. Bear this in mind, particularly if you are presented with an argument that seems logical and correct but which reaches a factually impossible or absurd result. This could indicate the existence of hidden assumptions that make the argument invalid.

FALLACIES

As mentioned earlier, the thought process that links the premise of an argument to its conclusion is called an inference. Errors may occur in any part of the argumentation process. These errors in reasoning are called *fallacies* or *flaws*.

Logicians have been studying flaws since Aristotle considered them in his *On Sophistical Refutations*. He wrote:

> That some reasonings are genuine, while others seem to be so but are not, is evident. This happens with arguments as also elsewhere, through a certain likeness between the genuine and the sham.

A fallacy is a form of reasoning that is illogical or violates the rules of argumentation. A fallacy is, in other words, an argument that seems to be sound but is not.

Scholars differ on the classification of fallacies. We shall discuss the most common types of fallacies and those that appear most often on the GMAT.

Guilt by Association

One type of fallacy is guilt by association. Suppose that one proves that educator John Doe is a dues-paying member of the Association for Fairy Teeth (A.F.T.), a fact not denied by Doe. Suppose that three members of the association have been found to be subversives. An argument may be:

1. John Doe is a member of the A.F.T.
2. X, Y, and Z are members of the A.F.T. and are subversives.

Therefore, (3) John Doe is a subversive.

This argument involves an invalid induction from premise (2) to a (missing) premise: all members of the A.F.T. are subversives. This has not been proven in the argument. It is left for the reader to draw his or her own—in this case, fallacious—conclusion, namely, that John Doe is a subversive.

A Venn diagram may be helpful. The largest circle represents all members of the A.F.T. A small circle within the larger one represents the three A.F.T. members that are known subversives. We are told in the statements that X, Y, and Z are known subversives, but we are not told that it is known that they are the *only* subversives in the A.F.T. membership. Therefore, we have no way of knowing whether or not John Doe is a subversive. In terms of a Venn diagram, we have no way of knowing whether or not the circle representing subversives should represent more than three members or whether or not the John Doe circle should overlap a larger circle representing all subversives.

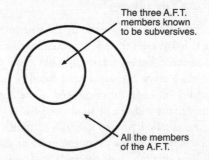

The three A.F.T. members known to be subversives.

All the members of the A.F.T.

Faulty Analogy

Another type of fallacy is that of faulty analogy. A faulty analogy assumes that things that are similar in one respect must be similar in other respects. In general, analogies may be a useful form of communication. They enable a speaker to convey concepts in terms already familiar to the audience. A statement such as "our civilization is flowering" may be helpful in making a point, but the generalization is faulty. May we conclude that civilizations are in need of fertilizer?

Suppose that an economist argues that a "tariff on textiles will help our textile industry, a tariff on steel will help the steel industry, a tariff on every imported product will benefit the economy."

The above analogy may be stated as:

1. Tariffs on textiles benefit the textile industry.
2. Tariffs on steel benefit the steel industry.

Therefore (3), a tariff on every imported product benefits the economy.

A Venn diagram of the above argument is:

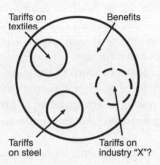

The analogy here assumes that because two industries benefit from tariffs, all others will also benefit. However, no proof for this argument is given.

Causal Fallacies

Some of the common causal fallacies are treating an insignificant relationship as a causal factor and assuming that a sequential relationship implies a causal relationship. That two events occur in sequence is not evidence of a causal relationship. For example, Herbert Hoover was elected President of the United States in 1928, an act followed by a recession in 1929. Did Hoover's policies cause the recession or were there other intervening factors? (There were.)

The following is an example of a causal fallacy.

Roni develops a rash whenever exposed to cactus weed. On his way home from a hike, he breaks out in a rash. Upon applying some ointment, he exclaims, "I must have brushed by cactus weed."

Roni's argument may be expanded as:

1. Rashes are caused by cactus weed.
2. I have a rash.

Therefore (3), I must have touched cactus weed.

Roni may be correct. However, other phenomena may have caused his rash: an allergy to certain food, contact with other plants, or many other things. Unless these can be ruled out, Roni's argument is fallacious.

Post Hoc Ergo Hoc ("After this, on account of this")

One type of fallacy of causality is a fallacy termed *post hoc ergo hoc*. This is the proposition that because events follow one another, one causes the other.

Consider the following scenario. In one of a company's five sales districts, the advertising budget was increased 20 percent, while in the other four districts, advertising expenditure was unchanged. Sales increased in the first district by nearly 20 percent, while sales remained unchanged in the other four districts. Did the increased advertising cause the sales increase?

This argument is in the form:

1. Event Y followed event X
2. So X is the cause of Y

The inference is weak. Y may be affected by a third factor Z. For example, in the sales district with the increase, a major competitor may have withdrawn from the market.

Fallacies of Relevance

Fallacies of relevance involve arguments wherein one or more of the premises are irrelevant to the conclusion. Some examples are as follows.

Ad Hominem (Personal attacks)

One type of fallacy of relevance is the *ad hominem* fallacy. In this type of fallacy, the person is attacked, not his or her argument. Attacking an opponent may well be easier than rebutting the merit of the argument. The role of the demagogue is to assasinate the character of his or her opponent, thereby casting doubt on his/her argument.

For example, an economics professor exclaims to her class: "Even a freshman knows that good economists don't necessarily have to be good mathematicians." Or, "Congressman Goodboy has argued eloquently in favor of increasing public spending in his district. Isn't he the same congressman who was accused of wasting taxpayers' money on new autobuses whose air conditioning systems didn't work?"

The fallacy in these examples is that arguments are not treated on their merit. The arguments follow the form:

1. Z asserts B.
2. Z would benefit if we accept B.
3. Z's assertion of B is insufficient to accept B as true.

This sort of argument attempts to show that B is not a reliable source because of some self-interest.

Another form of *ad hominem* argument is an appeal to the special position or vested interest of the person being argued with. Such arguments may include phrases such as "You, as members of the armed forces, can be counted on . . ." or "As a lover of the arts, you will be the first to agree that we need to raise taxes to support them."

Suppose that the listener does not agree to increased taxes. The argument then takes on the form:

1. You believe X (that taxes shouldn't be raised).
2. It is in your interest to reject X (your belief).
3. You should reject X.

The conclusion does not show that personal gain is evidence enough to reject the belief against increased taxes.

Tu Quoque (You Too)

This fallacy of relevance occurs when an argument is weakened by the assertion that its proponent is guilty by commission. A typical argument of this sort is, "You implore me not to drink, but you drink. Therefore, I can ignore your advice and do as I please." Here, the proponent's case is turned against him. This argument takes the form:

1. You assert not to do X.
2. But you do X.
3. I can ignore your advice not to do X.

The above argument is invalid because (2) is not relevant to the advice given. The behavior of the person giving the advice has nothing to do with the validity of the claim or advice.

Fallacies of Language (Ambiguity)

Ambiguity occurs when there are two or more meanings for a word, phrase, statement, or expression, especially when the meanings are easily confused. Another problem occurs when it is not clear in what context the meaning is being used. Words and expressions such as "democracy," "teamwork," "the American way," and "payoff" have different meanings to different people and may be used in different contexts. For example, is the United States government a democracy in the same sense as the Indian government? Does teamwork mean the same thing to Japanese and American workers? The only way to avoid ambiguity is to carefully define the meaning of words in context.

Let us look at some cases where ambiguity is used with intent to deceive or confuse.

Equivocation (Double Meaning)

The fallacy of equivocation occurs when words or phrases that have more than one meaning are used. An arguer using this fallacy relies on the fact that the audience fails to realize that some word or expression occurring more than once is used in different ways. The ambiguity may occur in both premises or in a premise and the conclusion. In the following for example, the structure of the argument is valid but an equivocation occurs.

1. Happiness is the end of life. (X is Y)
2. The end of life is death. (Y is Z)
3. So, happiness is death. (X is Z)

The fallacy is that the expression "end of life" has a different meaning in each premise. What has been asserted with one sense of the expression is then wrongly regarded as having been proved with respect to the other expression. An equivocation has been committed on the expression.

Amphiboly (Double Talk)

This fallacy results whenever there is ambiguity in sentence structure. For example:

"Can you spell backwards?"
"I have filled out the claim form for my damaged car which I enclose."

Most logic textbooks quote a story in Herodotus about Croesus and the oracle. Croesus asked the oracle what would be the outcome if he attacked Cyrus the Great of Persia. The oracle's reply was that, "He would destroy a great empire." Of course, the empire that was destroyed was his own. In both possible outcomes, the oracle would have been correct. Fallacies of these sorts can usually be corrected by changing the syntax or punctuation, as in the first example above: "Can you spell 'backwards'?"

Accent

The meaning of statements can change depending on which words are stressed. Placing stress on certain words can change the meaning from the original unaccented statement. See the following example:

"Throw away your food."
                  to:
"Throw away your *food*." (instead of something else).
"*Throw away* your food." (instead of eating it?).
"Throw away *your* food." (instead of someone else's?).

SOME FINAL HINTS

Sherlock Holmes once said, "When you have eliminated the impossible, whatever remains, *however improbable*, must be the truth." Can this statement be a true guide to critical reasoning problems? When taking the test, be sure to relate the possible answers to the actual statements, without drawing on prior conceptions or possible misconceptions. Each of us perceives a thing in his or her own way, but critical reasoning problems can only have one solution.

Some final tactics to consider:

1. Never rule out the blatantly obvious; it may just be the only solution possible.
2. Never rule out the blatantly ridiculous; it could also be the only reasonable conclusion to be drawn from a specific set of criteria.
3. Always treat each conclusion in isolation, since only one answer can be correct.

Mathematics Review

CHAPTER 8

For Problem Solving and Data Sufficiency Sections

The Problem Solving and Data Sufficiency areas of the GMAT require a working knowledge of mathematical principles, including an understanding of the fundamentals of algebra, geometry, and arithmetic, and the ability to interpret graphs. The following review covers these areas thoroughly and if used properly, will prove helpful in preparing for the mathematical parts of the GMAT.

Read through the review carefully. You will notice that each topic is keyed for easy reference. Use the key number next to each answer given in the Sample Tests to refer to those sections in the review that cover material you may have missed and therefore will need to spend more time on.

I. Arithmetic

I–1. INTEGERS

■ I–1.1

The numbers 0, 1, 2, 3, . . . are called the positive integers. –1, –2, –3, . . . are called the negative integers. An integer is a positive or negative integer or the number 0. The term whole number is also used to describe in integer.

■ I–1.2

If the integer k divides m evenly, then we say m is divisible by k or k is a factor of m. For example, 12 is divisible by 4, but 12 is not divisible by 5. The factors of 12 are 1, 2, 3, 4, 6, and 12.

If k is a factor of m, then there is another integer n such that $m = k \times n$; in this case, m is called a multiple of k.

Since $12 = 4 \times 3$, 12 is a multiple of 4 and also 12 is a multiple of 3. For example, 5, 10, 15, and 20 are all multiples of 5, but 15 and 5 are not multiples of 10.

Any integer is a multiple of each of its factors.

■ I–1.3

Any whole number is divisible by itself and by 1. If p is a whole number greater than 1, which has only p and 1 as factors, then p is called a *prime number*. 2, 3, 5, 7, 11, 13, 17, 19, and 23 are all primes. 14 is not a prime since it is divisible by 2 and by 7.

A whole number that is divisible by 2 is called an *even* number; if a whole number is not even, then it is an *odd* number. 2, 4, 6, 8, and 10 are even numbers, and 1, 3, 5, 7, and 9 are odd numbers.

A collection of integers is *consecutive* if each number is the successor of the integer which precedes it in the collection. For example, 7, 8, 9, and 10 are *consecutive*, but 7, 8, 10, 13 are not. 4, 6, 8, 10 are consecutive even numbers. 7, 11, 13, 17 are consecutive primes. 7, 13, 19, 23 are not consecutive primes since 11 is a prime between 7 and 13.

■ I–1.4

> Any integer greater than 1 is a prime or can be written as a product of primes.

To write a number as a *product of prime factors*:

A Divide the number by 2 if possible; continue to divide by 2 until the factor you get is not divisible by 2.

B Divide the result from (A) by 3 if possible; continue to divide by 3 until the factor you get is not divisible by 3.

C Divide the result from (B) by 5 if possible; continue to divide by 5 until the factor you get is not divisible by 5.

D Continue the procedure with 7, 11, and so on, until all the factors are primes.

EXAMPLE 1

Express 24 as a product of prime factors.

A $24 = 2 \times 12$, $12 = 2 \times 6$, $6 = 2 \times 3$ so $24 = 2 \times 2 \times 2 \times 3$. Since each factor (2 and 3) is prime, $24 = 2 \times 2 \times 2 \times 3$.

EXAMPLE 2

Express 252 as a product of primes.

A $252 = 2 \times 126$, $126 = 2 \times 63$ and 63 is not divisible by 2, so $252 = 2 \times 2 \times 63$.

B $63 = 3 \times 21$, $21 = 3 \times 7$ and 7 is not divisible by 3. Since 7 is a prime, then $252 = 2 \times 2 \times 3 \times 3 \times 7$ and all the factors are primes.

EXAMPLE 3

A class of 45 students will sit in rows with the same number of students in each row. Each row must contain at least 2 students and there must be at least 2 rows. A row is parallel to the front of the room. How many different arrangements are possible?

Since 45 = (the number of rows)(the number of students per row), the question can be answered by finding how many different ways to write 45 as a product of two positive integers each of which is larger than 1. (The integers must be larger than 1 since there must be at least 2 rows and at least 2 students per row.) So write 45 as a product of primes $45 = 3 \times 15 = 3 \times 3 \times 5$. Therefore 3×15, 5×9, 9×5, and 15×3 are the only possibilities. So, the correct answer is 4. The fact that a row is parallel to the front of the room means that 3×15 and 15×3 are different arrangements.

■ I–1.5

An integer, m, is a *common multiple* of two other integers k and j if it is a multiple of each of them. For example, 12 is a common multiple of 4 and 6, since $3 \times 4 = 12$ and $2 \times 6 = 12$. 15 is not a common multiple of 3 and 6, because 15 is not a multiple of 6.

An integer, k, is a *common factor* of two other integers m and n if k is a factor of m and k is a factor of n.

The *least common multiple* (L.C.M.) of two integers is the smallest integer that is a common multiple of both integers. To find the least common multiple of two numbers k and j:

Ⓐ Write k as a product of primes and j as a product of primes.

Ⓑ If there are any common factors *delete* them in *one* of the products.

Ⓒ Multiply the remaining factors; the result is the least common multiple.

EXAMPLE 1

Find the L.C.M. of 12 and 11.

Ⓐ $12 = 2 \times 2 \times 3, 11 = 11 \times 1$.

Ⓑ There are no common factors.

Ⓒ The L.C.M. is $12 \times 11 = 132$.

EXAMPLE 2

Find the L.C.M. of 27 and 63.

Ⓐ $27 = 3 \times 3 \times 3, 63 = 3 \times 3 \times 7$.

Ⓑ $3 \times 3 = 9$ is a common factor so delete it once.

Ⓒ The L.C.M. is $3 \times 3 \times 3 \times 7 = 189$.

You can find the L.C.M. of a collection of numbers in the same way except that if in step (B) the common factors are factors of more than two of the numbers, then delete the common factor in *all but one* of the products.

EXAMPLE 3

Find the L.C.M. of 27, 63, and 72.

Ⓐ $27 = 3 \times 3 \times 3, 63 = 3 \times 3 \times 7, 72 = 2 \times 2 \times 2 \times 3 \times 3$.

Ⓑ Delete 3×3 from two of the products.

Ⓒ The L.C.M. is $3 \times 7 \times 2 \times 2 \times 2 \times 3 \times 3 = 21 \times 72 = 1,512$.

EXAMPLE 4

It takes Eric 20 minutes to inspect a car. Jane only needs 15 minutes to inspect a car. If they both start inspecting cars at 9:00 A.M., what is the first time they will finish inspecting a car at the same time?

Since Eric will finish k cars after $k \times 20$ minutes and Jane will finish j cars after $j \times 15$ minutes, they will both finish inspecting a car at the same time when $k \times 20 = j \times 15$. Since k and j must be integers (they represent the number of cars finished), this question is asking you to find a common multiple of 20 and 15. The question asks for the first time they will finish at the same time, so you must find the least common multiple.

Ⓐ $20 = 4 \times 5 = 2 \times 2 \times 5$, $15 = 3 \times 5$

Ⓑ   Delete 5 from one of the products.

Ⓒ   So, the L.C.M. is $2 \times 2 \times 5 \times 3 = 60$.

So Eric and Jane will finish inspecting a car at the same time 60 minutes after they start, or at 10:00 A.M. (By that time, Eric will have inspected 3 cars and Jane will have inspected 4 cars.)

◼ I–1.6

The numbers 0, 1, 2, 3, 4, 5, 6, 7, 8, and 9 are called *digits*. The number 132 is a three-digit number. In the number 132, 1 is the first or hundreds digit, 3 is the second or tens digit, and 2 is the last or units digit.

EXAMPLE

Find x if x is a two-digit number whose last digit is 2. The difference of the digits of x is 5.

The two digit numbers whose last digits are 2 are 12, 22, 32, 42, 52, 62, 72, 82, and 92. The difference of the digits of 12 is either 1 or –1 so 12 is not x. Since $7 - 2$ is 5, x is 72.

I–2. FRACTIONS

◼ I–2.1

A *fraction* is a number that represents a ratio or division of two numbers. A fraction is written in the form $\frac{a}{b}$. The number on the top, a, is called the numerator; the number on the bottom, b, is called the denominator. The denominator tells how many equal parts there are (for example, parts of a pie); the numerator tells how many of these equal parts are taken. For example, $\frac{5}{8}$ is a fraction whose numerator is 5 and whose denominator is 8; it represents taking 5 of 8 equal parts, or dividing 8 into 5.

> A fraction cannot have 0 as a denominator since division by 0 is not defined.

A fraction with 1 as the denominator is the same as the whole number which is its numerator. For example, $\frac{12}{1}$ is 12, $\frac{0}{1}$ is 0.

If the numerator and denominator of a fraction are identical, the fraction represents 1. For example, $\frac{3}{3} = \frac{9}{9} = \frac{13}{13} = 1$. Any whole number, k, is represented by a fraction with a numerator equal to k times the denominator. For example, $\frac{18}{6} = 3$, and $\frac{30}{5} = 6$.

■ I–2.2

Mixed Numbers

A *mixed number* consists of a whole number and a fraction. For example, $7\frac{1}{4}$ is a mixed number; it means $7 + \frac{1}{4}$ and $\frac{1}{4}$ is called the fractional part of the mixed number $7\frac{1}{4}$. Any mixed number can be changed into a fraction:

(A) Multiply the whole number by the denominator of the fractional part.

(B) Add the numerator of the fraction to the result of step A.

(C) Use the result of step B as the numerator and use the denominator of the fractional part of the mixed number as the denominator. This fraction is equal to the mixed number.

EXAMPLE 1

Write $7\frac{1}{4}$ as a fraction.

(A) $4 \times 7 = 28$

(B) $28 + 1 = 29$

(C) So, $7\frac{1}{4} = \frac{29}{4}$.

A fraction whose numerator is larger than its denominator can be changed into a mixed number.

(A) Divide the denominator into the numerator; the result is the whole number of the mixed number.

(B) Put the remainder from step A over the denominator; this is the fractional part of the mixed number.

EXAMPLE 2

If a pizza pie has 8 pieces, how many pizzas pies have been eaten at a party where 35 pieces were eaten?

Since there are 8 pieces in a pie, $\frac{35}{8}$ pies were eaten. To find the number of pies, we need to change $\frac{35}{8}$ into a mixed number.

(A) Divide 8 into 35; the result is 4 with a remainder of 3.

(B) $\frac{3}{8}$ is the fractional part of the mixed number.

(C) So, $\frac{35}{8} = 4\frac{3}{8}$.

We can regard any whole number as a mixed number with 0 as the fractional part. For example, $\frac{18}{6} = 3$.

> In calculations with mixed numbers, change the mixed numbers into fractions.

■ I–2.3

Multiplying Fractions

To multiply two fractions, multiply their numerators and divide this result by the product of their denominators.

EXAMPLE

John saves $\frac{1}{3}$ of \$240. How much does he save? $\frac{1}{3} \times \frac{240}{1} = \frac{240}{3} = \$80$, the amount John saves.

■ I–2.4

Dividing Fractions

To divide one fraction (the dividend) by another fraction (the divisor), invert the divisor and multiply. To invert a fraction, turn it upside down; for example, if you invert $\frac{3}{4}$, the result is $\frac{4}{3}$.

EXAMPLE 1

$\frac{5}{6} \div \frac{3}{4} = \frac{5}{6} \times \frac{4}{3} = \frac{20}{18}$

EXAMPLE 2

A worker makes a basket in $\frac{2}{3}$ of an hour. If the worker works for $7\frac{1}{2}$ hours, how many baskets will he make?

We want to divide $\frac{2}{3}$ into $7\frac{1}{2}$, and $7\frac{1}{2} = \frac{15}{2}$, so we want to divide $\frac{15}{2}$ by $\frac{2}{3}$.

Thus, $\frac{15}{2} \div \frac{2}{3} = \frac{15}{2} \cdot \frac{3}{2} = \frac{45}{4} = 11\frac{1}{4}$ baskets.

■ I–2.5

Dividing and Multiplying by the Same Number

If you multiply the numerator and denominator of a fraction by the same nonzero number the fraction remains the same.

If you divide the numerator and denominator of any fraction by the same nonzero number, the fraction remains the same.

Consider the fraction $\frac{3}{4}$. If we multiply 3 by 10 and 4 by 10, then $\frac{30}{40}$ must equal $\frac{3}{4}$.

When we multiply fractions, if any of the numerators and denominators have a common factor (see Section I–1.2 for factors) we can divide each of them by the common factor and the fraction remains the same. This process is called *cancelling* and can be a great time-saver.

EXAMPLE

Multiply $\frac{4}{9} \times \frac{75}{8}$.

Since 4 is a common factor of 4 and 8, divide 4 and 8 by 4, getting $\frac{4}{9} \times \frac{75}{8} = \frac{1}{9} \times \frac{75}{2}$. Since

3 is a common factor of 9 and 75, divide 9 and 75 by 3 to get $\frac{1}{9} \times \frac{75}{2} = \frac{1}{3} \times \frac{25}{2}$.

So $\frac{4}{9} \times \frac{75}{8} = \frac{1}{3} \times \frac{25}{2} = \frac{25}{6}$.

This is denoted by striking or crossing out the appropriate numbers. For instance, the example

would be written as $\frac{\cancel{4}}{\cancel{9}} \times \frac{\cancel{75}}{\cancel{8}} = \frac{1}{3} \times \frac{25}{2} = \frac{25}{6}$.

Since you want to work as fast as possible on the GMAT exam, cancel whenever you can.

■ I–2.6

Equivalent Fractions

Two fractions are equivalent or equal if they represent the same ratio or number. In the last section, you saw that if you multiply or divide the numerator and denominator of a fraction by the same

nonzero number the result is equivalent to the original fraction. For example, $\frac{7}{8} = \frac{70}{80}$ since 70 = 10×7 and 80 = 10×8.

> In the test there will only be five choices, so your answer to a problem may not be the same as any of the given choices. You may have to express a fraction as an equivalent fraciton.

To find a fraction with a known denominator equal to a given fraction:

Ⓐ divide the denominator of the given fraction into the known denominator;

Ⓑ multiply the result of (A) by the numerator of the given fraction; this is the numerator of the required equivalent fraction.

EXAMPLE

Find a fraction with a denominator of 30 which is equal to $\frac{2}{5}$:

A 5 into 30 is 6;

B $6 \cdot 2 = 12$ so, $\frac{12}{30} = \frac{2}{5}$.

■ I–2.7

Reducing a Fraction to Lowest Terms

A fraction has been reduced to lowest terms when the numerator and denominator have no common factors.

For example, $\frac{3}{4}$ is reduced to lowest terms, but $\frac{3}{6}$ is not because 3 is a common factor of 3 and 6.

> To reduce a fraction to lowests terms, cancel all the common factors of the numerator and denominator. (Cancelling common factors will not change the value of the fraction.)

For example, $\dfrac{\overset{2}{\cancel{\underset{\cancel{100}}{}}}}{\underset{\underset{3}{\cancel{15}}}{\cancel{150}}} = \frac{2}{3}$. Since 2 and 3 have no common factors, $\frac{2}{3}$ is $\frac{100}{150}$ reduced to lowest terms. A fraction is equivalent to the fraction reduced to lowest terms.

If you aren't sure if there are any common factors, write the numerator and denominator as products of primes. Then it will be easy to cancel any common factors.

$$\frac{63}{81} = \frac{3 \cdot 3 \cdot 7}{3 \cdot 3 \cdot 3 \cdot 3} = \frac{7}{9}$$

■ I–2.8

Adding Fractions

If the fractions have the same denominator, then the denominator is called a *common denominator*. Add the numerators, and use this sum as the new numerator with the common denominator as the denominator of the sum.

EXAMPLE 1

$$\frac{5}{12} + \frac{3}{12} = \frac{5+3}{12} = \frac{8}{12} = \frac{2}{3}$$

EXAMPLE 2

A box of light bulbs contains 24 bulbs. A worker replaces 17 bulbs in the shipping department and 13 bulbs in the accounting department. How many boxes of bulbs did the worker use?

The worker used $\dfrac{17}{24}$ of a box in the shipping department and $\dfrac{13}{24}$ of a box in the accounting

department. So the total used was $\dfrac{17}{24} + \dfrac{13}{24} = \dfrac{30}{24} = 1\dfrac{1}{4}$ boxes.

If the fractions don't have the same denominator, you must first find a common denominator. One way to get a common denominator is to multiply all the denominators.

For example, to find $\dfrac{1}{2} + \dfrac{2}{3} + \dfrac{7}{4}$, note that $2 \bullet 3 \bullet 4 = 24$ which is a common denominator.

There are many common denominators; the smallest one is called the *least common denominator*. For the previous example, 12 is the least common denominator.

Once you have found a common denominator, express each fraction as an equivalent fraction with the common denominator, and add as you did for the case when the fractions had the same denominator.

EXAMPLE

$\dfrac{1}{2} + \dfrac{2}{3} + \dfrac{7}{4} = ?$

Ⓐ 24 is a common denominator.

Ⓑ $\dfrac{1}{2} = \dfrac{12}{24}, \dfrac{2}{3} = \dfrac{16}{24}, \dfrac{7}{4} = \dfrac{42}{24}.$

Ⓒ $\dfrac{1}{2} + \dfrac{2}{3} + \dfrac{7}{4} = \dfrac{12}{24} + \dfrac{16}{24} + \dfrac{42}{24} = \dfrac{12+16+42}{24} = \dfrac{70}{24} = \dfrac{35}{12}$

■ I–2.9

Subtracting Fractions

When the fractions have the same denominator, subtract the numerators and place the result over the denominator.

EXAMPLE

There are 5 tacos in a lunch box. Jim eats two of the tacos. What fraction of the original tacos are left in the lunch box?

Jim took $\dfrac{2}{5}$ of the original tacos, so $1 - \dfrac{2}{5}$ are left. Write 1 as $\dfrac{5}{5}$; then $\dfrac{5}{5} - \dfrac{2}{5} = \dfrac{(5-2)}{5} = \dfrac{3}{5}.$

So, $\dfrac{3}{5}$ are left in the lunch box.

When the fractions have different denominators:

A Find a common denominator.

B Express the fractions as equivalent fractions with the same denominator.

C Subtract.

EXAMPLE

$\dfrac{3}{5} - \dfrac{2}{7} = ?$

A A common denominator is $5 \cdot 7 = 35$.

B $\dfrac{3}{5} = \dfrac{21}{35}, \dfrac{2}{7} = \dfrac{10}{35}$.

C $\dfrac{3}{5} - \dfrac{2}{7} = \dfrac{21}{35} - \dfrac{10}{35} = \dfrac{21-10}{35} = \dfrac{11}{35}$.

■ I–2.10

Complex Fractions

A fraction whose numerator and denominator are themselves fractions is called a *complex fraction*.

For example $\dfrac{\frac{2}{3}}{\frac{4}{5}}$ is a complex fraction. A complex fraction can always be simplified by dividing the

fraction.

EXAMPLE 1

$\dfrac{2}{3} \div \dfrac{4}{5} = \dfrac{2}{3} \cdot \dfrac{5}{4} = \dfrac{1}{3} \cdot \dfrac{5}{2} = \dfrac{5}{6}$

EXAMPLE 2

It takes $2\dfrac{1}{2}$ hours to get from Buffalo to Cleveland traveling at a constant rate of speed. What

part of the distance is traveled in $\dfrac{3}{4}$ of an hour?

$\dfrac{\frac{3}{4}}{2\frac{1}{2}} = \dfrac{\frac{3}{4}}{\frac{5}{2}} = \dfrac{3}{4} \cdot \dfrac{2}{5} = \dfrac{3}{2} \cdot \dfrac{1}{5} = \dfrac{3}{10}$ of the distance.

I–3. DECIMALS

■ I–3.1

A collection of digits (the digits are 0, 1, 2, . . . 9) after a period (called the decimal point) is called a *decimal fraction*. For example, .503, .5602, .32, and .4 are all decimal fractions. A zero to the left of the decimal point is optional in a decimal fraction. So, 0.503 and .503 are equal.

Every decimal fraction represents a fraction. To find the fraction that a decimal fraction represents:

Ⓐ The denominator is $10 \times 10 \times 10 \times \ldots \times 10$. The number of copies of 10 is equal to the number of digits to the right of the decimal point.

Ⓑ The numerator is the number represented by the digits to the right of the decimal point.

EXAMPLE 1

What fraction does 0.503 represent?

Ⓐ There are 3 digits to the right of the decimal point, so the denominator is $10 \times 10 \times 10 = 1,000$.

Ⓑ The numerator is 503, so the fraction is $\dfrac{503}{1,000}$.

EXAMPLE 2

Find the fraction that .05732 represents.

Ⓐ There are five digits to the right of the decimal point, so the denominator is $10 \times 10 \times 10 \times 10 \times 10 = 100,000$.

Ⓑ The numerator is 5,732, so the fraction is $\dfrac{5,732}{100,000}$.

You can add any number of zeros to the right of a decimal fraction without changing its value.

EXAMPLE

$$.3 = \frac{3}{10} = \frac{30}{100} = .30 = .30000 = \frac{30,000}{100,000} = .300000000 \ldots$$

▪ I–3.2

We call the first position to the right of the decimal point the tenths place, since the digit in that position tells you how many tenths you should take. (It is the numerator of a fraction whose denominator is 10.) In the same way, we call the second position to the right the hundredths place, the third position to the right the thousandths, and so on. This is similar to the way whole numbers are expressed, since 568 means $5 \times 100 + 6 \times 10 + 8 \times 1$. The various digits represent different numbers depending on their position: the first place to the left of the decimal point represents units, the second place to the left represents tens, and so on.

The following diagram may be helpful:

```
T      H      T      O   •   T      H      T
H      U      E      N       E      U      H
O      N      N      E       N      N      O
U      D      S      S       T      D      U
S      R                     H      R      S
A      E                     S      E      A
N      D                            D      N
D      S                            T      D
S                                   H      S
                                    S      T
                                           H
                                           S
```

Thus, 5,342.061 means 5 thousands + 3 hundreds + 4 tens + 2 ones + 0 tenths + 6 hundredths + 1 thousandth.

▪ I–3.3

A *decimal* is a whole number plus a decimal fraction; the decimal point separates the whole number from the decimal fraction. For example, 4,307.206 is a decimal which represents 4,307 added to the decimal fraction .206. A decimal fraction is a decimal with zero as the whole number.

▪ I–3.4

A fraction whose denominator is a multiple of 10 is equivalent to a decimal. The denominator tells you the last place that is filled to the right of the decimal point. Place the decimal point in the numerator so that the last place to the right of the decimal point corresponds to the denominator. If the numerator does not have enough digits, add the appropriate number of zeros *before* the numerator.

EXAMPLE 1

Find the decimal equivalent of $\frac{5,732}{100}$.

Since the denominator is 100, you need two places to the right of the decimal point so,

$\frac{5,732}{100} = 57.32.$

EXAMPLE 2

What is the decimal equivalent of $\dfrac{57}{10,000}$?

The denominator is 10,000, so you need 4 decimal places to the right of the decimal point.

Since 57 only has two places, we add two zeros in front of 57; thus, $\dfrac{57}{10,000} = .0057$.

Do not make the error of adding the zeros to the right of 57 instead of the left.

.5700 is $\dfrac{5,700}{10,000}$, not $\dfrac{57}{10,000}$.

■ I–3.5

Adding Decimals

Decimals are much easier to add than fractions. To add a collection of decimals:

A Write the decimals in a column with the decimal points vertically aligned.

B Add enough zeros to the right of the decimal point so that every number has an entry in each column to the right of the decimal point.

C Add the numbers in the same way as whole numbers.

D Place a decimal point in the sum so that it is directly beneath the decimal points in the decimals added.

EXAMPLE 1

How much is 5 + 3.43 + 16.021 + 3.1?

A
```
    5
    3.43
   16.021
 +  3.1
```

B
```
    5.000
    3.430
   16.021
 +  3.100
```

C
```
    5.000
    3.430
   16.021
 +  3.100
```

D 27.551   The answer is 27.551.

EXAMPLE 2

If Mary has $.50, $3.25, and $6.05, how much does she have?

```
 $ .50
   3.25
 + 6.05
```
```
 $9.80     So, Mary has $9.80.
```

■ I–3.6

Subtracting Decimals

To subtract one decimal from another:

A Put the decimals in a column so that the decimal points are vertically aligned.

B Add zeros so that every decimal has an entry in each column to the right of the decimal point.

C Subtract the numbers as you would whole numbers.

D Place the decimal point in the result so that it is directly beneath the decimal points of the numbers you subtracted.

EXAMPLE 1

Solve 5.053 – 2.09.

A
$$\begin{array}{r} 5.053 \\ -\ 2.09 \\ \hline \end{array}$$

B
$$\begin{array}{r} 5.053 \\ -\ 2.090 \\ \hline \end{array}$$

C
$$\begin{array}{r} 5.053 \\ -\ 2.090 \\ \hline \end{array}$$

D   2.963   The answer is 2.963.

EXAMPLE 2

If Joe has $12 and he loses $8.40, how much money does he have left?

Since $12.00 – $8.40 = $3.60, he has $3.60 left.

■ I–3.7

Multiplying Decimals

Decimals are multiplied like whole numbers. *The decimal point of the product is placed so that the number of decimal places in the product is equal to the total of the number of decimal places in all of the numbers multiplied.*

EXAMPLE 1

What is (5.02)(.6)?

(502)(6) = 3012. There were 2 decimal places in 5.02 and 1 decimal place in .6, so the product must have 2 + 1 = 3 decimal places. Therefore, (5.02)(.6) = 3.012.

EXAMPLE 2

If eggs cost $.06 each, how much should a dozen eggs cost?

Since (12)(.06) = .72, a dozen eggs should cost $.72.

> **Computing Tip:** To multiply a decimal by 10, just move the decimal point to the right one place; to multiply by 100 or move the decimal point two places to the right and so on.

EXAMPLE 1

$9,983.456 \times 100 = 998,345.6$

◼ I–3.8

Dividing Decimals

To divide one decimal (the dividend) by another decimal (the divisor):

Ⓐ Move the decimal point in the divisor to the right until there is no decimal fraction in the divisor (this is the same as multiplying the divisor by a multiple of 10).

Ⓑ Move the decimal point in the dividend the same number of places to the right as you moved the decimal point in step (A).

Ⓒ Divide the result of (B) by the result of (A) as if they were whole numbers.

Ⓓ The number of decimal places in the result (quotient) should be equal to the number of decimal places in the result of step (B).

Ⓔ You may obtain as many decimal places as you wish in the quotient by adding zeros to the right in the dividend and then repeating step (C). For each zero you add to the dividend, you need one more decimal place in the quotient.

EXAMPLE 1

Divide .05 into 25.155.

Ⓐ Move the decimal point two places to the right in .05; the result is 5.

Ⓑ Move the decimal point two places to the right in 25.155; the result is 2515.5.

Ⓒ Divide 5 into 25155; the result is 5031.

Ⓓ Since there was one decimal place in the result of (B), the answer is 503.1.

Ⓔ There is no need to continue the division.

The work for this example might look like this:

$$.05\overline{)25.155} \to 503.1$$

You can always check division by multiplying.

$$(503.1)(.05) = 25.155 \text{ so our answer checks.}$$

If you write division as a fraction, example 1 would be expressed as $\dfrac{25.155}{.05}$.

You can multiply both the numerator and denominator by 100 without changing the value of the fraction. So,

$$\frac{25.155}{.05} = \frac{25.155 \times 100}{.05 \times 100} = \frac{2515.5}{5.}.$$

So steps (A) and (B) always change the division of a decimal by a decimal into the division of a decimal by a whole number.

To divide a decimal by a whole number, divide them as if they were whole numbers. Then place the decimal point in the quotient so that the quotient has as many decimal places as the dividend.

EXAMPLE 2

$\dfrac{100.11}{.8} = ?$

Ⓐ Move the decimal point one place to the right in .8; the result is 8.

Ⓑ Move the decimal point one place to the right in 100.11; the result is 1001.1.

Ⓒ Divide 8 into 10011; the result is 1251, with a remainder of 3. Since the division is not exact, we use step (E).

Ⓓ The result must have four decimal places (1 from step (B) and 3 from step (E)), so the answer is 125.1375.

Ⓔ Add 3 zeros to the right of 1001.1 and repeat (C). So we divide 8 into 10011000; the result is 1251375.

The work for this example might look like this:

$$.8\overline{)100.11000}\atop{125.1375}$$

CHECK: (.8)(125.1375) = 100.11000 = 100.11 so this is correct.

EXAMPLE 3

If oranges cost 42¢ each, how many oranges can you buy for $2.52? Make sure the units are compatible, so 42¢ is $.42. Therefore, the number of oranges is

$$\frac{2.52}{.42} = \frac{252}{42} = 6.$$

> **Computing Tip:** To divide a decimal by 10, move the decimal point *to the left* one place; to divide by 100, move the decimal point two places to the left, and so on.

EXAMPLE

Divide 5,637.6471 by 1,000.

The answer is 5.6376471, since to divide by 1,000 you move the decimal point 3 places to the left.

■ I–3.9

Converting a Fraction into a Decimal

To convert a fraction into a decimal, divide the denominator into the numerator. For example, $\frac{3}{4} = \frac{3.00}{4} = .75$. Some fractions give a repeating decimal when you divide the denominator into the numerator, for example,

$\frac{1}{3} = .333$ . . . where the three dots mean you keep on getting 3 with each step of division. .333 . . . is a *repeating decimal*.

  You should know the following decimal equivalents of fractions:

$\frac{1}{100} = 0.01$	$\frac{1}{10} = .1$	$\frac{2}{5} = .4$
$\frac{1}{50} = 0.2$	$\frac{1}{9} = .1\overline{11}$	$\frac{1}{2} = .5$
$\frac{1}{40} = 0.25$	$\frac{1}{8} = .125$	$\frac{5}{8} = .625$
$\frac{1}{25} = 0.4$	$\frac{1}{6} = .16\overline{66}$	$\frac{2}{3} = .6\overline{66}$
$\frac{1}{20} = 0.5$	$\frac{1}{5} = .2$	$\frac{3}{4} = .75$
$\frac{1}{16} = .0625$	$\frac{1}{4} = .25$	$\frac{7}{8} = .875$
$\frac{1}{15} = .06\overline{66}$	$\frac{1}{3} = .3\overline{33}$	$\frac{3}{2} = 1.5$
$\frac{1}{12} = 0.8\overline{33}$	$\frac{3}{8} = .375$	

Any decimal with a bar above is a repeating decimal.
If a fraction has a repeating decimal, use the fraction in any computation.

EXAMPLE 1

What is $\frac{2}{9}$ of $3,690.90?

  Since the decimal for $\frac{2}{9}$ is .2222 . . . use the fraction $\frac{2}{9}$.

  $\frac{2}{9} \times \$3,690.90 = 2 \times \$410.10 = \$820.20.$

I–4. PERCENTAGE

■ I–4.1

Percentage is another method of expressing fractions or parts of an object. Percentages are expressed in terms of hundredths, so 100% means 100 hundredths or 1, and 50% would be 50 hundredths or $\frac{1}{2}$.

A decimal is converted to a percentage by multiplying the decimal by 100. Since multiplying a decimal by 100 is accomplished by moving the decimal point two places to the right, *you convert a decimal into a percentage by moving the decimal point two places to the right.* For example, .134 = 13.4%.

If you wish to convert a percentage into a decimal, you divide the percentage by 100. There is a shortcut for this also. To divide by 100 you move the decimal point two places to the left.

Therefore, *to convert a percentage into a decimal, move the decimal point two places to the left.* For example, 24% = .24.

A fraction is converted into a percentage by changing the fraction to a decimal and then changing the decimal to a percentage. A percentage is changed into a fraction by first converting the percentage into a decimal and then changing the decimal to a fraction. *You should know the following fractional equivalents of percentages:*

$1\% = \frac{1}{100}$	$25\% = \frac{1}{4}$	$80\% = \frac{4}{5}$
$2\% = \frac{1}{50}$	$33\frac{1}{3}\% = \frac{1}{3}$	$83\frac{1}{3}\% = \frac{5}{6}$
$4\% = \frac{1}{25}$	$37\frac{1}{2}\% = \frac{3}{8}$	$87\frac{1}{2}\% = \frac{7}{8}$
$5\% = \frac{1}{20}$	$40\% = \frac{2}{5}$	$100\% = 1$
$8\frac{1}{3}\% = \frac{1}{12}$	$50\% = \frac{1}{2}$	$120\% = \frac{6}{5}$
$10\% = \frac{1}{10}$	$60\% = \frac{3}{5}$	$125\% = \frac{5}{4}$
$12\frac{1}{2}\% = \frac{1}{8}$	$62\frac{1}{2}\% = \frac{5}{8}$	$133\frac{1}{3}\% = \frac{4}{3}$
$16\frac{2}{3}\% = \frac{1}{6}$	$66\frac{2}{3}\% = \frac{2}{3}$	$150\% = \frac{3}{2}$
$20\% = \frac{1}{5}$	$75\% = \frac{3}{4}$	

Note, for example, that $133\frac{1}{3}\% = 1.33\frac{1}{3} = 1\frac{1}{3} = \frac{4}{3}$.

When you compute with percentages, it is usually easier to change the percentages to decimals or fractions.

EXAMPLE 1

A company has 6,435 bars of soap. If the company sells 20% of its bars of soap, how many bars of soap did it sell?

Change 20% into .2. Thus, the company sold (.2)(6,435) = 1287.0 = 1,287 bars of soap. An alternative method would be to convert 20% to $\frac{1}{5}$.

Then, $\frac{1}{5} \times 6,435 = 1,287$.

EXAMPLE 2

In a class of 60 students, 18 students received a grade of B. What percentage of the class received a grade of B?

$\frac{18}{60}$ of the class received a grade of B. $\frac{18}{60} = \frac{3}{10} = .3 = 30\%$, so 30% of the class received a grade of B.

EXAMPLE 3

If the population of Dryden was 10,000 in 1960 and the population of Dryden increased by 15% between 1960 and 1970, what was the population of Dryden in 1970?

The population increased by 15% between 1960 and 1970, so the increase was (.15)(10,000) which is 1,500. The population in 1970 was 10,000 + 1,500 = 11,500.

A quicker method: The population increased 15%, so the population in 1970 is 115% of the population in 1960. Therefore, the population in 1970 is 115% of 10,000 which is (1.15)(10,000) = 11,500.

■ I–4.2

Interest and Discount

Two of the most common uses of percentages are in interest and discount problems.
The rate of interest is usually given as a percentage. The basic formula for interest problems is:

$$\text{INTEREST} = \text{AMOUNT} \times \text{TIME} \times \text{RATE}$$

You can assume the rate of interest is the annual rate of interest unless the problem states otherwise; so you should express the time in years.

EXAMPLE 1

How much interest will $10,000 earn in 9 months at an annual rate of 6%?

9 months is $\dfrac{3}{4}$ of a year and 6% = $\dfrac{3}{50}$, so using the formula, the interest is

$10,000 $\times \dfrac{3}{4} \times \dfrac{3}{50}$ = 50×9 = $450.

EXAMPLE 2

What annual rate of interest was paid if $5,000 earned $300 in interest in 2 years?

Since the interest was earned in 2 years, $150 is the interest earned in one year.

$\dfrac{150}{5,000}$ = .03 = 3%, so the annual rate of interest was 3%.

The type of interest described above is called *simple interest.*

There is another method of computing interest called *compound interest*. In computing compound interest, the interest is periodically added to the amount (or principal) which is earning interest.

EXAMPLE 3

What will $1,000 be worth after three years if it earns interest at the rate of 5% compounded annually?

Compounded annually means that the interest earned during one year is added to the amount (or principal) at the end of each year. The interest on $1,000 at 5% for one year is $(1,000)(.05) = $50. So you must compute the interest on $1,050 (not $1,000) for the second year. The interest is $(1,050)(.05) = $52.50. Therefore, during the third year interest will be computed for $1,102.50. During the third year the interest is $(1,102.50)(.05) = $55.125 = $55.13. Therefore, after 3 years the original $1,000 will be worth $1,157.63.

If you calculated simple interest on $1,000 at 5% for three years, the answer would be $(1,000)(.05)(3) = $150. Therefore, using simple interest, $1,000 is worth $1,150 after 3 years. You earn more interest with compound interest.

You can assume that interest means simple interest unless a problem states otherwise. The basic formula for discount problems is:

DISCOUNT = COST × RATE OF DISCOUNT

EXAMPLE 1

What is the discount if a car which cost $3,000 is discounted 7%? The discount is $3,000 × .07 = $210 since 7% = .07.

If we know the cost of an item and its discounted price, we can find the rate of discount by using the formula

$$\text{rate of discount} = \frac{\text{cost} - \text{price}}{\text{cost}}$$

EXAMPLE 2

What was the rate of discount if a boat which cost $5,000 was sold for $4,800?

Using this formula, we find that the rate of discount equals

$$\frac{5,000 - 4,800}{5,000} = \frac{200}{5,000} = \frac{1}{25} = .04 = 4\%.$$

After an item has been discounted once, it may be discounted again. This procedure is called successive discounting.

EXAMPLE 3

A bicycle originally cost $100 and was discounted 10%. After three months it was sold after being discounted 15%. How much was the bicycle sold for?

After the 10% discount the bicycle was selling for $100(.90) = $90. An item which costs $90 and is discounted 15% will sell for $90(.85) = $76.50, so the bicycle was sold for $76.50.

Notice that if you added the two discounts of 10% and 15% and treated the successive discounts as a single discount of 25%, your answer would be that the bicycle sold for $75, which is incorrect. Successive discounts are *not* identical to a single discount of the sum of the discounts. The previous example shows that successive discounts of 10% and 15% are not identical to a single discount of 25%.

I–5. ROUNDING OFF NUMBERS

▉ I–5.1

Many times an approximate answer can be found more quickly and may be more useful than the exact answer. For example, if a company had sales of $998,875.63 during a year, it is easier to remember that the sales were about $1 million.

Rounding off a number to a decimal place means finding the multiple of the representative of that decimal place which is closest to the original number. Thus, rounding off a number to the nearest hundred means finding the multiple of 100 which is closest to the original number. Rounding off to the nearest tenth means finding the multiple of $\frac{1}{10}$ which is closest to the original number.

After a number has been rounded off to a particular decimal place, all the digits to the right of that particular decimal place will be zero.

To round off a number to the *r*th decimal place:

Ⓐ Look at the digit in the place to the right of the *r*th place;

Ⓑ *If the digit is 4 or less, change all the digits in places to the right of the rth place to 0 to round off the number.*

Ⓒ *If the digit is 5 or more, add 1 to the digit in the rth place and change all the digits in places to the right of the rth place to 0 to round off the number.*

For example, the multiple of 100 which is closest to 5,342.1 is 5,300.

EXAMPLE 1

Round off 3.445 to the nearest tenth.

The digit to the right of the tenths place is 4, so 3.445 is 3.4 to the nearest tenth.

Most problems dealing with money are rounded off to the nearest hundredth or cent if the answer contains a fractional part of a cent. This is common business practice.

EXAMPLE 2

If 16 cookies cost $1.00, how much should three cookies cost?

Three cookies should cost $\frac{3}{16}$ of $1.00. Since $\frac{3}{16} \times 1 = .1875$, the cost would be $.1875. In practice, you would round it up to $.19 or 19¢.

Rounding off numbers can help you get quick, approximate answers. Since some questions require only rough answers, you can save time on the test by rounding off numbers.

EXAMPLE 3

If 5,301 of the 499,863 workers employed at the XYZ factory don't show up for work on Monday, about what percentage of the workers don't show up?

(A) 1
(B) 2
(C) 3
(D) 4
(E) 5

You can quickly see that the answer is (A) by rounding off both numbers to the nearest thousand before you divide, because $\frac{5,000}{500,000} = \frac{1}{100} = .01 = 1\%$. The exact answer is

$\frac{5,301}{499,863} = .010604$, but it would take much longer to get an exact answer.

> ## EXAMPLE 4
>
> Round off 43.796 to the nearest tenth.
>
> The place to the right of tenths is hundredths, so look in the hundredths place. Since 9 is bigger than 5, add 1 to the tenths place. Therefore, 43.796 is 43.8 rounded off to the nearest tenth.
>
> If the digit in the *r*th place is 9 and you need to add 1 to the digit to round off the number to the *r*th decimal place, put a zero in the *r*th place and add 1 to the digit in the position to the left of the *r*th place. For example, 298 rounded off to the nearest 10 is 300; 99,752 to the nearest thousand is 100,000.

I–6. SIGNED NUMBERS

■ I–6.1

A number preceded by either a plus or a minus sign is called a *signed number*. For example, $+5$, -6, -4.2, and $+\frac{3}{4}$ are all signed numbers. If no sign is given with a number, a plus sign is assumed; thus, 5 is interpreted as $+5$.

Signed numbers can often be used to distinguish different concepts. For example, a profit of $10 can be denoted by $+\$10$ and a loss of $10 by $-\$10$. A temperature of 20 degrees below zero can be denoted $-20°F$.

■ I–6.2

Signed numbers are also called *directed numbers*. You can think of numbers arranged on a line, called a number line, in the following manner:

Take a line that extends indefinitely in both directions, pick a point on the line and call it 0, pick another point on the line to the right of 0 and call it 1. The point to the right of 1 which is exactly as far from 1 as 1 is from 0 is called 2, the point to the right of 2 just as far from 2 as 1 is from 0 is called 3, and so on. The point halfway between 0 and 1 is called $\frac{1}{2}$, the point halfway between $\frac{1}{2}$ and 1 is called $\frac{3}{4}$. In this way, you can identify any whole number or any fraction with a point on the line.

All the numbers that correspond to points to the right of 0 are called *positive numbers*. The sign of a positive number is $+$.

If you go to the left of zero the same distance as you did from 0 to 1, the point is called -1; in the same way as before, you can find -2, -3, $-\frac{1}{2}$, $-\frac{3}{2}$ and so on.

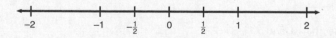

All the numbers that correspond to points to the left of zero are called *negative numbers*. Negative numbers are signed numbers whose sign is $-$. For example, -3, -5.15, $-.003$ are all negative numbers.

> Zero is neither positive nor negative; any
> nonzero number is positive or negative
> but not both.

■ I–6.3

Absolute Value

The absolute value of a signed number is the distance of the number from 0. The absolute value of any nonzero number is *positive*. For example, the absolute value of 2 is 2; the absolute value of −2 is 2. The absolute value of a number *a* is denoted by $|a|$, so $|-2| = 2$. The absolute value of any number can be found by dropping its sign, $|-12| = 12$, $|4| = 4$. *Thus $|-a| = |a|$ for any number a.* The only number whose absolute value is zero is zero.

■ I–6.4

Adding Signed Numbers

Case I. Adding numbers with the *same sign*:

A The sign of the sum is the same as the sign of the numbers being added.

B Add the absolute values.

C Put the sign from step (A) in front of the number you obtained in step (B).

EXAMPLE 1

What is $-2 + (-3.1) + (-.02)$?

A The sign of the sum will be −.

B $|-2| = 2$, $|-3.1| = 3.1$, $|-.02| = .02$, and $2 + 3.1 + .02 = 5.12$.

C The answer is −5.12.

Case II. Adding two numbers with *different signs*:

A The sign of the sum is the sign of the number that is largest in absolute value.

B Subtract the absolute value of the number with the smaller absolute value from the absolute value of the number with the larger absolute value.

C The answer is the number you obtained in step (B) preceded by the sign from part (A).

EXAMPLE 2

How much is $-5.1 + 3$?

A The absolute value of −5.1 is 5.1 and the absolute value of 3 is 3, so the sign of the sum will be −.

B 5.1 is larger than 3, and $5.1 - 3 = 2.1$.

C The sum is −2.1.

Case III. Adding *more than two* numbers with <u>*different signs*</u>:

Ⓐ Add all the positive numbers; the result is positive (this is Case I).

Ⓑ Add all the negative numbers; the result is negative (this is Case I).

Ⓒ Add the result of step (A) to the result of step (B), by using Case II.

EXAMPLE 3

Find the value of 5 + 52 + (−3) + 7 + (−5.1).

Ⓐ 5 + 52 + 7 = 64.

Ⓑ −3 + (−5.1) = −8.1.

Ⓒ 64 + (−8.1) = 55.9, so the answer is 55.9.

EXAMPLE 4

If a store made a profit of $23.50 on Monday, lost $2.05 on Tuesday, lost $5.03 on Wednesday, made a profit of $30.10 on Thursday, and made a profit of $41.25 on Friday, what was its total profit (or loss) for the week? Use + for profit and − for loss.

The total is 23.50 + (−2.05) + (−5.03) + 30.10 + 41.25 which is 94.85 + (−7.08) = 87.77. So the store made a profit of $87.77.

◼ I–6.5

Subtracting Signed Numbers

When subtracting signed numbers:

Ⓐ Change the sign of the number you are subtracting (the subtrahend).

Ⓑ Add the result of step (A) to the number being subtracted from (the minuend) using the rules of the preceding section.

EXAMPLE 1

Subtract 4.1 from 6.5.

Ⓐ 4.1 becomes −4.1.

Ⓑ 6.5 + (−4.1) = 2.4.

EXAMPLE 2

What is 7.8 − (−10.1)?

Ⓐ −10.1 becomes 10.1.

Ⓑ 7.8 + 10.1 = 17.9.

So we subtract a negative number by adding a positive number with the same absolute value, and we subtract a positive number by adding a negative number of the same absolute value.

■ **I–6.6**

Multiplying Signed Numbers

Case I. Multiplying two numbers:

Ⓐ Multiply the absolute values of the numbers.

Ⓑ If both numbers have the same sign, the result of step (A) is the answer—i.e. the product is positive. If the numbers have different signs, then the answer is the result of step (A) with a minus sign.

EXAMPLE 1

$(-5)(-12) = ?$

Ⓐ $5 \times 12 = 60$

Ⓑ Both signs are the same, so the answer is 60.

EXAMPLE 2

$(4)(-3) = ?$

Ⓐ $4 \times 3 = 12$

Ⓑ The signs are different, so the answer is –12.

You can remember the sign of the product in the following way:

$$(-)(-) = +$$
$$(+)(+) = +$$
$$(-)(+) = -$$
$$(+)(-) = -$$

Case II. Multiplying more than two numbers:

Ⓐ Multiply the first two factors using Case I.

Ⓑ Multiply the result of (A) by the third factor.

Ⓒ Multiply the result of (B) by the fourth factor.

Ⓓ Continue until you have used each factor.

EXAMPLE 3

$(-5)(4)(2)(-\dfrac{1}{2})(\dfrac{3}{4}) = ?$

Ⓐ $(-5)(4) = -20$

Ⓑ $(-20)(2) = -40$

Ⓒ $(-40)(-\dfrac{1}{2}) = 20$

Ⓓ $(20)(\dfrac{3}{4}) = 15$, so the answer is 15.

◼ I–6.7

Dividing Signed Numbers

Divide the absolute values of the numbers; the sign of the quotient is determined by the same rules as you used to determine the sign of a product. Thus,

$$\text{positive} \div \text{positive} = \text{positive}$$
$$\text{negative} \div \text{negative} = \text{positive}$$
$$\text{positive} \div \text{negative} = \text{negative}$$
$$\text{negative} \div \text{positive} = \text{negative}$$

EXAMPLE 1

Divide 53.2 by –4.

53.2 divided by 4 is 13.3. Since one of the numbers is positive and the other negative, the answer is –13.3.

EXAMPLE 2

$$\frac{-5}{-2} = \frac{5}{2} = 2.5$$

> The sign of the product or quotient is + if there are no negative factors or an even number of negative factors. The sign of the product or quotient is – if there are an odd number of negative factors.

I–7. DESCRIPTIVE STATISTICS AND PROBABILITY

◼ I–7.1

Mean

The *average* or *arithmetic mean* of N numbers is the sum of the N numbers divided by N.

EXAMPLE 1

The scores for 9 students on a test were 72, 78, 81, 64, 85, 92, 95, 60, and 55. What was the average score of the students?

Since there are 9 students, the average is the total of all the scores divided by 9.

So, the average is $\frac{1}{9}$ of (72 + 78 + 81 + 64 + 85 + 92 + 95 + 60 + 55), which is $\frac{1}{9}$ of 682

or $75\frac{7}{9}$.

EXAMPLE 2

The temperature at noon in Coldtown, U.S.A. was 5°F on Monday, 10°F on Tuesday, 2°F below zero on Wednesday, 5°F below zero on Thursday, 0°F on Friday, 4°F on Saturday, and 1°F below zero on Sunday. What was the average temperature at noon for the week?

Use negative numbers for the temperatures below zero. The average temperature is the average of 5, 10, –2, –5, 0, 4, and –1, which is $\dfrac{5+10+(-2)+(-5)+0+4+(-1)}{7} = \dfrac{11}{7} = 1\dfrac{4}{7}$.

Therefore, the average temperature at noon for the week is $1\dfrac{4}{7}$ °F.

EXAMPLE 3

If the average annual income of 10 workers is $15,665 and two of the workers each made $20,000 for the year, what is the average annual income of the remaining 8 workers?

The total income of all 10 workers is 10 times the average income which is $156,650. The two workers made a total of $40,000, so the total income of the remaining 8 workers was $156,650 – $40,000 = $116,650. Therefore, the average annual income of the 8 remaining workers is $\dfrac{\$116{,}650}{8} = \$14{,}581.25$.

■ I–7.2

The Median

If we arrange N numbers in order, the *median* is the middle number if N is odd and the average of the two middle numbers if N is even. In example 1 above, the median score was 78, and in example 2, the median temperature for the week was 0. Notice that the medians were different from the averages. In example 3, we don't have enough data to find the median although we know the average.

> In general the median and the average of
> a collection of numbers are different.

The average and the median are examples of descriptive statistics. Other statistics that you should know are the *mode, range,* and *standard deviation.*

■ I–7.3

The Mode

In a collection of numbers or measurements, the mode is the most frequent measurement in the collection.

EXAMPLE 1

The number of defects in 12 different production runs were 2, 5, 10, 0, 5, 3, 4, 3, 2, 2, 0, and 0. The mode(s) of the defects are 2 and 0 since both 2 and 0 occurred 3 times in the set of defects.

A set can have more than one mode.

■ I–7.4

Frequency Distributions

A set of numbers is often summarized compactly by a frequency distribution. A frequency distribution for a set of measurements or numbers is a table that gives each value in the collection along with the number of times it occurs in the collection.

EXAMPLE 1

The number of defects in 12 different production runs were 2 , 5, 10, 0, 5, 3, 4, 3, 2, 2, 0, and 0. This data can be summarized in a frequency distribution as follows :

(i) The values that occur in the set in increasing order are 0, 2, 3, 4, 5, and 10.

(ii) The frequency of 0 is 3 since it occurs 3 times in the set. The frequency of 2 is 3 since it occurs 3 times in the set. The frequency of 3 is 2 since it occurs twice in the set. The frequency of 5 is 2 since it occurs twice in the set. Both 4 and 10 have frequency 1 since they occur only once in the set.

(iii) So the set can be summarized in a table:

Measurement	Frequency
0	3
2	3
3	2
4	1
5	2
10	1

Notice that the frequencies add up to 12, which is the number of measurements in the set.

Calculations are easier if the data are given in a frequency distribution. If you have a large data set, it is better to organize the data into a frequency distribution before starting calculations.

EXAMPLE 2

Find the arithmetic mean, median, and mode of the set of defects in the 12 production runs given above.

Finding the mean:

(i) Multiply each measurement by its frequency ($3 \times 0 = 0$, $3 \times 2 = 6$, $2 \times 3 = 6$, $1 \times 4 = 4$, $2 \times 5 = 10$, and $1 \times 10 = 10$).

(ii) Add the results obtained in step (i) ($0 + 6 + 6 + 4 + 10 + 10 = 36$).

(iii) Add the frequencies ($3 + 3 + 2 + 1 + 2 + 1 = 12$).

(iv) Divide the results of step (ii), which is the sum of the measurements, by the result of step (iii), which is number of measurements, to obtain the average ($\frac{36}{12} = 3$). So 3 is the average number of defects per production run for the set.

Finding the median:

(i) Find the number of measurements by adding the frequencies ($3 + 3 + 2 + 1 + 2 + 1 = 12$).

(ii) Find the location of the median in the ordered set. (The median will be the average of the sixth and seventh values.)

(iii) Since the frequency distribution gives the values in order, pick out the appropriate value(s) and calculate the median. (The sixth measurement is 2 and the seventh measurement is 3, so the median is $\frac{(2+5)}{2} = 2.5$.)

Finding the mode:

(i) Find the largest frequency (3 is the largest frequency).

(ii) The entries corresponding to the largest frequencies are the modes. (2 and 0 have frequencies of 3, so they are the modes.)

The *average or mean*, *median*, and *mode* are statistics which are used to estimate a "typical" or "most likely" measurement in a set. Another way of thinking about this idea is to say these statistics are used to estimate the center or middle of a collection of numbers.

■ I–7.5

Range and Standard Deviation

In some situations we need to know the spread or dispersal of the values in a set. The *range* and *standard deviation* are two statistics used to measure how varied the measurements are.

Range. The range of a set of measurements is the difference of the largest and smallest measurements in the set.

Example: The range of defects in the production runs given in the previous section is $10 - 0 = 10$.

The range of a set of measurements depends only on the largest and smallest values in the set.

Standard Deviation. The standard deviation is a statistic used to measure the spread of a distribution that involves all the values in the set.

Example: Calculate the standard deviation of the set of defects in the 12 production runs.

   (i) Find the mean of the set (we know the mean is 3).
   (ii) Subtract the mean from each measurement, the results are called the deviations.
   (iii) Square each deviation.
   (iv) Add all the squares of the deviations. (Be sure to multiply the squared deviation by its frequency.)
   (v) Divide by the number of measurements. (In other words, find the average of the squared deviations.)
   (vi) Take the square root of the result of step (v). This is the standard deviation of the data.

We will calculate the standard deviation for the data. Much of the calculation can be done with the frequency distribution.

Measurement	Frequency	Deviation	Squared deviation
0	3	0 – 3	$(-3)^2 = 9$
2	3	2 – 3	$(-1)^2 = 1$
3	2	3 – 3	$0^2 = 0$
4	1	4 – 3	$1^2 = 1$
5	2	5 – 3	$2^2 = 4$
10	1	10 – 3	$7^2 = 49$

   (iv) The sum of the squared deviations is $3 \times 9 + 3 \times 1 + 2 \times 0 + 1 \times 1 + 2 \times 4 + 1 \times 49$, which is $27 + 3 + 0 + 1 + 8 + 49 = 88$.

   (v) Divide 88 by 12 to get 7 and $\frac{1}{3}$.

   (vi) The standard deviation is $\sqrt{7.333...} = 2.708...$

You will probably not be asked to calculate a standard deviation, however, there are often some questions that will involve understanding the standard deviation.

If one set has a smaller standard deviation than a second set, then the first set is less spread out than the second set.

If you multiply each number in a data set by the same constant to obtain a new data set, then the mean, median, mode, range, and standard deviation of the new set will be the statistics of the old set multiplied by the constant.

EXAMPLE 1

Each defect in a production run means that a box that contains six bottles must be discarded. For the productions runs given above find the mean, median, mode, range, and standard deviation of the number of bottles discarded.

   Do not recalculate the data and then recalculate the statistics. Simply multiply the statistics by 6. So the mean is $6 \times 3 = 18$, the median is $6 \times 3 = 18$, the modes are $6 \times 0 = 0$ and $6 \times 2 = 12$, the range is $6 \times 10 = 60$ and the standard deviation is $6 \times 2.708 = 16.248$.

If you add the same constant to each number in a data set to obtain a new data set, then the mean, median, mode of the new set can be found by adding the constant to the mean, median, and mode of the original set.

   However, the range and standard deviation will be unchanged since the new distribution has the same dispersal as the original distribution.

EXAMPLE 2

The compensation of the employees of the marketing department has a distribution with a mean of $51,000 and a standard deviation of $5,200. If every person in the department receives an increment of $1,000, find the mean and standard deviation of the compensations after the increments.

   The mean is increased by $1,000, so the new mean is $51,000 + $1,000 = $52,000.

   Since every compensation increased by $1,000 and the mean increased by $1,000, the deviations will be unchanged; so the standard deviation will remain $5,200.

EXAMPLE 3

The median of the daily high temperatures in a city for the month of June was 86° Fahrenheit with a range of 18° Fahrenheit. You can translate degrees Fahrenheit to degrees Celsius by the following formula:

$$\text{degrees Celsius} = \frac{5}{9}(\text{degrees Fahrenheit} - 32)$$

Find the median and the range of the daily high temperatures for June in degrees Celsius.

   The median high temperature will be $\left(\frac{5}{9}\right)(86 - 32) = \left(\frac{5}{9}\right)(54) = 30°$ Celsius.

   The range will be $\left(\frac{5}{9}\right)(18) = 10°$ Celsius. (Notice that you do not subtract 32 since adding or subtracting the same amount from each temperature will not change the range.

▪ I–7.6

Discrete Probability

Probability is a way to measure how likely an occurence is. Probabilities are measured by assigning values from 0 to 1 inclusive. A probability assignment of 0 means something will "never" happen, a probability assignment of 1 means that something "always" happens.

   The most common way of assigning probabilities is when each outcome is equally likely. If a question says a person is randomly chosen, that means each person has the same chance of being chosen. When outcomes are equally likely, then the probability of any particular outcome is 1 divided by the number of outcomes.

   For example, think of a jar that contains 10 red and 5 blue marbles. You reach in and take a marble without looking. There are 15 marbles in the jar, so there are 15 different outcomes when you pick the marble. Since you did not look when you picked the marble, each marble should have the same chance of being picked, and so we assign $\frac{1}{15}$ as the probability that any particular marble is picked. Since there are 10 red marbles in the jar, the probability that a red marble is picked is $10 \times \left(\frac{1}{15}\right) = \frac{10}{15}$ or $\frac{2}{3}$. Since there are 5 blue marbles in the jar the probability that a blue marble is picked is $5 \times \left(\frac{1}{15}\right) = \frac{5}{15}$ or $\frac{1}{3}$.

   We let R stand for the outcome that the marble picked is red and $p(R)$ stand for the probability that R occurs. So we showed $p(R) = \frac{10}{15}$ or $\frac{2}{3}$.

If B means that the marble picked was blue, then $p(B) = \frac{5}{15}$ or $\frac{1}{3}$.

If we picked a red marble from the jar and then picked a second marble without replacing the first marble, then the probability that the second marble is red if the first marble was red is $\frac{9}{14}$. The probability that the second marble is blue if the first marble was red is $\frac{5}{14}$.

Some simple facts that are useful when working with probability are the following:

1. The probability that an event does not happen is 1 minus the probability that the event does happen. This is often stated as *p(not A) = 1 − p(A)* (*not A* is also referred to as the negation of A.)

For example, when we picked the marble from the jar, there were 10 red marbles and 5 nonred marbles in the jar, so $p(\text{not B})$ = the probability that the marble picked is not blue = $\frac{10}{15} = 1 - \left(\frac{5}{15}\right) = 1 - p(B)$.

2. The probability that A is followed by B is the probability that A occurs times the probability that B occurs if A has occurred. This is often stated as *p(A and B) = p(A)p(B occurs if A occurred)*.

For example, the probability that the first two marbles drawn are red is $\left(\frac{10}{15}\right) \times \left(\frac{9}{14}\right)$.

3. If two outcomes cannot both occur, they are called *disjoint*. If events are disjoint, the probability that both events occur is 0. This is stated as *p(A and B) = 0 if A and B are disjoint*.

For example, the first marble picked is red and the first marble picked is blue are disjoint outcomes. However, the first marble is red and the second marble is blue are not disjoint outcomes since it is possible that the first marble is red and the second marble is blue.

4. To find the probability that at least one of two outcomes occurs add the probabilities of each outcome and then subtract the probability that both outcomes occur. You subtract the probability that both occur since any outcome that has both occurring will be counted in the probability that the first occurs and again in the probability that the second occurs. This is stated as *p(A or B) = p(A) + p(B) − p(A and B)*.

EXAMPLE 1

One marble is picked from the jar, and without replacing the first marble in the jar a second marble is picked from the jar. What is the probability that the marbles are not the same color?

This can happen two different ways: red followed by blue and blue followed by red. The probability of red followed by blue is $\left(\frac{10}{15}\right) \times \left(\frac{5}{14}\right) = \frac{5}{21}$ and the probability of blue followed by red is $\left(\frac{5}{15}\right) \times \left(\frac{10}{14}\right) = \frac{5}{21}$. So the probability that the marbles are different colors is $\left(\frac{5}{21}\right) + \left(\frac{5}{21}\right) = \frac{10}{21}$.

EXAMPLE 2

One marble is picked from the jar and without replacing the first marble in the jar a second marble is picked from the jar. What is the probability that both marbles are the same color?

You could answer this by finding the probability of red followed by red and then the probability of blue followed by blue and adding the two results. However, a much easier way is to notice that the negation of (both marbles are the same color) is when the two marbles are different colors. So the probability that the two marbles are the same color is

$$1 - \left(\frac{10}{21}\right) = \frac{11}{21}.$$

EXAMPLE 3

One marble is picked from the jar, and without replacing the first marble in the jar a second marble is picked from the jar. What is the probability that the second marble is blue?

The second marble is blue can happen in two different ways: (1) if the first marble is red and the second marble is blue or (2) if the first marble is blue and the second marble is blue.

The probability of red followed by blue is $\left(\frac{2}{3}\right) \times \left(\frac{5}{14}\right) = \frac{5}{21}$ and the probability of blue

followed by blue is $\left(\frac{1}{3}\right) \times \left(\frac{4}{14}\right) = \frac{2}{21}$. So the probability that the second marble is blue is

$$\left(\frac{5}{21}\right) + \left(\frac{2}{21}\right) = \frac{7}{21} = \frac{1}{3}.$$

EXAMPLE 4

One marble is picked from the jar, and without replacing the first marble in the jar a second marble is picked from the jar. What is the probability that at least one blue marble is picked?

Method 1 (Using property 1). The only way no blue marbles are picked is when both marbles are red. So the probability that at least one blue is picked is

$$1 - p(\text{both are red}) = 1 - \left[\left(\frac{2}{3}\right) \times \left(\frac{9}{14}\right)\right] = 1 - \left(\frac{3}{7}\right) = \frac{4}{7}.$$

Method 2 (Using property 4). Find the probability that the first marble is blue; then find the probability that the second marble is blue. If you add these two numbers, you will count the outcome blue followed by blue twice, so the correct answer is

$$p(\text{first is blue}) + p(\text{second is blue}) - p(\text{both are blue}) = \left(\frac{1}{3}\right) + \left(\frac{1}{3}\right) - \left(\frac{1}{3}\right) \times \left(\frac{4}{14}\right) =$$

$$\left(\frac{2}{3}\right) - \left(\frac{2}{21}\right) = \frac{12}{21} = \frac{4}{7}.$$

I–8. POWERS, EXPONENTS, AND ROOTS

■ I–8.1

If b is any number and n is a positive integer, b^n means the product of n factors each of which is equal to b. Thus,

$b^n = b \times b \times b \times \cdots \times b$ where there are n copies of b.

If $n = 1$, there is only one copy of b so $b^1 = b$. Here are some examples:

$$2^5 = 2 \times 2 \times 2 \times 2 \times 2 = 32, \ (-4)^3 = (-4) \times (-4) \times (-4) = -64, \ \frac{3^2}{4} = \frac{3 \times 3}{4} = \frac{9}{4},$$

$$1^n = 1 \text{ for any } n, \ 0^n = 0 \text{ for any } n.$$

b^n is read as "b raised to the nth power." b^2 is read "b squared." b^2 is always greater than 0 (positive) if b is not zero, since the product of two negative numbers is positive. b^3 is read "b cubed." b^3 can be negative or positive.

You should know the following squares and cubes:

$1^2 = 1$	$9^2 = 81$	$1^3 = 1$
$2^2 = 4$	$10^2 = 100$	$2^3 = 8$
$3^2 = 9$	$11^2 = 121$	$3^3 = 27$
$4^2 = 16$	$12^2 = 144$	$4^3 = 64$
$5^2 = 25$	$13^2 = 169$	$5^3 = 125$
$6^2 = 36$	$14^2 = 196$	
$7^2 = 49$	$15^2 = 225$	
$8^2 = 64$		

If you raise a fraction, $\frac{p}{q}$, to a power, then $\left(\frac{p}{q} \right)^n = \frac{p^n}{q^n}$. For example,

$$\left(\frac{5}{4} \right)^3 = \frac{5^3}{4^3} = \frac{125}{64}.$$

EXAMPLE

If the value of an investment triples each year, what percent of its value today will the investment be worth in 4 years?

The value increases by a factor of 3 each year. Since the time is 4 years, there will be four factors of 3. So the investment will be worth $3 \times 3 \times 3 \times 3 = 3^4$ as much as it is today. $3^4 = 81$, so the investment will be worth 8,100% of its value today in four years.

■ I–8.2

Exponents

In the expression b^n, b is called the *base* and n is called the *exponent*. In the expression 2^5, 2 is the base and 5 is the exponent. The exponent tells how many factors there are.

> The three basic formulas for problems involving exponents are:
>
> (A) $b^n \times b^m = b^{n+m}$
>
> (B) $a^n \times b^n = (a \cdot b)^n$
>
> (C) If $a^x = a^y$, then $x = y$, provided a is not 1
>
> (A) and (B) are called *laws of exponents*.

EXAMPLE 1

What is 6^3?

$$\text{Since } 6 = 3 \times 2, 6^3 = 3^3 \times 2^3 = 27 \times 8 = 216.$$
$$\text{or}$$
$$6^3 = 6 \times 6 \times 6 = 216.$$

EXAMPLE 2

Find the value of $2^3 \times 2^2$.

Using (A), $2^3 \times 2^2 = 2^{(2+3)} = 2^5$ which is 32. You can check this, since $2^3 = 8$ and $2^2 = 4$; $2^3 \times 2^2 = 8 \times 4 = 32$.

■ I–8.3

Negative Exponents

$b^0 = 1$ *for any nonzero number b.* If we want (A) to hold, then $b^n \times b^0$ should be b^{n+0} which is b^n. So b^0 must be 1. For example, $3^0 = 1$. (NOTE: 0^0 is not defined.)

Using the law of exponents once more, you can define b^{-n} where n is a positive number. If (A) holds, $b^{-n} \times b^n = b^{-n+n} = b^0 = 1$, so $b^{-n} = \dfrac{1}{b^n}$. *Multiplying by b^{-n} is the same as dividing by b^n.*

EXAMPLE 1

$$2^{-3} = \frac{1}{2^3} = \frac{1}{8}$$

EXAMPLE 2

$$\left(\frac{1}{2}\right)^{-1} = \frac{1}{\frac{1}{2}} = 2$$

EXAMPLE 3

Find the value of $\dfrac{6^4}{3^3}$.

$$\frac{6^4}{3^3} = \frac{(3 \cdot 2)^4}{3^3} = \frac{3^4 \cdot 2^4}{3^3} = 3^4 \times 2^4 \times 3^{-3} = 3^4 \times 3^{-3} \times 2^4 = 3^1 \times 2^4 = 48.$$

■ I–8.4

Roots

If you raise a number d to the nth power and the result is b, then d is called the nth root of b, which is usually written $\sqrt[n]{b} = d$. Since $2^5 = 32$, then $\sqrt[5]{32} = 2$. The second root is called the square root and is written $\sqrt{}$; the third root is called the cube root. If you read the columns of the table in Section I–8.1 from right to left, you have a table of square roots and cube roots. For example, $\sqrt{225} = 15$; $\sqrt{81} = 9$; $\sqrt[3]{64} = 4$.

There are two possibilities for the square root of a positive number; the positive one is called the square root. Thus, we say $\sqrt{9} = 3$ although $(-3) \times (-3) = 9$.

Since the square of any nonzero number is positive, *the square root of a negative number is not defined as a real number*. Thus $\sqrt{-2}$ is not a real number. There are cube roots of negative numbers. $\sqrt[3]{-8} = -2$, because $(-2) \times (-2) \times (-2) = -8$.

You can also write roots as exponents; for example,

$$\sqrt[n]{b} = b^{\frac{1}{n}} \text{ ; so } \sqrt{b} = b^{\frac{1}{2}} \text{ , } \sqrt[3]{b} = b^{\frac{1}{3}}.$$

Since you can write roots as exponents, formula (B) under Section I–8.2 is especially useful.

$$a^{\frac{1}{n}} \times b^{\frac{1}{n}} = (a \times b)^{\frac{1}{n}} \text{ or } \sqrt[n]{a \times b} = \sqrt[n]{a} \times \sqrt[n]{b}$$

This formula is the basic formula for simplifying square roots, cube roots, and so on. *On the test you must state your answer in a form that matches one of the choices given.*

EXAMPLE 1

$\sqrt{54} = ?$

Since $54 = 9 \times 6$, $\sqrt{54} = \sqrt{9 \times 6} = \sqrt{9} \times \sqrt{6}$. Since $\sqrt{9} = 3$, $\sqrt{54} = 3\sqrt{6}$.

You cannot simplify by adding square roots unless you are taking square roots of the same number. For example,

$$\sqrt{3} + 2\sqrt{3} - 4\sqrt{3} = -\sqrt{3}, \text{ but } \sqrt{3} + \sqrt{2} \text{ is not equal to } \sqrt{5}.$$

EXAMPLE 2

Simplify $6\sqrt{12} + 2\sqrt{75} - 3\sqrt{98}$.

Since $12 = 4 \times 3$, $\sqrt{12} = \sqrt{4 \times 3} = \sqrt{4} \times \sqrt{3} = 2\sqrt{3}$;

$75 = 25 \times 3$, so $\sqrt{75} = \sqrt{25} \times \sqrt{3} = 5\sqrt{3}$; and $98 = 49 \times 2$, so $\sqrt{98} = \sqrt{49} \times \sqrt{2} = 7\sqrt{2}$.

Therefore, $6\sqrt{12} + 2\sqrt{75} - 3\sqrt{98} = 6 \times 2\sqrt{3} + 2 \times 5\sqrt{3} - 3 \times 7\sqrt{2}$

$= 12\sqrt{3} + 10\sqrt{3} - 21\sqrt{2} = 22\sqrt{3} - 21\sqrt{2}$.

EXAMPLE 3

Simplify $27^{\frac{1}{3}} \times 8^{\frac{1}{3}}$.

$27^{\frac{1}{3}} = \sqrt[3]{27} = 3$ and $8^{\frac{1}{3}} = 2$, so $27^{\frac{1}{3}} \times 8^{\frac{1}{3}} = 3 \times 2 = 6$.

Notice that 6 is $\sqrt[3]{216}$ and $27^{\frac{1}{3}} \times 8^{\frac{1}{3}} = (27 \times 8)^{\frac{1}{3}} = 216^{\frac{1}{3}}$.

II. Algebra

II–1. ALGEBRAIC EXPRESSIONS

■ II–1.1

Often it is necessary to deal with quantities that have a numerical value that is unknown. For example, we may know that Tom's salary is twice as much as Joe's salary. If we let the value of Tom's salary be called T and the value of Joe's salary be J, then T and J are numbers that are unknown. However, we do know that the value of T must be twice the value of J, or $T = 2J$.

T and $2J$ are examples of algebraic expressions. An algebraic expression may involve letters in addition to numbers and symbols; however, *in an algebraic expression a letter always stands for a number.* Therefore, you can multiply, divide, add, subtract, and perform other mathematical operations on a letter. Thus, x^2 would mean x times x. Some examples of algebraic expressions are: $2x + y$, $y^3 + 9y$, $z^3 - 5ab$, $c + d + 4$, $5x + 2y(6x - 4y + z)$. When letters or numbers are written together without any sign or symbol between them, multiplication is assumed. Thus, $6xy$ means 6 times x times y. $6xy$ is called a term; terms are separated by + or − signs. The expression $5z + 2 + 4x^2$ has three terms, $5z$, 2, and $4x^2$. Terms are often called monomials (mono = one). If an expression has more than one term, it is called a *polynomial* (poly = many). The letters in an algebraic expression are called *variables* or *unknowns*. When a variable is multiplied by a number, the number is called the *coefficient* of the variable. So, in the expression $5x^2 + 2yz$, the coefficient of x^2 is 5, and the coefficient of yz is 2.

■ II–1.2

Simplifying Algebraic Expressions

Since there are only five choices of an answer given for the test questions, you must be able to recognize algebraic expressions that are equal. It will also save time when you are working problems if you can change a complicated expression into a simpler one.

Case I. Simplifying expressions which don't contain parentheses:

Ⓐ Perform any multiplications or divisions before performing additions or subtractions. Thus, the expression $6x + y \div x$ means add $6x$ to the quotient of y divided by x. Another way of writing the expression would be $6x + \dfrac{y}{x}$. This is not the same as $\dfrac{6x + y}{x}$.

Ⓑ The order in which you multiply numbers and letters in a term does not matter. So, $6xy$ is the same as $6yx$.

Ⓒ The order in which you add terms does not matter; for instance, $6x + 2y - x = 6x - x + 2y$.

Ⓓ If there are roots or powers in any terms, you may be able to simplify the term by using the laws of exponents. For example, $5xy \cdot 3x^2y = 15x^3y^2$.

Ⓔ Combine like terms. *Like terms* (or similar terms) are terms that have exactly the same letters raised to the same powers. So x, $-2x$, $\dfrac{1}{3}x$ are like terms. For example, $6x - 2x + x + y$ is equal to $5x + y$. In combining like terms, you simply add or subtract the coefficients of the like terms, and the result is the coefficient of that term in the simplified expression. In the example given, the coefficients of x were + 6, −2, and +1; since $6 - 2 + 1 = 5$ the coefficient of x in the simplified expression is 5.

Ⓕ Algebraic expressions that involve divisions or factors can be simplified by using the techniques for handling fractions and the laws of exponents. Remember dividing by b^n is the same as multiplying by b^{-n}.

EXAMPLE 1

$3x^2 - 4\sqrt{x} + \sqrt{4x} + xy + 7x^2 = ?$

D $\sqrt{4x} = \sqrt{4}\sqrt{x} = 2\sqrt{x}$.

E $3x^2 + 7x^2 = 10x^2, -4\sqrt{x} + 2\sqrt{x} = -2\sqrt{x}$.

The original expression equals $3x^2 + 7x^2 - 4\sqrt{x} + 2\sqrt{x} + xy$. Therefore, the simplified expression is $10x^2 - 2\sqrt{x} + xy$.

EXAMPLE 2

Simplify $\dfrac{21x^4y^2}{3x^6y}$.

F $\dfrac{21}{3}x^4y^2x^{-6}y^{-1}$.

B $7x^4x^{-6}y^2y^{-1}$.

D $7x^{-2}y$, so the simplified term is $\dfrac{7y}{x^2}$.

EXAMPLE 3

Write $\dfrac{2x}{y} - \dfrac{4}{x}$ as a single fraction.

F A common denominator is xy so $\dfrac{2x}{y} = \dfrac{2x \cdot x}{y \cdot x} = \dfrac{2x^2}{xy}$, and $\dfrac{4}{x} = \dfrac{4y}{xy}$.

Therefore, $\dfrac{2x}{y} - \dfrac{4}{x} = \dfrac{2x^2}{xy} - \dfrac{4y}{xy} = \dfrac{2x^2 - 4y}{xy}$.

Case II. Simplifying expressions that have parentheses:

The first rule is to perform the operations inside parentheses first. So $(6x + y) \div x$ means divide the sum of $6x$ and y by x. Notice that $(6x + y) \div x$ is different from $6x + y \div x$.

The main rule for getting rid of parentheses is the distributive law, which is expressed as $a(b + c) = ab + ac$. In other words, if any monomial is followed by an expression contained in a parenthesis, then *each* term of the expression is multiplied by the monomial. Once we have gotten rid of the parentheses, we proceed as we did in Case I.

> If an expression has more than one set of parentheses, remove the *inner parentheses first* and then work *out* through the rest of the parentheses.

EXAMPLE 4

$2x(6x - 4y + 2) = (2x)(6x) + (2x)(-4y) + (2x)(2) = 12x^2 - 8xy + 4x.$

EXAMPLE 5

$2x - (x + 6(x - 3y) + 4y) = ?$

To remove the inner parentheses we multiply $6(x - 3y)$ getting $6x - 18y$. Now we have $2x - (x + 6x - 18y + 4y)$ which equals $2x - (7x - 14y)$. Distribute the minus sign (multiply by -1), getting $2x - 7x - (-14y) = -5x + 14y$. Sometimes brackets are used instead of parentheses.

EXAMPLE 6

Simplify $-3x \left[\dfrac{1}{2}(3x - 2y) - 2(x(3 + y) + 4y) \right]$

$= -3x \left[\dfrac{1}{2}(3x - 2y) - 2(3x + xy + 4y) \right]$

$= -3x \left[\dfrac{3}{2}x - y - 6x - 2xy - 8y \right]$

$= -3x \left[-\dfrac{9}{2}x - 2xy - 9y \right]$

$= \dfrac{27}{2}x^2 + 6x^2y + 27xy.$

■ **II–1.3**

Adding and Subtracting Algebraic Expressions

Since algebraic expressions are numbers, they can be added and subtracted.

> The only algebraic terms that can be combined are like terms.

EXAMPLE 1

$(3x + 4y - xy^2) + (3x + 2x(x - y)) = ?$

The expression $= (3x + 4y - xy^2) + (3x + 2x^2 - 2xy)$, removing the inner parentheses;

$= 6x + 4y + 2x^2 - xy^2 - 2xy$, combining like terms.

EXAMPLE 2

$(2a + 3a^2 - 4) - 2(4a^2 - 2(a + 4)) = ?$

It equals $(2a + 3a^2 - 4) - 2(4a^2 - 2a - 8)$, removing inner parentheses;

$= 2a + 3a^2 - 4 - 8a^2 + 4a + 16$, removing outer parentheses;

$= -5a^2 + 6a + 12$, combining like terms.

■ II–1.4

Multiplying Algebraic Expressions

When you multiply two expressions, you multiply *each term of the first by each term of the second.*

EXAMPLE 1

$(b - 4)(b + a) = b(b + a) - 4(b + a) = ?$

$= b^2 + ab - 4b - 4a.$

EXAMPLE 2

$(2h - 4)(h + 2h^2 + h^3) = ?$

$= 2h(h + 2h^2 + h^3) - 4(h + 2h^2 + h^3)$

$= 2h^2 + 4h^3 + 2h^4 - 4h - 8h^2 - 4h^3$

$= -4h - 6h^2 + 2h^4$, which is the product.

If you need to multiply more than two expressions, multiply the first two expressions, then multiply the result by the third expression, and so on until you have used each factor. Since algebraic expressions can be multiplied, they can be squared, cubed, or raised to other powers.

EXAMPLE 3

$(x - 2y)^3 = (x - 2y)(x - 2y)(x - 2y)$.

Since $(x - 2y)(x - 2y)$

$$= x^2 - 2yx - 2yx + 4y^2$$

$$= x^2 - 4xy + 4y^2,$$

$(x - 2y)^3 = (x^2 - 4xy + 4y^2)(x - 2y)$

$$= x(x^2 - 4xy + 4y^2) - 2y(x^2 - 4xy + 4y^2)$$

$$= x^3 - 4x^2y + 4xy^2 - 2x^2y + 8xy^2 - 8y^3$$

$$= x^3 - 6x^2y + 12xy^2 - 8y^3.$$

The order in which you multiply algebraic expressions does not matter. Thus, $(2a + b)(x^2 + 2x) = (x^2 + 2x)(2a + b)$.

EXAMPLE 4

If a and b are two-digit numbers, and the last digit of a is 7 and the last digit of b is 8, what is the last digit of a times b?

The key to problems such as this is to think of a number in terms of its digits. So a must be written as $x7$, where x is a digit. This means $a = 10x + 7$. In the same way $b = 10y + 8$ for some digit y. So a times b is $(10x + 7)(10y + 8)$, which is $100xy + 80x + 70y + 56$. The digits x and y all are multiplied by 10 or 100 so they will not affect the units place. The only term that will affect the units place is 56. So the units digit or last digit of a times b is 6. This pattern works all the time and can be expressed by the following rule: the last digit of the product of two numbers is the last digit of the product of the last digits of the two numbers. For example, the last digit of 136 times 157 is 2 because the last digit of 6 times 7 is 2.

◼ II–1.5

Factoring Algebraic Expressions

If an algebraic expression is the product of other algebraic expressions, then the expressions are called factors of the original expression. For instance, we claim that $(2h - 4)$ and $(h + 2h^2 + h^3)$ are factors of $- 4h - 6h^2 + 2h^4$. We can always check to see if we have the correct factors by multiplying; so by example 2 above we see that our claim is correct. We need to be able to factor algebraic expressions in order to solve quadratic equations. It also can be helpful in dividing algebraic expressions.

First remove any monomial factor that appears in every term of the expression.

Some examples:

$3x + 3y = 3(x + y)$: 3 is a monomial factor.

$15a^2b + 10ab = 5ab(3a + 2)$: $5ab$ is a monomial factor.

$\frac{1}{2}hy - 3h^3 + 4hy = h\left(\frac{1}{2}y - 3h^2 + 4y\right), = h\left(\frac{9}{2}y - 3h^2\right)$: h is a monomial factor.

You may also need to factor expressions that contain squares or higher powers into factors that only contain linear terms. (Linear terms are terms in which variables are raised only to the first power.) The first rule to remember is that since $(a + b)(a - b) = a^2 + ba - ba - b^2 = a^2 - b^2$, the difference of two squares can always be factored.

EXAMPLE 1

Factor $(9m^2 - 16)$.

$9m^2 = (3m)^2$ and $16 = 4^2$, so the factors are $(3m - 4)(3m + 4)$.

Since $(3m - 4)(3m + 4) = 9m^2 - 16$, these factors are correct.

EXAMPLE 2

Factor $x^4y^4 - 4x^2$.

$x^4y^4 = (x^2y^2)^2$ and $4x^2 = (2x)^2$, so the factors are $x^2y^2 + 2x$ and $x^2y^2 - 2x$.

You also may need to factor expressions that contain squared terms and linear terms, such as $x^2 + 4x + 3$. The factors will be of the form $(x + a)$ and $(x + b)$. Since $(x + a)(x + b) = x^2 + (a + b)x + ab$, you must look for a pair of numbers a and b such that $a \bullet b$ is the numerical term in the expression and $a + b$ is the coefficient of the linear term (the term with exponent 1).

EXAMPLE 3

Factor $x^2 + 4x + 3$.

You want numbers whose product is 3 and whose sum is 4. Look at the possible factors of 3 and check whether they add up to 4. Since $3 = 3 \times 1$ and $3 + 1$ is 4, the factors are $(x + 3)$ and $(x + 1)$. Remember to check by multiplying.

EXAMPLE 4

Factor $y^2 + y - 6$.

Since -6 is negative, the two numbers a and b must be of opposite sign. Possible pairs of factors for -6 are -6 and $+1$, 6 and -1, 3 and -2, and -3 and 2. Since $-2 + 3 = 1$, the factors are $(y + 3)$ and $(y - 2)$. So $(y + 3)(y - 2) = y^2 + y - 6$.

EXAMPLE 5

Factor $a^3 + 4a^2 + 4a$.

Factor out a, so $a^3 + 4a^2 + 4a = a(a^2 + 4a + 4)$. Consider $a^2 + 4a + 4$; since $2 + 2 = 4$ and $2 \times 2 = 4$, the factors are $(a + 2)$ and $(a + 2)$. Therefore, $a^3 + 4a^2 + 4a = a(a + 2)^2$.

If the term with the highest exponent has a coefficient unequal to 1, divide the entire expression by that coefficient. For example, to factor $3a^3 + 12a^2 + 12a$, factor out a 3 from each term, and the result is $a^3 + 4a^2 + 4a$ which is $a(a + 2)^2$. Thus, $3a^3 + 12a^2 + 12a = 3a(a + 2)^2$.

There are some expressions that cannot be factored, for example, $x^2 + 4x + 6$. In general, if you can't factor something by using the methods given above, don't waste a lot of time on the question. Sometimes you may be able to check the answers given to find out what the correct factors are.

■ II–1.6

Division of Algebraic Expressions

The main things to remember in division are:

1. When you divide a sum, you can get the same result by dividing each term and adding quotients. For example, $\dfrac{9x + 4xy + y^2}{x} = \dfrac{9x}{x} + \dfrac{4xy}{x} + \dfrac{y^2}{x} = 9 + 4y + \dfrac{y^2}{x}$.

2. You can cancel common factors, so the results on factoring will be helpful. For example,
$\dfrac{x^2 - 2x}{x - 2} = \dfrac{x(x - 2)}{x - 2} = x$.

EXAMPLE 1

$\dfrac{2x + 2y + x^2 - y^2}{x + y} = ?$

$$\dfrac{2x + 2y + x^2 - y^2}{x + y} = \dfrac{2x + 2y}{x + y} + \dfrac{x^2 - y^2}{x + y}$$

$$= \dfrac{2(x + y)}{x + y} + \dfrac{(x - y)(x + y)}{x + y}$$

$$= 2 + x - y$$

You can also divide one algebraic expression by another using long division.

EXAMPLE 2

$(15x^2 + 2x - 4) \div (3x - 1) = ?$

$$
\begin{array}{r}
5x + 2 \\
3x - 1{\overline{\smash{\big)}\,15x^2 + 2x - 4}} \\
\underline{15x^2 - 5x} \\
7x - 4 \\
\underline{6x - 2} \\
x - 2
\end{array}
$$

So, the answer is $5x + 2$ with a remainder of $x - 2$. You can check by multiplying,

$$(5x + 2)(3x - 1) = 15x^2 + 6x - 5x - 2$$

$$= 15x^2 + x - 2;$$

now add the remainder $x - 2$ and the result is $15x^2 + x - 2 + x - 2 = 15x^2 + 2x - 4$.

Division problems where you need to use (1) and (2) are more likely than problems involving long division.

II–2. EQUATIONS

■ II–2.1

An *equation* is a statement that says two algebraic expressions are equal. $x + 2 = 3$, $4 + 2 = 6$, $3x^2 + 2x - 6 = 0$, $x^2 + y^2 = z^2$, $\frac{y}{x} = 2 + z$, and $A = LW$ are all examples of equations. We will refer to the algebraic expressions on each side of the equals sign as the left side and the right side of the equation. Thus, in the equation $2x + 4 = 6y + x$, $2x + 4$ is the left side and $6y + x$ is the right side.

■ II–2.2

If we assign specific numbers to each variable or unknown in an algebraic expression, then the algebraic expression will be equal to a number. This is called *evaluating* the expression. For example, if you evaluate $2x + 4y^2 + 3$ for $x = -1$ and $y = 2$, the expression is equal to $2(-1) + 4 \cdot 2^2 + 3 = -2 + 4 \cdot 4 + 3 = 17$.

If we evaluate each side of an equation and the number obtained is the same for each side of the equation, then the specific values assigned to the unknowns are called a *solution of the equation*. Another way of saying this is that the choices for the unknowns satisfy the equation.

EXAMPLE 1

Consider the equation $2x + 3 = 9$.

If $x = 3$, then the left side of the equation becomes $2 \cdot 3 + 3 = 6 + 3 = 9$, so both sides equal 9, and $x = 3$ is a solution of $2x + 3 = 9$. If $x = 4$, then the left side is $2 \cdot 4 + 3 = 11$. Since 11 is not equal to 9, $x = 4$ is not a solution of $2x + 3 = 9$.

EXAMPLE 2

Consider the equation $x^2 + y^2 = 5x$.

If $x = 1$ and $y = 2$, then the left side is $1^2 + 2^2$ which equals $1 + 4 = 5$. The right side is $5 \cdot 1 = 5$; since both sides are equal to 5, $x = 1$ and $y = 2$ is a solution.

If $x = 5$ and $y = 0$, then the left side is $5^2 + 0^2 = 25$ and the right side is $5 \cdot 5 = 25$, so $x = 5$ and $y = 0$ is also a solution.

If $x = 1$ and $y = 1$, then the left side is $1^2 + 1^2 = 2$ and the right side is $5 \cdot 1 = 5$. Therefore, since $2 \neq 5$, $x = 1$ and $y = 1$ is not a solution.

There are some equations that *do not have any solutions that are real numbers*. Since the square of any real number is positive or zero, the equation $x^2 = -4$ does not have any solutions that are real numbers.

■ II–2.3

Equivalence

One equation is *equivalent* to another equation, if they have exactly the same solutions. The basic idea in solving equations is to transform a given equation into an equivalent equation whose solutions are obvious.

> The two main rules for solving equations are:
>
> **A** If you add or subtract the same algebraic expression to or from *each side* of an equation, the resulting equation is equivalent to the original equation.
>
> **B** If you multiply or divide both sides of an equation by the same *nonzero* algebraic expression, the resulting equation is equivalent to the original equation.

The most common type of equation is the linear equation with only one unknown. $6z = 4z - 3$, $3 + a = 2a - 4$, $3b + 2b = b - 4b$, are all examples of linear equations with only one unknown.

Using (A) and (B), you can solve a linear equation in one unknown in the following way:

1. Group all the terms that involve the unknown on one side of the equation and all the terms that are purely numerical on the other side of the equation. This is called *isolating the unknown*.
2. Combine the terms on each side.
3. Divide each side by the coefficient of the unknown.

EXAMPLE 1

Solve $6x + 2 = 3$ for x.

1. Using (A) subtract 2 from each side of the equation. Then $6x + 2 - 2 = 3 - 2$ or $6x = 3 - 2$.

2. $6x = 1$.

3. Divide each side by 6. Therefore, $x = \dfrac{1}{6}$.

You should always check your answer in the original equation.

CHECK: Since $6\left(\dfrac{1}{6}\right) + 2 = 1 + 2 = 3$, $x = \dfrac{1}{6}$ is the solution.

EXAMPLE 2

Solve $3x + 15 = 3 - 4x$ for x.

1. Add $4x$ to each side and subtract 15 from each side; $3x + 15 - 15 + 4x = 3 - 15 - 4x + 4x$.

2. $7x = -12$.

3. Divide each side by 7, so $x = \dfrac{-12}{7}$ is the solution.

CHECK: $3\left(\dfrac{-12}{7}\right) + 15 = \dfrac{-36}{7} + 15 = \dfrac{69}{7}$ and $3 - 4\left(\dfrac{-12}{7}\right) = 3 + \dfrac{48}{7} = \dfrac{69}{7}$.

If you do the same thing to each side of an equation, the result is still an equation but it may not be equivalent to the original equation. Be especially careful if you square each side of an equation. For example, $x = -4$ is an equation; square both sides and you get $x^2 = 16$ which has both $x = 4$ and $x = -4$ as solutions. *Always check your answer in the original equation.*

If the equation you want to solve involves square roots, get rid of the square roots by squaring each side of the equation. Remember to check your answer since squaring each side does not always give an equivalent equation.

EXAMPLE 3

Solve $\sqrt{4x+3} = 5$.

Square both sides: $\left(\sqrt{4x+3}\right)^2 = 4x + 3$ and $5^2 = 25$, so the new equation is $4x + 3 = 25$. Subtract 3 from each side to get $4x = 22$ and now divide each side by 4. The solution is

$x = \dfrac{22}{4} = 5.5$. Since $4(5.5) + 3 = 25$ and $\sqrt{25} = 5$, $x = 5.5$ is a solution to the equation

$\sqrt{4x+3} = 5$.

If an equation involves fractions, multiply through by a common denominator and then solve. Check your answer to make sure you did not multiply or divide by zero.

EXAMPLE 4

Solve $\dfrac{3}{a} = 9$ for a.

Multiply each side by a: the result is $3 = 9a$. Divide each side by 9, and you obtain $\dfrac{3}{9} = a$ or $a = \dfrac{1}{3}$. Since $\dfrac{3}{\frac{1}{3}} = 3 \cdot 3 = 9$, $a = \dfrac{1}{3}$ is a solution.

■ II–2.4

Solving Two Equations in Two Unknowns

You may be asked to solve two equations in two unknowns. Use one equation to solve for one unknown in terms of the other; now change the second equation into an equation in only one unknown which can be solved by the methods of the preceding section.

EXAMPLE 1

Solve for x and y: $\begin{cases} \dfrac{x}{y} = 3 \\ 2x + 4y = 20. \end{cases}$

The first equation gives $x = 3y$. Using $x = 3y$, the second equation is $2(3y) + 4y = 6y + 4y$ or $10y = 20$, so $y = \dfrac{20}{10} = 2$. Since $x = 3y$, $x = 6$.

CHECK: $\dfrac{6}{2} = 3$, and $2 \cdot 6 + 4 \cdot 2 = 20$, so $x = 6$ and $y = 2$ is a solution.

EXAMPLE 2

If $2x + y = 5$ and $x + y = 4$, find x and y.

Since $x + y = 4$, $y = 4 - x$, so $2x + y = 2x + 4 - x = x + 4 = 5$ and $x = 1$. If $x = 1$, then $y = 4 - 1 = 3$. So, $x = 1$ and $y = 3$ is the solution.

CHECK: $2 \cdot 1 + 3 = 5$ and $1 + 3 = 4$.

Sometimes we can solve two equations by adding them or by subtracting one from the other. If we subtract $x + y = 4$ from $2x + y = 5$ in example 2, we have $x = 1$. However, the previous method will work in cases when the addition method does not work.

■ II–2.5

Solving Quadratic Equations

If the terms of an equation contain squares of the unknown as well as linear terms, the equation is called *quadratic*. Some examples of quadratic equations are $x^2 + 4x = 3$, $2z^2 - 1 = 3z^2 - 2z$, and $a + 6 = a^2 + 6$.

To solve a quadratic equation:

Ⓐ Group all the terms on one side of the equation so that the other side is *zero*.

Ⓑ Combine the terms on the nonzero side.

Ⓒ Factor the expression into linear expressions.

Ⓓ Set the linear factors equal to zero and solve.

The method depends on the fact that if a product of expressions is zero then at least one of the expressions must be zero.

EXAMPLE 1

Solve $x^2 + 4x = -3$.

(A) $x^2 + 4x + 3 = 0$

(C) $x^2 + 4x + 3 = (x + 3)(x + 1) = 0$

(D)   So $x + 3 = 0$ or $x + 1 = 0$. Therefore, the solutions are $x = -3$ and $x = -1$.

CHECK: $(-3)^2 + 4(-3) = 9 - 12 = -3$

         $(-1)^2 + 4(-1) = 1 - 4 = -3$, so $x = -3$ and $x = -1$ are solutions.

A quadratic equation will usually have 2 different solutions, but it is possible for a quadratic to have only one solution or even no real solution.

EXAMPLE 2

If $2z^2 - 1 = 3z^2 - 2z$, what is z?

(A) $0 = 3z^2 - 2z^2 - 2z + 1$

(B) $z^2 - 2z + 1 = 0$

(C) $z^2 - 2z + 1 = (z - 1)^2 = 0$

(D) $z - 1 = 0$ or $z = 1$

CHECK: $2 \cdot 1^2 - 1 = 2 - 1 = 1$ and $3 \cdot 1^2 - 2 \cdot 1 = 3 - 2 = 1$, so $z = 1$ is a solution.

Equations that may not look like quadratics may be changed into quadratics.

EXAMPLE 3

Find a if $a - 3 = \dfrac{10}{a}$.

Multiply each side of the equation by a to obtain $a^2 - 3a = 10$, which is quadratic.

(A) $a^2 - 3a - 10 = 0$

(C) $a^2 - 3a - 10 = (a - 5)(a + 2)$

(D)   So $a - 5 = 0$ or $a + 2 = 0$

   Therefore, $a = 5$ and $a = -2$ are the solutions.

CHECK: $5 - 3 = 2 = \dfrac{10}{5}$ so $a = 5$ is a solution. $-2 - 3 = -5 = \dfrac{10}{-2}$ so $a = -2$ is a solution.

You can also solve quadratic equations by using the *quadratic formula*. The quadratic formula states that the solutions of the quadratic equation

$$ax^2 + bx + c = 0 \text{ are } x = \frac{1}{2a}\left[-b + \sqrt{b^2 - 4ac}\right] \text{ and } x = \frac{1}{2a}\left[-b - \sqrt{b^2 - 4ac}\right]$$

This is usually written $x = \frac{1}{2a}\left[-b \pm \sqrt{b^2 - 4ac}\right]$

Use of the quadratic formula would replace steps (C) and (D).

EXAMPLE 4

Find x if $x^2 + 5x = 12 - x^2$.

Ⓐ $x^2 + 5x + x^2 - 12 = 0$

Ⓑ $2x^2 + 5x - 12 = 0$

So $a = 2$, $b = 5$ and $c = -12$. Therefore, using the quadratic formula, the solutions are

$$\frac{1}{4}\left[-5 \pm \sqrt{25 - 4 \cdot 2 \cdot (-12)}\right] = \frac{1}{4}\left[-5 \pm \sqrt{25 + 96}\right] = \frac{1}{4}\left[-5 \pm \sqrt{121}\right].$$

So, we have $x = \frac{1}{4}[-5 \pm 11]$. The solutions are $x = \frac{3}{2}$ and $x = -4$.

CHECK: $\left(\frac{3}{2}\right)^2 + 5 \cdot \frac{3}{2} = \frac{9}{4} + \frac{15}{2} = \frac{39}{4} = 12 - \frac{9}{4} = 12 - \left(\frac{3}{2}\right)^2 \quad (-4)^2 + 5(-4) = 16 - 20 = -4 = 12 - 16 =$

$12 - (-4)^2$

NOTE: If $b^2 - 4ac$ is negative, then the quadratic equation $ax^2 + bx + c = 0$ has no real solutions because negative numbers do not have real square roots.

The quadratic formula will always give you the solutions to a quadratic equation. If you can factor the equation, factoring will usually give you the solution in less time. Remember, you want to answer as many questions as you can in the time given. So factor if you can. If you don't see the factor immediately, then use the formula.

II-3. WORD PROBLEMS

■ II–3.1

The general method for solving word problems is to translate them into algebraic problems. The quantities you are seeking are the unknowns, which are usually represented by letters. The information you are given in the problem is then turned into equations. Words such as "is," "was," "are," and "were" mean equals, and words like "of" and "as much as" mean multiplication.

EXAMPLE 1

A coat was sold for $75. The coat was sold for 150% of the cost of the coat. How much did the coat cost?

You want to find the cost of the coat. Let C be the cost of the coat. You know that the coat was sold for $75 and that $75 was 150% of the cost. So $75 = 150% of $C or $75 = 1.5C$.

Solving for C you get $C = \dfrac{75}{1.5} = 50$, so the coat cost $50.

CHECK: $(1.5)\$50 = \$75$.

EXAMPLE 2

Tom's salary is 125% of Joe's salary; Mary's salary is 80% of Joe's salary. The total of all three salaries is $61,000. What is Mary's salary?

Let M = Mary's salary, J = Joe's salary and T = Tom's salary. The first sentence says $T = 125\%$ of J or $T = \dfrac{5}{4}J$, and M = 80% of J or $M = \dfrac{4}{5}J$. The second sentence says that $T + M + J = \$61,000$.

Using the information from the first sentence, $T + M + J = \dfrac{5}{4}J + \dfrac{4}{5}J + J = \dfrac{25}{20}J + \dfrac{16}{20}J + J = \dfrac{61}{20}J$.

So, $\dfrac{61}{20}J = 61,000$; solving for J you have $J = \dfrac{20}{61} \times 61,000 = 20,000$.

Therefore, $T = \dfrac{5}{4} \times \$20,000 = \$25,000$ and $M = \dfrac{4}{5} \times \$20,000 = \$16,000$.

CHECK: $\$25,000 + \$16,000 + \$20,000 = \$61,000$. So Mary's salary is $16,000.

EXAMPLE 3

Steve weighs 25 pounds more than Jim. The combined weight of Jim and Steve is 325 pounds. How much does Jim weigh?

Let S = Steve's weight in pounds and J = Jim's weight in pounds. The first sentence says $S = J + 25$, and the second sentence becomes $S + J = 325$. Since $S = J + 25$, $S + J = 325$ becomes $(J + 25) + J = 2J + 25 = 325$. So $2J = 300$ and $J = 150$. Therefore, Jim weighs 150 pounds.

CHECK: If Jim weighs 150 pounds, then Steve weighs 175 pounds and $150 + 175 = 325$.

EXAMPLE 4

A carpenter is designing a closet. The floor will be in the shape of a rectangle whose length is 2 feet more than its width. How long should the closet be if the carpenter wants the area of the floor to be 15 square feet?

The area of a rectangle is length times width, usually written $A = LW$, where A is the area, L is the length, and W is the width. We know $A = 15$ and $L = 2 + W$. Therefore, $LW = (2 + W)W = W^2 + 2W$; this must equal 15. So we need to solve $W^2 + 2W = 15$ or $W^2 + 2W - 15 = 0$. Since $W^2 + 2W - 15$ factors into $(W + 5)(W - 3)$, the only possible solutions are $W = -5$ and $W = 3$. Since W represents a width, -5 cannot be the answer; therefore the width is 3 feet. The length is the width plus two feet, so the length is 5 feet. Since $5 \times 3 = 15$, the answer checks.

■ II–3.2

Distance Problems

A common type of word problem is a distance or velocity problem. The basic formula is:

$$\text{DISTANCE TRAVELED} = \text{RATE} \times \text{TIME}$$

The formula is abbreviated $d = rt$.

EXAMPLE 1

A train travels at an average speed of 50 miles per hour for $2\frac{1}{2}$ hours and then travels at a speed of 70 miles per hour for $1\frac{1}{2}$ hours. How far did the train travel in the entire 4 hours?

The train traveled for $2\frac{1}{2}$ hours at an average speed of 50 miles per hour, so it traveled $50 \times \frac{5}{2} = 125$ miles in the first $2\frac{1}{2}$ hours. Traveling at a speed of 70 miles per hour for $1\frac{1}{2}$ hours, the distance traveled will be equal to $r \times t$ where $r = 70$ m.p.h. and $t = 1\frac{1}{2}$, so the distance is $70 \times \frac{3}{2} = 105$ miles. Therefore, the total distance traveled is $125 + 105 = 230$ miles.

EXAMPLE 2

The distance from Cleveland to Buffalo is 200 miles. A train takes $3\frac{1}{2}$ hours to go from Buffalo to Cleveland and $4\frac{1}{2}$ hours to go back from Cleveland to Buffalo. What was the average speed of the train for the round trip from Buffalo to Cleveland and back?

The train took $3\frac{1}{2} + 4\frac{1}{2} = 8$ hours for the trip. The distance of a round trip is $2(200) = 400$ miles. Since $d = rt$ then 400 miles $= r \times 8$ hours. Solve for r and you have $r = \dfrac{400 \text{ miles}}{8 \text{ hours}} = 50$ miles per hour. Therefore, the average speed is 50 miles per hour.

The speed in the formula is the average speed. If you know that there are different speeds for different lengths of time, then you must use the formula more than once, as we did in example 1.

■ II–3.3

Work Problems

In this type of problem you can always assume all workers in the same category work at the same rate. The main idea is: If it takes k workers 1 hour to do a job, then *each worker does $\frac{1}{k}$ of the job in an hour* or works at the rate of $\frac{1}{k}$ of the job per hour. If it takes m workers h hours to finish a job, then each worker does $\frac{1}{m}$ of the job in h hours or does $\frac{1}{h}$ of $\frac{1}{m}$ in an hour. Therefore, each worker *works at the rate of $\frac{1}{mh}$ of the job per hour.*

EXAMPLE 1

If 5 workers take an hour to dig a ditch, how long should it take 12 workers to dig a ditch of the same type?

Since 5 workers took an hour, each worker does $\frac{1}{5}$ of the job in an hour. So 12 workers will work at the rate of $\frac{12}{5}$ of the job per hour. Thus if T is the time it takes for 12 workers to do the job, $\frac{12}{5} \times T = 1$ job and $T = \frac{5}{12} \times 1$, so $T = \frac{5}{12}$ hours or 25 minutes.

EXAMPLE 2

Worker A takes 8 hours to do a job. Worker B takes 10 hours to do the same job. How long should it take worker A and worker B working together, but independently, to do the same job?

Worker A works at a rate of $\frac{1}{8}$ of the job per hour, since he takes 8 hours to finish the job.

Worker B finished the job in 10 hours, so he works at a rate of $\frac{1}{10}$ of the job per hour.

Therefore, if they work together they should complete $\frac{1}{8} + \frac{1}{10} = \frac{18}{80} = \frac{9}{40}$, so they work

at a rate of $\frac{9}{40}$ of the job per hour together. So if T is the time it takes them to finish the job,

$\frac{9}{40}$ of the job per hour $\times T$ hours must equal 1 job. Therefore, $\frac{9}{40} \times T = 1$ and $T = \frac{40}{9} =$

$4\frac{4}{9}$ hours.

EXAMPLE 3

There are two taps, tap 1 and tap 2, in a keg. If both taps are opened, the keg is drained in 20 minutes. If tap 1 is closed and tap 2 is open, the keg will be drained in 30 minutes. If tap 2 is closed and tap 1 is open, how long will it take to drain the keg?

Tap 1 and tap 2 together take 20 minutes to drain the keg, so together they drain the keg

at a rate of $\frac{1}{20}$ of the keg per minute. Tap 2 takes 30 minutes to drain the keg by itself, so it

drains the keg at the rate of $\frac{1}{30}$ of the keg per minute. Let r be the rate at which tap 1 will drain

the keg by itself. Then $\left(r + \frac{1}{30} \right)$ of the keg per minute is the rate at which both taps together

will drain the keg, so $r + \frac{1}{30} = \frac{1}{20}$. Therefore, $r = \frac{1}{20} - \frac{1}{30} = \frac{1}{60}$, and tap 1 drains the keg at

the rate of $\frac{1}{60}$ of the keg per minute, so it will take 60 minutes or 1 hour for tap 1 to drain the keg if tap 2 is closed.

II–4. COUNTING PROBLEMS

■ II–4.1

An example of one type of counting problem is: Fifty students signed up for both English and Math. Ninety students signed up for either English or Math. If 25 students are taking English but not taking Math, how many students are taking Math but not taking English?

In these problems, "either . . . or . . ." means you can take both, so the people taking both are counted among the people taking either Math or English.

You must avoid counting the same people twice in these problems. The formula is:

the number taking English or Math =
the number taking English + the number taking Math – the number taking both.

You have to subtract the number taking both subjects since they are counted once with those taking English and counted again with those taking Math.

A person taking English is either taking Math or not taking Math, so there are 50 + 25 = 75 people taking English, 50 taking English and Math and 25 taking English but not taking Math. Since 75 are taking English, 90 = 75 + number taking Math – 50; so there are 90 – 25 = 65 people taking Math. 50 of the people taking Math are taking English so 65 – 50 or 15 are taking Math but not English.

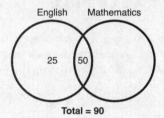

Total = 90

The figure shows what is given. Since 90 students signed up for English or Mathematics, 15 must be taking Mathematics but not English.

EXAMPLE 1

In a survey, 60% of those surveyed owned a car and 80% of those surveyed owned a TV. If 55% owned both a car and a TV, what percent of those surveyed owned a car or a TV or both?

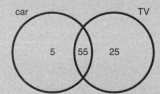

The basic formula is:

> people who own a car or a TV = people who own a car + people who own a TV – people who own both a car and a TV.

So the people who own a car or a TV = 60% + 80% – 55% = 85%. Therefore, 85% of the people surveyed own either a car or a TV.

If we just add 60% and 80% the result is 140% which is impossible. This is because the 55% who own both are counted twice.

This example could also be solved using probability. Let TV represent the outcome that the person surveyed owned a TV, so the probability that TV occurs is 80% = .8 or $p(TV) = .8$. In the same way let C stand for the outcome that the person surveyed owned a car, so $p(C) = .6$. You are told that $p(C \text{ and } TV) = .55$.

The question asks you to find the probability that at least one of C and TV occurs. So $p(C \text{ or } TV) = p(C) + p(TV) - p(C \text{ and } TV) = .6 + .8 - .55 = .85$. Therefore, 85 percent of the people surveyed owned a car or a TV or both, and the probability that a person surveyed owned a car or a TV or both is 85 percent.

This type of problem can involve three or more groups. The basic principle remains to avoid counting the same person more than once.

EXAMPLE 2

Seventy students are enrolled in Math, English, or German. Forty students are in Math, 35 are in English, and 30 are in German. Fifteen students are enrolled in all three of the courses. How many of the students are enrolled in exactly two of the courses: Math, English, and German?

If we add 40, 35, and 30, the people enrolled in exactly two of the courses will be counted twice and the people in all three courses will be counted three times. So if we let N stand for the number enrolled in exactly two courses, then we have the equation $70 = 40 + 35 + 30 - N - 2(15) = 75 - N$. Therefore, N is $75 - 70 = 5$. So there are 5 students enrolled in exactly two of the three courses.

■ II–4.2

> If an event can happen in m different ways,
> and each of the m ways is followed by a
> second event that can occur in k different
> ways, then the first event can be followed
> by the second event in $m \cdot k$ different ways.
> This is called the *fundamental principle
> of counting*.

EXAMPLE 1

If there are 3 different roads from Syracuse to Binghamton and 4 different roads from Binghamton to Scranton, how many different routes are there from Syracuse to Scranton that go
through Binghamton?

There are 3 different ways to go from Syracuse to Binghamton. Once you are in Binghamton,
there are 4 different ways to get to Scranton. So using the fundamental principle of counting,
there are $3 \times 4 = 12$ different ways to get from Syracuse to Scranton going through Binghamton.

EXAMPLE 2

A club has 20 members. They are electing a president and a vice-president. How many different
outcomes of the election are possible? (Assume the president and vice-president must be
different members of the club.)

There are 20 members, so there are 20 choices for president. Once a president is chosen,
there are 19 members left who can be vice-president. So, there are $20 \cdot 19 = 380$ different
possible outcomes of the election.

II–5. RATIO AND PROPORTION

■ II–5.1

Ratio

A ratio is a comparison of two numbers by division. The ratio of a to b is written as $a : b = \frac{a}{b} = a \div b$.

We can handle ratios as fractions, since a ratio is a fraction. In the ratio $a : b$, a and b are called the
terms of the ratio.

Since $a : b$ is a fraction, b can never be zero. The fraction $\frac{a}{b}$ is usually different from the fraction

$\frac{b}{a}$ $\left(\text{for example, } \frac{3}{2} \text{ is not the same as } \frac{2}{3}\right)$ *so the order of the terms in a ratio is important.*

EXAMPLE 1

If an orange costs 20¢ and an apple costs 12¢, what is the ratio of the cost of an orange to the cost of an apple?

The ratio is $\dfrac{20¢}{12¢} = \dfrac{5}{3}$ or $5 : 3$. Notice that the ratio of the cost of an apple to the cost of an

orange is $\dfrac{12¢}{20¢} = \dfrac{3}{5}$ or $3 : 5$. So the order of the terms is important.

A ratio is a number, so if you want to find the ratio of two quantities they must be expressed in the same units.

EXAMPLE 2

What is the ratio of 8 inches to 6 feet?

Change 6 feet into inches. Since there are 12 inches in a foot, 6 feet = 6×12 inches = 72

inches. So the ratio is $\dfrac{8 \text{ inches}}{72 \text{ inches}} = \dfrac{1}{9}$ or $1 : 9$.

If you regard ratios as fractions, the units must cancel out. In example 2, if you did not change units the ratio would be $\dfrac{8 \text{ inches}}{6 \text{ feet}} = \dfrac{4 \text{ inches}}{3 \text{ feet}}$, which is not a number.

If two numbers measure different quantities, their quotient is usually called a rate. For example, $\dfrac{50 \text{ miles}}{2 \text{ hours}}$, which equals 25 miles per hour, is a rate of speed.

▪ II–5.2

Proportion

A proportion is a statement that two ratios are equal. For example, $\dfrac{3}{12} = \dfrac{1}{4}$ is a proportion; it could also be expressed as $3 : 12 = 1 : 4$ or $3 : 12 :: 1 : 4$.

In the proportion $a : b = c : d$, the terms on the outside (a and d) are called the *extremes*, and the terms on the inside (b and c) are called the *means*. Since $a : b$ and $c : d$ are ratios, b and d are both different from zero, so $bd \neq 0$. Multiply each side of $\dfrac{a}{b} = \dfrac{c}{d}$ by bd; you get $(bd)\left(\dfrac{a}{b}\right) = ad$ and

$(bd)\left(\dfrac{c}{d}\right) = bc$. Since $bd \neq 0$, the proportion is equivalent to the equation $ad = bc$. This is usually expressed in the following way:

In a proportion, the product of the extremes is equal to the product of the means.

EXAMPLE 1

Find x if $\dfrac{4}{5} = \dfrac{10}{x}$.

In the proportion $\dfrac{4}{5} = \dfrac{10}{x}$, 4 and x are the extremes and 5 and 10 are the means, so

$4x = 5 \cdot 10 = 50$. Solve for x and we get $x = \dfrac{50}{4} = 12.5$.

Finding the products ad and bc is also called *cross multiplying the proportion*: $\dfrac{a}{b} \bowtie \dfrac{c}{d}$. So cross

multiplying a proportion gives two equal numbers. The proportion $\dfrac{a}{b} = \dfrac{c}{d}$ is read "a is to b as c is to d."

EXAMPLE 2

Two numbers are in the ratio 5 : 4 and their difference is 10. What is the larger number?

Let m and n be the two numbers. Then $\dfrac{m}{n} = \dfrac{5}{4}$ and $m - n = 10$. Cross multiply the

proportion and you get $5n = 4m$ or $n = \dfrac{4}{5}m$. So $m - n = m - \dfrac{4}{5}m = \dfrac{1}{5}m = 10$ and $m = 50$,

which means $n = \dfrac{4}{5} \cdot 50 = 40$. Therefore, the larger number is 50.

CHECK: $\dfrac{50}{40} = \dfrac{5}{4}$ and $50 - 40 = 10$.

Two variables, a and b, are *directly proportional* if they satisfy a relationship of the form $a = kb$, where k is a number. The distance a car travels in two hours and its average speed for the two hours are directly proportional, since $d = 2s$ where d is the distance and s is the average speed expressed in miles per hour. Here $k = 2$. Sometimes the word *directly* is omitted, so a and b are proportional means $a = kb$.

EXAMPLE 3

If *m* is proportional to *n* and *m* = 5 when *n* = 4, what is the value of m when *n* = 18?

There are two different ways to work the problem.

I. Since *m* and *n* are directly proportional, *m* = *kn*; and *m* = 5 when *n* = 4, so 5 = *k* · 4 which means $k = \frac{5}{4}$. Therefore, $m = \frac{5}{4}n$. So when *n* = 18, $m = \frac{5}{4} \cdot 18 = \frac{90}{4} = 22.5$.

II. Since *m* and *n* are directly proportional, *m* = *kn*. If *n*' is some value of *n*, then the value of *m* corresponding to *n*' we will call *m*', and *m*' = *kn*'. So $\frac{m}{n} = k$ and $\frac{m'}{n'}$ therefore, $\frac{m}{n} = \frac{m'}{n'}$, is a proportion. Since *m* = 5 when *n* = 4, $\frac{m}{n} = \frac{5}{4} = \frac{m'}{18}$. Cross multiply and we have

$4m' = 90$ or $m' \frac{90}{4} = 22.5$.

If two quantities are proportional, you can always set up a proportion in this manner.

EXAMPLE 4

If a machine makes 3 yards of cloth in 2 minutes, how many yards of cloth will the machine make in 50 minutes?

The amount of cloth is proportional to the time the machine operates. Let y be the number of yards of cloth the machine makes in 50 minutes; then $\frac{2 \text{ minutes}}{50 \text{ minutes}} = \frac{3 \text{ yards}}{y \text{ yards}}$, so $\frac{2}{50} = \frac{3}{y}$.

Cross multiply and you have 2*y* = 150, so *y* = 75. Therefore, the machine makes 75 yards of cloth in 50 minutes.

Since a ratio is a number, the units must cancel; so put the numbers that measure the same quantity in the same ratio.

Any two units of measurement of the same quantity are directly proportional.

EXAMPLE 5

How many ounces are there in $4\frac{3}{4}$ pounds?

Let *x* be the number of ounces in $4\frac{3}{4}$ pounds. Since there are 16 ounces in a pound,

$\frac{x \text{ ounces}}{16 \text{ ounces}} = \frac{4\frac{3}{4} \text{ pounds}}{1 \text{ pound}}$. Cross multiply to get $x = 16 \cdot 4\frac{3}{4} = 16 \cdot \frac{19}{4} = 76$; so $4\frac{3}{4}$ pounds = 76 ounces.

You can always change units by using a proportion. You should know the following measurements:

LENGTH:	1 foot = 12 inches 1 yard = 3 feet
AREA:	1 square foot = 144 square inches 1 square yard = 9 square feet
TIME:	1 minute = 60 seconds 1 hour = 60 minutes 1 day = 24 hours 1 week = 7 days 1 year = 52 weeks
VOLUME:	1 quart = 2 pints 1 gallon = 4 quarts
WEIGHT:	1 ounce = 16 drams 1 pound = 16 ounces 1 ton = 2,000 pounds

EXAMPLE 6

On a map, it is $2\frac{1}{2}$ inches from Harrisburg to Gary. The actual distance from Harrisburg to Gary is 750 miles. What is the actual distance from town A to town B if they are 4 inches apart on the map?

Let d miles be the distance from A to B; then $\dfrac{2\frac{1}{2} \text{ inches}}{4 \text{ inches}} = \dfrac{750 \text{ miles}}{d \text{ miles}}$. Cross multiply and

we have $\left(2\frac{1}{2}\right)d = 4 \times 750 = 3{,}000$, so $d = \dfrac{2}{5} \times 3{,}000 = 1{,}200$. Therefore, the distance from

A to B is 1,200 miles. Problems like this one are often called *scale problem*s.

Two variables, a and b, are *indirectly proportional* or *inversely proportional* if they satisfy a relationship of the form $k = ab$, where k is a number. So the average speed of a car and the time it takes the car to travel 300 miles are indirectly proportional, since $st = 300$ where s is the speed and t is the time.

EXAMPLE 7

m is indirectly proportional to n and $m = 5$ when $n = 4$. What is the value of m when $n = 18$?

Since m and n are indirectly proportional, $m \cdot n = k$, and $k = 5 \cdot 4 = 20$ because $m = 5$ when

$n = 4$. Therefore, $18m = k = 20$, so $m = \dfrac{20}{18} = \dfrac{10}{9}$ when $n = 18$.

Other examples of indirect proportion are work problems (see Section II–3.3).

> If two quantities are directly proportional, then when one increases, the other increases. If two quantitites are indirectly proportional, when one quantity increases, the other decreases.

■ II–5.3

It is also possible to compare three or more numbers by a ratio. The numbers A, B, and C are in the ratio $2 : 4 : 3$ means $A : B = 2 : 4$, $A : C = 2 : 3$, and $B : C = 4 : 3$. The order of the terms is important: $A : B : C$ is read A is to B is to C.

EXAMPLE 1

What is the ratio of Tom's salary to Martha's salary to Anne's salary if Tom makes \$15,000, Martha makes \$12,000 and Anne makes \$10,000?

The ratio is $15,000 : 12,000 : 10,000$ which is the same as $15 : 12 : 10$. You can cancel a factor that appears in *every* term.

EXAMPLE 2

The angles of a triangle are in the ratio $5 : 4 : 3$. How many degrees are there in the largest angle?

The sum of the angles in a triangle is $180°$. If the angles are $a°$, $b°$, and $c°$, then

$a + b + c = 180$, and $a : b : c = 5 : 4 : 3$. You could find b in terms of a, since $\dfrac{a}{b} = \dfrac{5}{4}$, and c in terms of a, since $\dfrac{a}{c} = \dfrac{5}{3}$, and then solve the equation for a.

A quicker method for this type of problem is:

1. Add all the numbers: $5 + 4 + 3 = 12$

2. Use each number as the numerator of a fraction whose denominator is the result of step (1), getting $\dfrac{5}{12}, \dfrac{4}{12}, \dfrac{3}{12}$.

3. Each quantity is the corresponding fraction (from step 2) of the total.

Thus, $a = \dfrac{5}{12}$ of 180 or 75, $b = \dfrac{4}{12}$ of 180 or 60, and $c = \dfrac{3}{12}$ of 180 or 45.

So the largest angle is $75°$.

CHECK: $75 : 60 : 45 = 5 : 4 : 3$ and $75 + 60 + 45 = 180$.

II-6. SEQUENCES AND PROGRESSIONS

■ II–6.1

A *sequence* is an ordered collection of numbers. For example, 2, 4, 6, 8, 10, . . . is a sequence. 2, 4, 6, 8, 10 are called the *terms* of the sequence. We identify the terms by their position in the sequence; so 2 is the first term, 8 is the 4th term and so on. The dots mean the sequence continues; you should be able to figure out the succeeding terms. In the example, the sequence is the sequence of even integers, and the next term after 10 would be 12.

EXAMPLE 1
What is the eighth term of the sequence 1, 4, 9, 16, 25, . . . ?
Since $1^2 = 1$, $2^2 = 4$, $3^2 = 9$, the sequence is the sequence of squares of integers, so the eighth term is $8^2 = 64$.

Sequences are sometimes given by a rule that defines an entry (usually called the *n*-th entry) in terms of previous entries of the sequence.

EXAMPLE 2
If a sequence is defined by the rule $a_n = (a_{n-1} - 3)^2$, what is a_4 (the fourth term of the sequence) if a_1 is 1?
Since a_1 is 1, a_2 is $(1-3)^2 = (-2)^2 = 4$. So a_3 is $(4-3)^2 = (1)^2 = 1$. Therefore, a_4 is $(1-3)^2 = 4$.

■ II–6.2

An *arithmetic progression* is a sequence of numbers with the property that the *difference* of any two consecutive numbers is always the same. The numbers 2, 6, 10, 14, 18, 22, . . . constitute an arithmetic progression, since each term is 4 more than the term before it. 4 is called the common difference of the progression.

If d is the common difference and a is the first term of the progression, then the nth term will be $a + (n - 1)d$. So a progression with common difference 4 and initial term 5 will have $5 + 6(4) = 29$ as its 7th term. You can check your answer. The sequence would be 5, 9, 13, 17, 21, 25, 29, . . . so 29 is the seventh term.

A sequence of numbers is called a *geometric progression* if the *ratio* of consecutive terms is always the same. So 3, 6, 12, 24, 48, . . . is a geometric progression since $\frac{6}{3} = 2 = \frac{12}{6} = \frac{24}{12} = \frac{48}{24}$, ...

The nth term of a geometric progression is ar^{n-1} where *a* is the first term and *r* is the common ratio. If a geometric progression started with 2 and the common ratio was 3, then the fifth term should be $2 \cdot 3^4 = 2 \cdot 81 = 162$. The sequence would be 2, 6, 18, 54, 162, . . . so 162 is indeed the fifth term of the progression.

We can quickly add up the first *n* terms of a geometric progression that starts with *a* and has common ratio *r*. *The formula for the sum of the first n terms is* $\frac{ar^n - a}{r - 1}$ when $r \neq 1$. (If $r = 1$ all the terms are the same so the sum is *na*.)

EXAMPLE

Find the sum of the first 7 terms of the sequence 5, 10, 20, 40, ... Since $\frac{10}{5} = \frac{20}{10} = \frac{40}{20} = 2$,

the sequence is a geometric sequence with common ratio 2. The first term is 5, so $a = 5$ and the common ratio is 2. The sum of the first seven terms means $n = 7$, thus the sum is

$$\frac{5 \cdot 2^7 - 5}{2 - 1} = 5(2^7 - 1) = 5(128 - 1) = 5 \cdot 127 = 635.$$

CHECK: The first seven terms are 5, 10, 20, 40, 80, 160, 320, and 5 + 10 + 20 + 40 + 80 + 160 + 320 = 635.

II–7. INEQUALITIES

■ II–7.1

A number is positive if it is greater than 0, so 1, $\frac{1}{1,000}$, and 53.4 are all positive numbers. Positive numbers are signed numbers whose sign is +. If you think of numbers as points on a number line (see Section I–6.1), positive numbers correspond to points to the right of 0.

A number is negative if it is less than 0. $-\frac{4}{5}$, –50, and –.0001 are all negative numbers. Negative numbers are signed numbers whose sign is –. Negative numbers correspond to points to the left of 0 on a number line.

Zero is the only number that is neither positive nor negative.

$a > b$ means the number a is greater than the number b; that is, $a = b + x$ where x is a positive number. If we look at a number line, $a > b$ means a is to the right of b. $a > b$ can also be read as b is less than a, which is also written $b < a$. For example, $-5 > -7.5$ because $-5 = -7.5 + 2.5$ and 2.5 is positive.

The notation $a \leq b$ means a is less than or equal to b, or b is greater than or equal to a. For example, $5 \geq 4$; also $4 \geq 4$. $a \neq b$ means a is not equal to b.

> If you need to know whether one fraction is greater than another fraction, put the fractions over a common denominator and compare the numerators.

EXAMPLE

Which is larger, $\frac{13}{16}$ or $\frac{31}{40}$?

A common denominator is 80. $\frac{13}{16} = \frac{65}{80}$, and $\frac{31}{40} = \frac{62}{80}$; since 65 > 62, $\frac{65}{80} > \frac{62}{80}$, so $\frac{13}{16} > \frac{31}{40}$.

■ II–7.2

Inequalities have certain properties that are similar to equations. We can talk about the left side and the right side of an inequality, and we can use algebraic expressions for the sides of an inequality. For example, $6x < 5x + 4$. A value for an unknown *satisfies an inequality*, if when you evaluate each side of the inequality the numbers satisfy the inequality. So if $x = 2$, then $6x = 12$ and $5x + 4 = 14$ and since $12 < 14$, $x = 2$ satisfies $6x < 5x + 4$. Two inequalities are equivalent if the same collection of numbers satisfies both inequalities.

The following basic principles are used in work with inequalities:

A   Adding the same expression to *each* side of an inequality gives an equivalent inequality (written $a < b \leftrightarrow a + c < b + c$ where $\leftrightarrow$ means equivalent).

B   Subtracting the same expression from *each* side of an inequality gives an equivalent inequality ($a < b \leftrightarrow a - c < b - c$).

C   Multiplying or dividing *each* side of an inequality by the same *positive* expression gives an equivalent inequality ($a < b \leftrightarrow ca < cb$ for $c > 0$).

D   Multiplying or dividing each side of an inequality by the same *negative* expression *reverses* the inequality ($a < b \leftrightarrow ca > cb$ for $c < 0$).

E   If both sides of an inequality have the same sign, inverting both sides of the inequality *reverses* the inequality.

$$0 < a < b \leftrightarrow 0 < \frac{1}{b} < \frac{1}{a}$$

$$a < b < 0 \leftrightarrow \frac{1}{b} < \frac{1}{a} < 0$$

F   If two inequalities are of the same type (both greater or both less), adding the respective sides gives the same type of inequality.

$$(a < b \text{ and } c < d, \text{ then } a + c < b + d)$$

Note that the inequalities are *not* equivalent.

G   If $a < b$ and $b < c$ then $a < c$.

EXAMPLE 1

Find the values of x for which $5x - 4 < 7x + 2$.

Using principle (B) subtract $5x + 2$ from each side, so $(5x - 4 < 7x + 2) \leftrightarrow -6 < 2x$. Now use principle (C) and divide each side by 2, so $-6 < 2x \leftrightarrow -3 < x$.

So any x greater than -3 satisfies the inequality. It is a good idea to make a spot check. -1 is > -3; let $x = -1$ then $5x - 4 = -9$ and $7x + 2 = -5$. Since $-9 < -5$, the answer is correct for at least the particular value $x = -1$.

Some inequalities are not satisfied by any real number. For example, since $x^2 \geq 0$ for all x, there is no real number x such that $x^2 < -9$.

You may be given an inequality and asked whether other inequalities follow from the original inequality. You should be able to answer such questions by using principles (A) through (G).

If there is any property of inequalities you can't remember, try out some specific numbers. If $x < y$, then what is the relation between $-x$ and $-y$? Since $4 < 5$ but $-5 < -4$, the relation is probably $-x > -y$, which is true by (D).

Probably the most common mistake is forgetting to reverse the inequalities if you multiply or divide by a negative number.

EXAMPLE 2

Find the values of a that satisfy $a^2 + 1 > 2a + 4$.

We will solve this using an alternate method:

Ⓐ Group all terms on one side, so that the other side will be 0. The result is $a^2 - 2a + 1 - 4 = a^2 - 2a - 3 > 0$.

Ⓑ Find all values of the variable that make the expression equal 0.

Since $a^2 - 2a - 3 = (a - 3)(a + 1)$, the result is $a = 3$ and $a = -1$. So the only possible solutions are: $a > 3$, $-1 < a < 3$, and $a < -1$.

Ⓒ Choose points other than those found in (B), and check whether the points are solutions. If $a = 0$, then $a^2 - 2a - 3 = -3$, which is less than 0, so $-1 < a < 3$ is not a solution. If $a = 4$, then $a^2 - 2a - 3 = 5$, which is greater than 0, so $a > 3$ is a solution. Use $a = -2$ to see that $a < -1$ is also a solution. So the solutions are $a > 3$ and $a < -1$.

This method is quicker for solving inequalities that are not linear.

III. Geometry

III–1. ANGLES

■ III–1.1

If two straight lines meet at a point they form an *angle*. The point is called the *vertex* of the angle and the lines are called the *sides* or *rays* of the angle. The sign for angle is ∠ and an angle can be denoted in the following ways:

A ∠ABC where B is the vertex, A is a point on one side, and C a point on the other side.

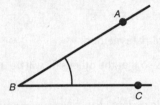

B ∠B where B is the vertex.

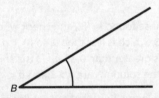

C ∠1 or ∠x where x or 1 is written inside the angle.

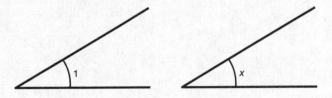

Angles are usually measured in degrees. We say that an angle equals x degrees, when its measure is x degrees. Degrees are denoted by °. An angle of 50 degrees is 50°. 60' = 1°, 60" = 1' where ' is read minutes and " is read seconds.

■ III–1.2

Two angles are *adjacent* if they have the same vertex and a common side and one angle is not inside the other.

A

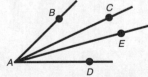

∠BAC and ∠CAD are adjacent, but ∠CAD and ∠EAD are not adjacent.

Where two lines intersect at a point, they form 4 angles. The angles opposite each other are called vertical angles. ∠1 and ∠3 are vertical angles. ∠2 and ∠4 are vertical angles.

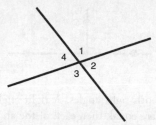

Vertical angles are equal,

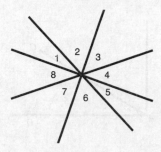

so, ∠1 = ∠5, ∠2 = ∠6, ∠3 = ∠7, ∠4 = ∠8.

■ III–1.3

A straight angle is an angle whose sides lie on a straight line. *A straight angle equals 180°.*

∠*ABC* is a straight angle.

If the sum of two adjacent angles is a straight angle, then the angles are *supplementary* and each angle is the supplement of the other.

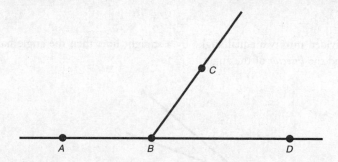

∠*ABC* and ∠*CBD* are supplementary.

If an angle of $x°$ and an angle of $y°$ are supplements, then $x + y = 180$.

If two supplementary angles are equal, they are both *right angles*. A right angle is half of a straight angle. A right angle = 90°.

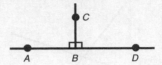

∠*ABC* = ∠*CBD* and they are both right angles. A right angle is denoted by ∟. When 2 lines intersect and all four of the angles are equal, then each of the angles is a right angle.

If the sum of two adjacent angles is a right angle, then the angles are *complementary* and each angle is the complement of the other.

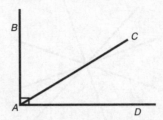

∠*BAC* and ∠*CAD* are complementary.

If an angle of $x°$ and an angle of $y°$ are complementary, then $x + y = 90$.

EXAMPLE

If the supplement of angle x is three times as much as the complement of angle x, how many degrees is angle x?

Let d be the number of degrees in angle x; then the supplement of x is $(180 - d)°$, and the complement of x is $(90 - d)°$. Since the supplement is 3 times the complement, $180 - d = 3(90 - d) = 270 - 3d$ which gives $2d = 90$, so $d = 45$.

Therefore, angle x is 45°.

If an angle is divided into two equal angles by a straight line, then the angle has been bisected and the line is called the *bisector* of the angle.

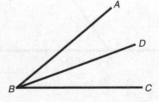

BD bisects ∠*ABC*; so ∠*ABD* = ∠*DBC*.

An *acute angle* is an angle less than a right angle. An obtuse angle is an angle greater than a right angle, but less than a straight angle.

∠1 is an acute angle, and ∠2 is an obtuse angle.

III–2. LINES

■ III–2.1

A line is understood to be a straight line. A line is assumed to extend indefinitely in both directions. *There is one and only one line between two distinct points.* There are two ways to denote a line:

1. by a single letter: *l* is a line;

2. by two points on the line:

AB is a line.

A *line segment* is the part of a line between two points called *endpoints*. A line segment is denoted by its endpoints.

AB is a line segment. If a point *P* on a line segment is equidistant from the endpoints, then *P* is called the *midpoint* of the line segment.

P is the midpoint of *AB* if the length of *AP* = the length of *PB*. Two line segments are equal if their lengths are equal; so *AP* = *PB* means the line segment *AP* has the same length as the line segment *PB*. When a line segment is extended indefinitely in one direction, it is called a ray. A ray has one endpoint.

AB is a ray that has *A* as its endpoint.

■ III–2.2

P is a *point of intersection* of two lines if *P* is a point which is on both of the lines. *Two different lines cannot have more than one point of intersection*, because there is only one line between two points.

P is the point of intersection of *m* and *n*. We also say *m and n intersect at P.*

Two lines are parallel if they do not intersect no matter how far they are extended.

m and *n* are parallel, but *k* and *l* are not parallel since if *k* and *l* are extended they will intersect. Parallel lines are denoted by the symbol ‖; so *m* ‖ *n* means m is parallel to *n*.

If two lines are parallel to a third line, then they are parallel to each other.

If a third line intersects two given lines, it is called a *transversal.* A transversal and the two given lines form eight angles. The four inside angles are called *interior* angles. The four outside angles are called *exterior* angles. If two angles are on opposite sides of the transversal they are called *alternate* angles.

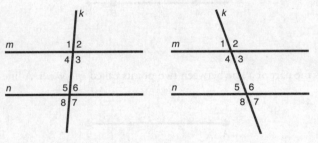

k is a transversal of the lines *m* and *n*. Angles 1, 2, 7, and 8 are the exterior angles, and angles 3, 4, 5, and 6 are the interior angles. ∠4 and ∠6 are an example of a pair of alternate angles. ∠1 and ∠5, ∠2 and ∠6, ∠3 and ∠7, and ∠4 and ∠8 are pairs of *corresponding* angles.

If two parallel lines are intersected by a transversal then:

1. Alternate interior angles are equal.
2. Corresponding angles are equal.
3. Interior angles on the same side of the transversal are supplementary.

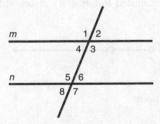

If we use the fact that vertical angles are equal, we can replace "interior" by "exterior" in 1. and 3.

m is parallel to *n* implies:

1. $\angle 4 = \angle 6$ and $\angle 3 = \angle 5$
2. $\angle 1 = \angle 5$, $\angle 2 = \angle 6$, $\angle 3 = \angle 7$ and $\angle 4 = \angle 8$
3. $\angle 3 + \angle 6 = 180°$ and $\angle 4 + \angle 5 = 180°$

The reverse is also true. Let *m* and *n* be two lines that have *k* as a transversal.

1. If a pair of alternate interior angles are equal, then *m* and *n* are parallel.
2. If a pair of corresponding angles are equal, then *m* and *n* are parallel.
3. If a pair of interior angles on the same side of the transversal are supplementary, then *m* is parallel to *n*.

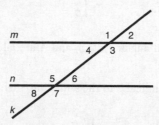

If $\angle 3 = \angle 5$, then $m \parallel n$. If $\angle 4 = \angle 6$ then $m \parallel n$. If $\angle 2 = \angle 6$ then $m \parallel n$. If $\angle 3 + \angle 6 = 180°$, then $m \parallel n$.

EXAMPLE

If *m* and *n* are two parallel lines and angle 1 is 60°, how many degrees is angle 2?

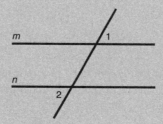

Let $\angle 3$ be the vertical angle equal to angle 2.

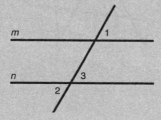

$\angle 3 = \angle 2$. Since *m* and *n* are parallel, corresponding angles are equal. Since $\angle 1$ and $\angle 3$ are corresponding angles, $\angle 1 = \angle 3$. Therefore, $\angle 1 = \angle 2$, and $\angle 2$ equals 60° since $\angle 1 = 60°$.

■ III–2.3

When two lines intersect and all four of the angles formed are equal, the lines are said to be *perpendicular*. If two lines are perpendicular, they are the sides of right angles whose vertex is the point of intersection.

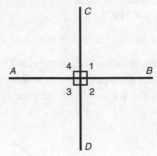

AB is perpendicular to *CD*, and angles 1, 2, 3, and 4 are all right angles. ⊥ is the symbol for perpendicular; so *AB* ⊥ *CD*.

If two lines in a plane are perpendicular to the same line, then the two lines are parallel.

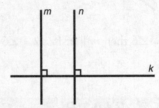

m ⊥ *k* and *n* ⊥ *k* imply that *m* ∥ *n*.

If *any one* of the angles formed when two lines intersect is a right angle, then the lines are perpendicular.

III–3. POLYGONS

A *polygon* is a closed figure in a plane that is composed of line segments that meet only at their endpoints. The line segments are called sides of the polygon, and a point where two sides meet is called a *vertex* (plural *vertices*) of the polygon.

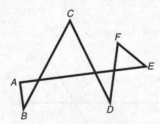

ABCDEF is not a polygon since the line segments intersect at points that are not endpoints.

Some examples of polygons are:

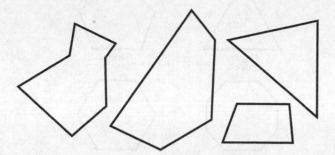

A polygon is usually denoted by the vertices given in order.

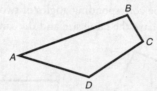

ABCD is a polygon.

A *diagonal* of a polygon is a line segment whose endpoints are nonadjacent vertices. The *altitude* from a vertex *P* to a side is the line segment with endpoint *P* which is perpendicular to the side. In the diagram below, *AC* is a diagonal, and *CE* is the altitude from *C* to *AD*.

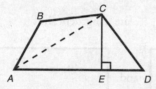

Polygons are classified by the number of angles or sides they have. A polygon with three angles is called a *triangle*; a four-sided polygon is a *quadrilateral*; a polygon with five angles is a *pentagon*; a polygon with six angles is a *hexagon*; an eight-sided polygon is an *octagon*. The number of angles is always equal to the number of sides in a polygon, so a six-sided polygon is a hexagon. The term *n*-gon refers to a polygon with *n* sides.

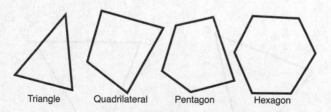

Triangle   Quadrilateral   Pentagon   Hexagon

If the sides of a polygon are all equal in length and if all the angles of a polygon are equal, the polygon is called a *regular* polygon.

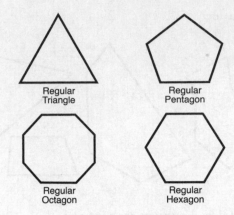

If the corresponding sides and the corresponding angles of two polygons are equal, the polygons are *congruent*. Congruent polygons have the same size and the same shape:

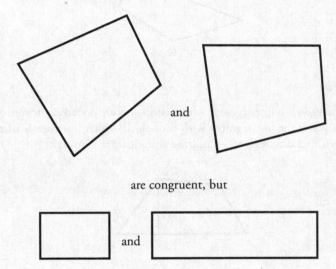

In figures for problems on congruence, sides with the same number of strokes through them are equal.

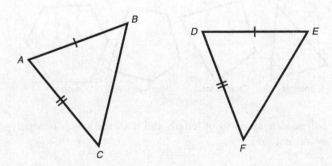

This figure indicates that $AB = DE$ and $AC = DF$.

If all the corresponding angles of two polygons are equal and the lengths of the corresponding sides are proportional, the polygons are said to be *similar*. Similar polygons have the same shape but need not be the same size.

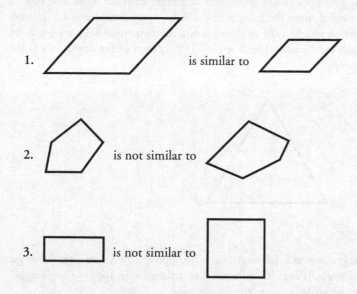

1. ⟋▱⟍ is similar to ▱

2. ⬠ is not similar to ⬡

3. ▭ is not similar to ▢

In 3. the corresponding angles are equal, but the corresponding sides are not proportional.

The sum of all the angles of an n-gon is $(n - 2)180°$. So the sum of the angles in a hexagon is $(6 - 2)180° = 720°$.

III–4. TRIANGLES

■ III–4.1

A *triangle* is a 3-sided polygon. If two sides of a triangle are equal, it is called *isosceles*. If all three sides are equal, it is an *equilateral* triangle. If all of the sides have different lengths, the triangle is *scalene*. When one of the angles in a triangle is a right angle, the triangle is a *right triangle*. If one of the angles is obtuse we have an *obtuse triangle*. If all the angles are acute, the triangle is an *acute triangle*.

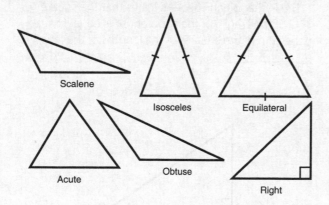

The symbol for a triangle is △; so △*ABC* means a triangle whose vertices are *A*, *B*, and *C*.

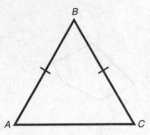

The sum of the angles in a triangle is 180°.

The sum of the lengths of any two sides of a triangle must be longer than the remaining side.

If two angles in a triangle are equal, then the lengths of the sides opposite the equal angles are equal. If two sides of a triangle are equal, then the angles opposite the two equal sides are equal. In an equilateral triangle all the angles are equal and each angle = 60°. If each of the angles in a triangle is 60°, then the triangle is equilateral.

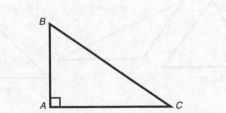

If $AB = BC$, then $\angle BAC = \angle BCA$.

If one angle in a triangle is larger than another angle, the side opposite the larger angle is longer than the side opposite the smaller angle. If one side is longer than another side, then the angle opposite the longer side is larger than the angle opposite the shorter side.

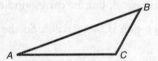

$AB > AC$ implies $\angle BCA > \angle ABC$.

If the side of a triangle is extended, then the resulting exterior angle is greater than either of the opposite and interior angles. So in the triangle above, if we had extended the side AC beyond C to a point D, then the angle BCD would be greater than the angle BAC and greater than the angle ABC.

In a right triangle, the side opposite the right angle is called the *hypotenuse*, and the remaining two sides are called *legs*.

The Pythagorean Theorem states that the square of the length of the hypotenuse is equal to the sum of the squares of the lengths of the legs.

$(BC)^2 = (AB)^2 + (AC)^2$

If $AB = 4$ and $AC = 3$ then $(BC)^2 = 4^2 + 3^2 = 25$ so $BC = 5$. If $BC = 13$ and $AC = 5$, then $13^2 = 169 = (AB)^2 + 5^2$. So $(AB)^2 = 169 - 25 = 144$ and $AB = 12$.

If the lengths of the three sides of a triangle are a, b, and c and $a^2 + b^2 = c^2$, then the triangle is a right triangle where c is the length of the hypotenuse.

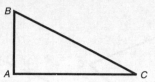

If $AB = 8$, $AC = 15$, and $BC = 17$, then since $17^2 = 8^2 + 15^2$, $\angle BAC$ is a right angle.

■ III–4.2

Congruence

Two triangles are congruent if two pairs of corresponding sides and the corresponding *included* angles are equal. This is called *Side-Angle-Side* and is denoted by S.A.S.

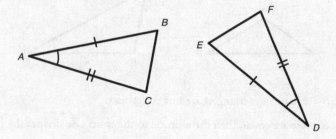

$AB = DE$, $AC = DF$ and $\angle BAC = \angle EDF$ imply that $\triangle ABC \cong \triangle DEF$. $\cong$ means congruent.

Two triangles are congruent if two pairs of corresponding angles and the corresponding *included* sides are equal. This is called *Angle-Side-Angle* or A.S.A.

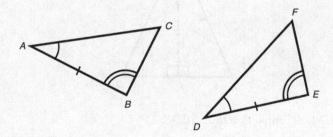

If $AB = DE$, $\angle BAC = \angle EDF$, and $\angle CBA = \angle FED$ then $\triangle ABC \cong \triangle DEF$.

If all three pairs of corresponding sides of two triangles are equal, then the triangles are congruent. This is called *Side-Side-Side* or S.S.S.

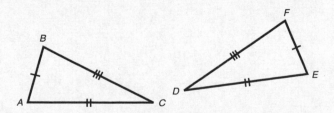

$AB = EF$, $AC = ED$, and $BC = FD$ imply that $\triangle ABC \cong \triangle EFD$.

Because of the Pythagorean Theorem, if any two corresponding sides of two right triangles are equal, the third sides are equal and the triangles are congruent.

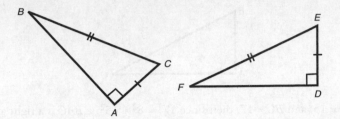

$AC = DE$ and $BC = EF$ imply $\triangle ABC \cong \triangle DFE$.

In general, if two corresponding sides of two triangles are equal, we cannot infer that the triangles are congruent.

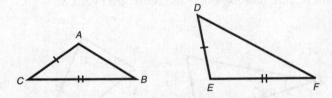

$AC = DE$ and $CB = EF$, but the triangles are not congruent.

If two sides of a triangle are equal, then the altitude to the third side divides the triangle into two congruent triangles.

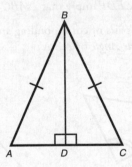

$AB = BC$ and $BD \perp AC$ imply $\triangle ADB \cong \triangle CDB$.

Therefore, $\angle ABD = \angle CBD$, so BD bisects $\angle ABC$. Since $AD = DC$, D is the midpoint of AC so BD is the median from B to AC. A *median* is the segment from a vertex to the midpoint of the side opposite the vertex.

EXAMPLE

If $AB = 4$, $AC = 4.5$ and $BC = 6$, $\angle BAC = \angle EDF$, $DE = 4$, and $DF = 4.5$, what is EF?

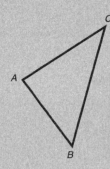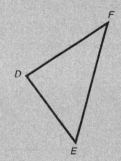

Since two pairs of corresponding sides (AB and DE, AC and DF) and the corresponding included angles ($\angle BAC$, $\angle EDF$) are equal, the triangles ABC and DEF are congruent by S.A.S. Therefore, $EF = BC = 6$.

■ III–4.3

Similarity

Two triangles are similar if all three pairs of corresponding angles are equal. Since the sum of the angles in a triangle is 180°, it follows that if two corresponding angles are equal, the third angles must be equal.

If you draw a line that passes through a triangle and is parallel to one of the sides of the triangle, the triangle formed is similar to the original triangle.

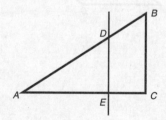

If $DE \parallel BC$ then $\triangle ADE \sim \triangle ABC$. The symbol ~ means similar.

EXAMPLE

A man 6 feet tall casts a shadow 4 feet long; at the same time a flagpole casts a shadow that is 50 feet long. How tall is the flagpole?

The man with his shadow and the flagpole with its shadow can be regarded as the pairs of corresponding sides of two similar triangles.

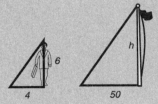

Let *h* be the height of the flagpole. Since corresponding sides of similar triangles are proportional, $\frac{4}{50} = \frac{6}{h}$. Cross multiply, getting $4h = 6 \cdot 50 = 300$; so $h = 75$. Therefore, the flagpole is 75 feet high.

III–5. QUADRILATERALS

A *quadrilateral* is a polygon with four sides. The sum of the angles in a quadrilateral is 360°. If both sets of opposite sides of a quadrilateral are parallel, the figure is a *parallelogram*.

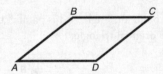

ABCD is a parallelogram.

In a parallelogram:

1. Opposite sides are equal.
2. Opposite angles are equal.
3. All diagonals divide the parallelogram into two congruent triangles.
4. The diagonals bisect each other. (A line *bisects* a line segment if it intersects the segment at the midpoint of the segment.)

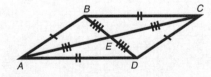

ABCD is a parallelogram.

1. $AB = DC$, $BC = AD$.
2. $\angle BCD = \angle BAD$, $\angle ABC = \angle ADC$.
3. $\triangle ABC \cong \triangle ADC$, $\triangle ABD \cong \triangle CDB$.
4. $AE = EC$ and $BE = ED$.

If *any* of the statements 1., 2., 3., and 4. are true for a quadrilateral, then the quadrilateral is a parallelogram.

If all of the sides of a parallelogram are equal, the figure is called a *rhombus*.

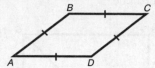

ABCD is a rhombus.

The diagonals of a rhombus are perpendicular.

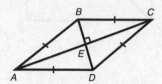

$BD \perp AC$; $\angle BEC = \angle CED = \angle AED = \angle AEB = 90°$.

If all the angles of a parallelogram are right angles, the figure is a *rectangle*.

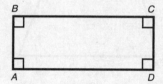

ABCD is a rectangle.

Since the sum of the angles in a quadrilateral is 360°, if *all* the angles of a quadrilateral are equal then the figure is a rectangle. The diagonals of a rectangle are equal. The length of a diagonal can be found by using the Pythagorean Theorem.

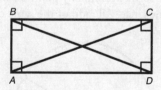

If *ABCD* is a rectangle, $AC = BD$ and $(AC)^2 = (AD)^2 + (DC)^2$.

If all the sides of a rectangle are equal, the figure is a *square*.

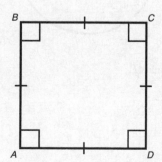

ABCD is a square.

If all the angles of a rhombus are equal, the figure is a square. The length of the diagonal of a square is $\sqrt{2}\,s$ where s is the length of a side.

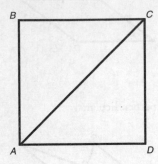

In square $ABCD$, $AC = (\sqrt{2})AD$.

A quadrilateral with two parallel sides and two sides that are not parallel is called a *trapezoid*. The parallel sides are called *bases*, and the nonparallel sides are called *legs*.

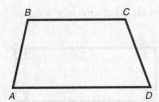

If $BC \parallel AD$ then $ABCD$ is a trapezoid; BC and AD are the bases.

III–6. CIRCLES

A *circle* is a figure in a plane consisting of all the points that are the same distance from a fixed point called the *center* of the circle. A line segment from any point on the circle to the center of the circle is called a *radius* (plural: *radii*) of the circle. All radii of the same circle have the same length.

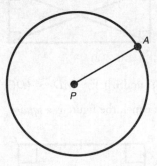

This circle has center P and radius AP.

A circle is denoted by a single letter, usually its center. Two circles with the same center are *concentric*.

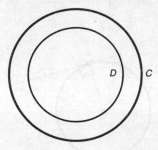

C and *D* are concentric circles.

A line segment whose endpoints are on a circle is called a *chord*. A chord that passes through the center of the circle is a *diameter*. *The length of a diameter is twice the length of a radius.* A diameter divides a circle into two congruent halves which are called *semicircles*.

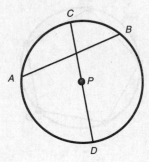

P is the center of the circle.

AB is a chord and *CD* is a diameter.

A diameter that is perpendicular to a chord bisects the chord.

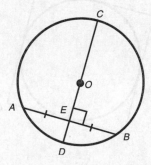

O is the center of this circle and *AB* ⊥ *CD*; then *AE* = *EB*.

If a line intersects a circle at one and only one point, the line is said to be a *tangent* to the circle. The point common to a circle and a tangent to the circle is called the *point of tangency*. The radius from the center to the point of tangency is perpendicular to the tangent.

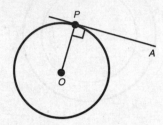

AP is tangent to the circle with center *O*. *P* is the point of tangency and *OP* ⊥ *PA*.

A polygon is *inscribed* in a circle if all of its vertices are points on the circle.

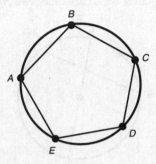

ABCDE is an inscribed pentagon.

A polygon circumscribes a circle if each side of the polygon is tangent to the circle.

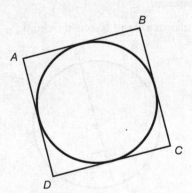

ABCD is a circumscribed quadrilateral.

An angle whose vertex is a point on a circle and whose sides are chords of the circle is called an *inscribed angle*. An angle whose vertex is the center of a circle and whose sides are radii of the circle is called a *central angle*.

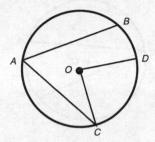

∠*BAC* is an inscribed angle.

∠*DOC* is a central angle.

An *arc* is a part of a circle.

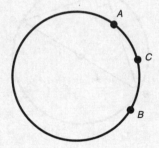

ACB is an arc. Arc *ACB* is written $\overset{\frown}{ACB}$.

If two letters are used to denote an arc, they represent the smaller of the two possible arcs. So $\overset{\frown}{AB}$ = $\overset{\frown}{ACB}$.

An arc can be measured in degrees. The entire circle is 360°; thus an arc of 120° would be $\frac{1}{3}$ of a circle.

A central angle is equal in measure to the arc it intercepts.

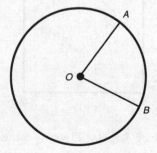

∠*AOB* = $\overset{\frown}{AB}$

An inscribed angle is equal in measure to $\frac{1}{2}$ the arc it intercepts.

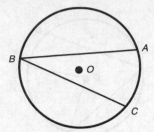

$\angle ABC = \frac{1}{2} \widehat{AC}$

An angle inscribed in a semicircle is a *right angle*.

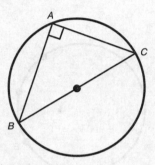

If *BC* is a diameter, then $\angle BAC$ is inscribed in a semicircle; so $\angle BAC = 90°$.

III–7. AREA AND PERIMETER

■ III–7.1

The area A of a square equals s^2, where s is the length of a side of the square. Thus, $A = s^2$.

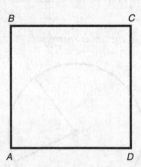

If $AD = 5$ inches, the area of square *ABCD* is 25 square inches.

The area of a rectangle equals length times width; if L is the length of one side and W is the length of a perpendicular side, then the area $A = LW$.

If $AB = 5$ feet and $AD = 8$ feet, then the area of rectangle $ABCD$ is 40 square feet.

The area of a parallelogram is base × height; $A = bh$, where b is the length of a side and h is the length of an altitude to that side.

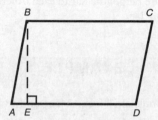

If $AD = 6$ yards and $BE = 4$ yards, then the area of the parallelogram $ABCD$ is 6 • 4 or 24 square yards.

The area of a trapezoid is the (average of the bases) × height. $A = \dfrac{(b_1 + b_2)}{2} h$ where b_1 and b_2 are the lengths of the parallel sides and h is the length of an altitude to one of the bases.

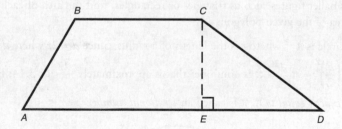

If $BC = 3$ miles, $AD = 7$ miles, and $CE = 2$ miles, then the area of trapezoid $ABCD$ is $\dfrac{(3+7)}{2}$ • 2 = 10 square miles.

The area of a triangle is $\frac{1}{2}$ (base $\times$ height); $A = \frac{1}{2}bh$, where b is the length of a side and h is the length of the altitude to that side.

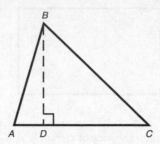

If AC = 5 miles and BD = 4 miles, then the area of the triangle is $\frac{1}{2} \times 5 \times 4 = 10$ square miles.

Since the legs of a right triangle are perpendicular to each other, the area of a right triangle is one-half the product of the lengths of the legs.

EXAMPLE

If the lengths of the sides of a triangle are 5 feet, 12 feet, and 13 feet, what is the area of the triangle?

Since $5^2 + 12^2 = 25 + 144 = 169 = 13^2$, the triangle is a right triangle and the legs are the sides with lengths 5 feet and 12 feet. Therefore, the area is $\frac{1}{2} \times 5 \times 12 = 30$ square feet.

If we want to find the area of a polygon that is not of a type already mentioned, we break the polygon up into smaller figures such as triangles or rectangles, find the area of each piece, and add these to get the area of the given polygon.

The area of a circle is πr^2 where r is the length of a radius. Since $d = 2r$ where d is the length of a diameter, $A = \pi\left(\frac{d}{2}\right)^2 = \pi\frac{d^2}{4}$. π is a number that is approximately $\frac{22}{7}$ or 3.14; however, *there is no fraction that is exactly equal to* π. π *is called an irrational number.*

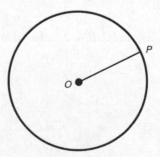

If OP = 2 inches, then the area of the circle with center O is $\pi 2^2$ or 4π square inches. The portion of the plane bounded by a circle and a central angle is called a *sector* of the circle.

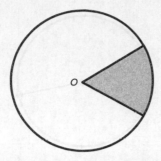

The shaded region is a sector of the circle with center O. The area of a sector with central angle $n°$ in a circle of radius r is $\frac{n}{360}\pi r^2$.

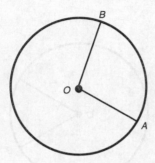

If $OB = 4$ inches and $\angle BOA = 100°$, then the area of the sector is $\frac{100}{360}\pi \cdot 4^2 = \frac{5}{18} \cdot 16\pi = \frac{40}{9}\pi$ square inches.

◼ III–7.2

The *perimeter* of a polygon is the sum of the lengths of the sides.

EXAMPLE 1

What is the perimeter of a regular pentagon whose sides are 6 inches long?

A pentagon has 5 sides. Since the pentagon is regular, all sides have the same length which is 6 inches. Therefore, the perimeter of the pentagon is 5×6 which equals 30 inches or 2.5 feet.

The *perimeter of a rectangle* is $2(L + W)$ where L is the length and W is the width.

The *perimeter of a square* is $4s$ where s is the length of a side of the square.

The *perimeter of a circle* is called the *circumference* of the circle. The *circumference of a circle* is πd or $2\pi r$, where d is the length of a diameter and r is the length of a radius.

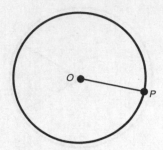

If O is the center of a circle and OP = 5 feet, then the circumference of the circle is $2 \times 5\pi$ or 10π feet.

The length of an arc of a circle is $\left(\dfrac{n}{360}\right)\pi d$ where the central angle of the arc is $n°$.

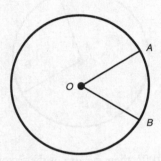

If O is the center of a circle where OA = 5 yards and $\angle AOB$ = 60°, then the length of arc AB is $\dfrac{60}{360}\pi \times 10 = \dfrac{10}{6}\pi = \dfrac{5}{3}\pi$ yards.

EXAMPLE 2

How far will a wheel of radius 2 feet travel in 500 revolutions? (Assume the wheel does not slip.)

The diameter of the wheel is 4 feet; so the circumference is 4π feet. Therefore, the wheel will travel $500 \times 4\pi$ or $2,000\pi$ feet in 500 revolutions.

III–8. VOLUME AND SURFACE AREA

■ III–8.1

The volume of a rectangular prism or box is length times width times height.

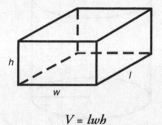

$$V = lwh$$

EXAMPLE 1

What is the volume of a box that is 5 feet long, 4 feet wide, and 6 feet high?

The volume is $5 \times 4 \times 6$ or 120 cubic feet.

If each of the faces of a rectangular prism is a congruent square, then the solid is a *cube*. The volume of a cube is the length of a side (or edge) cubed.

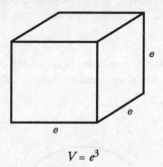

$$V = e^3$$

If the side of a cube is 4 feet long, then the volume of the cube is 4^3 or 64 cubic feet.

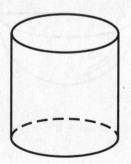

This solid is a circular cylinder. The top and the bottom are congruent circles. Most tin cans are circular cylinders. The volume of a circular cylinder is the product of the area of the circular base and the height.

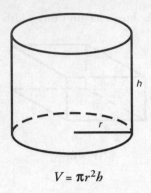

$$V = \pi r^2 h$$

EXAMPLE 2

A circular pipe has a diameter of 10 feet. A gallon of oil has a volume of 2 cubic feet. How many gallons of oil can fit into 50 feet of the pipe?

Think of the 50 feet of pipe as a circular cylinder on its side with a height of 50 feet and a radius of 5 feet. Its volume is $\pi \cdot 5^2 \cdot 50$ or $1{,}250\pi$ cubic feet. Since a gallon of oil has a volume of 2 cubic feet, 50 feet of pipe will hold $\dfrac{1250\pi}{2}$ or 625π gallons of oil.

A *sphere* is the set of points in space equidistant from a fixed point called the center. The length of a segment from any point on the sphere to the center is called the radius of the sphere. *The volume of a sphere of radius r is $\frac{4}{3}\pi r^3$.*

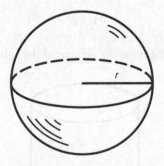

The volume of a sphere with radius 3 feet is $\frac{4}{3}\pi 3^3 = 36\pi$ cubic feet.

■ **III–8.2**

The surface area of a rectangular prism is $2LW + 2LH + 2WH$ where L is the length, W is the width, and H is the height.

> ### EXAMPLE 1
>
> If a roll of wallpaper covers 30 square feet, how many rolls are needed to cover the walls of a rectangular room 10 feet long by 8 feet wide by 9 feet high? There are no windows in the room.
>
> We have to cover the surface area of the walls which equals $2(10 \times 9 + 8 \times 9)$ or $2(90 + 72)$ or 324 square feet. (Note that the product omits the area of the floor or the ceiling.) Since a roll covers 30 square feet, we need $\dfrac{324}{30} = 10\dfrac{4}{5}$ rolls.

The surface area of a cube is $6e^2$ where e is the length of an edge.

The area of the circular part of a cylinder is called the lateral area. The lateral area of a cylinder is $2\pi rh$, since if we unroll the circular part, we get a rectangle whose dimensions are the circumference of the circle and the height of the cylinder. The total surface area is the lateral surface area plus the areas of the circles on top and bottom, so the total surface area is $2\pi rh + 2\pi r^2$.

> ### EXAMPLE 2
>
> How much tin is needed to make a tin can in the shape of a circular cylinder whose radius is 3 inches and whose height is 5 inches?
>
> The area of both the bottom and top is $\pi \cdot 3^2$ or 9π square inches. The lateral area is $2\pi \cdot 3 \cdot 5$ or 30π square inches. Therefore, we need $9\pi + 9\pi + 30\pi$ or 48π square inches of tin.

III–9. COORDINATE GEOMETRY

In coordinate geometry, every point in the plane is associated with an ordered pair of numbers called *coordinates*. Two perpendicular lines are drawn; the horizontal line is called the *x*-axis and the vertical line is called the *y*-axis. The point where the two axes intersect is called the *origin*. Both of the axes are number lines with the origin corresponding to zero (see I–6.2). Positive numbers on the *x*-axis are to the right of the origin, negative numbers to the left. Positive numbers on the *y*-axis are above the origin, negative numbers below the origin. The coordinates of a point P are (x, y) if P is located by moving x units along the *x*-axis from the origin and then moving y units up or down. *The distance along the x-axis is always given first.*

The numbers in parentheses are the coordinates of the point. Thus "$P = (3, 2)$" means that the coordinates of P are $(3, 2)$. *The distance between the point with coordinates (r, s) and the point with coordinates (a, b) is* $\sqrt{(r-a)^2 + (s-b)^2}$. You should be able to answer most questions by using the distance formula.

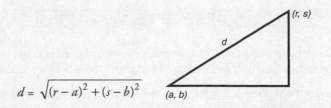

$$d = \sqrt{(r-a)^2 + (s-b)^2}$$

EXAMPLE

Is *ABCD* a parallelogram?

$A = (3, 2)$, $B = (1, -2)$, $C = (-2, 1)$, $D = (1, 5)$. The length of *AB* is $\sqrt{(3-1)^2 + (2-(-2))^2} = \sqrt{2^2 + 4^2} = \sqrt{20}$. The length of *CD* is $\sqrt{(-2-1)^2 + (1-5)^2} = \sqrt{(-3)^2 + (-4)^2} = \sqrt{25}$. Therefore, $AB \ne CD$, so *ABCD* cannot be a parallelogram, since in a parallelogram the lengths of opposite sides are equal.

You can often use coordinate geometry to solve problems that do not appear to involve coordinates.

EXAMPLE

City A is 5 miles north of City B and City C is 12 miles west of City B. How far is it between City A and City C?

Set up a coordinate axis with City B at the origin, east-west as the *x* axis, and north-south as the *y* axis, as in the diagram.

C (–12, 0)   A (0, 5)
                B (0, 0)

Then City A has coordinates (0, 5) and City C has coordinates (–12, 0). So the distance from A to C is the square root of $(-12 - 0)^2 + (5 - 0)^2$ or $\sqrt{144 + 25} = \sqrt{169}$, which is 13. So the answer is 13 miles.

Geometry problems occur frequently in the data sufficiency questions. *If you are not provided with a diagram, draw one for yourself.* Think of any conditions that will help you answer the question; perhaps you can see how to answer a different question that will lead to an answer to the original question. It may help to draw in some diagonals, altitudes, or other auxiliary lines in your diagram.

IV. Tables and Graphs

IV–1. TABLES

General Hints

1. Make sure to look at the *entire* table or graph.

2. Figure out what *units* the table or graph is using. Make sure to express your answer in the correct units.

3. Look at the possible answers before calculating. Since many questions only call for an approximate answer, it may be possible to round off (see I–5), saving time and effort.

4. Don't confuse decimals and percentages. If the units are percentages, then an entry of .2 means .2% which is equal to .002.

5. In inference questions, only the information given can be used.

6. See if the answer makes sense.

(Refer to the table on page 270 to answer these questions.)

1. What percent of the babies born in the U.S. in 1947 died before the age of 1 year?

(A) 3.22
(B) 4.7
(C) 26.7
(D) 32.2
(E) 47

To find a percentage, use the information given in the rate columns. The rate is given *per thousand.* In 1947 the rate was 32.2 per thousand which is $\frac{32.2}{1,000}$ = .0322 or 3.22%.

So the correct answer is (A). If you assumed incorrectly that the rate was per hundred, you would get the incorrect answer (D); if you looked in the wrong column you might get (B) or (E) as your answer.

2. Which state had the most infant deaths in 1940?

(A) California
(B) New Mexico
(C) New York
(D) Pennsylvania
(E) Texas

Look in the numbers column under 1940. Only Texas had more than 8,000 in 1940, so the correct answer is (E). New Mexico had a higher rate, but the question asked for the *highest amount. Make sure you answer the question that is asked.*

INFANT DEATHS (UNDER 1 YEAR OF AGE) AND RATES PER 1,000 LIVE BIRTHS, BY STATES: 1940 TO 1950

State	Number of Infant Deaths					Rate per 1,000 Live Births				
	1940	1947	1948	1949	1950	1940	1947	1948	1949	1950
United States	110,984	119,173	113,169	111,531	103,825	47.0	32.2	32.0	31.3	29.2
Alabama	3,870	3,301	3,228	3,345	3,044	61.5	37.5	37.8	39.6	36.8
Arizona	983	973	1,083	1,034	953	85.5	50.8	56.4	51.0	45.8
Arkansas	1,810	1,445	1,363	1,539	1,209	47.0	29.5	28.4	33.7	26.5
California	4,403	7,233	6,885	6,574	6,115	39.2	29.4	28.6	26.8	25.0
Colorado	1,270	1,234	1,267	1,153	1,167	60.4	37.5	38.4	35.1	34.4
Connecticut	868	1,150	1,026	943	886	34.0	25.2	24.3	23.1	21.8
Delaware	217	239	214	224	235	47.7	31.0	29.5	30.4	30.7
District of Columbia	554	691	531	576	603	49.3	31.9	25.5	29.1	30.4
Florida	1,818	2,285	2,103	2,088	2,078	53.8	38.2	35.3	33.8	32.1
Georgia	3,744	3,251	3,169	3,101	3,064	57.8	34.2	34.2	33.3	33.5
Idaho	506	478	481	431	434	42.9	29.4	29.8	27.0	27.1
Illinois	4,398	5,672	5,123	5,195	4,868	35.3	28.9	27.7	27.4	25.6
Indiana	2,595	2,949	2,760	2,746	2,520	42.1	30.6	29.8	29.1	27.0
Iowa	1,636	1,817	1,610	1,591	1,555	36.5	28.5	26.6	25.7	24.8
Kansas	1,106	1,251	1,151	1,136	1,130	38.3	28.1	26.9	25.9	25.7
Kentucky	3,387	2,971	3,073	3,139	2,616	53.1	37.1	39.8	41.2	34.9
Louisiana	3,268	2,773	2,779	2,810	2,639	64.3	37.2	37.9	37.2	34.6
Maine	810	853	706	713	650	53.2	35.7	32.0	32.5	30.9
Maryland	1,590	1,794	1,537	1,636	1,465	49.1	31.6	28.8	30.5	27.0
Massachusetts	2,458	3,027	2,613	2,347	2,240	37.5	28.1	26.8	24.5	23.3
Michigan	4,032	5,080	4,639	4,545	4,230	40.7	31.5	30.0	28.9	26.3
Minnesota	1,758	2,165	1,959	1,893	1,889	33.2	28.6	26.9	25.6	25.1
Mississippi	2,869	2,448	2,474	2,631	2,385	54.4	36.8	37.9	39.6	36.7
Missouri	2,885	2,929	2,585	2,563	2,510	46.9	32.5	30.3	30.0	29.2
Montana	537	484	461	457	441	46.5	32.1	30.7	29.7	28.2
Nebraska	792	894	835	761	796	36.0	27.8	26.8	24.1	25.0
Nevada	109	134	147	118	139	51.7	33.2	39.8	32.1	37.9
New Hampshire	341	399	361	333	282	40.9	30.1	29.1	27.9	24.5
New Jersey	2,121	2,965	2,585	2,534	2,467	35.5	27.9	26.5	26.0	25.2
New Mexico	1,488	1,379	1,438	1,408	1,211	100.6	67.9	70.1	65.1	54.8
New York	7,297	9,123	8,258	7,878	7,429	37.2	28.2	27.3	26.1	24.7
North Carolina	4,631	3,938	3,858	4,113	3,674	57.6	34.9	35.3	38.1	34.5
North Dakota	593	523	487	517	453	45.1	30.6	29.4	30.7	26.6
Ohio	4,744	5,817	5,693	5,315	4,990	41.4	29.5	30.5	28.1	26.8
Oklahoma	2,238	1,733	1,731	1,531	1,514	49.9	32.3	34.4	30.8	30.2
Oregon	585	895	897	869	812	33.2	24.7	25.5	24.6	22.5
Pennsylvania	7,404	7,741	6,442	6,567	6,126	44.7	31.1	28.4	29.2	27.6
Rhode Island	410	522	444	395	450	37.9	28.2	26.3	24.0	27.8
South Carolina	3,042	2,352	2,331	2,283	2,220	68.2	39.5	40.4	39.0	38.6
South Dakota	466	511	525	448	473	38.7	30.9	32.0	26.0	26.6
Tennessee	2,954	3,144	3,098	3,331	2,961	53.5	36.3	37.7	40.2	36.4
Texas	8,675	8,161	9,131	8,628	7,630	68.3	41.1	46.2	42.7	37.4
Utah	539	545	568	535	503	40.4	25.1	27.4	25.3	23.7
Vermont	309	303	271	301	221	44.5	31.2	28.9	32.4	24.5
Virginia	3,335	3,142	3,163	3,162	2,836	58.5	36.6	38.5	38.1	34.6
Washington	992	1,643	1,537	1,530	1,522	35.2	28.1	27.5	27.1	27.3
West Virginia	2,269	2,091	2,108	2,082	1,822	53.7	38.0	40.2	39.6	36.1
Wisconsin	2,046	2,476	2,148	2,202	2,121	37.3	29.5	26.3	26.5	25.7
Wyoming	232	249	293	280	247	44.7	34.0	39.5	37.4	32.5

SOURCE: Department of Health, Education, and Welfare, Public Health Service, National Office of Vital Statistics; annual report *Vital Statistics of the United States.*

3. Which of the following statements can be inferred from the table?

    I.   In 1950 less than $\frac{1}{20}$ of the babies born in the U.S. died before the age of 1 year.

    II.   The number of infant deaths in the U.S. decreased from 1945 to 1950.

  III. More than 5% of the infant deaths in the U.S. in 1950 occurred in California.

  IV. The number of infant deaths in North America in 1950 was less than 150,000.

(A) I only
(B) II only
(C) I and III only
(D) I, III, IV only
(E) I, II, III, IV

Analysis:

Statement I can be inferred since $\frac{1}{20}$ of 1,000 = 50 which exceeds the rate per thousand of 29.2 in 1950.

Statement II can't be inferred since the table has no information about 1945. Infant deaths decreased between 1940 and 1950, but that doesn't mean they decreased between 1945 and 1950.

Statement III can be inferred from the table. The total number of infant deaths in 1950 was 103,825, and 6,115 occurred in California. A calculation of $\frac{6,115}{103,825}$ could be made, but it is much quicker to find 5% of 103,825 which is 5,191. Since 6,115 is greater than 5,191, more than 5% of the infant deaths in the U.S. occurred in California.

Statement IV can't be inferred, because the table only gives information about the U.S. and there are other countries in North America.

So the correct answer is (C).

IV–2. CIRCLE GRAPHS

Circle graphs are used to show how various sectors share in the whole. Circle graphs are sometimes called pie charts. Circle graphs usually give the percentage that each sector receives.

(Refer to the graph that follows to answer these questions.)

EXPENDITURES OF GENERAL INDUSTRIES
(by major categories)

1960 ($3,087 million)

1970 ($4,851 million)

1. The amount spent on materials in 1960 was 120% of the amount spent on

   (A) research in 1960
   (B) compensation in 1960
   (C) advertising in 1970
   (D) materials in 1970
   (E) legal affairs in 1960

   When using circle graphs to find ratios of various sectors, don't find the amounts each sector received and then the ratio of the amounts. Find the *ratio of the percentages*, which is much quicker. In 1960, 18% of the expenditures were for materials. We want x where 120% of x = 18%; so x = 15%. Any category that received 15% of 1960 expenditures gives the correct answer, but only one of the five choices is correct. Here, the answer is (A) since research received 15% of the expenditure in 1960. Check the 1960 answers first since you need look only at the percentages, which can be done quickly. Notice that (C) is incorrect, since 15% of the expenditures for 1970 is different from 15% of the expenditures for 1960.

2. The fraction of the total expenditures for 1960 and 1970 spent on compensation was about

   (A) $\frac{1}{5}$

   (B) $\frac{1}{4}$

   (C) $\frac{1}{3}$

   (D) $\frac{3}{7}$

   (E) $\frac{1}{2}$

   In 1960, 26% of $3,087 million was spent on compensation and in 1970 compensation received 38% of $4,851 million. The total expenditures for 1960 and 1970 are

   $(3,087 + 4,851)$ million. So the exact answer is $\frac{[(.26)(3,087)+(.38)(4,851)]}{(3,087+4,851)}$. Actually

   calculating the answer, you will waste a lot of time. Look at the answers and think for a second.

   We are taking a weighted average of 26% and 38%. To find a weighted average, we multiply each value by a weight and divide by the total of all the weights. Here 26% is given a weight of 3,087 and 38% a weight of 4,851. The following general rule is often useful in average problems: The average or weighted average of a collection of values can *never* be:

   1. less than the smallest value in the collection, or
   2. greater than the largest value in the collection.

   Therefore, the answer to the question must be greater than or equal to 26% and less than or equal to 38%.

   Since $\frac{1}{5}$ = 20% and $\frac{1}{4}$ = 25%, which are both less than 26%, neither (A) nor (B) can

   be the correct answer. Since $\frac{3}{7}$ = $42\frac{6}{7}$% and $\frac{1}{2}$ = 50%, which are both greater than 38%,

   neither (D) nor (E) can be correct. Therefore, by elimination (C) is the correct answer.

3. The amount spent in 1960 for materials, advertising, and taxes was about the same as

   (A) $\frac{5}{4}$ of the amount spent for compensation in 1960

   (B) the amount spent for compensation in 1970
   (C) the amount spent on materials in 1970

   (D) $\frac{5}{3}$ of the amount spent on advertising in 1970

   (E) the amount spent on research and construction in 1970

   First calculate the combined percentage for materials, advertising, and taxes in 1960. Since 18% + 12% + 10% = 40%, these three categories accounted for 40% of the expenditures in 1960. You can check the one answer that involves 1960 now. Since $\frac{5}{4}$ of 26% =

   32.5%, (A) is incorrect. To check the answers that involve 1970, you must know the amount spent on the three categories above in 1960. 40% of 3,087 is 1,234.8; so the amount spent on the three categories in 1960 was $1,234.8 million. You could calculate the amount spent in each of the possible answers, but there is a quicker way. Find the *approximate* percentage that 1,234.8 is of 4,851, and check this against the percentages of the answers.

Since $\frac{12}{48} = \frac{1}{4}$, the amount for the 3 categories in 1960 is about 25% of the 1970 expenditures. Compensation received 38% of 1970 expenditures, so (B) is incorrect. Materials received 22% and research and construction together received 19%; since advertising received 15%, $\frac{5}{3}$ of the amount for advertising yields 25%. So (D) is probably correct.

You can check by calculating 22% of 4,851 which is 1,067.22, while 25% of 4,851 = 1,212.75. Therefore, (D) is correct.

In inference questions involving circle graphs, *do not compare different percentages.* Note in question 3 that the percentage of expenditures in 1960 for the three categories (40%) is *not equal* to 40% of the expenditures in 1970.

IV–3. LINE GRAPHS

Line graphs are used to show how a quantity changes continuously. Very often the quantity is measured as time changes. If the line goes up, the quantity is increasing; if the line goes down, the quantity is decreasing; if the line is horizontal, the quantity is not changing. To measure the height of a point on the graph, use your pencil or a piece of paper (for example, the admission card to the exam) as a straight edge.

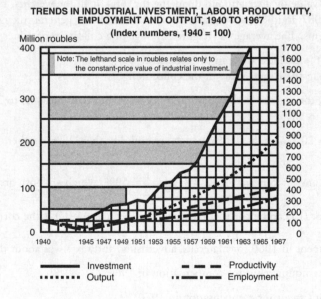

SOURCE: United Nations Economics Bulletin for Europe

(Refer to the graph above to answer these questions.)

1. The ratio of productivity in 1967 to productivity in 1940 was about

   (A) 1 : 4
   (B) 1 : 3
   (C) 3 : 1
   (D) 4 : 1
   (E) 9 : 1

   In 1967 productivity had an index number of 400, and the index numbers are based on 1940 = 100. So the ratio is 400 : 100 = 4 : 1. Therefore, the answer is (D). [If you used (incorrectly) output or employment (instead of productivity) you would get the wrong answer (E) or (C); if you confused the order of the ratio you would have incorrectly answered (A).]

2. If 1 rouble = $3, then the constant-price value of industrial investment in 1959 was about

   (A) $1.9 million
   (B) $200 million
   (C) $420,000,000
   (D) $570,000,000
   (E) $570,000 million

   In 1959, the value was about 190 million roubles. (It was a little below 200 million.) The answers are all in dollars, so multiply 190 by 3 to get $570 million or $570,000,000 (D). If you are not careful about units, you may answer (B) or (E), which are incorrect.

3. Employment was at its minimum during the years shown in

   (A) 1940
   (B) 1943
   (C) 1945
   (D) 1953
   (E) 1967

   The minimum of a quantity displayed on a line graph is the lowest place on the line. Thus in 1945, (C), the minimum value of employment was reached.

4. Between 1954 and 1965, output

   (A) decreased by about 10%
   (B) stayed about the same
   (C) increased by about 200%
   (D) increased by about 250%
   (E) increased by about 500%

   The line for output goes up between 1954 and 1965, so output increased between 1954 and 1965. Therefore, (A) and (B) are wrong. Output was about 200 in 1954 and about 700 in 1965, so the increase was 500. Since $\frac{500}{200}$ = 2.5 = 250%, the correct answer is (D).

IV–4. BAR GRAPHS

Quantities can be compared by the height or length of a bar in a bar graph. A bar graph can have either vertical or horizontal bars. You can compare different quantities or the same quantity at different times. Use your pencil or a piece of paper to compare bars that are not adjacent to each other.

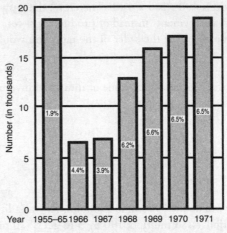

DISABILITY BENEFICIARIES REPORTED AS REHABILITATED
(number, as percent of all rehabilitated clients of state
vocational rehabilitation agencies, years 1955–1971)

SOURCE: Social Security Bulletin

(Refer to the graph above to answer these questions.)

1. Between 1967 and 1971, the largest number of disability beneficiaries were reported as rehabilitated in the year

    (A) 1967
    (B) 1968
    (C) 1969
    (D) 1970
    (E) 1971

    The answer is (E) since the highest bar is the bar for 1971. The percentage of disability beneficiaries out of all rehabilitated clients was higher in 1969, but the *number* was lower.

2. Between 1955 and 1965, about how many clients were rehabilitated by state vocational rehabilitation agencies?

    (A) 90,000
    (B) 400,000
    (C) 1,000,000
    (D) 1,900,000
    (E) 10,000,000

    1.9% of those rehabilitated were disability beneficiaries, and there were about 19,000 disability beneficiaries rehabilitated. So if T is the total number rehabilitated, then 1.9% of T = 19,000 or $.019T$ = 19,000. Thus, $T = \dfrac{19,000}{.019} = 1,000,000$ and the answer is (C).

IV–5. CUMULATIVE GRAPHS

You can compare several categories by a graph of the cumulative type. These are usually bar or line graphs where the height of the bar or line is divided up proportionately among different quantities.

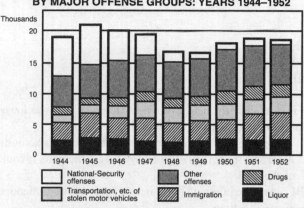

FEDERAL PRISONERS RECEIVED FROM THE COURTS, BY MAJOR OFFENSE GROUPS: YEARS 1944–1952

SOURCE: Statistical Abstract of the U.S. 1953

Refer to the graph above to answer these questions.

1. In 1946, roughly what percent of the federal prisoners received from the courts were national-security offenders?

   (A) 10
   (B) 15
   (C) 25
   (D) 30
   (E) 35

   The total number of prisoners in 1946 was about 20,000, and national-security offenders accounted for the part of the graph from just above 15,000 to just above 20,000. Therefore, there were about 20,000 – 15,000 = 5,000 prisoners convicted of national-security offenses. Since $\frac{5,000}{20,000} = \frac{1}{4} = 25\%$, the correct answer is (C).

2. Of the combined total for the four years 1947 through 1950, the largest number of offenders were in the category

   (A) national-security offenses
   (B) other offenses
   (C) drugs
   (D) immigration
   (E) liquor

   The correct answer is (B). Since other offenses had the most offenders in each year, that category must have the largest total number of offenders. [If you answered this question for the years 1944–1946, then (A) would be correct.]

3. Which of the following statements can be inferred from the graph?

    I. The number of federal prisoners received from the courts decreased each year from 1946 to 1948.

   II. More than 40% of the prisoners between 1944 and 1952 came from the other offenses category.

  III. 2% of the federal prisoners received in 1952 were convicted on heroin charges.

    (A) I only
    (B) III only
    (C) I and II only
    (D) I and III only
    (E) I, II, and III

Statement I is true, since the height of the bar for each year was lower than the height of the bar for the previous year in 1946, 1947, and 1948.

Statement II is not true. For most of the years, other offenses accounted for about 25–30%, and it never was more than 40% in any year. Therefore, it could not account for more than 40% of the total.

Statement III cannot be inferred. There is a category of drug offenders, but there is no information about specific drugs.

So, the correct answer is (A).

Review of Formulas

(Numbers next to the formulas refer to the section of the Math Review where the formula is discussed.)

Interest = Amount × Time × Rate — I–4

Discount = Cost × Rate of Discount — I–4

Price = Cost × (100% − Rate of Discount) — I–4

$x^2 - y^2 = (x + y)(x - y)$ — II–1

$x = \dfrac{1}{2a}\left[-b \pm \sqrt{b^2 - 4ac}\,\right]$ (quadratic formula) — II–2

Distance = Rate × Time — II–3

$a^2 + b^2 = c^2$ when a and b are the legs and c is the hypotenuse of a right triangle (Pythagorean Theorem) — III–4

Diameter of a circle = 2 × Radius — III–6

Area of a square = s^2 — III–7

Area of a rectangle = LW — III–7

Area of a triangle = $\dfrac{1}{2}bh$ — III–7

Area of a circle = πr^2 — III–7

Area of a parallelogram = bh — III–7

Area of a trapezoid = $\dfrac{1}{2}(b_1 + b_2)h$ — III–7

Circumference of a circle = πd — III–7

Perimeter of a square = $4s$ — III–7

Perimeter of a rectangle = $2(L + W)$ — III–7

Volume of a box = lwh — III–8

Volume of a cube = e^3 — III–8

Volume of a cylinder = $\pi r^2 h$ — III–8

Volume of a sphere = $\dfrac{4}{3}\pi r^3$ — III–8

Surface area of a box = $2LW + 2LH + 2WH$ — III–8

Surface area of a cube = $6e^2$ — III–8

Surface area of a cylinder = $2\pi rh + 2\pi r^2$ — III–8

Distance between points (x,y) and (a,b) is $\sqrt{(x - a)^2 + (y - b)^2}$ — III–9

The following are always equal:

Any two radii of the same circle.

The two sides opposite equal angles of a triangle.

The two angles opposite equal sides of a triangle.

Opposite angles formed by intersecting lines.

Alternate angles formed by parallel lines.

The four sides of a square.

The three sides of an equilateral triangle.

Opposite sides (and angles) of a parallelogram.

The sides (and angles) of any regular polygon.

Corresponding angles of similar polygons.

All right angles.

The square of the hypotenuse and the sum of the squares of two remaining sides of a right triangle.

The difference of two squares and the product of the sum and difference of their square roots.

The following are always right angles:

Any angle whose measure is 90 degrees.

Angles formed by perpendicular lines.

Any of four equal angles formed by intersection of two lines.

Any angle that is equal to its supplement.

All angles of a square, rectangle, or cube.

Any angle inscribed in a semi-circle.

The angle formed by a circle's radius and tangent.

The angle opposite the longest side of a right triangle.

The angles between north, south, east, and west.

Angle between the base and height of a triangle.

Angle between the base and height of a cylinder.

The angle between floor and wall or ceiling and wall.

If any of the following properties hold, two triangles are congruent:

Two corresponding angles and the corresponding included sides are equal.

Two corresponding sides and the corresponding included angles are equal.

All three corresponding sides are equal.

Two right triangles that have any two corresponding sides equal.

HINTS FOR ANSWERING MATHEMATICS QUESTIONS

1. Make sure you answer the question you are asked to answer.

2. Look at the answers before you start to work out a problem; you can save a lot of time.

3. Don't waste time on superfluous computations.

4. *Estimate* whenever you can to save time.

5. Budget your time so you can try all the questions. (Check the time box frequently.)

6. Don't make extra assumptions on inference questions.

7. Work efficiently; don't waste time worrying during the test.

8. Make sure you express your answer in the units asked for.

9. On data sufficiency questions, don't do any more work than is necessary. (Don't solve the problem; you only have to know that the problem can be solved.)

Practice Exercises

The four exercises that follow will give you an indication of your ability to handle both mathematics and data sufficiency questions. The time for each practice mathematics exercise is 30 minutes. Scoring for each of the mathematics exercises may be interpreted as follows:

22–25	EXCELLENT
18–21+	GOOD
13–17+	FAIR
0–12+	POOR

Your score should be determined by counting the number of correct answers minus ¼ the number of incorrect answers.

Mathematics

Exercise A

Directions: Solve each of the following problems.

NOTE: A figure that appears with a problem is drawn as accurately as possible unless the words "Figure not drawn to scale" appear next to the figure. Numbers in this test are real numbers.

1. In 1955, it cost \$12 to purchase one hundred pounds of potatoes. In 1975, it cost \$34 to purchase one hundred pounds of potatoes. The price of one hundred pounds of potatoes increased X dollars between 1955 and 1975 with X equal to:

    (A) 1.20
    (B) 2.20
    (C) 3.40
    (D) 22
    (E) 34

2. A house cost Ms. Jones C dollars in 1965. Three years later she sold the house for 25% more than she paid for it. She has to pay a tax of 50% of the gain. (The gain is the selling price minus the cost.) How much tax must Ms. Jones pay?

    (A) $\frac{1}{24}C$

    (B) $\frac{C}{8}$

    (C) $\frac{1}{4}C$

    (D) $\frac{C}{2}$

    (E) $.6C$

3. If the length of a rectangle is increased by 20%, and the width of the same rectangle is decreased by 20%, then the area of the rectangle

   (A) decreases by 20%
   (B) decreases by 4%
   (C) is unchanged
   (D) increases by 20%
   (E) increases by 40%

Use the following graph for questions 4–7.

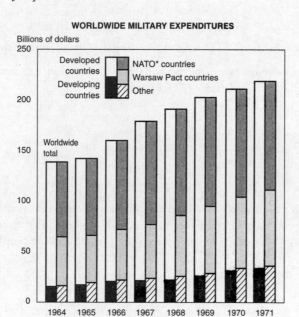

WORLDWIDE MILITARY EXPENDITURES

*North Atlantic Treaty Organization

SOURCE: Pocket Data Book U.S.A. 1973.

4. Between 1964 and 1969, worldwide military expenditures

   (A) increased by about 50%
   (B) roughly doubled
   (C) increased by about 150%
   (D) almost tripled
   (E) increased by 10%

5. The average yearly military expenditure by the developing countries between 1964 and 1971 was approximately how many billions of dollars?

   (A) 20
   (B) 50
   (C) 100
   (D) 140
   (E) 175

6. Which of the following statements can be inferred from the graph?

   I. The NATO countries have higher incomes than the Warsaw Pact countries.
  II. Worldwide military expenditures have increased each year between 1964 and 1971.
 III. In 1972 worldwide military expenditures were more than 230 billion dollars.

(A) I only
(B) II only
(C) I and II only
(D) II and III only
(E) I, II, and III

7. A speaker claims that the NATO countries customarily spend $\frac{1}{3}$ of their combined incomes on military expenditures. According to the speaker, the combined incomes of the NATO countries (in billions of dollars) in 1971 was about

(A) 100
(B) 200
(C) 250
(D) 350
(E) 500

8. 8% of the people eligible to vote are between 18 and 21. In an election 85% of those eligible to vote who were between 18 and 21 actually voted. In that election, people between 18 and 21 who actually voted were what percent of those people eligible to vote?

(A) 4.2
(B) 6.4
(C) 6.8
(D) 8
(E) 68

9. If n and p are both odd numbers, which of the following numbers *must* be an even number?

(A) $n + p$
(B) np
(C) $np + 2$
(D) $n + p + 1$
(E) $2n + p$

10. It costs g cents a mile for gasoline and m cents a mile for all other costs to run a car. How many *dollars* will it cost to run the car for 100 miles?

(A) $\dfrac{g + m}{100}$
(B) $100g + 100m$
(C) $g + m$
(D) $g + .1m$
(E) g

11. What is the length of the line segment that connects *A* to *B*?

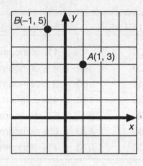

(A) $\sqrt{3}$
(B) 2
(C) $2\sqrt{2}$
(D) 4
(E) 8

12. A cabdriver's income consists of his salary and tips. His salary is $50 a week. During one week his tips were $\frac{5}{4}$ of his salary. What fraction of his income for the week came from tips?

(A) $\frac{4}{9}$

(B) $\frac{1}{2}$

(C) $\frac{5}{9}$

(D) $\frac{5}{8}$

(E) $\frac{5}{4}$

Use the following table for questions 13–17.

INCOME (IN DOLLARS)	TAX (IN DOLLARS)
0 – 4,000	1% of income
4,000 – 6,000	40 + 2% of income over 4,000
6,000 – 8,000	80 + 3% of income over 6,000
8,000 – 10,000	140 + 4% of income over 8,000
10,000 – 15,000	220 + 5% of income over 10,000
15,000 – 25,000	470 + 6% of income over 15,000
25,000 – 50,000	1,070 + 7% of income over 25,000

13. How much tax is due on an income of $7,500?

    (A) $75
    (B) $80
    (C) $125
    (D) $150
    (E) $225

14. Your income for a year is $26,000. You receive a raise so that next year your income will be $29,000. How much more will you pay in taxes next year if the tax rate remains the same?

    (A) $70
    (B) $180
    (C) $200
    (D) $210
    (E) $700

15. Joan paid $100 tax. If X was her income, which of the following statements is true?

    (A) $0 < X < 4,000$
    (B) $4,000 < X < 6,000$
    (C) $6,000 < X < 8,000$
    (D) $8,000 < X < 10,000$
    (E) $10,000 < X < 15,000$

16. The town of Zenith has a population of 50,000. The average income of a person who lives in Zenith is $3,700 per year. What is the total amount paid in taxes by the people of Zenith? Assume each person pays tax on $3,700.

    (A) $37
    (B) $3,700
    (C) $50,000
    (D) $185,000
    (E) $1,850,000

17. A person who has an income of $10,000 pays what percent (to the nearest percent) of his or her income in taxes?

    (A) 1
    (B) 2
    (C) 3
    (D) 4
    (E) 5

18. Given that x and y are real numbers, let $S(x, y) = x^2 - y^2$. Then $S(3, S(3, 4)) =$

    (A) −40
    (B) −7
    (C) 40
    (D) 49
    (E) 56

19. Eggs cost 90¢ a dozen. Peppers cost 20¢ each. An omelet consists of 3 eggs and $\frac{1}{4}$ of a pepper. How much will the ingredients for 8 omelets cost?

    (A) $.90
    (B) $1.30
    (C) $1.80
    (D) $2.20
    (E) $2.70

20. It is 185 miles from Binghamton to New York City. If a bus takes 2 hours to travel the first 85 miles, how long must the bus take to travel the final 100 miles in order to average 50 miles an hour for the entire trip?

    (A) 60 min
    (B) 75 min
    (C) 94 min
    (D) 102 min
    (E) 112 min

21. What is the area of this figure? *ABDC* is a rectangle and *BDE* is an isosceles right triangle.

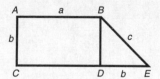

    (A) ab
    (B) ab^2
    (C) $b\left(a + \dfrac{b}{2}\right)$
    (D) cab
    (E) $\dfrac{1}{2}bc$

22. If $2x + y = 5$ then $4x + 2y$ is equal to

  (A) 5
  (B) 8
  (C) 9
  (D) 10
  (E) none of these

23. In 1967, a new sedan cost \$2,500; in 1975, the same type of sedan cost \$4,800. The cost of that type of sedan has increased by what percent between 1967 and 1975?

  (A) 48
  (B) 52
  (C) 92
  (D) 152
  (E) 192

24. What is the area of the square *ABCD*?

  (A) 10
  (B) 18
  (C) 24
  (D) 36
  (E) 48

25. If $x + y = 6$ and $3x - y = 4$, then $x - y$ is equal to

  (A) −1
  (B) 0
  (C) 2
  (D) 4
  (E) 6

Mathematics

Exercise B

Directions: Solve each of the following problems.

NOTE: A figure that appears with a problem is drawn as accurately as possible unless the words "Figure not drawn to scale" appear next to the figure. Numbers in this test are real numbers.

Use the graphs below for questions 1–5.

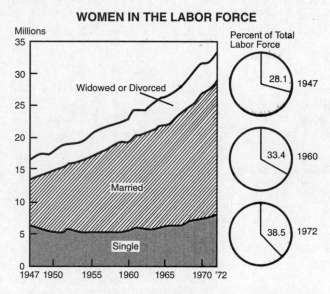

SOURCE: Pocket Data Book U.S.A. 1973. Bureau of the Census.

1. The total labor force in 1960 was about *y* million with *y* equal to about

   (A) 22
   (B) 65
   (C) 85
   (D) 95
   (E) 100

2. In 1947, the percentage of women in the labor force who were married was about

   (A) 28
   (B) 33
   (C) 38
   (D) 50
   (E) 65

3. What was the first year when more than 20 million women were in the labor force?

   (A) 1950
   (B) 1953
   (C) 1956
   (D) 1958
   (E) 1964

4. Between 1947 and 1972, the number of women in the labor force

    (A) increased by about 50%
    (B) increased by about 100%
    (C) increased by about 150%
    (D) increased by about 200%
    (E) increased by about 250%

5. Which of the following statements about the labor force can be inferred from the graphs?

    I.   Between 1947 and 1957, there were no years when more than 5 million widowed or divorced women were in the labor force.
    II.   In every year between 1947 and 1972, the number of single women in the labor force has increased.
    III.   In 1965, women made up more than $\frac{1}{3}$ of the total labor force.

    (A) I only
    (B) II only
    (C) I and II only
    (D) I and III only
    (E) I, II, and III

6. If $\frac{x}{y} = \frac{2}{3}$ then $\frac{y^2}{x^2}$ is equal to

    (A) $\frac{4}{9}$

    (B) $\frac{2}{3}$

    (C) $\frac{3}{2}$

    (D) $\frac{9}{4}$

    (E) $\frac{5}{2}$

7. In the figure, *BD* is perpendicular to *AC*. *BA* and *BC* have length *a*. What is the area of the triangle *ABC*?

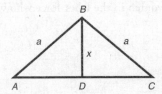

    (A) $2x\sqrt{a^2 - x^2}$

    (B) $x\sqrt{a^2 - x^2}$

    (C) $a\sqrt{a^2 - x^2}$

    (D) $2a\sqrt{x^2 - a^2}$

    (E) $x\sqrt{x^2 - a^2}$

8. If two places are one inch apart on a map, then they are actually 160 miles apart. (The scale on the map is one inch equals 160 miles.) If Seaton is $2\frac{7}{8}$ inches from Monroe on the map, how many miles is it from Seaton to Monroe?

    (A) 3
    (B) 27
    (C) 300
    (D) 360
    (E) 460

9. In the accompanying diagram $ABCD$ is a rectangle. The area of isosceles right triangle $ABE = 7$, and $EC = 3(BE)$. The area of $ABCD$ is

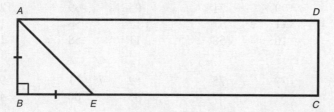

    (A) 21
    (B) 28
    (C) 42
    (D) 56
    (E) 84

10. An automobile tire has two punctures. The first puncture by itself would make the tire flat in 9 minutes. The second puncture by itself would make the tire flat in 6 minutes. How long will it take for both punctures together to make the tire flat? (Assume the air leaks out at a constant rate.)

    (A) $3\frac{3}{5}$ minutes

    (B) 4 minutes

    (C) $5\frac{1}{4}$ minutes

    (D) $7\frac{1}{2}$ minutes

    (E) 15 minutes

11. If n^3 is odd, which of the following statements are true?

    I. n is odd.
    II. n^2 is odd.
    III. n^2 is even.

    (A) I only
    (B) II only
    (C) III only
    (D) I and II only
    (E) I and III only

Use the table below for questions 12–15.

PARTICIPATION IN NATIONAL ELECTIONS

Persons in millions. Civilian noninstitutional population as of Nov. 1. Based on post-election surveys of persons reporting whether or not they voted.

Characteristic	1964		1968		1972	
	Persons of voting age	Percent voted	Persons of voting age	Percent voted	Persons of voting age	Percent voted
Total	111	69	117	68	136	63
Male	52	72	54	70	64	64
Female	58	67	62	66	72	62
White	99	71	105	69	121	64
Black and other	11	57	12	56	15	51
Black	10	58	11	58	13	52
Region:						
North and West	78	75	82	71	94	66
South	32	57	35	60	43	55
Age:						
18–24 years	10	51	12	50	25	50
25–44 years	45	69	46	67	49	63
45–64 years	38	76	40	75	42	71
65 years and over	17	66	18	66	40	63

Source: U.S. Bureau of the Census.

12. Which of the following groups had the highest voting percentage in 1968?

    (A) 18–24 years
    (B) Female
    (C) South
    (D) 25–44 years
    (E) Male

13. In 1972, what percent (to the nearest percent) of persons of voting age were female?

    (A) 52
    (B) 53
    (C) 62
    (D) 64
    (E) 72

14. In 1968, how many males of voting age voted?

    (A) 37,440,000
    (B) 37,800,000
    (C) 42,160,000
    (D) 54,000,000
    (E) 62,000,000

15. Let *X* be the number (in millions) of persons of voting age in the range 25–44 years who lived in the North and West in 1964. Which of the following includes all possible values and only possible values of *X*?

(A) $0 \leqq X \leqq 45$

(B) $13 \leqq X \leqq 45$

(C) $13 \leqq X \leqq 78$

(D) $45 \leqq X \leqq 78$

(E) $75 \leqq X \leqq 78$

16. There are 50 students enrolled in Business 101. Of the enrolled students, 90% took the final exam. Two-thirds of the students who took the final exam passed the final exam. How many students passed the final exam?

(A) 30
(B) 33
(C) 34
(D) 35
(E) 45

17. If *a* is less than *b*, which of the following numbers is greater than *a* and less than *b*?

(A) $\dfrac{(a+b)}{2}$

(B) $\dfrac{(ab)}{2}$

(C) $b^2 - a^2$
(D) ab
(E) $b - a$

18. In the figure, *OR* and *PR* are radii of circles. The length of *OP* is 4. If *OR* = 2, what is *PR*? *PR* is tangent to the circle with center *O*.

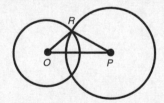

(A) 2

(B) $\dfrac{5}{2}$

(C) 3

(D) $2\sqrt{3}$

(E) $3\sqrt{2}$

19. A bus uses one gallon of gasoline to travel 15 miles. After a tune-up, the bus travels 15% farther on one gallon. How many gallons of gasoline (to the nearest tenth) will it take for the bus to travel 150 miles after a tune-up?

(A) 8.5
(B) 8.7
(C) 8.9
(D) 9.0
(E) 10.0

20. If $x + 2y = 4$ and $\dfrac{x}{y} = 2$, then x is equal to

(A) 0

(B) $\dfrac{1}{2}$

(C) 1

(D) $\dfrac{3}{2}$

(E) 2

Use the following table for questions 21–23.

SPEED OF A TRAIN OVER A 3-HOUR PERIOD								
TIMED PERIOD *(in minutes)*	0	30	45	60	90	120	150	180
SPEED AT TIME *(in m.p.h.)*	40	45	47.5	50	55	60	65	70

21. How fast was the train traveling $2\dfrac{1}{2}$ hours after the beginning of the timed period?

(A) 50 mph
(B) 55 mph
(C) 60 mph
(D) 65 mph
(E) 70 mph

22. During the three hours shown on the table the speed of the train

(A) increased by 25%
(B) increased by 50%
(C) increased by 75%
(D) increased by 100%
(E) increased by 125%

23. At time t measured in minutes after the beginning of the timed period, which of the following gives the speed of the train in accordance with the table?

   (A) $\frac{1}{6}t$

   (B) $10t$

   (C) $40 + t$

   (D) $40 + \frac{1}{6}t$

   (E) $40 + 10t$

24. It costs \$1,000 to make the first thousand copies of a book and x dollars to make each subsequent copy. If it costs a total of \$7,230 to make the first 8,000 copies of a book, what is x?

   (A) .89
   (B) .90375
   (C) 1.00
   (D) 89
   (E) 90.375

25. If 16 workers can finish a job in three hours, how long should it take 5 workers to finish the same job?

   (A) $3\frac{1}{2}$ hours

   (B) 4 hours

   (C) 5 hours

   (D) $7\frac{1}{16}$ hours

   (E) $9\frac{3}{5}$ hours

Mathematics

Exercise C

Directions: Solve each of the following problems.

NOTE: A figure that appears with a problem is drawn as accurately as possible unless the words "Figure not drawn to scale" appear next to the figure. Numbers in this test are real numbers.

---

1. A box contains 12 poles and 7 pieces of net. Each piece of net weighs .2 pounds; each pole weighs 1.1 pounds. The box and its contents together weigh 16.25 pounds. How much does the empty box weigh?

   (A) 1.2 pounds
   (B) 1.65 pounds
   (C) 2.75 pounds
   (D) 6.15 pounds
   (E) 16 pounds

2. If $a + b + c + d$ is a positive number, a minimum of x of the numbers a, b, c, and d must be positive where x is equal to

   (A) 0
   (B) 1
   (C) 2
   (D) 3
   (E) 4

3. Consider the accompanying diagram. Which of the following statements is true?

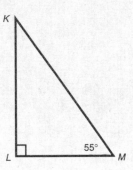

   (A) $KM < KL$
   (B) $KM < LM$
   (C) $KL + LM < KM$
   (D) $KL < LM$
   (E) $LM < KL$

Use the graphs below for questions 4–6.

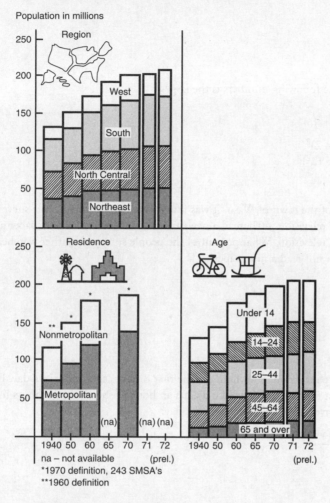

POPULATION CHARACTERISTICS

Population in millions

SOURCE: Pocket Data Book U.S.A. 1973. Bureau of the Census.

4. In 1970, the ratio of the population living in metropolitan areas to the population living in nonmetropolitan areas was approximately

   (A) 1 to 2
   (B) 2 to 3
   (C) 7 to 5
   (D) 2 to 1
   (E) 3 to 1

5. In 1950, the age group that had the fewest people was

   (A) under 14
   (B) 14–24
   (C) 25–44
   (D) 45–64
   (E) 65 and over

6. How many of the regions shown had a population increase of less than 5% between 1940 and 1972?

   (A) 0
   (B) 1
   (C) 2
   (D) 3
   (E) 4

7. Which of the following numbers is the largest?

   (A) $(2 + 2 + 2)^2$
   (B) $[(2 + 2)^2]^2$
   (C) $(2 \times 2 \times 2)^2$
   (D) $2 + 2^2 + (2^2)^2$
   (E) 4^3

8. In a survey of the town of Waso, it was found that 65% of the people surveyed watched the news on television, 40% read a newspaper, and 25% read a newspaper and watched the news on television. What percent of the people surveyed neither watched the news on television nor read a newspaper?

   (A) 0%
   (B) 5%
   (C) 10%
   (D) 15%
   (E) 20%

9. A worker is paid d dollars an hour for the first 8 hours she works in a day. For every hour after the first 8 hours, she is paid c dollars an hour. If she works 12 hours in one day, what is her average hourly wage for that day?

   (A) $\dfrac{(2d + c)}{3}$

   (B) $8d + 4c$

   (C) $\dfrac{(8d + 12c)}{12}$

   (D) $\dfrac{(4d + 8c)}{12}$

   (E) $d + \left(\dfrac{1}{3}\right)c$

10. A screwdriver and a hammer currently have the same price. If the price of a screwdriver rises by 5% and the price of a hammer goes up by 3%, how much more will it cost to buy 3 screwdrivers and 3 hammers?

    (A) 3%
    (B) 4%
    (C) 5%
    (D) 8%
    (E) 24%

11. If the radius of a circle is increased by 6%, then the area of the circle is increased by

   (A) .36%
   (B) 3.6%
   (C) 6%
   (D) 12.36%
   (E) 36%

12. Given that a and b are real numbers, let $f(a, b) = ab$ and let $g(a) = a^2 + 2$. Then $f[3, g(3)] =$

   (A) $3a^2 + 2$
   (B) $3a^2 + 6$
   (C) 27
   (D) 29
   (E) 33

13. A share of stock in Ace Enterprises cost D dollars on Jan. 1, 1999. One year later, a share increased to Q dollars. The fraction by which the cost of a share of stock has increased in the year is

   (A) $\dfrac{(Q-D)}{D}$

   (B) $\dfrac{(D-Q)}{Q}$

   (C) $\dfrac{D}{Q}$

   (D) $\dfrac{Q}{D}$

   (E) $\dfrac{(Q-D)}{Q}$

14. *ABCD* is a square, *EFGH* is a rectangle. *AB* = 3, *EF* = 4, *FG* = 6. The area of the region outside of *ABCD* and inside *EFGH* is

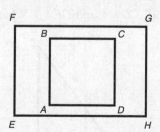

   (A) 6
   (B) 9
   (C) 12
   (D) 15
   (E) 24

Use the table below for questions 15–17.

	% OF PROTEIN	% OF CARBOHYDRATES	% OF FAT	COST PER 100 GRAMS
FOOD A	10	20	30	$1.80
FOOD B	20	15	10	$3.00
FOOD C	20	10	40	$2.75

15. If you purchase x grams of Food A, y grams of Food B, and z grams of Food C, the cost will be

   (A) $\left(\dfrac{9}{5}x + 3y + \dfrac{11}{4}z\right)¢$

   (B) $\$\left(\dfrac{9}{5}x + 3y + \dfrac{11}{4}z\right)$

   (C) $\$(1.8x + 3z + 2.75y)$
   (D) $(3x + 1.8y + 2.75z)¢$
   (E) $\$(x + y + z)$

16. Which of the following diets would supply the most grams of protein?

   (A) 500 grams of A
   (B) 250 grams of B
   (C) 350 grams of C
   (D) 150 grams of A and 200 grams of B
   (E) 200 grams of B and 200 grams of C

17. All of the following diets would supply at least 75 grams of fat. Which of the diets costs the least?

   (A) 200 grams of A, 150 grams of B
   (B) 500 grams of B, 100 grams of A
   (C) 200 grams of C
   (D) 150 grams of A, 100 grams of C
   (E) 300 grams of A

18. CD is parallel to EF. $AD = DF$, $CD = 4$, and $DF = 3$. What is EF?

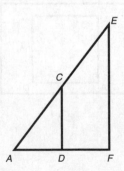

   (A) 4
   (B) 5
   (C) 6
   (D) 7
   (E) 8

19. Which of the following fractions is the largest?

    (A) $\frac{5}{6}$

    (B) $\frac{11}{14}$

    (C) $\frac{12}{15}$

    (D) $\frac{17}{21}$

    (E) $\frac{29}{35}$

20. How much simple interest will $2,000 earn in 18 months at an annual rate of 6%?

    (A) $120
    (B) $180
    (C) $216
    (D) $1,800
    (E) $2,160

21. If $x + y > 5$ and $x - y > 3$, then which of the following gives all possible values of x and only possible values of x?

    (A) $x > 3$
    (B) $x > 4$
    (C) $x > 5$
    (D) $x < 5$
    (E) $x < 3$

22. If the average (or arithmetic mean) of 6 numbers is 4.5, what is the sum of the numbers?

    (A) 4.5
    (B) 24
    (C) 27
    (D) 30
    (E) cannot be determined

23. A silo is filled to capacity with W pounds of wheat. Rats eat r pounds a day. After 25 days, what percentage of the silo's capacity have the rats eaten?

(A) $\dfrac{25r}{W}$

(B) $\dfrac{25r}{100W}$

(C) $2{,}500\left(\dfrac{r}{W}\right)$

(D) $\dfrac{r}{W}$

(E) $\dfrac{r}{25W}$

24. If $x^2 + 2x - 8 = 0$, then x is either -4 or

(A) -2
(B) -1
(C) 0
(D) 2
(E) 8

25. The interest charged on a loan is p dollars per \$1,000 for the first month and q dollars per \$1,000 for each month after the first month. How much interest will be charged during the first three months on a loan of \$10,000?

(A) $30p$
(B) $30q$
(C) $p + 2q$
(D) $20p + 10q$
(E) $10p + 20q$

Data Sufficiency

Exercise D

We have included one data sufficiency exercise to give you practice in answering this type of problem. The time allotted for this practice exercise is 18 minutes. Scoring may be interpreted as follows:

13–15	EXCELLENT
10–12+	GOOD
7–9+	FAIR
0–6+	POOR

Determine your score by counting the number of correct answers minus ¼ the number of incorrect answers. Before starting this practice exercise, refer to the system for answering data sufficiency questions as outlined on pages 38–43 of this book.

Directions: Each of the following problems has a question and two statements which are labeled (1) and (2). Use the data given in (1) and (2) together with other available information (such as the number of hours in a day, the definition of *clockwise*, mathematical facts, etc.) to decide whether the statements are *sufficient* to answer the question. Then fill in space

(A) If you can get the answer from (1) **ALONE** but not from (2) alone
(B) If you can get the answer from (2) **ALONE** but not from (1) alone
(C) If you can get the answer from **BOTH** (1) **and** (2) **TOGETHER** but not from (1) alone or (2) alone
(D) If **EITHER** statement (1) **ALONE OR** statement (2) **ALONE** suffices
(E) If you **CANNOT** get the answer from statements (1) and (2) **TOGETHER**, but need even more data

All numbers used in this section are real numbers. A figure given for a problem is intended to provide information consistent with that in the question, but not necessarily with the additional information contained in the statements.

---

1. Find the value of the expression $x^3y - \left(\dfrac{x^3}{y}\right)$.

   (1) $x = 2$
   (2) $y = 1$

2. If x is a two-digit number (so $x = ba$ with b and a digits), what is the last digit a of x?

   (1) The number $3x$ is a three-digit number whose last digit is a.
   (2) The digit a is less than 7.

3. Is the number $\dfrac{N}{3}$ an odd integer? (You may assume that $\dfrac{N}{3}$ is an integer.)

   (1) $N = 3K$ where K is an integer.
   (2) $N = 6J + 3$ where J is an integer.

4. How many families in Jaytown own exactly two phones?

   (1) 150 families in Jaytown own at least one telephone.
   (2) 45 families in Jaytown own at least three telephones.

5. Is the line *PQ* parallel to the line *SR?*

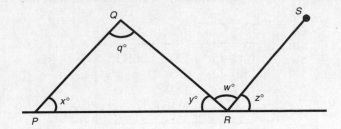

   (1) $w = q$
   (2) $y = z$

6. What is the value of $x^3 - y^3$?

   (1) $x^6 - y^6 = 0$
   (2) $y = 0$

7. How much does John weigh? Tim weighs 200 pounds.

   (1) Tim's weight plus Moe's weight is equal to John's weight.
   (2) John's weight plus Moe's weight is equal to twice Tim's weight.

8. Which triangle, *ADE* or *AEC*, has the larger area? *ABCD* is a rectangle.

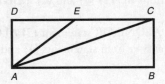

   (1) *DE* is longer than *EC*.
   (2) *AC* is longer than *AE*.

9. *ABCDEFGH* is a cube. What is the length of the line segment *AG?*

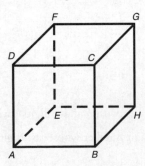

   (1) The length of the line segment *AB* is 4 inches.
   (2) The area of the square *BCGH* is 16 square inches.

10. Is the integer K an odd integer?

    (1) $K = 3M$ where M is an integer.
    (2) $K = 6J$ where J is an integer.

11. What was the value of the sales of the ABC Company in 2000?

    (1) The sales of the ABC Company increased by \$100,000 each year from 1990 to 2000.
    (2) The value of the sales of the ABC Company doubled between 1990 and 2000.

12. Is x greater than 2? (You may assume y is not equal to zero.)

    (1) $\left(\dfrac{x}{y}\right)$ is greater than 2.

    (2) $\left(\dfrac{1}{y}\right)$ is less than 1.

13. How many gallons of a chemical can be stored in a cylindrical tank if the radius of the tank is 15 feet? One gallon is equal to 231 cubic inches.

    (1) The height of the tank is 20 feet.
    (2) The temperature is 60 degrees Fahrenheit.

14. Is the area of the circle with center O larger than the area of the region outside the circle and inside the square $ABCD$? The straight line OEF is parallel to AB.

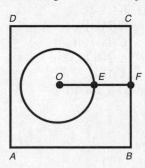

    (1) $OE < \left(\dfrac{1}{4}\right)AB$

    (2) $EF < \left(\dfrac{1}{4}\right)AB$

15. If $x^6 - y^6 = 0$, what is the value of $x^3 - y^3$?

    (1) x is positive.
    (2) y is greater than 1.

ANSWERS

The letter following each question number is the correct answer. The numbers in parentheses refer to the sections of this chapter that explain the necessary mathematics principles. A more detailed explanation of all answers follows.

Mathematics Exercise A

1. D (I-1)	10. C (II-1)	19. D (I-2)
2. B (I-4)	11. C (III-9, I-8)	20. D (II-3)
3. B (III-7, I-4)	12. C (I-2)	21. C (III-7, II-1, I-8)
4. A (IV-4, IV-5, I-4)	13. C (I-4)	22. D (II-2)
5. A (IV-4, I-7)	14. D (I-4)	23. C (I-4)
6. B (IV-4)	15. C (I-4)	24. D (III-9, III-7)
7. D (IV-4, I-2)	16. E (I-7, I-4)	25. A (II-2)
8. C (I-4)	17. B (I-4, I-5)	
9. A (I-1)	18. A (II-1)	

Mathematics Exercise B

1. B (IV-2, IV-3)	10. A (II-3)	19. B (I-4)
2. D (IV-3)	11. D (I-1)	20. E (II-2)
3. C (IV-3)	12. E (IV-1)	21. D (IV-1)
4. B (IV-3)	13. B (IV-1)	22. C (IV-1)
5. A (IV-3)	14. B (IV-1)	23. D (II-1)
6. D (I-8)	15. B (IV-1, II-7)	24. A (II-2)
7. B (III-4, III-7)	16. A (I-4, I-2)	25. E (II-3)
8. E (II-5)	17. A (II-7)	
9. D (III-7)	18. D (III-6, III-4)	

Mathematics Exercise C

1. B (I-3)	10. B (I-4)	19. A (I-1, I-2)
2. B (II-7, I-6)	11. D (III-7)	20. B (I-4)
3. E (III-4)	12. E (II-1)	21. B (II-7)
4. E (IV-5, II-5)	13. A (I-2)	22. C (I-7)
5. E (IV-5)	14. D (III-7)	23. C (I-4)
6. A (IV-5)	15. A (II-1)	24. D (II-1, II-2)
7. B (I-8)	16. E (I-4)	25. E (II-1)
8. E (II-4)	17. E (IV-1)	
9. A (I-7, II-I)	18. E (III-4)	

Data Sufficiency Exercise D

1. (B)	6. (C)	11. (C)
2. (E)	7. (C)	12. (E)
3. (B)	8. (A)	13. (A)
4. (E)	9. (D)	14. (A)
5. (A)	10. (B)	15. (C)

EXPLANATION OF ANSWERS

Mathematics Exercise A

Difficulty Level

1. **(D)** The price increased by 34 − 12 = 22 dollars.

Difficulty Level

2. **(B)** She sold the house for 125% of *C* or $\frac{5}{4}$ *C*. Thus, the gain is $\frac{5}{4}$ *C* − *C* = $\frac{C}{4}$. She must pay a

    tax of 50% of $\frac{C}{4}$ or $\frac{1}{2}$ of $\frac{C}{4}$. Therefore, the tax is $\frac{C}{8}$. Notice that the three years has nothing
    to do with the problem. Sometimes a question contains unnecessary information.

Difficulty Level

3. **(B)** The area of a rectangle is length times width. Let *L* and *W* denote the original length and
    width. Then the new length is 1.2*L* and the new width is .8*W*. Therefore, the new area is
    (1.2*L*)(.8*W*) = .96*LW* or 96% of the original area. So the area has decreased by 4%.

Difficulty Level

4. **(A)** In 1964 military expenditures were about 140 billion and by 1969 they had increased to

    about 200 billion. $\frac{60}{140}$ = $\frac{3}{7}$ which is almost 50%. By using a straight edge, you may see that

    the bar for 1969 is about half again as long as the bar for 1964.

Difficulty Level

5. **(A)** Since the developing countries' military expenditures for every year were less than 30 billion,
    choice A is the only possible answer. Notice that by reading the possible answers first, you save
    time. You don't need the exact answer.

Difficulty Level

6. **(B)** I. cannot be inferred since the graph indicates *only* the dollars spent on military expendi-
    tures, not the percent of income and not total income. II. is true since each bar is higher than
    the previous bar to the left. III. cannot be inferred since the graph gives no information about
    1972. So only statement II. can be inferred from the graph.

Difficulty Level

7. **(D)** In 1971 the NATO countries spent over 100 billion and less than 150 billion on military

    expenditures. Since this was $\frac{1}{3}$ of their combined incomes the combined income is between
    300 billion and 450 billion. Thus, choice D must be the correct answer.

Difficulty Level

8. **(C)** Voters between 18 and 21 who voted are 85% of the 8% of eligible voters. Thus, (.08)(.85)
    = .068, so 6.8% of the eligible voters were voters between 18 and 21 who voted.

Difficulty Level

9. **(A)** Odd numbers are of the form 2*x* + 1 where *x* is an integer. Thus, if *n* = 2*x* + 1 and *p* =
    2*k* + 1, then *n* + *p* = 2*x* + 1 + 2*k* + 1 = 2*x* + 2*k* + 2 which is even. Using *n* = 3 and *p* = 5, all the
    other choices give an odd number. In general, if a problem involves odd or even numbers, try
    using the fact that odd numbers are of the form 2*x* + 1 and even numbers of the form 2*y* where
    x and *y* are integers.

Difficulty Level

10. **(C)** To run a car 100 miles will cost 100(*g* + *m*) cents. Divide by 100 to convert to dollars.
    The result is *g* + *m*.

Difficulty Level

11. **(C)** Using the distance formula, the distance from *A* to *B* is $\sqrt{1-(-1))^2 + (3-5)^2}$ = $\sqrt{4+4}$ =
    $\sqrt{8}$ = $\sqrt{4 \times 2}$ = $\sqrt{4}\sqrt{2}$ = 2$\sqrt{2}$. You have to be able to simplify $\sqrt{8}$ in order to obtain the
    correct answer.

12. **(C)** Tips for the week were $\frac{5}{4} \cdot 50$ so his total income was $50 + \frac{5}{4}(50) = \frac{9}{4}(50)$. Therefore,

tips made up $\dfrac{\frac{5}{4}(50)}{\frac{9}{4}(50)} = \dfrac{\frac{5}{4}}{\frac{9}{4}} = \dfrac{5}{9}$ of his income. *Don't* waste time figuring out the total income

and the tip income. You can use the time to answer other questions.

13. **(C)** 7,500 is in the 6,000–8,000 bracket so the tax will be 80 + 3% of the income over 6,000. Since 7,500 – 6,000 = 1,500, the income over 6,000 is 1,500. 3% of 1,500 = (.03)(1,500) = 45, so the tax is 80 + 45 = 125.

14. **(D)** The tax on 26,000 is 1,070 + 7% of (26,000 – 25,000). Thus, the tax is 1,070 + 70 = 1,140. The tax on 29,000 is 1.070 + 7% of (29,000 – 25,000). Thus, the tax on 29,000 is 1,070 + 280 = 1,350. Therefore, you will pay 1,350 – 1,140 = $210 more in taxes next year. A faster method is to use the fact that the $3,000 raise is income over 25,000, so it will be taxed at 7%. Therefore, the tax on the extra $3,000 will be (.07)(3,000) = 210.

15. **(C)** If income is less than 6,000, then the tax is less than 80. If income is greater than 8,000, then the tax is greater than 140. Therefore, if the tax is 100, the income must be between 6,000 and 8,000. You *do not* have to calculate her exact income.

16. **(E)** Each person pays the tax on $3,700 which is 1% of 3,700 or $37. Since there are 50,000 people in Zenith, the total taxes are (37)(50,000) = $1,850,000.

17. **(B)** The tax on 10,000 is 220, so taxes are $\dfrac{220}{10,000} = .022 = 2.2\%$ of income. 2.2% is 2% after

rounding to the nearest percent.

18. **(A)** $S(3, 4) = 3^2 - 4^2 = 9 - 16 = -7$. Therefore, $S(3, S(3, 4)) = S(3, -7) = 3^2 - (-7)^2 = 9 - 49 = -40$.

19. **(D)** 8 omelets will use $8 \cdot 3 = 24$ eggs and $8 \cdot \frac{1}{4} = 2$ peppers. Since 24 is two dozen, the cost will be (2)(90¢) + (2)(20¢) = 220¢ or $2.20.

20. **(D)** In order to average 50 m.p.h. for the trip, the bus must make the trip in $\dfrac{185}{50} = 3\frac{7}{10}$ hours

which is 222 minutes. Since 2 hours or 120 minutes were needed for the first 85 miles, the final 100 miles must be completed in 222 – 120 which is 102 minutes.

21. **(C)** The area of a rectangle is length times width so the area of *ABDC* is *ab*. The area of a triangle is one half of the height times the base. Since *BDE* is an isosceles right triangle, the base

and height both are equal to *b*. Thus, the area of *BDE* is $\frac{1}{2}b^2$. Therefore, the area of the figure

is $ab + \frac{1}{2}b^2$ which is equal to $b\left(a + \frac{b}{2}\right)$. You have to express your answer as one of the possible

answers, so you need to be able to simplify.

22. **(D)** Since $4x + 2y$ is equal to $2(2x + y)$ and $2x + y = 5$, $4x + 2y$ is equal to 2(5) or 10.

23. **(C)** The cost has increased by \$4,800 minus \$2,500, or \$2,300, between 1967 and 1975.

So the cost has increased by $\frac{2,300}{2,500}$ which is .92 or 92%. Answer (E) is incorrect. The price

in 1975 is 192% of the price in 1967, but the *increase* is 92%.

24. **(D)** The distance from (−1, 2) to (5, 2) is 6. (You can use the distance formula or just count the blocks in this case.) The area of a square is the length of a side squared, so the area is 6^2 or 36.

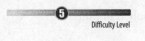

25. **(A)** Since $x + y = 6$ and $3x − y = 4$, we may add the two equations to obtain $4x = 10$, or $x = 2.5$. Then, because $x + y = 6$, y must be 3.5. Therefore, $x − y = −1$.

Mathematics Exercise B

1. **(B)** In 1960 women made up 33.4% or about $\frac{1}{3}$ of the labor force. The line graph shows there were about 22 million women in the labor force in 1960. So the labor force was about 3(22) or 66 million. The closest answer among the choices is 65 million.

2. **(D)** In 1947, there were about 16 million women in the labor force, and about 14 − 6 or 8 million of them were married. Therefore, the percentage of women in the labor force who

were married is $\frac{8}{16}$ or 50%.

3. **(C)** Look at the possible answers first. You can use scrap paper as straight edges.

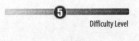

4. **(B)** In 1947, there were about 16 million women in the labor force. By 1972 there were about 32 million. Therefore, the number of women doubled which is an increase of 100%. (Not of 200%.)

5. **(A)** I. is true since the width of the band for widowed or divorced women was never more than 5 million between 1947 and 1957. II. is false since the number of single women in the labor force decreased from 1947 to 1948. III. cannot be inferred since there is no information about the total labor force or women as a percent of it in 1965. Thus, only I. can be inferred.

6. **(D)** If $\frac{x}{y}$ is $\frac{2}{3}$, then $\frac{y}{x}$ is $\frac{3}{2}$. Since $\left(\frac{y}{x}\right)^2$ is equal to $\frac{y^2}{x^2}$, $\frac{y^2}{x^2}$ is $\left(\frac{3}{2}\right)^2$ or $\frac{9}{4}$.

7. **(B)** The area of a triangle is $\frac{1}{2}$ altitude times base. Since BD is perpendicular to AC, x is the

altitude. Using the Pythagorean Theorem, $x^2 + (AD)^2 = a^2$ and $x^2 + (DC)^2 = a^2$.

Thus, $AD = DC$, and $AD = \sqrt{a^2 - x^2}$. So, the base is $2\sqrt{a^2 - x^2}$. Therefore, the area is

$\frac{1}{2}(x)(2\sqrt{a^2 - x^2})$ which is choice B.

8. **(E)** $1 : 160 = 2\frac{7}{8} : x.$ $x = 2\frac{7}{8}(160).$ $2\frac{7}{8}$ is $\frac{23}{8}$ so the distance from Seton to Monroe is

$\frac{23}{8}(160) = 460$ miles.

9. **(D)** Let $EF = FG = GC$. Therefore, $BE = EF = FG = GC$. Draw perpendiculars EH, FI, GJ. Draw diagonals HF, IG, JC. The 8 triangles are equal in area since they each have the same altitude (AB or DC) and equal bases (BE, EF, FG, GC, AH, HI, IJ, JD). Since the area of $ABE = 7$, the area of $ABCD = (8)(7)$ or 56.

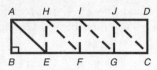

10. **(A)** In each minute the first puncture will leak $\frac{1}{9}$ of the air and the second puncture will leak

$\frac{1}{6}$ of the air. Together $\frac{1}{9} + \frac{1}{6} = \frac{5}{18}$. So, $\frac{5}{18}$ of the air will leak out in each minute. In $\frac{18}{5}$ or

$3\frac{3}{5}$ minutes the tire will be flat. Even if you can't solve the problem, you should be able to

eliminate choices D and E because the second puncture alone takes only 6 minutes.

11. **(D)** Since an even number times any number is even, and n times n^2 is odd, neither n nor n^2 can be even. Therefore, n and n^2 must both be odd for n^3 to be odd. I and II are true, and III is false.

12. **(E)** Look in the fourth column.

13. **(B)** In 1972 there were 72 million females out of 136 million persons of voting age. $\frac{72}{136} = $ .529 which is 53% to the nearest percent.

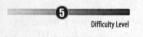

14. **(B)** In 1968, 70% of the 54 million males of voting age voted, and $(.7)(54,000,000) = $ 37,800,000.

15. **(B)** Since 78 million persons of voting age lived in the North and West in 1964, and there were 65 million persons of voting age not in the 25–44 year range, there must be at least $78 - 65 = 13$ million people in the North and West in the 25–44 year range. X must be greater than or equal to 13. Since there were 45 million people of voting age in the 25–44 year range, X must be less than or equal to 45.

16. **(A)** 90% of 50 is 45, so 45 students took the final. $\frac{2}{3}$ of 45 is 30. Therefore, 30 students passed the final.

17. (A) The average of two different numbers is always between the two. If $a = 2$ and $b = 3$, then $b^2 - a^2 = 5$, $ab = 6$, and $b - a = 1$ so C, D, and E must be false. If $a = \frac{1}{2}$ and $b = 1$, then $\frac{(ab)}{2} = \frac{1}{4}$, so B is also false.

18. (D) Since the radius to the point of tangency is perpendicular to the tangent OR must be perpendicular to PR. Therefore, ORP is a right triangle, and $(PO)^2 = (OR)^2 + (PR)^2$. Then,

$(PR)^2 = (PO)^2 - (OR)^2$. Thus $(PR)^2 = 4^2 - 2^2$, and $PR = \sqrt{16 - 4} = \sqrt{12} = \sqrt{4}\sqrt{3} = 2\sqrt{3}$.

19. (B) After the tune-up, the bus will travel $(1.15)(15) = 17.25$ miles on a gallon of gas. Therefore, it will take $(150) \div (17.25) = 8.7$ (to the nearest tenth) gallons of gasoline to travel 150 miles.

20. (E) If $\frac{x}{y} = 2$, then $x = 2y$, so $x + 2y = 2y + 2y = 4y$. But $x + 2y = 4$, so $4y = 4$, or $y = 1$. Since $x = 2y$, x must be 2.

21. (D) $2\frac{1}{2}$ hours is 150 minutes.

22. (C) The train's speed increased by $70 - 40$, which is 30 miles per hour. $\frac{30}{40}$ is 75%.

23. (D) When $t = 0$, the speed is 40, so A and B are incorrect. When $t = 180$, the speed is 70, so C and E are incorrect. Choice D gives all the values that appear in the table.

24. (A) The cost of producing the first 8,000 copies is $1,000 + 7,000x$. $1,000 + 7,000x = \$7,230$. Therefore, $7,000x = 6230$ and $x = .89$. You should be able to eliminate choices C, D, and E easily.

25. (E) Assume all workers work at the same rate unless given different information. Since 16 workers take 3 hours, each worker does $\frac{1}{48}$ of the job an hour. Thus, the 5 workers will finish $\frac{5}{48}$ of the job each hour. $\frac{5}{48}x = \frac{48}{48}$. It will take $\frac{48}{5} = 9\frac{3}{5}$ hours for them to finish the job.

Mathematics Exercise C

1. (B) The 12 poles weigh $(12)(1.1) = 13.2$ pounds and the 7 pieces of net weigh $7(.2) = 1.4$ pounds, so the contents of the box weigh $13.2 + 1.4 = 14.6$ pounds. Therefore, the box by itself must weigh $16.25 - 14.6 = 1.65$ pounds.

2. (B) If all the numbers were not positive, then the sum could not be positive so A is incorrect. If a, b, and c were all -1 and d were 5, then $a + b + c + d$ would be positive so C, D, and E are incorrect.

 3. **(E)** Since the measure of angle M is 55°, the measure of angle K is 35°. Therefore, $LM < KL$ since the larger side is opposite the larger angle.

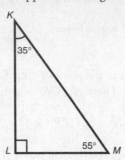

 4. **(E)** The population in metropolitan areas in 1970 was about 140 million, and the population in nonmetropolitan areas was about $190 - 140$ or 50 million. Therefore, the ratio was about 140 to 50 and 3 to 1 is the best choice.

 5. **(E)** Compare the segments of the second bar under "age."

 6. **(A)** All regions increased by at least 10%. Compare the segments of the first bar with those of the last bar under "Region."

 7. **(B)** Choice A gives 6^2 or 36. Choice B gives 4^4 or 256. Choice C is 8^2 or 64. Choice D is $2 + 4 + 16$ or 22. Choice E is 4^3 or 64.

 8. **(E)** Since 25% read the newspaper and watched the news on television and 40% read the newspaper, $40\% - 25\%$ or 15% read the newspaper but did not watch the news on television. Thus $65\% + 15\%$ or 80% read the newspaper or watched the news on television, so $100\% - 80\%$ or 20% neither read the newspaper nor watched the news on television.

 9. **(A)** For the first 8 hours, she is paid a total of $8d$. For the final 4 hours $(12 - 8)$, she is paid $4c$. Therefore, her total pay is $8d + 4c$. To find the average hourly pay, divide by 12. To find the correct answer among the choices, you have to reduce the fraction. Divide the numerator by four and the denominator by four.

 10. **(B)** If the price of one screwdriver increases by 5%, then the price of three screwdrivers increases by 5% (not 15%). The percentage change is the same regardless of the number sold. Since a screwdriver and a hammer currently cost the same, the screwdrivers and the hammers each cost one half of the total price. So one half of the total is increased by 5%. The other half is increased by 3%. Therefore, the total price is increased by $\frac{1}{2}(5\%) + \frac{1}{2}(3\%) = 4\%$.

 11. **(D)** After the radius is increased by 6%, the radius will be 1.06 times the original radius. Since the area of a circle is πr^2, the new area will be $\pi(1.06r)^2 = \pi(1.1236r^2)$ or $1.12361\pi r^2$. Thus, the area has been increased by .1236 or by 12.36%.

 12. **(E)** Since $g(a) = a^2 + 2$, $g(3)$ is $3^2 + 2$ or 11. So, $f[3, g(3)]$ is $f(3, 11) = 3 \times 11$ or 33.

 13. **(A)** The difference in the price is $Q - D$. So, the fraction by which it has increased is $\frac{(Q - D)}{D}$. Note that the denominator is the *original* price.

14. **(D)** Since *ABCD* is a square, the area of *ABCD* is 3^2 or 9. The area of the rectangle *EFGH* is *length* times *width* or $4 \times 6 = 24$. Thus, the area outside the square and inside the rectangle is $24 - 9$ or 15.

15. **(A)** The cost of food A is $1.80 per hundred grams or 1.8¢ a gram, so x grams cost $(1.8x)$¢ or $\left(\dfrac{9}{5}\right)x$¢. Each gram of food B costs 3¢ so y grams of food B will cost $3y$¢. Each gram of food C costs 2.75¢ or $\left(\dfrac{11}{4}\right)$¢; thus, z grams of food C will cost $\left(\dfrac{11}{4}\right)z$¢. Therefore, the total cost is $[\left(\dfrac{9}{5}\right)x + 3y + \left(\dfrac{11}{4}\right)z]$¢.

16. **(E)** Since food A is 10% protein, 500 grams of food A will supply 50 grams of protein. Food B is 20% protein so 250 grams of food B will supply 50 grams of protein. 350 grams of food C will supply 70 grams of protein. 150 grams of food A and 200 grams of food B will supply $15 + 40 = 55$ grams of protein. 200 grams of food B and 200 grams of food C will supply $40 + 40$ or 80 grams of protein. Choice E supplies the most protein.

17. **(E)** The diet of choice A will cost $2(\$1.80) + \left(\dfrac{3}{2}\right)(\$3) = \$3.60 + \$4.50 = \$8.10$. Choice B will cost $5(\$3) + \$1.80 = \$16.80$. Choice C costs $2(\$2.75) = \$5.50$. Choice D costs $\left(\dfrac{3}{2}\right)(\$1.80) + \$2.75 = \$2.70 + \$2.75 = \$5.45$. The diet of Choice E costs $3(\$1.80)$ or $5.40, so Choice E costs the least.

18. **(E)** Since *CD* is parallel to *EF*, the triangles *ACD* and *AEF* are similar. Therefore, corresponding sides are proportional. So *CD* is to *EF* as *AD* is to *AF*. Since $AD = DF$, $\dfrac{AD}{AF}$ is $\dfrac{1}{2}$. Therefore, *EF* is twice *CD* or 8.

19. **(A)** You need to find a common denominator for the fractions. One method is to multiply all the denominators. A quicker method is to find the least common multiple of the denominators. Since $6 = 3 \times 2$, $14 = 2 \times 7$, $15 = 3 \times 5$, $21 = 3 \times 7$, and $35 = 5 \times 7$, the least common multiple is $2 \times 3 \times 5 \times 7 = 210$. $\dfrac{5}{6}$ is $\dfrac{175}{210}$, $\dfrac{11}{14}$ is $\dfrac{165}{210}$, $\dfrac{12}{15}$ is $\dfrac{168}{210}$, $\dfrac{17}{21}$ is $\dfrac{170}{210}$, and $\dfrac{29}{35}$ is $\dfrac{174}{210}$. So $\dfrac{5}{6}$ is the largest.

20. **(B)** 18 months is $\dfrac{3}{2}$ of a year. Interest = Amount × Time × Rate. $(\$2,000)\left(\dfrac{3}{2}\right)(.06) = \$180$.

21. **(B)** If $x + y > 5$ and $x - y > 3$, then, since both inequalities are of the same type, the corresponding sides can be added to obtain $2x > 8$ or $x > 4$.

22. **(C)** The average of 6 numbers is the sum of the numbers divided by 6. Thus, the sum of the numbers is the average multiplied by 6 or 4.5×6 which is 27.

23. **(C)** After 25 days the rats have eaten $25r$ pounds of wheat. So $\frac{(25r)}{W}$ is the fraction of

the capacity eaten by the rats. To change this to percent, multiply by 100. $\frac{(25r)}{W} \times 100 =$
$2{,}500\left(\dfrac{r}{W}\right)$.

24. **(D)** Factor $x^2 + 2x - 8$ into $(x + 4)(x - 2)$. If x is either -4 or 2, $x^2 + 2x - 8 = 0$, and D is the correct answer.

25. **(E)** The interest on the \$10,000 for the first month will be 10p. For the next 2 months the interest will be 20q. The total interest is $10p + 20q$.

Data Sufficiency Exercise D

(Refer to pages 39–40 for an explanation of the system used in solving the following problems.)

1. **(B)** If statement (1) is true, then $x^3y - \left(\dfrac{x^3}{y}\right)$ is equal to $8y - \left(\dfrac{8}{y}\right)$, but the value of y is

    needed to find the value of the expression. Therefore, (1) alone is not sufficient. So the answer to question I is NO, and the only possible choices are B, C, or E.

    If STATEMENT (2) alone is true, then $x^3y - \left(\dfrac{x^3}{y}\right)$ is equal to $x^31 - \left(\dfrac{x^3}{1}\right)$, which is equal to 0.

    Therefore, (2) alone is sufficient, and the answer to question II is YES. So the correct choice is B.
        This problem illustrates the need to be careful. You might quickly infer that a value for x and a value for y are both needed and INCORRECTLY answer C. To understand the problem,

    you need to simplify the expression by factoring out an x^3 from each term. So $x^3y - \left(\dfrac{x^3}{y}\right)$ is

    equal to $x^3\left(y - \left(\dfrac{1}{y}\right)\right)$, which is equal to 0 if $x = 0$ or if $y - \left(\dfrac{1}{y}\right) = 0$. Thus, the expression's

    value is determined if $x = 0$ or if $y = 1$; otherwise, you need both a value for x and a value for y.

2. **(E)** If statement (1) is true, then since $x = ba$, $3x = 3(10b + a) = 30b + 3a$. Now, because b is multiplied by 10 in the expression for $3x$, the final digit of $3x$ must be the final digit of $3a$. Since a is a digit, $0 \le a \le 9$, which implies $0 \le 3a \le 27$. So for the last digit of $3a$ to be equal to a, $3a$ must equal a or $10 + a$ or $20 + a$. If $a = 3a$, then $a = 0$. If $10 + a = 3a$, then $10 = 2a$ or $a = 5$. If $20 + a = 3a$, then $20 = 2a$ or $a = 10$, but since 10 is not a digit this is not possible. So if (1) is true, then a is 0 or 5, and (1) alone is not sufficient. Thus the answer to question I is NO, and the only possible choices are B, C, or E.
        Now since 26 and 25 are both two-digit numbers whose last digits are less than 7, STATEMENT (2) alone is not sufficient. So the answer to question II is NO, and the only possible choices are C or E. Also, since (2) does not allow us to choose between 0 and 5, statements (1) and (2) together are not sufficient, so the correct choice is E.
        Many people would be able to see that STATEMENT (2) alone would be insufficient but might not be able to decide whether (1) is sufficient. You can use the strategy to make an intelligent guess. Since (2) alone is not sufficient, the answer to question II on the decision tree is NO. Since choices B and D need an answer of YES to II, the only possible choices are A, C, or E. Since you can eliminate two choices, it is worthwhile to guess.

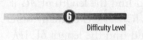

3. **(B)** STATEMENT (1) alone is not sufficient since then $\frac{N}{3} = \frac{(3K)}{3} = K$. Now if $K = 1$,

then $\frac{N}{3} = 1$, which is odd, but if $K = 2$, then $\frac{N}{3} = 2$, which is even. So the answer to question I is NO, and the only possible choices are B, C, or E.

STATEMENT (2) alone is sufficient since then $\frac{N}{3} = \frac{(6J+3)}{3} = 2J + 1$, which is always odd since J is an integer. So the answer to question II is YES, and the correct choice is B.

4. **(E)** If you use STATEMENTS (1) and (2) together, you can deduce that $150 - 45 = 105$ families own at least one telephone and less than three telephones. However, since this is the total of families with one phone and families with two phones, we cannot find the number of families with exactly two phones. So (1) and (2) together are not sufficient. Thus, the answer to question III is NO, and the correct choice is E.

5. **(A)** Since w and q are alternate interior angles, if STATEMENT (1) is true then PQ is parallel to SR. So (1) alone is sufficient. Thus, the answer to question I is YES and the only possible choices are A and D.

STATEMENT (2) alone is not sufficient since the line RS can be moved so that y is still equal to z but PQ and RS are not parallel. (See the diagram below.)

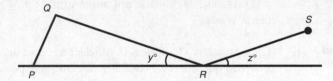

Therefore, the answer to question II is NO, and the correct choice is A.

6. **(C)** If STATEMENT (1) alone is true, then since $x^6 - y^6$ can be factored into $(x^3 + y^3)(x^3 - y^3)$, either $x^3 + y^3 = 0$ or $x^3 - y^3 = 0$. So (1) alone is not sufficient, and the answer to question I is NO. Thus, the only possible choices are B, C, or E.

STATEMENT (2) alone is insuffficient since if $y = 0$, then $x^3 - y^3 = x^3$, and we have no value for x. So the answer to question II is NO, and the only possible choices are C or E.

If (1) and (2) are both true, then we can deduce that x and y must both be equal to zero, which is sufficient. Thus, the answer to question III is YES, and the correct choice must be C.

7. **(C)** Let J, M, and T stand for the weights of John, Moe, and Tim respectively. We need to find J and we know $T = 200$. statement (1) gives the equation $200 + M = J$, but since we don't know M, (1) alone is not sufficient.

STATEMENT (2) alone gives the equation $J + M = 2T = 400$, and since we don't know M, (2) alone is insufficient.

However, if we use statements (1) and (2) together, then we have two linear equations in two unknowns, which we know can be solved to find J and M.

NOTE: Don't waste time actually solving the equations. You only have to decide if there is enough information to answer the question; you don't have to compute the actual answer.

8. **(A)** Since the area of a triangle is $\left(\frac{1}{2}\right)$(altitude)(base) and since both triangles have *DA* as an altitude, if the base (*DE*) of triangle *ADE* is larger than the base (*EC*) of triangle *AEC*, then the area of *ADE* is larger than the area of *AEC*. So statement (1) alone is sufficient, and the answer to question I is YES.

    STATEMENT (2) alone is not sufficient since for any point *E* between *D* and *C* (2) will be true, but, depending on whether *E* is closer to *D* or *C*, a different triangle will have the larger area. So the answer to question II is NO, and the correct choice is A.

9. **(D)** By using the distance formula (Pythagorean Theorem) you could find the length of *AG* if you knew the lengths of *AH* and *GH* (or if you knew the lengths of *AC* and *CG* or many other combinations). If you knew the lengths of *AB* and *BH*, then you could find the length of *AH*. Thus, it is sufficient to know the lengths of *AB*, *BH*, and *GH*. Since *ABCDEFGH* is a cube, *AB*, *BH*, and *GH* all have the same length since they are all edges of the cube. So it is sufficient to know the length of an edge of the cube. Now STATEMENTS (1) and (2) are equivalent since the area of a square face of the cube is 16 if and only if the length of an edge is 4. Therefore, (1) alone and (2) alone are sufficient, and the correct choice is D.

    Notice that, if you knew that (1) and (2) are equivalent, then the only possible choices are D or E, so you can make an intelligent guess.

10. **(B)** STATEMENT (2) alone is sufficient since if (2) is true, then $K = 2(3J)$, which means that *K* is even. Note this is sufficient to answer the question even though the answer is NO.

    STATEMENT (1) alone is not sufficient since if *M* is even, then *K* is even, but if *M* is odd, then *K* is odd.

11. **(C)** STATEMENT (1) alone is insufficient since we don't know the sales for any year. Thus, the answer to question I is NO. Therefore, the only possible choices are B, C, or E.

    STATEMENT (2) alone is not sufficient since we don't know the value of the sales in 1990. So the answer to question II is NO, and the only possible choices are C and E.

    Using (1), we can calculate the change in sales from 1990 to 2000, and then by using (2), we can find the value of the sales in 2000. Therefore, the answer to question III is YES, and the correct choice is C.

12. **(E)** Since $x = 3$, $y = 1$, and $x = 1$, $y = \left(\frac{1}{3}\right)$ both make STATEMENT (1) true, (1) alone is not sufficient. So the answer to question I is NO, and the only possible choices are B, C, or E.

    STATEMENT (2) alone is obviously not sufficient since it gives no information about *x*. Thus, the answer to question II is NO, and the only possible choices are C or E. (note: Even if you can't answer question I for this problem, you should be able to answer question II, and you would be able to guess either A, C, or E.)

    Now if *y* were positive, we could use statement (2) to deduce that $y > 1$ and then (1) would imply that $x > 2$. However, negative values of *y* can also satisfy (2) (for example, $y = -1$) and then (1) would have solutions with $x < 2$. So (1) and (2) together are not sufficient, and the answer to question III is NO. Thus the correct choice is E.

13. **(A)** STATEMENT (1) alone is sufficient since it will allow you to compute the volume of the tank in cubic feet. To actually find the answer, you would then change cubic feet into gallons using the fact that 231 cubic inches is one gallon. However, do not perform the calculation since it will only waste time.

    Since using statement (2) alone will not allow you to find the volume of the tank, the correct answer is A.

14. **(A)** The area of the circle plus the area of the region outside the circle and inside the square is equal to the area of the square, which is $(AB)^2$. Thus, if you can determine whether one area is larger (or smaller) than $\left(\frac{1}{2}\right)AB^2$, that is sufficient.

STATEMENT (1) alone is sufficient since the area of the circle is $\pi(OE)^2$, and if (1) holds, then $\pi(OE)^2 < \pi\left(\left(\frac{1}{4}\right)AB\right)^2 = \left(\frac{\pi}{16}\right)AB^2$. But since $\frac{\pi}{16}$ is less than $\left(\frac{1}{2}\right)$, we can answer the question. So the answer to question I is YES, and the only possible choices are A or D.

STATEMENT (2) alone is not sufficient since (2) does not give any information about the radius of the circle. Note you might think that $OE + EF = \left(\frac{1}{2}\right)AB$; however, that requires the additional information that O is also the center of the square, which is NOT given. So the answer to question II is NO, and the correct choice is A.

15. **(C)** The key to solving this problem is to relate $x^3 - y^3$ to the information $x^6 - y^6 = 0$. If you think of $x^6 - y^6$ as $(x^3)^2 - (y^3)^2$, then you can factor the equation into $(x^3 - y^3)(x^3 + y^3) = 0$. So if $x^3 + y^3$ is not zero, then $x^3 - y^3$ must be zero. Thus statements (1) and (2) together are sufficient because they imply that $x^3 + y^3$ is greater than zero.

However, (1) alone or (2) alone is not sufficient because the cube of a negative number is negative. We could have $x^3 + y^3$ equal zero, and then the value of $x^3 - y^3$ may not be determined. For example, $x = 1, y = 1$ and $x = 1, y = -1$ show (1) alone is not sufficient, and $x = 2, y = 2$ and $x = -2, y = 2$ show (2) alone is not sufficient.

PRE-TEST REVIEW

Answer Sheet
PRE-TEST

Quantitative Section

1 Ⓐ Ⓑ Ⓒ Ⓓ Ⓔ	11 Ⓐ Ⓑ Ⓒ Ⓓ Ⓔ	21 Ⓐ Ⓑ Ⓒ Ⓓ Ⓔ	31 Ⓐ Ⓑ Ⓒ Ⓓ Ⓔ
2 Ⓐ Ⓑ Ⓒ Ⓓ Ⓔ	12 Ⓐ Ⓑ Ⓒ Ⓓ Ⓔ	22 Ⓐ Ⓑ Ⓒ Ⓓ Ⓔ	32 Ⓐ Ⓑ Ⓒ Ⓓ Ⓔ
3 Ⓐ Ⓑ Ⓒ Ⓓ Ⓔ	13 Ⓐ Ⓑ Ⓒ Ⓓ Ⓔ	23 Ⓐ Ⓑ Ⓒ Ⓓ Ⓔ	33 Ⓐ Ⓑ Ⓒ Ⓓ Ⓔ
4 Ⓐ Ⓑ Ⓒ Ⓓ Ⓔ	14 Ⓐ Ⓑ Ⓒ Ⓓ Ⓔ	24 Ⓐ Ⓑ Ⓒ Ⓓ Ⓔ	34 Ⓐ Ⓑ Ⓒ Ⓓ Ⓔ
5 Ⓐ Ⓑ Ⓒ Ⓓ Ⓔ	15 Ⓐ Ⓑ Ⓒ Ⓓ Ⓔ	25 Ⓐ Ⓑ Ⓒ Ⓓ Ⓔ	35 Ⓐ Ⓑ Ⓒ Ⓓ Ⓔ
6 Ⓐ Ⓑ Ⓒ Ⓓ Ⓔ	16 Ⓐ Ⓑ Ⓒ Ⓓ Ⓔ	26 Ⓐ Ⓑ Ⓒ Ⓓ Ⓔ	36 Ⓐ Ⓑ Ⓒ Ⓓ Ⓔ
7 Ⓐ Ⓑ Ⓒ Ⓓ Ⓔ	17 Ⓐ Ⓑ Ⓒ Ⓓ Ⓔ	27 Ⓐ Ⓑ Ⓒ Ⓓ Ⓔ	37 Ⓐ Ⓑ Ⓒ Ⓓ Ⓔ
8 Ⓐ Ⓑ Ⓒ Ⓓ Ⓔ	18 Ⓐ Ⓑ Ⓒ Ⓓ Ⓔ	28 Ⓐ Ⓑ Ⓒ Ⓓ Ⓔ	
9 Ⓐ Ⓑ Ⓒ Ⓓ Ⓔ	19 Ⓐ Ⓑ Ⓒ Ⓓ Ⓔ	29 Ⓐ Ⓑ Ⓒ Ⓓ Ⓔ	
10 Ⓐ Ⓑ Ⓒ Ⓓ Ⓔ	20 Ⓐ Ⓑ Ⓒ Ⓓ Ⓔ	30 Ⓐ Ⓑ Ⓒ Ⓓ Ⓔ	

Verbal Section

1 Ⓐ Ⓑ Ⓒ Ⓓ Ⓔ	12 Ⓐ Ⓑ Ⓒ Ⓓ Ⓔ	23 Ⓐ Ⓑ Ⓒ Ⓓ Ⓔ	35 Ⓐ Ⓑ Ⓒ Ⓓ Ⓔ
2 Ⓐ Ⓑ Ⓒ Ⓓ Ⓔ	13 Ⓐ Ⓑ Ⓒ Ⓓ Ⓔ	24 Ⓐ Ⓑ Ⓒ Ⓓ Ⓔ	36 Ⓐ Ⓑ Ⓒ Ⓓ Ⓔ
3 Ⓐ Ⓑ Ⓒ Ⓓ Ⓔ	14 Ⓐ Ⓑ Ⓒ Ⓓ Ⓔ	25 Ⓐ Ⓑ Ⓒ Ⓓ Ⓔ	37 Ⓐ Ⓑ Ⓒ Ⓓ Ⓔ
4 Ⓐ Ⓑ Ⓒ Ⓓ Ⓔ	15 Ⓐ Ⓑ Ⓒ Ⓓ Ⓔ	26 Ⓐ Ⓑ Ⓒ Ⓓ Ⓔ	38 Ⓐ Ⓑ Ⓒ Ⓓ Ⓔ
5 Ⓐ Ⓑ Ⓒ Ⓓ Ⓔ	16 Ⓐ Ⓑ Ⓒ Ⓓ Ⓔ	27 Ⓐ Ⓑ Ⓒ Ⓓ Ⓔ	39 Ⓐ Ⓑ Ⓒ Ⓓ Ⓔ
6 Ⓐ Ⓑ Ⓒ Ⓓ Ⓔ	17 Ⓐ Ⓑ Ⓒ Ⓓ Ⓔ	28 Ⓐ Ⓑ Ⓒ Ⓓ Ⓔ	40 Ⓐ Ⓑ Ⓒ Ⓓ Ⓔ
7 Ⓐ Ⓑ Ⓒ Ⓓ Ⓔ	18 Ⓐ Ⓑ Ⓒ Ⓓ Ⓔ	29 Ⓐ Ⓑ Ⓒ Ⓓ Ⓔ	41 Ⓐ Ⓑ Ⓒ Ⓓ Ⓔ
8 Ⓐ Ⓑ Ⓒ Ⓓ Ⓔ	19 Ⓐ Ⓑ Ⓒ Ⓓ Ⓔ	30 Ⓐ Ⓑ Ⓒ Ⓓ Ⓔ	
9 Ⓐ Ⓑ Ⓒ Ⓓ Ⓔ	20 Ⓐ Ⓑ Ⓒ Ⓓ Ⓔ	31 Ⓐ Ⓑ Ⓒ Ⓓ Ⓔ	
10 Ⓐ Ⓑ Ⓒ Ⓓ Ⓔ	21 Ⓐ Ⓑ Ⓒ Ⓓ Ⓔ	32 Ⓐ Ⓑ Ⓒ Ⓓ Ⓔ	
11 Ⓐ Ⓑ Ⓒ Ⓓ Ⓔ	22 Ⓐ Ⓑ Ⓒ Ⓓ Ⓔ	34 Ⓐ Ⓑ Ⓒ Ⓓ Ⓔ	

Quantitative and Verbal Practice Sections

This part of the book contains two practice sections—one quantitative and one verbal—and two practice tests. Now that you've completed your review of the instructional chapters, use the quantitative and verbal practice sections to gauge how well you've mastered the different question types. Take the practice sections and review the answer explanations. If you discover that you still have some weak areas, review the relevant portions of the instructional chapters. Once you're confident that you've mastered all of the material in the instructional chapters, you can then move on to the practice tests in the next section of the book.

QUANTITATIVE SECTION

TIME: 75 MINUTES

37 QUESTIONS

This section consists of two types of questions: Problem Solving and Data Sufficiency.

Problem Solving
Directions: Solve each of the following problems; then indicate the correct answer.

NOTE: A figure that appears with a problem is drawn as accurately as possible so as to provide information that may help in answering the question.
Numbers in this test are real numbers.

Data Sufficiency
Directions: Each of the following problems has a question and two statements which are labeled (1) and (2). Use the data given in (1) and (2) together with other available information (such as the number of hours in a day, the definition of *clockwise*, mathematical facts, etc.) to decide whether the statements are *sufficient* to answer the question. Then fill in space

(A) If you can get the answer from (1) **ALONE** but not from (2) alone
(B) If you can get the answer from (2) **ALONE** but not from (1) alone
(C) If you can get the answer from **BOTH** (1) **and** (2) **TOGETHER** but not from (1) alone or (2) alone
(D) If **EITHER** statement (1) **ALONE OR** statement (2) **ALONE** suffices
(E) If you **CANNOT** get the answer from statements (1) and (2) **TOGETHER** but need even more data

All numbers used in this section are real numbers.

A figure given for a problem is intended to provide information consistent with that in the question, but not necessarily with the additional information contained in the statements.
All figures lie in the plane unless you are told otherwise.
Figures are drawn as accurately as possible; straight lines may not appear straight on the screen.

1. How many books are on the bookshelf?

    (1) The bookshelf is 12 feet long.
    (2) The average weight of each book is 1.2 pounds.

2. The equation of a straight line containing the points (10,100) and (15, 60) is

    (A) $y = -8x + 180$
    (B) $y = 8x - 180$
    (C) $y = (\frac{1}{8})x + 7.5$
    (D) $y = -8x - 180$
    (E) $y = (-\frac{1}{8})x + 22.5$

3. If $f(x) = x^3 - 4$ and $f(y) = 4$, then y is equal to

    (A) 0

    (B) $2^{\frac{1}{3}}$

    (C) $\sqrt{2}$
    (D) 2
    (E) 3

4. In triangle ABC, find z if $AB = 5$ and $y = 40$.

    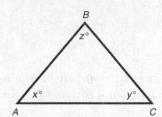

    (1) $BC = 5$
    (2) The bisector of angle B is perpendicular to AC.

> **(A)** If you can get the answer from **(1) ALONE** but not from **(2)** alone
> **(B)** If you can get the answer from **(2) ALONE** but not from **(1)** alone
> **(C)** If you can get the answer from **BOTH (1) and (2) TOGETHER** but not from **(1)** alone or **(2)** alone
> **(D)** If **EITHER** statement **(1) ALONE OR** statement **(2) ALONE** suffices
> **(E)** If you **CANNOT** get the answer from statements **(1)** and **(2) TOGETHER** but need even more data

5. How far is it from town A to town B? Town C is 12 miles east of town A.

    (1) Town C is south of town B.
    (2) It is 9 miles from town B to town C.

6. If $x + y + z + w = 15$, then at least k of the numbers x, y, z, w must be positive, where k is

    (A) 0
    (B) 1
    (C) 2
    (D) 3
    (E) 4

7. Is there a route from A to C that passes through B and is more than 8 miles long?

    (1) Two roads from A to B are at least 5 miles long.
    (2) Three roads from B to C are at least 5 miles long.

8. If you test 2 different lightbulbs from a box of 100 bulbs that contains 1 defective bulb what is the probability that both lightbulbs that you test are defective?

    (A) 0
    (B) 0.0001
    (C) $\dfrac{1}{9,900}$
    (D) 0.01
    (E) $\dfrac{1}{99}$

9. A company can sell $100x$ machine parts if it charges $10 - 0.1x$ dollars for each machine part. How many machine parts can the company sell if it charges \$4.00 for each machine part?

    (A) 6
    (B) 9.6
    (C) 60
    (D) 960
    (E) 6,000

10. A car goes 15 miles on a gallon of gas when it is driven at 50 miles per hour. When the car is driven at 60 miles per hour it only goes 80 percent as far. How many gallons of gas will it take to travel 120 miles driving at 60 miles per hour?

    (A) 2
    (B) 6.4
    (C) 8
    (D) 9.6
    (E) 10

11. Train X leaves New York at 1 A.M. and travels east at a speed of x miles per hour. If train Z leaves New York at 2 A.M. and travels east, at what rate of speed will train Z have to travel in order to catch train X at exactly 5:30 A.M.?

    (A) $\left(\dfrac{5}{6}\right)x$

    (B) $\left(\dfrac{9}{8}\right)x$

    (C) $\left(\dfrac{6}{5}\right)x$

    (D) $\left(\dfrac{9}{7}\right)x$

    (E) $\left(\dfrac{3}{2}\right)x$

12. A company makes a profit of 6 percent on its first $1,000 of sales each day, and 5 percent on all sales in excess of $1,000 for that day. How many dollars in profit will the company make on a day when sales are S dollars if S is greater than 1,000?

    (A) $0.05S$
    (B) $0.06S$
    (C) 110
    (D) $10 + 0.05S$
    (E) $60 + 0.05S$

13. Is x an even integer? Assume n and p are integers.

    (1) $x = (n + p)^2$
    (2) $x = 2n + 10p$

14. What is the value of *x*?

(1) $\dfrac{x}{y} = 3$

(2) $x - y = 9$

15. Two different holes, hole *A* and hole *B*, are put in the bottom of a full water tank.
If the water drains out through the holes, how long will it be before the tank
is empty?

(1) If only hole *A* is put in the bottom, the tank will be empty in 24 minutes.
(2) If only hole *B* is put in the bottom, the tank will be empty in 42 minutes.

16. How many pounds of fertilizer that is 10 percent nitrogen must be added to
12 pounds of fertilizer that is 20 percent nitrogen so that the resulting mixture is
18 percent nitrogen?

(A) 3
(B) 6
(C) 12
(D) 24
(E) 48

17. What is the probability that there is exactly 1 defective pen in a box of pens?

(1) The probability that all the pens in the box are not defective is 96 percent.
(2) The probability that there is more than 1 defective pen in the box is 3 percent.

18. The line *t* passes through the lines *l* and *k* and forms the angles *u, v, x, y, a, b, c,* and *d.*
Is line *l* parallel to line *k*?

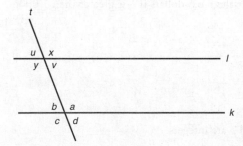

(1) $x = u$
(2) $u = a$

(A) If you can get the answer from (1) **ALONE** but not from (2) alone

(B) If you can get the answer from (2) **ALONE** but not from (1) alone

(C) If you can get the answer from **BOTH** (1) **and** (2) **TOGETHER** but not from (1) alone or (2) alone

(D) If **EITHER** statement (1) **ALONE OR** statement (2) **ALONE** suffices

(E) If you **CANNOT** get the answer from statements (1) and (2) **TOGETHER** but need even more data

19. Is there a route from *A* to *C* that passes through *B* and is more than 11 miles long?

    (1)   Two roads from *A* to *B* are at least 5 miles long.

    (2)   Three roads from *B* to *C* are at least 5 miles long.

20. Let $g(x) = 4^x$. If $g(a) = 32$, then *a* is

    (A) 2

    (B) 2.33

    (C) 2.5

    (D) 2.75

    (E) 3

21. In the figure, angles *A*, *B*, *C*, *D*, *E*, *F*, *G*, *H* are all 90° and *AB* = *AH* = *EF* = *DE*. Also, *BC* = *CD* = *HG* and the Cartesian coordinates of *A*, *C*, and *E* are (1, 2), (2, 5), and (5, 4), respectively. What is the area of figure *ABCDEFG*?

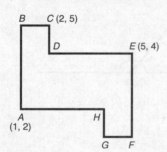

    (A) 6

    (B) 7

    (C) 8

    (D) 10

    (E) 12

(A) If you can get the answer from **(1) ALONE** but not from **(2)** alone
(B) If you can get the answer from **(2) ALONE** but not from **(1)** alone
(C) If you can get the answer from **BOTH (1) and (2) TOGETHER** but not from
(1) alone or (2) alone
(D) If **EITHER** statement **(1) ALONE OR** statement **(2) ALONE** suffices
(E) If you **CANNOT** get the answer from statements **(1)** and **(2) TOGETHER** but
need even more data

22. When an automobile is driven at 70 miles per hour, it uses 0.06 gallon of gas per
mile. When the car is driven at 50 miles per hour, it uses 0.04 gallon of gas per mile.
Which of the following relations are *possible* between the gallons of gas used per
mile and the speed at which the car is driven?

   I.   They are directly proportional.
  II.   They are indirectly proportional.
 III.   They are linearly related.

  (A) only I
  (B) only II
  (C) only III
  (D) I and III
  (E) I, II, and III

23. The points A and C are on the line l. Is line segment AB greater than line segment BC?

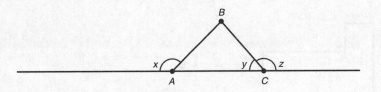

  (1) Angle x is greater than angle y.
  (2) Angle z is greater than angle x.

24. Is x positive?

  (1) $x^2 + 10\,x > 0$
  (2) $3^x > 1$

25.

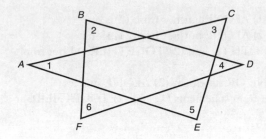

The sum of angles 1, 2, 3, 4, 5 and 6 is

(A) 180°
(B) 360°
(C) 480°
(D) 540°
(E) 720°

26. If $a + 2b = 6$ and $ab = 4$ what is $\dfrac{2}{a} + \dfrac{1}{b}$?

(A) $\dfrac{1}{2}$

(B) 1

(C) $\dfrac{3}{2}$

(D) 2

(E) $\dfrac{5}{2}$

27. Ms. Jones has twice as much invested in stocks as in bonds. Last year, the stock investments paid 7.5 percent of their value and the bonds paid 10 percent of their value. If the total that both investments paid last year was $1,000, how much did Ms. Jones have invested in stocks?

(A) $3,636
(B) $4,000
(C) $7,500
(D) $8,000
(E) $10,000

28. A pair of skis originally cost \$160. After a discount of x percent, the skis were
    discounted y percent. Do the skis cost less than \$130 after the discounts?

    (1) $x = 20$
    (2) $y = 15$

29. Is $xy < 0$?

    (1) $\dfrac{1}{x} < \dfrac{1}{y}$

    (2) $x > 0$

30. What is the mean (average) number of defective pens in a box of pens? The probability
    that there is exactly 1 defective pen in a box is 1 percent.

    (1) The probability that all the pens in the box are not defective is 96 percent.
    (2) The probability that there is more than 1 defective pen in the box is 3 percent.

31. Two-thirds of the roads from A to B are at least 5 miles long, and $\dfrac{1}{4}$ of the roads from
    B to C are at least 5 miles long. If you randomly pick a road from A to B and then
    randomly pick a road from B to C, what is the probability that at least one of the roads
    you pick is at least 5 miles long?

    (A) $\dfrac{1}{6}$

    (B) $\dfrac{1}{4}$

    (C) $\dfrac{2}{3}$

    (D) $\dfrac{3}{4}$

    (E) $\dfrac{11}{12}$

(A) If you can get the answer from (1) **ALONE** but not from (2) alone
(B) If you can get the answer from (2) **ALONE** but not from (1) alone
(C) If you can get the answer from **BOTH** (1) **and** (2) **TOGETHER** but not from (1) alone or (2) alone
(D) If **EITHER** statement (1) **ALONE OR** statement (2) **ALONE** suffices
(E) If you **CANNOT** get the answer from statements (1) and (2) **TOGETHER** but need even more data

32. *ABC* and *AED* are triangles with *BC* and *ED* perpendicular to *AB*. Find the length of *ED* if the area of *ABC* is 16.

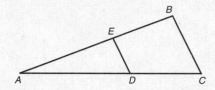

(1) $AB = 8$
(2) $AE = 5$

33. There are 30 socks in a drawer. Sixty percent of the socks are red, and the rest are blue. What is the minimum number of socks that must be taken from the drawer without looking in order to be certain that at least 2 blue socks have been chosen?

(A) 2
(B) 3
(C) 14
(D) 19
(E) 20

34. Are two triangles congruent?

(1) Both triangles are right triangles.
(2) Both triangles have the same perimeter.

35. *C* is a circle with center *D* and radius 2. *E* is a circle with center *F* and radius *R*. Are there any points that are on both *E* and *C*?

(1) The distance from *D* to *F* is $1 + R$.
(2) $R = 3$.

(A) If you can get the answer from (1) **ALONE** but not from (2) alone

(B) If you can get the answer from (2) **ALONE** but not from (1) alone

(C) If you can get the answer from **BOTH** (1) **and** (2) **TOGETHER** but not from
     (1) alone or (2) alone

(D) If **EITHER** statement (1) **ALONE OR** statement (2) **ALONE** suffices

(E) If you **CANNOT** get the answer from statements (1) and (2) **TOGETHER** but
     need even more data

36. *ABC* and *AED* are triangles with *BC* parallel to *ED*. Find the area of *BCDE* if the area
     of *ABC* is 16.

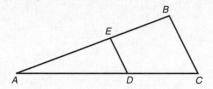

     (1)   *BC* = 8
     (2)   *ED* = 5

37. A car traveled 75 percent of the way from town *A* to town *B* at an average speed of
     50 miles per hour. The car travels at an average speed of *S* miles per hour for the
     remaining part of the trip. The average speed for the entire trip was 40 miles per hour.
     What is *S*?

     (A) 10
     (B) 20
     (C) 25
     (D) 30
     (E) 37.5

STOP

*IF THERE IS STILL TIME REMAINING, YOU MAY
REVIEW YOUR ANSWERS. AFTER YOU HAVE CONFIRMED
YOUR ANSWERS, YOU CANNOT RETURN TO THESE QUESTIONS.*

VERBAL SECTION

TIME: 75 MINUTES

41 QUESTIONS

Reading Comprehension
Directions: This section contains three reading passages. You are to read each one carefully. When answering the questions, you *will* be allowed to refer back to the passages. The questions are based on what is *stated* or *implied* in each passage.

Critical Reasoning
Directions: For each question in this section, choose the best answer from among the listed alternatives.

Sentence Correction
Directions: This part of the section consists of a number of sentences for each of which some part or the whole is underlined. Each sentence is followed by five alternative versions of the underlined portion. Select the alternative you consider both most correct and most effective according to the requirements of standard written English. Answer (A) is the same as the original version; if you think the original version is best, select answer (A).

In considering the answer choices, be attentive to matters of grammar, diction, and syntax, as well as clarity, precision, and fluency. Do not select an answer that alters the meaning of the original sentence.

1. Lavoisier, the 18th-century scientist, became more influential and famous than most
    of his contemporaries because not only did he discover and isolate many of the chemical
    elements but he also gave them names that both described the element in terms of
    its power and function and came to be accepted by other scientists in subsequent
    generations.

    Which of the following can be inferred from the above passage?

    (A) Lavoisier strived for fame and influence in the 18th century.
    (B) All elements found in the 18th century were named after Lavoisier.
    (C) Some of the elements that Lavoisier isolated were given names that described
         their properties.
    (D) Lavoisier was the most influential and famous scientist of his time.
    (E) Lavoisier became famous only because the names that he gave the chemicals
         became accepted.

2. The disaster that followed the earthquake in Armenia was tragic and serious, not just
    because of the fatalities and injuries, but because such widespread and severe damage
    was avoidable. The earthquake was less than 6 on the open-ended Richter scale, but its
    effects and aftermath matched the scene of events after much stronger quakes. What
    caused the casualty figures to reach such horrendous heights was that the buildings in
    the area were generally of a design that could not be expected to withstand anything
    more than a minor tremor.

    Which of the following statements can best be inferred from the passage?

    (A) People were not killed and injured by the earthquake, but by the falling masonry.
    (B) Resources should be invested in predicting the location, incidence, and strength
         of earthquakes.
    (C) Emergency evacuation procedures should be introduced in areas where earthquakes
         tend to occur frequently.
    (D) It would be better if earthquakes occurred only in areas far away from large centers
         of population.
    (E) The rescue aid provided by international organizations and other countries after
         the earthquake will hopefully improve relations.

3. In 1896, Henri Bequerel found that uranium salts emitted penetrating radiations
    similar to those which Roentgen produced only a year earlier with a gas discharge tube.

    (A) similar to those which Roentgen
    (B) like those which Roentgen
    (C) similar to those that Roentgen had
    (D) similar to them that Roentgen
    (E) similar to those Roentgen

4. Unless they reverse present policies immediately, the world may suffer permanent dam-
    age from the unregulated use of pesticides.

    (A) Unless they reverse present policies
    (B) Unless present policies are reversed
    (C) Unless present policies will be reversed
    (D) If it will not reverse present policies
    (E) If present policies will not be reversed

5. John <u>wanted to have gone</u> to the movies.

    (A) wanted to have gone
    (B) had wanted to have gone
    (C) wanted to go
    (D) wanted to have went
    (E) had wanted to have went

Questions 6–9 are based on the following passage.

       Despite the early protectionist moves, such as introducing steel tariffs, the Bush admin-
istration has pushed hard for trade liberalization in the past few years. In contrast, the
European Union has appeared divided and ineffective. Its trade commissioner, Peter Man-
Line delson, has so far failed to persuade skeptical member states that the benefits of new export
(5) markets will outweigh the costs of allowing greater competition at home, especially in agri-
culture. Though some members, notably Britain and other north Europeans, favor a more
liberal approach, it has proved all but impossible to get agreement from France and other
more protected economies with vociferous farmers. Europe's general position has been to
refuse any more lowering of agricultural barriers until poorer countries agree to liberalize
(10) trade in goods and services.

       Nor is the G20 group of developing nations giving much impetus to the talks. Led by
India and Brazil, the G20 is refusing to negotiate without deeper concessions on agricul-
ture. India, with its large population, may turn out to be a big problem. Its government
worries that competition from Chinese factories and American farms represents too great
(15) a threat, while gaining more access to world markets is only of limited attraction.

       Other poor countries are also unsure what they would gain. There is general talk of
hopeful prospects for poor farmers gaining greater access to rich-world markets. But the
benefits will not flow evenly from rich to poor. The World Bank estimates that removing
current agricultural distortions would produce a general benefit of more than $300 billion
(20) a year. Relative to national income, poor countries would enjoy a third more of this benefit than rich, industrialized ones. However, nearly half of that benefit would come from
reforms by the developing countries themselves, something governments might do anyway
were it not for the serious problem of the political pain the reforms are bound to cause.

       The impasse first led to the deadline for an agreement, which was originally supposed
(25) to be settled at the Hong Kong ministerial meeting in December 2005, to slip to the end
of April 2006. Now, in theory, this is to be resolved by the middle of summer 2006.
Missed deadlines may be nothing new for the World Trade Organization (WTO), but
these deadlines matter. There is no further room to slide from them. The American government's fast-track negotiating authority, which forces Congress to accept or reject a trade
(30) bill without introducing amendments, is thought to be essential if America is to take part
in talks. The authority expires in 2007 and few expect it to be renewed. Too many American politicians are once again turning protectionist. Congress only barely passed the Bush
administration's Central America Free Trade Agreement, even though its impact on the
American economy will be tiny compared to the ambitions for Doha. And as it will take
(35) roughly a year to work out the finer details of any world trade agreement, the outstanding
issues must be resolved early enough so the Bush administration to get a deal through
Congress.

6. It can be inferred that a removal of agricultural distortions would provide gains to poor countries of approximately

   (A) $300 million per year.
   (B) $500 million per year.
   (C) $100 billion per year.
   (D) $300 billion per year.
   (E) $500 billion per year.

7. The Indian government aims to

   (A) penetrate Chinese consumer markets.
   (B) reduce barriers to the sale of its farm produce.
   (C) impose more restrictive trade policies.
   (D) improve its bargaining position.
   (E) protect its farmers against foreign competition.

8. According to the passage, the American legislature is

   (A) liberalizing its policy toward foreign trade.
   (B) sensitive to the demands of third-world countries.
   (C) becoming more protectionist.
   (D) pushing hard for trade liberalization.
   (E) opposing any amendment to existing world trade agreements.

9. Achieving an agreement at the lateest round of trade talks seems doubtful because

   (A) the EU trade commissioner has failed to persuade India and China to liberalize exports of farm produce.
   (B) America's fast-track negotiating authority is soon to expire.
   (C) poorer countries refuse to lower agricultural barriers until developed countries open their markets to manufactured goods.
   (D) both the EU and G20 groups are unsure of the gains that might accrue from an agreement.
   (E) Britain and France are steadfastly against a new agreement.

10. Scientists believe they have discovered the wreck of the *USS Harvard*, sunk by Japanese torpedoes during World War II. Their conclusions are drawn from underwater searches by mini-submarines of the area about 4 miles west of Midway Island in the Pacific Ocean during what started out as offshore oil platform accident procedures. There are some military historians that are skeptical about the scientists' claim, on the basis that sophisticated sonar equipment has not identified the ship as, indeed, the *Harvard*.

    Which of the following, if true, would weaken the historians' arguments?

    (A) Thorough searching by divers and bathyscopes has not located the wreck.
    (B) Three other ships were sunk in this area during World War II.
    (C) The ship's last known position was 20 miles east of Midway.
    (D) The use of sonar only enables the user to identify the shape and dimension of a wreck.
    (E) It is not known whether the *Harvard* suffered much structural damage before being sunk.

11. In Great Britain, the problem of violence among spectators at soccer games has become more and more serious, with hardly a weekend passing without many arrested and many injured from among those who supposedly came to see a sport.

    Many suggestions have been made to combat this problem, most of them involving the introduction of more restrictions on the freedom of the crowds. Increased police presence at all games, enclosing supporters of opposing teams in pens, preventing the two groups from coming into contact with each other, and the use of membership cards with photographs which must be presented in order to gain access have all been tried.

    What is needed now is a deterrent factor. Increased fines, Saturday afternoon detention centers, and even jail terms must be introduced speedily and rigorously if we are going to solve this problem.

    Which of the following, if true, would most strengthen the present view of the writer?

    (A) The British Government has just passed legislation outlawing alcoholic drink to be sold at or brought into soccer matches.
    (B) Last week there were 36 arrested and 50 injured in fighting among the top soccer matches. This was an increase of 25% over the figures for the previous week.
    (C) The soccer clubs should do more to encourage families to attend their games by improving facilities and making special enclosures.
    (D) Violence is on the increase at soccer matches, and the authorities must get tougher.
    (E) Closed-circuit television has been set up to monitor trouble-making elements in the crowd.

12. Either you transfer the data that was demanded or file a report explaining why you did not submit the overall annual figures.

    (A) Either you transfer the data which was demanded
    (B) You either transfer the data, which was demanded,
    (C) You either transfer the data that were demanded
    (D) Either you transfer the data, which was demanded,
    (E) Either you transfer the data, which were demanded,

13. On entering the stadium, cheers greeted them as a sign of universal approval of their great achievement.

    (A) On entering the stadium, cheers greeted them
    (B) On entering the stadium, they were greeted by cheers
    (C) While entering the stadium, cheers greeted them
    (D) On entering the stadium cheers greeted them
    (E) On entering the stadium: cheers greeted them

14. The set of propositions which was discussed by the panel have been published in the society journal.

    (A) which was discussed by the panel have
    (B) which were discussed by the panel have
    (C) that was discussed by the panel has
    (D) which were discussed by the panel has
    (E) which was discussed, by the panel, has

Questions 15–18 are based on the following passage.

He began his long and transcendent career in a nondescript laboratory on the Adriatic Sea, dissecting eels. "Since eels do not keep diaries," the investigator, 19-year-old Sigmund Freud, wrote to a friend in the spring of 1876, the only way to detect gender was to cut and
Line slice, "but in vain, all the eels which I cut open are of the fairer sex."
(5)   Beginning May 11, 2006, the New York Academy of Medicine will exhibit the largest collection of Freud's drawings ever assembled, including several pieces from private collectors that have not been displayed in public. The drawings, some embedded in letters and scientific essays, chart the evolution of the Austrian neurologist's thinking, from his early and lesser known devotion to marine anatomy to the psychological theory that would alter
(10)   forever humans' conception of themselves and launch a discipline, psychoanalysis, that dominated psychiatry for half a century. The American Psychoanalytic Association and the New York Psychoanalytic Society and Institute collaborated in the exhibition.

Freud's methods have fallen from favor in recent decades, but science historians say that his investigation of the unconscious more than a century ago stands as a revolutionary
(15)   achievement that still informs many therapists' understanding of memory, trauma, and behavior.

Freud's drawings were serious science, the eel doodle notwithstanding. In the latter part of the 19th century, German researchers considered drawing to be instrumental to scientific discovery, both as a way to capture the microscopic detail of nerve cells, for example,
(20)   and to illustrate theories of how the brain might work, said Lynn Gamwell, curator of the exhibit and director of the Art Museum at the State University of New York at Binghamton. "Einstein once said that when he thought about science, he thought visually, he thought in pictures, and this appears to be the case with Freud," said Dr. Gamwell, a professor of science history.

(25)   Freud's drawings tell a story in three acts, from biology to psychology, from the microscope to the couch. The first, from Freud's college years into his mid-twenties, took place in laboratories, where he examined the nervous systems of crayfish and lamprey, among other animals. The 21 drawings from this period would look familiar to anyone who used a microscope in high school but on deeper inspection betray compulsive detail.

(30)   One, titled "On the Structure of the Nerve Fibers and Nerve Cells of the River Crayfish," depicts four types of nerve cells and minutely details the elements in the nuclei, the cell bodies shaded so carefully that they appear three-dimensional, alive, alien eyeballs bobbing in space. In another sketch, of the spinal anatomy of the lamprey, nerve fibers braid together like climbing vines, with cells hung throughout like clusters of ripening grapes.

(35)   By his late twenties, Freud had gained some experience with patients and, in a second phase of his career, he began to focus on brain function rather than descriptive anatomy. One drawing from this period, meant to illustrate the brain's auditory system, is as spare and geometric as a Calder sculpture, with fibers running between neural regions. The sketch is meant to represent scientific pathways in the brain, but the depiction is dramati-
(40)   cally more abstract than his earlier work. In another, from an unpublished essay titled "Introduction to Neuropathology," looping lines connect several nodes in a diagram intended to show how areas of the brain represent body, arms, face, hands.

At the time these drawings appeared, many neurologists presumed the body was somehow mirrored in the brain, perhaps altered in form but recognizable, intact. Yet in this
(45)   sketch and others like it, Freud said the brain worked differently; that is, fibers and cells "contain the body periphery in the same way as a poem contains the alphabet, in a complete arrangement" based on a body part's function, not its location. Later research supported Freud's contention.

15. In the late 19th century, it was believed that drawings were important to scientific discovery because they

    (A) helped researchers relax during times of stress.
    (B) charted the evolution of scientific thinking.
    (C) illustrated how the brain functions.
    (D) helped to determine gender.
    (E) were more accurate than photographs.

16. Freud began his career as a

    (A) neurologist.
    (B) psychologist.
    (C) biologist.
    (D) laboratory assistant.
    (E) artist.

17. In a career change, Freud switched from anatomy to a study of

    (A) brain functions.
    (B) unconscious behavior.
    (C) neuropathology.
    (D) nervous systems.
    (E) pathology.

18. The best possible title for the passage is

    (A) *"Freud as an Artist."*
    (B) *"On the Structure of Nerve Fibers."*
    (C) *"From Microscope to Couch."*
    (D) *"Elementary Psychoanalysis."*
    (E) *"From Dissection to Introspection."*

19. There are three main factors that control the risks of becoming dependent on drugs. These factors are the type of drug, the personality of the individual, and the circumstances in which the drug is taken. Indeed, it could be said that the majority of the adult population have taken alcohol, yet few have become dependent on it. Also, many strong drugs that have been used for medical purposes have not caused the patient to become addicted.

    However, it can be demonstrated that people who have taken drugs for fun are more likely to become dependent on the drug. The dependence is not always physiological but may remain psychological, although the effects are still essentially the same. Those at greatest risk appear to be personalities that are psychopathic, immature, or otherwise unstable.

    Psychological dependence is very strong with heroin, morphine, cocaine, and amphetamines. Physiological dependence is great with heroin and morphine, but less with amphetamines, barbiturates, and alcohol.

    Which of the following conclusions can be drawn from the text?

    (A) One cannot become addicted to certain drugs if one has a strong personality.
    (B) Taking drugs for "kicks" increases the possibility of becoming dependent on drugs.
    (C) Psychological dependence is greatest with heroin.
    (D) Alcohol is a safe drug since very few people become dependent on it.
    (E) Long-term use of certain drugs for medical purposes does not cause addiction.

20. In 1985 there were 20 deaths from automobile accidents per 1,000 miles traveled. A total of 20,000 miles were traveled via automobiles in 1985. In the same year, 800 people died in airplane crashes and 400 people were killed in train disasters. A statistician concluded from these data alone that it was more dangerous to travel by plane, train, and automobile, in that order.

Which of the following refutes the statistician's conclusion?

(A) There is no common denominator by which to compare the number of deaths resulting from each mode of travel.
(B) One year is insufficient to reach such a conclusion.
(C) More people travel by car than any other mode of transport, therefore, the probability of a car accident is greater.
(D) The number of plane flights and train trips is not stated.
(E) The probability of being killed in a train disaster and as a result of a car crash is the same.

21. From a letter to the commercial editor of a newspaper: Your article of January 9 drew attention to the large deficit in Playland's balance of payments that has worsened over the past three years. Yet, you favor the recent trade treaty signed between Playland and Workland. That treaty results in a lowering of our import duties that will flood us with Workland's goods. This will only exacerbate our balance of trade. How can you be in favor of the treaty?

Which of the following considerations would weaken the letter writer's argument?

(A) import diversion versus import creation
(B) prices paid by importers versus prices paid by consumers
(C) economic goals versus political goals
(D) duties levied increase government revenue
(E) free trade versus protectionism

22. In 1930, there were, on the average 10 deaths at birth (infant mortality) per 10,000 population. By 1940 there were 8.5, and by 1950, 7.0. Today there are 5.5 deaths at birth per 10,000 population, and it is anticipated that the downward trend will continue.

Each of the following, if true, would help to account for this trend *except*

(A) Medical care is more widespread and available.
(B) More effective birth control methods have been implemented.
(C) Sanitary conditions have improved.
(D) The number of pediatricians per 10,000 population has increased.
(E) Midwifery has declined in favor of medical doctors.

23. Product shipments of household appliances are expected to rise to $17 billion next year, an average annual increase of 8.0 percent over the past five years. The real growth rate, after allowing for probable price increases, is expected to be about 4.3 percent each year, resulting in shipments this year of $14 billion in 1987 dollars.

Each of the following, if true, could help to account for this trend *except*

(A) Consumer spending for durable products has increased.
(B) Household formations have increased.
(C) Consumer disposable income has increased.
(D) The consumer price of electricity has decreased.
(E) Individual tax advantages have decreased.

24. In this particular job we have discovered that <u>to be diligent is more important than being bright</u>.

    (A)   to be diligent is more important than being bright
    (B)   for one to be diligent is more important than being bright
    (C)   diligence is more important than brightness
    (D)   being diligent is more important than to be bright
    (E)   by being diligent is more important than being bright

25. No one but <u>him could have told them that the thief was I</u>.

    (A)   him could have told them that the thief was I
    (B)   he could have told them that the thief was I
    (C)   he could have told them that the thief was me
    (D)   him could have told them that the thief was me
    (E)   he could have told them the thief was me

26. 1.   All members of Group IV include all members of Group II.
    2.   All members of Group III include all members of Group I.
    3.   All members of Group IV include all members of Group I.
    4.   All members of Group II include all members of Group I.
    5.   All members of Group III include all members of Group IV.

Which of the following statements must be true in order to establish that Group III is the all-embracing group, that is, includes Groups I, II, and IV?

    (A)   Statement 1 is a vital piece of information.
    (B)   Statement 2 is a vital piece of information.
    (C)   Statement 3 is a vital piece of information.
    (D)   Statement 4 is a vital piece of information.
    (E)   None of the above statements is a vital piece of information.

27. Before the middle of the 14th century, there were no universities north of Italy, except in France and England. By the end of the 15th century, there were 23 universities in this region, from Louvain and Mainz to Rostock, Cracow, and Bratislava, and the number of universities in Europe as a whole had more than doubled.

Given the above information, which of the following statements is correct?

    (A)   Until the age of university expansion in the 15th century, there were perhaps 11 universities in the whole of Europe.
    (B)   South of Italy there were 23 universities in the 14th century.
    (C)   In the 13th century, France and England were the only countries in Europe with universities.
    (D)   After the great age of university expansion in the 14th and 15th centuries, France and England were not the only northern European countries to have such centers of learning.
    (E)   Italy was the cradle of university expansion.

28. After a careful evaluation of the circumstances surrounding the incident, we decided that we <u>neither have the authority nor</u> the means to cope with the problem.

    (A) neither have the authority nor
    (B) neither have authority or
    (C) have neither the authority nor
    (D) have neither the authority or
    (E) have not either the authority nor

29. <u>Everyone of us have understood that without him helping us</u> we would not have succeeded in our program over the past six months.

    (A) Everyone of us have understood that without him helping us
    (B) Everyone of us has understood that without his helping us
    (C) Everyone of us have understood that without his help
    (D) Everyone of us has understood that without him helping us
    (E) Every single one of us have understood that without him helping us

30. On the African continent, the incidence of vitamin <u>deficiencies correlates positively with</u> the level of solar radiation

    (A) deficiencies correlates positively with
    (B) deficiencies correlate positively with
    (C) deficiencies, correlate positively with,
    (D) deficiencies correlate positively to
    (E) deficiencies correlates positively to

31. <u>A thoroughly frightened child was seen by her cowering in the corner of the room.</u>

    (A) A thoroughly frightened child was seen by her cowering in the corner of the room.
    (B) Cowering in the corner of the room a thoroughly frightened child was seen by her.
    (C) She saw, cowering in the corner of the room, a thoroughly frightened child.
    (D) A thoroughly frightened child, cowering in the corner of the room, was seen by her.
    (E) She saw a thoroughly frightened child who was cowering in the corner of the room.

32. <u>If they would have taken greater care</u> in the disposal of the nuclear waste, the disaster would not have occurred.

    (A) If they would have taken greater care
    (B) Unless they took greater care
    (C) Had they not taken greater care
    (D) If they had taken greater care
    (E) If they took greater care

33. <u>Neither the judge nor I am ready to announce who the winner is.</u>

    (A) Neither the judge nor I am ready to announce who the winner is.
    (B) Neither the judge nor I are ready to announce who the winner is.
    (C) Neither the judge nor I are ready to announce who is the winner.
    (D) Neither the judge nor I am ready to announce who is the winner.
    (E) Neither I or the judge are ready to announce who is the winner.

34. One major obligation of the social psychologist is to provide his own discipline, the other social sciences, and interested laymen with conceptual tools that will increase the range and the reliability of their understanding of social phenomena. Beyond that, responsible government officials are today turning more frequently to the social scientist for insights into the nature and solution of the problems with which they are confronted.

The above argument assumes that

(A) social psychologists must have a strong background in other sciences as well as their own.

(B) a study of social psychology should be a part of the curriculum of government officials.

(C) the social scientist has an obligation to provide the means by which social phenomena may be understood by others.

(D) social phenomena are little understood by those outside the field of social psychology.

(E) a good social psychologist is obligated principally by the need to solve interdisciplinary problems.

35. Administrators and executives are members of the most stable occupation.

The stability mentioned in the above statement could be dependent on each of the following factors *except*

(A) training and skills.

(B) nature of the occupation.

(C) status.

(D) relatively high income.

(E) rate of turnover.

36. Between 1979 and 1983, the number of unincorporated business self-employed women increased five times faster than the number of self-employed men and more than three times faster than the number of women wage-and-salary workers. Part-time self-employment among women increased more than full-time self-employment.

Each of the following, if true, could help to account for this trend *except*

(A) Owning a business affords flexibility to combine work and family responsibilities.

(B) The proportion of women studying business administration courses has grown considerably.

(C) There are more self-employed women than men.

(D) Unincorporated service industries have grown by 300 percent over the period; the ratio of women to men in this industry is three to one.

(E) The financial reward of having a second wage earner in the household has taken on increased significance.

37. <u>More than any animal</u>, the wolverine exemplifies the unbridled ferocity of "nature red in tooth and claw."

    (A) More than any animal,
    (B) More than any other animal,
    (C) More than another animal,
    (D) Unlike any animal,
    (E) Compared to other animals,

Questions 38–41 are based on the following passage.

Literature is at once the most intimate and the most articulate of the arts. It cannot impart its effect through the senses or the nerves as the other arts can; it is beautiful only through the intelligence; it is the mind speaking to the mind; until it has been put into
Line absolute terms, of an invariable significance, it does not exist at all. It cannot awaken this
(5) emotion in one, and that in another; if it fails to express precisely the meaning of the author, if it does not say *him*, it says nothing, and is nothing. So that when a poet has put his heart, much or little, into a poem, and sold it to a magazine, the scandal is greater than when a painter has sold a picture to a patron, or a sculptor has modeled a statue to order. These are artists less articulate and less intimate than the poet; they are more exterior to their work;
(10) they are less personally in it; they part with less of themselves in the dicker. It does not change the nature of the case to say that Tennyson and Longfellow and Emerson sold the poems in which they couched the most mystical messages their genius was charged to bear mankind. They submitted to the conditions which none can escape; but that does not justify the conditions, which are none the less the conditions of hucksters because they are
(15) imposed upon poets. If it will serve to make my meaning a little clearer, we will suppose that a poet has been crossed in love, or has suffered some real sorrow, like the loss of a wife or child. He pours out his broken heart in verse that shall bring tears of sacred sympathy from his readers, and an editor pays him a hundred dollars for the right of bringing his verse to their notice. It is perfectly true that the poem was not written for these dollars, but it is
(20) perfectly true that it was sold for them.

38. The author implies that writers are

    (A) incompetent in business.
    (B) not sufficiently paid for their work.
    (C) greedy.
    (D) hucksters.
    (E) profiting against their will.

39. A possible title that best expresses the meaning of the passage would be

    (A) *"The Man of Letters as a Man of Business"*
    (B) *"Literature and the Arts"*
    (C) *"Progress in Literature"*
    (D) *"Poets and Writers"*
    (E) *"The State of the Arts"*

40. By accepting payment for works of literature or art, its creators are

    I. writing and painting solely for monetary gain.
    II. justifying the practice of art.
    III. exchanging their work for remuneration.

    (A) I only
    (B) III only
    (C) I and II only
    (D) II and III only
    (E) I, II, and III

41. The author of the passage proposes that writers and artists

    (A) make the best out of a bad situation.
    (B) attempt to induce society to change its values.
    (C) withhold their work until they gain recognition.
    (D) adopt the principles of commercialism.
    (E) adopt the value system of society.

STOP

IF THERE IS STILL TIME REMAINING, YOU MAY REVIEW YOUR ANSWERS. AFTER YOU HAVE CONFIRMED YOUR ANSWERS, YOU CANNOT RETURN TO THESE QUESTIONS.

Answer Key
PRE-TEST

Quantitative Section

1. E	11. D	21. D	31. D
2. A	12. D	22. C	32. C
3. D	13. B	23. B	33. E
4. D	14. C	24. B	34. E
5. C	15. C	25. B	35. C
6. B	16. A	26. C	36. C
7. C	17. C	27. D	37. C
8. A	18. C	28. A	
9. E	19. E	29. C	
10. E	20. C	30. E	

Verbal Section

1. C	12. C	23. E	34. C
2. A	13. B	24. C	35. E
3. C	14. D	25. A	36. C
4. B	15. C	26. A	37. B
5. C	16. C	27. D	38. E
6. C	17. A	28. C	39. A
7. B	18. C	29. B	40. B
8. C	19. B	30. A	41. A
9. D	20. A	31. C	
10. D	21. A	32. D	
11. B	22. B	33. A	

ANSWERS EXPLAINED

Quantitative Section

1. **(E)** STATEMENT (1) would be sufficient if there were information about the width of each book. Since STATEMENT (2) gives information only about the *weight* of each book, both statements together are not sufficient.

2. **(A)** The slope of the line is $\frac{(y_1 - y_2)}{(x_1 - x_2)}$, which is $\frac{(100 - 60)}{(10 - 15)} = \frac{40}{-5} = -8$. So the equation of the line is $y = -8x + b$. Use either point to find b. Using (10,100), we have $100 = y = -8x + b = -8(10) + b$, so $100 = -80 + b$, which gives us $b = 180$. So the equation of the line is $y = -8x + 180$.

3. **(D)** Since $f(y) = y^3 - 4$ and $f(y) = 4$, we know that $y^3 - 4 = 4$. Solve the equation for y, which gives $y^3 = 8$, and so $y = 2$.

4. **(D)** STATEMENT (1) alone is sufficient since $BC = AB$ implies $x = y = 40$. Since the sum of the angles in a triangle is 180°, z must equal 100. STATEMENT (2) alone is sufficient. Let D be the point where the bisector of angle B meets AC. Then according to (2), triangle BDC is a right triangle. Since angle y is 40°, the remaining angle in triangle BDC is 50° and equals $\frac{1}{2}z$; so $z = 100$.

5. **(C)** STATEMENT (2) alone is insufficient since you need to know what direction town B is from town C.

   STATEMENT (1) alone is insufficient since you need to know how far it is from town B to town C.

   Using both STATEMENTS (1) and (2), A, B, and C form a right triangle with legs of 9 miles and 12 miles. The distance from town A to town B is the hypotenuse of the triangle, so the distance from town A to town B is $\sqrt{9^2 + 12^2}$ = 15 miles.

6. **(B)** If three of the numbers are negative, then as long as the fourth is greater than the absolute value of the sum of the other three, the sum of all four is positive. For example, $(-50) + (-35) + (-55) + 155 = 15$.

7. **(C)** STATEMENT (1) alone is not sufficient since you have no information about the distance from B to C. STATEMENT (2) alone is not sufficient since you have no information about the distance from A to B. The two statements together are sufficient since they show that there are at least six routes from A to C that pass through B and are at least 10 miles long.

8. **(A)** Since the question says you test 2 *different* bulbs and there is only 1 defective bulb in the box, there is no possibility that both bulbs will be defective.

9. **(E)** If the company sells the parts for \$4.00 each, then $4 = 10 - 0.1x$. Solve $4 = 10 - 0.1x$ for x. The result is $x = 60$. The company will sell $100x$ parts; so they will sell $100(60) = 6,000$ machine parts.

10. **(E)** Let x be the number of miles the car travels on a gallon of gas when driven at 60 mph. Then 80 percent of 15 is x; so $(0.80)(15) = x$ and $x = 12$. So it will take $\frac{120}{12} = 10$ gallons of gas to travel 120 miles at 60 mph. Notice that many of the other choices correspond to misconceptions. If you divide $\frac{120}{15}$, you get 8, which is choice (C), but this is the number of gallons needed to travel 120 miles at 50 mph. If you take 80 percent of 8 gallons, you get choice (B), and if you take 120 percent of 8, you get choice (D). So the fact that your answer matches one of the given choices does not mean it is correct.

11. **(D)** By 5:30 A.M. train X will have traveled $(4\frac{1}{2})x$ miles. So train Z must travel $(4\frac{1}{2})x$ miles in $3\frac{1}{2}$ hours. The average rate of speed necessary is $\dfrac{4\frac{1}{2}x}{3\frac{1}{2}}$ which equals $\left(\frac{9}{7}\right)x$.

12. **(D)** Since S is greater than 1,000, the profit is 6 percent of $1,000 plus 5 percent of $(S - 1,000)$ dollars, which is $60 + (0.05S - 50)$ dollars. Therefore, the profit equals $(10 + 0.05S)$ dollars.

13. **(B)** An even integer is an integer divisible by 2. Since $2n + 10p$ is $2(n + 5p)$, using STATEMENT (2) lets you deduce that x is even. STATEMENT (1) by itself is not sufficient. If n were 2 and p were 3, $(n + p)^2$ would be 25, which is not even, but by choosing n to be 2 and p to be 4, $(n + p)^2$ is 36, which is even.

14. **(C)** STATEMENT (1) alone implies $x = 3y$. Since there is no more information about y, STATEMENT (1) alone is insufficient.

STATEMENT 2 alone gives $x = 9 + y$ but there is no information about y, so STATEMENT (2) alone is not sufficient.

STATEMENTS (1) and (2) together are sufficient. If $x = 9 + y$ and $x = 3y$, then $3y = 9 + y$ which gives $y = \frac{9}{2}$; so $x = (3)\left(\frac{9}{2}\right) = \frac{27}{2}$.

15. **(C)** In each minute, hole A drains $\frac{1}{24}$ of the tank according to STATEMENT (1). Since we have no information about B, STATEMENT (1) alone is not sufficient. In each minute, hole B drains $\frac{1}{42}$ of the tank according to STATEMENT (2), but STATEMENT (2) gives no information about hole A. So STATEMENT (2) alone is not sufficient. If we use STATEMENTS (1) and (2), then both holes together will drain $\frac{1}{24} + \frac{1}{42}$ or $\frac{11}{168}$ of the tank each minute. Therefore, it will take

$\frac{168}{11}$ or $15\frac{3}{11}$ minutes for the tank to empty. So STATEMENTS (1) and (2) together are sufficient, but neither statement alone is sufficient. (*Note*: Don't bother working out how long it will take to drain the tank.)

16. **(A)** Let x be the amount of 10 percent nitrogen fertilizer that is needed. Then the amount of nitrogen in the mixture will be 10% of x + 20% of 12 = $0.1x + 2.4$. The percentage of nitrogen in the mixture will be $\dfrac{(0.1x + 2.4)}{(x + 12)}$, which must equal 0.18. Solve this equation for x by multiplying each side by $x + 12$ to obtain

$$0.1x + 2.4 = 0.18(x + 12)$$
$$= 0.18x + 2.16$$
$$2.4 - 2.16 = 0.18x - 0.1x$$
$$0.24 = 0.08x$$
$$x = \frac{0.24}{0.8} = 3$$

17. **(C)** STATEMENT (1) alone is not sufficient since we can only deduce that $100\% - 96\% = 4\%$ is the probability that there is *at least 1* defective pen in the box. STATEMENT (2) alone is not sufficient since we can only deduce that $100\% - 3\% = 97\%$ is the probability that there are 0 or 1 defective pen in the box. Using STATEMENTS (1) and (2) together, we can see that $4\% - 3\% = 1\%$ is the probability that there is exactly 1 defective pen in the box.

18. **(C)** STATEMENT (1) alone is not sufficient since it tells you that l and t are perpendicular but gives no information about t and k. STATEMENT (2) alone is not sufficient. If the angles u and a are right angles, then l and k are parallel; but if the angles are not right angles, then the lines are not parallel. STATEMENTS (1) and (2) together are sufficient since together they prove that l and k are parallel.

19. **(E)** STATEMENT (1) alone is not sufficient since you have no information about the distance from B to C. STATEMENT (2) alone is not sufficient since you have no information about the distance from A to B. The two statements together are not sufficient. For instance if the longest road from A to B is 5.2 miles long and the longest road from B to C was 5.6 miles long, then the longest route from A to C through B is 10.8 miles. But if the longest road from A to B is 7 miles long and the longest road from B to C is 5.6 miles long, then the longest route from A to C through B is 12.6 miles.

20. **(C)** We must solve $4^a = 32$. The key to this problem is the fact that 4 and 32 are both powers of 2, and so we can rewrite the equation as $4^a = (2^2)^a = 2^{2a} = 32 = 2^5$. So $2a$ must equal 5 since $2^x = 2^y$ if and only if $x = y$. Solve $2a = 5$ to obtain $a = 2.5$.

Another method: Since $4 = 16$, we have $2(4^2) = 32$. Since $2 = \sqrt{4} = 4^{\frac{1}{2}}$, $32 = (4^2)(4^{0.5}) = 4^{2.5}$.

21. **(D)** Since the angle at B is 90°, the coordinates of B are (1, 5), so $AB = 3$ and $BC = 1$. To find the area, break the figure into three smaller figures by extending the line CD until it meets AH at point J and extending line GH until it meets DE at point K. Then the area sought is the sum of the areas of $ABCJ$, $JDKH$, and $KEFG$. All three figures are rectangles because all their angles are 90°. The area of $ABCJ$ is 3×1 since AB is 3 and BC is 1. The area of $JDKH$ is $JD \times JH$. Since the coordinates of D, J, and K are (2, 4), (2, 2), and (4, 4), respectively, the area of $JDKH$ is $2 \times 2 = 4$. Finally, since $EF = AB = 3$ and $KE = 1$, the area of $EFGK$ is $3 \times 1 = 3$. Therefore, the area of the figure is $3 + 4 + 3 = 10$.

6 Difficulty Level   22.   **(C)** Let G be the gallons of gas per mile and S be the speed at which the car is driven. The two quantities G and S are directly proportional if $G = kS$ for some constant k. So if G and S are directly proportional, then $70 = k(0.06)$ and $50 = k(0.04)$. Solve both equations for k. The first equation gives $k = \dfrac{70}{0.06}$, but the second equations give $k = \dfrac{50}{0.04}$, which is not equal to $\dfrac{70}{0.06}$. So G and S are not directly proportional, and I is impossible. The two quantities G and S are indirectly proportional if $GS = k$ for some constant k. So $70(0.06)$ and $50(0.04)$ should both equal k. Since $50(0.04)$ is not equal to $70(0.06)$, G and S are not indirectly proportional, and II is impossible. Since two points determine a straight line, it is possible for G and S to be linearly related. You can find the equation of the line through the two points $(70, 0.06)$ and $(50, 0.04)$. *Don't waste time doing this. You already know enough to answer the question, so don't spend any more time on the problem.* Therefore, the correct answer is III only.

6 Difficulty Level   23.   **(B)** STATEMENT (1) is always true since the exterior angle of one vertex is equal to the sum of the other two interior angles of a triangle. So STATEMENT (1) alone is not sufficient. STATEMENT (2) alone is sufficient since it implies that angle BAC is greater than angle BCA. This implies that the side opposite angle BAC (which is BC) is greater than the side opposite angle BCA (which is AB.)

6 Difficulty Level   24.   **(B)** Since $x^2 + 10x = x(x + 10)$, STATEMENT (1) is true for $x > 0$ or $x < -10$. So STATEMENT (1) alone is not sufficient. STATEMENT (2) alone is sufficient since $3^0 = 1$ and as x increases 3^x increases.

7 Difficulty Level   25.   **(B)** Since ACE is a triangle with angles 1, 3 and 5, the sum of angles 1, 3, and 5 is 180°. Since BDF is a triangle with angles 2, 4, and 6, the sum of angles 2, 4, and 6 is 180°. So the sum of angles 1, 2, 3, 4, 5, and 6 is 180° + 180° = 360°.

7 Difficulty Level   26.   **(C)** Convert $\dfrac{2}{a} + \dfrac{1}{b}$ into a single fraction. The fact that you are given the value of ab, which is a common denominator, is a clue. So $\dfrac{2}{a} + \dfrac{1}{b} = \dfrac{(2b + a)}{ab} = \dfrac{6}{4} = \dfrac{3}{2}$.

7 Difficulty Level   27.   **(D)** Let S be the amount invested in stocks and B be the amount invested in bonds. Then $0.75S + 0.1B = 1{,}000$ and $S = 2B$. So $0.075(2B) + .1B = .25B = 1000$, which means that $B = \dfrac{1{,}000}{0.25}$ or $B = \$4{,}000$. Finally, $S = 2B$; so $S = \$8{,}000$.

7 Difficulty Level   28.   **(A)** Since 80 percent of \$160 = \$128, we know that after the first discount the skis cost less than \$130. Any further discount will only lower the price. So (1) alone is sufficient. STATEMENT (2) alone is not sufficient since if x were 10 percent, (2) would tell us the price is less than \$130; but if x were 1 percent, (2) would imply that the price is greater than \$130.

7 Difficulty Level   29.   **(C)** STATEMENT (1) alone is not sufficient; x could be negative or positive with y positive, and (1) would be true.
STATEMENT (2) alone is not sufficient since it gives no information about y.
STATEMENT (1) and (2) together are sufficient. If $x > 0$, then (1) implies y is > 0; so $xy > 0$.

30. **(E)** We need to know the probability of each number of defective pens to calculate the mean. STATEMENT (1) alone is not sufficient since we can only deduce that 100% − 97% = 3% is the probability that *there are more than 1* defective pen in the box. STATEMENT (2) alone is not sufficient since more than 1 could mean 2, 3, and so on. Using STATEMENTS (1) and (2) together, we still don't have the information needed to calculate the mean.

31. **(D)** Two-thirds of your choices for the road from *A* to *B* are at least 5 miles long. One-third of your choices of the road from *A* to *B* are less than 5 miles long, but for these choices $\frac{1}{4}$ of your choices from *B* to *C* will be at least 5 miles long. So $\frac{2}{3} + \left(\frac{1}{3}\right)\left(\frac{1}{4}\right) = \frac{9}{12} = \frac{3}{4}$ of your choices will give at least one road that is at least 5 miles long.

    Another method: Let *E* be the event that the road from *A* to *B* is at least 5 miles long and let *F* be the event that the road from *B* to *C* is at least 5 miles long. The question asks for the probability of the union of *E* and *F* $[(P(E \cup F)]$, which is equal to $P(E) + P(F) − P(E \cap F)$.

    This is $\frac{2}{3} + \frac{1}{4} - \left(\frac{2}{3}\right)\left(\frac{1}{4}\right) = \frac{9}{12} = \frac{3}{4}$.

32. **(C)** STATEMENT (1) alone is not sufficient since *ED* can be moved inside the triangle *ABC* without changing *AB*. STATEMENT (2) is insufficient because *BC* can be moved and its length changed without changing STATEMENT (2). Since *BC* and *ED* are perpendicular to the same line, they are parallel. So the triangles *AED* and *ABC* are similar, and so $\frac{ED}{BC} = \frac{AE}{AB} = \frac{5}{8}$ using STATEMENT (1) and STATEMENT (2). Using the fact that the area of *ABC* is 16 will let you find that the altitude from *C* to *AB* (which is *BC*) has length 4. Since $\frac{ED}{BC} = \frac{5}{8}$ you can find *ED* so STATEMENTS (1) and (2) together are sufficient.

33. **(E)** The key word in this problem is *certain.* If you pick only 2 socks, you might get a pair of blue socks, but this is not certain. If the question asked for a pair of socks the same color, then after only 3 socks have been picked, 2 socks will have to be the same color—but the 2 socks might be red. Since 60 percent of the 30 socks, or 18 socks, are red, it is possible, although unlikely, that you could pick 18 reds and only 1 blue after 19 picks. However, if you pick 20 socks, you will get at least 2 blue socks. So the correct choice is (E).

34. **(E)** A triangle with sides of lengths 3, 4, and 5 is a right triangle since $3^2 + 4^2 = 5^2$, and its perimeter is 12. A triangle with sides of lengths 2, 4.8, and 5.2 also has a perimeter of 12. And since $2^2 + (4.8)^2 = (5.2)^2$, it too is a right triangle. Therefore, two triangles can satisfy STATEMENTS (1) and (2) yet not be congruent. On the other hand, any pair of congruent right triangles satisfies STATEMENTS (1) and (2). Thus, STATEMENTS (1) and (2) together are not sufficient to answer the question.

35. **(C)** STATEMENT (2) alone is not sufficient since we must know how close the circles are and we know only the radius of each circle.

    STATEMENT (1) alone is not sufficient. If *R* is less than 0.5, then the circle with center *F* is completely inside the circle with center *D*, and so there are no points on both circles.

    STATEMENTS (1) and (2) together are sufficient since STATEMENT (2) means that *R* is greater than 0.5. The centers of the two circles are closer than the sum of the radii. (So we can form a triangle with *DF* as one side and the two other sides with lengths 2 and *R*, respectively; but this means that the third vertex of the triangle will be on both circle *E* and circle *C*.)

36. **(C)** Since *ED* can be moved inside the triangle, which will change the area of *BCDE* without changing STATEMENT (1), STATEMENT (1)) alone is not sufficient. STATEMENT (2) by itself is insufficient since it gives no information about the other three sides of *BCDE*. Since *ED* and *BC* are parallel, triangles *ABC* and *AED* are similar, and the ratio of corresponding sides such as $\frac{ED}{BC}$ will be $\frac{5}{8}$ using STATEMENTS (1) and (2). Since the triangles are similar, their altitudes from *A* to *ED* and from *A* to *BC* must also have the same ratio, $\frac{5}{8}$, which means that the ratio of the area of *AED* to the area of *ABC* is $\left(\frac{5}{8}\right)\left(\frac{5}{8}\right) = \frac{25}{64}$. Since you are given the area of *ABC*, you can find the area of *AED*. Subtract the area of *AED* from the area of *ABC* to get the area of *BCDE*. (*Note*: Don't bother to do the calculations because you only have to decide if there is enough information to solve the problem.)

37. **(C)** This problem can be worked out by some complicated algebra if you let *D* be the distance between the towns and let *T* be the total time of the trip. However, it is much easier to work it out if you simply choose a convenient number for the distance. So assume the distance between town *A* and town *B* is 1,000 miles. Then 75 percent of the distance is 750 miles, so the car traveled for $\frac{750}{50} = 15$ hours at 50 mph. If the car averaged 40 mph for the entire trip, then the entire trip took $\frac{1,000}{40} = 25$ hours. So the car must have taken 25 – l5 = 10 hours for the part of the trip it traveled at *S* miles per hours. It traveled 1,000 – 750 = 250 miles at *S* miles per hour, so *S* is $\frac{250}{10} = 25$. A common mistake is to solve the equation $0.75(50) + 0.25S = 40$ for *S*. This approach would be correct if the car traveled 75 percent of the time at 50 miles per hour and 25 percent of the time at *S* miles per hour. However, you are given that the car traveled 75 percent of the distance at 50 miles per hour and since speed changes the time it takes to travel a certain distance, 75 percent of the distance will not be 75 percent of the time.

Verbal Section

1. **(C)** That Lavoisier strived for fame and influence may be a statement of fact, but not one that may be concluded from the passage. We learn from the passage only that he became famous and influential; therefore, choice (A) is inappropriate. Certainly, some of the elements discovered in the 1700s were named after Lavoisier, as can be learned from the passage, but not all of them. Therefore, choice (B) is also not appropriate. Choice (D) can be ruled out because of the presence in the passage of the key words "more influential than most of his contemporaries" and not, as choice (D) states, "the most influential scientist of his time." There is a comparison between Lavoisier and the other scientists, but that is as far as the passage goes. Choice (E) is not appropriate because the passage does not give as fact that the names he allocated to the chemicals he discovered were accepted as the only reason for his subsequent fame. The word *only* rules it out. Choice (C) correctly states the conclusion, which can be drawn from the passage and is, therefore, the appropriate answer.

2. **(A)** The main inference in the whole paragraph is that an earthquake by itself—that is, a movement of the earth's crust that on the surface is felt as a series of sudden jerks—will not necessarily cause human casualties. It is only when quakes occur in heavily populated areas wherein there are many buildings and the buildings collapse that people are injured and killed by being hit by falling bricks and masonry. (A), therefore, is the appropriate answer. The proposal in choice (B), however laudable, does not emanate from the passage. Choice (C) proposes another alternative measure that cannot be inferred from the passage. (D) presents an opinion with which probably nobody would disagree, but again, this view is not taken from the text. (E) can be ruled out for the same reason: It is not contained in and cannot be inferred from the passage.

3. **(C)** The past perfect tense *had produced* is required in this sentence to show that Roentgen's work preceded that of Bequerel.

4. **(B)** Choice (A) suffers from the use of the ambiguous pronoun *they*. It is not clear whom *they* is supposed to refer to. The use of the future tense in choices (C), (D), and (E) is incorrect.

5. **(C)** The sequence of tenses is incorrect. According to the meaning of the sentence, John's wanting comes *before*, not *after*, John's going.

6. **(C)** See paragraph 3. It is estimated that removing agricultural distortions will amount to $300 billion a year, of which poor countries sould gain one-third, that is, $100 billion.

7. **(B)** The Indian government, like many other "poorer" countries, wants developed countries to reduce barriers to imports of farm produce. See paragraph 2.

8. **(C)** See paragraph 4. "Too many American politicians are once again turning protectionist." The next sentence also exemplifies the difficulty in getting trade legislation passed.

9. **(D)** Paragraphs 1 and 3 illustrate that both some EU countries and the G20 group of developing nations are unsure of the costs and gains resulting from a new trade agreement. Note that (C) is just the opposite of what is contained in the passage, at the end of the first paragraph.

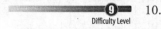

10. **(D)** The statement in choice (A) would strengthen the historians' arguments, so (A) is incorrect. The additional information provided in statement (B) could also be used to strengthen the historian's argument since if there is a wreck of a ship in the location in question, it may not be that of the *Harvard* but rather could be that of any of several ships known to have been sunk in the area during the War. Therefore, (B) is inappropriate. The statement in (E) does not help to determine whether what has been found is or is not a wreck or whether it is or is not the *Harvard*; it is not relevant to the argument, and therefore (E) is incorrect. The fact that the *Harvard*'s last known position was not close to the area where the wreck has been found may strengthen the historian's conclusion. It certainly does not weaken his argument. To weaken

the historian's argument most effectively, counterevidence that shows that their method of investigation or study produces results that are inconclusive must be provided. Statement (D) does this. It points out shortcomings in the method employed—that is, sonar equipment—thereby making the conclusions reached more tenuous. This is the statement that would most effectively weaken the historians' arguments, and thus (D) is the correct answer.

11. **(B)** The question asks which statement would most strengthen the present view of the writer. Choice (D) is simply a summation of the author's opinion and is not necessarily likely to strengthen his view. While the writer may agree with the sentiments expressed in (C), it by itself will not reinforce his views. Choices (D) and (C), therefore, cannot be correct. What will harden the author's viewpoint is learning more facts that are not to his liking. Presumably, the developments noted in (A) and (E) will meet with his approval and are therefore not appropriate. On the other hand, the information conveyed by (B) will serve to increase his anger and resolve and strengthen his present view. (B), therefore, is the appropriate answer.

12. **(C)** *Either . . . or* connect *transfer* and *file*. *Data* here is plural and requires the verb *were*.

13. **(B)** A participial phrase at the beginning of a sentence must be followed by the word it modifies.

14. **(D)** The *set has been* published, while the *propositions* (individually) *were* discussed.

15. **(C)** See paragraph 4. Drawings were considered intrumental to scientific discovery to illustrate how the brain functions.

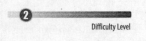

16. **(C)** Freud started his career as a marine biologist. Evidence of this is given in the second and fifth paragraphs.

17. **(A)** While Freud eventually studied unconscious behavior (paragraph 3); his career change was from descriptive anatomy to a focus on brain functions (paragraph 8).

18. **(C)** The microscope represents the biologist's tool, while the couch is the psychoanalyst's tool. These illustrate the career change that Freud made.

19. **(B)** Although a strong personality might have some resistance to the psychological dependence factors of drug use, it cannot be stated with any certainty that a strong personality can prevent physiological dependence. In this way, (A) is not a reasonable conclusion.

Psychological dependence on heroin is greater than that of drugs such as alcohol and marijuana, but it is not stated to be the greatest since psychological dependence is also great with cocaine and amphetamines. There is no conclusive evidence in the text to support this view. (C) is not, therefore, a reasonable conclusion.

A safe drug implies no danger of addiction, and since it cannot be shown that there is no danger of addiction to alcohol, statement (D) is also not valid.

Although short-term use of certain drugs for medical purposes rarely produces dependence, long-term use of certain drugs often causes physiological dependence; in this respect (E) is not a valid assumption.

(B) is the only conclusion that can probably be true. Statistics show that many hard-drug addicts and regular users started their habit by taking drugs for "kicks." Also the search for drugs to be used for kicks almost inevi?tably causes exposure to localities where harder and more addictive drugs are available, thus increasing the chances of attempting more addictive drugs for kicks. The passage states that the circumstances in which the drug is taken is one factor controlling the risk of becoming dependent and also that it can be demonstrated that people who have taken drugs for fun are more likely to become dependent on the drug.

Difficulty Level ⑦

20. **(A)** Note that the casualty figure for automobile deaths is given as the ratio of number of deaths to miles traveled. In order to make a comparison with other modes of transport, the same denominator (miles traveled) would have to be used.

Difficulty Level ⑦

21. **(A)** If the treaty results in increased Workland exports to Playland at the expense of local producers (import creation), Playland's balance of payments will show a larger deficit. If however, increased Workland exports to Playland merely replace imports from other countries (import diversion), the trade balance will not change. Alternative (C) is a second-best consideration; that is, that political objectives supersede economic goals. The remaining alternatives have no bearing on Playland's balance of trade.

Difficulty Level ③

22. **(B)** There is no association between birth control and infant mortality. Birth control can prevent pregnancies but not death after birth.

Difficulty Level ②

23. **(E)** If tax advantages (deductions, etc.) decrease, less disposable income is available for spending. All other alternatives explain why total shipments of appliances have increased.

Difficulty Level ⑧

24. **(C)** Parallelism: a similar form is required on either side of the comparison.

Difficulty Level ⑨

25. **(A)** *But* meaning *except* is always followed by the objective pronoun, and the copula *was* takes the subjective *I*.

Difficulty Level ⑨

26. **(A)** If you did not have statement 4, you would still know that Group I is in Group III (from statement 2) and Group IV (from statement 3) and that Group II is in Group IV (from statement 1). Because you know Group IV is in Group III (from statement 5), you can still infer that Group III includes all the other groups. Therefore, (D) is inappropriate. Similarly, if you lacked the information in statement 2, or that in statement 3, you would still have sufficient information to conclude what Group II includes. So choices (B) and (C) are inappropriate. Statement 1, however is vital, as without it one cannot be certain if Group III includes Group II or vice versa. Therefore, (A) is the appropriate answer. Choice (E) is not appropriate since (A) is vital.

Difficulty Level ⑥

27. **(D)** The passage states that university expansion—north of Italy and outside France and England—took place between the mid-14th century and the end of the 15th century. There is nothing in the passage about the number of universities in the whole of Europe, so we have no way of knowing if (A) is correct. Statement (B) is not substantiated by what is in the passage—namely, that "by the end of the 15th century, there were 23 universities" in a wide region. There is nothing in the passage that states that France and England were the only countries with universities in the 13th century, so (C) is not appropriate. Similarly, nothing in the passage states or implies that Italy was the cradle of university expansion (E).

Difficulty Level ⑤

28. **(C)** *Neither . . . nor* apply to *authority* and *means* and must precede them directly.

Difficulty Level ③

29. **(B)** *Everyone* is singular and requires the singular *has*. The preposition *without* requires the gerund *helping* preceded by the possessive *his*.

Difficulty Level ③

30. **(A)** The *incidence* (singular) *correlates*. The preposition *with* is correct.

Difficulty Level ⑨

31. **(C)** This is a suspenseful sentence since what *She saw* is held off to the very last word in the sentence. Also, an active verb, *saw*, is preferable to the passive *was seen*.

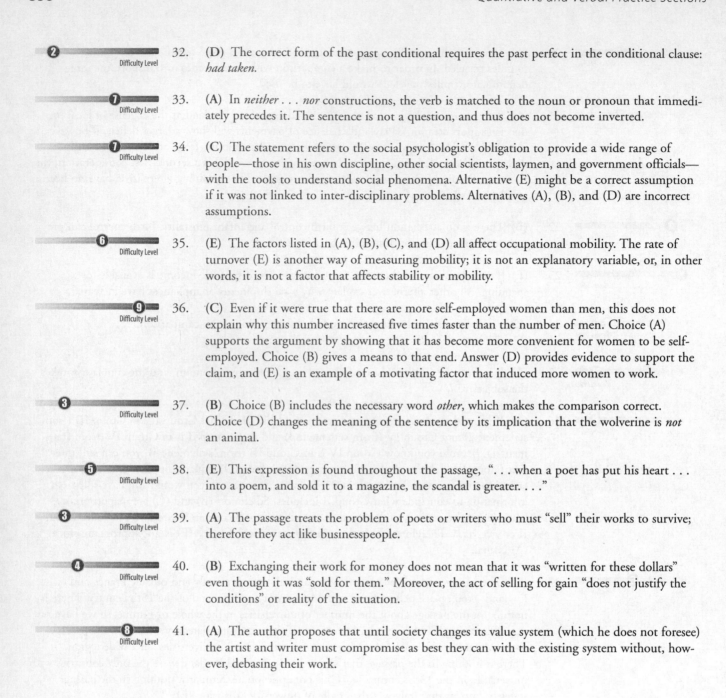

2 Difficulty Level   32. **(D)** The correct form of the past conditional requires the past perfect in the conditional clause: *had taken.*

7 Difficulty Level   33. **(A)** In *neither . . . nor* constructions, the verb is matched to the noun or pronoun that immediately precedes it. The sentence is not a question, and thus does not become inverted.

7 Difficulty Level   34. **(C)** The statement refers to the social psychologist's obligation to provide a wide range of people—those in his own discipline, other social scientists, laymen, and government officials—with the tools to understand social phenomena. Alternative (E) might be a correct assumption if it was not linked to inter-disciplinary problems. Alternatives (A), (B), and (D) are incorrect assumptions.

6 Difficulty Level   35. **(E)** The factors listed in (A), (B), (C), and (D) all affect occupational mobility. The rate of turnover (E) is another way of measuring mobility; it is not an explanatory variable, or, in other words, it is not a factor that affects stability or mobility.

9 Difficulty Level   36. **(C)** Even if it were true that there are more self-employed women than men, this does not explain why this number increased five times faster than the number of men. Choice (A) supports the argument by showing that it has become more convenient for women to be self-employed. Choice (B) gives a means to that end. Answer (D) provides evidence to support the claim, and (E) is an example of a motivating factor that induced more women to work.

3 Difficulty Level   37. **(B)** Choice (B) includes the necessary word *other*, which makes the comparison correct. Choice (D) changes the meaning of the sentence by its implication that the wolverine is *not* an animal.

5 Difficulty Level   38. **(E)** This expression is found throughout the passage, ". . . when a poet has put his heart . . . into a poem, and sold it to a magazine, the scandal is greater. . . ."

3 Difficulty Level   39. **(A)** The passage treats the problem of poets or writers who must "sell" their works to survive; therefore they act like businesspeople.

4 Difficulty Level   40. **(B)** Exchanging their work for money does not mean that it was "written for these dollars" even though it was "sold for them." Moreover, the act of selling for gain "does not justify the conditions" or reality of the situation.

8 Difficulty Level   41. **(A)** The author proposes that until society changes its value system (which he does not foresee) the artist and writer must compromise as best they can with the existing system without, however, debasing their work.

TEST YOURSELF

Answer Sheet

SAMPLE TEST 1

Quantitative Section

1 Ⓐ Ⓑ Ⓒ Ⓓ Ⓔ	11 Ⓐ Ⓑ Ⓒ Ⓓ Ⓔ	21 Ⓐ Ⓑ Ⓒ Ⓓ Ⓔ	31 Ⓐ Ⓑ Ⓒ Ⓓ Ⓔ
2 Ⓐ Ⓑ Ⓒ Ⓓ Ⓔ	12 Ⓐ Ⓑ Ⓒ Ⓓ Ⓔ	22 Ⓐ Ⓑ Ⓒ Ⓓ Ⓔ	32 Ⓐ Ⓑ Ⓒ Ⓓ Ⓔ
3 Ⓐ Ⓑ Ⓒ Ⓓ Ⓔ	13 Ⓐ Ⓑ Ⓒ Ⓓ Ⓔ	23 Ⓐ Ⓑ Ⓒ Ⓓ Ⓔ	33 Ⓐ Ⓑ Ⓒ Ⓓ Ⓔ
4 Ⓐ Ⓑ Ⓒ Ⓓ Ⓔ	14 Ⓐ Ⓑ Ⓒ Ⓓ Ⓔ	24 Ⓐ Ⓑ Ⓒ Ⓓ Ⓔ	34 Ⓐ Ⓑ Ⓒ Ⓓ Ⓔ
5 Ⓐ Ⓑ Ⓒ Ⓓ Ⓔ	15 Ⓐ Ⓑ Ⓒ Ⓓ Ⓔ	25 Ⓐ Ⓑ Ⓒ Ⓓ Ⓔ	35 Ⓐ Ⓑ Ⓒ Ⓓ Ⓔ
6 Ⓐ Ⓑ Ⓒ Ⓓ Ⓔ	16 Ⓐ Ⓑ Ⓒ Ⓓ Ⓔ	26 Ⓐ Ⓑ Ⓒ Ⓓ Ⓔ	36 Ⓐ Ⓑ Ⓒ Ⓓ Ⓔ
7 Ⓐ Ⓑ Ⓒ Ⓓ Ⓔ	17 Ⓐ Ⓑ Ⓒ Ⓓ Ⓔ	27 Ⓐ Ⓑ Ⓒ Ⓓ Ⓔ	37 Ⓐ Ⓑ Ⓒ Ⓓ Ⓔ
8 Ⓐ Ⓑ Ⓒ Ⓓ Ⓔ	18 Ⓐ Ⓑ Ⓒ Ⓓ Ⓔ	28 Ⓐ Ⓑ Ⓒ Ⓓ Ⓔ	
9 Ⓐ Ⓑ Ⓒ Ⓓ Ⓔ	19 Ⓐ Ⓑ Ⓒ Ⓓ Ⓔ	29 Ⓐ Ⓑ Ⓒ Ⓓ Ⓔ	
10 Ⓐ Ⓑ Ⓒ Ⓓ Ⓔ	20 Ⓐ Ⓑ Ⓒ Ⓓ Ⓔ	30 Ⓐ Ⓑ Ⓒ Ⓓ Ⓔ	

Verbal Section

1 Ⓐ Ⓑ Ⓒ Ⓓ Ⓔ	12 Ⓐ Ⓑ Ⓒ Ⓓ Ⓔ	23 Ⓐ Ⓑ Ⓒ Ⓓ Ⓔ	35 Ⓐ Ⓑ Ⓒ Ⓓ Ⓔ
2 Ⓐ Ⓑ Ⓒ Ⓓ Ⓔ	13 Ⓐ Ⓑ Ⓒ Ⓓ Ⓔ	24 Ⓐ Ⓑ Ⓒ Ⓓ Ⓔ	36 Ⓐ Ⓑ Ⓒ Ⓓ Ⓔ
3 Ⓐ Ⓑ Ⓒ Ⓓ Ⓔ	14 Ⓐ Ⓑ Ⓒ Ⓓ Ⓔ	25 Ⓐ Ⓑ Ⓒ Ⓓ Ⓔ	37 Ⓐ Ⓑ Ⓒ Ⓓ Ⓔ
4 Ⓐ Ⓑ Ⓒ Ⓓ Ⓔ	15 Ⓐ Ⓑ Ⓒ Ⓓ Ⓔ	26 Ⓐ Ⓑ Ⓒ Ⓓ Ⓔ	38 Ⓐ Ⓑ Ⓒ Ⓓ Ⓔ
5 Ⓐ Ⓑ Ⓒ Ⓓ Ⓔ	16 Ⓐ Ⓑ Ⓒ Ⓓ Ⓔ	27 Ⓐ Ⓑ Ⓒ Ⓓ Ⓔ	39 Ⓐ Ⓑ Ⓒ Ⓓ Ⓔ
6 Ⓐ Ⓑ Ⓒ Ⓓ Ⓔ	17 Ⓐ Ⓑ Ⓒ Ⓓ Ⓔ	28 Ⓐ Ⓑ Ⓒ Ⓓ Ⓔ	40 Ⓐ Ⓑ Ⓒ Ⓓ Ⓔ
7 Ⓐ Ⓑ Ⓒ Ⓓ Ⓔ	18 Ⓐ Ⓑ Ⓒ Ⓓ Ⓔ	29 Ⓐ Ⓑ Ⓒ Ⓓ Ⓔ	41 Ⓐ Ⓑ Ⓒ Ⓓ Ⓔ
8 Ⓐ Ⓑ Ⓒ Ⓓ Ⓔ	19 Ⓐ Ⓑ Ⓒ Ⓓ Ⓔ	30 Ⓐ Ⓑ Ⓒ Ⓓ Ⓔ	
9 Ⓐ Ⓑ Ⓒ Ⓓ Ⓔ	20 Ⓐ Ⓑ Ⓒ Ⓓ Ⓔ	31 Ⓐ Ⓑ Ⓒ Ⓓ Ⓔ	
10 Ⓐ Ⓑ Ⓒ Ⓓ Ⓔ	21 Ⓐ Ⓑ Ⓒ Ⓓ Ⓔ	32 Ⓐ Ⓑ Ⓒ Ⓓ Ⓔ	
11 Ⓐ Ⓑ Ⓒ Ⓓ Ⓔ	22 Ⓐ Ⓑ Ⓒ Ⓓ Ⓔ	34 Ⓐ Ⓑ Ⓒ Ⓓ Ⓔ	

Sample Test 1 with Answers and Analysis

WRITING ASSESSMENT

Part I   TIME: 30 MINUTES

Directions: Write a clear, logical, and well-organized response to the following issue or argument. Your response should be in the form of a short essay, following the conventions of standard written English. Your answer should fit on three pages of lined 8½" × 11" paper or equivalent on your PC. Write legibly. Essays that are illegible or that are written on a topic other than the one outlined in the question will not be scored.

The fear is widespread among environmentalists that free trade increases economic growth and that growth harms the environment. That fear is misplaced. Growth enables governments to tax and to raise resources for a variety of objectives, including the abatement of pollution and the general protection of the environment. Without such revenues, little can be achieved, no matter how pure one's motives may be.

Which do you find more compelling, the fear of free trade or the response to it? Explain the position you take by using appropriate reasons, examples from your experience, reading, and study.

STOP

IF THERE IS STILL TIME REMAINING, YOU MAY REVIEW YOUR ANSWER. AFTER YOU HAVE CONFIRMED YOUR ANSWER, YOU CANNOT RETURN TO THIS QUESTION.

Part II TIME: 30 MINUTES

Directions: Write a clear, logical, and well-organized response to the following issue or argument. Your response should be in the form of a short essay, following the conventions of standard written English. Your answer should fit on three pages of lined 8½" × 11" paper or equivalent on your PC. Write legibly. Essays that are illegible or that are written on a topic other than the one outlined in the question will not be scored.

The installation of electronic high-speed scanning devices at the entrances and exits of toll roads will obviate the need for toll booths. Automobiles will have scanner-sensitive license plates—like the bar codes on consumer packaged products—so that the scanner devices will record the license numbers of cars entering and exiting the toll road. Car owners will be billed monthly by the highway authorities.

Discuss how logically persuasive you find the above argument. In presenting your point of view, analyze the sort of reasoning used and supporting evidence. In addition, state what further evidence, if any, would make the argument more sound and convincing or would make you better able to evaluate its conclusion.

STOP

IF THERE IS STILL TIME REMAINING, YOU MAY REVIEW YOUR ANSWER. AFTER YOU HAVE CONFIRMED YOUR ANSWER, YOU CANNOT RETURN TO THIS QUESTION.

QUANTITATIVE SECTION

TIME: 75 MINUTES

37 QUESTIONS

This section consists of two types of questions: Problem Solving and Data Sufficiency.

Problem Solving
Directions: Solve each of the following problems; then indicate the correct answer.

NOTE: A figure that appears with a problem is drawn as accurately as possible so as to provide information that may help in answering the question.
Numbers in this test are real numbers.

Data Sufficiency
Directions: Each of the following problems has a question and two statements which are labeled (1) and (2). Use the data given in (1) and (2) together with other available information (such as the number of hours in a day, the definition of *clockwise*, mathematical facts, etc.) to decide whether the statements are *sufficient* to answer the question. Then fill in space

(A) If you can get the answer from (1) **ALONE** but not from (2) alone
(B) If you can get the answer from (2) **ALONE** but not from (1) alone
(C) If you can get the answer from **BOTH** (1) **and** (2) **TOGETHER** but not from (1) alone or (2) alone
(D) If **EITHER** statement (1) **ALONE OR** statement (2) **ALONE** suffices
(E) If you **CANNOT** get the answer from statements (1) and (2) **TOGETHER** but need even more data

All numbers used in this section are real numbers.

A figure given for a problem is intended to provide information consistent with that in the question, but not necessarily with the additional information contained in the statements.
All figures lie in the plane unless you are told otherwise.
Figures are drawn as accurately as possible; straight lines may not appear straight on the screen.

(A) If you can get the answer from (1) **ALONE** but not from (2) alone
(B) If you can get the answer from (2) **ALONE** but not from (1) alone
(C) If you can get the answer from **BOTH (1) and (2) TOGETHER** but not from (1) alone or (2) alone
(D) If **EITHER** statement (1) **ALONE OR** statement (2) **ALONE** suffices
(E) If you **CANNOT** get the answer from statements (1) and (2) **TOGETHER** but need even more data

1. It takes 30 days to fill a laboratory dish with bacteria. If the size of the bacteria colony doubles each day, how long did it take for the bacteria to fill one half of the dish?

   (A) 10 days
   (B) 15 days
   (C) 24 days
   (D) 29 days
   (E) 29.5 days

2. If the ratio of the areas of two squares is 2 : 1, then the ratio of the perimeters of the squares is

   (A) 1 : 2
   (B) 1 : $\sqrt{2}$
   (C) $\sqrt{2}$: 1
   (D) 2 : 1
   (E) 4 : 1

3. Are two triangles congruent?

   (1) Both triangles are right triangles.
   (2) Both triangles have the same perimeter.

4. Is x greater than zero?

   (1) $x^4 - 16 = 0$
   (2) $x^3 - 8 = 0$

5. If both conveyer belt A and conveyer belt B are used, they can fill a hopper with coal in 1 hour. How long will it take for conveyer belt A to fill the hopper without conveyer belt B?

   (1) Conveyer belt A moves twice as much coal as conveyer belt B.
   (2) Conveyer belt B would take 3 hours to fill the hopper without conveyer belt A.

(A) If you can get the answer from (1) **ALONE** but not from (2) alone
(B) If you can get the answer from (2) **ALONE** but not from (1) alone
(C) If you can get the answer from **BOTH** (1) **and** (2) **TOGETHER** but not from (1) alone or (2) alone
(D) If **EITHER** statement (1) **ALONE OR** statement (2) **ALONE** suffices
(E) If you **CANNOT** get the answer from statements (1) and (2) **TOGETHER** but need even more data

6. There are three types of tickets available for a concert: orchestra, which cost $12 each; balcony, which cost $9 each; and box, which cost $25 each. There were P orchestra tickets, B balcony tickets, and R box tickets sold for the concert. Which of the following expressions gives the percentage of ticket proceeds due to the sale of orchestra tickets?

(A) $100 \times \dfrac{P}{(P+B+R)}$

(B) $100 \times \dfrac{12P}{(12P+9B+25R)}$

(C) $\dfrac{12P}{(12P+9B+25R)}$

(D) $100 \times \dfrac{(9B+25R)}{(12P+9B+25R)}$

(E) $100 \times \dfrac{(12P+9B+25R)}{(12P)}$

7. City B is 5 miles east of city A. City C is 10 miles southeast of city B. Which of the following is the closest to the distance from city A to city C?

(A) 11 miles
(B) 12 miles
(C) 13 miles
(D) 14 miles
(E) 15 miles

8. There are 30 socks in a drawer. What is the probability that if 2 socks are picked from the drawer without looking both socks are blue?

(1) 40 percent of the socks in the drawer are blue.
(2) The ratio of blue socks to red socks in the drawer is 2 : 1.

9. If $3x - 2y = 8$, then $4y - 6x$ is

(A) −16
(B) −8
(C) 8
(D) 16
(E) cannot be determined

(A) If you can get the answer from (1) **ALONE** but not from (2) alone
(B) If you can get the answer from (2) **ALONE** but not from (1) alone
(C) If you can get the answer from **BOTH** (1) **and** (2) **TOGETHER** but not from (1) alone or (2) alone
(D) If **EITHER** statement (1) **ALONE OR** statement (2) **ALONE** suffices
(E) If you **CANNOT** get the answer from statements (1) and (2) **TOGETHER** but need even more data

10. It costs 10¢ a kilometer to fly and 12¢ a kilometer to drive. If you travel 200 kilometers, flying x kilometers of the distance and driving the rest, then the cost of the trip in dollars is

(A)   20
(B)   24
(C) $24 - 2x$
(D) $24 - .02x$
(E) $2,400 - 2x$

11. Is y larger than 1?

(1) y is larger than 0.
(2) $y^2 - 4 > 0$.

12. A worker is hired for 6 days. He is paid $2 more for each day of work than he was paid for the preceding day of work. How much was he paid for the first day of work?

(1)   His total wages for the 6 days were $150.
(2)   He was paid 150 percent of his first day's pay for the sixth day.

13. Let $^*y$ be the operation given by $^*y = \dfrac{4}{y} - y$. Which of the following statements are true?

   I.   If $0 < y$, then $^*y$ is negative.
   II. If $0 < y < z$, then $^*y > {^*z}$.
   III. If $0 < y$ then $y(^*y)$ is less than 5.

(A)   I only
(B)   II only
(C)   III only
(D)   II and III
(E)   I, II, and III

14. A car originally sold for $3,000. After a month, the car was discounted x percent, and a month later the car's price was discounted y percent. Is the car's price after the discounts less than $2,600?

(1) $y = 10$
(2) $x = 15$

15. How likely is a bird to be classified as positive?

(1)   80 percent of birds with avian flu are classified as positive.
(2)   5 percent of birds without avian flu are classified as positive.

16. If the area of a square increases by 69 percent, then the side of the square increases by

    (A) 13%
    (B) 30%
    (C) 39%
    (D) 69%
    (E) 130%

17. Which of the following statements can be inferred from the table?

    Distribution of Work Hours in a Factory

Number of Workers		Number of Hours Worked
20		45–50
15		40–44
25		35–39
16		30–34
4		0–29
80	TOTAL	3,100

    I.   The average number of hours worked per worker is less than 40.
    II. At least 3 workers worked more than 48 hours.
    III. More than half of all the workers worked more than 40 hours.

    (A) I only
    (B) II only
    (C) I and II only
    (D) I and III only
    (E) I, II, and III

18. When a truck travels at 60 miles per hour, it uses 30 percent more gasoline to travel any distance than it does when it travels at 50 miles per hour. The truck can travel 20 miles on a gallon of gas if it is traveling at 50 miles per hour. The truck has only 10 gallons of gas and is 160 miles from its destination. It takes 20 minutes for the truck to stop for gas. How long will it take the truck to reach its final destination if it is driven at 60 miles per hour?

    (A) 160 minutes
    (B) 180 minutes
    (C) 190 minutes
    (D) 192 minutes
    (E) 195 minutes

19. Company *A* owns 40 percent of the stock in the XYZ Corporation. Company *B* owns 15,000 shares. Company *C* owns all the shares not owned by company *A* or *B*. How many shares of stock does company *A* own if company *C* has 25 percent more shares than company *A*?

    (A) 45,000
    (B) 50,000
    (C) 60,000
    (D) 75,000
    (E) 90,000

(A) If you can get the answer from (1) **ALONE** but not from (2) alone

(B) If you can get the answer from (2) **ALONE** but not from (1) alone

(C) If you can get the answer from **BOTH** (1) **and** (2) **TOGETHER** but not from (1) alone or (2) alone

(D) If **EITHER** statement (1) **ALONE OR** statement (2) **ALONE** suffices

(E) If you **CANNOT** get the answer from statements (1) and (2) **TOGETHER** but need even more data

20. How many squares with sides $\frac{1}{2}$ inch long are needed to cover a rectangle that is 4 feet long and 6 feet wide?

    (A) 24
    (B) 96
    (C) 3,456
    (D) 13,824
    (E) 14,266

21. How much cardboard will it take to make an open cubical box with no top?

    (1) The area of the bottom of the box is 4 square feet.
    (2) The volume of the box is 8 cubic feet.

22. Is the integer x divisible by 3?

    (1) The last digit in x is 3.
    (2) $x + 5$ is divisible by 6.

23. Is the figure *ABCD* a rectangle?

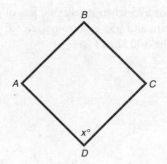

    (1) $x = 90$
    (2) $AB = CD$

24. A sequence of numbers is given by the rule $a_n = (a_{n-1})^2$. What is a_5?

    (1) $a_1 = -1$
    (2) $a_3 = 1$

25. In a group of people solicited by a charity, 30 percent contributed $40 each, 45 percent contributed $20 each, and the rest contributed $12 each. What percentage of the total contributed came from people who gave $40?

    (A) 25%
    (B) 30%
    (C) 40%
    (D) 45%
    (E) 50%

26. A trapezoid *ABCD* is formed by adding the isosceles right triangle *BCE* with base 5 inches to the rectangle *ABED*, where *DE* is *t* inches. What is the area of the trapezoid in square inches?

    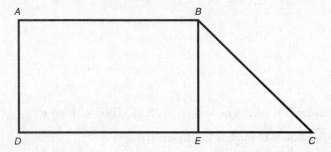

    (A) $5t + 12.5$
    (B) $5t + 25$
    (C) $2.5t + 12.5$
    (D) $(t + 5)^2$
    (E) $t^2 + 25$

27. A manufacturer of jam wants to make a profit of $75 when it sells 300 jars of jam. It costs 65¢ each to make the first 100 jars of jam and 55¢ each to make each jar after the first 100. What price should it charge for the 300 jars of jam?

    (A) $75
    (B) $175
    (C) $225
    (D) $240
    (E) $250

28. A car traveled 75 percent of the distance from town *A* to town *B* by traveling for *T* hours at an average speed of *V* miles per hour. The car traveled at an average speed of *S* miles per hour for the remaining part of the trip. Which of the following expressions represents the time the car traveled at *S* miles per hour?

    (A) $\dfrac{VT}{S}$

    (B) $\dfrac{VS}{4T}$

    (C) $\dfrac{4VT}{3S}$

    (D) $\dfrac{3S}{VT}$

    (E) $\dfrac{VT}{3S}$

(A) If you can get the answer from (1) **ALONE** but not from (2) alone
(B) If you can get the answer from (2) **ALONE** but not from (1) alone
(C) If you can get the answer from **BOTH** (1) **and** (2) **TOGETHER** but not from (1) alone or (2) alone
(D) If **EITHER** statement (1) **ALONE OR** statement (2) **ALONE** suffices
(E) If you **CANNOT** get the answer from statements (1) and (2) **TOGETHER** but need even more data

29. How much is John's weekly salary?

    (1) John's weekly salary is twice as much as Fred's weekly salary.
    (2) Fred's weekly salary is 40 percent of the total of Chuck's weekly salary and John's weekly salary.

30. Find $x + 2y$.

    (1) $x + y = 4$
    (2) $2x + 4y = 12$

31. Is angle *BAC* a right angle?

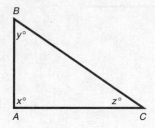

    (1) $x = 2y$
    (2) $y = 1.5z$

32. If a, b, and c are digits, is $a + b + c$ a multiple of 9? A digit is one of the integers 0, 1, 2, 3, 4, 5, 6, 7, 8, 9.

    (1) The three-digit number *abc* is a multiple of 9.
    (2) $(a \times b) + c$ is a multiple of 9.

33. In Teetown 50 percent of the people have blue eyes and blond hair. What percent of the people in Teetown have blue eyes but do not have blond hair?

    (1) 70 percent of the people in Teetown have blond hair.
    (2) 60 percent of the people in Teetown have blue eyes.

34. Thirty-six identical chairs must be arranged in rows with the same number of chairs in each row. Each row must contain at least 3 chairs, and there must be at least 3 rows. A row is parallel to the front of the room. How many different arrangements are possible?

    (A) 2
    (B) 4
    (C) 5
    (D) 6
    (E) 10

35. Which of the following solids has the largest volume? (*Figures are not drawn to scale.*)

   I. A cylinder of radius 5 millimeters and height 11 millimeters

   II. A sphere of radius 6 millimeters (the volume of a sphere of radius r is $\frac{4}{3}\pi r^3$)

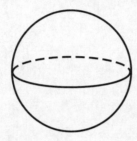

   III. A cube with edge of 9 millimeters.

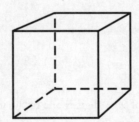

   (A) I
   (B) II
   (C) III
   (D) I and II
   (E) II and III

(A) If you can get the answer from (1) **ALONE** but not from (2) alone

(B) If you can get the answer from (2) **ALONE** but not from (1) alone

(C) If you can get the answer from **BOTH** (1) **and** (2) **TOGETHER** but not from (1) alone or (2) alone

(D) If **EITHER** statement (1) **ALONE OR** statement (2) **ALONE** suffices

(E) If you **CANNOT** get the answer from statements (1) and (2) **TOGETHER** but need even more data

36. The pentagon *ABCDE* is inscribed in a circle with center *O*. How many degrees is angle *ABC*?

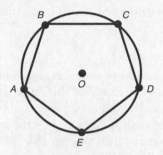

   (1)   The pentagon *ABCDE* is a regular pentagon, which means that all sides are the same length and all interior angles are the same size.

   (2)   The radius of the circle is 5 inches.

37. Is $k^2 + k - 2 > 0$?

   (1) $k < 1$

   (2) $k > -1$

STOP

*IF THERE IS STILL TIME REMAINING, YOU MAY
REVIEW YOUR ANSWERS. AFTER YOU HAVE CONFIRMED
YOUR ANSWERS, YOU CANNOT RETURN TO THESE QUESTIONS.*

VERBAL SECTION

TIME: 75 MINUTES

41 QUESTIONS

Reading Comprehension
Directions: This section contains three reading passages. You are to read each one carefully. When answering the questions, you *will* be allowed to refer back to the passages. The questions are based on what is *stated* or *implied* in each passage.

Critical Reasoning
Directions: For each question in this section, choose the best answer among the listed alternatives.

Sentence Correction
Directions: This part of the section consists of a number of sentences in each of which some part or the whole is underlined. Each sentence is followed by five alternative versions of the underlined portion. Select the alternative you consider both most correct and most effective according to the requirements of standard written English. Answer (A) is the same as the original version; if you think the original version is best, select answer (A).

In considering the answer choices, be attentive to matters of grammar, diction, and syntax, as well as clarity, precision, and fluency. Do not select an answer that alters the meaning of the original sentence.

1. Farmers in the North have observed that heavy frost is usually preceded by a full moon. They are convinced that the full moon somehow generates the frost.

   Which of the following, if true, would weaken the farmers' conviction?

   (A) The temperature must fall below 10 degrees Celsius (50 degrees Fahrenheit) for frost to occur.
   (B) Absence of a cloud cover cools the ground which causes frost.
   (C) Farmers are superstitious.
   (D) No one has proven that the moon causes frost.
   (E) Farmers are not experts in meteorology.

2. Professor Tembel told his class that the method of student evaluation of teachers is not a valid measure of teaching quality. Students should fill out questionnaires at the end of the semester when courses have been completed.

   Which of the following, if true, provides support for Professor Tembel's proposal?

   (A) Professor Tembel received low ratings from his students.
   (B) Students filled out questionnaires after the midterm exam.
   (C) Students are interested in teacher evaluation.
   (D) Teachers are not obligated to use the survey results.
   (E) Student evaluation of teachers is voluntary.

3. If she was to decide to go to college, I, for one, would recommend that she plan to go to Yale.

   (A) If she was to decide to go to college,
   (B) If she were to decide to go to college,
   (C) Had she decided to go to college,
   (D) In the event that she decides to go to college,
   (E) Supposing she was to decide to go to college,

4. Except for you and I, everyone brought a present to the party.

   (A) Except for you and I, everyone brought
   (B) With exception of you and I, everyone brought
   (C) Except for you and I, everyone had brought
   (D) Except for you and me, everyone brought
   (E) Except for you and me, everyone had brought

Questions 5–8 are based on the following passage.

The domestic economy expanded in a remarkably vigorous and steady fashion. . . . The resurgence in consumer confidence was reflected in the higher proportion of incomes spent for goods and services and the marked increase in consumer willingness to take on install-
Line   ment debt. A parallel strengthening in business psychology was manifested in a stepped-up
(5)   rate of plant and equipment spending and a gradual pickup in outlays for inventory. Confidence in the economy was also reflected in the strength of the stock market and in the stability of the bond market. . . . For the year as a whole, consumer and business sentiment benefited from rising public expectations that a resolution of the conflict in Vietnam was in prospect and that East-West tensions were easing.
(10)   The United States balance of payments deficit declined sharply. Nevertheless, by any other test, the deficit remained very large, and there was actually a substantial deterioration in our trade account to a sizable deficit, almost two thirds of which was with Japan. . . .

The underlying task of public policy for the year ahead—and indeed for the longer run—remained a familiar one: to strike the right balance between encouraging healthy eco-
(15)   nomic growth and avoiding inflationary pressures. With the economy showing sustained and vigorous growth, and with the currency crisis highlighting the need to improve our competitive posture internationally, the emphasis seemed to be shifting to the problem of inflation. The Phase Three program of wage and price restraint can contribute to dampening inflation. Unless productivity growth is unexpectedly large, however, the expansion of
(20)   real output must eventually begin to slow down to the economy's larger run growth potential if generalized demand pressures on prices are to be avoided. Indeed, while the unemployment rates of a bit over five percent were still too high, it seems doubtful whether the much lower rates of four percent and below often cited as appropriate definitions of full employment do in fact represent feasible goals for the United States economy—unless there
(25)   are improvements in the structure of labor and product markets and public policies influencing their operation. There is little doubt that overall unemployment rates can be brought down to four percent or less, for a time at least, by sufficient stimulation of aggregate demand. However, the resultant inflationary pressures have in the past proved exceedingly difficult to contain.

5. The passage was most likely published in a

    (A) popular magazine
    (B) general newspaper
    (C) science journal
    (D) financial journal
    (E) textbook

6. Confidence in the economy was expressed by all of the following except

    (A) a strong stock market
    (B) a stable bond market
    (C) increased installment debt
    (D) increased plant and equipment expenditures
    (E) rising interest rates

7. According to the passage, a major problem is how to

    (A) sustain economic growth
    (B) improve labor productivity
    (C) balance growth with low inflation
    (D) stimulate demand
    (E) avoid large increases in imports

8. Most of the trade deficit in the balance of payments was attributed to trade with which country?

(A) United Kingdom
(B) Japan
(C) Germany
(D) France
(E) Saudi Arabia

9. When one reads the poetry of the seventeenth century, you find a striking contrast between the philosophy of the Cavalier poets such as Suckling and the attitude of the Metaphysical poets such as Donne.

(A) When one reads the poetry of the seventeenth century, you find
(B) When you read the poetry of the seventeenth century, one finds
(C) When one reads the poetry of the seventeenth century, he finds
(D) If one reads the poetry of the 17th century, you find
(E) As you read the poetry of the 17th century, one finds

10. Because of his broken hip, John Jones has not and possibly never will be able to run the mile again.

(A) has not and possibly never will be able to run
(B) has not and possibly will never be able to run
(C) has not been and possibly never would be able to run
(D) has not and possibly never would be able to run
(E) has not been able to run and possibly never will be able to run

11. The President lobbied for passage of his new trade bill which would liberalize trade with industrialized countries such as Japan, members of the European Community, and Canada.

Each of the following, if true, could account for the above, except:

(A) The President is up for re-election and needs to show results.
(B) Labor unions have petitioned the President to provide more local jobs.
(C) The trade agreement could bring a *quid pro quo* on pending negotiations.
(D) Economists claimed that the passage of the bill would increase the country's trade deficit.
(E) It was politically desirable for a trade bill at the present time.

12. If we are doomed to have local drug rehabilitation centers—and society has determined that we are—then society ought to pay for them.

Which of the following, if true, would weaken the above argument?

(A) Drug rehabilitation centers are too expensive to be locally funded.
(B) Many neighborhood groups oppose rehabilitation centers.
(C) Drug rehabilitation centers are expensive to maintain.
(D) Drug addicts may be unwilling to receive treatment.
(E) A government committee has convinced many groups that local rehabilitation centers are ineffective.

Questions 13–16 are based on the following passage.

These huge waves wreak terrific damage when they crash on the shores of distant lands or continents. Under a perfectly sunny sky and from an apparently calm sea, a wall of water may break twenty or thirty feet high over beaches and waterfronts, crushing houses and
Line drowning unsuspecting residents and bathers in its path.
(5)   How are these waves formed? When a submarine earthquake occurs, it is likely to set up a tremendous amount of shock, disturbing the quiet waters of the deep ocean. This distur-bance travels to the surface and forms a huge swell in the ocean many miles across. It rolls outward in all directions, and the water lowers in the center as another swell looms up. Thus, a series of concentric swells are formed similar to those made when a coin or small pebble is
(10)   dropped into a basin of water. The big difference is in the size. Each of the concentric rings of basin water traveling out toward the edge is only about an inch across and less than a quarter of an inch high. The swells in the ocean are sometimes nearly a mile wide and rise to several multiples of ten feet in height.
Many of us have heard about these waves, often referred to by their Japanese name of
(15)   "tsunami." For ages they have been dreaded in the Pacific, as no shore has been free from them. An underwater earthquake in the Aleutian Islands could start a swell that would break along the shores and cause severe damage in the southern part of Chile in South America. These waves travel hundreds of miles an hour, and one can understand how they would crash as violent breakers when caused to drag in the shallow waters of a coast.
(20)   Nothing was done about tsunamis until after World War II. In 1947 a particularly bad submarine earthquake took place south of the Aleutian Islands. A few hours later, people bathing in the sun along the quiet shores of Hawaii were dashed to death and shore-line property became a mass of shambles because a series of monstrous, breaking swells crashed along the shore and drove far inland. Hundreds of lives were lost in this catastrophe, and
(25)   millions upon millions of dollars' worth of damage was done.

13.   One surprising aspect of the waves discussed in the passage is the fact that they

(A)   are formed in concentric patterns
(B)   often strike during clear weather
(C)   arise under conditions of cold temperature
(D)   are produced by deep swells
(E)   may be forecast scientifically

14.   The waves discussed in the passage often strike

(A)   along the coasts of the Aleutian Islands
(B)   in regions outside the area monitored by the Coast and Geodetic Survey
(C)   at great distances from their place of origin
(D)   at the same time as the occurrence of earthquakes
(E)   in areas outside the Pacific region

15.   It is believed that the waves are caused by

(A)   seismic changes
(B)   concentric time belts
(C)   atmospheric conditions
(D)   underwater earthquakes
(E)   storms

16. A possible title for the passage could be

    (A) How Submarine Waves Are Formed
    (B) How to Locate Submarine Earthquakes
    (C) Underwater Earthquakes
    (D) "Tsunami" Waves
    (E) How to Prevent Submarine Earthquakes

17. Had I realized how close I was to failing, I would not have gone to the party.

    (A) Had I realized how close
    (B) If I would have realized
    (C) Had I had realized how close
    (D) When I realized how close
    (E) If I realized how close

18. The football team's winning it's first game of the season excited the student body.

    (A) The football team's winning it's first game of the season
    (B) The football team having won it's first game of the season
    (C) The football team's having won it's first game of the season
    (D) The football team's winning its first game of the season
    (E) The football team winning it's first game of the season

19. Anyone interested in the use of computers can learn much if you have access to a state-of-the-art microcomputer.

    (A) if you have access to
    (B) if he has access to
    (C) if access is available to
    (D) by access to
    (E) from access to

20. No student had ought to be put into a situation where he has to choose between his loyalty to his friends and his duty to the class.

    (A) No student had ought to be put into a situation where
    (B) No student had ought to be put into a situation in which
    (C) No student should be put into a situation where
    (D) No student ought to be put into a situation in which
    (E) No student ought to be put into a situation where

21. Being a realist, I could not accept her statement that supernatural beings had caused the disturbance.

    (A) Being a realist,
    (B) Since I am a realist,
    (C) Being that I am a realist,
    (D) Being as I am a realist,
    (E) Realist that I am,

22. Surviving this crisis is going to take everything we've got. In addition to … massive retraining, we may also need subsidies—direct or channeled through the private sector—for a radically expanding service sector. Not merely things like environmental clean-up, but basic human services. (Alvin Toffler, *Previews and Premises* (New York: Bantam Books, 1985), p. 57.)

Which of the following statements is inconsistent with the above?

(A) Subsidies are needed to overcome the crisis.
(B) Environmental controls will be loosened.
(C) The service sector is going to expand to such an extent that many more workers will be needed.
(D) The private sector will play a role in retraining workers.
(E) Before the crisis can end, an environmental clean-up will have to take place.

23. Per-capita income last year was $25,000. Per-capita income is calculated by dividing total aggregate cash income by the total population. Real median income for families headed by a female, with no husband present, was $29,000. Therefore, women wage-earners earned more than the national average.

Which of the following would, if true, weaken the above conclusion?

(A) Per-capita income is calculated in real terms.
(B) In 99 percent of the cases, families headed by a female included no other wage-earner.
(C) Average income is not significantly different from median income.
(D) The overall average and per-capita income were the same.
(E) Only a small proportion of the total wage earners are women family heads.

Questions 24–27 are based on the following passage.

I decided to begin the term's work with the short story since that form would be the easiest for [the police officers], not only because most of their reading up to then had probably been in that genre, but also because a study of the reaction of people to various situations was something they relied on in their daily work.

Line
(5)
The officer must remain neutral and clearly try to present a picture of the facts, while the artist usually begins with a preconceived message or attitude which is then transmitted through the use of carefully selected details of action described in words intended to provoke associations and emotional reactions in the reader. Only at the end of the term did the officer point out to me that he and his men also try to evaluate the events they describe and
(10) that their description of a sequence of events must of necessity be structured and colored by their understanding of what has taken place.

The policemen's reactions to events and characters in the stories were surprisingly unprejudiced . . . . They did not object to writers whose stories had to do with their protagonist's rebellion against society's accepted values. Nor did stories in which the strong father
(15) becomes the villain and in which our usual ideals of manhood are turned around offend them. The many hunters among my students readily granted the message in those hunting tales in which sensitivity triumphs over male aggressiveness, stories that show the boy becoming a man because he fails to shoot the deer, goose, or catbird. The only characters they did object to were those they thought unrealistic. As the previous class had done, this
(20) one also excelled in interpreting the ways in which characters reveal themselves, subtly manipulate and influence each other; they, too, understood how the story usually saves its insight, its revelation, for the end.

This almost instinctive grasp of the writing of fiction was revealed when the policemen volunteered to write their own short stories. . . . They not only took great pains with plot
(25) and character, but with style and language. The stories were surprisingly well written,

revealing an understanding of what a solid short story must contain: the revelation of character, the use of background description and language to create atmosphere and mood, the need to sustain suspense and yet make each event as it occurs seem natural, the insight achieved either by the characters in the story or the reader or both. They tended to favor
(30) surprise endings. Some stories were sheer fantasies, or derived from previous reading, films, or television shows. Most wrote stories, obviously based on their own experiences, that revealed the amazing distance they must put between their personal lives and their work. These stories demonstrated how clearly, almost naively, these policemen wanted to continue to believe in some of the so-called American virtues—that courage is worth the
(35) effort and will be admired; that hard work will be rewarded; that life is somehow good; and that, despite the weariness, boredom, and occasional ugliness and danger, despite all their dislike of most of their routine and despite their own occasional grousing and complaints, they somehow did like being cops; that life, even in a chaotic and violent world, is worth it after all.

24. Compared to the artist, the policeman is

    (A) ruled by action, not words
    (B) factual and not fanciful
    (C) neutral and not prejudiced
    (D) stoic and not emotional
    (E) aggressive and not passive

25. Policemen reacted to story events and characters

    (A) like most other people
    (B) according to a policeman's stereotyped image
    (C) like dilettantes
    (D) unrealistically
    (E) without emotion

26. To which sort of characters did policemen object?

    I. Unrealistic
    II. Emotional
    III. Sordid

    (A) I only
    (B) II only
    (C) I and II only
    (D) II and III only
    (E) I, II, and III

27. The instructor chose the short story because

    I. it was easy for the students
    II. students had experience with it
    III. students would enjoy it

    (A) I only
    (B) II only
    (C) I and II only
    (D) II and III only
    (E) I, II, and III

Sample Test 1

28.   Foreign investment is composed of direct investment transactions (investment in plant, equipment and land) and securities investment transactions. Throughout the post-World War II period, net increases in U.S. direct investment in Europe (funds outflows) exceeded net new European direct investment in the U.S.

Each of the following, if true, could help to account for this trend except:

(A)   Land values in Europe were increasing at a faster rate than in the United States.
(B)   Duties on imported goods in Europe were higher than those imposed by the United States.
(C)   The cost of labor (wages) was consistently lower in Europe than in the United States.
(D)   Labor mobility was much higher in the United States than in Europe.
(E)   Corporate liquidity was lower in Europe than in the United States.

29.   Most large retail stores hold sales in the month of January. The original idea of price reduction campaigns in January became popular when it was realized that sales of products would generally slow down following the Christmas rush, were it not for some incentive. The lack of demand could be solved by the simple solution of reducing prices.

There is now an increasing tendency among major department stores in large urban centers to have their "January sales" begin before Christmas, some time before the end of the calendar year. The idea behind this trend is to endeavor to sell the maximum amount of stock at a profit, even if that may not be at the maximum profit.

Which of the following conclusions cannot be drawn from the above?

(A)   The incidence of "early" January sales results in the lower holdings of stocks with the corollary of lower stock holding costs.
(B)   Demand is a function of price; as you lower price, demand increases.
(C)   Major stores seem to think it makes sense to have the January sales campaigns pre-Christmas.
(D)   It is becoming less popular to start the January sales in the New Year.
(E)   The major department stores do not worry as much about profit maximization as they do about sales maximization.

30.   The reason <u>I came late to class today is because</u> the bus broke down.

(A)   I came late to class today is because
(B)   why I came late to class today is because
(C)   I was late to school today is because
(D)   that I was late to school today is because
(E)   I came late to class today is that

31. The grocer <u>hadn't hardly any of those kind</u> of canned goods.

    (A) hadn't hardly any of those kind
    (B) hadn't hardly any of those kinds
    (C) had hardly any of those kind
    (D) had hardly any of those kinds
    (E) had scarcely any of those kind

32. <u>Having stole the money, the police searched the thief.</u>

    (A) Having stole the money, the police searched the thief.
    (B) Having stolen the money, the thief was searched by the police.
    (C) Having stolen the money, the police searched the thief.
    (D) Having stole the money, the thief was searched by the police.
    (E) Being that he stole the money, the police searched the thief.

33. The child is <u>neither encouraged to be critical or to examine</u> all the evidence for his opinion.

    (A) neither encouraged to be critical or to examine
    (B) neither encouraged to be critical nor to examine
    (C) either encouraged to be critical or to examine
    (D) encouraged either to be critical nor to examine
    (E) not encouraged either to be critical or to examine

34. The process by which the community <u>influence the actions of its members</u> is known as social control.

    (A) influence the actions of its members
    (B) influences the actions of its members
    (C) had influenced the actions of its members
    (D) influences the actions of their members
    (E) will influence the actions of its members

35. Of the world's largest external-debt countries in 1999, three had the same share of world external-debt as they had in 1990. These three countries may serve as examples of countries that succeeded in holding steady their share of world external-debt.

    Which of the following, if true, would most seriously undermine the idea that these countries serve as examples as described above?

    (A) Of the three countries, two had a much larger share of world external-debt in 1995 than in 1999.
    (B) Some countries strive to reduce their share of world external-debt, not keep it steady.
    (C) The three countries have different rates of economic growth.
    (D) The absolute value of debt of the three countries is different.
    (E) Some countries are more concerned with internal budgets than with external debt.

36. The director of the customs service suggested that customs taxes on automobiles not be reduced as planned by the government because of the high incidence of traffic accidents last year.

Which of the above statements weakens the argument above?

I. Although the traffic accident rate last year was high, it was not appreciably higher than previous years and anyway, compulsory insurance covered most physical damage to automobiles and property.

II. A Commerce Department report showed that the demand for automobiles was highly inelastic. That is, as dealers lowered their prices, sales did not increase appreciably.

III. A study by the Economics Department at Classics University found that most traffic accidents had been caused by human error although it also concluded that an inadequate road network contributed to at least 40 percent of passenger injuries.

(A) I, but not II and not III.
(B) II, but not I and not III.
(C) I and III, but not II.
(D) II and III, but not I.
(E) I, II and III.

37. Significant beneficial effects of smoking occur primarily in the area of mental health, and the habit originates in a search for contentment. The life expectancy of our people has increased greatly in recent years; it is possible that the relaxation and contentment and enjoyment produced by smoking has lengthened many lives. Smoking is beneficial.

Which of the following, if true, weaken the above conclusion?

(A) That cigarettes are a major health hazard cannot be traced to the willfull act of any human or organization.
(B) The government earns millions of dollars from the tobacco tax and tens of thousands of civilians are employed in the tobacco industry.
(C) The evidence cited in the statement covers only one example of the effects of cigarette smoking.
(D) No mention is made of possible harmful side-effects of smoking.
(E) No statistical evidence has proven a link between smoking and longevity.

38. An economist was quoted as saying that the Consumer Price Index (CPI) will go up next month because of a recent increase in the price of fruit and vegetables.

Which of the following cannot be inferred from the statement?

(A) The cost of fruits and vegetables has risen sharply.
(B) Consumers have decreased their consumption of fruits and vegetables.
(C) The cost of fruit and vegetables is a major item in the CPI.
(D) Food cost changes are reflected quickly in the CPI.
(E) Other items that make up the CPI have not significantly decreased in price.

39. At a political rally at Jefferson Stadium, candidate Smith exclaimed: "Nearly everyone at the rally is behind me. It looks like I am going to be elected."

   Which of the following statements, if true, best supports the above conclusion?

   (A)   Smith's opponent also appeared at the rally.
   (B)   The rally was attended by almost all the residents of Smith's constituency.
   (C)   Smith was never defeated in an election.
   (D)   Smith was supported by the local mayor.
   (E)   People always vote their emotions.

40. <u>Depending on skillful suggestion, argument is seldom used in advertising</u>.

   (A)   Depending on skillful suggestion, argument is seldom used in advertising.
   (B)   Argument is seldom used by advertisers, who depend instead on skillful suggestion.
   (C)   Skillfull suggestion is depended on by advertisers instead of argument.
   (D)   Suggestion, which is more skillful, is used in place of argument by advertisers.
   (E)   Instead of suggestion, depending on argument is used by skillful advertisers.

41. In a famous experiment by Pavlov, when a dog smelled food, it salivated. Subsequently, a bell was rung whenever food was placed near the dog. After a number of trials, only the bell was rung, whereupon the dog would salivate even though no food was present.

   Which of the following conclusions may be drawn from the above experiment?

   (A)   Dogs are easily fooled.
   (B)   Dogs are motivated only by the sound of a bell.
   (C)   The ringing of a bell was associated with food.
   (D)   A conclusion cannot be reached on the basis of one experiment.
   (E)   Two stimuli are stronger than one.

STOP

IF THERE IS STILL TIME REMAINING, YOU MAY REVIEW YOUR ANSWERS. AFTER YOU HAVE CONFIRMED YOUR ANSWERS, YOU CANNOT RETURN TO THESE QUESTIONS.

Answer Key

SAMPLE TEST 1

Quantitative Section

1. D	11. C	21. D	31. C
2. C	12. D	22. B	32. A
3. E	13. D	23. E	33. B
4. B	14. B	24. D	34. C
5. D	15. E	25. E	35. B
6. B	16. B	26. A	36. A
7. D	17. A	27. E	37. C
8. A	18. B	28. E	
9. A	19. C	29. E	
10. D	20. D	30. B	

Verbal Section

1. B	12. E	23. E	34. B
2. B	13. B	24. C	35. A
3. B	14. C	25. A	36. B
4. D	15. D	26. A	37. E
5. D	16. A	27. C	38. B
6. E	17. A	28. D	39. B
7. C	18. D	29. A	40. B
8. B	19. B	30. E	41. C
9. C	20. D	31. D	
10. E	21. A	32. B	
11. D	22. B	33. E	

Analysis

Self-Scoring Guide—Analytical Writing

Evaluate your writing tests (or have a friend or teacher evaluate them for you) on the following basis. Read each essay completely, paying special attention to its logical organization and use of examples and facts to buttress its claims or position. Assign a holistic score between 0 and 6, using the scale below. Your writing score will be the average of the scores of the two essays.

6 Outstanding   Cogent, well-articulated analysis of the issue or critique of the argument. Develops a position with insightful reasons and persuasive examples. Well organized. Superior command of language and variety of syntax. Only minor flaws in grammar, usage, and mechanics.

5 Strong   Well-developed analysis or critique. Develops a position with well-chosen examples or reasons. Generally well organized. Clear control of language and variety of syntax. Minor flaws in grammar, usage, and mechanics.

4 Adequate   Competent analysis or critique. Develops a position with relevant reasons or examples. Adequately organized. Adequate control of language, but may lack syntactic variety. May have some flaws in grammar, usage, and mechanics.

3 Limited   Competent but clearly flawed analysis or critique. Vague or limited in developing a position. Poorly organized. Weak in using relevant examples or reasons. Language used imprecisely or lacking in sentence variety. Contains major errors or frequent minor errors in grammar, usage, and mechanics.

2 Seriously Flawed   Serious weaknesses in analysis and organization. Unclear or seriously limited in presenting or developing a position. Disorganized. Few relevant examples or reasons. Frequent serious problems in language and sentence structure. Numerous errors in grammar, usage, or mechanics that interfere with meaning.

1 Fundamentally Deficient   Little evidence of ability to organize and develop a coherent response to issue or argument. Severe and persistent errors in language and sentence structure. Pervasive pattern of errors in grammar, usage, and mechanics that severely interfere with meaning.

0 Unscorable   Illegible or not written in the assigned topic.

ANSWERS EXPLAINED

Quantitative Section

1. **(D)** Since the size of the bacteria colony doubles each day, the dish must be half full 1 day before it is full. So the correct answer is 29 days, or choice (D). A common mistake is to choose (B), but that gives half the time it takes to fill the dish, not the time when the dish is half full. If the question had asked when the dish was one-quarter full, the correct answer would be 28 days. (II–6)

2. **(C)** If s and t denote the sides of the two squares, then $s^2 : t^2 = 2 : 1$. or Thus, $\left(\dfrac{s}{t}\right)^2 = \dfrac{2}{1}$ and

$\dfrac{s}{t} = \dfrac{\sqrt{2}}{1}$. Since the ratio of the perimeters is $4s : 4t = s : t$, (C) is the correct answer. (II-5, III-7)

3. **(E)** A triangle with sides of lengths 3, 4, and 5 is a right triangle since $3^2 + 4^2 = 5^2$, and its perimeter is 12. A triangle with sides of lengths 2, 4.8, and 5.2 also has a perimeter of 12. And since $2^2 + (4.8)^2 = (5.2)^2$, it too is a right triangle. Therefore, two triangles can satisfy STATEMENTS (1) and (2) yet not be congruent. On the other hand, any pair of congruent right triangles satisfy STATEMENTS (1) and (2). Thus, STATEMENTS (1) and (2) together are not sufficient to answer the question. (III-4)

4. **(B)** $x^3 - 8 = 0$ has only $x = 2$ as a real solution. And 2 is greater than 0, so STATEMENT (2) alone is sufficient.
Since $x = 2$ and $x = -2$ are both solutions of $x^4 - 16 = 0$, STATEMENT (1) alone is not sufficient. (II-2)

5. **(D)** STATEMENT (1) is sufficient since it implies that conveyer belt A loads $\dfrac{2}{3}$ of the hopper while conveyer belt B loads only $\dfrac{1}{3}$ with both working. Since conveyer belt A loads $\dfrac{2}{3}$ of the hopper in a hour, it will take $1 \div \left(\dfrac{2}{3}\right)$ or 1.5 hours to fill the hopper by itself.

STATEMENT (2) is also sufficient since it implies that conveyer belt B fills $\dfrac{1}{3}$ of the hopper in 1 hour. Thus, conveyer belt A loads $\dfrac{2}{3}$ in 1 hour, and that means conveyer belt A would take 1.5 hours by itself. (II-3)

6. **(B)** First find an expression for the proceeds from orchestra tickets, which is $12P$. Next, find an expression for the total proceeds, which is $12P + 9B + 25R$. So $\dfrac{12P}{(12P + 9B + 25R)}$ gives the part of the total proceeds due to the sale of orchestra tickets. However, this is not a percentage. You need to multiply this expression by 100 to get a percentage. So the correct choice is (B). (II-3, I-4)

7. **(D)** Set up a coordinate system with A at $(0, 0)$. Then B is at $(5, 0)$. Since C is southeast of B, then BCD is an isosceles right triangle whose hypotenuse is 10 miles. So $BD^2 + CD^2 = 10^2 = 100$ and $BD = CD$, so $BD^2 = 50$. Therefore, $BD = \sqrt{50} = \sqrt{25}\sqrt{2} = 5\sqrt{2}$. So the coordinates of C are $(5 + 5\sqrt{2}, -5\sqrt{2})$. Remember, the distance between two points whose coordinates are (x, y) and (a, b) is $\sqrt{(x-a)^2 + (y-b)^2}$. So the distance from A to C is the square root of

$(5 + 5\sqrt{2})^2 + (-5\sqrt{2})^2$. You can work with these numbers, but it will be messy. It is much faster to use the fact that $\sqrt{2}$ is about 1.4. Remember, the question asks for only an approximate answer. So $5\sqrt{2}$ is about 7; thus, the distance is the square root of $(5 + 7)^2 + (-7)^2$. This is equal to the square root of $144 + 49$ or 193. *Do not try to find the square root of this number if you don't know it.* Simply square each answer and see which is closest to 193. Since $14^2 = 196$, the correct choice is 14 miles or (D). (III-9)

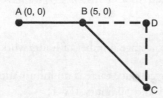

8. **(A)** If 40 percent of the socks are blue, then we can see that there are $12(.4 \times 30)$ blue socks in the drawer. So the probability that both socks are blue is $\left(\dfrac{12}{30}\right)\left(\dfrac{11}{29}\right)$ and STATEMENT 1 is sufficient. STATEMENT 2 is not sufficient since it does not tell us how many blue socks are in the drawer. You don't know that all the socks are either red or blue because there could be socks of other colors in the drawer. (I-7)

9. **(A)** $4y - 6x = -2(3x - 2y) = -2(8) = -16$. (II-2)

10. **(D)** Since the total distance is 200 kilometers, of which you fly x kilometers, you drive $(200 - x)$ kilometers. Therefore, the cost is $10x + (200 - x)12$, which is $10x - 12x + 2,400$ or $2,400 - 2x$ cents. The answer in dollars is obtained by dividing by 100, which is $(24 - .02x)$ dollars. (II-1)

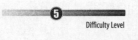

11. **(C)** (2) alone is not sufficient since both $y = 3$ and $y = -3$ satisfy $y^2 - 4 > 0$. (1) alone is not sufficient, since $\dfrac{1}{2}$ is larger than 0 but less than 1, while 3 is larger than 0 and larger than 1. If $y^2 - 4 > 0$, then either y is > 2 or $y < -2$. If (1) and (2) both hold, then y must be >2, which is >1. (II-7)

12. **(D)** Let \$$x$ be the amount he was paid the first day. Then he was paid $x + 2$, $x + 4$, $x + 6$, $x + 8$, and $(x + 10)$ dollars for the succeeding days. (1) alone is sufficient since the total he was paid is $(6x + 30)$ dollars, and we can solve $6x + 30 = 150$ (to find that he was paid \$20 for the first day). (2) alone is also sufficient. He was paid $(x + 10)$ dollars on the sixth day, so (2) means that $(1.5)x = x + 10$ (which is the same as $x = 20$). (II-6)

13. **(D)** I is not true for all positive y since *1 = 4 − 1 = 3, which is not negative. The question asks which statements are true for *all positive y*, not just some positive y. II is true since if $0 < y < z$, then $\dfrac{4}{y} > \dfrac{4}{z}$ and $-y > -z$, so $\left(\dfrac{4}{y}\right) - y$ is $> \left(\dfrac{4}{z}\right) - z$. So *y > *z. Since $y(*y) = y\left[\left(\dfrac{4}{y}\right) - y\right] = 4 - y^2$, which is less than 5 for any positive y, III is always true. So the correct answer is (D). (II-7)

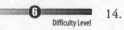

14. **(B)** Since 85 percent of \$3,000 is \$2,550, (2) alone is sufficient. (1) alone is not sufficient since if x were 5 percent, (1) would tell us that the price of the car is less than \$2,600. But if x were 1 percent, (1) would imply that the price of the car is greater than \$2,600. (I-4)

5 Difficulty Level

15. **(E)** Even assuming (1) and (2), you would still need to know what percentage of birds have avian flu in order to answer the question. Since that information is not available, both statements together are not sufficient. (I-7)

6 Difficulty Level

16. **(B)** If A_1 denotes the increased area and A the original area, then $A_1 = 1.69A$ since A_1 is A increased by 69 percent. Thus, $s_1{}^2 = A_1 = 1.69A = 1.69s^2$, where s_1 is the increased side and s the original side. Since the square root of 1.69 is 1.3, we have $s_1 = 1.3s$ so s is increased by .3 or 30 percent. (I-4)

5 Difficulty Level

17. **(A)** I can be inferred since the average number of hours worked is $\dfrac{3,100}{80} = 38.75$, which is less than 40. II cannot be inferred since there is no information given beyond the fact that 20 workers worked between 45 and 50 hours. (IV-1)

7 Difficulty Level

18. **(B)** To calculate the driving time, simply divide 160 miles by 60 miles per hour to obtain $2\dfrac{2}{3}$ hours, or 160 minutes. However, you need to decide whether or not the truck must stop for gasoline. At a speed of 60 miles per hour, the truck will use 30 percent more fuel, so it will need 1.3 gallons to travel 20 miles. Thus x (the amount of fuel needed to travel 160 miles) must satisfy the proportion $\dfrac{160}{20} = \dfrac{x}{1.3}$ or $x = 8(1.3) = 10.4$ gallons. So, if the truck is driven at 60 miles per hour, it will have to stop for gas since it has only 10 gallons. Therefore, the total time needed is $160 + 20 = 180$ minutes. (II-3)

8 Difficulty Level

19. **(C)** If company C owns 25 percent more than company A and A owns 40 percent of XYZ Corporation, then company C must own $1.25 \times .4 = .5$, or 50 percent of XYZ Corporation. Since B owns all that A and C do not own, then B must own $100\% - 40\% - 50\% = 10\%$.

If 10 percent of the shares is 15,000 shares, then there must be 150,000 shares in XYZ Corporation. Since company A owns 40 percent, it owns $150,000 \times 0.40 = 60,000$ shares. So (C) is the correct answer. Remember: Always answer the question asked. If you picked (D), you found only how many shares company C owns. (I-4, II-2)

7 Difficulty Level

20. **(D)** The area of the rectangle is $4 \times 6 = 24$ square feet. Since 1 square foot is 144 square inches, the area of the rectangle is 3,456 square inches. Each square has an area of $\left(\dfrac{1}{2}\right)^2$ or $\dfrac{1}{4}$ square inches. Therefore, the number of squares needed $= 3,456 \div \dfrac{1}{4} = 3,456 \times 4 = 13,824$. (III-7)

6 Difficulty Level

21. **(D)** Since there are a bottom and 4 sides, each a congruent square, the amount of cardboard needed will be $5e^2$, where e is the length of an edge of the box. So we need to find e.

(1) alone is sufficient. Since the area of the bottom is e^2, (1) means $e^2 = 4$ with $e = 2$ feet.
(2) alone is also sufficient. Since the volume of the box is e^3, (2) means $e^3 = 8$ and $e = 2$ feet. (III-8)

8 Difficulty Level

22. **(B)** STATEMENT (1) is not sufficient. If x is 33, then (1) is true and x is divisible by 3, but if x is 23, then (1) is true but x is not divisible by 3.

STATEMENT (2) is sufficient. According to (2) there must be an integer k such that $x + 5 = 6k$, so x is $6k - 5$. But this means that x divided by 3 will be $2k - \left(\dfrac{5}{3}\right)$, so x is not divisible by 3.

So (B) is the correct choice. (I-1)

Answers Explained

23. **(E)** If *ABCD* has the pairs of opposite sides equal and each angle is 90°, then it is a rectangle. But there are many quadrilaterals that have two opposite sides equal with one angle a right angle. For example, the figure below has $AB = DC$ and $x = 90$, but it is not a rectangle. Therefore, (1) and (2) together are insufficient. (III-5)

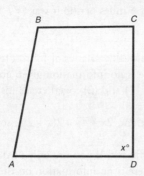

24. **(D)** (2) alone is sufficient since if $a_3 = 1$, then $a_4 = (a_3)^2 = 1^2 = 1$; then $a_5 = (a_4)^2 = 1^2 = 1$. (1) alone is also sufficient. If $a_1 = -1$, then $a_2 = (a_1)^2 = 1$ and $a_3 = (a_2)^2 = 1$, but $a_3 = 1$ is given by (2), which we know is sufficient. (II-6)

25. **(E)** Those who gave $12 were 25 percent (100% − 30% − 45% = 25%) of the group. Let x, y, and z stand for the number of people who contributed $40, $20, and $12, respectively. Then, the total number of people (n) who contributed is $x + y + z = n$. The total amount (T) contributed is

$$\$40x + \$20y + \$12z = T$$

Since 30 percent contributed $40, we know that $x = .3n$; in the same way, we know that $y = .45n$ and $z = .25n$. Therefore, the total contributed was

$$
\begin{aligned}
T &= \$40(.3n) &+& \$20(.45n) &+& \$12(.25n) \\
&= 12n &+& 9n &+& 3n \\
&= 24n
\end{aligned}
$$

The amount contributed by those who gave $40 was, therefore,

$$\$40\,(.3n) = 12n$$

So the percentage contributed by the $40 donors is $100(12n/24n)$ or 50 percent. (II-2)

26. **(A)** The area of trapezoid *ABCD* equals the area of rectangle *ABED*, which is $t \times 5$ (since $BE = BC = 5$), plus the area of triangle *BEC*, which is $\frac{(5 \times 5)}{2}$. The answer is thus $5t + 12.5$. (III-7)

27. **(E)** The selling price of the jars should equal cost plus $75. The cost of making 300 jars = $(100)65¢ + (200)55¢ = \$65 + \$110 = \$175$. So the selling price should be $175 + $75 or $250. (II-3)

28. **(E)** You need to find the total distance traveled in order to find the total time. Since the car traveled $V \times T$ miles when it averaged V miles per hour, then VT is 75 percent of the total distance. Therefore, the total distance traveled is $\frac{VT}{.75} = \frac{4VT}{3}$.

The distance that was traveled at S miles per hour is the total distance minus the distance at V miles per hour, which is

$$\left(\frac{4}{3}\right)VT - VT = \frac{VT}{3}$$

So the time spent traveling at S miles per hour was $(VT)/3 \div S = \dfrac{VT}{3S}$. (II-3)

29. **(E)** Let J, F, and C stand for the weekly salaries of John, Fred, and Chuck. (1) says $J = 2F$, and (2) says $F = .4(C + J)$. Since there is no information given about the value of C or F, we cannot deduce the value of J. Therefore, (1) and (2) together are insufficient. (II-3)

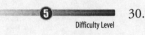

30. **(B)** STATEMENT (2) alone is sufficient. $2x + 4y = 2(x + 2y)$, so if $2x + 4y = 12$, then $2(x + 2y) = 12$ and $x + 2y = 6$.

    STATEMENT (1) alone is insufficient. If you use only STATEMENT (1), then you can get $x + 2y = x + y + y = 4 + y$, but there is no information on the value of y. (II-2)

31. **(C)** Since the sum of the angles in a triangle is 180°, $x + y + z = 180$. Using STATEMENT (1) alone, we have $2y + y + z = 3y + z = 180$, which is insufficient to determine y or z.

    Using STATEMENT (2) alone, we have $x + 1.5z + z = x + 2.5z = 180$, which is not sufficient to determine x or z.

    However, if we use both STATEMENTS (1) and (2) we obtain $3y + z = 4.5z + z = 5.5z = 180$, so $z = \dfrac{2}{11}$ of 180. Now $y = \dfrac{3}{2}$ of z, so $y = \dfrac{3}{11}$ of 180, and $x = \dfrac{6}{11}$ of 180. Therefore, angle BAC is not a right angle and STATEMENTS (1) and (2) are sufficient. (II-2, III-4)

32. **(A)** The three-digit number abc is $(100 \times a) + (10 \times b) + c$. If abc is a multiple of 9, then there is an integer k such that $k9 = (100 \times a) + (10 \times b) + c$. Divide this equation by 9 and you have

$$k = \left[\left(\frac{100}{9}\right) \times a\right] + \left[\left(\frac{10}{9}\right) \times b\right] + \frac{c}{9}$$

$$= \left[11a + \left(\frac{a}{9}\right)\right] + \left[b + \left(\frac{b}{9}\right)\right] + \frac{c}{9}$$

$$= 11a + b + \left(\frac{a}{9}\right) + \left(\frac{b}{9}\right) + \left(\frac{c}{9}\right)$$

$$= 11a + b + \left[\left(\frac{a+b+c}{9}\right)\right]$$

So (1) alone is sufficient. (2) is not sufficient since choosing $a = 0 = b$ and $c = 9$ makes (2) valid and $a + b + c$ is 9, but choosing $a = 4 = b$ and $c = 2$ also makes (2) valid with $a + b + c$ equal to 10. (I-1)

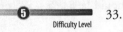

33. **(B)** STATEMENT (2) alone is sufficient. 60 percent of the people have blue eyes and 50 percent of the people have blue eyes and blond hair, so $60\% - 50\% = 10\%$ of the people have blue eyes but do not have blond hair.

    STATEMENT (1) alone is not sufficient. Using STATEMENT (1) alone we can only find out how many people have blond hair and do not have blue eyes, in addition to what is given. (II-4)

34. **(C)** Let c be the number of chairs in a row and r be the number of rows. Since each row must have the same number of chairs, c times r must equal 36. We need to know how many ways we can write 36 as a product of two integers each greater than or equal to 3, since each way to write 36 corresponds to an acceptable arrangement of the room. (c must be greater than or equal to 3 since each row must contain at least 3 chairs. In the same way, r must be greater than or equal to 3 because there must be at least 3 rows.) Writing 36 as a product of primes, we obtain $36 = 2 \times 18 = 2 \times 2 \times 9 = 2 \times 2 \times 3 \times 3$. So 36 can be written as 1×36, 2×18, 3×12, 4×9, 6×6, 9×4, 12×3, 18×2, and 36×1. Of these possibilities, five (3×12, 4×9, 6×6, 9×4, and 12×3) satisfy the requirements. Therefore, there are five arrangements. (I-1)

35. **(B)** The volume of the cube is $9 \times 9 \times 9 = 729$ cubic millimeters. The sphere has volume $\frac{4}{3}\pi 6 \times 6 \times 6 = 288\pi$. Since π is greater than 3, 288π is greater than 729. The volume of the cylinder is $5 \times 5 \times 11\pi = 275\pi$. So the sphere has the largest volume.

    You can save a lot of time in doing this problem if you do not change π to a decimal and then multiply the answers out. (III-8)

36. **(A)** The sum of the angles of the pentagon is 540°. [The sum of the angles of a polygon with n sides that is inscribed in a circle is $(n-2)180°$.]

    STATEMENT (1) alone is sufficient. If the polygon is regular, all angles are equal, and so angle ABC is $\frac{1}{5}$ of 540° or 108°.

    STATEMENT (2) alone is insufficient because the radius of the circle does not give any information about the angles of the pentagon. (III-3)

37. **(C)** The key to this problem is to factor $k^2 + k - 2$ into $(k + 2)(k - 1)$. The product of the two expressions is positive if and only if both expressions have the same sign. When (1) holds, then $k - 1$ is negative, but $k + 2$ can be positive or negative, so (1) alone is not sufficient. When (2) holds, then $k + 2$ is positive, but $k - 1$ can be positive or negative, so (2) alone is not sufficient. However, if both (1) and (2) are true, then k is between –1 and 1 and, so $k + 2$ is positive and $k - 1$ is negative, which means $(k + 2)(k - 1)$ is negative. This is sufficient to answer the question. (II-1)

Verbal Section

1. **(B)** The argument represents a fallacy in causality. Absence of cloud cover enables the moon to be seen. And, it is the absence of cloud cover—not a full moon—that causes the ground to cool and produce frost. Answer choice (A) may be a necessary but insufficient condition for frost to occur; that is, there may be an absence of frost even below 10 degrees Celsius. Farmers may be superstitious, but there is nothing in the statement that links superstition with the farmers' conviction (alternative C). Alternative (D) is inappropriate because, even if true, it could not change the farmers' convictions. Farmers do not have to be experts in meteorology (E) to hold a conviction.

2. **(B)** The question concerns Professor Tembel's proposal to improve the validity of the method used to measure teacher quality. Alternative (B) supports the proposal. Students relate only partial experience with a teacher if the questionnaires are completed at midterm. Alternative (A) suggests that Professor Tembel's motive for questioning the present evaluation method stems from his low ratings. It is questionable whether handing out questionnaires at the end of the semester would improve his ratings. Alternatives (C), (D), and (E) are not related to the validity of the evaluation method.

3. **(B)** This corrects the misuse of the subjunctive.

4. **(D)** This corrects the error in the case of the pronoun. Choice E corrects the error in case but introduces an error in tense.

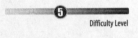

5. **(D)** This is clearly a passage dealing with the economy and economic policy. Note that (E) is too vague; an *economic policy* textbook might have been a correct answer.

6. **(E)** All of the others are given in paragraph 1.

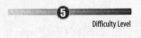

7. **(C)** See paragraph 3. The task is to obtain high economic growth without stimulating high inflation.

8. **(B)** See paragraph 2: ". . . there was actually a substantial deterioration in our trade account to a sizable deficit, almost two thirds of which was with Japan."

9. **(C)** The improper use of the pronouns one and you is corrected in Choice C.

10. **(E)** The omission of the past participle been is corrected in Choice E.

11. **(D)** All of the facts except (D) would be consonant with the President's actions. Fact (D) would be against passage of such a bill.

12. **(E)** The argument is in the form of a conditional syllogism: (1) *If* we must have drug rehabilitation centers, *then* society ought to pay for them. (2) We must have drug rehabilitation centers. (3) Society ought to pay for them. Alternative (E) falsifies the minor premise 2. Whether or not neighborhood groups oppose the centers (B) or drug addicts will go to them to receive treatment (D) is not relevant to the argument concerning who will pay for them. The level of government funding (A) or the amount of expense (C) are not mentioned in the passage and are not relevant to the argument. However, a government statement that local rehabilitation centers are ineffective would seriously weaken the premise upon which the argument rests.

5 Difficulty Level

13. **(B)** See paragraph 1: "Under a perfectly sunny sky and from an apparently calm sea . . ." None of the other answer choices is particularly surprising.

4 Difficulty Level

14. **(C)** See the first sentence of the passage: ". . . distant lands or continents."

3 Difficulty Level

15. **(D)** See paragraph 2: "How are these waves formed? When a submarine earthquake occurs . . ."

6 Difficulty Level

16. **(A)** While (B) and (E) suggest desirable actions, they are not mentioned in the passage. (C) and (D) provide far less information than alternative (A).

6 Difficulty Level

17. **(A)** No error.

7 Difficulty Level

18. **(D)** Misuse of word. The pronoun is *its*.

5 Difficulty Level

19. **(B)** This corrects the unnecessary switch in the pronouns, *anyone—you*.

4 Difficulty Level

20. **(D)** This corrects the error in tense and in the use of adjective or adverbial clauses.

5 Difficulty Level

21. **(A)** No error.

8 Difficulty Level

22. **(B)** The "crisis" which is alluded to in the statement refers to a need for environmental clean-up and basic human services (the latter mentioned in alternative (E)). In order to provide these services more workers will be needed (C), many of whom will have to be retrained. This retraining will have to be financed by subsidies (A), which may be provided by the private sector (D). Alternative (B) is inconsistent with the statement which calls for more environmental controls (clean-up), not less.

9 Difficulty Level

23. **(E)** Total per-capita income includes salaries and wages earned by women. In order to determine if women wage-earners earned more than the overall average, the salaries of all women—not just women heading families with no husband present—would have to be calculated separately. Alternative (E) states that women family heads are not representative of all women wage earners. Thus, the conclusion in the statement is a fallacy of relevance or representativeness. All other alternatives would buttress the conclusion.

6 Difficulty Level

24. **(C)** The correct answer is given in paragraph 2. The policeman must be neutral and present the facts, while the "artist usually begins with a preconceived message or attitude . . . ," i.e., prejudiced. While artists are "emotional," no mention is made that policemen are stoic (D).

7 Difficulty Level

25. **(A)** The writer explains that the policemen's reactions were "surprisingly unprejudiced." The rest of paragraph 3 explains that policemen reacted to story events and characters according to alternative (A).

6 Difficulty Level

26. **(A)** The only characters that policemen objected to were unrealistic. See paragraph 3.

6 Difficulty Level

27. **(C)** Alternatives I and II may be found in the first paragraph.

5 Difficulty Level

28. **(D)** Land values were higher in Europe, attracting U.S. capital (A); higher duties on U.S. exports to Europe (B) brought a substitution of foreign production for U.S. exports; lower labor costs in Europe (C) meant it was cheaper to produce there. Higher liquidity (E) in the U.S. provided the capital for foreign investment. Only (D) is irrelevant as an explanation of direct investment.

9 Difficulty Level

29. **(A)** A number of points are made in the paragraph, and a number of conclusions can be drawn. One is (B), the simple law of economics—that demand varies with price. Also, since it is stated that there is now an increasing tendency to have the January sales in December, it must be becoming less popular to start the sales in January itself. Therefore, the conclusions in (C) and (D) can be drawn, and so choices (C) and (D) are not appropriate. Further, the hypothesis in (C) and also in (E) can be inferred from what is stated in the paragraph about the stores' policies on end-of-year sales. Answer choice (A) introduces a new idea that may be correct and valid, but which cannot be inferred or concluded from what is stated in the paragraph; (A), therefore is the correct answer.

8 Difficulty Level

30. **(E)** *The reason is that* is preferable to *The reason is because.*

5 Difficulty Level

31. **(D)** This corrects the double negative (*hadn't hardly*) and the misuse of *those* with *kind.*

7 Difficulty Level

32. **(B)** This corrects the dangling participle and the misuse of *stole* for *stolen.*

7 Difficulty Level

33. **(E)** This question involves two aspects of correct English. *Neither* should be followed by *nor*; *either* by *or*. Choices A and D are, therefore, incorrect. The words *neither . . . nor* and *either . . . or* should be placed before the two items being discussed—*to be critical* and *to criticize.* Choice E meets both requirements.

3 Difficulty Level

34. **(B)** This question tests agreement. Agreement between subject and verb and pronoun and antecedent are both involved. *Community* (singular) needs a singular verb, *influences.* Also, the pronoun which refers to *community* should be singular (*its*). Choice B is best.

7 Difficulty Level

35. **(A)** Two of the three countries actually experienced shifts in their share of world external-debt from 1990 to 1999, hardly an example of stability. Answer choice (B) may be true for some countries, but it does not weaken the statement. Answer choices (C) and (D) skirt the issues: rates of economic growth and absolute debt are not related to external debt in the statement. Answer choice (E) may be so, but the example in the statement deals with external, not internal, debt.

9 Difficulty Level

36. **(B)** The argument claims that fewer cars on the road will lead to fewer accidents. In order to hold down the existing number of cars, it is suggested that custom taxes not be reduced so as not to lower the price to the consumer. Statement I does not weaken the claim because it does not refute the fact of a high incidence of traffic accidents. Statement III strengthens the claim. A higher volume of cars on an inadequate road network should lead to more accidents. Statement II weakens the argument because it provides evidence that even if car prices were reduced it would not lead to increased purchases, which, of course, is the argument in the passage.

7 Difficulty Level

37. **(E)** Statements (A) and (B) do not address themselves to the premise or conclusion. The conclusion in the statement is that smoking is beneficial. Why? Because it leads to longevity through greater relaxation as a result of smoking. Statement (C) is true, but it does not attack the premise. Statement (D) does attack the premise of the beneficiality of smoking, but it does not give evidence of harm. Statement (E) throws doubt on the major premise, and thus on the conclusion.

38. **(B)** The claim in the statement is that the CPI will go up. The reasoning behind the claim is based on the premise that the cost of fruit and vegetables has risen sharply (A). Since these commodities are major items in the CPI (C) and because food cost changes are reflected quickly in the index (D), the index will go up. A premise that could weaken the claim might be (E) if other items included in the index and weighted at least as much decreased in price, thus offsetting the cost increases for fruits and vegetables. However, alternative (E) gives evidence to the contrary. Alternative (B) may not be inferred. If consumers reduced consumption of fruits and vegetables, the prices of these items would be expected to drop. In any case, the rate of consumption cannot be inferred.

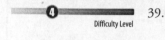

39. **(B)** If the behavior at the rally is indicative of how people will vote *and* the rally attendance was representative of the voters, then the conclusion is valid. The argument is thus: (1) The rally is representative of all voters. (2) Most at the rally are for me. (3) Most rally attendees will vote for me. Alternative (A) might also support the conclusion since even with the appearance of the opponent, Smith says "Nearly everyone at the rally is behind me," but this support depends on whether or not the people at the rally are voters in the election, so this is not the best answer. Smith's previous election results (C) or support from the mayor (D) are not relevant to the conclusion. Alternative (E) is also irrelevant; support at a rally does not imply only emotional support.

40. **(B)** As presented, the sentence contains a dangling participle, *depending*. Choice B corrects this error. The other choices change the emphasis presented by the author.

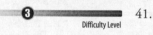

41. **(C)** In this experiment, the dog was conditioned to associate the ringing of a bell with food. Therefore, when the dog heard the bell, it expected to be fed, even though it could not smell food. Alternative (A) cannot be inferred. Alternative (B) and (D) are incorrect, and there is no proof for (E).

EVALUATING YOUR SCORE

Tabulate your score for each section of the Diagnostic Test according to the directions on page 12 and record the results in the Self-Scoring Table below. Then find your rating for each score on the Self-Scoring Scale and record it in the appropriate blank.

Self-Scoring Table

Section	Score	Rating
Quantitative		
Verbal		

Self-Scoring Scale—RATING

Section	Poor	Fair	Good	Excellent
Quantitative	0–15	15–25	26–30	31–37
Verbal	0–15	15–25	26–30	31–41

Study again the Review sections covering material in Sample Test 1 for which you had a rating of FAIR or POOR. Then go on to Sample Test 2.

Answer Sheet

SAMPLE TEST 2

Quantitative Section

1 Ⓐ Ⓑ Ⓒ Ⓓ Ⓔ	11 Ⓐ Ⓑ Ⓒ Ⓓ Ⓔ	21 Ⓐ Ⓑ Ⓒ Ⓓ Ⓔ	31 Ⓐ Ⓑ Ⓒ Ⓓ Ⓔ
2 Ⓐ Ⓑ Ⓒ Ⓓ Ⓔ	12 Ⓐ Ⓑ Ⓒ Ⓓ Ⓔ	22 Ⓐ Ⓑ Ⓒ Ⓓ Ⓔ	32 Ⓐ Ⓑ Ⓒ Ⓓ Ⓔ
3 Ⓐ Ⓑ Ⓒ Ⓓ Ⓔ	13 Ⓐ Ⓑ Ⓒ Ⓓ Ⓔ	23 Ⓐ Ⓑ Ⓒ Ⓓ Ⓔ	33 Ⓐ Ⓑ Ⓒ Ⓓ Ⓔ
4 Ⓐ Ⓑ Ⓒ Ⓓ Ⓔ	14 Ⓐ Ⓑ Ⓒ Ⓓ Ⓔ	24 Ⓐ Ⓑ Ⓒ Ⓓ Ⓔ	34 Ⓐ Ⓑ Ⓒ Ⓓ Ⓔ
5 Ⓐ Ⓑ Ⓒ Ⓓ Ⓔ	15 Ⓐ Ⓑ Ⓒ Ⓓ Ⓔ	25 Ⓐ Ⓑ Ⓒ Ⓓ Ⓔ	35 Ⓐ Ⓑ Ⓒ Ⓓ Ⓔ
6 Ⓐ Ⓑ Ⓒ Ⓓ Ⓔ	16 Ⓐ Ⓑ Ⓒ Ⓓ Ⓔ	26 Ⓐ Ⓑ Ⓒ Ⓓ Ⓔ	36 Ⓐ Ⓑ Ⓒ Ⓓ Ⓔ
7 Ⓐ Ⓑ Ⓒ Ⓓ Ⓔ	17 Ⓐ Ⓑ Ⓒ Ⓓ Ⓔ	27 Ⓐ Ⓑ Ⓒ Ⓓ Ⓔ	37 Ⓐ Ⓑ Ⓒ Ⓓ Ⓔ
8 Ⓐ Ⓑ Ⓒ Ⓓ Ⓔ	18 Ⓐ Ⓑ Ⓒ Ⓓ Ⓔ	28 Ⓐ Ⓑ Ⓒ Ⓓ Ⓔ	
9 Ⓐ Ⓑ Ⓒ Ⓓ Ⓔ	19 Ⓐ Ⓑ Ⓒ Ⓓ Ⓔ	29 Ⓐ Ⓑ Ⓒ Ⓓ Ⓔ	
10 Ⓐ Ⓑ Ⓒ Ⓓ Ⓔ	20 Ⓐ Ⓑ Ⓒ Ⓓ Ⓔ	30 Ⓐ Ⓑ Ⓒ Ⓓ Ⓔ	

Verbal Section

1 Ⓐ Ⓑ Ⓒ Ⓓ Ⓔ	12 Ⓐ Ⓑ Ⓒ Ⓓ Ⓔ	23 Ⓐ Ⓑ Ⓒ Ⓓ Ⓔ	35 Ⓐ Ⓑ Ⓒ Ⓓ Ⓔ
2 Ⓐ Ⓑ Ⓒ Ⓓ Ⓔ	13 Ⓐ Ⓑ Ⓒ Ⓓ Ⓔ	24 Ⓐ Ⓑ Ⓒ Ⓓ Ⓔ	36 Ⓐ Ⓑ Ⓒ Ⓓ Ⓔ
3 Ⓐ Ⓑ Ⓒ Ⓓ Ⓔ	14 Ⓐ Ⓑ Ⓒ Ⓓ Ⓔ	25 Ⓐ Ⓑ Ⓒ Ⓓ Ⓔ	37 Ⓐ Ⓑ Ⓒ Ⓓ Ⓔ
4 Ⓐ Ⓑ Ⓒ Ⓓ Ⓔ	15 Ⓐ Ⓑ Ⓒ Ⓓ Ⓔ	26 Ⓐ Ⓑ Ⓒ Ⓓ Ⓔ	38 Ⓐ Ⓑ Ⓒ Ⓓ Ⓔ
5 Ⓐ Ⓑ Ⓒ Ⓓ Ⓔ	16 Ⓐ Ⓑ Ⓒ Ⓓ Ⓔ	27 Ⓐ Ⓑ Ⓒ Ⓓ Ⓔ	39 Ⓐ Ⓑ Ⓒ Ⓓ Ⓔ
6 Ⓐ Ⓑ Ⓒ Ⓓ Ⓔ	17 Ⓐ Ⓑ Ⓒ Ⓓ Ⓔ	28 Ⓐ Ⓑ Ⓒ Ⓓ Ⓔ	40 Ⓐ Ⓑ Ⓒ Ⓓ Ⓔ
7 Ⓐ Ⓑ Ⓒ Ⓓ Ⓔ	18 Ⓐ Ⓑ Ⓒ Ⓓ Ⓔ	29 Ⓐ Ⓑ Ⓒ Ⓓ Ⓔ	41 Ⓐ Ⓑ Ⓒ Ⓓ Ⓔ
8 Ⓐ Ⓑ Ⓒ Ⓓ Ⓔ	19 Ⓐ Ⓑ Ⓒ Ⓓ Ⓔ	30 Ⓐ Ⓑ Ⓒ Ⓓ Ⓔ	
9 Ⓐ Ⓑ Ⓒ Ⓓ Ⓔ	20 Ⓐ Ⓑ Ⓒ Ⓓ Ⓔ	31 Ⓐ Ⓑ Ⓒ Ⓓ Ⓔ	
10 Ⓐ Ⓑ Ⓒ Ⓓ Ⓔ	21 Ⓐ Ⓑ Ⓒ Ⓓ Ⓔ	32 Ⓐ Ⓑ Ⓒ Ⓓ Ⓔ	
11 Ⓐ Ⓑ Ⓒ Ⓓ Ⓔ	22 Ⓐ Ⓑ Ⓒ Ⓓ Ⓔ	34 Ⓐ Ⓑ Ⓒ Ⓓ Ⓔ	

Sample Test 2 with Answers and Analysis

WRITING ASSESSMENT

Part I   TIME: 30 MINUTES

Directions: Write a clear, logical, and well-organized response to the following issue or argument. Your response should be in the form of a short essay, following the conventions of standard written English. Your answer should fit on three pages of lined 8½" × 11" paper or equivalent on your PC. Write legibly. Essays that are illegible or that are written on a topic other than the one outlined in the question will not be scored.

Forced obsolescence is a strategy that manufacturers use to limit the useful life of some consumer products in order to increase sales. Some commentators complain that this practice results in a waste of resources. What they do not understand is that by shortening the life cycle of products, manufacturers are able to both improve them and lower the cost to the consumer.

Which do you find more convincing: that forced obsolescence wastes resources or that it benefits consumers? State your position using relevant reasons from your own experience, observation, or reading.

STOP

IF THERE IS STILL TIME REMAINING, YOU MAY REVIEW YOUR ANSWER. AFTER YOU HAVE CONFIRMED YOUR ANSWER, YOU CANNOT RETURN TO THIS QUESTION.

Sample Test 2

Part II TIME: 30 MINUTES

Directions: Write a clear, logical, and well-organized response to the following issue or argument. Your response should be in the form of a short essay, following the conventions of standard written English. Your answer should fit on three pages of lined 8½" × 11" paper or equivalent on your PC. Write legibly. Essays that are illegible or that are written on a topic other than the one outlined in the question will not be scored.

Women are more fashion-conscious than men. Women's clothing styles change ever year, forcing them update their wardrobes so as not to appear behind the times.

Discuss how logically persuasive you find the above argument. In presenting your point of view, analyze the sort of reasoning used and supporting evidence. In addition, state what further evidence, if any, would make the argument more sound and convincing or would make you better able to evaluate its conclusion.

IF THERE IS STILL TIME REMAINING, YOU MAY REVIEW YOUR ANSWER. AFTER YOU HAVE CONFIRMED YOUR ANSWER, YOU CANNOT RETURN TO THIS QUESTION.

QUANTITATIVE SECTION

TIME: 75 MINUTES

37 QUESTIONS

This section consists of two types of questions: Problem Solving and Data Sufficiency.

Problem Solving
Directions: Solve each of the following problems; then indicate the correct answer.

NOTE: A figure that appears with a problem is drawn as accurately as possible so as to provide information that may help in answering the question.

Numbers in this test are real numbers.

Data Sufficiency
Directions: Each of the following problems has a question and two statements which are labeled (1) and (2). Use the data given in (1) and (2) together with other available information (such as the number of hours in a day, the definition of *clockwise*, mathematical facts, etc.) to decide whether the statements are *sufficient* to answer the question. Then fill in space

(A) If you can get the answer from (1) **ALONE** but not from (2) alone
(B) If you can get the answer from (2) **ALONE** but not from (1) alone
(C) If you can get the answer from **BOTH (1)** and **(2) TOGETHER** but not from (1) alone or (2) alone
(D) If **EITHER** statement (1) **ALONE OR** statement (2) **ALONE** suffices
(E) If you **CANNOT** get the answer from statements (1) and (2) **TOGETHER** but need even more data

All numbers used in this section are real numbers.

A figure given for a problem is intended to provide information consistent with that in the question, but not necessarily with the additional information contained in the statements.

All figures lie in the plane unless you are told otherwise.

Figures are drawn as accurately as possible; straight lines may not appear straight on the screen.

1. Water has been poured into an empty rectangular tank at the rate of 5 cubic feet per minute for 6 minutes. The length of the tank is 4 feet and the width is $\frac{1}{2}$ of the length. How deep is the water in the tank?

   (A)   7.5 inches
   (B)   3 feet 7.5 inches
   (C)   3 feet 9 inches
   (D)   7 feet 6 inches
   (E)   30 feet

2. If x, y, z are chosen from the three numbers -3, $\frac{1}{2}$, and 2, what is the largest possible value of the expression $\left(\dfrac{x}{y}\right)z^2$?

   (A) $-\dfrac{3}{8}$

   (B)   16
   (C)   24
   (D)   36
   (E)   54

3. A survey of n people found that 60 percent preferred brand A. An additional x people were surveyed who all preferred brand A. Seventy percent of all the people surveyed preferred brand A. Find x in terms of n.

   (A) $\dfrac{n}{6}$

   (B) $\dfrac{n}{3}$

   (C) $\dfrac{n}{2}$

   (D) n
   (E) $3n$

4. Is x greater than y?

   (1) $3x = 2k$
   (2) $k = y^2$

(A) If you can get the answer from **(1) ALONE** but not from **(2)** alone
(B) If you can get the answer from **(2) ALONE** but not from **(1)** alone
(C) If you can get the answer from **BOTH (1) and (2) TOGETHER** but not from (1) alone or (2) alone
(D) If **EITHER** statement **(1) ALONE OR** statement **(2) ALONE** suffices
(E) If you **CANNOT** get the answer from statements (1) and (2) **TOGETHER** but need even more data

5. Is *ABCD* a parallelogram?

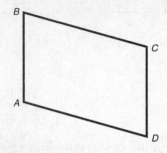

    (1) $AB = CD$
    (2) *AB* is parallel to *CD*

6. The hexagon *ABCDEF* is regular. That means all its sides are the same length and all its interior angles are the same size. Each side of the hexagon is 2 feet. What is the area of the rectangle *BCEF*?

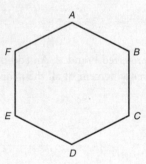

    (A)   4 square feet
    (B) $4\sqrt{3}$ square feet
    (C)   8 square feet
    (D) $4 + 4\sqrt{3}$ square feet
    (E)   12 square feet

7. In Motor City 90 percent of the population own a car, 15 percent own a motorcycle, and everybody owns one or the other or both. What is the percentage of motorcycle owners who own cars?

    (A)   5%
    (B)   15%
    (C) $33\frac{1}{3}$%
    (D)   50%
    (E)   90%

(A) If you can get the answer from (1) **ALONE** but not from (2) alone
(B) If you can get the answer from (2) **ALONE** but not from (1) alone
(C) If you can get the answer from **BOTH (1) and (2) TOGETHER** but not from (1) alone or (2) alone
(D) If **EITHER** statement (1) **ALONE OR** statement (2) **ALONE** suffices
(E) If you **CANNOT** get the answer from statements (1) and (2) **TOGETHER** but need even more data

8. Jim's weight is 140 percent of Marcia's weight. Bob's weight is 90 percent of Lee's weight. Lee weighs twice as much as Marcia. What percentage of Jim's weight is Bob's weight?

    (A) $64\frac{2}{7}$

    (B) $77\frac{7}{9}$

    (C) 90

    (D) $128\frac{4}{7}$

    (E) $155\frac{5}{9}$

9. What is the two-digit number whose first digit is a and whose second digit is b? The number is greater than 9.

    (1) $2a + 3b = 11a + 2b$
    (2)   The two-digit number is a multiple of 19.

10. A chair originally cost $50.00. The chair was offered for sale at 108 percent of its cost. After a week, the price was discounted 10 percent and the chair was sold. The chair was sold for

    (A) $45.00
    (B) $48.60
    (C) $49.00
    (D) $49.50
    (E) $54.00

11. k is a positive integer. Is k a prime number?

    (1)   No integer between 2 and $\sqrt{k}$ inclusive, divides k evenly.

    (2)   No integer between 2 and $\frac{k}{2}$ inclusive, divides k evenly, and k is greater than 5.

12. Towns A and C are connected by a straight highway that is 60 miles long. The straight-line distance between town A and town B is 50 miles, and the straight-line distance from town B to town C is 50 miles. How many miles is it from town B to the point on the highway connecting towns A and C that is closest to town B?

    (A) 30
    (B) 40
    (C) $30\sqrt{2}$
    (D) 50
    (E) 60

13. A worker is paid *x* dollars for the first 8 hours he works each day. He is paid *y* dollars per hour for each hour he works in excess of 8 hours. During one week he works 8 hours on Monday, 11 hours on Tuesday, 9 hours on Wednesday, 10 hours on Thursday, and 9 hours on Friday. What is his average daily wage in dollars for the 5-day week?

(A) $x + 1.4y$

(B) $2x + y$

(C) $\dfrac{(5x + 8y)}{5}$

(D) $8x + 1.4y$

(E) $5x + 7y$

14. A club has 8 male and 8 female members. The club is choosing a committee of 6 members. The committee must have 3 male and 3 female members. How many different committees can be chosen?

(A) 112,896

(B) 3,136

(C) 720

(D) 112

(E) 9

15. The towns *A*, *B*, and *C* lie on a straight line. *C* is between *A* and *B*. The distance from *A* to *B* is 100 miles. How far is it from *A* to *C*?

(1) The distance from *A* to *B* is 25 percent more than the distance from *C* to *B*.

(2) The distance from *A* to *C* is $\dfrac{1}{4}$ of the distance from *C* to *B*.

16. A club has 10 male and 5 female members. Each member of the club writes their name on a ticket, and the tickets are deposited in a box. The club chooses 2 members to go to a national meeting by drawing 2 tickets from the box. What is the probability that both members picked for the trip are female?

(A) $\dfrac{2}{21}$

(B) $\dfrac{1}{10}$

(C) $\dfrac{2}{7}$

(D) $\dfrac{5}{15}$

(E) $\dfrac{2}{5}$

(A) If you can get the answer from **(1) ALONE** but not from **(2)** alone

(B) If you can get the answer from **(2) ALONE** but not from **(1)** alone

(C) If you can get the answer from **BOTH (1) and (2) TOGETHER** but not from (1) alone or (2) alone

(D) If **EITHER** statement **(1) ALONE OR** statement **(2) ALONE** suffices

(E) If you **CANNOT** get the answer from statements **(1)** and **(2) TOGETHER** but need even more data

17. The distribution of scores on a math test had a mean of 82 percent with a standard deviation of 5 percent. The score that is exactly 2 standard deviations above the mean is

    (A) 72%
    (B) 82%
    (C) 92%
    (D) 95%
    (E) cannot be determined

18. What is the value of $x - y$?

    (1) $x + 2y = 6$
    (2) $x = y$

19. The number of eligible voters is 100,000. How many eligible voters voted?

    (1) 63 percent of the eligible men voted.
    (2) 67 percent of the eligible women voted.

20. A motorcycle costs \$2,500 when it is brand new. At the end of each year it is worth 80 percent of what it was worth at the beginning of the year. What is the motorcycle worth when it is 3 years old?

    (A) \$1,000
    (B) \$1,200
    (C) \$1,280
    (D) \$1,340
    (E) \$1,430

21. Which of the following inequalities is the solution to the inequality $7x - 5 < 12x + 18$?

    (A) $x < -\dfrac{13}{5}$

    (B) $x > -\dfrac{23}{5}$

    (C) $x < -\dfrac{23}{5}$

    (D) $x > \dfrac{23}{5}$

    (E) $x < \dfrac{23}{5}$

(A) If you can get the answer from (1) **ALONE** but not from (2) alone
(B) If you can get the answer from (2) **ALONE** but not from (1) alone
(C) If you can get the answer from **BOTH** (1) **and** (2) **TOGETHER** but not from (1) alone or (2) alone
(D) If **EITHER** statement (1) **ALONE OR** statement (2) **ALONE** suffices
(E) If you **CANNOT** get the answer from statements (1) and (2) **TOGETHER** but need even more data

22. The hexagon *ABCDEF* is inscribed in the circle with center *O*. What is the length of *AB*?

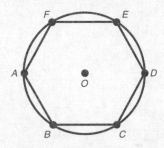

(1) The radius of the circle is 4 inches.
(2) The hexagon is a regular hexagon. That means all its sides are the same length and all its interior angles are the same size.

23. What was the percentage of defective items produced at a factory?

(1) The total number of defective items produced was 1,234.
(2) The ratio of defective items to nondefective items was 32 to 5,678.

24. On a list of peoples ages the tabulator made an error that resulted in 20 years being added to each person's age. Which of the following statements is true.

   I. The mean of the listed ages and the mean of the actual ages are the same.
  II. The standard deviation of the listed ages and the actual ages are the same.
 III. The range of the listed ages and the actual ages are the same.

(A) only II
(B) I and II
(C) I and III
(D) II and III
(E) I, II, and III

25.   Is *ABC* a right triangle? *AB* = 5; *AC* = 4.

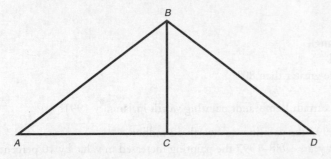

(1)   *BC* = 3

(2)   *AC* = *CD*

26.   Did the price of energy rise last year?

(1)   If the price of energy rose last year, then the price of food would rise this year.

(2)   The price of food rose this year.

27.   Mary, John, and Karen ate lunch together. Karen's meal cost 50 percent more than John's meal, and Mary's meal cost $\frac{5}{6}$ as much as Karen's meal. If Mary paid $2 more than John, how much was the total that the three of them paid?

(A) $28.33

(B) $30.00

(C) $35.00

(D) $37.50

(E) $40.00

28.   A group of 49 consumers were offered a chance to subscribe to three magazines: *A*, *B*, and *C*. Thirty-eight of the consumers subscribed to at least one of the magazines. How many of the 49 consumers subscribed to exactly two of the magazines?

(1)   Twelve of the 49 consumers subscribed to all three of the magazines.

(2)   Twenty of the 49 consumers subscribed to magazine *A*.

29.   Is *k* an odd integer?

(1)   *k* is divisible by 3.

(2)   The square root of *k* is an integer divisible by 3.

(A) If you can get the answer from (1) **ALONE** but not from (2) alone
(B) If you can get the answer from (2) **ALONE** but not from (1) alone
(C) If you can get the answer from **BOTH** (1) **and** (2) **TOGETHER** but not from
   (1) alone or (2) alone
(D) If **EITHER** statement (1) **ALONE OR** statement (2) **ALONE** suffices
(E) If you **CANNOT** get the answer from statements (1) and (2) **TOGETHER** but
   need even more data

30. If the angles of a triangle are in the ratio 1 : 2 : 2, the triangle

   (A) is isosceles
   (B) is obtuse
   (C) is a right triangle
   (D) is equilateral
   (E) has one angle greater than 80°

31. How much was a certain Rembrandt painting worth in January 1991?

   (1) In January 1997 the painting was worth $2 million.
   (2) Over the ten years 1988–1997 the painting increased in value by 10 percent
        each year.

32. A sequence of numbers a_1, a_2, a_3, . . . is given by the rule $a_n^2 = a_{n+1}$. Does 3 appear in
   the sequence?

   (1) $a_1 = 2$
   (2) $a_3 = 16$

33. A wall with no windows is 11 feet high and 20 feet long. A large roll of wallpaper
   costs $25 and will cover 60 square feet of wall. A small roll of wallpaper costs $6 and
   will cover 10 square feet of wall. What is the least cost for enough wallpaper to cover
   the wall?

   (A) $75
   (B) $99
   (C) $100
   (D) $120
   (E) $132

34. A jar is filled with 60 marbles. All the marbles in the jar are either red or green. What is
   the smallest number of marbles that must be drawn from the jar in order to be certain
   that a red marble is drawn?

   (1) The ratio of red marbles to green marbles is 2 : 1.
   (2) There are 20 green marbles in the jar.

35. Is $\frac{1}{x}$ greater than $\frac{1}{y}$?

   (1) x is greater than 1.
   (2) x is less than y.

(A) If you can get the answer from **(1) ALONE** but not from **(2)** alone

(B) If you can get the answer from **(2) ALONE** but not from **(1)** alone

(C) If you can get the answer from **BOTH (1)** and **(2) TOGETHER** but not from (1) alone or (2) alone

(D) If **EITHER** statement **(1) ALONE OR** statement **(2) ALONE** suffices

(E) If you **CANNOT** get the answer from statements (1) and (2) **TOGETHER** but need even more data

36. Plane *X* flies at *r* miles per hour from *A* to *B*. Plane *Y* flies at *S* miles per hour from *B* to *A*. Both planes take off at the same time. Which plane flies at a faster rate? Town *C* is between *A* and *B*.

    (1)   *C* is closer to *A* than it is to *B*.
    (2)   Plane *X* flies over *C* before plane *Y*.

37. Is $\frac{x}{12} > \frac{y}{40}$?

    (1) $10x > 3y$
    (2) $12x < 4y$

STOP

IF THERE IS STILL TIME REMAINING, YOU MAY REVIEW YOUR ANSWERS. AFTER YOU HAVE CONFIRMED YOUR ANSWERS, YOU CANNOT RETURN TO THESE QUESTIONS.

Sample Test 2

VERBAL SECTION

TIME: 75 MINUTES

41 QUESTIONS

Reading Comprehension
Directions: This section contains three reading passages. You are to read each one carefully. When answering the questions, you *will* be allowed to refer back to the passages. The questions are based on what is *stated* or *implied* in each passage.

Critical Reasoning
Directions: For each question in this section, choose the best answer among the listed alternatives.

Sentence Correction
Directions: This part of the section consists of a number of sentences in each of which some part or the whole is underlined. Each sentence is followed by five alternative versions of the underlined portion. Select the alternative you consider both most correct and most effective according to the requirements of standard written English. Answer (A) is the same as the original version; if you think the original version is best, select answer (A).

In considering the answer choices, be attentive to matters of grammar, diction, and syntax, as well as clarity, precision, and fluency. Do not select an answer that alters the meaning of the original sentence.

Questions 1–4 are based on the following passage.

Line
(5)

The main burden of assuring that the resources of the federal government are well managed falls on relatively few of the five million men and women whom it employs. Under the department and agency heads there are 8,600 political, career, military, and foreign service executives—the top managers and professionals—who exert major influence on the manner in which the rest are directed and utilized. Below their level there are other thousands with assignments of some managerial significance, but we believe that the line of demarcation selected is the best available for our purposes in this attainment.

There is no complete inventory of positions or people in federal service at this level. The lack may be explained by separate agency statutes and personnel systems, diffusion among so many special services, and absence of any central point (short of the President himself) with jurisdiction over all upper-level personnel of the government.

(10)

Top Presidential appointees, about 500 of them, bear the brunt of translating the philosophy and aims of the current administration into practical programs. This group includes the secretaries and assistant secretaries of cabinet departments, agency heads and their deputies, heads and members of boards and commissions with fixed terms, and chiefs and directors of major bureaus, divisions, and services. Appointments to many of these politically sensitive positions are made on recommendation by department or agency heads, but all are presumably responsible to Presidential leadership.

(15)

One qualification for office at this level is that there be no basic disagreement with Presidential political philosophy, at least so far as administrative judgments and actions are concerned. Apart from the bi-partisan boards and commissions, these men are normally identified with the political party of the President, or are sympathetic to it, although there are exceptions.

(20)

There are four distinguishable kinds of top Presidential appointees, including:

(25)

— Those whom the President selects at the outset to establish immediate and effective control over the government (e.g., Cabinet secretaries, agency heads, his own White House staff and Executive Office Personnel).

— Those selected by department and agency heads in order to establish control within their respective organizations (e.g.—assistant secretaries, deputies, assistants to, and major line posts in some bureaus and divisions).

(30)

— High-level appointees who—though often requiring clearance through political or interest group channels, or both—must have known scientific or technical competence (e.g.—the Surgeon General, the Commissioner of Education).

— Those named to residual positions traditionally filled on a partisan patronage basis.

(35)

These appointees are primarily regarded as policy makers and overseers of policy execution. In practice, however, they usually have substantial responsibilities in line management, often requiring a thorough knowledge of substantive agency programs.

1. No complete inventory exists of positions in the three highest levels of government service because

   (A) no one has bothered to count them
   (B) computers cannot handle all the data
   (C) separate agency personnel systems are used
   (D) the President has never requested such information
   (E) the Classification Act prohibits such a census

2. Top Presidential appointees have as their central responsibility the

    (A) prevention of politically motivated interference with the actions of their agencies
    (B) monitoring of government actions on behalf of the President's own political party
    (C) translation of the aims of the administration into practical programs
    (D) investigation of charges of corruption within the government
    (E) maintenance of adequate controls over the rate of government spending

3. One exception to the general rule that top Presidential appointees must be in agreement with the President's political philosophy may be found in

    (A) most cabinet-level officers
    (B) members of the White House staff
    (C) bipartisan boards and commissions
    (D) those offices filled on a patronage basis
    (E) offices requiring scientific or technical expertise

4. Applicants for Presidential appointments are usually identified with or are members of

    (A) large corporations
    (B) the foreign service
    (C) government bureaus
    (D) academic circles
    (E) the President's political party

5. Richard is a terrible driver. He has had at least five traffic violations in the past year.

    Which of the following can be said about the above claim?

    (A) This is an example of an argument that is directed against the source of the claim rather than the claim itself.
    (B) The statement is fallacious because it contains an illegitimate appeal to authority.
    (C) The above argument obtains its strength from a similarity of two compared situations.
    (D) The argument is built upon an assumption that is not stated but rather is concealed.
    (E) In the above statements, there is a shifting in the meaning of terms, causing a fallacy of ambiguity.

6. The exchange rate is the ruling official rate of exchange of dollars for other currencies. It determines the value of American goods in relation to foreign goods. If the dollar is devalued in terms of other currencies, American exports (which are paid for in dollars) become cheaper to foreigners and American imports (paid for by purchasing foreign currency) become more expensive to holders of dollars.

    What conclusion can be drawn from the above?

    (A) There are certain disadvantages for the United States economy attached to devaluation.
    (B) The prospect of devaluation results in a speculative outflow of funds.
    (C) By encouraging exports and discouraging imports, devaluation can improve the American balance of payments.
    (D) The difference between imports and exports is called the Trade Gap.
    (E) It is possible that inflation neutralizes the beneficial effects of devaluation.

7. <u>Although I calculate that he will be here</u> any minute, I cannot wait much longer for him to arrive.

    (A) Although I calculate that he will be here
    (B) Although I reckon that he will be here
    (C) Because I calculate that he will be here
    (D) Although I think that he will be here
    (E) Because I am confident that he will be here

8. <u>The fourteen-hour day not only has been reduced</u> to one of ten hours but also, in some lines of work, to one of eight or even six.

    (A) The fourteen-hour day not only has been reduced
    (B) Not only the fourteen-hour day has been reduced
    (C) Not the fourteen-hour day only has been reduced
    (D) The fourteen-hour day has not only been reduced
    (E) The fourteen-hour day has been reduced not only

9. In the human body, platelets promote blood clotting by clumping together. Aspirin has been found to prevent clotting by making platelets less sticky. Research has now shown that heart attacks and strokes caused by blood clots could be avoided by taking one aspirin a day. Statistics show that the incidence of second heart attacks has been reduced by 21% and overall mortality rates by 15% as a result of taking aspirin.

    Unfortunately, the drug has several unpleasant side effects, including nausea, gastric bleeding, and, in severe cases, shock. In children, it has been linked to Reye's Syndrome, a rare, but occasionally fatal, childhood illness.

    On balance, however, for men aged 40 and over, an aspirin a day may present an excellent prophylactic measure for a disease that affects 1.5 million Americans yearly and claims the lives of about 540,000.

Which of the following conclusions can most properly be drawn from the information above?

    (A) All people should take an aspirin a day to prevent heart attacks.
    (B) Painkillers prevent heart attacks.
    (C) Smokers can safely continue smoking, provided that they take at least one aspirin a day.
    (D) The majority of people suffering second subsequent cardiac arrests could have been saved by taking an aspirin a day.
    (E) Aspirin can be used to reduce mortality rates in patients who have already suffered heart attacks.

Sample Test 2

10. In the past, to run for one's country in the Olympics was the ultimate achievement of any athlete. Nowadays, an athlete's motives are more and more influenced by financial gain, and consequently we do not see our best athletes in the Olympics, which is still only for amateurs.

Which of the following will most weaken the above conclusion?

(A) The publicity and fame that can be achieved by competing in the Olympics makes athletes more "marketable" by agents and potential sponsors, while allowing the athletes to retain their amateur status.
(B) The winning of a race is not as important as participating.
(C) There is a widely held belief that our best Olympic athletes already receive enough in terms of promotion and sponsorship.
(D) It has been suggested that professional athletes should be allowed to compete in the games.
(E) Athletics as an entertainment is like any other entertainment job and deserves a financial reward.

11. <u>We want the teacher to be him</u> who has the best rapport with the students.

(A) We want the teacher to be him
(B) We want the teacher to be he
(C) We want him to be the teacher
(D) We desire that the teacher be him
(E) We anticipate that the teacher will be him

12. <u>If she were to win the medal,</u> I for one would be disturbed.

(A) If she were to win the medal,
(B) If she was to win the medal,
(C) If she wins the medal,
(D) If she is the winner of the medal,
(E) In the event that she wins the medal,

13. The function of a food technologist in a large marketing chain of food stores is to ensure that all foodstuffs which are offered for sale in the various retail outlets meet certain standard criteria for nonperishability, freshness, and fitness for human consumption.

It is the technologist's job to visit the premises of suppliers and food producers (factory or farm), inspect the facilities and report thereon. Her responsibility also includes receiving new products from local and foreign suppliers and performing exhaustive quality control testing on them. Finally, she should carry out surprise spot-checks on goods held in the marketing chain's own warehouses and stores.

What conclusion can best be drawn from the preceding paragraph?

(A) A university degree in food technology is a necessary and sufficient condition for becoming a food technologist.
(B) Imported products, as well as home-produced goods, must be rigorously tested.
(C) The food technologist stands between the unhygienic producer and the unsuspecting consumer.
(D) Home-produced foodstuffs are safer to eat than goods imported from abroad because they are subject to more regular and closer inspection procedures.
(E) Random checking of the quality of goods stored on the shelves in a foodstore is the best way of ensuring that foodstuffs of an inferior quality are not purchased by the general public.

14. The scouts were told to take an overnight hike, pitch camp, prepare dinner, and that they should be in bed by 9 P.M.

   (A) to take an overnight hike, pitch camp, prepare dinner, and that they should be in bed by 9 P.M.
   (B) to take an overnight hike, to pitch camp, to prepare dinner, and that they should be in bed by 9 P.M.
   (C) to take an overnight hike, pitch camp, prepare dinner, and be in bed by 9 P.M.
   (D) to take an overnight hike, pitching camp, preparing dinner and going to bed by 9 P.M.
   (E) to engage in an overnight hike, pitch camp, prepare dinner, and that they should be in bed by 9 P.M.

Questions 15–18 are based on the following passage.

In the past, American colleges and universities were created to serve a dual purpose—to advance learning and to offer a chance to become familiar with bodies of knowledge already discovered to those who wished it. To create and to impart, these were the hallmarks of
Line American higher education prior to the most recent, tumultuous decades of the twentieth
(5) century. The successful institution of higher learning had never been one whose mission could be defined in terms of providing vocational skills or as a strategy for resolving societal problems. In a subtle way Americans believed postsecondary education to be useful, but not necessarily of immediate use. What the student obtained in college became beneficial in later life—residually, without direct application in the period after graduation.
(10) Another purpose has now been assigned to the mission of American colleges and universities. Institutions of higher learning—public or private—commonly face the challenge of defining their programs in such a way as to contribute to the service of the community.

One need only be reminded of the change in language describing the two-year college to appreciate the new value currently being attached to the concept of a service-related uni-
(15) versity. The traditional two-year college has shed its pejorative "junior" college label and is generally called a "community" college, a clearly value-laden expression representing the latest commitment in higher education.

This novel development is often overlooked. Educators have always been familiar with those parts of the two-year college curriculum that have a "service" or vocational orienta-
(20) tion. Knowing this, otherwise perceptive commentaries on American postsecondary education underplay the impact of the attempt of colleges and universities to relate to, if not resolve, the problems of society. Whether the subject under review is student unrest, faculty tenure, the nature of the curriculum, the onset of collective bargaining, or the growth of collegiate bureaucracies, in each instance the thrust of these discussions obscures the larger
(25) meaning of the emergence of the service-university in American higher education. Even the highly regarded critique of Clark Kerr, formerly head of the Carnegie Foundation, which set the parameters of academic debate around the evolution of the so-called "multiversity," failed to take account of this phenomenon.

Taken together the attrition rate (from known and unknown causes) was 48 percent, but
(30) the figure for regular students was 36 percent while for Open Admissions categories it was 56 percent. The most important statistics, however, relate to the findings regarding Open Admissions students, and these indicated as a projection that perhaps as many as 70 percent would not graduate from a unit of the City University.

15. The dropout rate among regular students in Open Admissions was approximately

   (A) 35%
   (B) 45%
   (C) 55%
   (D) 65%
   (E) 75%

16. According to the passage, in the past it was *not* the purpose of American higher education to

    (A) advance learning
    (B) solve societal problems
    (C) impart knowledge
    (D) train workers
    (E) prepare future managers

17. One of the recent, important changes in higher education relates to

    (A) student representation on college boards
    (B) faculty tenure requirements
    (C) curriculum updates
    (D) service-education concepts
    (E) cost constraints

18. The attrition rate for Open Admissions students was greater than the rate for regular students by what percent?

    (A) 10%
    (B) 20%
    (C) 36%
    (D) 40%
    (E) 46%

19. The government's failing to keep it's pledges will earn the distrust of all the other nations in the alliance.

    (A) government's failing to keep it's pledges
    (B) government failing to keep it's pledges
    (C) government's failing to keep its pledges
    (D) government failing to keep its pledges
    (E) governments failing to keep their pledges

20. Most students like to read these kind of books during their spare time.

    (A) these kind of books
    (B) these kind of book
    (C) this kind of book
    (D) this kinds of books
    (E) those kind of books

21. In the normal course of events, John will graduate high school and enter college in two years.

    (A) John will graduate high school and enter
    (B) John will graduate from high school and enter
    (C) John will be graduated from high school and enter
    (D) John will be graduated from high school and enter into
    (E) John will have graduated high school and enter

22. The daily journey from his home to his office takes John Bond on average an hour and 35 minutes by car. A friend has told him of a different route that is longer in mileage, but will only take an hour and a quarter on average, because it contains stretches of roads where it is possible to drive at higher speeds.

    John Bond's only consideration apart from the time factor is the cost, and he calculates that his car will consume 10% less gasoline if he takes the suggested new route. John decides to take the new route for the next two weeks as an experiment.

    If the above were the only other considerations, which one of the following may have an effect on the decision John has made?

    (A) Major road work is begun on the shorter (in distance) route, which holds up traffic for an extra 10 minutes. The project will take six months, but after it, the improvements will allow the journey to be made in half an hour less than at present.
    (B) There is to be a strike at local gas stations and the amount of gasoline drivers may purchase may be rationed.
    (C) John finds a third route which is slightly longer then his old route, but shorter than the suggested route.
    (D) The old route passes the door of a work colleague, who without a ride, would have to go to work by bus.
    (E) None of the above.

23. All elephants are gray.
    And all mice are gray.
    Therefore, I conclude that all elephants are mice.

    The argument above is invalid because

    (A) the writer bases her argument on another argument that contains circular reasoning.
    (B) the writer has illogically classified two disparate groups together when there is no relationship between them, except that they both have the same attribute.
    (C) the writer has made a mistaken analogy between two dissimilar qualities.
    (D) the writer has used a fallacy which involves the ambiguous description of animals by their color.
    (E) the writer has failed to express her reasoning fully.

24. Sally overslept. Therefore, she did not eat breakfast. She realized that she was late for school, so she ran as fast as she could and did not see a hole in the ground which was in her path. She tripped and broke her ankle. She was then taken to the hospital and while lying in bed was visited by her friend, who wanted to know why she had got up so late.

    Which of the following conclusions can be made from the above passage?

    (A) Because Sally did not eat her breakfast, she broke her ankle.
    (B) Sally's friend visited her in the hospital because she wanted to know why she was late for school.
    (C) Sally did not notice the hole because she overslept.
    (D) Sally broke her ankle because she went to bed late the previous night.
    (E) Sally's broken ankle meant she did not go to school that day.

Sample Test 2

Questions 25–30 are based on the following passage.

For those of a certain age and educational background, it is hard to think of higher education without thinking of ancient institutions. Some universities are a venerable age—the University of Bologna was founded in 1088 and Oxford University in 1096—and many of
Line them have a strong sense of tradition. The truly old ones make the most of their pedigrees,
(5) and those of a more recent vintage work hard to create an aura of antiquity.

And yet these tradition-loving (or -creating) institutions are currently ending a thunderstorm of changes so fundamental that some say the very idea of the university is being challenged. Universities are experimenting with new ways of funding (most notably through student fees), forging partnerships with private companies, and engaging in mergers and
(10) acquisitions. Such changes are tugging at the ivy's roots.

This is happening for four reasons. The first is the democratization of higher education— "massification," in the language of the educational profession. In the rich world, massification has been going on for some time. The proportion of adults with higher educational qualifications in the OECD countries almost doubled between 1975 and 2000, from 22
(15) percent to 41 percent. But most of the rich countries are still struggling to digest this huge growth in numbers. And now massification is spreading to the developing world. China doubled its student population in the late 1990s, and India is trying to follow suit.

The second reason is the rise of the knowledge economy. The world is in the grips of a "soft revolution" in which knowledge is replacing physical resources as the main driver of
(20) economic growth. The OECD calculates that between 1985 and 1997, the contribution of knowledge-based industries to total value added increased from 51 percent to 59 percent in Germany and from 45 percent to 51 percent in Britain. The best companies are now devoting at least a third of their investment to knowledge-intensive intangibles, such as R&D, licensing, and marketing. Universities are among the most important engines of the knowl-
(25) edge economy. Not only do they produce the brain workers who man it, they also provide much of its backbone, from laboratories to libraries to computer networks.

The third factor is globalization. The death of distance is transforming academia just as radically as it is transforming business. The number of people from OECD countries studying abroad has doubled over the past 20 years, to 1.9 million; universities are opening cam-
(30) puses all around the world; and a growing number of countries are trying to turn higher education into an export industry.

The fourth is competition. Traditional universities are being forced to compete for students and research grants, and private companies are trying to break into a sector that they regard as "the new health care." The World Bank calculates that global spending on higher
(35) education amounts to $300 billion a year, or 1 percent of global economic output. There are more than 80 million students worldwide, and 3.5 million people are employed to teach them or look after them.

25. Changes in tradition-oriented universities' education are caused by

    (A) increased enrollments
    (B) lack of financing
    (C) online education
    (D) more qualified students
    (E) lack of resources

26. The best possible title for the passage would be

    (A) *"Massification"*
    (B) *"The Brains Business"*
    (C) *"The Decline of Tradition-Loving Universities"*
    (D) *"Downfall of Academic Dogma"*
    (E) *"Globalization of Higher Education"*

27. According to the passage, mass higher education is forcing universities to become

    (A) more democractic
    (B) better managed
    (C) more liberal
    (D) more teaching-oriented
    (E) more competitive

28. Younger universities try to

    (A) compete with older ones
    (B) create an image like that of more traditional ones
    (C) diversify their student bodies
    (D) rely less on outside financing
    (E) diversify income sources

29. Universities have had to reexamine their mission because

    (A) there are more and better-educated high school graduates
    (B) state funding is declining
    (C) state-run universities are being privatized
    (D) good faculty is in short supply
    (E) of the rise in distance learning

30. In business terms, it can be said that higher education has become

    (A) more profitable
    (B) an export industry
    (C) better managed
    (D) bottom line-oriented
    (E) customer-oriented

31. The owners of a local supermarket have decided to make use of three now-redundant checkout counters. They believe that they will attract those customers who lately have been put off by the long checkout lines during the mid-morning and evening rush hours. The owners have concluded that in order to be successful, the increased revenue from existing and added counters will have to be more than the increase in maintenance costs for the added counters.

    The underlying goal of the owners can be summarized thus:

    (A) To improve services to all customers.
    (B) To attract people who have never been to the store.
    (C) To make use of the redundant counters.
    (D) To keep maintenance costs on the added counters as low as possible.
    (E) To increase monthly profits.

32. The cost of housing in many parts of the United States has become so excessive that many young couples, with above-average salaries, can only afford small apartments. Mortgage commitments are so huge that they cannot consider the possibility of starting a family. A new baby would probably mean either the mother or father giving up a well-paid position. The lack of or great cost of child-care facilities precludes the return of both parents to work.

Which of the following adjustments could practically be made to the situation described above which would allow young couples to improve their housing prospects?

(A) Encourage couples to remain childless.
(B) Encourage couples to have one child only.
(C) Encourage couples to postpone starting their families until a later age than previously acceptable to society.
(D) Encourage young couples to move to cheaper areas of the United States.
(E) Encourage fathers to remain at home while mothers return to work.

33. With the exception of <u>Frank and I, everyone in the class finished</u> the assignment before the bell rang.

(A) Frank and I, everyone in the class finished
(B) Frank and me, everyone in the class finished
(C) Frank and me, everyone in the class had finished
(D) Frank and I, everyone in the class had finished
(E) Frank and me everyone in the class finished

34. Many middle-class individuals find that they cannot obtain good medical attention, <u>despite they need it badly.</u>

(A) despite they need it badly
(B) despite they badly need it
(C) in spite of they need it badly
(D) however much they need it
(E) therefore, they need it badly

35. Unless new reserves are found soon, the world's supply of coal is being depleted in such a way that with demand continuing to grow at present rates, reserves will be exhausted by the year 2050.

Which of the following, if true, will most weaken the above argument?

(A) There has been a slowdown in the rate of increase in world demand for coal over the last 5 years from 10% to 5%.
(B) It has been known for many years that there are vast stocks of coal under Antarctica which have yet to be economically exploited.
(C) Oil is being used increasingly in place of coal for many industrial and domestic uses.
(D) As coal resources are depleted more and more marginal supplies, which are more costly to produce and less efficient in use are being mined.
(E) None of the above.

36. In accordance with their powers, many state authorities are introducing fluoridation of drinking water. This follows the conclusion of 10 years of research that the process ensures that children and adults receive the required intake of fluoride that will strengthen teeth. The maximum level has been set at one part per million. However, there are many who object, claiming that fluoridation removes freedom of choice.

Which of the following will weaken the claim of the proponents of fluoridation?

(A) Fluoridation over a certain prescribed level has been shown to lead to a general weakening of teeth.
(B) There is no record of the long-term effects of drinking fluoridated water.
(C) The people to be affected by fluoridation claim that they have not had sufficient opportunity to voice their views.
(D) Fluoridation is only one part of general dental health.
(E) Water already contains natural fluoride.

37. When one eats in this restaurant, you often find that the prices are high and that the food is poorly prepared.

(A) When one eats in this restaurant, you often find
(B) When you eat in this restaurant, one often finds
(C) As you eat in this restaurant, you often find
(D) If you eat in this restaurant, you often find
(E) When one ate in this restaurant, he often found

38. Ever since the bombing, there has been much opposition from they who maintain that it was an unauthorized war.

(A) from they who maintain that it was an unauthorized war
(B) from they who maintain that it had been an unauthorized war
(C) from those who maintain that it was an unauthorized war
(D) from they maintaining that it was unauthorized
(E) from they maintaining that it had been unauthorized

39. I am not to eager to go to this play because it did not get good reviews.

(A) I am not to eager to go to this play because it did not get good reviews.
(B) Because of its poor reviews, I am not to eager to go to this play.
(C) Because of its poor revues, I am not to eager to go to this play.
(D) I am not to eager to go to this play because the critics did not give it good reviews.
(E) I am not too eager to go to this play because of its poor reviews.

40. In 1980, global service exports totaled about $370 billion, approximately 20 percent of world trade. Still, no coherent system of rules, principles, and procedures exists to govern trade in services.

    Which of the following best summarizes the argument?

    (A) Regulatory systems lag behind reality.
    (B) A regulatory system ought to reflect the importance of service exports.
    (C) World trade totaled $1850 billion in 1980.
    (D) Service trade legislation is a veritable wasteland.
    (E) While trade legislation exists, it is uncoordinated.

41. <u>It was decided by us that the emphasis would be placed on the results that might be attained.</u>

    (A) It was decided by us that the emphasis would be placed on the results that might be attained.
    (B) We decided that the emphasis would be placed on the results that might be attained.
    (C) We decided to emphasize the results that might be attained.
    (D) We decided to emphasize the results we might attain.
    (E) It was decided that we would place emphasis on the results that might be attained.

STOP

Answer Key
SAMPLE TEST 2

Quantitative Section

1. C	11. D	21. B	31. C
2. D	12. B	22. C	32. D
3. B	13. A	23. B	33. B
4. E	14. B	24. D	34. D
5. C	15. D	25. A	35. C
6. B	16. A	26. E	36. E
7. C	17. C	27. B	37. A
8. D	18. B	28. E	
9. A	19. E	29. E	
10. B	20. C	30. A	

Verbal Section

1. C	12. A	23. B	34. D
2. C	13. C	24. C	35. E
3. C	14. C	25. D	36. B
4. E	15. A	26. B	37. C
5. D	16. B	27. E	38. C
6. C	17. D	28. B	39. E
7. D	18. B	29. A	40. B
8. E	19. C	30. B	41. C
9. E	20. C	31. E	
10. A	21. B	32. C	
11. B	22. C	33. C	

Analysis

	Self-Scoring Guide—Analytical Writing

Evaluate your writing tests (or have a friend or teacher evaluate them for you) on the following basis. Read each essay completely, paying special attention to its logical organization and use of examples and facts to buttress its claims or position. Assign a holistic score between 0 and 6, using the scale below. Your writing score will be the average of the scores of the two essays.

6 Outstanding — Cogent, well-articulated analysis of the issue or critique of the argument. Develops a position with insightful reasons and persuasive examples. Well organized. Superior command of language and variety of syntax. Only minor flaws in grammar, usage, and mechanics.

5 Strong — Well-developed analysis or critique. Develops a position with well-chosen examples or reasons. Generally well organized. Clear control of language and variety of syntax. Minor flaws in grammar, usage, and mechanics.

4 Adequate — Competent analysis or critique. Develops a position with relevant reasons or examples. Adequately organized. Adequate control of language, but may lack syntactic variety. May have some flaws in grammar, usage, and mechanics.

3 Limited — Competent but clearly flawed analysis or critique. Vague or limited in developing a position. Poorly organized. Weak in using relevant examples or reasons. Language used imprecisely or lacking in sentence variety. Contains major errors or frequent minor errors in grammar, usage, and mechanics.

2 Seriously Flawed — Serious weaknesses in analysis and organization. Unclear or seriously limited in presenting or developing a position. Disorganized. Few relevant examples or reasons. Frequent serious problems in language and sentence structure. Numerous errors in grammar, usage, or mechanics that interfere with meaning.

1 Fundamentally Deficient — Little evidence of ability to organize and develop a coherent response to issue or argument. Severe and persistent errors in language and sentence structure. Pervasive pattern of errors in grammar, usage, and mechanics that severely interfere with meaning.

0 Unscorable — Illegible or not written in the assigned topic.

ANSWERS EXPLAINED

Quantitative Section

1. **(C)** The volume of water that has been poured into the tank is 5 cubic feet per minute for 6 minutes, or 30 cubic feet. The tank is rectangular, so its volume is length times width times height, with the answer in cubic units. The width is $\frac{1}{2}$ the length, or $\frac{1}{2}$ of 4 feet which is 2 feet. The volume, which we already know is 30 cubic feet, is, therefore, 4 feet × 2 feet × the height. The height (depth of the water in the tank) is, therefore, $\frac{30}{8} = 3\frac{3}{4}$ feet = 3 feet 9 inches. (III-8)

2. **(D)** Since –3 has the largest absolute value of the three given numbers, using z as –3 will make z^2 as large as possible. Since $\frac{x}{y}$ is a quotient, to make it as large as possible use the smallest positive number for y and the largest positive number for x. So if you use $x = 2$ and $y = \frac{1}{2}$, then $\frac{x}{y}$ is as large as possible. Therefore, the largest value of the expression is $\frac{2}{\frac{1}{2}}(-3)^2 =$ 4(9) = 36. (I-2).

3. **(B)** The total number of people surveyed was $n + x$. Since 70 percent of the total preferred brand A, that means $.7(n + x)$ preferred brand A. However, 60 percent of the n people and all of the x people preferred brand A. So $.6n + x$ preferred brand A. Therefore, $.7(n + x)$ must equal $.6n + x$. So we have $.7n + .7x = .6n + x$. Solving for x gives $0.1n = 0.3x$ or $x = \frac{n}{3}$. (I-4)

4. **(E)** Since STATEMENT (1) describes only x and STATEMENT (2) describes only y, both are needed to get an answer. Using STATEMENT (2), STATEMENT (1) becomes $3x = 2k = 2y^2$, so $x = \frac{2}{3}y^2$.

However, this is not sufficient since if $y = -1$, then $x = \frac{2}{3}$ and x is greater than y, but if $y = 1$, then again $x = \frac{2}{3}$ but now x is less than y.

    Therefore, STATEMENTS (1) and (2) together are not sufficient. (II-7)

5. **(C)** $ABCD$ is a parallelogram if AB is parallel to CD and BC is parallel to AD. STATEMENT (2) tells you that AB is parallel to CD, but this is not sufficient since a trapezoid has only one pair of opposite sides parallel. Thus, STATEMENT (2) alone is not sufficient.

    STATEMENT (1) alone is not sufficient since a trapezoid can have the two nonparallel sides equal.

    However, using STATEMENTS (1) and (2) together we can deduce that BC is parallel to AD since the distance from BC to AD is equal along two different parallel lines. (III-5)

6. **(B)** A diagram always helps. You are given that *BC* and *EF* are each 2 feet. Since the area of a rectangle is length times width, you must find the length (*CE* or *BF*). Look at the triangle *ABF*. It has two equal sides (*AB* = *AF*), so the perpendicular from *A* to the line *BF* divides *ABF* into two congruent right triangles, *AHF* and *AHB*, each with hypotenuse 2.

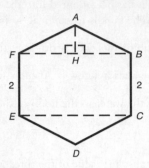

The angle *FAB* is 120° since the total of all the angles of the hexagon is 720°. So each of the two triangles is a 30° – 60° – 90° right triangle with hypotenuse 2. So *AH* = 1, and *FH* and *HB* must equal $\sqrt{3}$. Therefore, *BF* is $2\sqrt{3}$ and the area is $2 \times 2\sqrt{3} = 4\sqrt{3}$ square feet.

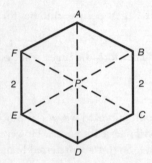

(You can find the sum of the angles of any convex polygon by connecting all vertices to a fixed interior point, *P*. In the case of the hexagon this will give 6 triangles. The total of all the triangles' angles is $6 \times 180° = 1,080°$. Since the angles at the fixed point, which are not part of the hexagon angles, will add up to 360°, the sum of the hexagon's angles is $1,080° - 360° = 720°$.) (III-3, III-4)

7. **(C)** You want the ratio of the percentage who own both a car and a motorcycle to the percentage who own a motorcycle. You know that 15 percent own a motorcycle, so you need to find the percentage who own both a car and a motorcycle. Let *A* stand for the percentage who own both a car and a motorcycle. Then (the percentage who own a car) plus (the percentage who own a motorcycle) minus *A* must equal the percentage who own one or the other or both. Since 100 percent own one or the other or both, we obtain $90\% + 15\% - A = 105\% - A = 100\%$. So $A = 5\%$. Since 15 percent own motorcycles, the percentage of motorcycle owners who own

cars is $\dfrac{5\%}{15\%} = \dfrac{1}{3} = 33\dfrac{1}{3}\%$. (II-4)

8. **(D)** To do computations, change percentages to decimals. Let *J*, *M*, *B*, and *L* stand for Jim's, Marcia's, Bob's, and Lee's respective weights. Then we know $J = 1.4M$, $B = .9L$, and $L = 2M$. We need to know *B* as a percentage of *J*. Since $B = .9L$ and $L = 2M$, we have $B = .9(2M) = 1.8M$.

$J = 1.4M$ is equivalent to $M = \left(\dfrac{1}{1.4}\right)J$. So $B = 1.8M = 1.8\left(\dfrac{1}{1.4}\right)J = \left(\dfrac{9}{7}\right)J$. Converting to a

percentage, we have $\dfrac{9}{7} = 1.28\left(\dfrac{4}{7}\right) = 128\dfrac{4}{7}\%$, so (D) is the correct answer. (Once you know

$B = \frac{9}{7}J$, this means the correct answer must be greater than 100 percent so you should guess (D) or (E) if you can't finish the problem). (II-2, I-4)

9. **(A)** Two-digit numbers are the integers from 10 to 99. Since you are told that the number is greater than 9, the only possible choices are integers 10, 11, . . ., 99.

STATEMENT (1) alone is sufficient since (1) is equivalent to $9a = b$. In this case if a is greater than 1, then $9a$ is not a digit, and if a is 0, then the number is not greater than 9. Thus there is only one possible choice, $a = 1$, which yields the number 19, which satisfies (1).

STATEMENT (2) alone is not sufficient since 19, 38, 57, 76, and 95 satisfy (2) and are two-digit numbers greater than 9.

So (A) is the correct choice. (I-1)

10. **(B)** Since 108 percent of $50 = (1.08)(50) = \$54$, the chair was offered for sale at $54.00. It was sold for 90 percent of $54 since there was a 10 percent discount. Therefore, the chair was sold for $(.9)(\$54)$ or $48.60. (I-4)

11. **(D)** k is a prime if none of the integers 2, 3, 4, . . . up to $k - 1$ divide k evenly. STATEMENT (1) alone is sufficient since if k is not a prime, then $k = (m)(n)$, where m and n must be integers less than k. But this means either m or n must be less than or equal to $\sqrt{k}$ since if m and n are both larger than $\sqrt{k}$, $(m)(n)$ is larger than $\left(\sqrt{k}\right)\left(\sqrt{k}\right)$ or k. So STATEMENT (1) implies k is a prime.

STATEMENT (2) alone is also sufficient since if $k = (m)(n)$ and m and n are both larger than $\frac{k}{2}$, then $(m)(n)$ is greater than $\frac{k^2}{4}$, but $\frac{k^2}{4}$ is greater than k when k is larger than 5.

Therefore, if no integer between 2 and $\frac{k}{2}$, inclusive divides k evenly, then k is a prime. (I-1)

12. **(B)** The towns can be thought of as the vertices of a triangle.

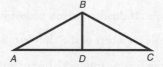

Since the distance from A to B is equal to the distance from B to C, the triangle is isosceles. The point D on AC that is closest to B is the point on AC such that BD is perpendicular to AC. (If BD were not perpendicular to AC, then there would be a point on AC closer to B than D; in the diagram, E is closer to B than D is.)

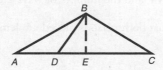

So the triangles ABD and CBD are right triangles with two corresponding sides equal. Therefore, ABD is congruent to CBD. Thus, $AD = DC$, and since AC is 60, AD must be 30. Since ABD is a right triangle with hypotenuse 50 and another side equal to 30, the remaining side (BD) must be 40. (III-4)

13. **(A)** Here's a table of the hours worked:

	Mon.	Tues.	Wed.	Thurs.	Fri.	Wages for week
Hours worked	8	8	8	8	8	$5x$
Excess worked over 8 hr	0	3	1	2	1	$(0 + 3 + 1 + 2 + 1)y = 7y$

The average daily wage equals $\dfrac{(5x + 7y)}{5}$ or $x + \dfrac{7}{5}y = x + 1.4y$. (II-3, I-7).

14. **(B)** There are 8 choices for the first female, then 7 choices for the second female, and 6 choices for the third female on the committee. So there are $8 \times 7 \times 6$ different ways to pick the 3 females in order. However, if member A is chosen first, then member B, and then member C, the same 3 females are chosen as when C is followed by A and B is chosen last. In fact, the same 3 members can be chosen in $3 \times 2 \times 1$ different orders. So to find the number of different groups of 3 females, DIVIDE $(8 \times 7 \times 6)$ by $(3 \times 2 \times 1)$ to obtain 56.

In the same way, there are $8 \times 7 \times 6 = 336$ ways to choose the 3 males in order, but any group of 3 males can be put in order $3 \times 2 \times 1 = 6$ different ways. So there are $\dfrac{336}{6} = 56$ different groups of 3 males. Therefore, there are $56 \times 56 = 3{,}136$ different committees. (II-4)

15. **(D)** Since we are given the fact that 100 miles is the distance from A to B, it is sufficient to find the distance from C to B. This is so because 100 minus the distance from C to B is the distance from A to C. STATEMENT (1) says that 125 percent of the distance from C to B is 100 miles. Thus, we can find the distance from C to B, which is sufficient. Since the distance from A to C plus the distance from C to B is the distance from A to B, we can use STATEMENT (2) to set up the equation 5 times the distance from A to C equals 100 miles.

Therefore, STATEMENTS (1) and (2) are each sufficient. (II-3)

16. **(A)** Each member has a $\dfrac{1}{15}$ chance to be the first one picked. So the probability that the first person picked is female is $\dfrac{5}{15}$. If the first person picked is female, then there are 14 tickets left in the box with only 4 female members of the club left. So the probability that the second person picked is female if the first person picked was female is $\dfrac{4}{14}$. In order for both persons to be female, the first person must be female and then the second person must be female, so the probability that both persons are female is $\left(\dfrac{5}{15}\right)\left(\dfrac{4}{14}\right) = \dfrac{2}{21}$.

Another method of solving the problem follows. The number of ways the 2 tickets can be picked in order is 15×14, and the number of ways 2 females can be picked in order is 5×4. So the probability that both persons picked are female is $\left(\dfrac{5 \times 4}{15 \times 14}\right) = \left(\dfrac{1}{3}\right)\left(\dfrac{2}{7}\right) = \dfrac{2}{21}$.

(I-7 or II-4)

17. **(C)** Since the standard deviation is 5 percent, 2 standard deviations is 10 percent. The mean is 82 percent, so the score that is 2 standard deviations above the mean is 82% + 10% = 92 percent. Notice that this problem really has nothing to do with statistics because all you need to do is plug in the values. (II-3)

18. **(B)** STATEMENT (2) alone is sufficient since $x = y$ implies $x - y = 0$.

STATEMENT (1) alone is not sufficient. An infinite number of pairs satisfy STATEMENT (1), for example, $x = 2$, $y = 2$, for which $x - y = 0$, and $x = 4$, $y = 1$, for which $x - y = 3$. (II-2)

19. **(E)** Since there is no information on how many of the eligible voters are men or how many are women, STATEMENTS (1) and (2) together are not sufficient. (II-4)

20. **(C)** Let x_n be what the motorcycle is worth after n years. Then we know $x_0 = \$2,500$ and $x_{n+1} = .8x_n$. So $x_1 = .8 \times 2,500$, which is \$2,000. x_2 is $.8 \times 2,000$, which is 1,600, and finally x_3 is $.8 \times 1,600$, which is 1,280. Therefore, the motorcycle is worth \$1,280 at the end of three years *or* $x_3 = .8x_2 = .8(.8x_1) = .8(.8)(.8\ x_0) = .512 \times 2,500 = 1,280$. (II-6)

21. **(B)** Simply use the properties of inequalities to solve the given inequality. Subtract $12x$ from each side to get $-5x - 5 < 18$. Next add 5 to each side to obtain $-5x < 23$. Finally, divide each side by -5 to get $x > -23/5$. Remember that if you divide each side of an inequality by a negative number, the inequality is reversed. You can make a quick check of your answer by using $x = -5$, which is not greater than $-\dfrac{23}{5}$, and $x = -4$, which is greater than $-\dfrac{23}{5}$ in the original inequality. Since $x = -5$ does not satisfy the original inequality (-40 is not less than -42) and $x = -4$ does satisfy the inequality (-33 is less than -30), the answer is correct. You could use the method of checking values to find the correct answer, but it would take longer. (II-7)

22. **(C)** Draw the radii from O to each of the vertices. These lines divide the hexagon into six triangles. STATEMENT (2) says that all the triangles are congruent since each of their pairs of corresponding sides is equal. Since there are 360° in a circle, the central angle of each triangle is 60°. And, since all radii are equal, each angle of the triangle equals 60°. Therefore, the triangles are equilateral, and AB is equal to the radius of the circle. Thus, if we assume STATEMENT (1), we know the length of AB. Without STATEMENT (1), we can't find the length of AB.

Also, STATEMENT (1) alone is not sufficient since AB need not equal the radius unless the hexagon is regular. (III-4)

23. **(B)** STATEMENT (2) alone is sufficient. If (2) holds, then $\dfrac{32}{(32 + 5,678)}$ represents the ratio of defective items to total items produced. Since any fraction can be changed into a percentage by multiplying by 100, STATEMENT (2) alone is sufficient.

STATEMENT (1) alone is not sufficient since the total number of items produced is also needed to find the percentage of defective items.

Therefore, (B) is the correct choice. (II-5, I-4)

24. **(D)** Since 20 was added to each age, the mean of the listed ages will be 20 more than the mean of the actual ages. [Note that this means you can eliminate (B), (C), and (E) and that you should guess (A) or (D) if you can't solve the problem.] The standard deviation and the range of a list measure how spread out the data is; adding the same number to every measurement in the list will not change either of these, so the correct answer is (D). (I-7)

25. **(A)** STATEMENT (1) alone is sufficient. Since $3^2 + 4^2 = 5^2$, ABC is a right triangle by the Pythagorean theorem.

STATEMENT (2) alone is not sufficient since you can choose a point D so that $AC = CD$ for *any* triangle ABC. (III-4)

26. **(E)** (1) and (2) are not sufficient. The price of food could rise for other reasons besides the price of energy rising.

27. **(B)** Let M, J, and K be the amounts paid by Mary, John, and Karen, respectively. Then

$K = 1.5J$, $M = \left(\dfrac{5}{6}\right)K$, and $M = J + 2$. So M, which is $\dfrac{5}{6}K$, must be $\left(\dfrac{5}{6}\right)(1.5)J = \left(\dfrac{5}{6}\right)\left(\dfrac{3}{2}\right)J = \dfrac{5}{4}J$.

Therefore, we have $\left(\dfrac{5}{4}\right)J = J + 2$ or $\left(\dfrac{1}{4}\right)J = 2$, which means $J = 8$. So $K = 1.5J$, or 12, and

$M = J + 2$, or 10. So the total is $8 + 12 + 10 = \$30$. (II-2)

28. **(E)** The number who subscribed to at least one magazine is the sum of the numbers who subscribed to exactly one, two, and three magazines. So $38 = N1 + N2 + N3$, where $N1$, $N2$, and $N3$ are the number who subscribed to 1, 2, and 3 magazines, respectively. We need to find $N2$. STATEMENT (1) is not sufficient since it gives the value of $N3$ but $N1$ and $N2$ are still both unknown. Even if we also use STATEMENT (1), we cannot find $N2$ since we have no information about the number of subscribers to magazines B and C. (II-4)

29. **(E)** STATEMENT (1) is insufficient since 9 (which is odd) and 6 (which is even) are both divisible by 3.

STATEMENT (2) is also insufficient since $\sqrt{81}$ and $\sqrt{36}$ are both divisible by 3. Both 81 and 36 are divisible by 3, so (1) and (2) together are still insufficient.

30. **(A)** The angles are in the ratio 1 : 2 : 2, so two angles are equal to each other and both are twice as large as the third angle of the triangle. Since a triangle with two equal angles must have the sides opposite equal, the triangle is isosceles. (Using the fact that the sum of the angles of a triangle is 180°, you can see that the angles of the triangle are 72°, 72°, and 36°, so only (A) is true.) (III-4)

31. **(C)** (1) alone is obviously insufficient. To use (2) you need to know what the painting was worth at some time between 1988 and 1997. So (2) alone is insufficient, but by using (1) and (2) together you can figure out the worth of the painting in January 1991. NOTE: You should not waste time actually figuring out the value. (II-6)

32. **(D)** (1) alone is sufficient since the rule enables you to compute all successive values once you know a_1. Also, the rule and (1) tell you that the numbers in the sequence will always increase. Thus, since $a_2 = 4$, 3 will never appear. In the same way, by using (2) and the rule for the sequence, you can determine that $a_2 = 4$ and a_1 is 2 or -2, so the reasoning used above shows that 3 will never appear. (II-6)

33. **(B)** The area of the wall is 11 feet × 20 feet = 220 square feet. Since a large roll of wallpaper gives more square feet per dollar, you should try to use large rolls. Since $\dfrac{220}{60} = 3$ with a remainder of 40, if you buy 3 large rolls, which cost $3 \times \$25 = \$75$, you will have enough to cover the entire wall, except for 40 square feet. You can cover 40 square feet by either buying 1 large roll or 4 small rolls. A large roll costs \$25 but 4 small rolls cost only \$24. So the minimum cost is $\$75 + \$24 = \$99$. (II-3)

34. **(D)** If there are x red marbles and y green marbles in the jar, then $(y + 1)$ marbles must contain at least one red marble. So it is sufficient to know the number of red marbles and the number of green marbles. Since you are given that $x + y = 60$, STATEMENT (2) is obviously sufficient. Also, STATEMENT (1) is sufficient since it implies that $x = 2y$, which enables you to find x and y. Therefore, the correct answer choice is (D).

35. **(C)** STATEMENT (2) alone is not sufficient. −1 is less than 2, and $\frac{1}{-1}$ is less than $\frac{1}{2}$, but 1 is less than 2 and $\frac{1}{1}$ is greater than $\frac{1}{2}$.

STATEMENT (1) alone is insufficient since there is no information about y.

STATEMENT (1) and (2) together imply that x and y are both greater than 1, and for two positive numbers x and y, if x is less than y, then $\frac{1}{x}$ is greater than $\frac{1}{y}$.

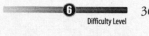

36. **(E)** Since C is closer to A, if plane X is flying faster than plane Y, it will certainly fly over C before plane Y. However, if plane X flies slower than plane Y, and C is very close to A, plane X will still fly over C before plane Y does. Thus, STATEMENTS (1) and (2) together are not sufficient. (II-3)

37. **(A)** To compare two fractions, the fractions must have the same denominator. The least common denominator for both fractions is 120. Using this fact, $\frac{x}{12} = \frac{10x}{120}$ and $\frac{y}{40} = \frac{3y}{120}$. So the relation between the fractions is the same as the relation between $10x$ and $3y$. Therefore, STATEMENT (1) alone is sufficient. STATEMENT (2) alone is not sufficient. Using $y = 13$ and $x = 4$, STATEMENT (2) is true and $\frac{x}{12}$ is greater than $\frac{y}{40}$. However, using $y = 10$ and $x = 2$, STATEMENT (2) is still true, but now $\frac{x}{12}$ is less than $\frac{y}{40}$. (I-2)

Answers Explained

Verbal Section

1. **(C)** See paragraph 2.

2. **(C)** See paragraph 3: "Top Presidential appointees, . . . bear the brunt of translating the philosophy and aims of the current administration into practical programs."

3. **(C)** See paragraph 4, sentence 2.

4. **(E)** See paragraph 4, last line.

5. **(D)** Analysis of the two sentences indicates the presence of an assumption that anyone who has had at least five traffic violations in a year is a terrible driver. This assumption is understood but is not stated. Rather, it is a hidden assumption, making (D) the appropriate answer. Alternative (A) is incorrect because there is no attack on the source of the claim. (B) is wrong because there is no appeal to authority—illegitimate or not. (C) is not the correct answer because there is no comparison of two similar situations in the statement. (E) is incorrect because there is no term with a confusing or double meaning.

6. **(C)** The best conclusion that can be drawn from the statement is one that sums up the facts that are given in one sentence; thus, (C) is the best answer. Although the given paragraph states that if there is devaluation of the dollar, American imports will become more expensive, this will not necessarily be a disadvantage for the U.S. economy. Hence, (A) is not appropriate. Alternative (B) is also inappropriate, because it highlights a disadvantage that may arise from the expectation of devaluation, but which is not dealt with in the paragraph. Alternatives (D) and (E) are both helpful pieces of information, but they cannot be concluded from the given text.

7. **(D)** Do not use *calculate* or *reckon* when you mean *think*.

8. **(E)** Since the words *but also* precede a phrase, to *one of eight or even six*, the words *not only* should precede a phrase, *to one of ten hours*. This error in parallel structure is corrected in choice E.

9. **(E)** According to the passage, all people cannot take aspirin without undesirable side effects, and in some cases, the danger caused by aspirin itself outweighs its benefits. The passage, by saying "On balance, however, for men aged 40 and over, an aspirin a day may present. . . ." also implies that not all, but only some people (men over 40) should take an aspirin a day. Alternative answer (A) clearly cannot be concluded from the passage. Answer alternative (B) is also inappropriate. No painkiller other than aspirin is mentioned in the passage, and it cannot be inferred that all painkillers reduce the "stickiness" of platelets. (C) is incorrect. Smoking is not mentioned in the passage and since studies of the effects of smoking and aspirin have not been reported, no conclusions can be drawn. (D) is wrong because the statistics given in the passage say that 15% of second heart attack victims were saved from death by taking aspirin, and 15% does not constitute a majority. (E) is the correct choice since it simply states that mortality rates can be reduced in patients who have already suffered a heart attack (as stated in the passage), without giving any specific statistics.

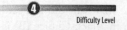

10. **(A)** It is fact that athletes can attract sponsorship and make money and that participation in the Olympics can aid this process. On the basis that it is true that athletes are more and more attracted by the profit motive, the conclusion that the best athletes do not compete in the Olympics is weakened. Therefore, A is the appropriate answer. Alternative (B) is an oft-stated maxim, but in this case, it is not relevant to the argument. The fact that people believe that amateur athletes are receiving adequate alternative remuneration does not bear on the argument for allowing genuine professional athletes into the games. So, (C) is inappropriate. Choice (D) comes close to weakening the argument, because if professional (as well as amateur) athletes were allowed to compete, presuming the participants were selected on merit, then the best athletes would be seen. However, it has only been a suggestion, perhaps in the past, (in which case it was not adopted) or in the future (in which case its adoption is not certain). Choice (E) represents an opinion that might or might not be held by the writer, but, whether or not the author agrees, it does not weaken the argument; therefore (E) is inappropriate.

11. **(B)** "He" is the subject of the sentence which takes who as the relative pronoun.

12. **(A)** No error.

13. **(C)** The paragraph demonstrates from beginning to end that the function of the food technologist is to prevent unfit foodstuffs from being marketed by the stores and passed on to the consumer, who relies on the store's control procedures. (C), therefore, is the most appropriate answer. Answer alternative (A) is inappropriate because it cannot be inferred from the text (even if it were true). Answer (B) and possibly answer (D) are factually correct, but these conclusions cannot be drawn from the text itself. (E) is not a correct interpretation of the facts; random checking is not the best way, since below-standard goods are caught in the net only by chance.

14. **(C)** This choice does not violate parallel structure.

15. **(A)** The dropout rate on average for all Open Admissions students was 48%; for regular students, 36%; and for Open Admissions categories, 56%.

16. **(B)** See paragraph 1: "The successful institution of higher learning had never been one whose mission could be defined in terms of providing vocational skills or . . . resolving societal problems." This is the sort of question that must be read carefully; it asks for an answer that is not among the alternatives given in the passage.

17. **(D)** The idea that a university must relate to the problems of society is given in paragraph 2.

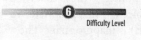

18. **(B)** The attrition rate for Open Admissions students was 56 percent, and that for regular students 36 percent, a difference of 20 percent.

19. **(C)** Choice C corrects errors in the possessive form of *government* (needed before a verbal noun) and *it*.

20. **(C)** This is also an error in agreement: *Kind* is singular and requires a singular modifier (*this*).

21. **(B)** The correct idiom is *graduate from*. The active case is preferred to the passive used in choice C. Choice D adds an unnecessary word, *into*.

22. **(C)** John's decision is to experiment with the new longer (in mileage) route for two weeks, and it is this decision that we have to consider. Choice (C), by offering a third alternative, gives John another possibility and, therefore, another outcome. It may affect his decision, and therefore, is the appropriate answer. Alternatives (A), (B), and (D) alter factors within the calculation affecting the decision, but taken individually and not making any other changes, will definitely not result in a different decision being made. These three are, therefore, not appropriate answers. The existence of a definite answer—in this case, (C)—means that alternative (E) is not appropriate.

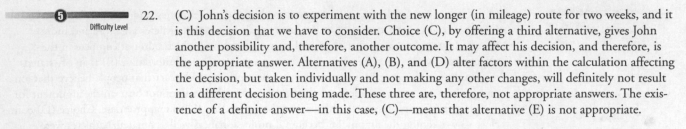

23. **(B)** There is only one argument in the passage based on two separate premises upon which the writer has based his conclusion. Choice (A) is inappropriate because there is no other argument. Choice (C) is incorrect because the qualities are the same (grey). (D) is inappropriate because the description is not ambiguous, and (E) is wrong because the writer has stated an argument—albeit invalid.

24. **(C)** Here we have a chain of events where the conclusion of one argument becomes the premise for another. Only (C) can be concluded from the facts given in the passage—that is, because Sally overslept she ran toward school, and because she ran, she did not notice the hole. Choice (A) is inappropriate because the chain of events is not linked by the fact that Sally did not eat her breakfast. The passage does not include a consequence emanating from that fact. Choice (B) is not appropriate because there is no way to link Sally's friend to the events in the passage. Similarly, facts not included preclude (D) from being the appropriate answer. Finally, (E) cannot be inferred, as we do not know what Sally did later that day; she may have been released from the hospital and gone to school.

25. **(D)** Massification, as it is termed in paragraph 3. While there are increased enrollments (A), these are a function of massification. None of the other alternatives is mentioned.

26. **(B)** The passage is about the business of education, or "brains." Alternatives (A) and (E) are mentioned, but they don't touch on the central idea. There is no basis for (C) or (D). Oxford University and other tradition-oriented universities are not in decline. (D) is not mentioned at all.

27. **(E)** Traditional universities are being forced to compete for students (last paragraph). There is no mention of the other alternatives.

28. **(B)** See paragraph 1. The old universities' attempt to maintain their image, whereas younger ones try to "create an aura of antiquity" (paragraph 1). It is true that younger universities compete with older ones, but that is the second-best answer.

29. **(A)** See paragraph 3. There are better-educated high school graduates, forcing universities to undergo change (paragraph 3).

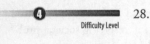

30. **(B)** This answer is given in paragraph 5. One of the major forces for change in higher education is the globalization of the industry. None of the other alternatives is mentioned.

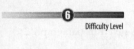

31. **(E)** Services will be improved, it is hoped, for a certain segment of customers—those that shop during the rush hours—but not for all customers. This fact makes choice (A) inappropriate. To attract new customers is not stated in the passage as an objective, so (B) is inappropriate. The utilization of excess capacity, as in (C) is a useful byproduct of the new system, but it is not the main goal. If maintenance costs are kept low, it will probably make the achievement of the main goal that much easier, but this is not the major objective so choice (D) is not appropriate. The principal purpose of the owners is to make more money from the change, by increasing income more than the added costs. Therefore, (E) is the appropriate answer.

6 Difficulty Level

32. **(C)** Encouraging couples to remain childless would have a negative social effect and would not be practical, so answer alternative (A) is not a reasonable suggestion. The income loss involved in having one child is not much more than that involved in having two or more children (assuming the loss of the income of one parent or the expense of child care), so suggestion (B) is also invalid. If couples move to cheaper areas in the country, as suggested in (D), the chances are that work would be less available or possibly that the couple would have a less positive economic future, so the change may not necessarily be financially advantageous. If fathers stayed at home rather than mothers, there would be no improvement in financial status, so suggestion (E) is invalid. Suggestion (C) is the only sensible solution, since financial stability is likely to increase with the length of time in employment.

4 Difficulty Level

33. **(C)** This corrects the two errors in this sentence—the error in case (*me* for *I*) and the error in tense (*had finished* for *finished*).

8 Difficulty Level

34. **(D)** *Despite* should be used as a preposition, not as a word joining clauses.

8 Difficulty Level

35. **(E)** Even if the rate of increase in demand has slowed from 10% per annum to 5% per annum over the last five years, that means that demand is still increasing at 5% per annum. If, as the passage states, demand continues to grow at the present rate—that is, by 5% per annum—the world's resources will be used up by the year 2050. Therefore, the argument is not weakened by the statement in answer alternative (A). Choice (B) introduces the matter of supply, but apparently the reserves in Antarctica have been known for some time, and this, therefore, does not affect the argument that stocks will be depleted unless new reserves are found. Choice (C) informs us that there is an alternative to coal which is being used increasingly. However, the questions of the supply of and the rate of growth of demand for oil do not affect the argument in the paragraph. Choice (D) states an economic fact of life that will have to be faced if the statements in the paragraph are true. It may lead to a search for alternative fuels and consequent decrease in demand for coal, but this is uncertain and cannot be inferred. So, neither (A), (B), (C), or (D) are appropriate. Choice (E) is, therefore, the correct answer.

4 Difficulty Level

36. **(B)** Choice (A) contains an important point which would have been considered in setting the maximum treatment level. So it does not weaken the argument of the authorities and is inappropriate. Choice (C) is incorrect as the passage states that the authorities are carrying out this policy in accordance with their powers. Choice (D) is a fact that would be acknowledged by both sides and weakens neither's case, while choice (E) is also a well-known fact, which like the fact in (A), would have been taken into consideration by the researchers, so it is also not appropriate. The fact that the authorities have no record of the long-term good or damage of fluoridation is a significant weakness in their case, and therefore, (B) is the appropriate answer.

5 Difficulty Level

37. **(C)** This was an unnecessary shift of pronoun. Do not shift from *you* to *one*. Choice D changes the meaning unnecessarily.

3 Difficulty Level

38. **(C)** The demonstrative pronoun *those* is needed here—*from those* (persons).

3 Difficulty Level

39. **(E)** Choice E corrects the misuse of the word *too*.

3 Difficulty Level

40. **(B)** Choice (A) is vague, while (D) equates service trade with legislation. Choice (C) is irrelevant to the argument. (E) comes close to summarizing the argument, but it is incomplete; uncoordinated is not an antonym for coherent.

8 Difficulty Level

41. **(C)** Active verbs are preferred to passive verbs.

EVALUATING YOUR SCORE

Tabulate your score for each section of the Diagnostic Test according to the directions on page 12 and record the results in the Self-Scoring Table below. Then find your rating for each score on the Self-Scoring Scale and record it in the appropriate blank.

Self-Scoring Table

Section	Score	Rating
Quantitative		
Verbal		

Self-Scoring Scale—RATING

Section	Poor	Fair	Good	Excellent
Quantitative	0–15	15–25	26–30	31–37
Verbal	0–15	15–25	26–30	31–41

Study again the Review sections covering material in Sample Test 2 for which you had a rating of FAIR or POOR.

BUSINESS SCHOOL BASICS

Why Go to Graduate Business School?

CHAPTER 12

Going to a graduate school of business is a considerable investment of time and money. For a full-time student, the cost will be anywhere from $30,000 to $125,000 for two years of study. A part-time student may expect to pay less, but he or she will have to spend as many as four years or more to complete the degree.

Despite the cost and time involved, a growing number of students feel that attending graduate business school is worthwhile. About 275,000 students are enrolled in MBA courses. Each year about 120,000 students receive a master's in business—more than any other advanced degree except for the master's in education. Applications for admission to graduate business schools continue to increase.

Why is a master's in business, and the MBA in particular, so popular? The main reason is that it is so highly regarded by the business world. Business firms are anxious to hire these graduates, and they are willing to pay higher salaries to those who have the degree. In a growing number of major firms that have extensive management development programs, such programs are open only to those with a relevant master's.

Businesses are concentrating more and more on these graduates because they find that graduate business training gives them valuable background and sophistication in business subjects. Companies have discovered that these graduates learn new jobs more quickly, are able to shoulder responsibilities sooner, and earn promotions faster than those lacking graduate business preparation. Therefore, with a variety of candidates having business backgrounds to choose from, many business firms would rather hire someone with a master's in business than someone with only an undergraduate degree in business. Talk to the personnel directors of many large firms, and they will point out that those with a master's in business not only can move into initial jobs easily but also have the skills and background necessary to learn new fields and deal with new business techniques and strategies. The complexity of business has increased enormously in recent years. Growth of multinational corporations and the radical changes brought about by computers, and the emphasis on total quality management are important new developments on the business scene, and these are usually part of the curriculum of any graduate business school. Graduate business students also learn the latest theories in finance, organizational structure and behavior, marketing theory, international trade, and dozens of other subjects that have immediate or future application in the business world. Companies want people with backgrounds that include such knowledge.

Companies are also willing to pay a premium for those with a graduate business degree. Starting salaries for those holding master's degrees in business administration often average $15,000 to $60,000 a year more than for those who graduate with just a bachelor's degree. In some cases, if you go to a prestigious graduate business school, job offers can run as much as $75,000 a year more than what you would receive with only a bachelor's degree in business.

Statistical records on the achievements of these students are still sketchy, so it is difficult to determine how all do financially or employment-wise over a period of time. However, some business schools do keep track of their graduates' job success. Twenty-five years out of school, one third of the Harvard MBAs are CEOs, managing directors, partners, or owners of companies. Obviously, Harvard is not a typical business school. However, even though most other business schools cannot boast of such a record, most placement directors can cite dozens of their graduates who have moved into top jobs in business. In a recent *Business Week* magazine list of the 1,000 largest companies in the United States, over 25 percent of the chief executive officers had MBAs.

Looking at a master's in business from a student's point of view, here are the advantages:

- The courses give you a broad background and training in business and sophisticated business skills.
- In a tight job market, you might have an advantage in finding a job that a person with only a bachelor's degree does not have. (It is important to keep in mind that the better the business school you attend, the better your chances of getting a job and at higher pay.)
- The odds are substantial that you will get a higher starting salary than you would with only a bachelor's degree.
- If you are interested in being chosen for a management development program by any of the country's top corporations, it is very advantageous to have a relevant master's (usually from a leading business school).
- If you are interested in going into your own business, you will find that your graduate courses will help you very much in your own business.
- If you are interested in getting chosen for a "fast track" program at some companies—which permits you to bypass or speed through the typical entry-level jobs—you will find a master's degree quite useful in most cases.
- Minority group members will find many companies anxious to locate and hire them for managerial positions if they have completed a graduate business program. Most companies are under great pressure from federal government agencies to increase the number of minority group employees in their management ranks. These firms intensively recruit minority students with graduate business degrees.
- Business is under considerable pressure to hire women for managerial posts, and companies are looking mainly for those with graduate business degrees. Currently, more than one third of all MBA students are women. Women who have graduate business degrees will find job and pay opportunities much better today. This doesn't mean that women will get paid the same as men holding identical degrees, but they will have greater job leverage than they have had before. Part of the current difference in starting pay between male and female graduates may result from job experience. Many men have had several years of prior work experience, and business firms are willing to pay more for this extra experience.
- Getting a graduate business degree at night or through distance learning is often a valuable alternative for individuals who find themselves stifled in their present situations. It can help them move out of dead-end jobs in their present firms, or into growth positions with other firms.
- If you aren't seeking a career in the business world, but plan a career in law, health administration, public administration, or a variety of other fields, possession of an advanced business degree and the knowledge it represents can be valuable. Even in creative fields or health care, a growing number of people desiring to become managers of opera companies or art museums find this training helpful. This is one reason more students are deciding to take joint programs that combine the study of business with that of law, architecture, or other disciplines.
- There are also a growing number of situations where "career changers," individuals who decide they want to make a major career change in their 30s and 40s, are enrolling as MBA students. A number of doctors, lawyers, and other professionals, as well as artists and teachers, have decided that entering the business world is a smart move.

YOUR DEGREE

Master of Business Administration (MBA)

Most graduate schools of business award the MBA degree, but many schools award other graduate business degrees. Some of these degrees are equivalent to the MBA, while others are not.

Basically, most full-time MBA programs are designed to be two-year courses of study that give students a broad background in a wide range of business subjects. MBA programs usually require students to take a substantial number of core courses in basic business areas such as accounting, finance, marketing, and management. MBA candidates also take other required general and specialized courses in business and are often permitted to take electives from the business school curriculum or from that of other schools within the university. In terms of credits, the MBA program usually requires from 36 to 60 semester hours. Students with strong undergraduate business backgrounds may be able to finish an MBA program by taking as few as 30 credit hours. (Most other master's degrees offered by business schools are either degrees that require fewer courses than the MBA or degrees that are quite specialized.) Only a small number of schools grant the MBA after only one year's graduate study. But there seems to be a trend in that direction as costs of getting an MBA grow. Notre Dame, Babson, Pittsburgh, Rollins, Kellogg, University of Georgia, and Pepperdine are among the more than 40 schools that offer one-year MBA programs. Texas A & M has a 16-month program.

Specific degree requirements vary from school to school. Some programs require the student to take only specified courses, while others grant considerable leeway in the courses each student can select. The same is true of research requirements and examinations at the completion of the course work. A large number of schools require a student to pass either an oral or a written comprehensive examination before he or she is eligible for the degree. Some schools require that each student submit a thesis.

The thesis represents a considerable body of research and usually counts as six hours of credit. It provides the opportunity for intensive study of a problem selected by the student, who then works under the supervision of a faculty adviser or committee. At many schools, course work is submitted in lieu of a thesis requirement.

Also, many schools require that students earn a minimum grade-point average of B (3.0 on a 4.0 scale). Other schools require them to show proficiency in various fields or topics related to the study of business. For example, at Boston University, information systems is a required part of the curriculum. There is generally a time limit on how long a student can take to finish any graduate business degree; this usually varies from five to seven years.

As a potential MBA student, you should study the differences in program requirements very carefully. If you think that writing a thesis would be too difficult an undertaking, concentrate on those schools that don't require one. You should also see if the school is strong in the business field you are most interested in. For example, the University of Illinois and Wharton are outstanding in accounting. Kellogg is a leader in marketing. MIT and Carnegie Mellon are leaders in production and operation management; Thunderbird, NYU, and University of South Carolina in international business; and Wharton, Chicago, and NYU in finance. Babson is a leader in entrepreneurship. The University of Texas offers 15 courses in entrepreneurship. If you are interested in getting your MBA as quickly as possible, look into those schools whose degree requirements are less demanding.

The same careful study of graduation requirements is important for those who plan to get their degrees as part-time students. It normally takes at least three to five years to earn an MBA on a part-time basis. This means that the number of required courses is an important consideration in determining the length of time you will have to attend school to earn your degree.

Alternatives to the MBA

The MBA is a very popular degree, but it isn't the only worthwhile one. There are other graduate business degrees, such as the Master of Science in Business (MSB) or the Master of Science in Business Administration (MSBA), which can usually be earned with only 30 hours of course work. This type of alternative program may give you the business courses you want without forcing you to take additional courses required by the MBA. Master's degrees are also offered in a variety of business subjects such as accounting and management science. Such programs are undertaken by those students who want to concentrate in a specific field and are not interested in the broader requirements of the MBA.

While the great majority of degrees awarded are MBAs, here are some of the special business- or management-related master's programs offered in addition to the MBA. The University of California at Los Angeles (UCLA) has a Master of Science in Management (MSM) program that prepares students to conduct substantial research in management science. The Master of Science in Accounting (MSA) degree at DePaul University offers a heavy concentration in accounting. The University of Southern California offers a Master of Business Taxation (MBT) or a Master of Accounting (MAcc). The University of Denver has an International MBA and a Master of Taxation (MT) through its law school. Fordham University in New York offers an MBA in Communications and Media Management. The Stuart School at Illinois Institute of Technology (IIT) now offers an MS in Financial Markets and Trading, an MS in Environmental Management, and an MS in Marketing Communications. Carnegie offers an MS in Electronic Commerce.

In 2004 more than 12,000 students received their graduate degrees in public administration. This increasingly popular alternative to the MBA is finding favor with students seeking professional positions in various levels of government. Many public administration programs throughout the country have changed their curricula to include more business skills materials.

Basically, the degrees just mentioned are for those students who already know what field of business they want and who desire a more specialized business education. The disadvantage of those degree programs is the fact that most companies seeking job candidates with a well-rounded business education want MBA graduates, not those with the more specialized master's degrees. Also, although the MBA commands a sizable salary differential over a bachelor's degree in business, the same differential is not always commanded by the master of science degree in business or its equivalent. However, some special degrees, such as the Master in Taxation, are in heavy demand.

Special Programs

Joint MBA Programs

If you are interested in combining business training with another professional discipline, a growing number of universities offer MBA programs (and sometimes other master's in business degrees) in conjunction with other professional degrees. The major advantage here is that the combined programs usually enable a student to save both time and money. For example, the combined MBA/JD (business/law) degree program takes four years of full-time study; separately, the programs would normally take five years.

Probably the MBA/JD is the most popular combined program, and this is offered by more than 40 universities, including Michigan, Pennsylvania (Wharton), Columbia, Virginia, Stanford, Harvard, Cornell, Chicago, Washington (St. Louis), and Boston. But there are other combination programs as well, and one may be perfectly suited to your career needs. Several schools offer MBAs combined with architecture and urban planning. Columbia Business School has a three-year program with its School of Architecture that grants a degree in urban planning along with the MBA. At Washington University, there are joint MBA/MSW (social work) and MBA/MArch programs. Boston University offers an MBA in combination with a Master of Science in Manufacturing Engineering. Columbia offers the MBA combined with journalism, and the Wharton School (University of Pennsylvania) offers the MBA/MSE (engineering) among other programs. Boston also offers an MBA/MS in Television Management with the School of Public Communication and an MBA/MA in Economics with the Graduate School. The University of Michigan has initiated joint degree programs with the Institute of Public Policy Studies (MBA/MPP), the Music School (MBA/MM), and 14 other schools or units within the university. Washington University also offers an MBA/MA Eastern Asian Studies degree. A decade ago, 10 graduate business schools made an arrangement with several nursing schools to offer a joint MBA/MSN degree program. Some of the graduate business schools taking part are Michigan, Texas, Virginia, Vanderbilt, and Columbia. Dartmouth's Tuck School and Medical School offer a joint MBA/MD program. Each year, the number of joint programs increases substantially.

The actual structures of the combined programs vary widely. For instance, take the business/law program. At many schools you spend the first year in law school, then go to business school for the second year. You then take the third and fourth years in the law school while squeezing in some business courses during these two years. In other joint programs, each semester offers almost equal numbers of business courses and courses in the other degree field.

The major advantage of the joint program, as indicated earlier, is that it can be completed in a shorter time than by taking the two degree programs separately. However, by pursuing a joint program, you might find yourself becoming academically overqualified for your career needs. An MBA is advantageous for a lawyer if he or she plans to go into corporate work. However, an individual might find it better to go to law school, decide on what legal specialty he or she wants, and then pursue a graduate business degree part time if it will be helpful in the chosen field of concentration. Before deciding on a joint program, it is wise to discuss it with prospective employers.

Still another problem with some of the joint programs is the fact that you usually have to apply and be admitted separately to each of the graduate schools. In other words, if you want to get into a joint MBA/JD program you will have to be admitted to both the law school and the business school separately. This means that if you are contemplating going into a joint program, you will have to do more planning when you are a college senior. Since it is difficult now to gain admission to law schools, you might have to send out a great many applications. Also, since law school is the harder school to get into, the quality of the business school you attend will be determined by the law schools that accept you. If you were going to business school alone, you might have a chance to be admitted by a number of leading ones, but if you can only get into a mediocre law school, chances are that the university's business school may also be mediocre.

For part-time students, a joint MBA program seems out of the question because of the great amount of time involved. On a part-time basis a joint program might run as long as 10 years, and few schools would encourage a part-time student to get involved in such a long-range undertaking.

Foreign Study

If you would like to combine graduate business study at a foreign university with study at an American business school, you will find a number of programs that offer foreign study. The reason is that most American graduate business programs are only one or two years long, and schools want to provide the complete program rather than share it with a foreign university where there may be substantial problems of coordination and supervision of programs between campuses located thousands of miles apart.

However, a substantial number of graduate business schools do offer programs that involve study abroad. For example, the Wharton School has exchange programs of one semester each. Students go in the fall semester to the London Business School, the Delft (Holland) Graduate Management School, the Institut Supérieur des Affaires in Paris, Stockholm School of Economics, or Universidad de Navarra at Barcelona. There is an MBA program at the NYU Stern School of Business in which second-year students may study one term at any one of 31 schools in 24 countries. The University of Chicago and Cornell University have long-standing, formal exchange programs, and the University of California at Berkeley, the University of Washington, and the Tuck School at Dartmouth College also have exchange programs. Washington now has 14 exchange partners in 13 countries. The Kellogg School of Management at Northwestern participates in numerous exchange programs with European and Asian graduate schools and also offers global issues courses that culminate in two-week trips abroad to meet business leaders in the country or region studied. Boston University offers an International Management Program in Kobe, Japan, and Shanghai, China, where selected MBA students may complete specific MBA coursework. The University of Hawaii has a cooperative program with the Institute for International Studies and Training in Fujinomiya, Japan, and an exchange program with Keio University's Graduate School of Business in Yokohama, Japan. At the University of California at Berkeley, students can spend the fall term of their second year at one of seven leading business schools abroad and Columbia University in New York. A number of U.S. graduate business schools are members of the Programme International de Management to facilitate exchange programs with business schools worldwide.

Dartmouth now offers an exchange program with the International University of Japan, which has recently established an MBA program in Niigata, Japan. The program, taught in English, is the first such business school in Japan and has been modeled after the program at Tuck.

The University of Michigan now has 14 different foreign exchange programs. The University of Chicago has recently opened a campus in Singapore and already has one in Barcelona. It now has exchange programs with 33 schools in 21 countries and in seven languages.

Interestingly, Arthur D. Little, the management consulting firm in Cambridge, Massachusetts, has the accredited Arthur D. Little School of Management, which offers an 11-month Master of Science in Management degree to a class that is usually 90 percent international, typically representing dozens of countries.

Actually, most of these foreign study programs are mainly for those students who have already decided upon their careers and feel it is to their advantage to be able to speak a foreign language fluently, get to know a foreign country fairly well, and be aware of the special business practices and philosophies of a specific foreign country. Usually, though, students don't have overseas work as their career goal. For them, spending time at a university overseas may provide an interesting experience, but it could lengthen the time needed to get the graduate business degree. Also, it is often true that the student usually does not have access to the same business courses he or she would have by completing all graduate business work at an American business school. So, for most students, the disadvantages of such programs seem to outweigh the advantages.

Nevertheless, a small but growing number of American students want to study abroad part time or full time and receive their degree from a graduate business school overseas. Foreign business schools usually are less expensive and quite a few offer a one-year MBA. They are not interested in the typical exchange program between an American graduate business school and a foreign graduate business school.

These students may have such an interest because they plan to live and work abroad or because their families are living overseas, and it is convenient to attend a local graduate business school. One interesting development is that a few American schools have started satellite schools overseas. For example, St. Xavier College in Chicago has an executive MBA program in Paris. This way students living abroad can get an American-type MBA program.

Obviously, the first choice for foreign students living abroad would be a business school in their own country or in a nearby country. Enrollments at foreign business schools are increasing, and many of these graduate business schools have achieved outstanding reputations. Interestingly, China now has more than 50 graduate business schools, and India has several hundred.

Americans wishing to attend foreign business schools should be aware that if courses are not taught in English, they should be fluent in the foreign language used. Also, many foreign business schools charge considerably more tuition for overseas students than for residents of their own countries. For example, the London Business School charges more than two times the tuition for overseas students than for those from Great Britain and the European Economic Community (EEC) countries. The same is true at Canada's York University, which has an outstanding graduate business school. Tuition there is more than two times as much for non-Canadians as for Canadian residents. However, even with this premium, the cost at York is not high compared to major competitive U.S. schools.

Executive Programs

Executive programs are designed for those who already have middle management jobs and, generally, the endorsement and financial backing of their employers. A big advantage of these executive programs is that often students can complete the program in two years of study or less—a good deal shorter than the usual four years it takes to earn the degree as a part-time student. Students in executive programs are generally considered full-time students and take about the same courses as students in the regular MBA programs. Today more than 200 colleges offer such programs and more than 10,000 students are enrolled in executive MBA programs.

In most schools, enrollment in the executive MBA programs is limited to outstanding middle management men and women between the ages of 30 to 45 who are sponsored by their firms. The cost of these programs—generally paid for by the employer—is usually a flat fee that includes tuition, books, and meals on campus. A typical program is the one at Fairleigh Dickinson, which is designed to handle a group of 25 students who go through the two-year program as a group in which they develop close working relationships.

Normally, an executive program has the same curriculum as a university's regular MBA program, except that some electives are eliminated. In a number of these programs, students spend the first week or two in September going to school full time. After that they have classes all day Friday of one week followed by all day Saturday of the next week. Or, they may go to class both Friday and Saturday of alternate weeks. This means that the employer must let them take off one day of work every two weeks, and the employee must give up one Saturday every two weeks.

The University of Chicago is considered the pioneer in the executive program, having started its own program more than 50 years ago. More than 5,000 executives have received degrees in this program. Among the graduate business schools offering an executive program are those at Rochester, Columbia, Wake Forest, Southern Methodist (Cox School), Pittsburgh, Pace, Illinois (at its Urbana-Champaign campus), New Mexico, Denver (Daniels), Kellogg, the University of Washington, and Florida Atlantic University.

If you can get in on an executive program, by all means do so. By selecting you for an executive program your company has shown that it feels you are promising enough to warrant investing a substantial amount of money in furthering your education. And you will be going to class with an elite group of students who may turn out to be valuable future business contacts and social acquaintances.

The executive programs discussed above lead to MBA degrees, and they should not be confused with another type of executive program that is also becoming popular.

These executive programs are usually one or two weeks in duration and are given by graduate business schools for company executives. They are usually tailored by the graduate school and the sponsoring company to meet the specific needs of the sponsor corporation. For example, USG Corporation has sponsored a one-week course on strategic planning at the Kellogg School of Management at Northwestern.

Today, more than 200 graduate business schools offer these courses that are sponsored by a growing number of companies. General Motors, in particular, has been a major sponsor of such courses and has sent its executives to a number of graduate business schools.

A few graduate schools have built excellent facilities to hold these courses and house the executives. For example, the James L. Allen Center at Northwestern, in addition to classrooms, has attractive sleeping room accommodations, as well as dining facilities, athletic facilities, and most of the other amenities available at a small hotel. Kellogg also provides customized executive education programs for companies including Microsoft and Boeing.

Doctoral Programs

While most students who attend graduate business school are interested only in earning an MBA or other master's degree, some go on to earn their doctoral degrees. These can include the traditional Doctor of Philosophy (PhD), the Doctor of Business Administration (DBA), the Doctor of Commercial Science (DCS), and the Doctor of Professional Studies (DPS). More than 1,000 doctoral degrees in business were awarded in 2004, more than 30 percent of which were earned by women. If you are considering a doctoral degree program, here are some facts to keep in mind:

- A doctoral degree usually takes twice as long to earn as a master's, and sometimes the MBA is not the logical path to follow toward the doctorate.
- Earning a doctoral degree involves far more than taking additional courses and spending a longer period of time in school. Many schools require that their doctoral candidates be proficient in statistics, and students usually have to pass comprehensive tests in this area. Sometimes, proficiency in a foreign language is required.
- You probably will have to take comprehensive oral and written examinations in three or more fields of business to demonstrate that you have an overall grasp of these areas.
- You must write a research dissertation, which can easily run 200 to 500 pages and take one or two years to write. Even after you've finished writing the dissertation, you have to defend it before a faculty committee, and this can be an awesome hurdle for some students.

Because getting a doctoral degree is a very difficult task for most graduate students, many schools discourage a student from trying to earn a doctorate unless they feel that he or she has the necessary scholastic abilities and plans to go into the academic world or some research field after graduation.

One area of major demand for PhDs is for teachers at graduate business schools. While salaries in the academic world usually don't compare to what is available in the business world, salaries have increased. It is estimated that there is currently a PhD vacancy rate of more than 10 percent at business schools. Starting salaries for instructors or associate professors with a PhD can run $45,000 to $110,000 for a nine-month year. Many professors with specialties like finance or accounting earn annual salaries of $80,000 to $150,000; some "superstar" professors earn as much as $300,000 to $400,000 a year. A great deal of "raiding" has taken place lately as graduate business schools vie for top talent. Several years ago, Wharton wooed away a professor from Princeton for a package estimated at $250,000 a year. Professors can also supplement their teaching income with consulting work. Consulting fees of $1,000 to $4,000 a day are possible for outstanding specialists. Business schools face a shortage of qualified teachers. While business school enrollments have grown sharply since 1985, the number of new doctoral graduates has increased only by a very small amount. One reason is that it has been estimated that it costs $180,000 to $300,000 in extra tuition and lost income to gain a doctoral degree in business.

Only a few schools encourage business-oriented students to take the doctoral program. Pace University, for example, offers a doctoral program in business that is designed for qualified executives who want to experience a rigorous study program while continuing their professional careers. This program has been considered unusually successful.

Another key point to consider in evaluating the pros and cons of a doctoral degree is that there may be very little difference between what some companies would pay, for example, an MBA applicant and an applicant with a doctorate. In fact, in some cases a company might shy away from hiring a young job candidate with a doctorate who wants to get into a regular management training program. Companies often feel that doctoral applicants are overqualified or simply too academically oriented.

On the positive side, there are some jobs in the business world where the doctorate is regarded as a plus—particularly jobs in the economic and business research fields. Investment banking firms over the past five years have been hiring PhDs from the academic world at very high salaries. In recent years, an increasing number of newly minted PhDs in Business have opted for careers in the business world. Also, you might be the sort of person who wants the prestige, self-satisfaction, and joy of learning that one can get by undertaking such a course of study. If that's what you want, go full steam ahead.

A fairly recent development is the hiring of so-called "clinical professors" by a number of business schools. These professors are recruited from the ranks of corporate executives and the goal is to bring more real world business experience into the classroom. These clinical professors usually don't have the same academic credentials as their colleagues nor are they usually on the typical tenure track. More often they sign three- or five-year contracts and are rarely asked to do formal research. However, they often are full time and participate in most faculty activities.

How to Choose a Business School

There are a number of things you should consider when choosing a business school. Obviously, your range of selectivity depends on such factors as your undergraduate grades, the type of program you wish to pursue, whether you plan to go to school full time or part time, and your finances. If you live in a small city where there is only one university that offers a graduate business program, and you want to go to school in that city, your decision is somewhat limited. If you want to go to school in New York City, however, you have a choice of 10 or more schools that offer graduate business programs. In the Chicago area, there are more than 20 schools offering the MBA program. If you are a good student with the financial resources to go to any school in the country, you have an even more difficult choice to make. A major new factor in the decision to go to graduate business schools is the increasing number of schools offering MBAs through "distance learning" courses. The sections that follow describe some of the criteria you should consider when deciding on your preference in schools.

FACTORS TO TAKE INTO ACCOUNT

Accreditation

When you evaluate a school, accreditation is an important consideration. Accreditation is the process of recognizing educational institutions whose performance and integrity entitle them to the confidence of the educational community and the public. Accreditation of business schools usually comes about through two types of organizations.

The first type of accreditation group is a regional nongovernmental or voluntary organization. Currently, there are six major regional organizations: the Middle States Commission on Higher Education (MSCHE), the New England Association of Schools and Colleges (NEASC), the Northwest Commission on Schools and Universities (NWCCU), the North Central Association of Colleges and Schools (NCA), the Southern Association of Colleges and Schools (SACS), and the Western Association on Schools and Colleges (WASC). These organizations establish criteria, evaluate institutions at their request, and extend approval to those colleges and universities whose purposes, resources, and performance the pertinent accrediting organization feels deserve such recognition.

Most universities are accredited by one of these six major regional groups. For you, this accreditation is a guarantee that the university, of which the business school is a part, has met the minimum standards set by the accrediting organization. In practical terms, it also means that, if you transfer from an accredited school, the chances are good that another school will accept your transfer courses and grades. If you transferred from a school that was not accredited, chances of getting credit for most of your previous work would be slim.

In addition to these regional organizations that provide general accreditation, there are accreditation groups set up to accredit specialized schools in areas such as architecture, journalism, medicine, and business. There are currently 37 professional fields where there are recognized accreditation agencies. In the business school area, the accreditation agency is the AACSB, the Association to Advance Collegiate Schools of Business.

One very good yardstick to measure the quality of a graduate business school is to determine whether it is accredited by AACSB. Founded in 1916, AACSB is dedicated to furthering the quality of education at schools of business. It does this through an accreditation program at both undergraduate and graduate schools of business. As of December 2004, AACSB had accredited the master's degree programs at about 448 of the more than 750 schools offering the MBA degree or its equivalent in the United States.

Just about all the major graduate schools of business have their programs accredited by AACSB, and many who lack accreditation are busily seeking it. To be accredited, a school must conform to a high level of standards. Up until 1982, these standards were pretty rigidly defined. For example, at least 75 percent of the faculty had to have their terminal degrees (usually the doctorate), and student-faculty ratios and the number of part-time and full-time faculty members were also precisely defined. In 1982, the AACSB made a sweeping revision in its accreditation standards to give its evaluators more leeway in judging the quality of a school's programs. The changes were adopted to reduce reliance on purely quantitative factors. In 1991, AACSB made some radical changes in its accreditation standards. These were the result of a two-year study by AACSB members and in response to criticism that there should be more flexibility in the accreditation process and more emphasis on teaching and preparing students for the needs of the business world.

Under the new standards, schools have flexibility in determining their mission, or market niche, and to develop programs to accomplish their goals. They have more freedom to package their courses and to assemble faculty.

This new flexibility as applied to faculty means they are freer to use faculty members who have doctorates in fields other than business and that some professors may need only master's degrees as long as they have relevant professional experience.

On the other hand, there is emphasis on student standards, and students must be able to demonstrate skills in written and oral communications, quantitative analysis, and computer usage.

Many schools have already made changes in their curriculum to match the new requirements, but a substantial number still have changes coming. The new standards are now in place.

Usually, if a school desires accreditation, the process will take two years—assuming the school passes the various hurdles.

A new Candidacy Partnership program establishes stable, ongoing, and helpful partnerships between AACSB and institutions working toward AACSB accreditation. "Candidacy" status signifies that the candidate institution is demonstrating reasonable progress toward attainment of accreditation.

Keep in mind that normally you needn't concern yourself with whether the school you are considering is called a graduate school, a graduate division, an MBA program, or another master's business degree program. As long as the school is an autonomous degree-recommending unit that reports to the central administration, it is eligible to be considered for accreditation by AACSB.

Obviously, the fact that a school is accredited by AACSB should give you added confidence about the quality of its business program—a guarantee that a number of minimum standards have been met or surpassed. If you want complete details on the accrediting procedure, write to AACSB, 177 South Harbor Island Boulevard, Suite 750, Tampa, FL 33602.

One problem area that would-be graduate business students should be alert to is the fact that dozens of new MBA programs have sprung up to attract students and enhance a school's enrollments and finances. *Business Week* magazine reported that a number of schools now offering the MBA have seemed to relax academic standards to make their courses appealing to students who want a degree in the shortest amount of time and with the least amount of work. There has also been a growing number of for-profit schools that are offering MBA degrees through total distance learning programs. Some of these schools may not have a long life due to increased competition. So a word of warning: It's safest to choose a graduate school that has been offering the MBA degree for at least 15 to 20 years. There are exceptions, of course. A new MBA program was recently offered at the University of California at San Diego.

The overall coordinating agency for accreditation programs is the Commission on Recognition of Postsecondary Accreditation (CORPA), the private sector oversight body for postsecondary accreditation.

Teaching Methods

Most graduate schools of business organize their curricula around three basic elements: the core, the concentration, and electives. Core courses—usually finance, marketing, management, and accounting—provide an introduction to fundamental business concepts. The field of concentration is generally intended to provide advanced knowledge and specialized intensive preparation in an area of the student's major interest. Electives then offer a broad range of optional subjects.

However, there are wide differences in the ways various schools balance these three elements. Some schools offer a fixed curriculum with no field of specialization and no electives. Others either encourage or discourage specialization in areas such as finance and accounting. Many schools spend a good deal of time on broad management courses that cut across many business disciplines. Some schools give students the opportunity to sample courses from a wide variety of areas in the business curriculum and sometimes even outside the business school; others don't. In a few schools, students can design programs that fit their personal interests or career goals.

There are constant shifts taking place in the schools and in their curricula, and this is being accelerated by the change in policies by AACSB several years ago. Harvard reduced both classroom time and reading materials by about 15 percent. The reduction was made after the faculty concluded that the school had been trying to deal with too many topics in too little time and in not enough depth. However, the workload still makes for a 65-hour week. At Stanford, professors may choose whatever methods suit their personal style and the materials they use. There has been a noticeable increase in team teaching and also bringing in professors from other disciplines, including history, religion, politics, and law.

There's also a shift to more production, operations management, and productivity information systems, E-commerce, entrepreneurship, and international business courses, a reaction to business's growing need for managers who can run factories efficiently and compete with the growing inroads made by productivity-minded foreign manufacturers. MIT's Sloan School now offers majors in technology. Northeastern University has an MBA program specializing in high technology designed primarily for managers already in highly technical businesses. Rensselaer and Georgia Tech's DuPree School have an MBA concentration in the Management of Technology and Entrepreneurship. Quality control management is another area growing in popularity and is offered at a number of MBA schools such as IIT's Stuart School.

The international business course has become extremely popular in recent years and many new programs and courses have been developed to meet perceived needs. Courses in ethics and communications skills have also been added by many schools. This has been accelerated due to scandals in 2001 involving executives at such major companies as Enron and World Com.

Business schools are now working on ways to involve business executives in the curriculum and teaching assignments. This has been aided by the appointments of some top former executives to dean positions at major business schools. This has been the case at Rice, Stanford, Fordham, Indiana, Boston, and other schools.

Teaching methods also vary from school to school, with each program emphasizing different elements. Harvard and the University of Virginia utilize the case method, which calls for the study and solution of problems actually faced by companies. Other schools, such as Carnegie Mellon, are very involved in simulated "management games," where students work through business problems. The University of Chicago stresses economic and financial theory and recently became an innovator in business leadership programs, offering students courses that bridge the gap between classroom and marketplace. Some schools offer a great many seminars; others have lectures before large class groups. Many have role-playing; some utilize small group projects. Some schools are very practical in their approach and utilize primarily business executives holding MBAs and other advanced degrees who have a commitment to excellence in teaching and who provide a practitioner's orientation to business management theories and concepts.

In a number of schools, students must undertake a substantial amount of research and writing; in others, oral presentations are emphasized. At one time, many graduate business schools required a thesis for an MBA. A recent survey shows that most schools do not require either a formal thesis or a written or oral examination for completion of the degree.

At the University of Buffalo (State University of New York), graduate business students coordinate their classroom efforts with the real business world by working on problems that involve local business concerns while earning credit for this experience. The Fuqua School (Duke) has a student consulting group that assists small North Carolina business firms as well as minority-owned businesses in the state.

At the University of Pennsylvania, students may do consulting projects for companies such as Continental Can Company, INA, and Chase Manhattan Bank. Many schools integrate course work with practical experience by encouraging students to work during summers or as part of the curriculum.

At Emory and the University of Texas, students work with managers of companies such as Procter & Gamble, Motorola, and 3M in customer development work. General Electric and the University of Connecticut operate an E-commerce laboratory on the college's Stamford, Connecticut, campus.

In an effort to bring more realism into school work, a number of business schools offer special, innovative programs. At Texas Christian University, students taking the Seminar in Investments have total investment control of the university's Educational Investment Fund, which has $1.5 million in portfolio assets. Similar programs are offered at the Kenan Flagler Business School (University of North Carolina), the University of Wisconsin at Madison, and Indiana University. At Wisconsin, the students invest $12 million through three different funds. At Florida Atlantic University, at least one course utilizes prominent businessmen and -women as lecturers. Loyola of Chicago has a Center for Family Business.

The Yale graduate school employs standard teaching methods but bases them on some rather unique concepts. Yale's plan is to educate leaders not only for corporations but for government, the military, and private foundations. The school wants to produce a versatile executive with a broad knowledge of how a variety of organizations operate. At the same time, students are trained in the full set of hard-edged management skills they might acquire in a more traditional MBA program.

How does a student decide what type of program will be best for him or her? There are no hard-and-fast guidelines, but most students will be served best by the more traditional program structure. A good solid grounding in business fundamentals is a must. The opportunity to concentrate on a special field of interest is also an advantage to the student. Most graduates will have to indicate some preference for a particular field of specialty to prospective employers. They should, therefore, get enough of a taste of each of these areas while in graduate school so that they will (1) be sure they like a particular field, and (2) have taken enough courses in a specific field to step into a management training program or initial job without feeling they are in over their heads.

Regarding electives, their major advantage is in providing the opportunity to gain some insight into new fields—fields into which students might want to delve further when they enter the job world. Another advantage is that these electives can give the students a "rounding out" that may have ultimate value in their later careers.

As for teaching emphasis, if a student is practical-minded rather than theoretical, it is best for him or her to stay away from some of the business schools that place major stress on economic and business theory courses or the mathematical approach to business decision-making. Schools that offer practical courses such as investment decision-making—utilizing actual investment funds—can be very advantageous. Likewise, taking courses that give you on-the-job training or consulting experience in the real business world can be very useful. Often, such experiences may provide the spark to put you on a future career path or give you the contacts that eventually result in a job offer.

A growing number of schools concentrate on developing the concept of teamwork among the MBA students. These schools believe that such courses will better prepare students for the job world. Keep in mind that MBA programs change with the times and with the needs of business and industry. In a number of schools, students work as a team on course work and projects and are graded as a team.

Full Time Versus Part Time

The last time the federal government counted, for every two students attending full-time graduate business programs, there were three going to school part time. Indications are that the percentage of part-time students will probably increase in the next few years. The advent of distance learning courses will help accelerate this trend. The reason is simple: Many people decide to get their master's in business after they are already out in the job world. They don't want to give up their jobs to go to school full time. Also, a large number of men and women who would like to go to school full time simply can't afford to, and attending on a part-time basis is their only alternative.

As a result, many universities have MBA or other graduate business programs that make special provisions for and, in some cases, even cater to part-time students. Courses are given at night, in the early morning, on weekends, and over closed-circuit television or computer by means of distance learning.

Students who do have the choice of going to school full time or part time should take a hard look at the pros and cons. Here are some advantages of being a part-time student:

- The costs will probably be much less.
- It indicates to your employer that you are ambitious, hardworking, and well motivated.
- If you are an employee and a part-time student, many companies will pay all or part of your tuition.
- You can often better comprehend the practical implications of the material being taught in the classroom if you hold a full-time job and go to school part time.
- You won't lose as much as two years' earnings or two years' work experience and promotion possibilities that you would if you attended school full time.

However, there are some substantial reasons for not opting for a part-time schedule:

- If you work full time, you might find yourself very tired and your attention span limited when you attend classes at night or on weekends.
- If you are working and raising a family, going to school puts additional pressure on your job, family, and marriage. Taking six hours of courses per semester can take a big slice of your time—as much as 18 hours a week; on the other hand, part-time programs are more flexible today.
- As a part-time student, you usually are unable to spend the same amount of preparation time for your classes, tests, and term papers that you could as a full-time student. Generally, you are expected to study two to three hours for each classroom hour. Also, you don't have the same access to library facilities, faculty members, or student advisers for research and discussion.
- You will have little chance to meet and spend time with your fellow students, to get to know them, or to make friendships, because you will generally arrive at school after work, with little time to spare, and will then leave as soon as class is over. It also means you rarely have time to participate in any extracurricular or social activities of the university, so you could miss what is generally called "the campus experience."
- It is difficult to build close relationships with your professors. You are usually under substantial time pressures, and many professors don't have office hours in the late afternoons or evenings, which are the times during which most part-time students can visit.
- There is also a question about the quality of many of the business programs geared to part-time students. A number of business programs that specialize in night school students, for example, rely heavily on part-time teachers. Others don't provide adequate library or computer resources at night. On the other hand, at a school like Fordham's Graduate School of Business, which offers primarily evening courses, but also has sizeable full-time and daytime programs, some 80 to 85 percent of all courses are taught by full-time faculty, and the program is accredited by AACSB. The same is true at many other MBA schools.

Some of the best business schools in the country do not offer evening or part-time courses. This list includes Harvard, Columbia, Dartmouth, and Stanford. It is also true that some leading corporations recruit for prospective employers solely among graduate business schools that have only full-time students.

On the other hand, some very fine graduate business schools do offer graduate business programs to part-time students, and their number is increasing. Two top business schools that offer programs geared to working students are NYU's Stern School of Business and the University of Chicago, which both offer prestigious day and evening programs. The schools treat the two programs as one, and offer the same faculty to night students as they do to full-time day students. The schools have only one set of admissions standards. Once admitted, students at Chicago can transfer between day and evening classes without losing credit or continuity. Some Chicago professors even prefer the evening students because they feel they are more mature and dedicated.

More and more universities are providing not only evening courses but a variety of other schedules to accommodate part-time students. Some universities hold classes all day Friday or Saturday. The University of New Mexico, for example, offers a Friday-Saturday program.

Some programs even permit students to take graduate business courses right in their employers' offices or plants. More and more such programs are cropping up because they save commuting time for working students. Also, employers sometimes allow such courses to begin on their premises in the late afternoon because it cuts down on the amount of time their employees have to spend attending school. Distance learning courses offer the opportunity to take courses at your office, home, or almost anywhere.

The University of South Carolina offers students a unique opportunity to earn the business master's via television while living and working almost anywhere in the state. This program is a joint effort of the university and the South Carolina Educational Television Network (SCETV) and is being emulated by other business schools. SCETV transmits lectures in each course to cities and towns throughout the state. Students simply go to the "classroom" nearest their home once or twice a week, where they watch lectures that are broadcast "live" from the system's parent classroom in Columbia, South Carolina. The students sit at desks equipped with talk-back capability with the instructor or fellow students. An average three-unit course consists of 30 hours of tele-vision instruction, usually in two-hour segments one night a week. In addition, four visits to the campus are required—on Saturdays, usually once each month—for computer work, counseling, and examinations.

Other schools set up satellite campuses to reach where students live and work. Illinois Institute of Technology, for example, opened minicenters in the Chicago suburbs of Wheaton and Schaumburg. The programs in Wheaton reach engineers who want to get their MBAs at nearby companies.

Distance Learning

Probably the most important development taking place in graduate business schools is the trend toward establishing distance learning programs. Distance learning utilizes many techniques and equipment such as radio, TV, computers, CDs, video, chat rooms, and so on to bring courses to students no matter where they are—at home, in the office, and across continents. The challenge for the student is to evaluate the schools, their programs, and classes.

There are a number of Internet sites that provide information on programs: EarnMyDegree.com (*www.earnmydegree.com*) offers free information on distance learning programs in a wide range of fields and degree programs, including MBA programs with a number of specializations, including accounting, e-commerce, finance, human resource management, marketing, and technology management to name only a few; GetEducated.com (*www.geteducated.com*) offers a free down-loadable e-book that provides information, including accreditation status, on 120 online MBA programs; Degree.net (*www.degree.net*) provides information on 79 online programs in business, management, and related fields. Since 2000 *Business Week* magazine has provided a list of universities with online MBA programs and detailed profiles on each program. To review the latest lists and profiles go to: *www.businessweek.com/bschools/03/distance.htm*.

The universities and programs listed on these sites are not only nontraditional schools, such as Capella University or Nova Southeastern University, but highly recognized old-line schools, such as Auburn University, Carnegie-Mellon University, Colorado State University, and Syracuse University. The schools generally have regional accreditation, although an increasing number are also AACSB accredited, such as the Virtual MBA Program at Florida Atlantic University.

The student should be concerned about the accreditation of the schools offering distance learning programs. In addition to traditional accreditation bodies, such as the Southern Association of Colleges and Schools and the AACSB, distance learning programs may be accredited by the Distance Education and Training Council (DETC) (*detc.org*). DETC not only looks at program content and delivery, but also outcomes assessment. DETC believes that students should feel their decision to pursue a degree program through distance learning is evidenced through program completion and validated through goal attainment as a key element of program outcomes assessment.

Today, in addition to the many universities offering full distance learning degree programs, most graduate business schools are offering at least some distance learning courses as part of their curriculum, and this trend is gaining momentum each semester. Distance learning opens the door for thousands of students to get their MBAs, usually at their convenience and in many cases with reduced campus residency.

The students enrolled in online programs and courses tend to be in their thirties and forties and generally hold middle management positions in business. They tend to be self-disciplined, ambitious, serious, and well motivated. They are taking these courses because it is more convenient than going to a campus, and because they can take the course material usually on a very flexible schedule and do not have to commit to given days, nights, or weekends. Such courses may cost more than the standard courses or carry additional fees. They can easily run to $500 a credit hour at private universities, but the offset is that in most cases their companies pay part or all of the cost. And, of course, students are spending little or no time away from their families and jobs in residence on campus.

Are students who get their MBAs through distance learning any better or worse than those who do not? So far, the research has been minimal, but to date some schools report that they seem to be on par. Indeed, with many business schools offering their students a mix of classes delivered in the traditional *live* lecture-discussion-case study format, as well as through a distance learning format, there would appear to be no difference, except for self-selection on the part of students, related to enrollment in such classes. As such, the dropout rate for some distance learning students might be higher than regular part-time students if they are not fully disciplined to manage their online study time.

While there are a number of advantages for students through distance learning, there are a number of obvious drawbacks. A student does *not* have a "campus experience," nor does he or she usually have much or any contact with fellow students and professors. While there are chat rooms and other means of getting involved with students and teachers, it is not comparable to being in a classroom.

It is also not clear how corporate recruiters will regard the distance learning MBA. Will they regard it as the equivalent of a traditional MBA and "hire" accordingly? Only time will tell. As a practical matter, the MBA earned through distance learning looks the same as a regular MBA diploma and looks the same when put on a resume. In today's economy employers are increasingly evaluating the skills and creativity of new hires and existing employees separate from their educational credentials, so the educational format may not be a significant factor for the student who earned a degree through distance learning.

Distance learning also poses a number of concerns for graduate business schools. Will they pay extra, and perhaps premiums, to professors who develop and teach such courses? Do the professors who develop such courses own the courses or does the college? Will the college utilize tapes and material of prestigious professors at other colleges or utilize their own faculty exclusively? Can smaller business colleges survive the threat of major business schools offering their degrees through distance learning?

Clearly there are many concerns and problems as well as opportunities, but it seems obvious that distance learning will change the face of graduate business education in the years to come.

How Long Does It Take?

While many graduate business degree programs require two academic years if pursued on a full-time basis, some programs can run as short as one year if the student has had substantial undergraduate work in business. At Babson, you can earn your degree in one year. Some schools allow advanced standing on the basis of undergraduate courses, but usually these decisions are made only upon an individual review of the student's records. To qualify for advanced standing, the best bet is to have an undergraduate degree in business administration and to get the master's degree from the same university.

How Long It Can Take You to Earn Your Master's in Business as a Part-time Student

Semester Hours Required for Degree	Two Courses per Term, Three Terms a Year	Two Courses per Semester, Two Semesters a Year	One Course per Term, Three Terms a Year	One Course per Semester, Two Semesters a Year
60	3⅓ years	5 years	6⅔ years	10 years
48	2⅔ years	4 years	5⅓ years	8 years
36	2 years	3 years	4 years	6 years
30	1⅔ years	2½ years	3⅓ years	5 years

A substantial number of graduate business schools allow students to accelerate their studies by offering year-round programs and by permitting them to enter school in the spring and summer as well as in the fall. Pace offers four terms a year, and a student can start in any term. The Columbia Graduate School of Business offers two terms a year and a student can start in any term. But at many graduate schools, such as Carnegie Mellon and Cornell, students may begin only in the fall. So, if you are interested in getting your master's degree in the shortest possible time, concentrate on those schools that offer year-round courses and permit you to enter during any term.

If you are a part-time student, it is important to check admissions policies carefully, because you probably will want to earn your degree in the shortest time, and you may want to study all year round. It is also important to see what sequences of courses and electives are offered each semester so you don't have to wait out a semester until a course you need is given.

Most part-time programs run four years, but this, too, varies considerably. If you plan to go part-time, figure that at most you can take two courses per semester. Going to school three semesters per year, you could take 18 semester hours per year. If the degree requirement is 48 hours, you could finish in two and two-third years' time. On the other hand, if you need 60 hours for your degree, it will take five years at six hours a semester, two semesters a year, and three and one-third years if you go three semesters a year.

Fields of Specialization

At those schools where students can specialize in one or more areas of business, the most popular fields are accounting, finance, marketing, management, and information systems. A study by Korn/Ferry International and The Anderson School at UCLA surveyed business executives several years ago to find out what specialities they thought were the fastest route to the top. Some 25 percent of the respondents felt that the financial/accounting route was the best way to get to the top; 35 percent said that marketing/sales was the best; 23 percent said general management; 7 percent said professional/technical; and 6 percent indicated that production/manufacturing was the best route. Currently the very popular areas are international business, E-commerce, entrepreneurship, and marketing.

These trends often are a reflection of what employers are looking for in graduates and what fields offer the highest starting pay. For example, banks and insurance companies are usually interested in students who concentrate on finance, whereas accounting firms are interested in accounting and finance majors, and retail firms look for marketing majors.

Keep in mind that these patterns always tend to be in a state of flux. Don't jump into a major field just because it is "hot" for the time being. You are better off picking a field that you like and for which you feel you have special aptitude and talent.

School Rankings

Most graduate business candidates are part-time students who mainly choose their graduate business schools on the basis of accessibility to where they live and work, courses offered, and the reputation of the institution. Accessibility may become less of a factor as distance learning courses become more widespread and accepted.

For most full-time students, other key criteria include the cost of attending and the length of time it will take to get the degree. Full-time students with average grades and test scores will find many schools that meet their needs and must simply figure out what criteria to weigh the heaviest. Those students who want to attend full time, who have excellent grades, and for whom the location and cost of attending graduate business school are not serious problems really have a difficult decision in selecting a school. Most students in this situation opt for the best business school.

This brings us to the question of which is the best graduate business school in the country and which schools are the runners-up. The quick answer is that no one can be sure of just which school is the "best," but we can determine fairly well a number of schools that are considered among the best. Actually, there are about 20 to 30 graduate business schools that are considered to be "top drawer" schools and that have the reputation of being national business schools. By "national," we mean that the student enrollment is drawn from a very wide geographic area and that major companies from all over the country recruit on their campuses.

With regard to ranking these schools, there are countless arguments about which one is best; in fact, every time a ranking study is made it triggers off dozens of letters from the schools, their graduates, and faculty, all complaining that the particular study and its results are invalid. As a result, while there have been a number of studies done in recent years attempting to rank business schools, there have been serious reservations about the results of a number of those studies. Some of the ratings are based on rather unscientific samplings and highly subjective judgments.

So, just which is the best business school? This is a question that continually comes up but is very difficult to answer. There is no one universally accepted rating standard, but the results of several surveys seem to indicate that Harvard, Chicago, Stanford, University of Pennsylvania, Northwestern, and MIT are at the very top of the heap.

In fact the ratings of graduate business schools in recent years by *Business Week* magazine, *U.S. News & World Report*, and *The Wall Street Journal* have resulted in a great deal of nail biting by the deans of many business schools. It is a fact that the ratings by those publications—particularly the *Business Week* rankings—have resulted in a substantial increase in applications to the business schools that have ranked high on the lists. These ratings have also put pressure on the administration of a substantial number of business schools to improve their ratings. This has resulted in some changes in business school curricula, and also in extensive communications programs to the business world and prospective students touting the advantages of the various schools. A number of graduate business schools have hired public relations firms, at fees in excess of $100,000 a year, to help tell their stories and improve their image.

The first point regarding ratings is that there are many ways to rank schools, and it is hard to say which one is the best way. The second point is that if you want to go *to* one of the best schools, you will find the names of the same schools appearing on almost any list of the top 20, but they don't always rank the same way in each survey.

A third point is that the major schools are in fierce competition for bright students and believe that the various surveys ranking the schools can influence students' choices. Many graduate schools wish that such ranking surveys would disappear, but since they will not, the schools are anxious to make sure they show up well on such rankings.

Once you get beyond the top national schools, you have about 100 regional schools that draw students mainly from the regional areas. The remaining schools, which total more than 600, usually draw on students from a more limited geographic area.

One other key fact to consider that will have a great impact on these schools' future ratings and program quality are their current development efforts. Many schools have recently received or plan to obtain substantial new funds to help them recruit outstanding faculty and provide improved facilities and new programs. Such funds include $50 million to the University of Texas, $60 million to the University of Virginia, $40 million to Houston University, $25 million to Fairfield University, and $35 million to Notre Dame. The Walton family gave $300 million to the University of Arkansas; Carnegie Mellon recently received $55 million.

Suitability of Undergraduate Business Majors Versus Undergraduate Nonbusiness Majors

Most schools do not insist that those wanting to enroll in graduate business programs must have majored in business as undergraduates; in fact, one recent trend among those entering graduate business schools is to major in engineering. Currently, the combination of an undergraduate engineering degree plus an MBA is highly prized by many companies. However, if you have not had a sizable number of undergraduate business courses, you may have to attend graduate school longer than the student with undergraduate business training. The major disadvantage for nonbusiness majors is that they may be asked to take a number of prerequisite courses before commencing the actual master's program. In some cases, deficiencies in mathematics or economics might have to be remedied before admittance is possible as a regular student.

At some graduate schools, there are distinct disadvantages for those who have not taken a great number of undergraduate business courses. On the other hand, at Carnegie Mellon and other schools that put special emphasis on quantitative courses, mathematics, and computer skills, it is felt that students with undergraduate business courses do not have the most desirable backgrounds.

Costs: State Versus Private

One important consideration if you are on a budget is the fact that tuition at city and state universities is usually much lower than that at most private universities. On average, tuition at a state university is about two and a half to three times less than the cost at a private university. The difference can be as much as $20,000 a year, so for a two-year graduate program you could save as much as $40,000 by going to the business school of a state university in your own state rather than attending a private university. Also, keep in mind that even if you go to a state university as a non-state resident, the tuition costs will probably be less than those of a good private university. There are a number of state universities with excellent graduate schools of business, including the University of Michigan/Ann Arbor, the University of Virginia, Georgia Tech, the University of California/Berkeley and Los Angeles, Purdue University (Krannert), the University of Texas at Austin, the University of Illinois, Indiana University, and a number of others.

YOUR ADMISSION CHANCES

Your chances of being admitted depend primarily on your undergraduate grade-point average (GPA) and on your GMAT score (if the graduate school requires a GMAT score). Other factors enter into the admissions decision, but these two are of prime importance. In some cases, there is an advantage if you have work or military experience. If you are a woman or a member of a minority, this, too, may increase your chances of gaining admission. You are also at an advantage if you are a resident applying to a graduate business school in your home state.

As an Immediate College Graduate

Here you are staking your chances almost exclusively on your undergraduate record and your GMAT test score. Generally speaking, a growing number of schools are using the AACSB-recommended method of combining GPA with GMAT score. The formula is to take your overall undergraduate GPA, multiply it by 200, and then add the GMAT score. Or, you can take your upper-division GPA, multiply it by 200, and add the GMAT score. In any case, the AACSB recommends that the graduate school only accept students who have a minimum of 950 if they use the overall GPA, or 1000 if they use the upper-division GPA. If you don't meet these minimums, you will have a difficult time getting into an AACSB-accredited school. However, you will find a substantial number of non-AACSB-accredited schools that will accept students with C averages and fairly low GMAT scores.

As a College Graduate with Work Experience

If you have your undergraduate degree and several years of business or military experience, you will find that at many schools you will have an edge over candidates fresh out of college. A growing number of graduate schools prefer students who have full-time business experience of two to five years. This work experience can demonstrate job proficiency and interest in business, and students with such experience are often more serious and can relate class work better with the real business world. At Stanford, nearly 100 percent of the entering students had at least two years of full-time work experience before coming to Stanford. At Harvard, most entering students have two or more years of work experience. At Wharton, the average student has four years of work experience. At the University of Texas at Austin, work experience is assuming increased importance in the admissions practice. The trend is for MBA students to have an increasing amount of work experience before starting their MBA program.

There are some disadvantages to going back to school full-time after an interruption of several years, but most of them are personal. Often, you make a greater financial sacrifice by going back to college once you have been working in the business world. Also, relearning study habits and the knack of taking tests might be difficult.

As a Minority Group Member

If you are a member of a minority group, your chances of getting into a graduate school of business are better now than at almost any point in the past. Many graduate schools are spending considerable effort to increase their representation of African-Americans, Native Americans, Hispanics, Asian-Americans, and other minority groups.

In 2004, the percentage of ethnic minorities, including Hispanics, Asians, Native Americans, and African-Americans, was estimated at about 10 percent of all MBA students. The enrollment of African-American students is estimated to be around the 7 percent level and has stayed around that level for several years.

Several organizations are trying to reverse this trend. The National Black MBA Association is developing a series of programs designed to attract minority MBA students. Coca-Cola, General Motors, Ford, Citicorp, and others have signed up as partners of the National Black MBA Association in a drive to get more African-Americans enrolled in MBA programs. Michigan and MIT have the highest percentage of minority students among the top 10 business schools according to a recent survey.

Some of the recruitment programs are done under special consortium arrangements, with funding provided by major nonprofit foundations. The Consortium of Graduate Study in Management recruits minority students, using funds from foundations and businesses. Consortium schools include the Universities of Southern California, Wisconsin, Rochester, Michigan, North Carolina, Texas (Austin), Virginia, and California (Berkeley); Indiana and Washington (St. Louis) Universities; and NYU's Stern School of Business. Consortium fellowships provide free tuition. More than 3,000 students have graduated using this program.

As a Woman

The number of women attending graduate business schools has been on the increase for quite a few years now, and at many schools they comprise more than 35 percent of the student body. Many graduate business schools are making an effort to increase the enrollment of women students. This is in keeping with the revolution in attitudes toward women executives that is taking place in American business. In contrast to the situation only 10 to 15 years ago, women executives have become well accepted by top executives in most major corporations. In most large companies, top executives are focusing on performance whether they are assessing a man or a woman executive.

The present effort that graduate business schools are making to recruit women may include special financial aid funds and placement services. Other sources women might want to check for aid or programs are the Business and Professional Women's Foundation, 2012 Massachusetts Avenue, N.W., Washington, DC 20036 (for both scholarships and loan programs), and local chapters of the American Association of University Women (AAUW).

While there has been an increase of women in the MBA program, there still seem to be some problems concerning how women MBAs fare once they go into the job world. The woman MBA at the entry level usually feels quite welcome in her first job. After three or five years she may get somewhat frustrated and feel that her hard work and talent are not being recognized in pay and promotion the way her male colleagues' work and talent are.

So, while the influx of women MBAs has helped make a great deal of progress in increasing the position of women in the business world, there are still sizable roadblocks that have to be overcome.

As an International Student

One major development in recent years is the heavy influx of foreign students to American graduate business schools. They come mainly from Europe and the Far East—Japan, China, South Korea, India, Malaysia, and Taiwan. The reasons are many. In the Far East, there are no graduate business schools with the high reputation of the American schools. A degree in the United States is a bargain for many foreign students. Many students go to school in the United States and then return to top posts in their native countries armed with the prestigious American MBA degree. Others are interested in learning American business techniques and also in getting a better sense of American thinking. More than one third of the applications to top business schools are filed by foreign students and they comprise more than 10 percent of the student body at graduate business schools.

Many graduate business schools, like the Stern School at NYU, have had about one-third of their student body from outside the United States. Yale, Stanford, Chicago, and Northwestern (Kellogg) also have high percentages; however, this trend suffered a sharp setback in 2004, and applications from foreign students have declined sharply. The reasons are mainly twofold: much tighter visa regulations regarding these students, and the fact that there has been growing anti-American sentiment in a large number of foreign countries.

International students are generally expected to meet the same admission standards as those set for everyone else. One major concern business schools have regarding international students is their proficiency in English. Usually the school's admissions committee will want to see evidence that a student can understand rapidly spoken idiomatic English, participate in class discussions, and be able to write reports and other required materials.

Because of this concern, most business schools require international students whose university training was not conducted in English to demonstrate their proficiency through the Test of English as a Foreign Language (TOEFL). TOEFL is administered by the Educational Testing Service (ETS) in hundreds of cities throughout the world. You can obtain the information bulletin describing the test and the examination procedures by writing: TOEFL/TSE Services, P.O. Box 6151, Princeton, NJ 08541-6151. The Bulletin can also be ordered or downloaded from the TOEFL web site (*www.toefl.org*). Barron's *How to Prepare for the TOEFL* provides special help to those who plan to take the TOEFL exam. International students should also keep in mind that the Graduate Management Admission Test (GMAT) is given only in English. The test may not be taken more than once a month.

One problem schools have had in evaluating the applications of international students is determining the quality and caliber of their undergraduate work. Their transcripts are usually written in a foreign language, and course titles, contents, and the semester credit systems at foreign universities can be totally different from those of American schools. This is one reason why it is important for international students to submit their applications to business schools at least one year in advance.

Another way admissions policies toward international students differ from those accorded American students is that business schools often require them to finish *all* their undergraduate academic work before considering them for admission.

It would be advisable for international students to determine well in advance just how much special assistance they can get from the business schools in which they are interested. Some schools have special advisers and programs for international students; others have no special programs, and international students are left to more or less fend for themselves. Typical of the school that offers special services to international students is the University of Michigan. Its International Center helps foreign students with housing, immigration problems, and personal adjustment. Students should also keep in mind that most business schools won't make financial aid available to them during their first year of graduate school. However, there are some outstanding overseas MBA schools, and both foreign and American students are now finding these schools increasingly attractive.

International students who want more specific information on graduate study opportunities as well as on how to cope with special problems they will face at American schools should write or visit the U.S. Information Service educational advising center(s) in their home countries. International students may get useful information from the Institute of International Education, 809 United Nations Plaza, New York, NY 10017. The Institute cannot provide research assistance by mail or phone, but offer several books that may be purchased from the address above, on the web site *www.IIEbooks.org*.

The Application Procedure

CHAPTER 14

ADMISSION REQUIREMENTS

The number of applications for admission to graduate business schools continue to be impressive. Currently it is estimated that for every opening in a quality graduate business school there are almost two applicants, and at some of the more prestigious schools such as Harvard, Stanford, Chicago, and Michigan, there are six to ten or more applicants for each available opening.

Basically, there are four requirements for admission to a graduate school of business:

- A bachelor's degree from a recognized educational institution.
- An acceptable test score on the Graduate Management Admission Test (GMAT).
- An academic standing that meets the school's criteria. This can range from the upper half of your undergraduate class to the top 10 percent, depending on the graduate school to which you apply. Some schools also have specific grade-point averages they require as a minimum.
- Most international students must have an acceptable score on the Test of English as a Foreign Language (TOEFL).

While not all colleges will supply specific information on the minimum GMAT scores required, most will provide average scores and ranges of scores from their last admissions group.

The same is true of your undergraduate grades. Many graduate schools have fixed ideas of the minimum grade-point average (GPA) they will accept—or the minimum class standing. Again, this may not be indicated in the college catalogs, but admission officials will supply this information if you speak with them. Schools tend to avoid putting such information in print because there are a great many intangibles they consider when looking at an applicant's record. For example, a B average from Princeton will probably carry more weight with an admissions committee than a B+ from a less prestigious university. The committee also looks at more than grades. They take note of the courses and course load you took to see if you had a "heavy" or "light" load, and easy or difficult courses. They will also look at the trend of your grades. Did you start as a C student and wind up an A student by the time you graduated? Or, did you start as a B student and stay a B student for four years? They may look at your grades in your major field and see how long it has been since you finished your college work.

Most graduate business schools do not require undergraduate courses in business administration or other specific fields and will consider applicants who have majored in a wide range of fields. Some business schools, however, may require college mathematics, calculus, and statistics, and if you did not take such courses, you may have to take them before being fully admitted to the graduate school. Other schools may require some minimal business or economics undergraduate courses. Here again you may be admitted without them but will have to make up this deficiency before you are classified as a regular student.

Most admissions committees look with favor upon applicants who have a good grounding in an experimental science or in psychology. They also are interested to see if an applicant has the ability to speak and write English well. A substantial number of schools, such as Harvard, emphasize work experience before beginning a graduate business program. In almost every case, work experience is given substantial consideration in evaluating candidates.

In many schools, special admissions criteria are used in evaluating applicants from minority groups or from distant countries (colleges often like to publicize the fact that their student body comes from so many different states and countries). On the other hand, state university business schools favor state residents, and private schools may look favorably at relatives of alumni.

Keep in mind that there may be substantial differences in admissions standards within the same business school depending on the type of program. Admission standards for part-time students may be different from those for full-time students. The requirements for a specialized degree program, say an MBA with a specialty in taxation, may be more or less stringent than the regular MBA program at the same school, depending on whether the school is trying to increase or hold down enrollments.

Also, remember that admissions policies are formulated by different groups at the various universities, and this can mean sizable variations. Generally, the key people involved in admissions decisions are the faculty committee, dean, director of admissions, and a governing board or central graduate school advisory board. The admissions officer is usually the person responsible for administering and carrying out the admissions policies.

To apply to a graduate school, there are several documents you must usually submit. These include:

- The completed application form.
- One or more transcripts of your undergraduate courses and grades. Grades for any course in progress at the time the admissions decision is made must usually be reported to the school prior to enrollment. However, unless you completely fail your final semester, chances are that once you are admitted, the business school won't reverse that decision.
- Letters of recommendation.
- GMAT score.
- Rank in class.
- Application fee.

ADVANCED STANDING AND TRANSFER

If you feel there is a chance you might be eligible for advanced standing for courses taken at undergraduate or graduate school or for work experience, apply for it. The worst that can happen is that you don't get it. Most university catalogs will tell you whether or not transfer credit is accepted. Keep in mind that regulations vary considerably between one school and another. For example, at the Kenan Flagler Business School (University of North Carolina) there is no waiver of program requirements on the basis of undergraduate work. At the University of Michigan, students may waive some required courses by passing a placement exam and then can take an elective course in its place. At the University of Chicago, transfer credits can't reduce the required number of hours, but students are able to take more electives.

At Boston University, students may accelerate their programs by transferring graduate credit from other accredited schools and having course requirements waived. The Illinois Institute of Technology (IIT) will waive up to three courses for students who took undergraduate courses in equivalent areas. At the University of Southern California, students can transfer a maximum of four units of graduate work at the A or B level, but only from approved graduate schools.

The point is that if you have done graduate work already or have had a heavy concentration of business administration and economics courses as an undergraduate, it is worthwhile to try to get credit for these courses.

WHEN TO APPLY

Most school catalogs indicate the deadline for admission applications. Usually it is anywhere from March 1 to August 1 (and most likely before June 1) for those planning to enter graduate school in the fall. However, some admissions officers will advise that applying as much as a year in advance can be advantageous. This is particularly true for international students. And, if you intend to apply for financial aid or for some type of assistantship or scholarship, applying one year in advance may also be to your advantage. In addition, by applying early you can sometimes avoid the complicated and embarrassing negotiations of delaying reply dates to one graduate school while you are waiting to hear about admission to another school.

It is important to keep in mind that it takes time for your credentials and other materials to reach the various schools for their evaluation. You will also need to plan ahead to prepare for and take the GMAT examination that most business schools require.

HOW TO HELP YOUR CHANCES OF BEING ADMITTED

Once you are a college senior and have taken your GMAT, you can't do much to alter your academic standing or your test scores. But that doesn't mean your application has to stand or fall simply on the basis of these statistics. The way you fill out your application and handle items such as letters of recommendation and personal interviews can be very important, particularly if you are a borderline admissions case.

The Application Form

Regardless of what the instructions say about it being permissible to fill out the form in ink, don't do it. Type it or have a professional type it. One good tip is to make a copy of the application form or get two application forms and use one as your rough draft. A neatly typed, good-looking application form can be a plus in admissions.

Make sure you respond to all the questions. Your grammar and punctuation should be impeccable. If you are a poor speller or grammarian, have someone who is good at these skills look over your application before it is typed. If you have to write an essay, make sure it is your best effort. You may have to rewrite it several times before it is ready to be typed. Again, it pays to show the essay to friends, relatives, or anyone who has an eye for good, clear writing. There are now computer software programs available that can cut down on the time required if you are submitting multiple applications.

Where you list extracurricular activities on the application, be sure to put your best foot forward. The admissions committee wants to know whether you are well-rounded, versatile, a self-starter, or an innovator. List those activities that show you have some or all of these traits. Unique activities always catch the eye. Are you a tournament bridge player, a sky diver, an astronomer, or a commodities speculator? If so, be sure to mention it.

Work experience does count heavily, so list your previous jobs and responsibilities carefully. The admissions committee looks at this item closely to see if you are a hard worker, are willing to assume responsibility, and have a record of job achievements. The student who went to college and held a job simultaneously is often given positive consideration. If you have had full-time work experience, play it up. If you have done only part-time work, list your jobs in a way that indicates the value of such experience.

If the school wants you to write one or more essays, try to be creative but not cute. Show them by the way you write your essay that you are keenly interested in getting an MBA, giving your reason, and that you believe you have the attributes to be successful in the business world. It is recommended that you spend five to ten hours on your application, particularly your essays.

Letters of Recommendation

Letters of recommendation can be important, so you should give considerable attention to deciding whom to list as references. Consider those people you know who will give the time and attention necessary in writing a reference or in filling out the recommendation form the school sends them. Also, choose people who you feel will complete the recommendations by the deadline dates, so their letters will be reviewed.

You probably have a wide range of references to choose from—professors, business acquaintances, family friends, and alumni of the business school. Don't bother to list millionaires, ministers, congressmen, or judges as references unless you are sure they will write a favorable and individualized reference for you. You don't want mediocre or routine letters of recommendation. You don't want letters that say what a great athlete or social charmer you are. You do want letters that say you have the character, talent, and intelligence to do well at business school and in the business world.

If you are out of ideas about whom to list as a reference, ask the professor who gave you your highest grades. Another approach is to look to the younger professors; some of the older ones may be tired of writing recommendations and their letters may look tired, too. Generally, avoid the most popular professors; they may be swamped.

Before you finally decide on whom to list as references, call or write and ask them if they will agree to help you. At the same time, it might be a good idea to suggest to these persons that you would be pleased to send them some material on the criteria the school uses in screening students, as well as a summary sketch of your background and accomplishments. This way, you will be providing your references with material they can use in their letters. If a reference asks that you write the first draft of the letter that he or she will then edit, jump at the chance. Also, keep in mind that if you are writing summaries for three different references, give each of them some unique and different material. This will prevent their reference letters from commenting on almost identical traits using the same illustrations.

Obviously, collecting the right references and getting them to write recommendations that are super takes a lot of work, but if you want to be a success in the business world, this is the kind of project you'll be engaged in continuously. So, you might as well start now.

Is it worthwhile to ask business acquaintances and others to try to "pull some strings" to help get you into a good business school? In answering this question, you have to be guided by some knowledge of the particular graduate school involved and also by common sense. For example, if you are asked to give three recommendations and you give three, but then you ask a dozen people to write letters to the college urging that they admit you, you are asking for trouble because you have applied overkill. On the other hand, it is usually good if one or two prominent businesspeople or others write unsolicited letters to the admissions committee urging your admission. Keep in mind that if the director of admissions or dean thinks that you and your family are applying unusual pressure to gain admittance, it might trigger a negative reaction and work to your disadvantage.

The people who probably carry the most weight with admissions groups are members of the business school's faculty, members of the university's faculty, prominent alumni of the business school, and prominent businessmen or -women. If you can't use any of these people as references but you do have a chance to contact them, indicate that you are very much interested in being admitted to the specific business school. These professors and businesspeople are smart enough to know that you have given them this information with the hope that they can be helpful. If they want to help they will, but if they don't want to for one reason or another, your informal request hasn't put them under any pressure.

SHOULD YOU VISIT THE CAMPUS?

By all means visit the schools you are interested in if you have the time and can afford the trip. Nothing takes the place of a personal visit. It gives you a feel for the school and its environment and the personality of the students, and enables you to meet school officials and ask them questions. If you can arrange an interview and you do well in interview situations, it might help your chances of getting admitted. But if interviews are optional and you have found you don't come across well in interviews, skip it.

When you narrow down your list of prospective schools, you might find that you can save on airfare and other expenses by getting a great deal of information about the prospective schools on a computer. Most business schools offer through their web sites a virtual tour of their school and campus. Some of these web sites allow you to see physical facilities, classes, assignments, lists of required readings, etc. Often, business schools make videotapes available to prospective students.

If you do decide to visit, there's a good deal of homework you should do. First, you should read the catalog carefully and jot down any questions you have. When you have done this preliminary work, write to the admissions office and tell them you would like to spend the day visiting the campus. Suggest several possible dates, and let the admissions people indicate which date is best. Keep in mind that there are different officers in charge of various areas so you may have to see three or four people to get all your questions answered. Also, ask if the school has a guided tour you can take to see what the campus is like.

Here are some questions that should be mandatory for any campus visit:

1. What are your chances of being admitted?

2. What majors are possible?

3. What is a recommended first-year program?

4. How much campus recruiting is done by companies?

5. What social activities and cultural events are available?

6. What financial aid and scholarships or assistantship opportunities are offered?

Also, be sure to:

1. See the classroom and lecture facilities.

2. Visit the business library.

3. Check on student living and dining accommodations.

4. Check on college guidance and placement facilities.

Another way to size up the various schools is to attend one of the MBA forums or similar events that are held in cities throughout the country. MBA forums are also held in Europe. In addition, forums have been held in Hong Kong, Tokyo, Seoul, and Shanghai. Prospective students have a chance to talk with the admissions staff from many schools all at one location. It represents a substantial savings in time and money for the would-be graduate student. The Kellogg School of Management offers foreign students the chance to talk to school officials through their worldwide alumni network.

Another good idea is to see if you can locate alumni of the school from among your family's friends and acquaintances. However, try to talk to fairly recent graduates. If you discuss the school with alumni who are 20 to 30 years out of school, they may be out of touch with the philosophy and methods their alma mater now follows.

Personal Interviews

If you decide to go on an interview, it could be the opportunity you need. If you are interviewed regarding admission, be sure not to ask questions that you could easily have answered by reading the college catalog. These types of questions can be a liability. Concentrate on questions that are important. In the process, be sure to give the interviewer enough insight as to your interests, academic record, and job goals to make a favorable impression.

Prior to the interview, be prepared to articulate your reasons for pursuing a graduate business degree and your interest in that particular school. It turns off many admissions officers if it appears you are interested in getting into any one of several graduate business schools and not just the one for which you are being interviewed. When asked about goals, have some clearly in mind. School officials know that everybody won't become president of a major corporation, but they would like to have some idea of your aspirations.

Finally, dress can be an important factor in the impression you make on the interviewer. Go on the assumption that dressing like a businessperson is appropriate at a business school interview.

Financing Your Education

CHAPTER 15

HOW MUCH WILL IT REALLY COST?

The primary difference in the cost of going to graduate business school versus undergraduate school is slightly higher tuition. Naturally, the source of funds to pay for tuition, books, fees, housing, food, and transportation may be significantly different depending upon whether you are still a dependent of your parents or not. If you are a part-time student, your major expenses will be limited to tuition, books, fees, and transportation to and from school. The rest of your living expense would be the same even if you were not going to school. If you will be a full-time student attending a university away from home, you will have the added costs of room and board, periodic transportation from home to school, and other miscellaneous living expenses.

The entry section of this book provides you with an accurate estimate of the costs at different schools. The two items that represent the most substantial variations between one school and another are tuition and transportation. For example, if you go to a publicly supported city or state university, the tuition could be as low as $6,000 a year for a student meeting residency requirements. If, on the other hand, you go to a private school, the tuition could be as high as $25,000 to $40,000 a year. There may be incremental costs associated with urban versus more rural locations as well.

A state university with an outstanding, highly accredited business school can represent a very good bargain. For example, a resident of Virginia will pay more than $5,000 less than a nonresident to attend the University of Virginia graduate business school. In Ohio, a resident will pay about $11,000 less than a nonresident to attend Ohio State University business school. In Indiana, a resident will pay more than $13,000 less than a nonresident to attend the Krannert School of Business at Purdue University. When you consider total expense for a year, in California, a resident will spend more than $23,000 less than a nonresident to attend the Business School at the University of California at Berkeley. While the actual numbers vary and do change annually, tuition at other fine state universities throughout the country, such as the Darden School at the University of Virginia, the Mays School of Business at Texas A&M University, and the Kenan Flagler Business School at the University of North Carolina, for students who meet state residency requirements, is quite modest. In fact, the tuition rate for nonresident students at these schools can be viewed also as a bargain when compared to comparably rated private universities. For example, costs for one year at the Zicklin School at Baruch College of the City University of New York come to approximately $18,000 for in-state students and $34,635 for out-of-state students, compared to the costs at these private universities: Kogod School at American University, $53,132; the Fuqua School at Duke University, $72,798; and the Graduate Business School at Harvard University, $78,200.

The variable costs of room and board and other living expenses for graduate students can be managed the same way they are managed for undergraduate students. Living in campus housing is usually cheaper than living in an off-campus apartment; eating in campus cafeterias is cheaper than eating in off-campus restaurants, and so on. By the time a student has spent four years as an under-graduate, he or she should know how to budget these expenses.

No matter how you figure it, however, a full-time graduate will probably have to spend from $25,000 to $50,000 a year—considerably more at the very top-rated schools. If you are married, you can increase the cost by at least $10,000. If you have children, add $5,000 to $7,000 per child. Of course, having a spouse might mean that you have an additional source of income to help defray the cost of graduate school.

There is a very good web site available to assist students in estimating their total costs. The site is called "FinAid" and includes an interactive financial aid form as well as a calculator designed to enable students to compare costs of attending different schools.

The site can be accessed at *www.finaid.org/calculators/finaidestimate.phtml*.

WHAT TYPES OF FINANCIAL AID ARE AVAILABLE?

Financial assistance to graduate business students breaks down into four categories:

> Scholarships and fellowships
> Teaching and research assistantships
> Loans
> Tax-qualified tuition plans

Scholarships and Fellowships

Scholarships and fellowships, covering tuition expenses and often providing additional money to help defray living expenses, are usually awarded on the basis of merit. In nearly all cases, such awards are *not* considered income for tax purposes. Some awards are given directly by the schools; others are given by the government, nonprofit organizations, business groups, and individual firms. The Ford Foundation, Sears, Roebuck and Co., and General Electric are just a few of the hundreds of large organizations that provide sizable awards to graduate business students. Some of these grants are based on financial need, but many are awarded on the basis of merit alone. The awards are generally terminated if students fail to maintain a satisfactory level of scholarship. There are a number of computer programs and Internet web sites that can help you search out scholarship and fellowship information.

If you want to apply for a scholarship or fellowship—and it makes good sense to apply even if you think your chances of being successful are slim—make sure to get your business school application in early. You must be accepted for admission before your application for a grant will be considered. Check the financial aid offices at the schools to which you are applying to find out how to apply for the assistance available.

Teaching and Research Assistantships

Many business schools employ dozens of students as teaching or research assistants. Usually these assistantships require a specified number of work hours a week. Typically, a student will work 20 hours per week and will earn $8 to $12 per hour and receive a remission of tuition.

If you are taking a teaching assistantship, the work may include grading undergraduate quizzes, tutoring undergraduates, conducting "lab" sessions for large lecture classes, or being a computer lab instructor. Teaching assistantships are particularly good if you want to gain insight and experience into the education process. Research assistants generally help faculty members on research projects. These assistantships are often advantageous because they involve close collaboration with faculty members on projects that can be both interesting and rewarding.

The major drawback of assistantships is that they can take so much time from your work week that you might find it difficult to handle the job in addition to a full course load. In that case, it may take you longer to complete your degree. As with fellowships and scholarships, you usually have to be accepted into the graduate program before the school will consider your application for an assistantship.

Loans

As schools compete for good students, they are trying to increase their financial aid packages. If you have explored all the preceding forms of aid without success, you might consider a loan. Loans are approved by the school and by the lending institution. Terms, interest rates, and the repayment features of loans can vary substantially. Seek a low-interest loan that at the start does not carry interest charges and that you need not begin repaying until you graduate. Some lending institutions will let you pay your bills on the installment plan.

If you want to borrow through the federal loan program, you must file a Free Application for Federal Student Aid (FAFSA), which calculates your financial need. This form may be obtained from the institution to which you are applying. Or you may use the FAFSA Express on the Internet that allows you to fill out your application on the computer from the FAFSA web site *www.fafsa.ed.gov.* Complete one FAFSA with the Title IV school codes of all the institutions to which you are applying. Links on this web site provide you with additional information. You can also contact the Federal Student Aid Information Center for additional information on the web at contact *studentaid.ed.gov* or call 1-800-433-3243 Monday through Friday during normal business hours. You should contact those institutions to which you are applying for specific deadlines and any other additional information required.

Here are a few major programs:

- The Federal Stafford Loan Program is available in two forms: subsidized and unsubsidized. Both forms are low-interest loans that are insured by the federal government. Both forms also require that you are at least a half-time student. The subsidized Federal Stafford Loan is a need-based loan in which interest is deferred and subsidized by the federal government as long as you are enrolled at least half time as a student.

  The unsubsidized Federal Stafford Loan is not based on financial need and is used to meet unmet financial need and/or replace an expected family contribution. Interest on the unsubsidized Federal Stafford Loan is *not* paid by the federal government at any time, and thus must be paid by the borrower—the student. Students can pay the interest when billed quarterly or allow it to accrue and capitalize (be added to the principal) while in college.

  The maximum subsidized Federal Stafford Loan per year is currently $8,500 or the amount of your unmet need, whichever is less. The current combined annual maximum for the subsidized and unsubsidized Federal Stafford Loan program is $18,500. Therefore, the maximum unsubsidized Federal Stafford Loan you can borrow per year is the difference between the combined annual maximum (or $18,500) and your subsidized Federal Stafford Loan eligibility. The cumulative maximum is $138,500 with only $65,500 as subsidized loans.

  The interest rate for all Federal Stafford Loans, both subsidized and unsubsidized, granted after July 1, 1994, is variable with a cap of 8.25 percent. The rate is adjusted annually on July 1. Interest may be tax deductible. If you are eligible to deduct interest on your Stafford Loans there is a limit of $2,500 per year. Refer to the IRS Publication 970, Tax Benefits for Higher Education, for an explanation of this and other tax benefits for which you might be eligible. You can contact the IRS at 1-800-829-1040.

  For more information on the Federal Stafford Loan program consult the following web site: *www.studentaid.ed.gov/students/publications/student_guide/2003_2004/english/types-stafford.htm*
- The Federal Perkins Loan is both a federally insured and federally subsidized loan program administered by the various schools. You must be enrolled at least half time in order to be eligible for a Perkins Loan. It is designed to provide need-based, low-interest financial assistance to students demonstrating high financial need. The exact loan amount offered to students depends on the availability of funds and the amount of their financial need, but cannot exceed *$6,000* per year. The cumulative maximum for this program is $40,000 and includes both undergraduate and graduate borrowing. Principal and interest are deferred during the in-school years. Repayment begins following a grace period of either six or nine months depending upon when the student received his or her first Federal Perkins Loan. The interest rate is 5 percent during the repayment period, which can last up to 10 years. Deferments are available under certain situations once repayments start.

For more information on the Federal Perkins Loan *pro*gram consult the following web site: *www.studentaid.ed.gov/students/publications/student_guide/2003_2004/english/types-fedperkinsloan.htm*

There are a number of state loan programs. Some schools also have special programs for minority students. (See also the earlier section "As a Minority Group Member.")

You or your family may also be able to take advantage of the lifetime learning tax credit approved by Congress. The tax credit is available to individuals who file a tax return and owe taxes. This is either for a student filing his or her own return or, if the student is a dependent, it can be utilized when his or her family files a return. It is subtracted directly from an individual's or family's actual tax liability rather than being a tax deduction that reduces taxable income. The credit covers such items as room and board, transportation, and other living expenses.

Also, look into the new student loan interest deduction, which permits a deduction from interest paid on educational loans. There are restrictions and qualifiers for both programs, so check these out with a knowledgeable tax person.

Keep these pointers in mind when applying for loans:

- First, do not automatically assume you do not qualify for a loan because of your family income, and, as a result, decide not to apply for a specific college. Rules and regulations for loan programs constantly change, and such changes may make you eligible.
- Second, contact the financial aid office at each of the schools to which you plan to apply, because each office may require different forms to be completed.
- Third, make sure you apply early. Most schools have deadlines in early spring for the upcoming year.
- Fourth, keep copies of everything you send and send it by certified mail with return receipt requested.

Work-Study

The Federal Government Work-Study Program (FWS) allows financial aid directors to include summer and part-time jobs in student aid packages. The job will be with a public or private nonprofit agency, and the student can work 10 to 20 hours a week during regular semesters; more in summers and vacations periods; however, the student must go through an interview process in order to secure an FWS job. Check with your school's Office of Financial Aid to find out what deadlines apply for first-year and returning graduate students. FWS uses the federal minimum wage rate. However, many colleges subsidize this amount, paying between $8 and $12 per hour for graduate students.

For more information on the Federal Government Work-Study Program consult the following web site: *www.studentaid.ed.gov/students/publications/student_guide/2003_2004/english/types-fed-workstudy.htm*

Tax-qualified Tuition Programs

States remain the sole sponsor of tax-exempt plans. These usually take the form of prepaid tuition for undergraduate study, although some states will permit some of the funds to be used for graduate study. However, so-called Section 529 plans—Qualified Tuition Programs (QTP)—enable families and individuals to participate in college savings plans that can be beneficial for graduate students. The Section 529 plans are set up in the name of a beneficiary to be used any time in his or her lifetime for educational expenses. QTP contributors can "gift" up to $50,000 per year into an account. The maximum amount that can be contributed per beneficiary is dependent upon one's state of residence.

QTP contributors remain in control of the funds, so if they are not used up they can regain them. Nevertheless, when made, the payments are considered completed gifts for IRS purposes and are removed from the contributor's estate. Earnings in the account accumulate tax-deferred until withdrawn. This tax-free status will expire after 2010 unless Congress extends this benefit. The beneficiary has access to the funds for educational expenses, including graduate study. Individuals can even set up Section 529 accounts whereby they are the beneficiary at some future time.

Another investment program to consider is the Cloverdell Education Savings Account in which individuals can establish educational accounts for persons under the age of 18. All contributions must cease at age 18; however, the funds can be used by a designated beneficiary until the age of 30. *There is an annual $2,000 contribution limit, as well as an income ceiling of $190,000 for a married couple filing jointly. Families with incomes between $190,000 and $220,000 are eligible to make partial contributions.* This type of program may benefit graduate students in the future, but is probably too late to be an option for persons pursuing an MBA at this time. It is a good idea to recheck with the school's financial aid office for any change in these programs, which occur from time to time.

Other Options

If you are unable to get financial assistance in any of the ways just outlined, do not give up. There are many types of part-time jobs you might get. At some schools, graduate students take jobs as dormitory or residence hall counselors or advisors, earning free room and sometimes other benefits, such as full or partial tuition remission. Many students work part time in the library, mailroom, or computer center, or as waiters in residence halls and fraternities. Still others have come up with more unique jobs, such as stringing tennis rackets or working as hospital orderlies, substitute firefighters, lifeguards, or security personnel. In the past few years, some students have successfully started Internet companies and other start-up firms while still in school. Many universities and their graduate business schools now have affiliations with business research and development parks in which graduate business students can find paid employment as research assistants, management interns, and business consultants.

Married students should check on employment opportunities for their spouses. Sometimes such jobs are fairly easy to qualify for, but it may be difficult for a spouse to get a campus job because of the abundance of well-educated spouses who want jobs in campus communities.

Here are a number of general tips regarding scholarships and financial aid:

- Check all possible sources, including reference books and web sites, which provide information on scholarships and financial aid.
- Keep in mind that most schools that have the highest tuition and costs generally offer the greatest amount of financial assistance.
- Start your search for financial aid early.
- If you get an offer from one school and there are competing schools, do not hesitate to let the other schools know of the offer and see whether they will come up with an even better offer. It does not hurt to show your interest and negotiate!

What Employers Seek

The qualities employers favor in business master's graduates emerge with some clarity based on a number of studies done over the recent years. The results of these studies can be summarized as follows:

- Broad administrative skills are preferred over technical skills. For example, companies want MBAs to be potential marketing managers, not technicians in marketing research or advertising layout; they want managers of the accounting function, not work-a-day accountants.
- Employment needs are based on long-range executive potential rather than immediate job needs.
- Considerable work experience is preferred by most companies.
- Students who have strong backgrounds in the traditional functional areas of information systems, finance, management, marketing, and accounting are preferred.
- Employers want graduates with strong written and communications skills.

There has been a swing to practicality in most business schools. That's because a growing number of employers have indicated they want graduates who have taken "meat and potato" courses. A number of studies indicate this.

Some time ago, AACSB surveyed academicians and businesspeople and asked them to rank the 13 traditional business school subjects in terms of how much time and effort should be spent on each one of them. The initial analysis showed that most master's degree candidates should spend more time on finance, human behavior, and organization theory. There was a difference between academicians and businesspeople as to the subjects graduate business schools should teach. The academic respondents placed their main emphasis on economics, whereas businesspeople put accounting first and economics third. Many of these responses would be different today.

JOB PLACEMENT

It should be very important to you that the business school you attend has a good placement staff. Most graduate business schools have sizable job counseling and placement services and many are trying to improve their career counseling and placement assistance to graduates.

You should take a hard look at the placement center, which can be second in importance only to academics in terms of your career. The number of companies recruiting on many campuses has been reduced so it is important that you ask questions about what companies have been and will be recruiting at the schools in which you are interested. Some MBAs may find it difficult to get jobs particularly if they aren't a graduate of one of the top 20 or more "national" business schools or major regional schools where recruiters from major employers concentrate.

The placement service is the focal point of requests from corporations who want to do job interviews on campus and from other employers who are seeking applicants for jobs. If you are interested in getting the best job possible when you graduate, make sure to use the resources of your school's job placement service to the fullest extent.

Like everything else, there are good, mediocre, and poor placement offices, and you should have some idea as to the effectiveness of the one at your school. (Schools that have close links to the business community have a major advantage in placing students.) One way to do this is to visit it and gauge, firsthand, the staff and their method of operation. Try to determine whether the department provides individual counseling about the type of job you might be interested in, and if it has wide contacts with prospective employers. The office should have fairly extensive data on various local companies as well as those with headquarters elsewhere. It also should have data on current pay scales for most starting and junior management positions.

The placement office can play an important role in arranging job interviews for students. It alerts students to company recruiters who plan to be on campus and provides both parties with information about each other before and after the interviews. Placement officers can help students fill out the standardized application forms that they make available to prospective employers. The placement office might even prepare for distribution to prospective employers a special brochure listing key information about graduates' interests, backgrounds, and types of employment being sought. Schools often participate in job fairs, where prospective employers have booths and students can sign up if they want more information on the company or are interested in arranging a job interview.

The school's objective is to get good jobs for as many graduates as possible. In the interest of fairness, there are two basic restrictions for companies that are recruiting. First, students sign up for interviews on a first-come, first-served basis, so that companies cannot pick the students they want to talk with ahead of time. Second, academic records aren't available to the recruiters, so there isn't any way of knowing whether the student who walks through the door is at the top or the bottom of his or her class.

Most schools also offer special seminars on job possibilities, how to prepare résumés, and how to handle interviews and job negotiations. In addition to counseling students, the placement staff may also assist alumni who are seeking new positions.

At some schools, particularly those not in the top 30 ranked schools, students and placement officers have embarked on vigorous marketing programs to attract recruiters to visit their schools. The universities of Tennessee, Texas, and Georgia all have had unique programs to lure corporate recruiters to their campuses.

A growing number of graduate schools publish a detailed account every year of the types of jobs obtained by its graduating class and the salaries received. This can be very useful information for prospective students as they try to decide which schools they should consider.

Because of growing competition for students, many business schools are putting a great deal of emphasis on their placement offices. This has led to an increase in placement staff and to schools making more efforts to get national and regional companies to send recruiters to their campuses. There is a growing number of regional conferences where prospective graduates can meet with dozens of recruiters in one location.

Some schools are even coming up with some unique ways to market their graduates. A while back, at the Olin School at Washington University, the school printed up 50,000 mock baseball cards with profiles of their MBA graduates and sent them to 4,800 corporate human resource departments. Other schools send out videotapes of their graduates. Another way business schools are trying to improve job prospects for their new graduates is to tap the various alumni clubs they have set up, urging older MBA graduates to see if they can find jobs for the new MBAs.

The big national firms such as Citibank and others tend to concentrate on the top-tier schools and the big regional corporations often stick to the top-tier regional business schools. It generally means that schools that are not on the list of top 100 or so business schools have a much harder time placing their MBA students because the recruiting efforts by companies at those schools tend to be much less than at the bigger, better-known, and higher ranking schools.

Career Outlook

Figures published by a number of organizations that analyze job trends indicate that the needs of businesses for college graduates will continue to grow in the forseeable future. As a result, there are growing enrollments in undergraduate business schools as well as graduate business schools.

The major reason that businesses are seeking college-trained men and women is simply that the business world is becoming increasingly complex and needs employees who are trained in the basics of such fields as accounting, information science, and marketing. Business also needs people who have broad backgrounds in general management and are able to put all the elements of a problem together so it can be solved. Also, many college students are going into business careers because they are becoming more job oriented than they have been in the recent past. Education majors, for example, who may find job opportunities slim, are now turning to business as a major or second major to give them job flexibility.

While the demand for college business graduates is on the increase, the demand for business master's graduates is even greater. An interesting study done some time ago by the Association of MBA Executives showed the relative financial advantages of an MBA. This study was done on the assumption that students earn the MBA to enhance their chances of career success and increased salary. The survey measured the value of the MBA by comparing it in salary increments to the bachelor's degree. The conclusion was that there is a significant difference in measurable income between the MBA graduate and the bachelor's degree holder. Among the findings: Over a lifetime of work, an MBA degree can yield $500,000 or more compared to a bachelor's degree.

This study was done years ago. Today, most experts in the field would agree that this figure has at least doubled since then.

There are not only differences between the lifetime earnings of those with MBA degrees compared to those with only bachelor's degrees, but there can be sizable differences in average earnings between graduates of various business schools.

Starting Salaries

Starting salaries offered to business master's graduates are a widely discussed topic. For many, the salary is the tangible payoff at the end of their graduate work, but there are substantial variations. Salaries are based on many factors, including academic standing, age, previous experience, school attended, major field, the geographic area where you plan to work (the East and West Coast, for example, tend to pay higher starting salaries), the size of the company you start with, and the industry in which you are working.

It is clear that starting salaries for MBAs have gone up sharply in recent years. For graduates of some of the top business schools with several years of work experience, it was not unusual for some of them to receive salaries of more than $100,000 a year, plus sign-on bonuses that could be in the $10,000 to $25,000 range. Major corporations are the ones that hire most of the MBAs. For example, Procter & Gamble, Citicorp, and General Motors each have employed more than 100 MBAs in a single year. However, interest is growing on the part of graduate business students to work for small companies or the government. In general, the graduates of the prestigious national business schools command higher starting salaries than those from lesser-known schools.

While there are some sizable differences in pay between those with technical and nontechnical undergraduate degrees and those with work experience, there are also differences based on the industry a graduate enters. Management consulting, commercial banking, investment banking, automotive, and chemicals tend to be the industries that pay the highest; government agencies and nonprofit organizations pay the lowest.

Starting salaries, of course, will also vary between cities. To be realistic, you must weigh the salary offered by a company in one city against the cost of living in that city as compared with the salary offered by a firm in another city and the cost of living there. One way to do this is to get the Cost of Living Index comparisons of large cities, published by the Bureau of Labor Statistics. Then multiply the index ratio by the starting salary offered in one city and compare this result with offers received to work in other cities.

Several publications run articles on the companies for which MBAs would like to work. The same names seem to appear on most lists. They include

1. McKinsey
2. Goldman Sachs
3. Morgan Stanley
4. Merrill Lynch
5. Boston Consulting Group
6. Citicorp
7. Microsoft
8. Coca-Cola
9. Cisco
10. Amazon
11. A. T. Kearney
12. J. P. Morgan
13. GE Capital
14. Johnson and Johnson
15. Disney
16. Intel
17. Hewlett Packard

As you can see, consulting firms, investment banking, high-tech companies, and blue-chip firms dominate the list.

FUTURE TRENDS

A number of trends in graduate business schools and in industry are already discernable.

First, the number of new schools using traditional methods will slow down. On the other hand, for-profit schools offering the MBA through distance learning will continue to show sharp gains.

Competition for students will become keener, and schools will become more market-oriented as they position themselves to be of greater appeal to prospective students. Students will become more demanding of the quality of teaching, the utilization of new teaching methods, and how current and relevant the instruction is. Team teaching, cross-functional teaching, utilization of television, cable TV, computers, and distance learning will be very common.

As for courses, E-commerce, manufacturing and technology, entrepreneurial courses, and ethics courses have taken on new importance. A growing number of schools are also increasing the use of business executives to help teach these courses since changes in many of these fields are coming so rapidly that it is difficult for many of the full-time faculty to keep up with them.

Interest in international business has been dramatic. Many schools are offering special courses to cover this area or are integrating material on international business into existing courses. Several schools offer students the opportunity to work on projects overseas for which they are given credit toward their degree. In fact, foreign language study is being encouraged among those students who have an interest in international business. China (and Chinese), in particular, has become the focus of many students who are interested in having a career that involves international business.

There will also be an increased effort to better prepare MBAs for the business world they will enter. Business schools are making special efforts to paint a realistic picture of the business world and the realities of how to be successful in that world. A continual reassessment of the curriculum is being made by many business schools and existing courses changed and new ones added. There will be changes in the way students learn. In addition to the "core courses," such as accounting, finance, and marketing, students will be learning other skills, such as teamwork, cultural sensitivity, human interaction, foreign languages, and the ability to communicate well both in writing and speaking.

Appendix

A List of Schools Requiring the GMAT

Listed below are graduate schools of business that *require* the GMAT as part of their admissions procedure.

UNITED STATES

ALABAMA

Alabama Agricultural and Mechanical University
School of Business
Normal, AL 35762

Auburn University
Auburn School of Business
Graduate School
Auburn, AL 36830

Samford University
School of Business
Birmingham, AL 35229

Spring Hill College
MBA Program
Mobile, AL 36608

Troy State University
School of Business and Commerce
Troy, AL 36081

Troy State University at Dothan
Fort Rucker School of Business and Commerce
Dothan, AL 36301

Troy State University at Montgomery
MBA Program
Montgomery, AL 36082

University of Alabama/Birmingham
Graduate School of Management
Birmingham, AL 35294

University of Alabama/Huntsville
School of Administrative Science
Huntsville, AL 35899

University of Alabama/Tuscaloosa
Graduate School of Business
Tuscaloosa, AL 35487

University of North Alabama
School of Business
Florence, AL 35630

University of South Alabama Graduate School
College of Business and Management Studies
Mobile, AL 36688

ALASKA

University of Alaska/Anchorage
School of Business and Public Affairs
Anchorage, AK 99508

University of Alaska/Fairbanks
School of Management
MBA Program
Fairbanks, AK 99701

University of Alaska/Juneau
Division of Business
Juneau, AK 99801

ARIZONA

American Graduate School of International Management
Graduate Business Program
Glendale, AZ 85306

Arizona State University
College of Business Administration
Tempe, AZ 85287

Grand Canyon University
College of Business
Phoenix, AZ 85017

Northern Arizona University
College of Business Administration
Flagstaff, AZ 86011

University of Arizona
College of Business and Public Administration
Graduate Programs
Tucson, AZ 85721

ARKANSAS

Arkansas State University
College of Business
Graduate Programs
State University, AR 72467

Harding University
Graduate School of Business
Searcy, AR 72143

University of Arkansas/Fayetteville
College of Business Administration
Fayetteville, AR 72701

University of Arkansas/Little Rock
The Graduate School
Little Rock, AR 72204

University of Central Arkansas
Graduate Business Programs
Conway, AR 72032

CALIFORNIA

Azusa Pacific University
Division of Business Administration
Azusa, CA 91702

California Lutheran College
Graduate Program in Business Administration
Thousand Oaks, CA 91360

California Polytechnic State University/San Luis Obispo
School of Business
San Luis Obispo, CA 93407

California State Polytechnic University/Pomona
School of Business Administration
Graduate Programs
Pomona, CA 91768

California State University/Bakersfield
School of Business and Public Administration
Graduate Programs
Bakersfield, CA 93309

California State University/Chico
School of Business
MBA Program
Chico, CA 95929

California State University/Dominguez Hills
School of Management
Carson, CA 90747

California State University/Fresno
School of Business
Graduate Program
Fresno, CA 93740

California State University/Fullerton
School of Business Administration and Economics
Fullerton, CA 92634

California State University/Hayward
School of Business and Economics
Graduate Programs
Hayward, CA 94542

California State University/Long Beach
School of Business Administration
Graduate Programs
Long Beach, CA 90801

California State University/Los Angeles
School of Business and Economics
Graduate Programs
Los Angeles, CA 90032

California State University/Northridge
School of Business Administration and Economics
Northridge, CA 91330

California State University/Sacramento
School of Business and Public Administration
Sacramento, CA 95819

California State University/San Bernardino
School of Administration
Graduate Programs
San Bernardino, CA 92346

California State University/Stanislaus
Division of Business Administration
MBA Program
Turlock, CA 95380

Chapman College
School of Business and Management
MBA Programs
Orange, CA 92666

Claremont Graduate School
Business Administration Department
Claremont, CA 91711

College of Notre Dame
Graduate School
Belmont, CA 94002

Golden Gate University
Graduate College and School of Accounting
San Francisco, CA 94105

Holy Names College
The MBA in Weekend College
Oakland, CA 94619

Humboldt State University
College of Business and Economics/MBA Program
Arcata, CA 95521

La Sierra University
School of Business and Management
Riverside, CA 92515

Lincoln University
Department of Business Administration
San Francisco, CA 94118

Loyola Marymount University
College of Business Administration
MBA Program
Los Angeles, CA 90045

Monterey Institute of International Studies
Division of International Management
Graduate Programs
Monterey, CA 93940

Northrop University
College of Business and Management
Graduate Programs
Inglewood, CA 90306

Pacific Christian College
Graduate School of Business
San Diego, CA 92111

Pacific States University
College of Business Administration
Los Angeles, CA 90006

Pepperdine University
School of Business and Management
Graduate Programs
Los Angeles, CA 90044

Saint Mary's College of California
Graduate Business Programs
Moraga, CA 94575

San Diego State University
College of Business Administration
San Diego, CA 92182

San Francisco State University
School of Business
San Francisco, CA 94132

San Jose State University
School of Business
MBA Program
San Jose, CA 95192

Santa Clara University
Leavey School of Business and Administration
Santa Clara, CA 95053

Sonoma State University
School of Business and Economics
Rohnert Park, CA 94928

Stanford University
Graduate School of Business
Stanford, CA 94305

United States International University
School of Business and Management
Graduate Programs
San Diego, CA 92131

University of California/Berkeley
Graduate School of Business Administration
Berkeley, CA 94720

University of California/Davis
Graduate School of Administration
Davis, CA 95616

University of California/Irvine
Graduate School of Management
Irvine, CA 92717

University of California/Los Angeles
Graduate School of Management
Los Angeles, CA 90024

University of California/Riverside
Graduate School of Administration
Riverside, CA 92521

University of California/San Diego
Graduate School of Business Administration
San Diego, CA 92110

University of Judaism
Graduate School of Management
Public Management and Administration
Los Angeles, CA 90077

University of La Verne
School of Business and Economics
La Verne, CA 91750

University of San Diego
School of Business Administration
Alcala Park
San Diego, CA 92110

University of San Francisco
McLaren College of Business
MBA Program
San Francisco, CA 94117

University of Southern California
Graduate School of Business Administration
Los Angeles, CA 90007

University of the Pacific
School of Business and Public Administration
Stockton, CA 95211

COLORADO

Colorado State University
College of Business
MBA Program
Fort Collins, CO 80523

Regis College/Colorado Springs Campus
Graduate Program
Colorado Springs, CO 80904

Regis College/Denver Campus
Special Programs
MBA Program
Denver, CO 80221

University of Colorado
Graduate School of Business Administration
Boulder, CO 80309

University of Colorado at Colorado Springs
Graduate School of Business Administration
Colorado Springs, CO 80933

University of Colorado at Denver
Graduate School of Business
Denver, CO 80202

University of Denver
Graduate School of Business and Public Management
Denver, CO 80208

University of Southern Colorado
Graduate School of Business
Pueblo, CO 81001

CONNECTICUT

Central Connecticut State University
Organization and Management
New Britain, CT 06050

Fairfield University
School of Business
Graduate Program
Fairfield, CT 06430

Quinnipiac College
Graduate Studies
School of Business
Hamden, CT 06518

Sacred Heart University
Division of Graduate Studies
Bridgeport, CT 06606

Southern Connecticut State University
School of Business Economics
New Haven, CT 06515

University of Bridgeport
Graduate School of Management
Bridgeport, CT 06601

University of Connecticut
School of Business Administration
Storrs, CT 06269
(Note: The MBA program is offered at the Stamford and
     Hartford campuses.)

University of Hartford
Austin Dunham Barney School of Business and Public
     Administration
West Hartford, CT 06117

Western Connecticut State University
Ancell School of Business
Danbury, CT 06810

Yale University
School of Organization and Management
New Haven, CT 06520

DELAWARE

Delaware State College
Graduate School of Business
Dover, DE 19901

Goldey-Beacom College
Office of Graduate Studies
Wilmington, DE 19808

University of Delaware
College of Business and Economics
Newark, DE 19711

Wilmington College
MBA Program
New Castle, DE 19720

DISTRICT OF COLUMBIA

American University
The Kogod College of Business Administration
Washington, DC 20016

George Washington University
School of Government and Business Administration
Washington, DC 20052

Georgetown University
School of Business Administration
Washington, DC 20057

Howard University
School of Business and Public Administration
Washington, DC 20001

Southeastern University
School of Business and Public Administration
Washington, DC 20024

Strayer College
Graduate School, Business Administration
Washington, DC 20005

University of the District of Columbia
College of Business and Public Management
Washington, DC 20004

FLORIDA

Barry University
School of Business
Graduate Division
Miami Shores, FL 33161

Florida Agricultural and Mechanical University
Graduate Business Program
Tallahassee, FL 32307

Florida Atlantic University
College of Business and Public Administration
Boca Raton, FL 33431

Florida International University
Graduate Business Program
Miami, FL 33199

Florida State University
College of Business
Tallahassee, FL 32306

Jacksonville University
College of Business Administration
Jacksonville, FL 32211

Nova University
Center for the Study of Administration
Fort Lauderdale, FL 33314

Palm Beach Atlantic College
School of Graduate Studies
West Palm Beach, FL 33416

Rollins College
Roy E. Crummer Graduate School of Business
Winter Park, FL 32789

Saint Thomas University
Division of Human Resources
Program in Advanced Accounting
Miami, FL 33054

Stetson University
School of Business Administration
DeLand, FL 32720

University of Central Florida
College of Business Administration
Orlando, FL 32816

University of Florida
Graduate School of Business Administration
Gainesville, FL 32611

University of Miami
School of Business Administration
Graduate Studies
Coral Gables, FL 33124

University of North Florida
College of Business Administration
Jacksonville, FL 32216

University of South Florida
College of Business Administration
Tampa, FL 33620

GEORGIA

Albany State College
School of Business
Albany, GA 31705

Augusta College
School of Business Administration
Augusta, GA 30910

Berry College
Graduate Studies
Mount Berry, GA 30149

Clark Atlanta University
School of Business Administration
Atlanta, GA 30314

Columbus College
School of Business
Columbus, GA 31993

Emory University
Graduate School of Business Administration
Atlanta, GA 30322

Georgia College
School of Business
Milledgeville, GA 31061

Georgia Institute of Technology
College of Management
Atlanta, GA 30332

Georgia Southern College
Graduate School of Business
Statesboro, GA 30460

Georgia State University
Graduate Division
College of Business Administration
Atlanta, GA 30303

Kennesaw College
Graduate School of Business
Marietta, GA 30061

LaGrange College
MBA Program
LaGrange, GA 30240

Mercer University/Atlanta
Division of Business and Economics
MBA Program
Atlanta, GA 30341

Mercer University/Macon
School of Business and Economics
MBA Program
Macon, GA 31207

Savannah State College
School of Business
MBA Program
Savannah, GA 31404

Southern College of Technology
School of Management
Marietta, GA 30060

University of Georgia
Graduate School of Business Administration
Athens, GA 30602

Valdosta State College
School of Business Administration
Valdosta, GA 31698

West Georgia College
School of Business
Carrollton, GA 30118

HAWAII

Chaminade University of Honolulu
Business Administration Division
MBA Program
Honolulu, HI 96816

University of Hawaii at Hilo
Graduate School of Business
Hilo, HI 96720

University of Hawaii at Manoa
College of Business Administration
Honolulu, HI 96822

IDAHO

Boise State University
College of Business
Graduate Programs
Boise, ID 83725

Idaho State University
College of Business
MBA Program
Pocatello, ID 83209

ILLINOIS

Aurora University
Graduate Management Center
Aurora, IL 60506

Bradley University
College of Business Administration
MBA Program
Peoria, IL 61625

DePaul University
Graduate School of Business
Chicago, IL 60604

Eastern Illinois University
School of Business
Graduate Business Studies
Charleston, IL 61920

Governors State University
College of Business and Public Administration
Graduate Programs
Park Forest South, IL 60466

Illinois Benedictine College
MBA Program
Lisle, IL 60532

Illinois Institute of Technology
Stuart School of Management and Finance
Chicago, IL 60616

Illinois State University
College of Business
Graduate Programs
Normal, IL 61761

Lake Forest Graduate School of Management
Graduate Business Program
Lake Forest, IL 60045

Lewis University
College of Business
Romeoville, IL 60441

Loyola University of Chicago
Graduate School of Business
Chicago, IL 60611

North Central College
MBA Program
Naperville, IL 60566

Northeastern Illinois University
College of Business and Management
Chicago, IL 60625

Northern Illinois University
The Graduate School
College of Business
DeKalb, IL 60115

North Park College
MBA Programs
Chicago, IL 60625

Northwestern University
J.L. Kellogg Graduate School of Management
Evanston, IL 60201

Olivet Nazarene University
MBA Program
Kankakee, IL 60901

Quincy College
Graduate School of Business
Quincy, IL 62301

Roosevelt University
Walter E. Heller College of Business Administration
Graduate Programs
Chicago, IL 60605

Rosary College
Graduate Business Programs
River Forest, IL 60305

Saint Xavier College
Graham School of Management
Chicago, IL 60655

Sangamon State University
Graduate Programs
Springfield, IL 62708

Southern Illinois University/Carbondale
Graduate School and College of Business Administration
Carbondale, IL 62901

Southern Illinois University/Edwardsville
School of Business
Graduate Programs
Edwardsville, IL 62026

University of Chicago
Graduate School of Business
Chicago, IL 60637

University of Illinois at Chicago
Graduate School of Business
Chicago, IL 60680

University of Illinois at Urbana
Graduate School of Business
Urbana, IL 61801

Western Illinois University
College of Business
Graduate Programs
Macomb, IL 61455

INDIANA

Anderson University
School of Business
Anderson, IN 46012

Ball State University
College of Business
Graduate Programs
Muncie, IN 47306

Butler University
College of Business Administration
Graduate Programs
Indianapolis, IN 46208

Indiana State University
School of Business
Graduate Programs
Terre Haute, IN 47809

Indiana University/Bloomington
Graduate School of Business
Bloomington, IN 47401

Indiana University/Gary
Division of Business and Economics
Gary, IN 46408

Indiana University/Purdue University
Division of Business and Economics
Graduate Program
Fort Wayne, IN 46805

Indiana University/Purdue University
School of Business
Indianapolis, IN 46202

Indiana University/South Bend
Division of Business and Economics
Graduate Program
South Bend, IN 46615

Indiana University Southeast
Division of Business and Economics
New Albany, IN 47150

Manchester College
Graduate Program
North Manchester, IN 46962

Purdue University
Graduate School
Department of Management
Hammond, IN 46323

Purdue University
Krannert Graduate School of Management
West Lafayette, IN 47907

Saint Francis College
Department of Business Administration
Fort Wayne, IN 46808

University of Evansville
Graduate School of Business Administration
Evansville, IN 47702

University of Indianapolis
Graduate Business Programs
Indianapolis, IN 46227

University of Notre Dame
College of Business Administration
Graduate Division
Notre Dame, IN 46556

University of Southern Indiana
Office of Graduate Studies/School of Business
Evansville, IN 47712

IOWA

Drake University
College of Business Administration
Graduate Programs
Des Moines, IA 50311

Iowa State University
College of Business Administration
Ames, IA 50011

Maharishi International University
Department of Business Administration
Fairfield, IA 52556

Saint Ambrose College
MBA Program
Davenport, IA 52803

University of Dubuque
MBA Program
Dubuque, IA 52001

University of Iowa
College of Business Graduate Programs
Iowa City, IA 52242

University of Northern Iowa
School of Business
Graduate Programs
Cedar Falls, IA 50614

KANSAS

Emporia State University
Division of Business
Graduate Programs
Emporia, KS 66801

Fort Hays State University
School of Business
MBA Program
Hays, KS 67601

Friends University
College of Business Graduate Programs
Wichita, KS 67213

Kansas State University
College of Business Administration
Graduate Programs
Manhattan, KS 66506

Pittsburg State University
Kelce School of Business and Economics
MBA Program
Pittsburg, KS 66762

University of Kansas
School of Business
Graduate Programs
Lawrence, KS 66045

Washburn University
School of Business
MBA Program
Topeka, KS 66621

Wichita State University
College of Business Administration
Graduate Studies in Business
Wichita, KS 67208

KENTUCKY

Bellarmine College
Graduate Business Program
Louisville, KY 40205

Eastern Kentucky University
Graduate School
College of Business
Richmond, KY 40475

Morehead State University
School of Business and Economics
Morehead, KY 40351

Murray State University
College of Business and Public Affairs
Murray, KY 42071

Northern Kentucky University
Master of Business Administration
Highland Heights, KY 41076

University of Kentucky
College of Business and Economics
Lexington, KY 40506

University of Louisville
School of Business
Louisville, KY 40292

Western Kentucky University
Graduate College
Bowling Green, KY 42101

LOUISIANA

Centenary College of Louisiana
School of Business
MBA Program
Shreveport, LA 71104

Grambling State University
Graduate School of Business
Grambling, LA 71245

Louisiana State University/Baton Rouge
College of Business Administration
Graduate Division
Baton Rouge, LA 70803

Louisiana State University/Shreveport
College of Business Administration
MBA Program
Shreveport, LA 71115

Louisiana Tech University
College of Administration and Business
Graduate Programs
Ruston, LA 71272

Loyola University
College of Business Administration
Graduate Programs
New Orleans, LA 70118

McNeese State University
The Graduate School
MBA Program
Lake Charles, LA 70609

Nicholls State University
College of Business Administration
MBA Program
Thibodaux, LA 70310

Northeast Louisiana University
College of Business Administration
MBA Program
Monroe, LA 71209

Northwestern State University of Louisiana
Division of Business
Natchitoches, LA 71497

Southeastern Louisiana University
School of Graduate Studies
MBA Program
Hammond, LA 70402

Southern University
Graduate Accountancy Program
Baton Rouge, LA 70813

Tulane University
School of Business
MBA Program
New Orleans, LA 70118

University of New Orleans
College of Business Administration
Graduate Programs
New Orleans, LA 70112

University of Southwestern Louisiana
College of Business Administration
MBA Program
Lafayette, LA 70504

MAINE

Husson College
Graduate Studies Division
Bangor, ME 04401

Thomas College
Graduate School of Management
Waterville, ME 04901

University of Maine
College of Business Administration
The Graduate School
Orono, ME 04469

University of Southern Maine
School of Business Economics and Management
Portland, ME 04103

MARYLAND

Loyola College
School of Business and Management
Baltimore, MD 21210

Morgan State University
School of Graduate Studies
Baltimore, MD 21239

Mount Saint Mary's College
Graduate School of Business
Emmitsburg, MD 21727

Salisbury State College
School of Business
Salisbury, MD 21801

University of Baltimore
School of Business
Baltimore, MD 21201

University of Maryland/College Park
College of Business and Management
College Park, MD 20742

MASSACHUSETTS

American International College
School of Business Administration
Graduate Program
Springfield, MA 01109

Anna Maria College for Men and Women
Graduate Division, Department of Business Administration
Paxton, MA 01612

Assumption College
Graduate School
MBA Program
Worcester, MA 01609

Babson College
Graduate School of Business
Wellesley, MA 02157

Bentley College
Graduate School
Waltham, MA 02254

Boston College
Graduate School of Management
Chestnut Hill, MA 02167

Boston University
School of Management
Graduate Programs
Boston, MA 02215

Boston University
MBA Program
Boston, MA 02215

Brandeis University
Heller School
Waltham, MA 02254

Clark University
Graduate School of Management
Worcester, MA 01610

Fitchburg State College
Program in Management
Fitchburg, MA 01420

Massachusetts Institute of Technology
Alfred P. Sloan School of Management
Cambridge, MA 02139

Nichols College
MBA Program
Dudley, MA 01570

Northeastern University
Graduate School of Business Administration
Boston, MA 02115

Salem State College
Program in Business Administration
Salem, MA 01970

Simmons College
Graduate School of Management
Boston, MA 02115

Suffolk University
Graduate School of Management
Boston, MA 02108

University of Massachusetts at Amherst
School of Business Administration
Graduate School
Amherst, MA 01003

University of Massachusetts at Boston
Graduate Business School
Boston, MA 02105

University of Massachusetts at Dartmouth
MBA Program
North Dartmouth, MA 02747

University of Massachusetts at Lowell
College of Management
Lowell, MA 01854

University of Massachusetts/Worcester Medical Center
Graduate School of Nursing
Worcester, MA 01605

Western New England College
School of Business
Springfield, MA 01119

Worcester Polytechnic Institute
Evening School
MBA and MSA Programs
Worcester, MA 01609

MICHIGAN

Andrews University
School of Business
Berrien Springs, MI 49104

Aquinas College
Graduate Management Program
Grand Rapids, MI 49506

Central Michigan University
School of Business Administration
Graduate Programs
Mt. Pleasant, MI 48859

Eastern Michigan University
College of Business
Graduate Programs
Ypsilanti, MI 48197

GMI Engineering and Management Institute
Master of Science in Manufacturing Management Program
Flint, MI 48504

Grand Valley State Colleges
F.E. Seidman Graduate School of Business and Administration
Allendale, MI 49401

Lake Superior State College
Department of Business and Economics
MBA Program
Sault Ste. Marie, MI 49783

Madonna College
Graduate Studies Program
Livonia, MI 48150

Michigan State University
Graduate School of Business Administration
East Lansing, MI 48824

Michigan Technological University
School of Business and Engineering Administration
Graduate Program
Houghton, MI 49931

Northern Michigan University
School of Business and Management
MBA Program
Marquette, MI 49855

Oakland University
School of Economics and Management
Rochester, MI 48063

Saginaw Valley State College
School of Business and Management
University Center, MI 48710

University of Detroit
College of Business and Administration
Graduate Programs
Detroit, MI 48207

University of Michigan/Ann Arbor
Graduate School of Business Administration
Ann Arbor, MI 48109

University of Michigan/Dearborn
School of Management
MBA Program
Dearborn, MI 48128

University of Michigan/Flint
School of Management
MBA Program
Flint, MI 48503

Wayne State University
School of Business Administration
MBA Program
Detroit, MI 48202

Western Michigan University
College of Business
Kalamazoo, MI 49008

MINNESOTA

Mankato State University
College of Business Administration
Graduate Programs
Mankato, MN 56001

Metropolitan State University
Program in Management and Administration
St. Paul, MN 55101

Moorhead State University
MBA Program
Moorhead, MN 56560

Saint Cloud State University
College of Business
Graduate Programs
St. Cloud, MN 56301

University of Minnesota/Duluth
School of Business and Economics
MBA Program
Duluth, MN 55812

University of Minnesota/Minneapolis/St. Paul
Graduate School of Management
Minneapolis, MN 55455

University of St. Thomas
Graduate Programs in Management
St. Paul, MN 55105

Winona State University
Department of Business Administration and Economics
MBA Program
Winona, MN 55987

MISSISSIPPI

Delta State University
School of Business
Graduate School
Cleveland, MS 38732

Jackson State University
School of Business and Economics
The Graduate School
Jackson, MS 39217

Millsaps College
School of Management
Jackson, MS 39210

Mississippi College
School of Business and Public Administration
Clinton, MS 39058

Mississippi State University
College of Business and Industry
Division of Graduate Studies
Mississippi State, MS 39762

University of Mississippi
School of Business and Administration
University, MS 38677

University of Southern Mississippi/Hattiesburg
College of Business Administration
Graduate Studies
Hattiesburg, MS 39401

University of Southern Mississippi/Long Beach
Coordinator of Graduate Business Studies
Long Beach, MS 39560

William Carey College
Graduate Center for Management Development
Hattiesburg, MS 39401

MISSOURI

Avila College
Department of Business and Economics
MBA Program
Kansas City, MO 64145

Central Missouri State University
College of Business and Economics
Warrensburg, MO 64093

Drury College
Breech School of Business Administration
MBA Program
Springfield, MO 65802

Lincoln University
School of Graduate Studies
MBA Program
Jefferson City, MO 65101

Maryville College
Division of Management
St. Louis, MO 63141

Northeast Missouri State University
Division of Business
Graduate Programs
Kirksville, MO 63501

Northwest Missouri State University
School of Business Administration
Graduate Programs
Maryville, MO 64468

Rockhurst College
Graduate Business Program
Kansas City, MO 64110

Saint Louis College of Pharmacy
Director of Graduate Studies
St. Louis, MO 63110

Saint Louis University
MBA Program
St. Louis, MO 63108

Southwest Missouri State University
School of Business
Graduate Programs
Springfield, MO 65802

University of Missouri/Columbia
College of Business and Public Administration
Graduate Programs
Columbia, MO 65211

University of Missouri/Kansas City
School of Administration
Kansas City, MO 64110

University of Missouri/St. Louis
School of Business Administration
Graduate Programs
St. Louis, MO 63121

Washington University
Graduate School of Business Administration
St. Louis, MO 63130

MONTANA

University of Montana
School of Business Administration
Graduate Programs
Missoula, MT 59812

NEBRASKA

Bellevue College
Masters of Art in Management
Bellevue, NE 68005

Chadron State College
School of Graduate Studies
Chadron, NE 69337

Creighton University
College of Business Administration
Graduate Programs
Omaha, NE 68178

University of Nebraska/Lincoln
College of Business Administration
Lincoln, NE 68588

University of Nebraska/Lincoln at Offutt Air Force Base
MBA Program
Offutt Air Force Base, NE 68113

University of Nebraska/Omaha
College of Business Administration
Graduate Programs
Omaha, NE 68182

Wayne State College
Division of Business
Wayne, NE 68787

NEVADA

University of Nevada/Las Vegas
College of Business and Economics
Las Vegas, NV 89154

University of Nevada/Reno
College of Business Administration
Reno, NY 89557

NEW HAMPSHIRE

Dartmouth College
Amos Tuck School of Business Administration
Hanover, NH 03755

Plymouth State College
Master of Business Administration Program
Plymouth, NH 03264

Rivier College
Graduate Department of Business Administration
Nashua, NH 03060

University of New Hampshire
Whittemore School of Business and Economics
Durham, NH 03824

NEW JERSEY

Fairleigh Dickinson University
Samuel J. Silberman College of Business Administration
Madison, NJ 07940

Fairleigh Dickinson University
Graduate School of Business
Rutherford, NJ 07070

Fairleigh Dickinson University
Graduate School of Business
Teaneck, NJ 07666

Glassboro State College
Department of Business Administration
Graduate Studies
Glassboro, NJ 08028

Monmouth College
MBA Program
West Long Branch, NJ 07764

Montclair State College
School of Business Administration
MBA Program
Upper Montclair, NJ 07043

Rider College
Division of Graduate Studies School of Business
Lawrenceville, NJ 08648

Rowan College of New Jersey
Graduate Office
Glassboro, NJ 08028

Rutgers University/Camden
Master of Business Administration Program
Camden, NJ 08102

Rutgers University/Newark
Graduate School of Business Administration
Newark, NJ 07102

Seton Hall University
W. Paul Stillman School of Business
South Orange, NJ 07079

Stevens Institute of Technology
Department of Management Science
Hoboken, NJ 07030

William Paterson College of New Jersey
School of Management
MBA Program
Wayne, NJ 07470

NEW MEXICO

College of Santa Fe
Graduate School of Business
Santa Fe, NM 87501

Eastern New Mexico University
College of Business
Graduate Programs
Portales, NM 88130

New Mexico Highlands University
Division of Business and Economics
MBA Program
Las Vegas, NM 87701

New Mexico State University
College of Business Administration and Economics
Graduate Programs
Las Cruces, NM 88003

University of New Mexico
Robert O. Anderson Graduate School of Management
Albuquerque, NM 87131

Western New Mexico University
Department of Business and Public Administration
Silver City, NM 88061

NEW YORK

Adelphi University
School of Business Administration
Garden City, NY 11530

Canisius College
School of Business Administration
Buffalo, NY 14214

City University of New York/Baruch College
School of Business and Public Administration
Graduate Studies
New York, NY 10010

City University of New York/Graduate School and University Center
Program in Business
New York, NY 10036

Clarkson University
School of Management
Potsdam, NY 13676

College of Insurance
Graduate Program
Business Division
New York, NY 10038

College of Saint Rose
Graduate School
Social Science Division
Albany, NY 12203

Columbia University
Graduate School of Business
New York, NY 10027

Cornell University
Graduate School of Management
Ithaca, NY 14853

Cornell University
Graduate School, Hotel Administration
Ithaca, NY 14853

Dowling College
Master of Business Administration Program
Oakdale, NY 11769

Fordham University
Martino Graduate School of Business Administration
New York, NY 10023

Hofstra University
School of Business
Hempstead, NY 11550

Iona College
Hagan Graduate School of Business
New Rochelle, NY 10801

Iona College at Orangeburg
MBA Program
Orangeburg, NY 10962

Long Island University/Brooklyn Center
Graduate School of Business and Public Administration
Brooklyn, NY 11201

Long Island University/C.W. Post Center
Graduate Programs
Greenvale, NY 11548

Long Island University/Westchester
School of Business and Public Administration
Graduate Studies
Dobbs Ferry, NY 10522

Manhattan College
Graduate Division
School of Business
Riverdale, NY 10471

Marist College
Graduate Programs
Poughkeepsie, NY 12601

Mercy College
Master of Science Program in Human Resource Management
Dobbs Ferry, NY 10522

Mount Saint Mary College
MBA Program
Newburgh, NY 12550

New York Institute of Technology
Center for Business and Economics
Old Westbury, NY 11568

New York University
Leonard N. Stern School of Business
New York, NY 10006

Niagara University
College of Business Administration
MBA Program
Niagara University, NY 14109

Pace University
Lubin Graduate School of Business
New York, 10038

Pace University at White Plains
Graduate School of Business
White Plains, NY 10603

Polytechnic University
Division of Management
Brooklyn, NY 11201

Rensselaer Polytechnic Institute
School of Management
Troy, NY 12181

Rochester Institute of Technology
College of Business, Graduate Business Program
Rochester, NY 14623

Russell Sage College
MBA Program
Albany, NY 12208

Saint Bonaventure University
School of Business Administration
School of Graduate Studies
St. Bonaventure, NY 14778

Saint John Fisher College
Graduate School of Business
Rochester, NY 14618

Saint John's University
Graduate Division, College of Business Administration
Jamaica, NY 11439

Saint John's University
College of Business Administration
Staten Island, NY 10300

State University of New York at Albany
School of Business
Albany, NY 12222

State University of New York at Binghamton
School of Management
Binghamton, NY 13905

State University of New York at Buffalo
School of Management
Buffalo, NY 14214

State University of New York/College at Oswego
Graduate Program in Business Administration/Management
Oswego, NY 13126

State University of New York/Institute of Technology at Utica/Rome
P.O. Box 3050
Utica, NY 13504

State University of New York, Maritime College
Office of Continuing Education
Throgs Neck, NY 10465

Syracuse University
School of Management
Syracuse, NY 13210

Syracuse University at Corning Center
College Center of Finger Lakes
Corning, NY 14830

Union College and University
Institute of Administration and Management
Schenectady, NY 12308

University of Rochester
Graduate School of Management
Rochester, NY 14627

NORTH CAROLINA

Appalachian State University
John A. Walker College of Business
Boone, NC 28608

Campbell University
Department of Business
Buies Creek, NC 27506

Duke University
Fuqua School of Business
Durham, NC 27706

East Carolina University
School of Business
Greenville, NC, 27834

Elon College
Graduate Program in Business
Elon College, NC 27244

Fayetteville State University
Graduate School of Business
Fayetteville, NC 28301

High Point University
School of Business
High Point, NC 27262

Meredith College
Department of Business and Economics
Raleigh, NC 27607

North Carolina Central University
School of Business
Durham, NC 27707

Pfeiffer College
MBA Program
Charlotte, NC 28204

Queens College
The Graduate School
MBA Program
Charlotte, NC 28274

University of North Carolina/Chapel Hill
Graduate School of Business Administration
Chapel Hill, NC 27514

University of North Carolina/Charlotte
College of Business Administration
Charlotte, NC 28223

University of North Carolina/Greensboro
School of Business and Economics
Greensboro, NC 27412

University of North Carolina/Wilmington
MBA Program
Wilmington, NC 28406

Wake Forest University
Babcock Graduate School of Management
Winston-Salem, NC 27109

Western Carolina University
School of Business
Graduate School
Cullowhee, NC 28723

Wingate College
School of Business
Wingate, NC 28174

NORTH DAKOTA

North Dakota State University
MBA Program
Fargo, ND 58105

University of North Dakota
Graduate Business Programs
Grand Forks, ND 58202

OHIO

Air Force Institute of Technology
Director of Admissions
Wright Patterson, OH 45433

Ashland College
MBA Program
Ashland, OH 44805

Baldwin-Wallace College
Master of Business Administration Program
Berea, OH 44017

Bowling Green State University
College of Business Administration
Bowling Green, OH 43403

Case Western Reserve University
Weatherhead School of Management
Cleveland, OH 44106

Cleveland State University
James J. Nance College of Business Administration
Cleveland, OH 44115

Franciscan University of Steubenville
MBA Program
Steubenville, OH 43952

John Carroll University
School of Business
Cleveland, OH 44118

Kent State University
Graduate School of Management
Kent, OH 44242

Miami University
School of Business Administration
Oxford, OH 45056

Ohio State University
College of Administrative Science
Columbus, OH 43210

Ohio University
College of Business Administration
Athens, OH 45701

Tiffin University
Division of Business
Tiffin, OH 44883

University of Akron
College of Business Administration
Akron, OH 44325

University of Cincinnati
College of Business Administration
Cincinnati, OH 45221

University of Dayton
MBA Program
School of Business Administration
Dayton, OH 45469

University of Toledo
College of Business Administration
Toledo, OH 43606

Walsh University
Graduate Program
North Canton, OH 44720

Wright State University
College of Business Administration
School of Graduate Studies
Dayton, OH 45435

Xavier University
Graduate Programs
Cincinnati, OH 45206

Youngstown State University
Graduate School of Business
Youngstown, OH 44555

OKLAHOMA

Northeastern State University
The Graduate College
Tahlequah, OK 74464

Oklahoma City University
School of Management and Business Sciences
Graduate Programs
Oklahoma City, OK 73106

Oklahoma State University
College of Business Administration
Graduate Programs
Stillwater, OK 74078

Oral Roberts University
School of Business
Tulsa, OK 74171

Phillips University
Center of Business and Communication
MBA Program
Enid, OK 73702

Southern Nazarene University
Graduate Management Program
Bethany, OK 73008

University of Central Oklahoma
College of Business Administration
Edmond, OK 73034

University of Oklahoma
College of Business Administration
Graduate Programs
Norman, OK 73019

University of Tulsa
College of Business Administration
Graduate Programs
Tulsa, OK 74104

OREGON

Oregon State University
School of Business
Graduate Programs
Corvallis, OR 97331

Portland State University
School of Business Administration
Graduate Programs
Portland, OR 97207

Southern Oregon State College
School of Business
Graduate Programs
Ashland, OR 97520

University of Oregon
Graduate School of Management
Eugene, OR 97403

University of Portland
School of Business Administration
MBA Program
Portland, OR 97203

Willamette University
Geo. H. Atkinson Graduate School of Management
Salem, OR 97301

PENNSYLVANIA

Bloomsburg University of Pennsylvania
School of Graduate Studies
Bloomsburg, PA 17815

Bucknell University
Department of Management
Graduate Program
Lewisburg, PA 17837

California University of Pennsylvania
Department of Business and Economics
California, PA 15419

Carnegie-Mellon University
Graduate School of Industrial Administration
Pittsburgh, PA 15213

Clarion University of Pennsylvania
School of Business Administration
Graduate School
Clarion, PA 16214

Drexel University
College of Business and Administration
Philadelphia, PA 19104

Duquesne University
Graduate School of Business and Administration
Pittsburgh, PA 15282

Eastern College
Graduate Program in Business Administration
St. Davids, PA 19087

Gannon University
Master of Business Administration Program
Erie, PA 16541

Indiana University of Pennsylvania
School of Business
Graduate School
Indiana, PA 15705

Kings College
Graduate Office
Wilkes Barre, PA 18711

Kutztown University of Pennsylvania
College of Graduate Studies
Kutztown, PA 19530

La Roche College
Graduate Studies
Pittsburgh, PA 15237

La Salle University
School of Business Administration
Philadelphia, PA 19141

Lebanon Valley College
MBA Program
Annville, PA 17003

Lehigh University
College of Business and Economics
Bethlehem, PA 18015

Marywood College
Graduate Program in Business and Managerial Science
Scranton, PA 18509

Moravian College
MBA Program
Bethlehem, PA 18017

Pennsylvania State University at Erie, Behrend College
Graduate Admissions
Erie, PA 16563

Pennsylvania State University/The Capitol Campus
Master of Administration Program
Middletown, PA 17057

Pennsylvania State University/University Park
Graduate Studies
College of Business Administration
University Park, PA 16802

Philadelphia College of Textiles and Science
MBA Program
Philadelphia, PA 19144

Point Park College
MIBM Program
Pittsburgh, PA 15222

Robert Morris College
Graduate School
Coraoplis, PA 15108

Saint Joseph's University
MBA Program
Philadelphia, PA 19131

Temple University
School of Business Administration
Graduate School
Philadelphia, PA 19122

University of Pennsylvania
The Wharton School, Graduate Division
Philadelphia, PA 19104

University of Pittsburgh
Graduate School of Business
Pittsburgh, PA 15260

University of Scranton
School of Management, Graduate School
Pittsburgh, PA 18510

Villanova University
College of Commerce and Finance
MBA Program
Villanova, PA 19085

Waynesburg College
Graduate Program in Business
Waynesburg, PA 15370

West Chester University of Pennsylvania
School of Administration and Public Affairs
West Chester, PA 19380

Widener University
Graduate Program in Business Administration
Chester, PA 19013

Wilkes University
MBA Program
Wilkes Barre, PA 18766

York College of Pennsylvania
Department of Business Administration
York, PA 17405

RHODE ISLAND

Bryant College
Graduate School
Smithfield, RI 02917

Providence College
Graduate School
Department of Business Administration
Providence, RI 02918

University of Rhode Island
College of Business Administration
Kingston, RI 02881

SOUTH CAROLINA

Central Wesleyan College
Leadership Education for Adult Professionals
Central, SC 29630

Charleston Southern University
Director of Graduate Studies in Business
Charleston, SC 29423

Citadel, The
MBA Program
Department of Business Administration
Charleston, SC 29409

Clemson University
College of Industrial Management and Textile Science
Clemson, SC 29631

Clemson University-Furman University
MBA Program
Greenville, SC 29613

Francis Marion University
School of Business
Florence, SC 29501

University of South Carolina
College of Business Administration
Columbia, SC 29208

Winthrop College
School of Business Administration
Rock Hill, SC 29733

SOUTH DAKOTA

Huron University
Master of Business Administration
Huron, SD 57350

Northern State University
MBA Program
Aberdeen, SD 57401

University of South Dakota
School of Business
Graduate Programs
Vermillion, SD 57069

TENNESSEE

Belmont College
The Jack C. Massey Graduate School of Business
Nashville, TN 37212

Christian Brothers College
Graduate School of Business
Memphis, TN 38104

East Tennessee State University
College of Business
The School of Graduate Studies
Johnson City, TN 37601

Memphis State University
Fogelman College of Business and Economics
Graduate School
Memphis, TN 38152

Middle Tennessee State University
Graduate Studies
School of Business
Murfreesboro, TN 37132

Rhodes College
Department of Economics and Business Administration
Memphis, TN 38112

Tennessee State University
School of Business
Nashville, TN 37203

Tennessee Technological University
The Graduate School, Division of MBA Studies
Cookeville, TN 38501

Trevecca Nazarene College
Graduate Studies in Organizational Management
Nashville, TN 37210

University of Tennesse/Chattanooga
School of Business Administration
Chattanooga, TN 37402

University of Tennessee/Knoxville
College of Business Administration
Knoxville, TN 37916

University of Tennessee/Martin
School of Business Administration
Martin, TN 38238

Vanderbilt University
Owen Graduate School of Management
Nashville, TN 37203

TEXAS

Abilene Christian University
College of Business Administration
Abilene, TX 79699

Angelo State University
MBA Program
San Angelo, TX 76909

Baylor University
Hankamer School of Business
Graduate Programs
Waco, TX 76798

Corpus Christi State University
College of Business
Corpus Christi, TX 78412

East Texas State University/Commerce
College of Business and Technology
Commerce, TX 75428

East Texas State University/Texarkana
College of Business Administration
Master's Programs
Texarkana, TX 75501

Houston Baptist University
College of Business and Economics
Graduate Programs
Houston, TX 77074

Lamar University
College of Business
MBA Program
Beaumont, TX 77710

Prairie View A&M University
College of Business
Graduate Program
Prairie View, TX 77445

Rice University
Jesse H. Jones Graduate School of Administration
Houston, TX 77001

Saint Mary's University
School of Business and Administration
Graduate Programs
San Antonio, TX 78284

Sam Houston State University
College of Business Administration
Graduate Programs
Huntsville, TX 77341

Southern Methodist University
Edwin L. Cox School of Business
Graduate Programs
Dallas, TX 75275

Southwest Texas State University
School of Business, Graduate Division
San Marcos, TX 78666

Stephen F. Austin State University
Graduate School of Business
Nacogdoches, TX 75962

Sul Ross State University
Division of Business Administration
MBA Program
Alpine, TX 79830

Texas A&M University
College of Business Administration
Graduate Programs
College Station, TX 77843

Texas Christian University
M.J. Neeley School of Business
Fort Worth, TX 76129

Texas Southern University
School of Business
Graduate Programs
Houston, TX 77004

Texas Tech University
College of Business Administration
Graduate Programs
Lubbock, TX 79409

University of Dallas
Graduate School of Management
Irving, TX 75062

University of Houston/Clear Lake
School of Business and Public Administration
Graduate Programs
Houston, TX 77058

University of Houston/University Park
College of Business Administration
Graduate Programs
Houston, TX 77004

University of Mary Hardin-Baylor
Graduate Program—Business
Belton, TX 76513

University of North Texas
College of Business Administration
Graduate Programs
Denton, TX 76203

University of St. Thomas
Cameron School of Business
MBA Program
Houston, TX 77006

University of Texas/Arlington
College of Business Administration
Graduate Programs
Arlington, TX 76019

University of Texas/Austin
Graduate School of Business
Austin, TX 78712

University of Texas/Brownsville
Graduate School
Brownsville, TX 78520

University of Texas/Dallas
School of Management and Administration
Graduate Programs
Richardson, TX 75080

University of Texas/Pan American
School of Business Administration
Edinburg, TX 78539

University of Texas/San Antonio
College of Business
Graduate Program
San Antonio, TX 78285

University of Texas/Tyler
School of Business Administration
MBA Program
Tyler, TX 75701

West Texas State University
School of Business
Graduate Programs
Canyon, TX 79016

UTAH

Brigham Young University
Graduate School of Management
Provo, UT 84602

Southern Utah State College
Graduate School of Business
Cedar City, UT 84720

University of Utah
Graduate School of Business
Salt Lake City, UT 84112

Utah State University
College of Business
Graduate Programs
Logan, UT 84322

Weber State College
Graduate School of Business
Ogden, UT 84408

VERMONT

University of Vermont
Division of Engineering
Mathematics and Business Administration
Burlington, VT 05405

VIRGINIA

College of William and Mary in Virginia
School of Business Administration
Williamsburg, VA 23185

George Mason University
Graduate School
School of Business Administration
Fairfax, VA 22030

Hampton University
Graduate Studies in Business
Hampton, VA 23668

James Madison University
School of Business
Harrisonburg, VA 22807

Liberty University
School of Business and Government
MBA Program
Lynchburg, VA 24501

Lynchburg College
Department of Business Administration
Lynchburg, VA 24501

Mary Washington College
Graduate Business Programs
Fredericksburg, VA 22401

Marymount University
MBA Program
Arlington, VA 22207

Old Dominion University
School of Business Administration
Norfolk, VA 23508

Radford University
College of Business and Economics
Radford, VA 24142

Regent University
College of Administration and Management
Virginia Beach, VA 23464

Shenandoah College and Conservatory
MBA Program
Winchester, VA 22601

University of Richmond
Graduate Division
Richmond, VA 23173

University of Virginia
Colgate Darden Graduate School of Business
Charlottesville, VA 22906

Virginia Commonwealth University
School of Business
Richmond, VA 23284

Virginia Polytechnic Institute and State University
College of Business
Blacksburg, VA 24061

WASHINGTON

Eastern Washington University
MBA Program Office, School of Business
Cheney, WA 99004

Gonzaga University
School of Business Administration
Graduate Programs
Spokane, WA 99258

Pacific Lutheran University
School of Business Administration
MBA Program
Tacoma, WA 98447

Saint Martin's College
Graduate Studies in Management
Lacey, WA 98503

Seattle Pacific University
Master of Business Administration Program
Seattle, WA 98119

Seattle University
Albers School of Business
MBA Program
Seattle, WA 98122

University of Washington, Seattle
Graduate School of Business Administration
Seattle, WA 98195

Washington State University
College of Business and Economics
Graduate Programs
Pullman, WA 99163

Western Washington University
College of Business and Economics
Graduate Programs
Bellingham, WA 98225

WEST VIRGINIA

Marshall University
Graduate School
College of Business
Huntington, WV 25701

University of Charleston
Graduate School of Business
Charleston, WV 25304

West Virginia University
College of Business and Economics
Morgantown, WV 26506

West Virginia Wesleyan College
MBA Program
Buckhannon, WV 26201

Wheeling Jesuit College
Graduate Business Program
Wheeling, WV 26003

WISCONSIN

Marquette University
Robert A. Johnston College of Business Administration
Graduate Programs
Milwaukee, WI 53233

University of Wisconsin/Eau Claire
School of Business
MBA Program
Eau Claire, WI 54701

University of Wisconsin/La Crosse
College of Business Administration
MBA Program
La Crosse, WI 54601

University of Wisconsin/Madison
Graduate School of Business
Madison, WI 53706

University of Wisconsin/Milwaukee
Milwaukee School of Business Administration
Milwaukee, WI 53201

University of Wisconsin/Oshkosh
College of Business Administration
Oshkosh, WI 54901

University of Wisconsin/Parkside
Division of Business and Administrative Science
MBA Program
Kenosha, WI 53141

University of Wisconsin/Whitewater
College of Business and Economics
Whitewater, WI 53190

WYOMING

University of Wyoming
College of Commerce and Industry
Graduate Business Programs
Laramie, WY 82071

GUAM

University of Guam
College of Business and Public Administration
Mangilao, GU 96913

PUERTO RICO

Universidad del Turabo
Program in Accounting
Caguas, PR 00626

University of Puerto Rico, Mayaguez
College of Business Administration
Mayaguez, PR 00708

University of Puerto Rico/Rio Piedras
Graduate School of Business Administration
Rio Piedras, PR 00931

World University
Graduate School of Management and Accounting
Carolina, PR 00628

VIRGIN ISLANDS

University of the Virgin Islands
Division of Business Administration
St. Thomas, VI 00801

CANADA

Carleton University
Graduate School of Business
Ottawa, ON K1S5B

Concordia University
Faculty of Commerce and Administration
Montreal, PQ H3G1M

Dalhousie University
Faculty of Graduate Studies
International Business
Halifax, NS B3H31

Lakehead University
School of Business Administration
Thunder Bay, ON P7B5E

McGill University
Faculty of Management
Montreal, PQ H3A2T

McMaster University
Faculty of Business Program in Management Science
Hamilton, ON L8S4M

Memorial University of Newfoundland
Faculty of Business Administration
St. John's, NF A1B3X

Queen's University at Kingston
School of Business
Kingston, ON K7L3N

Saint Mary's University
Faculty of Commerce
Halifax, NS B3H3C

Simon Fraser University
Faculty of Business Administration/Finance
Burnaby, BC V5A1S

University College of Cape Breton
Sydney, NS B1P 6L2

Université de Sherbrooke
School of Business
Sherbrooke, PQ J1K2R

University of Guelph
Office of Graduate Studies
Guelph, ON N1G 2WI

University of Alberta
Faculty of Business
Edmonton, AB T6G2R

University of British Columbia
Faculty of Commerce and Business Administration
Vancouver, BC V6T1Z

University of Calgary
Faculty of Management
Calgary, AB T2N1N

Université du Québec à Montréal
Département des sciences administratives
Montréal, PQ H3C 3P8

University of Manitoba
Faculty of Administrative Studies
Winnipeg, ON R3T2N

University of New Brunswick
Graduate School of Business
Fredericton, NB E3B5A

University of Ottawa
MBA Program
Ottawa, ON K1N 6N5

University of Saskatchewan
College of Commerce
Saskatoon, SK S7NOW

University of Toronto
School of Graduate Studies
Department of Management
Toronto, ON M5SMB

University of Victoria
School of Business
Victoria, BC V8W 3P2

Index

NOTES

NOTES

NOTES